WHERE TO WATCH BIRDS IN

France

SECOND EDITION

WHERE TO WATCH BIRDS IN

France

SECOND EDITION

Compiled by Philippe J. Dubois
on behalf of La Ligue pour la Protection des Oiseaux

Translated and edited by Tony Williams and Ken Hall

Christopher Helm
London

First published 1992 by Christopher Helm, London.
Second edition published 2006 by Christopher Helm
an imprint of A&C Black Publishers Ltd,
38 Soho Square, London W1D 3HB

ISBN-10: 0-7136-6980-2
ISBN-13: 978-0-7136-6980-0

A CIP catalogue record for this book is available from the British Library.

A&C Black uses paper produced with elemental chlorine-free pulp, harvested from managed sustainable forests.

www.acblack.com

Printed and bound in France

10 9 8 7 6 5 4 3 2 1

Preface

Is looking up into the sky all it takes in order to see birds?

Of course not. To discover the secrets of the avian world takes patience and the accumulation of experience. It is probably because of this that we appreciate the eventual appearance of a sought-after bird so much. But that is no reason why the task for all who like watching birds for pleasure should not be simplified as far as possible.

For many years, the regional representatives and the many active members of the LPO (the Ligue Française pour la Protection des Oiseaux, the Birdlife partner for France) have provided information to birdwatchers on a regular basis. Then, published in 1989, came the first French edition of *Où voir les Oiseaux en France* [the English edition, *Where to Watch Birds in France*, appeared in 1992]. This proved a great success, and was the fruit of contributions from the whole of the ornithological community of France. Now, over a decade later, these experts in their field have been consulted once more and again they have shared their considerable knowledge with us. Benefiting from their knowledge and experience, we have a privileged insight into the diversity of habitats and rich bird life of France.

The book covers some 337 sites, the location and study of which has involved many thousands of hours of birdwatching time, in order to provide accurate and useful instructions that allow everyone to go into the field with profit at any season, whether for a couple of hours, or for days at a time! However, the use of the itineraries proposed here for enjoyable birdwatching should be tempered with care and respect for the fragile natural world in which we all live. In providing information to make it easier to find birds, the LPO hopes to change attitudes in a positive way. The aim of the authors of this book is simple: the more people there are that discover the fascinating world of birds, the more there are who will understand the need to protect them.

So let us all go out looking for birds, treating the places visited with the appropriate respect, but enjoying the real pleasure to be gained from spending unforgettable hours looking at those beings that are such a symbol of liberty – the birds.

Allain Bougrain-Dubourg
President of the LPO

LPO

Contents

Preface	5
Introduction	11
How to use this guide	12
Alsace	18
Aquitaine	28
Auvergne	42
Bourgogne / Burgundy	56
Bretagne / Brittany	70
Centre	86
Champagne-Ardenne	106
Corse / Corsica	120
Franche-Comté	132
Île-de-France / Paris	146
Languedoc-Roussillon	170
Limousin	188
Lorraine	196
Midi-Pyrénées	212
Nord-Pas-de-Calais	228
Basse-Normandie	250
Haute-Normandie	262
Pays de la Loire	270
Picardie	292
Poitou-Charentes	304
Provence-Alpes-Côte d'Azur	326
Rhône-Alpes	358
Glossary	380
Index of species	381
Index of sites	392

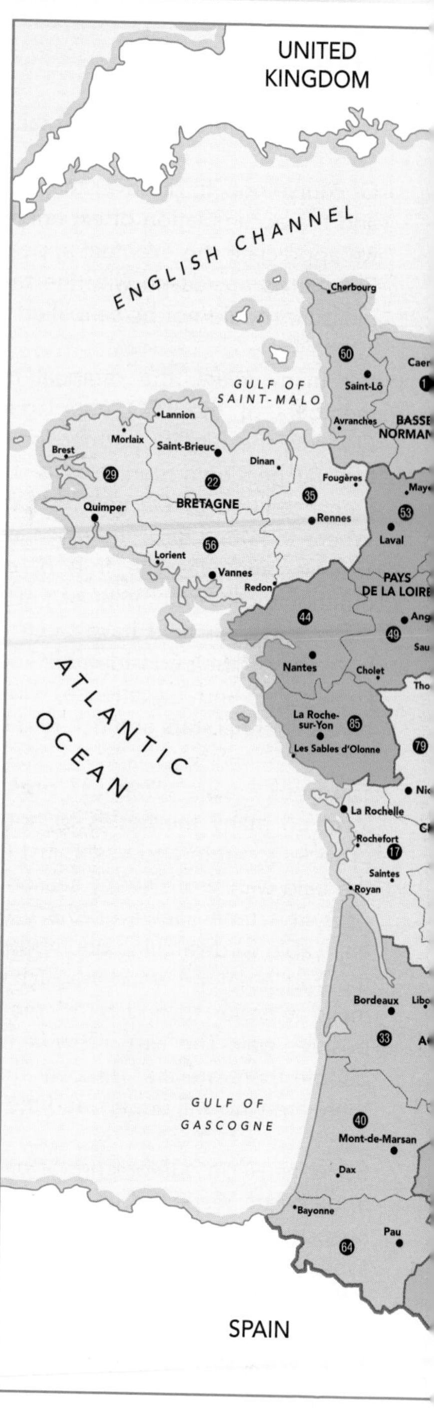

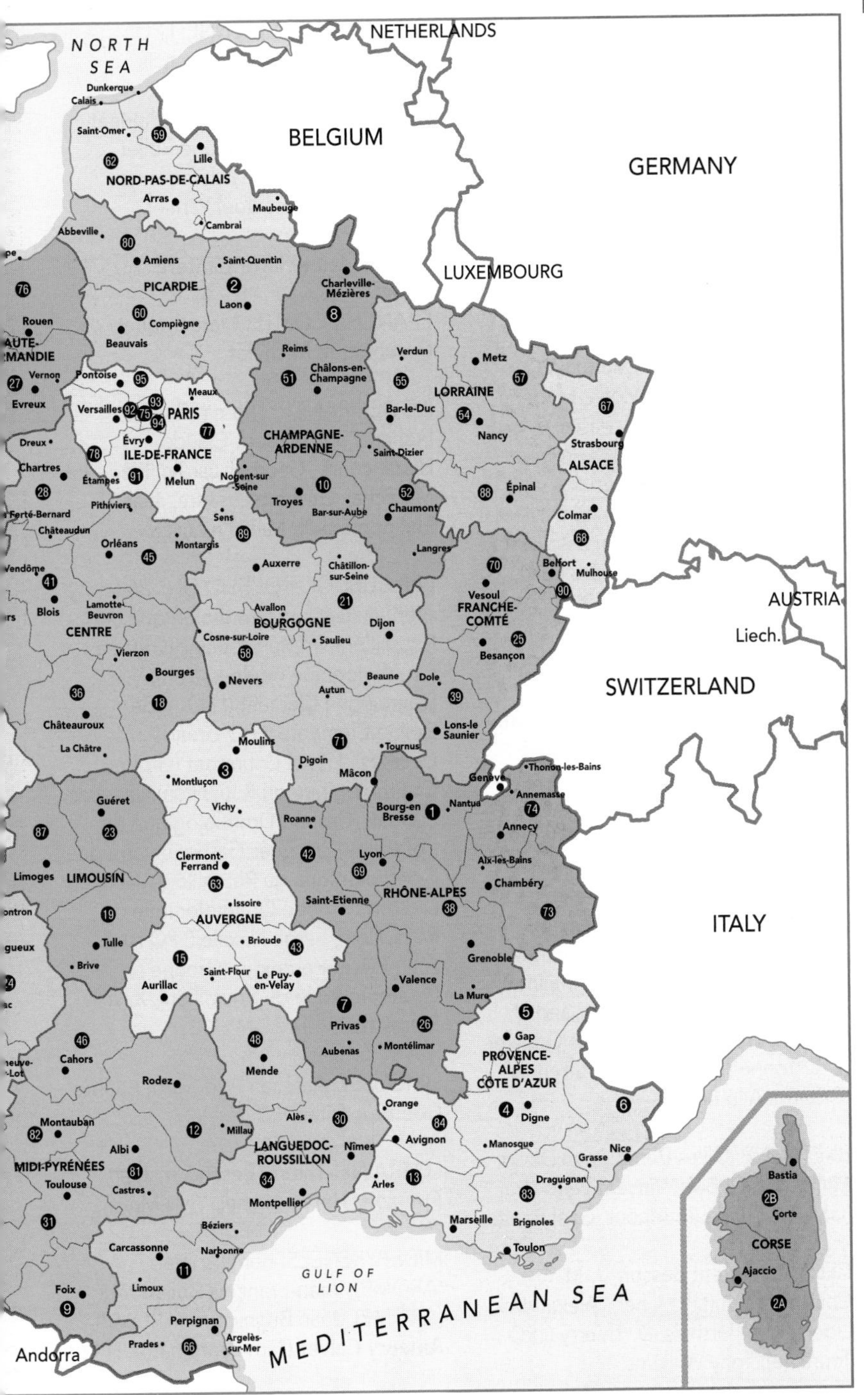
NETHERLANDS
NORTH SEA
Dunkerque
Calais
Saint-Omer
59
BELGIUM
GERMANY
62
Lille
NORD-PAS-DE-CALAIS
Arras
Maubeuge
Cambrai
Abbeville
80
Amiens
Saint-Quentin
Charleville-Mézières
LUXEMBOURG
76
PICARDIE
2
Laon
8
Rouen
60
Compiègne
Beauvais
Reims
Verdun
Metz
57
Châlons-en-Champagne
51
55
LORRAINE
Vernon
Pontoise
95
Meaux
27
Evreux
93
Versailles
92
75
PARIS
94
Bar-le-Duc
54
Nancy
67
77
CHAMPAGNE-ARDENNE
Strasbourg
Dreux
Évry
ILE-DE-FRANCE
Saint-Dizier
ALSACE
78
Chartres
Étampes
91
Melun
Nogent-sur-Seine
10
52
88
Épinal
28
Troyes
Bar-sur-Aube
Chaumont
Pithiviers
Colmar
Ferté-Bernard
Sens
Châteaudun
89
68
Orléans
45
Montargis
Langres
70
Auxerre
Châtillon-sur-Seine
Belfort
Mulhouse
Vendôme
41
90
AUSTRIA
21
Vesoul
Lamotte-Beuvron
Avallon
Blois
FRANCHE-COMTÉ
BOURGOGNE
Dijon
CENTRE
Liech.
Cosne-sur-Loire
Saulieu
25
Besançon
Vierzon
58
Bourges
SWITZERLAND
Nevers
Beaune
Dole
36
Autun
39
18
Châteauroux
Lons-le Saunier
Moulins
La Châtre
71
Tournus
Digoin
3
Thonon-les-Bains
Montluçon
Mâcon
Genève
Annemasse
Guéret
Vichy
Bourg-en Bresse
1
Nantua
74
Roanne
Annecy
87
23
42
Lyon
Clermont-Ferrand
Aix-les-Bains
69
Limoges
LIMOUSIN
Chambéry
63
Saint-Etienne
RHÔNE-ALPES
Issoire
38
73
19
AUVERGNE
ITALY
Brioude
43
Tulle
Grenoble
Brive
15
Saint-Flour
Le Puy-en-Velay
Aurillac
Valence
La Mure
5
7
Privas
26
Gap
46
48
Aubenas
Montélimar
Cahors
PROVENCE-ALPES CÔTE D'AZUR
Mende
Rodez
6
Orange
Montauban
4
Digne
82
12
Millau
Alès
30
84
Avignon
Albi
LANGUEDOC-ROUSSILLON
Nîmes
Manosque
Nice
MIDI-PYRÉNÉES
81
Grasse
Bastia
Toulouse
Castres
34
Arles
13
Draguignan
2B
Montpellier
83
Corte
31
Béziers
Marseille
Brignoles
CORSE
Carcassonne
Narbonne
Toulon
Ajaccio
11
GULF OF LION
Foix
Limoux
2A
9
MEDITERRANEAN SEA
Perpignan
Prades
66
Argelès-sur-Mer
Andorra

Contributing editors

The main contributors to the information in this book are listed below, by region. The names of the regional and departmental coordinators are given in bold type.

ALSACE: **Christian Dronneau** (LPO Alsace), Yves Muller (LPO Alsace).

AQUITAINE: Laurent Cousin (LPO Aquitaine), Alain Dal Molin, Frédéric Dupuy (LPO Aquitaine), Pascal Grisser (LPO Aquitaine/SEPANSO), Robert Guélin (LPO Aquitaine), Erick Kobierzycki (LPO Aquitaine), Olivier Le Gall (LPO Aquitaine), Yvan Letellier (SEPANSO), **Frédéric Revers** (LPO Aquitaine).

AUVERGNE: LPO Auvergne - Réné Auclair, Cathy Duvaut, Franck Chastagnol, Philippe J. Dubois, **Jean-Christophe Gigault**, Jean-Jacques Lallemant.

BOURGOGNE: Thomas Barral (LPO Yonne), Annie and Claude Chapalain (SOBA), **Didier Dagnas** (Yonne coordinateur, LPO Yonne), Pierre Durlet (CEOB L'Aile Brisée), Jean-Marc Frolet (AOMSL), Christian Gentilin (AOMSL), S. Merle, C. Neyer and N. Pointecouteau (SOBA), Alexis Queyrel (LPO Yonne), Y. Rivière, Luc Strenna (CEOB L'Aile Brisée).

BRETAGNE: Gilles Bentz, Jean David, Philippe J. Dubois, Vincent Liéron (GEOCA), Jacques Maout, Gaël Rault.

CENTRE: Florent Besson, J.-M. Chartendrault (LPO Cher), Alexandre Liger, Alain Perthuis, D. Thierry (LPO Touraine), Tony Williams.

CHAMPAGNE-ARDENNE: LPO Champagne-Ardenne - **Francis Desjardins**, Michel Goubault, Emmanuel Le Roy, Aymeric Mionnet, Christian Riols, Jean-Marie Rollet, Alain Sauvage, Bernard Theveny, Bernard Vacheret, Joël Varnier.

CORSE: **Jean-Pierre Cantera**.

FRANCHE-COMTÉ: Marc Duquet, **Domonique Michelat**.

ÎLE-DE-FRANCE: Thomas Biéro, François Bouzendorf, Claude Hadancourt , Georges Jardin, Pierre Le Maréchal, Guilhem Lesaffre, Jean-Philippe Siblet, Maxime Zucca.

LANGUEDOC-ROUSSILLON: Yves Aleman (Groupe Ornithologique du Roussillon), Frédérick Blanc (Groupe Ornithologique du Roussillon), Domonique Clément (LPO Aude), Céline Clémente (LPO Grands Causses), Lionel Courmont (Groupe Ornithologique du Roussillon), Jacques Dalmau (Groupe Ornithologique du Roussillon), Jacques Garrigue (Groupe Ornithologique du Roussillon), Jacques Laurens (Groupe Ornithologique du Roussillon), Serge Nicolle (LPO Aude), Jean-Pierre Pompidor (Groupe Ornithologique du Roussillon), Xavier Rufray (GRIVE).

LIMOUSIN: Aurélien Audevard, Karim Guerbaa, Gilles Pallier.

LORRAINE: Thierry Besançon, **Jean François, Hervé Michel**, Yves Muller.

MIDI-PYRÉNÉES: Bernard Alet (AROMP), **Jean-François Bousquet** (AROMP), Jean Bugnicourt (AROMP), **Amaury Calvet** (Tarn coordinator, LPO

Tarn), Céline Clémente (LPO Grands Causses), Araud Comby (LPO Aveyron), Jean Joachim (AROMP), Michel Malaterre (LPO Tarn), Claude Pichel (LPO Tarn).

NORD / PAS-DE-CALAIS: Christian Boutrouille (Groupe Ornithologique et Naturaliste Nord/Pas-de-Calais - GON), Philippe J. Dubois (GON), Guy Flohart (GON), Jacques Leclercq, Pierre-René Legrand (GON), Quentin Spriet (GON), Jean-Charles Tombal (GON), Alain Ward (GON).

BASSE-NORMANDIE: Gérard Debout, Philippe J. Dubois, Dominique Loir and Alain Verneau.

HAUTE-NORMANDIE: **Fréderic Malvaud** (LPO Haute-Normandie).

PAYS DE LA LOIRE: Patrick Berthelot (LPO Loire-Atlantique), Joël Bourlès (LPO Loire-Atlantique), Didier Desmots (LPO Vendée), Christophe Dougé (LPO Loire-Atlantique), Hubert Dougé (LPO Loire-Atlantique), Alain Gentric (LPO Loire-Atlantique), **Christian Gonin** (LPO Vendée), Julien Gonin (Vendée coordinator, LPO Vendée), Lucien Grillet (LPO Vendée), **Éric Lapous** (Sarthe coordinator), Jean-Paul Mérot (LPO Loire-Atlantique), **Franck Noël** (Maine-et-Loire coordinator, LPO Anjou), Jean-Paul Paillat (LPO Vendée), **Mickaël Potard** (Loire-Atlantique coordinator, LPO Loire-Atlantique), Jo Pourreau (LPO Loire-Atlantique), Frédéric Signoret (LPO Vendée), **Dominique Tavenon** (Mayenne coordinator).

PICARDIE: D. Baverel (LPO Aisne), **Laurent Gavory** (Somme coordinator), **Alain Rouge** (Oise coordinator).

POITOU-CHARENTES: Alain Armouet (Groupe Ornithologique des Deux-Sèvres - GODS), Christophe Bouchet (LPO), Frédéric Corre (LPO), Thomas de Cornulier (GODS), Philippe Delaporte (LPO), Thibault Dieuleveult (GODS), Alain Doumeret (LPO), Michel Fouquet (GODS), Nicolas Gendre (LPO), **Michel Granger** (Vienne coordinator, LPO Vienne), **Pascal Lavoué** (Charente coordinateur), Fabien Mercier (LPO), Hervé Roques (LPO), Paul Trotignon (LPO Charente-Maritime), **Jean-Marc Villalard** (Deux-Sèvres coordinator, GODS).

PROVENCE-ALPES-CÔTE D'AZUR: Arnica Montana, Christophe Baudoin (LPO PACA), Michel Blanchet, Didier Brugot (CRAVE), Cédric Denis, Amine Flitti (LPO PACA), Roger Garcin, Claire Grellet-Aumont (LPO PACA), Jean-Jacques Guitard (LPO PACA), Sylvain Henriquet (LPO PACA), Yves Kayser, Patrice Lafont (LPO PACA), **Matthieu Lascève**, **Georges Olioso** (Vaucluse coordinator), Philippe Pilard (LPO Mission Rapaces), André Zammit (LPO PACA).

RHÔNE-ALPES: Patrick Balluet (LPO Loire), **Samuel Blanc** (Isère coordinator, CORA), Didier Brugot, **Pierre Crouzier** (Ain coordinator), Francis Grunert (LPO Loire), Jean-Pierre Jordan (LPO Savoie), Boris Juillard (LPO Loire), **Alain Ladet** (Ardèche coordinator), **Georges Olioso** (Drôme coordinator), **Alexandre Renaudier** (Rhône coordinateur), Antoine Rouillon, André Ulmer (LPO Loire).

The Ligue pour la Protection des Oiseaux

The foundation of the Ligue pour la Protection des Oiseaux (LPO), the French equivalent of the RSPB, dates back to 1912. Like the RSPB, it started with a single-issue campaign, not in this case protesting against the use of heron plumes in the millinery trade, but trying to stop the indiscriminate shooting of auks breeding on the Brittany coast. This successful campaign resulted in the LPO's first reserve - Les Sept-Îles - and the adoption of the Puffin for their logo.

The LPO has since grown steadily, with membership currently around 35,000. It is the French representative of BirdLife International.

The LPO is always glad of new members, and is very happy to welcome those from the UK. If you wish to join, or even just to subscribe to the publications, more information is available on their web site (http://www.lpo.fr). The headquarters of the LPO is La Corderie Royale, BP 90263, 17305 Rochefort, France (Tel: +33 (0)5 46 82 12 34).

The current contact in the UK is Ken Hall, The Anchorage, The Chalks, Chew Magna BS40 8SN (Tel: 01275 332980). He runs an English-language website (http://www.kjhall.org.uk/lpo.html) which includes news items with a French slant, and can also arrange membership.

Introduction to the second edition

The first edition of *Où voir les oiseaux en France* appeared in 1989[1]. It enjoyed rapid success, and there can be few birdwatchers or ornithologists in France who have never used the book to find out about the different regions and their birds. It was the first work of its type in France, and at the time I coordinated the work of 98 authors who wrote about 278 sites spread right across the country. For this new edition no fewer than 160 people have worked on the description of 337 sites! Suffice it to say that the contents of this new volume are more diverse than ever.

It has to be said that the study of ornithology in France has changed a great deal over the past fifteen years. New reserves have been created, new sites discovered, others less well known in the past (and not included in the earlier edition) have on further investigation been found to be of great value for birds. On the other hand, over the same period, some sites have become less interesting, or have simply disappeared, whilst others are, for one reason or another, now inaccessible. Moreover, the network of birdwatchers out there looking has expanded and is much better organised than before. Knowledge spreads more quickly today due to the use of modern communication techniques by many keen naturalists, something which has also helped to make the book what it is today, an indispensable aid for birdwatchers venturing out into the field.

It is also worth emphasising the progress made by local authorities and voluntary organisations in promoting the wildlife interest of many sites. The remarkable development of 'green tourism' in France over the past decade has helped in France's very rich natural heritage being appreciated by many more people. This enthusiasm shows no sign of abating, and means, no doubt, that future editions of this book will be even more voluminous.

For the moment, this present edition offers an extraordinary panorama of France's wide diversity of birds and their habitats. Not only should we be aware of this but we should try to communicate to others the importance of preserving this natural heritage, as it is surely our duty to leave it in as good a state, if not better, that when we first found it, for our children and grand-children to enjoy in their turn.

So, enjoy reading the book and ... enjoy the birding!

Philippe J. Dubois

1. The first English language edition, *Where to Watch Birds in France*, was published by Christopher Helm (Publishers) Ltd in 1992.

How to use this guide

This book is intended for the use of anyone who enjoys birds, not just the ultra-keen birder. Its aim is to allow the birdwatcher – whether out for a walk, away for a weekend, or on holiday – to find those birds that breed or spend the winter in France or occur as passage migrants.

The sites chosen all allow the observer to watch birds in safety without causing undue disturbance. However, for the benefit both of the observers and of the birds, the access directions given in the book should be carefully adhered to, in addition to any instructions that are posted locally at the site itself.

Please note that this book does not pretend to be an identification guide, but is rather an adjunct to help with locating birds in different parts of the country. A good field-guide is therefore another essential purchase for those venturing out to look for birds in France.

The itineraries

There are **337** different sites in the book, classified according to the main administrative regions of France. In most cases the French version of the name of the region (e.g. Bourgogne, rather than Burgundy) is given, as these are what will be used on the maps that are an essential companion to a book such as this. Within each region each site is numbered, and grouped by 'département', the administrative units of France that approximate to 'counties' in the UK. Each of these départements has a two-digit number, which, incidentally, also features at the start of the five-digit postcode attached to any French postal address. When travelling through France and when searching for accommodation, it is useful to be aware of this number to locate roughly where you are. The map opposite the contents list at the start of the book shows the boundaries of the various départements, the code for each one, and the principal administrative centre.

At the start of each chapter there is a map showing the region covered relative to its neighbours, with the boundaries and codes of the départements within it. Within each region the sites covered are numbered in groups by département, and this name and code appears at the start of every entry. In general, the site name given is the French one, as again this is the name that will appear on printed maps. A Glossary at the end of the book gives English equivalents of some of the more common geographical terms that are used. For most sites the most useful map to refer to is the IGN 1:100,000 series that covers the whole of France, and the relevant map number is given at the start of every site account.

Not every one of the 337 sites treated here warrants equal treatment, and the itineraries have been divided into two main classes.

The principal itineraries cover **124** sites, chosen to be a representative sample of the most important birdwatching spots spread across the whole of France, each presented in the same format. This allows for a certain homogeneity between sites making direct comparisons of one site with another relatively easy.

These itineraries are described in three parts:

• A brief description of the site, its biogeographical and ecological context, its particular interest within the region (natural and historic) and usually an outline of some of the more important species to be found, particularly if they can be found anywhere within the site being treated, rather than at specific points (treated in the next section).

• Access details. Directions to get to the site are given, from the nearest large town; this information should be used in conjunction with the map that appears at the start of the chapter. Suitably sited car parks are also mentioned, and access by public transport given in some cases. For many remote sites, access by car is, however, the only practicable method within the usual time constraints available. Each site includes a map (see example below) with a suggested itinerary clearly marked. Wherever possible some idea of the distance covered is indicated. Access restrictions, where known, are given, and also suggestions for the time of day or season that will produce the best sightings. The route given is often just one of several possibilities, and is intended as a guide not as a limitation!

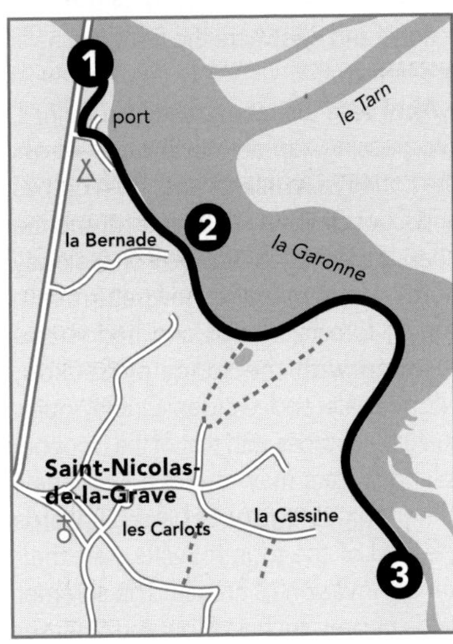

The numerals on the map correspond to the observation points described in the text, and species particularly associated with each part of the route are given here. Of course, many of the same species may well be encountered elsewhere along the itinerary. A drawing of a species typical of the itinerary is often included in the text.

• A third paragraph lists some of the most typical species that may be seen at each season and allows for an easy appreciation of the ornithological value of the site and the proposed itinerary; not all of the species will necessarily have been mentioned in the previous two paragraphs. Of course, it would be difficult – but maybe not impossible – to see all the species cited for any season during a single visit. And, of course, many species not mentioned could be seen, including some pleasant surprises.

The secondary itineraries, of which there are **213**, are presented in less detail, but again their position relative to the nearest large town is given, their more interesting natural features are described briefly and some of the more interesting birds that can be seen are listed. Some of these species may be visible year-round, while others are seasonal visitors; the details given will need to be interpreted accordingly. The list of bird species is by no means complete and many other species may well be seen. These secondary itineraries are thus perhaps more useful for those with a bit more birdwatching experience behind them.

The maps

The maps illustrated with each site account are to different scales, depending on the size of the site itself. They therefore need to be interpreted in conjunction with the description and distances given in the texts. Obviously for a small site, the details given as to the likely position of any particular bird species will be more precise than those for a more extensive area. For those new to birdwatching, the smaller sites are likely to lead to a more productive visit.

Some of the itineraries are intended to be made on foot throughout, whereas others will need some form of transport to get from one observation point to another. As mentioned above, the IGN 1:100,000 scale maps (1 cm = 1 km) is probably the most useful map to use, but a motoring atlas (e.g. the Michelin 1:200,000) may well be perfectly adequate for some. For more detail, the IGN 1:25,000 scale maps (1 cm = 250 metres) are recommended, particularly in mountainous terrain where in fact they may be essential for safety reasons. The whole of France is covered by these, and the more popular tourist areas have special versions covering larger areas than the standard ones. They are usually available in local bookshops, or can be ordered in advance from one of the specialist booksellers.

The seasons

Each season – even each month – has its own ornithological events. Thus a visit to a site in January may reveal a very different selection of species from a visit in July. Certain species are only present in France in the breeding season, most passing the winter in Africa, whereas others from Scandinavia or Siberia come for the winter. Some species only move short distances, whilst yet others are virtually sedentary. This diversity means that any site is usually worth visiting many times a year – even once a week – to look for species that may occur there for several months, a week or two, or for only a few hours. Each month has its highlights.

• As early as **February**, spring returns. This is the time when Greylag Geese, Lapwings and the first Golden Plovers start moving north. In wooded areas Buzzard and Goshawk may already be displaying over the treetops. Blackbirds, Song Thrushes and Dunnocks will already be singing in towns and gardens.

• In **March**, dabbling ducks will have started migrating, with large flocks occurring particularly along the Atlantic seaboard. This spring movement northwards seems to be happening earlier and earlier each year (perhaps a sign of global warming?) and now starts in February. Cormorants also leave, Black-tailed Godwits, Snipe and Ruffs stop off for a time before flying on farther north; the woodpeckers are very active, drumming and displaying in the still-bare woodland. In Mediterranean areas Sardinian Warblers start to sing in the maquis and elsewhere the first Chiffchaffs are heard.

• **April** sees the return of the hirundines, progressing rapidly northwards across the country. On inland lakes both grebes and Coot can be seen displaying and the coast is teeming with waders on their way north. Many migrants now return from Africa; forests, woods and hedgerows resound with the songs of Cuckoo, Nightingale and Golden Oriole, open sunny landscapes with that of the Hoopoe. Inland waters may attract a Garganey, either on passage or to breed. Towards the end of the month Swifts start their annual invasion of France. The summer birds of prey such as Montagu's Harrier and Short-toed Eagle also return. At high altitudes Black Grouse are displaying and Fieldfare are active.

• Early **May** and some terns are still on migration whereas others are starting to breed on islands, in rivers or lakes. Reedbeds are full of the song of Reed, Sedge and perhaps Savi's Warblers, and the Honey Buzzards start arriving. Coastal mudflats provide essential feeding grounds for Knot, Sanderling, Grey Plover and Turnstone on their way to Siberian breeding sites. This is the time of year to learn the various warblers' songs – the Midi, with its Mediterranean climate, has a particularly varied selection of species. Noisy colonies of Black-headed Gulls on inland lakes are a contrast to the discreet families of duck that start to appear out of the cover of wetland vegetation. By the end of May, late migrants such Marsh Warbler and Spotted Flycatcher eventually arrive. Owls are now well into their breeding cycle and become less vocal. This is a good month for finding rarer species – Red-rumped Swallow or Red-throated Pipit on the Mediterranean coast, Collared Flycatcher in Lorraine.

• **June** is the month when most species are breeding. The spring migration has finished; the very end of the month may see the first flocks of Lapwing, the first Green Sandpipers or Black-tailed Godwits returning south. Avocet, Black-winged Stilt and Kentish Plover are breeding on the saltpans of the Atlantic and Mediterranean coasts. France's only Greater Flamingo colony, in the Camargue, is under close surveillance to keep it free of disturbance. Bee-eaters and Black-eared Wheatears in the south, Kittiwakes and Icterine Warblers in the north, all are busily rearing young.

• **July** sees larger numbers of Arctic breeding waders on the move southwards. The early part of the month is perhaps the best time to explore the high mountains to find Ptarmigan, Snow Finch, Rock Thrush and Wallcreeper on their breeding grounds. Swallows and House Martins are still rearing young, but towards the end of this summer month many Swifts start moving back to Africa; for many birds autumn has begun.

• In **August** the coast abounds with species that only make a brief halt on their migrations. Curiously, even though the weather is often very good, the forests are silent, void of all bird song. Most of the White Storks and the early Black Storks pass through the country and the Black Kites leave. Over the sea are flocks of terns, also moving south.

• **September** and the autumn migration is at its height. Waders, various herons and birds of prey are seen almost everywhere. Seawatching is very good: shearwaters, Gannet, skuas, terns and sometimes Sabine's Gull are seen in impressive numbers at privileged sites along the Channel and Atlantic coasts. Many insectivorous passerines (Whinchat, Wheatear, Redstart, Spectacled Warbler, Bee-eater...) are noted by their absence on the breeding grounds as they leave discreetly, often migrating at night. And, of course, this is a good month for finding rarities – waders from the north (Dotterel) or North America (Pectoral and Buff-breasted Sandpipers ...), mainly along the western seaboard.

• **October** is another month when many birds are on the move. Cormorants, many ducks and birds of prey (including Sparrowhawk and Buzzard as well as more well-known migrant species) have returned for the winter, along with Redwings, Fieldfares, Chaffinches, Bramblings, Siskins and Redpolls. Petrels, skuas and Little Gulls occur out at sea, especially after strong winds. Starlings invade the country from east to west, and large flocks of Rooks arrive on ploughed fields. To the delight of many birdwatchers stray passerines arrive from Siberia, the best known being the Yellow-browed Warbler, these to be looked for at a few notable exposed sites along the Channel or Atlantic coasts.

• In early **November**, Red Kites and Cranes are two of the last species to pass south. Various wildfowl from farther north (divers, grebes, Eider, Common and Velvet Scoters, Red-breasted Merganser) occur in coastal waters. There is now a good chance of coming across a Woodcock in any wood, where mixed passerine flocks comprising mostly the various tits also include the occasional Short-toed or Common Treecreeper (depending on the region), Nuthatch, Goldcrest or Firecrest. The southern parts of France receive influxes of Robins, Blackbirds, thrushes, Chiffchaffs and Blackcaps.

• **December** is usually calm, unless there is a cold snap. The north and east of the country may see the arrival of small groups of Bean Geese or wild swans. Ducks are in their winter quarters, as are the coastal waders. Now is a good month to see them, and groups of Brent Geese on the Atlantic coast can be also be very impressive. Thrushes and finches are seen almost anywhere, and rarer species such as Crossbill, Grey Phalarope or Long-tailed Duck are always possible. This is also a good time for looking for northern passerines along the Channel shore – Shore Lark, Snow and Lapland Bunting.

• **January** is much like the previous month. However, if hard weather hits western Europe, France sees the arrival of wildfowl that normally winter in Great Britain or Holland. Hundreds of Goldeneye, Smew, Goosander and Eider occur along the coast and on open inland waters; with them may also occur geese – Bean, Greylag and White-fronted – and wild swans. Waders, particularly Oystercatchers, Curlews, Grey and Golden Plovers and Lapwings also arrive to avoid freezing conditions. A few Rough-legged Buzzards or White-tailed Eagles occur, mainly in the north-east of the country. If, however, there is a warm spell towards the end of the month, Tawny and Eagle Owls can be heard calling and Song Thrushes will start singing ... announcing spring!

Habitats

Once you have been out in the field a few times and gained some experience of what can be seen where, it becomes easier to make the link between any particular habitat and the bird species that you can expect to see. Looking for birds automatically involves looking at the habitat that they live in. Thus conifer forests contain certain species, such as Goldcrest, Coal and Crested Tits and Crossbill, that are less likely to be found elsewhere. Willow thickets are home to numbers of insectivorous passerines in autumn, whilst later in the season elder, mountain ash and blackthorn attract other species. Lakeside reedbeds are the preferred habitat for herons, Bittern, rails, Coot and various warblers, exposed muddy shores provide feeding grounds for waders, wagtails and pipits, and ducks and grebes are usually found on open water, etc. Using the itineraries proposed in this book it is possible not only to discover new sites with familiar species but to target other habitats that might be home to a desired species.

Be prepared!

Before going on the walks included in this book it is best to be well prepared in order to avoid disappointments and to take the terrain into account. Here are a few essential rules:

- Have warm clothing with you (in winter and/or at altitude) and maybe a change of clothes in case of bad weather. Hat, sun-glasses, compass, etc., should all be considered.
- Do wear waterproof boots, especially on the sea shore, around lakes and other wetland areas (lined boots in winter). Elsewhere use comfortable walking boots, not town shoes. A mobile telephone is always a good idea, especially if going alone or far from habitation. And of course it can always be used to inform others if the observer happens to come across an interesting species!
- Binoculars are a must (8 x 30, 8 x 40 or 10 x 40 are the most popular). A telescope is more than useful if looking at ducks, waders or sea-watching.
- Don't forget your field-guide. Remember that the present book in no way helps to identify birds, but is rather a complementary tool.
- Having a notebook is a great help. It allows the observer to take detailed notes of an unfamiliar bird seen in the field. Once back home, it is possible to compare these notes with reference books. Good photos or even a 'record shot' (in the case of a rare species) can be taken using a digital camera placed on or fixed to a telescope (digiscoping).
- A detailed map is always useful, especially in more remote areas or rugged terrain, or in extensive woodland areas. Not only does it help you not to get lost, but also allows you to place the itinerary in a wider geographical context.
- Don't forget drink and food if going out for half a day or more.
- Lastly and most importantly, please show respect for the habitat and for private property. Do not block any public or private entrances, tracks, access to fields etc., when parking. Remember the "Birdwatchers' code" – it all helps towards the success of a walk.

The birdwatchers' code (for more details see www.surfbirds.com or www.rspb.org)

Following the birdwatchers' code is good practice, common sense and should enable us all to enjoy seeing birds, whether in the UK, France or elsewhere in the world

- Avoid disturbing birds and their habitats - the birds' interests should always come first.
- Be an ambassador for birdwatching.
- Know the law and the rules for visiting the countryside, and follow them.
- Send your sightings to the local representative.[1]
- Think about the interests of wildlife and local people before passing on news of a rare bird, especially during the breeding season.

1. All sightings of rare species should be sent, with a detailed description, to the national rarities committee: Comité d'Homologation National, La Corderie Royale, BP 90263, 17305 Rochefort Cedex, France.

SITES

1 *The Île de Rhinau*

2 *Bruch de l'Andlau*

3 *Forêt d'Erstein*

4 *Île du Rohrschollen*

5 *Krafft reservoir at Plobsheim*

6 *Le Hohneck*

7 *Les Îles du Rhin*

8 *Barrage de Michelbach*

Alsace

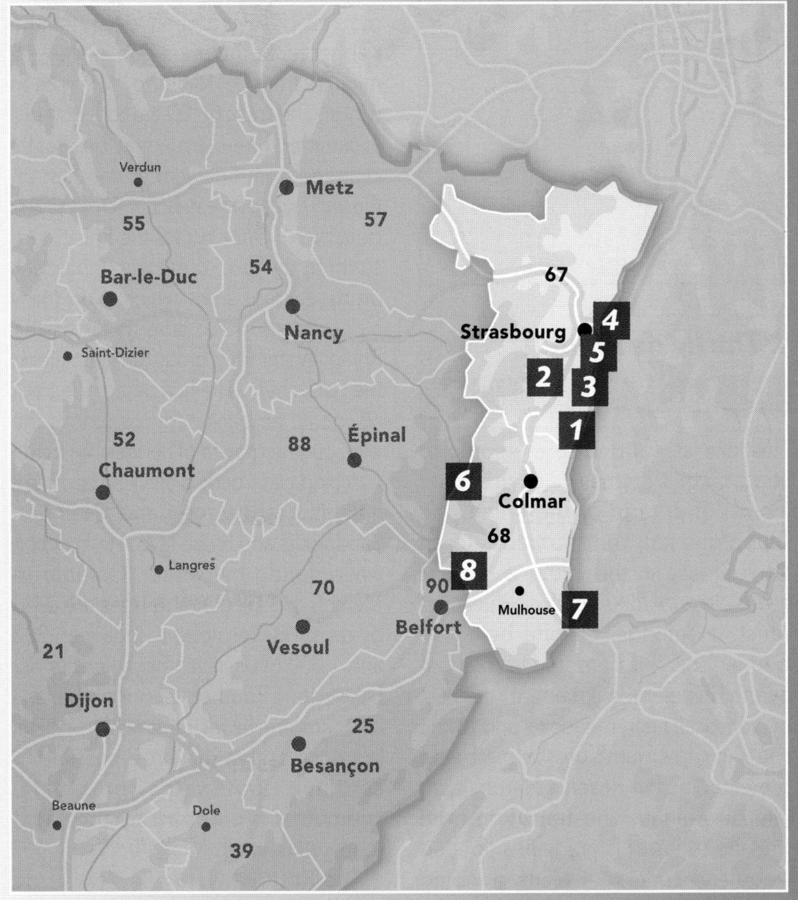

Verdun
Metz
55
57
Bar-le-Duc
54
67
Nancy
Strasbourg
4
5
Saint-Dizier
2
3
1
52
88
Épinal
Chaumont
6
Colmar
68
Langres
8
70
90
Mulhouse
7
Belfort
Vesoul
21
Dijon
25
Besançon
Beaune
Dole
39

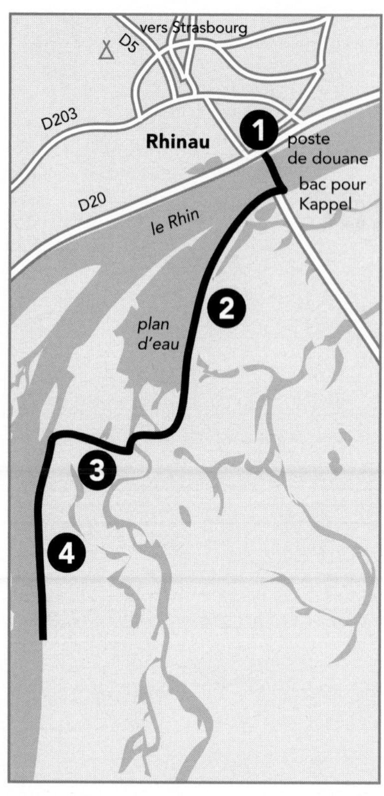

1. The Île de Rhinau

BAS-RHIN (67) *IGN 31*

The lake at Kappel, to the south of Strasbourg, is on the site of an ancient mouth of an arm of the Rhine, the Taubergiessen, transformed into an artificial lake in the 1960s as part of hydro-electric works south of Rhinau, to which it belongs, despite being on German soil. It is bordered to the west by the Rhine embankment, to the east by floristically rich meadows and to the south by luxuriant forest, this being protected as the Réserve Naturelle de l'Île de Rhinau. The transition from wetland to forest is gradual, a flooded woodland zone with many standing dead trees separating the two. The whole of this area is important for passage and wintering duck, with large flocks of Tufted Duck and Pochard, as well as Goldeneye and Goosander, to be seen. In summer there are good numbers of moulting Mute Swans on the river, while breeding species in the woodland include no fewer than six species of woodpecker.

■ Access

From Benfeld, on the N83 south of Strasbourg, take the D5 via Herbsheim and Boofzheim to Rhinau. Here park on the French side of the Rhine just after the customs post (1) and on foot catch the Kappel ferry: there are boats every 15 minutes from 06.15 am to 19.00 pm in winter, and from 06.00 am to 21.00 pm in summer (times given may be greatly changed from one year to another: on the way out ask the exact time of the last boat back). Once across the Rhine, turn south to the lake: there is a good track on its eastern side, which then turns along its southern side as far as the Rhine. Water Rails are often seen along the banks here. The first part of the track (2), on an embankment, overlooks the lake, but the growth of hedges has made watching waterbirds difficult. In late summer, migrant Green and Common Sandpipers and Snipe favour this section while during the winter (October to March), the surrounding trees are used by roosting Cormorants (between 500 and 1,000 birds in January). Farther on, beyond the southern shore of the lake (3) there are fewer observation points but once at the Rhine it is possible to continue southwards for several kilometres (4). Return by the same route, 8 km in all.

The Reserve Naturelle de l'Île de

MUTE SWAN

Rhinau can be reached by taking the D20 south from Rhinau, and following the west bank of the Rhine towards Diebolsheim. After about 4 km turn left towards the Central Hydroélectrique de Rhinau-Sundhouse, and cross the river to reach the island itself. From here on the area is best explored on foot. A road runs south between the river and the woodland all the way to the southern end of the island. Various tracks and paths provide access to the woodland, dense and wet in many places, but sheltering all the woodpeckers of the area, with Icterine Warbler also present in summer.

Calendar

Spring and autumn: Osprey, a few waders (Snipe, Green and Common Sandpipers), Little Gull and Black Tern.

Breeding season: summering Mute Swans (moulting ground), Common Tern. Green, Grey-headed, Black, Great Spotted, Middle Spotted and Lesser Spotted Woodpeckers.

Winter: Great Crested and Little Grebes, Cormorant, Great White Egret, Grey Heron, Mute Swan, Greylag Goose (especially October to December; increasing), dabbling ducks (all species wintering in France), Pochard, Tufted Duck, Goldeneye, Goosander, Water Rail, Moorhen, Coot, Black-headed, Common and Yellow-legged Gulls, Kingfisher. Other less regular species include: Bean Goose, Shelduck, Red-crested Pochard and White-tailed Eagle (which has become more regular of late).

2. *Bruch de l'Andlau*

BAS-RHIN (67) *IGN 12/31*

The Bruch de l'Andlau, south-west of Strasbourg, is an area of wet hay meadows (of great botanical interest) mixed with cultivated fields, separated by woods, thickets and hedgerows. Formerly it was a vast marsh (the word 'bruch' means marshland), but over the years has been drained and unfortunately many of the meadows are now being replaced by fields of maize. Nevertheless, in spite of recent damage, these are the best flood meadows in Alsace, and some protection has recently been afforded parts of the area. It is an important breeding site for Curlew, many birds of prey occur (notably Honey Buzzard, Sparrowhawk, Goshawk and Hobby, as well as Hen Harrier in winter) and there are some interesting passerines (Willow Tit, Icterine and Marsh Warblers).

■ ACCESS

From Strasbourg, either take the N83 south to Erstein or the N422 to Obernai. The D426 between these two towns cuts across the meadows via Schaeffersheim and Meistratzheim. There is unrestricted access to the whole area along the various farm tracks but the meadows themselves should not be entered, particularly in spring and summer when birds are breeding.

3. *Forêt d'Erstein*

BAS-RHIN (67) *IGN 12/31*

The riverine forests of this part of the Rhine valley are exceptional in Europe because of their complex structure, with a wide diversity of woodland species and an abundance of creepers such as ivy and clematis giving them an almost tropical jungle appearance. The Forêt d'Erstein, just south of Strasbourg, is a good example, and although it has partially been spoilt by forestry activities (logging, conifer planting, etc.), a significant area is protected as a Réserve Naturelle. There is an abundance of hole-nesting birds including Tawny Owl, various tits, Nuthatch, Short-toed Treecreeper and several species of woodpecker: Great Spotted, Lesser Spotted and Black Woodpeckers all occur and Middle Spotted is particularly abundant.

CURLEW

Access

From Strasbourg take the D468 through Plobsheim to Krafft. Turn left (eastwards) on the first tarmac road after the canal at Krafft (the réserve naturelle is signposted) and after about 1 km of narrow road, park in the car park. A track eastwards from here leads into the forest where a good network of tracks allows for easy exploration. The most productive visits will be in spring when breeding birds will be singing and setting up territory.

4. Île du Rohrschollen

Bas-Rhin (67) IGN 12

This wooded island bordered to the west by a canal and to the east by the Vieux Rhin, on the outskirts of Strasbourg, is now protected as a réserve naturelle. It is regularly flooded by the river, and this has lead to a particularly rich mix of woodland trees. Red-backed Shrike, Penduline Tit and six species of woodpecker are among the breeding species to be found. In the summer there is a colony of Black-headed Gulls and Common Terns on the German side of the river, and in winter the river holds significant numbers of wildfowl (see next site).

Access

From Strasbourg take the road towards Germany (the Route du Rhin). Turn right at the traffic-lights just before the Vauban bridge, going to 'Zone Portuaire Sud' (Route du Havre). Turn left at the second set of traffic-lights, some 5 or 6 km along this road, following signs to 'Usine Hydroélectrique de Strasbourg'. Once past the power-station fork right along a tarmac road, where a wooden sign indicates the reserve, and park on the embankment. Access is limited to the following times: 08.00 am to 17.00 pm in winter, 05.00 am to 19.00 pm in summer (a movable bollard blocks the road at other times).

5. Krafft reservoir at Plobsheim

Bas-Rhin (67) IGN 12

This compensation reservoir, situated between the previous two sites, is used to regulate the flow of the rivers Ill and Rhine, and is partially protected as a reserve. It is an extremely important area for wintering wildfowl: between 5,000 and 10,000 depending on the winter. Among the commoner species can be found divers, grebes, Red-crested Pochard, Scaup, scoters and Long-tailed Duck on a fairly regular basis. There is also a large winter gull roost, which includes a few Caspian Gulls as well as the more numerous Yellow-legged. Migrants in spring and autumn regularly include Black-necked and Red-necked Grebes, Osprey, Little Gull and Black Tern.

Access

Leave Strasbourg south on the D468 towards Plobsheim, turn left at the traffic-lights in the village, following signs to Rhinland, where it is possible to park. A track leads to the reservoir's edge.

6. Le Hohneck

Haut-Rhin (68)/ Vosges (88) IGN 31

Lying to the west of Colmar, the Hohneck, at 1,363 metres is the second highest point in the Vosges, dominating the woodland and valleys either side of what is essentially a north-south ridge of hills separating Lorraine from Alsace. The famous 'route des crêtes' trail follows its western flank. From the top, looking west, it is possible to look over the classic succession of woodland types from mixed beech and spruce forest, through high altitude beech woodland to alpine meadows. The eastern side is much more rugged: there are two rocky, glacial cirques, the Frankenthal to the north and the Wormspel to the south. Apart from birds, chamois can be seen fairly easily here, especially at Frankenthal.

RING OUZEL

Access

The suggested route will take a full day, and covers 12 km. The more detailed maps, IGN 3618OT and 3619OT, 1:25,000, may be helpful. From Colmar the D417 leads through Munster to the Col de la Schlucht (1), where there is a car park. The 'sentier des roches' way-marked footpath (marked with a blue rectangle) starts 200 metres east from the top of the pass. Along the trail look out for passerines such as Ring Ouzel, Coal and Crested Tits, Goldcrest and Firecrest and Crossbill. It is a good area for Black Woodpeckers, which can be heard calling noisily in early spring. The trail continues for 2 km through several rocky outcrops and 'natural' stands of spruce. Beyond this it runs through mixed beech/spruce woodland and leads to a wide forest track which climbs to the right to the Frankenthal cirque. Look for Alpine Accentor (1 or 2 pairs) in the cirque on the walk up, especially on the northern slopes. On the upper moors look for Meadow and Water Pipits. Pass the farm on the moraine (2) and skirt the peat bog (of great botanical interest), then take the steep track that climbs to the Col de Falimont pass, where Wheatear occur. Skirt the side of the cirque towards the Col du Schaeferthal pass (3). This affords views of moorland to the right and the southern side of the cirque to the left. In late May/early June, when the young have left the nest, Peregrines are often seen here, and other birds of prey such as Kestrel, Sparrowhawk or Honey Buzzard also occur. From the pass there are two possibilities: either (a) return directly westwards by skirting the northern edge of the Wormspel cirque as far as the Col du Fond, and, on the way, stop at one of the outcrops to look into the cirque. Rock Bunting may be seen in areas of rocky scrub. Citril Finch occurs on the moorland edge, as do Dunnock and Ring Ouzel. Alternatively (b) descend towards the lac de Schiessrothried (4), and skirt the right-hand side of this before climbing to the pass via the 'Fond-du-Cirque' footpath. Either way, from the Col

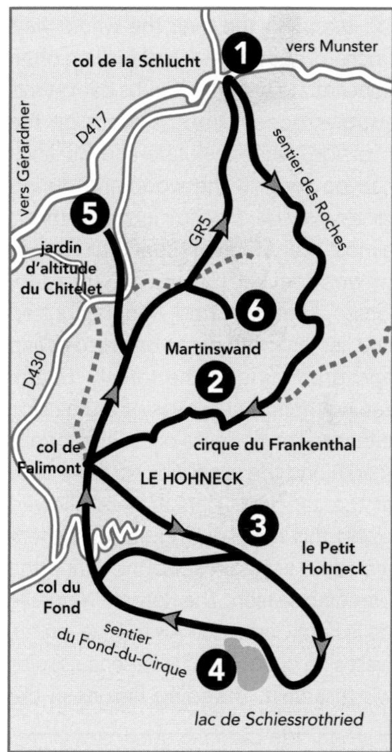

du Fond head directly north via the western side of the Hohneck (GR5 footpath, marked with red rectangles) to the Col de Falimont. Beyond here the Chitelet high altitude garden (5) is worth a visit, time permitting. Later, a short detour via the high ground of Martinswand (6) is worthwhile for a splendid view over the Hohneck and the Frankenthal. From here follow the ridge northwards, still on the GR5, back to the starting point.

Calendar

Spring and autumn: on the high, bare alpine meadows of the Hohneck and the Kastelberg to the south, Dotterel and Snow Bunting are regular migrants. *Breeding season*: Peregrine, Black Woodpecker, Water, Meadow and Tree Pipits, Alpine Accentor (rare), Wheatear, Ring Ouzel, Raven, Nutcracker, Citril Finch, Crossbill, Rock Bunting. Rock Thrush nested in 1991.

7. Les Îles du Rhin

Haut-Rhin (68) *IGN 31*

Despite the use of the plural, this site, between Mulhouse and Basel, comprises just one island, with the Rhine on one side and the Grand Canal d'Alsace (created in 1928) on the other. Much of the island's 100 hectares is deciduous woodland, with a few maize fields and dry meadows as well. On the French side the Rhine is bordered with willows. In 1870 the river was canalised and deep dredging gave rise to the appearance of two rocky bars (Barres d'Istein) which were responsible for the water course being no longer navigable. When the river is low, as in winter, these bars slow the flow of water, and this encourages the growth of aquatic plants and the presence of zebra mussels. However cold the winter, the Rhine never freezes over, and in some years this may be the only available open water in Alsace. Consequently it is an important refuge for wintering wildfowl, both diving ducks and surface feeders, with a good chance of a rarity under such conditions in cold winters. Note that the light makes for easier watching on the canal in the morning and the Rhine in the afternoon.

Access

From Mulhouse take the A35 motorway south towards Basel/Bâle, leave at the St.-Louis exit (No. 35) and take the D468 northwards towards Kembs. Turn right at Loéchlé and continue past the power-station to reach the canal-side car park and lock (1). From here walk down to the causeway (2), a good observation point. In winter Mute Swans are numerous, there are also many ducks on the canal, particularly Pochard and Tufted Duck. By walking upstream along the old towpath by the Rhine the river can be viewed easily. In winter wildfowl include Mallard, Pochard and Tufted Duck, but also Goldeneye, Goosander and a variety of rarer species. On autumn migration a good range of waders passes through, and Common Sandpipers sometimes remain through the winter. From Barres d'Istein (3) a track cuts back across to the other side of the island (4) for a shorter circuit of about 4 km back to the car park. The jetty (5) provides a viewpoint along the canal. At the end of the jetty, there is often a flock of Gadwall, Wigeon and Pintail and a large roost of Cormorants and Black-headed Gulls occurs each winter on the end of the island. For a longer circuit (12 km) continue along the towpath (4) to the far end of the island (6), scanning the river the whole way. Pochard, Tufted Duck and Mallard often concentrate near the Kembs dam at this southern end. Dippers occur on the riverside, while Fieldfare and Bullfinch can be seen in the woodland during winter. Grey Herons occur in small numbers almost everywhere. In spring six species of woodpecker (Black, Grey-headed, Green, Great Spotted, Middle Spotted and Lesser Spotted) can be heard calling and drumming in the forest, though seeing them is never easy. Return using either the same route or use the tarmac road along the canal side to arrive back at the car park. Cars are not allowed along this road, and in addition there are some access restrictions during the breeding season. The Réserve Naturelle de la Petit Camargue Alsacienne, on the west side of the canal at Rosenau, is also worth a visit. Breeding herons in the

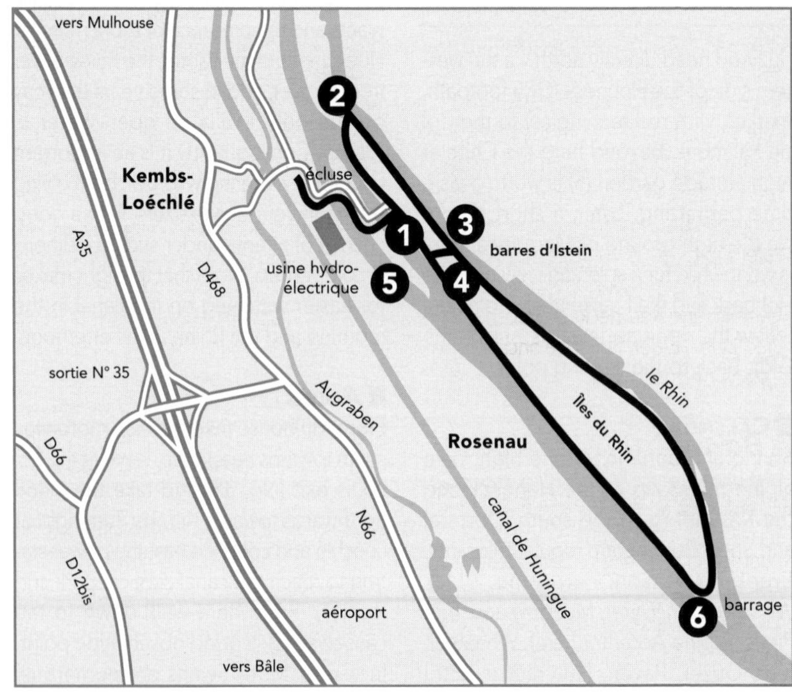

TUFTED DUCK

damp woodland here include Little Bittern, and there is a rich mix of dragonflies, amphibians and wetland flora.

Calendar

Spring: Nesting Grey Heron, Black Kite, six species of woodpecker, Nightingale, Golden Oriole.
Autumn: migrant waders, Osprey, Swift, hirundines, warblers, Firecrest, Song Thrush and roaming tit flocks throughout the day.
Winter. Great Crested and Little Grebes, Mute Swan, Teal, Mallard, Pintail, Wigeon, Pochard, Tufted Duck, Goldeneye, Goosander, Coot, Snipe, Common Sandpiper, Black-headed Gull, Kingfisher, Water Pipit, White Wagtail, Dipper. Rarer birds each year may include: divers, Slavonian and Red-necked Grebes, Long-tailed Duck, Eider. Fieldfare and Bullfinch in areas of buckthorn.

8. Barrage de Michelbach

HAUT-RHIN (68) *IGN 31*

Situated at the foot of the Vosges, about halfway between Mulhouse and Belfort, this artifical lake, 90 hectares in area, was built in 1982 to regulate the flow of the nearby River Doller. It has recently been given the status of réserve naturelle, and with no sailing or fishing allowed, has become an important refuge with a steadily increasing list of birds recorded. It is worth a visit at any time of year, although it may freeze over in winter. Both diving and surface-feeding ducks occur, along with grebes, Cormorant and Grey Heron. Ospreys occur on both spring and autumn passage, and Hobbies come to feed on dragonflies during the summer. There is a small colony of Black-headed Gulls on a raft, common woodland species nearby and various waders occur on both spring and autumn migration. From Mulhouse take the N66 west towards Thann, from where various minor roads lead south via Aspach-le-Haut to Michelbach. There is a car park and information board by the lake; from here a track on the embankment runs around the lake, passing through an orchard and woodland, making a nice walk and enabling the whole area to be scanned easily.

SITES

1 *Bassin d'Arcachon north: Audenge*

2 *Marais de Bruges*

3 *Pointe de Grave and the Gironde estuary*

4 *Bassin d'Arcachon south: Le Teich*

5 *Pointe du Cap-Ferret*

6 *Hossegor and Capbreton*

7 *Barthes de l'Adour*

8 *Captieux and Arjuzanx*

9 *Réserve naturelle de la Mazière-Villeton*

10 *Les Landes: Forêt de Campet*

11 *Retinues de la Ganne and du Brayssou*

12 *The Lot and Garonne valleys near Aiguillon*

13 *Lac d'Artix*

14 *Hendaye and the bay of Txingudi*

15 *Col d'Organbidexka*

16 *Vallée d'Ossau*

Aquitaine

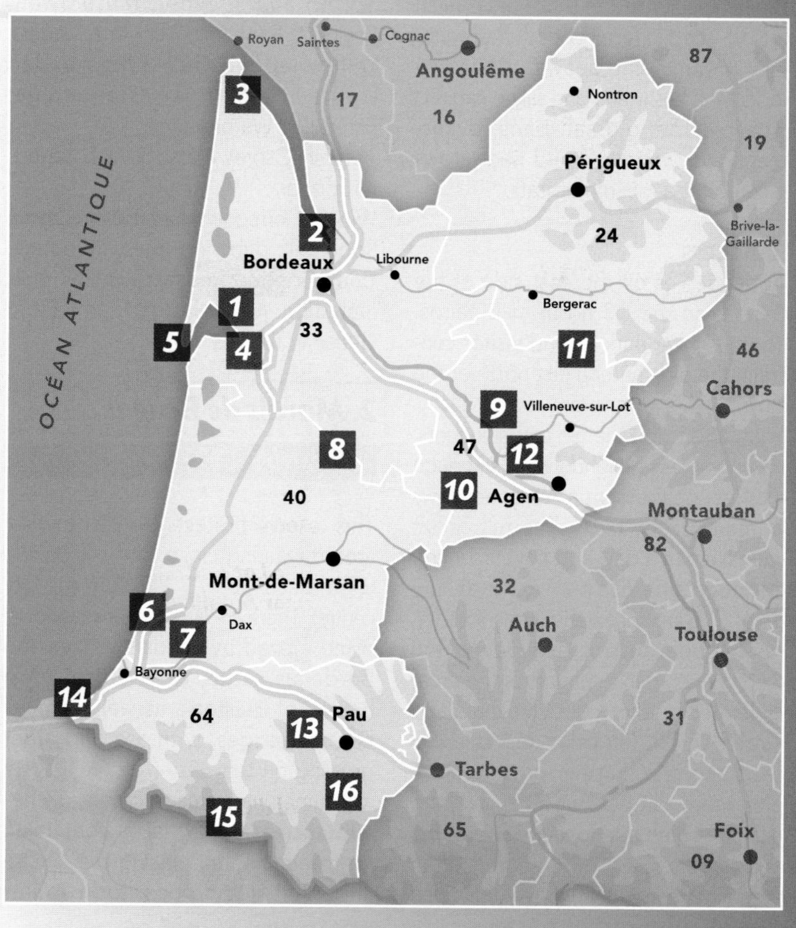

Royan
Saintes
Cognac
Angoulême
87
17
16
Nontron
19
OCÉAN ATLANTIQUE
Périgueux
Brive-la-Gaillarde
24
Bordeaux
Libourne
Bergerac
33
46
Cahors
Villeneuve-sur-Lot
47
40
Agen
Montauban
82
Mont-de-Marsan
32
Dax
Auch
Toulouse
Bayonne
64
Pau
31
Tarbes
65
Foix
09
1
2
3
4
5
6
7
8
9
10
11
12
13
14
15
16

1. Bassin d'Arcachon north: Audenge

Gironde (33) IGN 46/55

The huge tidal inlet of the Bassin d'Arcachon is one of the most significant wetland sites on the west coast of France, the vast mud-flats and eel-grass beds in the bay providing food for a profusion of waders and wildfowl. The former salt-pans of the 'Domaine de Certes' at Audenge, covering some 400 hectares, is one of the largest areas of embanked marsh remaining, with a similar species mix to those of Le Teich (site 4). The site receives both freshwater (via streams) and seawater (via sea locks) with freshwater and saline habitats side-by-side: old salt-pans, dykes, meadows, woodland and hedgerows making for a mix of habitats.

Access

Audenge lies on the east side of the Bassin, on the D3 north of Biganos. There is a car park (1) and visitor centre in the old château just north of the town, with a Cormorant roost nearby. Footpaths follow the old embankments, making access straightforward, although a telescope is essential for good views of many of the birds. The full circuit will take half a day, and covers 14 km, although one can turn back at any point. The area of extensive marshes (2), formed from ancient meanders of the Certes river, is in the heart of the area. Here grebes, diving duck (Pochard and Tufted Duck), Shoveler and Gadwall feed and rest. Farther on, the large elongated salt-pans at (3) and (5) are used as a high tide roost by Spoonbills and waders. Great White Egrets often feed and Peregrine hunt over this open area. The tamarisk hedges (4) and (7) are used by passerines. From April onwards White-spotted Bluethroat, Nightingale, Whitethroat and Blue-headed Wagtail can be found singing. The eel-grass beds of the Bassin (6), uncovered at low tide, provide a feeding ground for many waders and food for Brent Goose, Wigeon and Mute Swan. Black Kites are omnipresent in summer, with 60 pairs nesting in the pine wood (8) north of the chateau, although there is no public access here.

Calendar

Spring and summer: Mute Swan, Shelduck, Spoonbill, Black Kite, waders, Yellow-legged Gull, Blue-headed Wagtail, Bluethroat, Nightingale, Fan-tailed Warbler.
Autumn: Osprey, Marsh Harrier, waders, Kingfisher.
Winter: Cormorant, Great White Egret, Spoonbill, dabbling duck, Peregrine, Coot, Spotted Redshank, many gulls including Yellow-legged; and Brent Geese in the bay.

2. Marais de Bruges

Gironde (33) IGN 46/55

This reserve protects the last marshy area remaining close to the outskirts of Bordeaux (only 7 km from the city centre). There are large water-meadows, some grazed by Landais ponies and Bordelais cattle, two ancient local breeds of livestock, as well as many natural hedges, with ash and alder growing on the wetter ground. There are numerous drainage canals, ditches and ancient oxbow lakes containing permanent water, making the site an important staging post for migrants

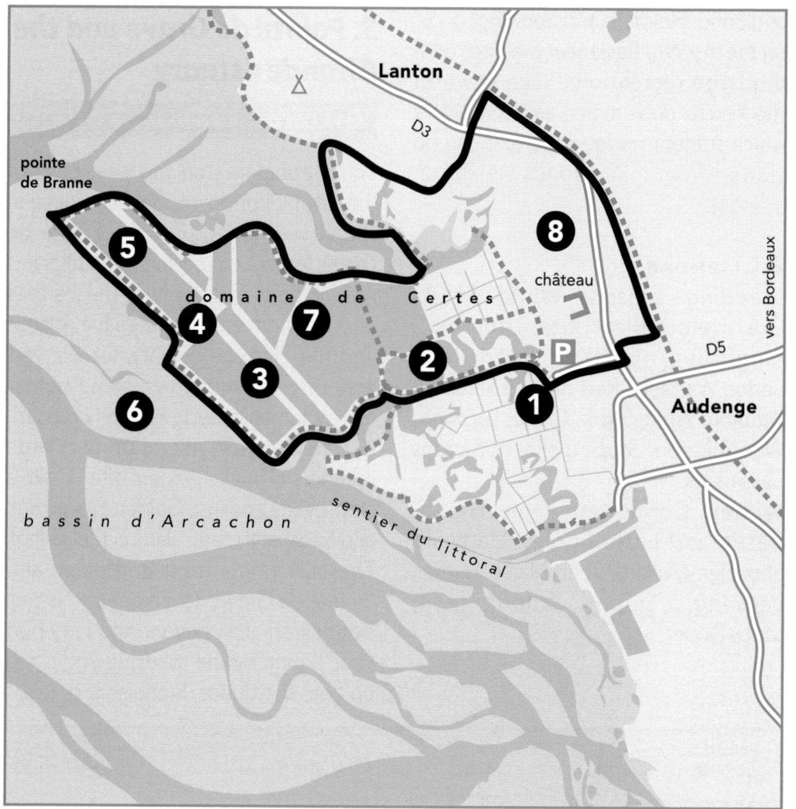

and a breeding site for a number of interesting species.

■ Access

The reserve is just north of Bordeaux, close to the ring-road. Leave this at exit 6 and take the D210 towards Blanquefort – the 'réserve naturelle' is signposted from the first junction, with its entrance on the right just before the village. There is room to park just before the level crossing (1). Cross with care, and walk along the track between woodland on one side and meadows on the other to reach the warden's office in some old farm buildings. The reserve, managed by SEPANSO, is officially open from 10.00 am to 18.00 pm, closed on Thursday and Friday. An information board beyond the farm gives details of access, though essentially this is a linear track of about 1 km in length out into the reserve, passing several hides that overlook various pools and damp woodland. There is a large heronry in the trees beyond the third hide. It is a good place in spring and summer for Black Kite, Buzzard, Honey Buzzard, Short-toed Eagle and Kestrel, and Red-backed Shrikes nest in the more natural hedgerows. White Stork, Purple and Night Herons often feed in the ponds. During the autumn migration period many species of waders may be seen. Golden Plover, Lapwing, Snipe and Jack Snipe are found on the meadows in winter and four species of thrush (Mistle and Song, Fieldfare and Redwing) occur on the reserve. Back near the ring road, the large recreational lake is worth checking for ducks, egrets and Cormorants which sometimes feed there. It can be viewed from minor roads which run round it.

Calendar

Breeding season: White Stork, Grey Heron, Black Kite, Little Owl, Kingfisher, Cetti's, Reed and Sedge Warblers, Red-backed Shrike.
Autumn: White Stork, Crane, Lapwing, Woodpigeon, Stock Dove, numerous passerines.
Winter: Cormorant, Grey Heron, Cattle and Little Egrets, Gadwall, Shoveler, Mallard, Teal, Marsh Harrier, Lapwing, Snipe, Woodpigeon, Stock Dove.

3. Pointe de Grave and the Gironde estuary

Gironde (33) *IGN 46*

The Medoc area on the west bank of the River Gironde, roughly triangular in shape with its apex at the Pointe de Grave, forms a natural funnel for migrants moving north in the spring. The marshes at its northern end, between the Atlantic and the Gironde estuary, form a vast area of water-meadows, some bordered by tamarisk hedges. Many passerines are seen on migration and large numbers of inland waders often make a stop-over: Lapwing, Golden Plover, Ruff and Redshank (particularly in the spring). The N215 runs from Bordeaux, and 'Pointe de Grave/Royan par bac' is well signposted. Just beyond the ferry port ('bac'), park by the roadside and climb up onto the dunes. In the spring, this is

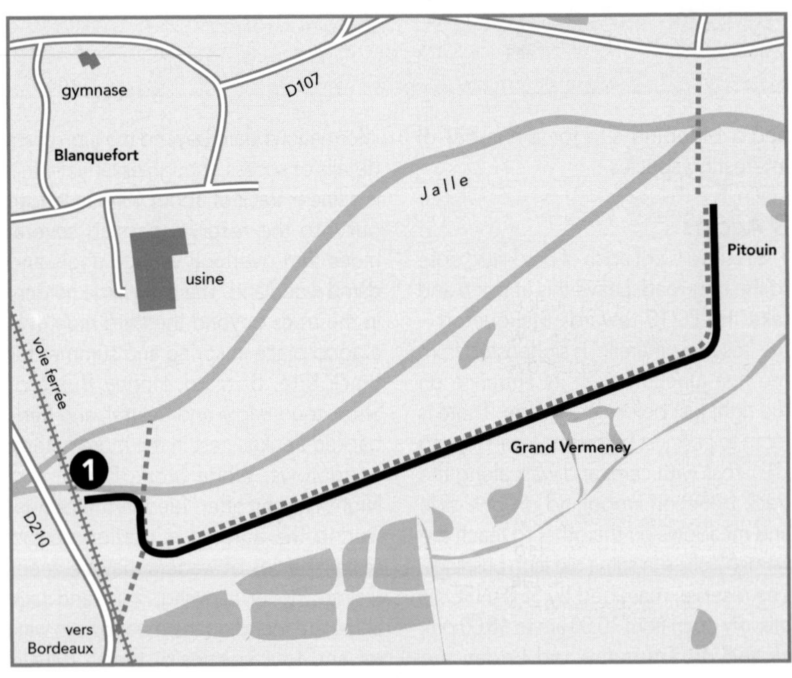

where watchers gather to count the birds passing overhead and out across the river. For the estuary, return through the town and keep left at the Soulac-sur-Mer turning and head towards the 'zone portuaire', where there is a good mixture of wetland habitat either side. The minor road from Neyran through Talais, St.-Vivien and on to Valeyrac crosses more of the same, with the 'port de Neyran' affording good views over the extensive mudflats sheltered behind the port area. Cattle and Little Egrets, Blue-headed Wagtails and Fan-tailed Warblers are typical of the fields throughout. The area is particularly interesting in spring for the following species: Marsh, Hen and Montagu's Harriers, Short-toed Eagle and Hobby, all of which nest nearby and come to the marshes to hunt.

4. Bassin d'Arcachon south: Le Teich

GIRONDE (33) IGN 46/55

The Parc Ornithologique du Teich is one of the most impressive bird reserves in France – over 260 species have been recorded. The area was once salt marshes, dyked in the 18th century for fish farming, and the lagoons have been converted into a whole range of wetland habitats. Dabbling and diving duck of every sort occur on migration and in winter, many waders including Avocet over-winter, as do Spoonbill and White Stork. There is a large Cormorant roost and a mixed heron colony (Grey and Night Herons, Little and Cattle Egrets). White Stork, Shelduck, Bluethroat and various other wetland passerines also nest. The A63/A660 (toll-free) and the N250 both bring you quickly from Bordeaux to the south side of the Bassin. Just west of Biganos, the D650 crosses the Eyre, and there is an information centre here, the Maison de la Nature, with footpaths taking you through riverine woodland (Firecrest, Short-toed Treecreeper, etc.) as far as Le Teich itself, with other loops through wet meadows and marshes. Alternatively continue on the road for another 3 km, and the reserve is well signposted to the right. The centre is open from 10.00 am to 19.00 pm, and is very well worth the entrance fee. It covers some 120 hectares with 6 km of trails and twenty hides. For more information, consult: http://www.parc-ornithologique-du-teich.com.

5. Pointe du Cap-Ferret

GIRONDE (33) IGN 46/55

This is another migration watch-point, like the Pointe de Grave, only this time of more interest in the autumn. Between September and November, more than 100 different species can be seen. It is a very good place for passage passerines (wagtails, larger thrushes including Ring Ouzel, large numbers of finches, Ortolan Bunting). More than a dozen species of birds of prey occur regularly including both kites, Hobby, Peregrine, Merlin, Kestrel, Osprey and the three harriers. Other species include storks, Spoonbill, Bee-eater and hirundines and the sea-watching can be good (Cory's and Balearic Shearwaters, Gannet, gulls and terns). Cap-Ferret is at the end of the D106 west from Bordeaux, with a public car park next to the Restaurant le Mirador. An interpretive trail from here leads through the dunes, whose fragile vegetation is under constant threat of erosion, so please keep to the paths. During the summer, Sandwich Terns from the huge colony on the Banc d'Arguin out to the south-west can be seen feeding offshore. This sandy island reserve can be visited by boat trips running out of Arcachon.

6. Hossegor and Capbreton

LANDES (40) *IGN 62*

The Lac d'Hossegor is a natural tidal lake among coastal sand dunes, the latter mostly occupied by rather up-market houses and hotels, which add variety and a degree of tranquillity to the area. Hunting is forbidden. At low tide, extensive mud and sand banks are exposed, especially at the southern end. A narrow stone-banked channel joins the lake to the marina at Capbreton, where the breakwaters at the river mouth are one of the better spots for sea-watching along this stretch of coast. The lake attracts a wide range of waders on both spring and autumn passage, and ducks and grebes through the winter. It is also a noted site for gulls, Mediterranean being especially common throughout the winter, but it is also one of the more regular sites for Ring-billed Gull.

BLACK-HEADED GULL

ACCESS

From exit 7 on the A62, head for Hossegor, where the lake is well-signposted. A road runs close to the shore along the east side, rather more distantly on the west. There are several parking places, and a footpath by the water's edge allows easy access. One possible route (covering some 4½ km) starts from the car park (1), a good place for looking over the northern part of the lake, favoured by Great Northern and Red-throated Divers. Go southwards as far as Les Mimosas (2): smaller waders congregate here on the mudflats. During a rising or receding tide many gulls pass between the lake and the sea and there is a gull roost at high tide. Cross the bridge (3) (check the channel for ducks) to reach the northern breakwater (4). For the southern breakwater (5), return to the port and follow signs for the Vieux Port and the casino. There is ample parking here, and the flat roof of the shopping arcade on the seafront provides an excellent viewpoint. Although gale conditions at Capbreton provide the most exciting birding, you have a much better chance of seeing feeding divers, grebes and ducks if the sea is calm.

CALENDAR

Spring and autumn: numerous waders, including Black-winged Stilt, and various ducks. From the breakwater: Greylag Geese, sometimes Spoonbill and Sabine's Gull (in autumn), flocks of migrant passerines.

Winter: On the lake, divers, Cormorant, Golden Plover, Dunlin, godwits, Curlew, various other waders, Black-headed, Little, Mediterranean, Herring, Yellow-legged, Lesser and Great Black-backed and Common Gulls. From the breakwaters: Black-throated and

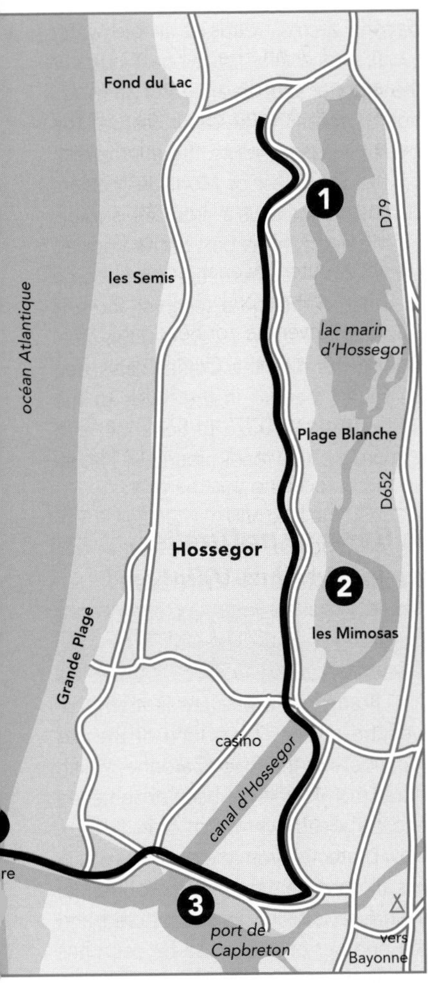

Great Northern Divers, Eider, Kittiwake, Razorbill, sometimes Gannet, shearwaters and petrels.

7. Barthes de l'Adour

LANDES (40) *IGN 62/69*

The lower part of the River Adour between Dax and Bayonne winds its way though a wide valley which is liable to flooding in winter, these flood meadows being called 'barthes' locally. In places these form vast open meadows, while in others they are more enclosed with damp woodland. The most important site, the Reserve des Barthes, is usually known under the name of the nearest village to it, St.-Martin-de-Seignanx, just north-east of Bayonne. From St.-Martin take the D126 south to where it drops down to the River Adour floodplain, and turn left along a lane signposted 'reserve de faune'. The narrow road winds past several damp fields, then makes a sharp right-hand bend, a short way after which a muddy track to the left brings you to the reserve entrance. Alternatively, take the D74 out of Bayonne, following the bank of the River Adour, until a sign 'maison de retraite' indicates a minor lane to the left which takes you to the same spot. A public tower hide provides excellent views over the main area. The star species here is Spotted Eagle, up to three of which have been seen in recent years, generally between late November and early March. Other wintering raptors include Hen and Marsh Harriers, Peregrine and the occasional White-tailed Eagle, in addition to resident Buzzard, Kestrel and Sparrowhawk. Osprey are regular on passage. Greylag Geese, Wigeon, Teal, Shoveler, Gadwall, Pintail, Curlew and Lapwing are all present in good numbers throughout the winter. There is a winter roost of several hundred Cattle Egrets. Crane, Spoonbill, Great White Egret and even one or two White Storks are regular winter visitors, the latter nesting at the reserve.

A second area worth visiting is around Saubusse, south-west of Dax, accessed along the N124 and then left along the D17 to the river bridge. From here, it is possible to follow the right bank of the river downstream as far as the N117 near Port-de-Lanne (though the last section is best covered on foot). Alternatively, various tracks lead out into the fields between Saubusse and Rivière, just to the north-east. Again, Cattle and Little Egret, White Stork, Black Kite, Hobby and Golden Oriole are among breeding species, with Lapwing, Curlew and other waders on passage.

8. Captieux and Arjuzanx

Landes (40) *IGN 62*

Over the past few years, the maize fields of the Landes have become France's most important area for wintering Cranes, sometimes hosting over 20,000 birds, thanks in part to the availability of secure roosting sites at the former Arjuzanx lignite mine and the military camp at Captieux. They are usually present from mid October through to early March, with numbers swelled during the migration periods. Along with them are large numbers of seed-eating passerines, Fieldfares, Redwings and other thrushes, with predators such as Hen Harrier, Buzzard, Sparrowhawk and Merlin all attracted by the wealth of prey. There have also been recent reports of White-tailed Eagle here.

Access

Coming south from the A62 at Langon, through Captieux on the D932, the military camp is obvious on the right, and a short distance south a minor road opposite the D24 turning to Bourriot-Bergonce leads to the fields where the Cranes often feed. An information board marks the start of the best area, but the birds can be dispersed quite widely. There is a hide on the left-hand side of the road before you reach some silos (Coop de Pau, Sicapan). Further on, beyond a cross-roads at an old water tower, another information board indicates the importance of the area, and warns you not to enter the fields or disturb the birds. Arjuzanx lies to the south-west, on the D38 west of Mont-de-Marsan. Just before the town a large lake is visible on the right; this is part of the flooded mine-workings where the Cranes come to roost. Although a reserve, there is currently little or no access into this area. During the day, the Cranes can often be found feeding in the fields to the north; take the D325 to Solferino, and explore the side roads around Le Platiet.

9. Réserve naturelle de la Mazière-Villeton

Lot-et-Garonne (47) *IGN 56*

The Étang de la Mazière is a strip of wetland on the line of one of the old meanders of the River Garonne, which like so many others has been straightened and canalised over much of its length. Now protected from the drainage which has affected the surrounding countryside, the habitat is being carefully restored, and the number of species to be seen has steadily increased. In summer there is a small heronry, mainly Grey Heron, but Purple and Night Heron also occur, and passerines include Woodchat Shrike. Winter visitors and passage migrants include Little and Great White Egrets, Little Grebe, various surface-feeding ducks, Snipe and Jack Snipe, Spotted Crake, and both Penduline and Bearded Tits. There is an active ringing programme, with around 20,000 birds ringed here. The reserve lies between the A62 and the Garonne at Tonneins. From here, take the D120 over the river, then the second right, signposted 'réserve naturelle'. The reserve centre lies a short distance to the right of this road. However, as the habitat is very fragile, all visits need to be arranged in advance (Tel. 05 53 88 02 57), and very little can be seen without entering the reserve itself.

10. Les Landes: Forêt de Campet

LOT-ET-GARONNE (47) *IGN 56*

Les Landes is a vast triangle of former marsh, heath and dunes bounded by the 230 km of coast from the Pointe de Grave to Bayonne, and stretching 100 km inland. Despite many attempts, it was not until the 19th century that the dunes were finally stabilised and the land drained, most of it to be replanted with conifers, at 950,000 hectares the largest forest in western Europe. Although seemingly a wild and undisturbed area, much of the forest can be unproductive as far as birds are concerned, and it is best to look for areas where large clearings interspersed with varied age woodland have been opened up. One such area is the Forêt de Campet, in the eastern part of the forest. Species such as Hen and Montagu's Harrier, Dartford Warbler, Nightjar and Tree Pipit occur and it is also worth keeping an eye out for

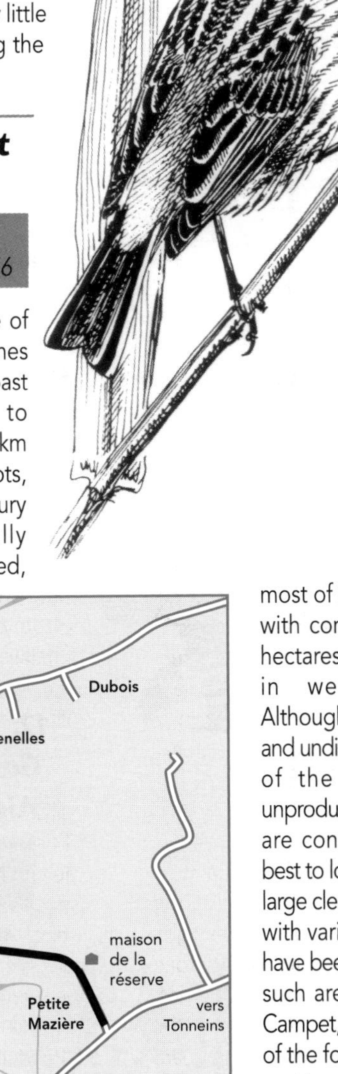

REED BUNTING

Borde Vieille
l'Ourbise
Dubois
Senelles
Grande Mazière
maison de la réserve
Petite Mazière
vers Tonneins
ruisseau de la Mazière
chalet d'accueil
P
Castagnon
Castets
vers Villeton

Short-toed Eagle here as elsewhere in the forest. The D655 south-east from Casteljaloux passes the eastern edge of this area, and the D8 west from exit 6 on the A62 crosses the northern side; minor roads and forest paths can be used for further exploration.

11. Retinues de la Ganne and du Brayssou

Lot-et-Garonne (47)

IGN 56

These two relatively new reservoirs, in the hilly countryside about 30 km south-east of Bergerac, although not of outstanding interest, can turn up some surprises, especially during migration periods and in the winter. In the summer there is a small nesting population of Great Crested Grebes (15-20 pairs), and Hobby is one of the breeding raptors of the surrounding wooded farmland. Numbers of dabbling ducks are dominated by Mallard, of course, but diving ducks such as Pochard also make an appearance in winter. The lakes are quite shallow, and the muddy shoreline attracts waders, gulls, herons and egrets on occasion when the water levels are low.

From Bergerac take the N21 south to Castillonnès, then the D2 east to Villeréal. From here take the D626 north-east for about 3 km, and take the second lane right after crossing the River Dropt. Both lakes are signposted from here. The smaller (45 hectare) Retinue de la Ganne is just east of Bariats, and can be viewed from its western shore. The larger Retinue du Brayssou (78 hectares) lies just to the east. It is possible to park near the dam at the western end and a footpath from here leads to a hide about halfway along the southern shore.

HOBBY

12. The Lot and Garonne valleys near Aiguillon

Lot-et-Garonne (47)

IGN 56

The valleys of the Lot and Garonne are important spring and autumn migration routes, the two rivers joining at Aiguillon, on the N113 south of Tonneins. An excellent viewpoint is the Pech de Berre, the southernmost point a range of calcareous hillsides, mostly covered with woodland and scrub. It is accessed by leaving the

Aiguillon to Tonneins road into the village of Nicole, then taking a minor road marked 'panorama' which winds steeply up to plateau dominated by a crucifix. During the summer, Black Kites are ever-present, but other birds of prey can be seen on migration, when it is a focus for birds moving along the escarpment, both in spring and autumn. Woodlark and Cirl Bunting breed in the area, and the wide range of other species recorded here has included Bee-eater and Great Spotted Cuckoo.

13. *Lac d'Artix*

PYRÉNÉES-ATLANTIQUES (64) *IGN 69*

The Gave de Pau, one of the larger Pyrenean rivers, has been dammed at Artix for hydro-electric purposes, and the resulting lake is now an important protected zone, of interest throughout the year. There are large areas of wet woodland, mingled with islands, mudflats and open channels, (difficult to penetrate), which hold large numbers of ducks and waders during the winter and times of migration. There is also an important mixed heronry. Access to either the lake or the reserve is forbidden. The best birdwatching is from the reinforced embankments, in the morning or evening.

ACCESS

Artix is a small town on the N117 about halfway between Pau and Orthez. Where the D281 south to Mourenx crosses the river, there is a small car park (1) on the left-hand side of the road, with a signboard explaining what can be seen at the reserve. Either scan from the car park, or walk back over the bridge (2) and along the path by the riverside to explore the edges of the damp woodland, passing the main heronry (3) – a walk of 2 km there and back.

East of Artix, two artificial lakes a short way from the river are also worth checking, particularly during migration periods. The Lac d'Uzein is immediately northwest

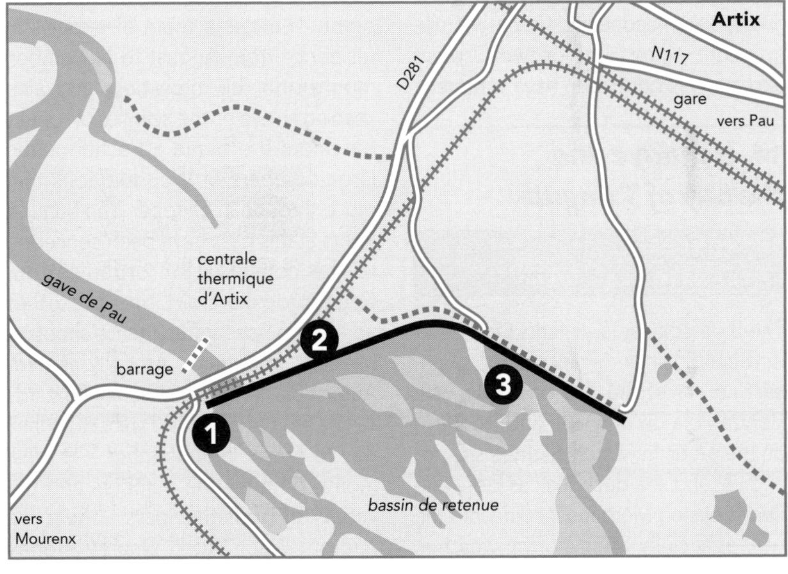

of Pau-Pyrénées airport, and a second lake lies further along the same valley near Mazerolles and Momas. West of Artix, and close to Orthez, is a réserve ornithologique at Biron, just east of exit 8 on the A64. This is a reserve very much aimed at the general public, but Black-winged Stilts have bred recently, and again is good for migrants.

Calendar

Spring: several mixed heron colonies (Grey and Night Herons, Little and Cattle Egrets), Gadwall, Black-headed and Yellow-legged Gulls. Many migrants, particularly ducks and waders. The willows often hold migrant passerines. Black Kite, Osprey, Marsh Harrier and Hobby also occur.

Autumn: large numbers of herons, waders and Spoonbill: sometimes White Stork and Crane on migration as well as many raptors and passerines.

Winter: Little Grebe, Cormorant, Grey Heron, Little Egret, many Mallard, Shoveler, Pintail, Wigeon, Gadwall, Teal, Tufted Duck and Pochard, Lapwing, Snipe, Black-headed and Common Gulls. In recent winters one or two Ospreys and a few Night Heron have wintered.

14. Hendaye and the bay of Txingudi

Pyrénées-Atlantiques (64) *IGN 69*

The Bidassoa estuary marks the border between Spain and France at the south-east corner of the Bay of Biscay, with Hondarribia on one side and Hendaye on the other. In winter, all three species of diver and sea-duck such as Eider and Red-breasted Merganser come into the bay, especially after stormy weather. Mediterranean Gulls are present throughout the winter in good numbers, with Little Gulls on passage and after winter gales. Offshore passage can be good in autumn, especially when the wind is from the north-west. The marshy areas attract migrants at both seasons, not just ducks and waders, but egrets, Spoonbills, Bluethroat and Penduline Tit. The river can be viewed from the roadside in Hendaye town in several places and there is a viewing platform by a roundabout at the end of the Boulevard du Général Leclerc which looks across to the small sandy Île des Oiseaux, which has reserve status. This is the best area for waders, gulls and terns which gather here to roost at high tide.

15. Col d'Organbidexka

Pyrénées-Atlantiques (64) *IGN 69*

The Col d'Organbidexka, at the western end of the Pyrenees, is probably France's best known raptor migration watch-point. There is a team of experts in residence from August to November, monitoring the migration, and also keeping an eye on the activities of hunters for whom the prime attraction is the large numbers of Woodpigeons that move through in October. The hunting rights at this pass have been conceded to the conservation organisation, Organbidexka Col Libre, but other adjacent passes suffer intense shooting pressure in autumn. As early as mid-August Black Kites and Honey Buzzards can be seen crossing the Pyrenees on their way to Africa. In September – an ideal month both for the numbers and the variety of birds that pass – there are migrant Black Stork, Osprey, Honey

RED KITE

Buzzard, Hobby, Marsh Harrier and large numbers of Swallows, particularly in the second half of the month. In October it is the turn of Red Kite, Buzzard and Sparrowhawk, accompanied, from the middle of the month onwards, by large numbers of Woodpigeons and many passerines such as Skylark, Meadow Pipit and Chaffinch. At the end of the month and especially in early November the migration season ends with the passage of the Cranes on their way to Spain.

The nearest village is Larrau, at the foot of one of the passes into Spain. However, from the village take the D19 towards St.-Jean-Pied-de-Port, Bayonne and Orthez. The pass is about 10 km from Larrau, before the Chalets d'Iraty. For more information contact OCL, 11, rue Bourgneuf, 64100 Bayonne (Tel: 05 59 25 62 03). They always welcome volunteer watchers, and also organise counts at two other passes, Lindux and Lizarrieta, further to the west.

16. Vallée d'Ossau

PYRÉNÉES-ATLANTIQUES (64) *IGN 69*

The Ossau is one of the most beautiful and ornithologically interesting valleys of the Pyrenees, running directly south from Pau to cross the border at the Col du Portalet. All the large raptors are there: Red and Black Kites, Golden Eagle, Griffon and Egyptian Vultures, Lammergeier, and Peregrine. The best place to start is the 'Falaise aux Vautours' visitor centre, well signposted at Aste-Béon, between Arudy and Laruns. CCTV cameras at the nests beam pictures live to the centre, while the birds themselves can be seen soaring all along this stretch of the valley. There are many footpaths in this general area for further exploration. The road west from Bielle over the Col de Marie Blanque is worth taking, and the high ground around the Spanish border can be accessed in several places from the Portalet pass and the nearby Pic du Midi d'Ossau.

SITES

1 *The Val d'Allier near Moulins*

2 *Forêt de Tronçais*

3 *Montilly*

4 *The Narse de Lascols*

5 *Prat-de-Bouc/ Plomb du Cantal*

6 *Gorges de la Dordogne*

7 *Gorges de la Truyère*

8 *Planèze de St.-Flour*

9 *Rocher de Prades*

10 *Massif du Mezenc*

11 *Narses de La Sauvetat*

12 *Montagne de la Serre*

13 *Chaîne des Dômes*

14 *Val d'Allier*

15 *Vallée de Chaudefour*

Auvergne

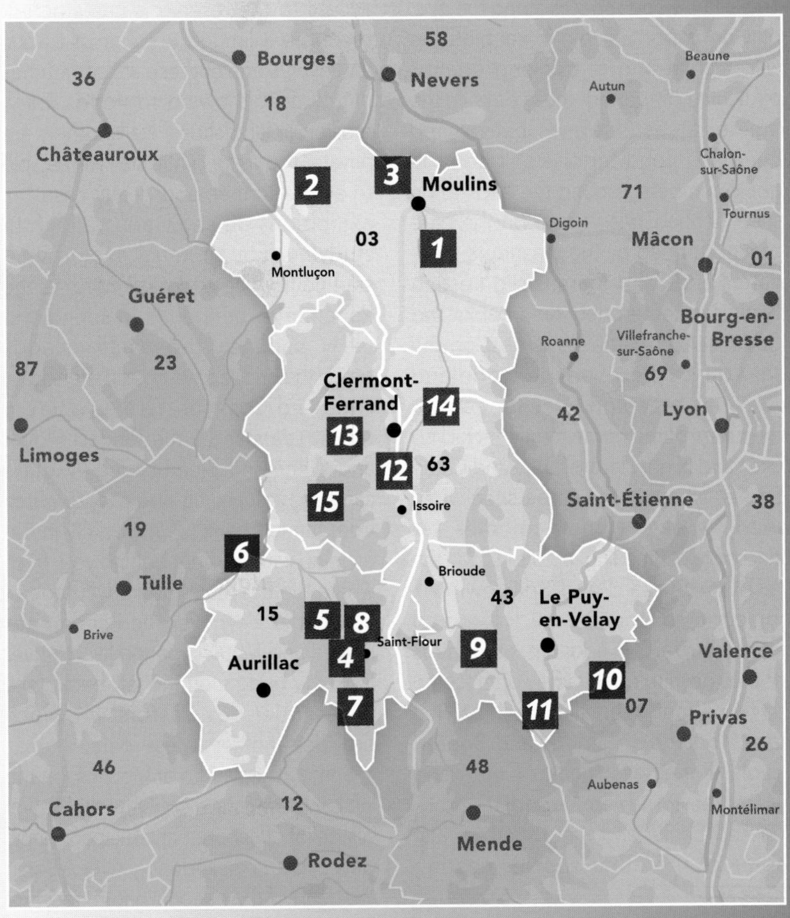

58
Bourges
Nevers
Beaune
36
18
Autun
Châteauroux
Chalon-sur-Saône
2
3
Moulins
71
Tournus
Digoin
03
1
Mâcon
01
Montluçon
Guéret
Bourg-en-Bresse
Roanne
Villefranche-sur-Saône
69
87
23
Clermont-Ferrand
14
42
Lyon
13
Limoges
12
63
15
Issoire
Saint-Étienne
38
19
6
Brioude
Tulle
43
Le Puy-en-Velay
15
5
8
Brive
Saint-Flour
9
Valence
Aurillac
4
10
7
11
07
Privas
26
46
48
Aubenas
Montélimar
12
Cahors
Mende
Rodez

1. The Val d'Allier near Moulins

ALLIER (03) *IGN 42*

The Allier has suffered less from canalisation and management than some of the other rivers of France; from Vichy it winds its way reasonably freely northwards through a flood-plain, before joining the Loire near Nevers. Its many ox-bow lakes or 'boires', its remarkable meanders, its banks and sandbars, all form an ever changing mosaic of natural habitats that harbour a rich fauna and flora. These large open spaces along the river play an important role in keeping the water clear and of drinking quality, particularly important these days. In the quieter areas European beaver and European pond tortoise still occur in good numbers. Among the birds to be seen, Stone Curlews nest on the bare ground formed by the meanders, Bee-eaters and Sand Martins dig nesting tunnels in the eroded sand banks and Common and Little Terns nest on the sandbars. The riverside woodland provides breeding sites for several members of the heron family, including Grey and Night Herons, Little and Cattle Egrets, all of which can be seen when feeding, even if their colonies are inaccessible. Breeding raptors include the resident Buzzard and Sparrowhawk joined in summer by Black Kite and Honey Buzzard. In addition, other birds of prey nesting not far away often come to feed along the valley, such as Hen and Montagu's Harriers, and Booted Eagle. Passerines such as Cetti's and Melodious Warblers, Woodlark, Red-backed Shrike and Kingfisher are just some of the other species nesting here also.

The Réserve Naturelle du Val d'Allier, stretching for 21 km to the south of Moulins, is especially interesting for birds; more than 250 species have been seen on its 1,450 hectares. Created in 1994, the reserve is managed jointly by the Office National des Forêts (ONF) and the LPO.

ACCESS

For up-to-date information about the area it is well worth stopping off at the Espace Nature du Val d'Allier visitor centre in Moulins, in the middle of this section of the river. Although in general access to the reserve is unrestricted, there are a limited number of tracks, and even some of these are sometimes impracticable owing to floods, bank erosion or land-slides, whilst others are private. The visitor centre staff will be able to advise further, and in any case the exhibitions on show are well worth studying. For an initial exploration, starting from here (1), walk north to the Règemortes bridge (2). In spring and early summer the small islands below the bridge have hosted significant Little and Common Tern colonies in recent years and Little Ringed Plover and White and Blue-headed Wagtails can also be seen. It is also easy to watch from the left bank (3), especially in the evening with the light behind you, from where there is the added advantage of a splendid view over the Règemortes bridge and Moulins generally. Up-river from the bridge, on the left bank, take the 'sentier des Castors' (4) which provides another access route.

Some 20 km south of Moulins, on the left bank, the church at Châtel-de-Neuvre village (5) offers a remarkable panoramic view over the meandering River Allier in the heart of the national nature reserve.

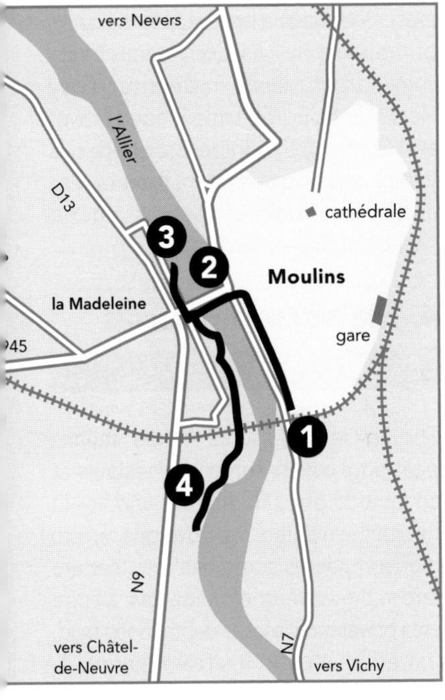

Either with a splendid setting sun or early morning mist, the Allier is a grand and living river which looks particularly impressive in the landscape here. During times of migration, the church can be a good point for viewing migrants moving along the Allier valley: Black and White Storks, Red Kite, Osprey, Woodpigeon and Stock Dove and many passerines (thrushes, hirundines, finches, larks, etc.) all occur. Various waders can be seen on the islands, especially in autumn, Greenshank, Dunlin, Curlew and Lapwing among others. In winter, duck often concentrate in the valley upstream (6), Mallard and Teal in particular with Gadwall on occasions as well. Grey Heron and Cormorant occur, and there are sometimes Curlew and both Little and Great Crested Grebes. Great White Egrets are increasing as a winter visitor, and can sometimes be seen in good

STONE CURLEW

numbers here, especially early in the morning. Cranes have recently started over-wintering farther down-river should be looked for in the surrounding maize fields.

Calendar

Spring and summer: most of the wetland birds that breed in this part of France can be found here – Little and Cattle Egrets, Night Heron, White Stork, Little Ringed Plover, Stone Curlew, Common and Little Terns, Bee-eater, Sand Martin. House Martins nest on the bridge over the river. Ospreys are quite numerous during both migrations.

Winter: Cormorant, Great White Egret, Mallard and Gadwall, Teal, Crane, Curlew, sometimes White-tailed Eagle or Peregrine.

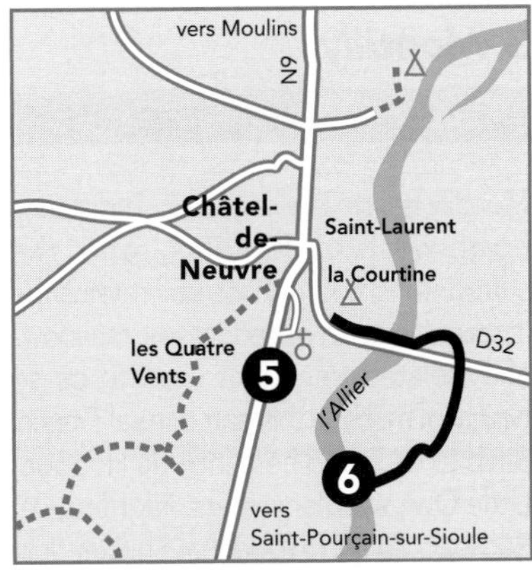

2. *Forêt de Tronçais*

ALLIER (03) *IGN 35*

The Forêt de Tronçais, between Moulins and Bourges, is one of the best oak woodlands in Europe, with many full-grown trees and much natural regeneration. The type of forestry practised here has created a diverse habitat with natural re-growth alongside old, mature trees (some 250 years old and protected), interspersed with many clearings. A good mix of woodland birds includes several woodpeckers (Great, Middle and Lesser Spotted, Black, Green and Grey-headed), birds of prey (Booted Eagle, Honey Buzzard, Black Kite, Goshawk and Hobby), Nightjar and breeding passerines such as Grasshopper, Wood and Bonelli's Warblers. The N953 from Moulins runs through the forest, which can be explored along the many woodland rides. The are several lagoons in the woodland which add to the variety of birds to be seen. Great Crested and Little Grebes both breed, along with Reed Warblers. Little Bitterns have been seen at the Étang de St.-Bonnet, in the northern part of the forest, but breeding records have been rather irregular.

3. *Montilly*

ALLIER (03) *IGN 36*

Montilly is a small village a short distance north-west of Moulins, and the surrounding countryside still retains the 'bocage' features of hedgerows, meadows and isolated trees that used to be so typical of much of this part of rural France. Birds to be found here include Hoopoe, Little Owl, warblers, chats, Nightingale, Red-backed and Woodchat Shrikes. Just east of the village a lane leads to the banks of the Allier at 'Les Coqueteaux', with some larger islands in the river. Grey Heron, Little Egret, Little Ringed Plover and Common Sandpiper are all species to be found here at different times of year, and in late summer there is a good chance of Bee-eaters also.

4. *The Narse de Lascols*

CANTAL (15) *IGN 49*

The Narse de Lascols ('narse' means peat bog) covers some 110 hectares at an altitude of 1,000 metres, and lies in the southern part of the Auvergne region. It encompasses some habitats that are rare in the Auvergne mountains: a large area of water of variable depth, open mud, grazed heath and a stream that feeds the bog. Hunted over during the autumn, Lascols along with other wetlands in the St.-Flour area is of most interest during the spring. Thanks to its European classification as an IBA (Important Bird Area) it benefits from special departmental protection.

ACCESS

The nearest large town is St.-Flour, just west of the A75 motorway (nearest exit is No. 29). From St.-Flour take the D921 south, and in a few kilometres turn right, between Bouzentes and Les Ternes, towards Cussac on the D57. Between Alleuzet and Cussac a turning to the right leads to the public car park (1) at Lascols. It is easy to view the peat bog and lake from the road, especially when the water levels are high. Otherwise, from the farm next to the bog, follow the track, wet in places, which runs by its boundary bank. The widest part of the lake is viewable from beyond the farm;

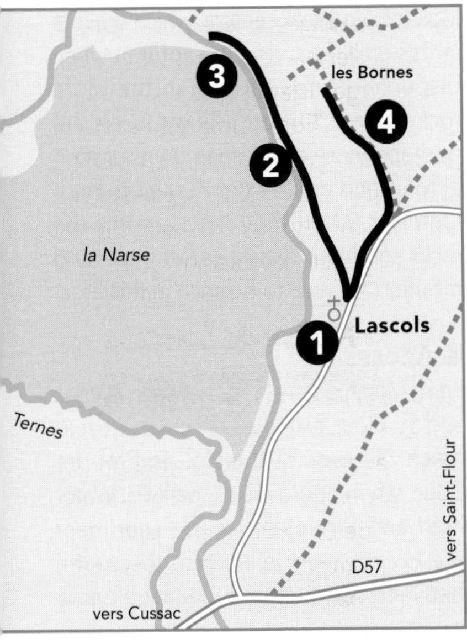

continue beyond here (2) to the far end of the narse (3) where there are mudflats that attract waders on passage, particularly in the spring: in February and early March there may be thousands of Lapwing and many Golden Plover here. Black and Whiskered Terns also occur on migration along with a few gulls. During March, all of the regular species of dabbling duck can be seen and both Mallard and Teal nest. As there have been several sightings of Red-footed Falcon on passage, especially in May, it is worth checking every fence post for this charismatic bird of prey at this time of year. June is the best month for seeing the breeding species: Lapwing, Curlew and a few Snipe, the latter best located during its drumming display flights. White and, more recently, Blue-headed Wagtails nest in the area, along with Whinchat and Wheatear. Both Spotted Crake and Water Rail also breed here, and although it is almost impossible to see them, it is worth making a visit at dusk to listen out for their distinctive and strange calls. In late summer, Montagu's and Hen Harriers both arrive in the evening to roost on the bog, which is also a favoured hunting ground for Black and Red Kites, migrant Marsh Harriers and Hobby, with Peregrine sometimes present in winter. An alternative route, also starting from the car park (1) follows the road through the village and past some animal rearing units to another viewpoint (4). Throughout the area, take care not to disturb the birds which are often not far away from the tracks, and do not try to penetrate the bog itself.

Calendar

Spring: all the commoner dabbling duck and many waders (including sandpipers, Greenshanks, Lapwing, Curlew, Golden Plover, Black-tailed Godwit), Yellow-legged and Black-headed Gulls. Also Marsh Harrier, Merlin, Hobby, Red-footed Falcon, Red-throated Pipit (regularly seen). Four breeding species are at their western European altitudinal limit: Spotted Crake, Lapwing, Snipe, Curlew.
Autumn: (mid-August to mid-September) waders, Montagu's and Hen Harrier roost, Grey Heron, sometimes White Stork, Crane, Blue-headed Wagtail, chats and Wheatear.

5. Prat-de-Bouc/ Plomb du Cantal

Cantal (15) IGN 49

Dominated by traditional summer pastures in the southern part of the volcanic Cantal range, the area

WHEATEAR

around the Prat-de-Bouc (1,386 metres) and the Plomb du Cantal (1,855 metres) is known for its rich flora and has a wide variety of natural habitats: sloping peat bogs, heath, stunted scrub, subalpine meadows and rocky outcrops. Because of its position on one of the Massif Central's autumn migration routes, it has been (since 1982) in a group of seven sites in southern France concerned with the protection and observation of migrating birds. Raptors to be seen here in autumn include Red and Black Kites, Honey Buzzard, Buzzard, Montagu's, Hen and Marsh Harriers, Sparrowhawk, Peregrine and Merlin. Water Pipits nest near the summits and Wheatears are common in areas of short grass. The best time to look for Alpine Accentors, which are rare in this area, is during the autumn when dispersing birds turn up in the more rocky areas. Similarly, Ring Ouzels are perhaps more easily seen on migration in May, and again from August to mid-October, when they feed among the rocks and bilberry bushes. Marmots and mouflon are also to be seen in this area.

Access

From Murat, on the N122 between Aurillac and St.-Flour, take the D39 south-west to reach the pass of the Col de Prat-de-Bouc, where there is a car park (1). Water Pipit and Wheatear can be seen near the houses here. A track to the south, between two buildings, heads along a

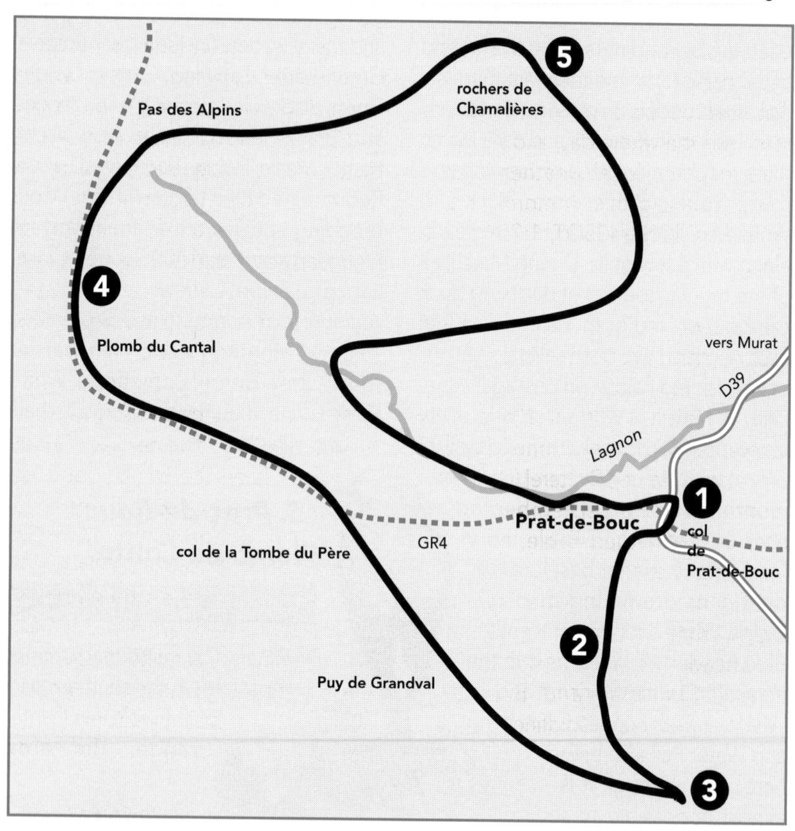

MONTAGU'S HARRIER

ridge, and after a quarter-of-an-hour's walk you come to the autumn migration watch-point (2), the best spot for watching birds of prey passing south overhead. Then head to the source of the River Épie (3) before turning west via the Puy de Grandval (a good area for migrant Dotterel in late August/early September) to eventually reach the Plomb du Cantal, the highest point in the range (4). Then descend via the ridge towards the Cirque de Chamalières (5). Raven, Kestrel and Mistle Thrush are all typical birds of this splendid cirque and with a little luck Rock Thrush can also be seen. From here the path runs through a series of peat-bogs, with a good selection of the typical flora of this sort of habitat, and eventually leads back to the Prat-de-Bouc pass. The circuit of about 11 km, including stops for birdwatching, can take the whole day, and it is worth checking the local weather forecast before setting out. A more detailed map (e.g. IGN 2435OT, 1:25,000) will be useful here.

CALENDAR

Spring and summer: breeding species include Rock Thrush, Ring Ouzel, Water Pipit, Crossbill. From late July onwards: Black Kite, Honey Buzzard, Montagu's Harrier, Dotterel (rare), Swift, warblers. From September: storks, Osprey, Short-toed Eagle, hirundines and Ring Ouzel.

Autumn: From October onwards: Red Kite, Peregrine, Merlin, Sparrowhawk, Woodpigeon, Stock Dove, Chaffinch and Brambling, Siskin, Greenfinch, Goldfinch.

6. *Gorges de la Dordogne*

CANTAL (15) *IGN 49*

The River Dordogne, rising in the Massif Central, winds it way through some spectacular scenery on its way to the Atlantic, and can provide some excellent birdwatching opportunities. In the area south of Bort-les-Orgues (named for its curious crystalline rock formations in the shape of organ pipes), the valley is steep-sided and wooded, with many cliffs and areas of heath. The river has been dammed in several places for hydro-electric purposes, forming long sinuous lakes. The whole area is well worth exploring, but two of the more interesting sites are Madic and Gratte-Bruyère. The first is on the left bank of the river, a short way downstream from Bort-les-Orgues, where there is a lake and marsh, an excellent area for breeding passerines such as Melodious Warbler, various *Sylvia* and *Phylloscopus* warblers, Reed Warbler and Whinchat, with a hirundine and Starling roost in July and August. The Belvédère de Gratte-Bruyère viewpoint is on the D168 ('Route des Ajustants') further downstream on the right bank, at the junction with the Sumène river. This is a particularly good spot for viewing the various raptors which either breed here or pass through on migration: Black and Red Kites, Honey Buzzard, Goshawk, Booted and Short-toed Eagles and Osprey. (See also site 2 in chapter on Limousin.)

7. Gorges de la Truyère

CANTAL (15) *IGN 49*

The section of the River Truyère immediately south of St.-Flour has been dammed for hydro-electric generation, but nevertheless the wooded slopes and heathland continue to provide excellent feeding and nesting opportunities for birds of prey. There are many potential observation points, the following being just a few suggestions. Longevialle, on the D48, is accessible from exit 31 on the A75 which crosses the valley just south of St.-Flour. This is an ideal spot for migrant Ospreys, both in spring and autumn, and pigeons and waders also pass through this area in autumn. A little further downstream, the D13 runs from the Viaduc de Gabarit through Faverolles to Fridefont. There is a good viewpoint at the Belvédère de Mallet, where duck can be seen in the spring, and raptors include Booted and Short-toed Eagles, plus both kites. Continuing to Chaudes-Aigues and then on the D11 brings you to the Pont de Tréboul. Again this is a good spot during autumn migration for raptors and pigeons, whilst in spring and summer Hen and Montagu's Harriers can be seen quartering the nearby heaths. Grey Herons can be seen along the river, and breeding species of owl include Little, Tawny, Long-eared and Eagle Owl.

8. Planèze de St.-Flour

CANTAL (15) *IGN 49*

Although Lascols (site 4 above) is the Cantal's best known wetland, there are others, natural or man-made, that are also good for migrant or nesting birds. The lake between Pierrefitte and Talizat, on the D697 north of St.-Flour, is home to the Cantal's only Black-headed Gull colony, and has many nesting Little Grebes and a few Garganey. There are many migrants in spring and Whiskered Tern has even tried to nest. The narse de Nouvialle lies within a triangle delimited by the villages of Nouvialle, Latga and Liozargues (south of the D926 between St.-Flour and Murat) and has nesting Curlew every year. Montagu's Harrier is regular, as well as Lapwing in early spring. At this time, in wet areas, migrants such as various duck, Crane and waders make a halt. A small lake at Sériers, off the D921 south of St.-Flour near Ternes, can also be very interesting. Little Grebe, Coot and Moorhen nest and there are duck in spring and autumn. Various migrants occur in spring, including marsh terns and a few waders. Throughout the whole of this general area it is possible to see such species as Hoopoe, Whinchat, Wheatear, Red-backed and Great Grey Shrikes (although this last is quite rare now) as well as both kites and Montagu's and Hen Harriers.

9. Rocher de Prades

HAUTE-LOIRE (43) *IGN 50*

The basaltic outcrop of the Rocher de Prades is more than 200 metres high and dominates this stretch of the fast-flowing River Allier near Langeac.

SHORT-TOED EAGLE

Between the granitic and volcanic plateaus either side of the river there are many different habitats: pebble banks, riverside woods, heathland, dry meadows and the rocky outcrops so characteristic of the Allier gorges. The area is a haven for a wide diversity of birds of prey during the breeding season, including good populations of several rare species. Eagle Owl, Short-toed Eagle, Red Kite and Hobby all breed here and Hen Harriers occur in the autumn. Ravens are resident, and the cliffs provide breeding sites for Alpine Swift and both Crag and House Martins. The woodland has a good mix of the commoner species, and Rock Buntings occur in more open areas. The shingle banks attract Common Sandpipers as breeding birds in summer, Kingfishers also occur, and Dippers are resident in the faster-flowing stretches. The area is not to be ignored in winter, as both Wallcreeper and Alpine Accentor have been seen at this time.

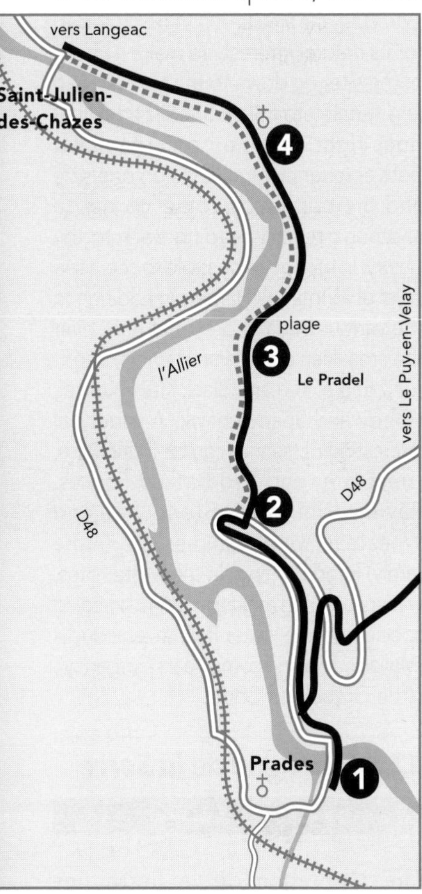

Access

From Langeac, on the Allier south of Brioude, follow the river upstream on the D585 to St.-Arcons-d'Allier, then take the D48 to Prades. There is a car park at the bridge over the Allier. From the foot of the rock (1), follow the road as far as the first hairpin bend (2) and then take the surfaced track marked as a walking route by red and white stripes in places. Beyond the small village of Le Pradel (3) it is possible to look over the banks of the Allier and the heathland on the other side. Continue past the church of Sainte-Marie (4); the riverside here sometimes holds Alpine Accentor in winter. The path rejoins the road at the St.-Julien-des-Chazes bridge. You can return by the same track or along the road on the other side of the river, about 6 km in all. It is also well worth climbing the mule trail from the foot to the summit of the rock: by doing this you get an idea of the general layout of the area, and also have a chance to see the birds of the plateau. The D48 continues beyond Prades, and then joins the D301 to St.-Privat-d'Allier. This road offers more views of the valley and access to other habitats away from the river itself. North of Langeac, on the D585 to Brioude, the Maison des Oiseaux du Haut-Allier information centre at Lavoûte-Chilhac is well worth a visit. LPO staff are on hand to provide details about the wildlife of the area, and organise different guided outings covering a variety of topics.

■ **Calendar**

Spring and summer: various raptors breed: Short-toed Eagle, Red and Black Kites, Honey Buzzard, Sparrowhawk, Kestrel and Hobby. On the rock itself there is a mixed colony of Crag and House Martins, with a few pairs of Alpine Swift, Raven and Rock Bunting. On the banks of the River Allier: Dipper, Common Sandpiper, Grey Wagtail.

Winter: Red-legged Partridge, Raven, Great Grey Shrike, Dipper, occasionally Wallcreeper and Alpine Accentor.

10. *Massif du Mezenc*

Haute-Loire (43)/ Ardèche (07) *IGN 50/52*

The 'Massif du Mezenc', volcanic hills on the Haute Loire/Ardèche border south-east of Le Puy-en-Velay, dominate the Parc Régional des Monts d'Ardèche which lies to the east. At its base, Les Estables (one of the highest villages in the Massif Central) is the gateway to a habitat typical of mid-altitude mountains, with a remarkable animal and plant community. In winter it is possible to see Black Woodpecker, Crossbill, Coal and Crested Tits, Fieldfare and Siskin, along with a few Snow Finches and Alpine Accentors. Ravens can be seen displaying during the first fine days of spring, but it is not until the end of May that all the nesting species will have returned: Water Pipit, Ring Ouzel, Rock Thrush, Citril Finch, and probably Woodcock. A few birds of prey hunt over the slopes: Short-toed Eagle, Red Kite and Hen Harrier, whilst Golden Eagle and Peregrine are seen from time to time. Since 1993 a few Nutcrackers have been seen regularly in this area, the only one in the Auvergne where they occur year round, but breeding, although suspected, has not as yet been proved.

11. *Narses de La Sauvetat*

Haute-Loire (43) *IGN 50*

La Sauvetat is a small village on the N88, about 20 km south of Le Puy-en-Velay. The 'narse' or peatbog, is accessed about 200 metres along the road that leads from here towards Les Soulis and Arlempdes. Park next to the quarry, from where there is a fine view over the bog, in the bottom of an ancient volcano crater. Although the peat here has been extracted, the area is due to be protected for its natural interest. To make a circuit of the site, go down to the tarmac road and turn left to follow the dirt track that goes right into the bog. Then skirt between agricultural fields on one side and the bog on the other to get to another dirt track leading back to the quarry. In spring it is possible to see a few pairs of Montagu's Harriers in addition to the various birds of prey that hunt over the area: Hen and Marsh Harriers, Short-toed Eagle, Red and Black Kites, Kestrel, Hobby and Sparrowhawk. A variety of interesting passerines can be found here: Great Grey and Red-backed Shrikes, Raven, Whinchat, Stonechat and Wheatear, Yellowhammer and (more rarely) Reed Bunting. In the wetter sites, waders occur on migration, while breeding species include Water Rail, several ducks (Mallard, Teal and some years Garganey), Little Grebe and Coot.

12. *Montagne de la Serre*

Puy-de-Dôme (63) *IGN 49*

The Montagne de la Serre lies

immediately south of Clermont-Ferrand, and consists of basaltic lava which, many millions of years ago, issued from Mont Vigeral and descended as far as the village of Crest at its eastern end. The rock has been worn down through erosion and now takes the form of a volcanic ridge. It has long been used by man (for grazing and crops) but nowadays only part is farmed, the rest having returned to its former 'natural' state (grass and scrub with wooded valley sides). On the south side the Chadrat sedimentary plateau is still cultivated. This diverse countryside shelters a wide variety of bird species, particularly birds of prey and some uncommon passerines. In the woods nearby there are Coal and Crested Tits and both Firecrest and Goldcrest, especially in the autumn, whilst Bonelli's Warbler arrives in summer to breed. Mixed thrush flocks (Redwing, Mistle and Song Thrushes) can often be found in autumn. Montagu's Harriers nest in the area and can be seen hunting over the crops. The Nightjar's strange song can be heard on warm summer evenings around woodland clearings, and Red-backed Shrikes also breed here. In autumn the central part of the Massif Central forms a natural bottle-neck for migrants and as the Montagne de la Serre is situated at the exit of this funnel, it is thus a good point for observing hundreds of thousands of birds both in spring and autumn: raptors, storks, Cranes, pigeons and passerines. Migration has been studied here since 1986, and counters are regularly present from August to October. The larger species such as the raptors, including both Red and Black Kites and Hen Harrier are a big attraction, but there is also a good mix of passerines: Ortolan Buntings in September, Tawny, Tree and Meadow Pipits, Woodlark and White Wagtail in October, whilst flocks of Hawfinches are also regularly seen in the autumn. Great Grey Shrikes have declined but are still sometimes seen on autumn passage. There is unrestricted access, with easy signposted paths.

■ Access

From Clermont-Ferrand take the A75 south towards Issoire, but leave on exit 5 near Veyre-Monton, along the D213 towards St.-Saturnin/St.-Amant-Tallende. Turn right on the D96 through Chadrat and continue another 1½ km as far as the car park (1) on the right. The road continues through Nadaillat to join the N89 at Theix for an alternative route to or from Clermont-Ferrand. From the car park take the track north for 100 metres, to the main migration viewpoint at the water-tower. Watchers are regularly here from 1st August to 31st October, counting birds heading south. Continue along the track for 1½ km, turn right at (2) and continue as far as the road, scanning both the woodland and the crops. Follow the road for about 50 metres and take the track on the right as far as the small chapel (3), then go back up to the car park. It is also possible to go on to (4): in the surrounding woods there are many nesting passerines including all four west European *Phylloscopus* warblers.

■ Calendar

Spring: on migration, Black Stork, Honey Buzzard, Black Kite, Montagu's Harrier, Tawny Pipit and Ortolan Bunting.
Summer: Short-toed Eagle, Montagu's Harrier, Buzzard, Honey Buzzard, Black and Red Kites, Sparrowhawk, Goshawk, Kestrel and Hobby all nest, as do Quail, Hoopoe, Woodlark, Red-backed Shrike, Chiffchaff, Willow,

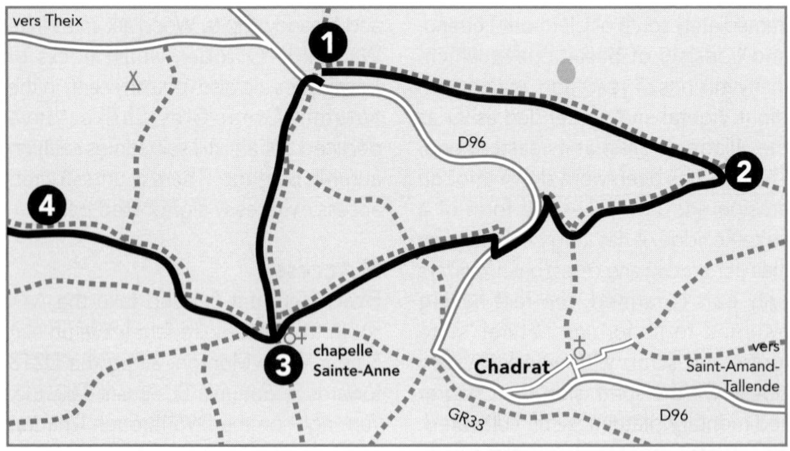

Wood and Bonelli's Warblers and Hawfinch.

Autumn: Osprey, Hen and Marsh Harriers, Red Kite and very large numbers of Woodpigeons (mid-October) and passerines (especially in the morning and evenings on active migration or stopping for a rest), sometimes Cranes (early November). Also some Great Spotted and especially Lesser Spotted Woodpeckers plus Great Grey Shrike.

13. Chaîne des Dômes

Puy-de-Dôme (63) *IGN 42*

The Dômes range of hills, one of the most beautiful volcanic complexes in Europe, lies to the west of Clermont-Ferrand. It is a vast area of peaks covered with forest and moor. Many typical mountain species occur, notably Tengmalm's Owl, Common Treecreeper (not always easy to find in France), Black Woodpecker and Crossbill, as well as both Firecrest and Goldcrest in the more wooded parts. It is sometimes possible to see six species of tit simultaneously! Birds of prey occur on the woodland edge, especially on the slopes descending towards the Limagne area to the east (Honey Buzzard, Short-toed Eagle, Goshawk, Red Kite). Hen Harriers breed on the heaths and grassy areas, along with Nightjar, Meadow Pipit, Whinchat and a few pairs of Great Grey Shrikes. Spring, from mid May, is the best time for birdwatching, but autumn can also be very good with many Red Kites and Hen Harriers. The Parc Régional des Volcans d'Auvergne is a huge area, but a good perspective of the area can be had by visiting the Puy de la Vache and Puy de Lassolas area, south-west of Clermont-Ferrand, where there is a visitor centre at the Château de Montlosier. There are various paths through the nearby surrounding woodland of the Cheire d'Aydat.

14. Val d'Allier

Puy-de-Dôme (63) *IGN 42/43*

Although the valley of the River Allier between Clermont-Ferrand and Vichy has often been much spoilt by human activities, a good variety of interesting habitats still remain, including riverside forests of differing ages, pebble banks, oxbow lakes, meadows, plus abandoned or working sand quarries. One of the better sections is that between the village of Limons and the Bec de Dore, the confluence with the River Dore. More than 180 species of birds characteristic of the Allier valley have been seen here, including breeding Grey and Night Herons, Little Egret, Canada Goose, Black Kite, Hobby, Stone Curlew, Common Sandpiper, Common Tern and Bee-eater, as well as Great, Middle and Lesser Spotted Woodpeckers. Many species of wader, gulls, terns, duck and passerines appear during times of migration, including Osprey at both seasons. Flooding during the spring regularly makes for good watching, including rarities. In winter Cormorant, Mallard, Teal and Black-headed Gull occur on the river.

15. *Vallée de Chaudefour*

Puy-de-Dôme (63) *IGN 49*

The Mont Dore massif, south-west of Clermont-Ferrand, has been much developed for skiing, and only two sites in the region have escaped relatively lightly: the Cirque de la Fontaine Salée and the Vallée de Chaudefour. This last site is now a réserve naturelle, of high botanical and geological interest, and various marked trails make visiting easier. Classification as a reserve has brought about an increased number of visitors at certain times of the year, and so it is best to avoid the busiest periods and visit early in the morning. Starting from Chambon-sur-Lac, to the east of Mont Dore, follow the D637 south-west to reach the visitor centre, which is signposted. More detailed maps are available here (e.g. IGN 2432ET, 1:25,000). The most interesting circuit goes around the valley and leaves from the reserve visitor centre. A track leads into the meadows at the bottom of the cirque. Early in the day, mouflon sometimes occur in this area. The left-hand fork leads to the 'cascade de la Biche', next to which Wallcreepers have very occasionally nested. However, instead of (or after) going there, take the track that climbs eastwards through the forest, checking for Coal Tit, Common Treecreeper and Black Woodpecker. Once out of the forest you are back in mouflon territory, but also Tree, Meadow and Water Pipits all may be seen. From the 'Puy Ferrand', the highest point on the circuit (1,854 metres), the trail arrives at the 'Col de la Cabane', descends to the 'Pan de la Grange' and, via the ridges, arrives at the 'Puy des Crebasses' (1,762 metres). Both in spring and autumn many birds of prey are easily seen on migration (e.g., kites, harriers, Honey Buzzard, Osprey), while Peregrine and Raven can be seen throughout the year. Crag Martins often hunt over south-facing slopes, and the rocky areas should be checked for Rock Thrush. Ring Ouzel should be looked for on the northern slopes of the ridge. This part of the circuit, botanically very interesting in June and July, is the best area for chamois. Halfway down the slope, above the end of the Chambon ski resort ski-lift, the trail leads off to the right, back to the bottom of the Chaudefour valley and the reserve centre. This itinerary is long, at least a five hour walk, covering an altitude range of more than 800 metres; to do it it is best to be physically fit, to wait for good weather and to be well equipped (correct footwear, warm clothing, a hat in summer and a good map).

SITES

1 *Lac de Marcenay*

2 *Gravière des Maillys*

3 *La combe de Lavaux, Gevrey-Chambertin*

4 *Lac Kir/Dijon*

5 *The Loire valley between Nevers and Neuvy-sur-Loire*

6 *Étangs de Baye and Vaux*

7 *Nevers*

8 *The River Doubs at Charette-Varennes*

9 *The River Saône at Marnay*

10 *Lac de la Sorme*

11 *Lac de Bas-Rebourseaux*

12 *Yonne valley gravel pits*

13 *Rochers du Saussois*

Bourgogne

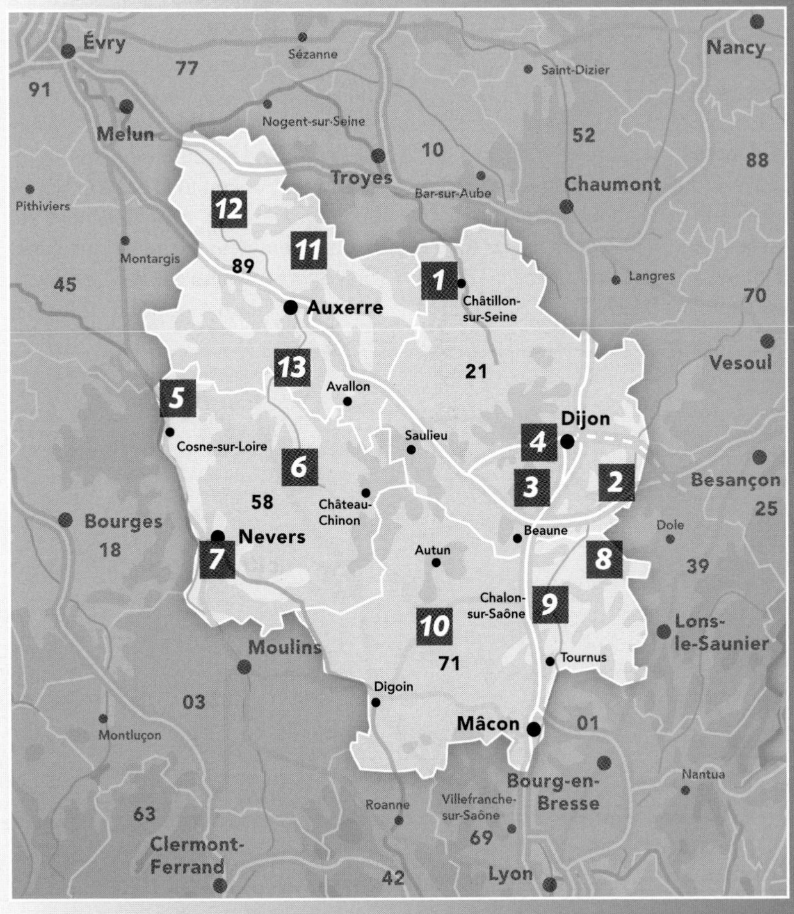

Évry
77
Sézanne
Saint-Dizier
Nancy
91
Nogent-sur-Seine
Melun
52
10
88
Troyes
Chaumont
Bar-sur-Aube
Pithiviers
12
11
Montargis
89
1
Langres
45
Châtillon-
sur-Seine
70
Auxerre
13
21
Vesoul
5
Avallon
Dijon
Saulieu
4
Cosne-sur-Loire
6
3
2
Besançon
58
Château-
Chinon
25
Bourges
Beaune
Dole
18
Nevers
7
Autun
8
39
Chalon-
sur-Saône
9
Lons-
le-Saunier
10
Moulins
71
Tournus
Digoin
03
Mâcon
01
Montluçon
Bourg-en-
Bresse
Nantua
Roanne
Villefranche-
sur-Saône
63
69
Clermont-
Ferrand
42
Lyon

1. Lac de Marcenay

Côte-d'Or (21) *IGN 28*

With its wooded limestone hillsides to the west and alternating hedgerows and crops to the east, the artificial Lac de Marcenay is situated in the centre of a mosaic of countryside typical of the north of the Côte-d'Or. Most of the northern edge of the lake is extensively wooded, while there are beaches on the south-east shore. About half of the total of 92 hectares is occupied by a reedbed. Because of the mix of habitats the area is of interest for woodland and open country species, in addition to the aquatic birds associated with the lake itself.

Access

Leave Châtillon-sur-Seine west on the D965 and after about 10 km turn right to the village of Marcenay. Park in the 'Le Santenoy' restaurant car park (1) and walk onto the beach. This is a good spot for a general scan for any waders, wagtails or pipits that may be present. A footpath runs right round the lake, passing through woodland and close to the reeds, but is wet and muddy in places, so be prepared to wear water-proof boots if necessary. First, turn right along the lake shore to cross a park where Fieldfares can seen throughout the year and which holds various other passerines such as Short-toed Treecreeper. Continuing along the track, you eventually cross the largest stream feeding the lake (2). A track to the right crosses a cultivated area to reach, after about 650 metres, another small lake, the Petit Étang de Larrey (3). In spring, Golden Oriole and Nightingale occupy the copses around the lake and Marsh Harriers hunt over the reedbeds. While crossing the cultivated area it is worth looking up for Short-toed Eagle or Hobby hunting overhead. In winter there are flocks of thrushes in this area, and Great Grey Shrike may also occur. Alternatively, at (2) a trail in the opposite direction

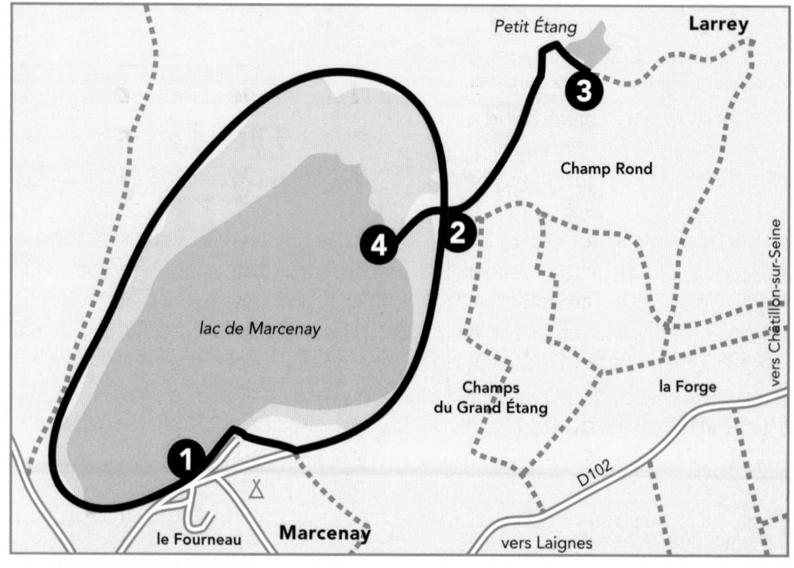

leads to the hides (4), which overlook both the lake and the reeds. If possible, visit here in the morning, with the sun at one's back, for better visibility. This is the best spot for good views of ducks, Water Rail and Kingfisher; and for watching Marsh Harrier and Hobby hunting over the reeds. The willows have a small Grey Heron colony. The main track from (2) continues right round the lake, a walk of about 5½ km, passing through woodland, where the six commoner species of woodpecker can be seen.

Calendar

Spring and autumn migration: Black-necked Grebe, Bittern, Garganey, Red-crested Pochard, Red Kite, Hen and Marsh Harriers, Osprey, Crane, Lapwing and various other waders, Black-headed and Little Gulls, Whiskered and Black Terns, Woodpigeon, Siskin.
Breeding season: Great Crested and Little Grebes, Mute Swan, Mallard, Honey Buzzard, Marsh, Hen and Montagu's Harriers, Sparrowhawk, Goshawk, Short-toed Eagle, Red and Black Kites, Hobby, Kestrel, Kingfisher, Woodpigeon, Stock Dove, six species of woodpecker (Green, Grey-headed, Black; Great, Middle and Lesser Spotted), Fieldfare, Song and Mistle Thrushes, Nightingale; Savi's, Reed, Sedge and Great Reed Warblers, Golden Oriole, Red-backed Shrike; Reed and Corn Buntings, Yellowhammer.
Winter: Great Crested and Little Grebes, Cormorant, Grey Heron, Great White Egret, Pochard, Tufted Duck with the occasional Ferruginous Duck or Scaup, Mallard, Gadwall, Shoveler, sometimes Wigeon and Pintail, Teal, Goldeneye and Smew, Coot and Water Rail, Kingfisher. Less regular are: Shelduck, other sawbills, scoters, gulls. Around the lake there are usually: Water Pipit, Fieldfare, Redwing and Great Grey Shrike.

2. *Gravière des Maillys*

Côte-d'Or (21) *IGN 37*

These gravel pits lie close to the River Saône, to the south-east of Dijon, and can be viewed from the D20, between Auxonne and Les Maillys. The gravel pits are of most interest for aquatic birds during the winter and migration periods, when Pochard, Tufted Duck, Teal and Goldeneye are often seen. From time to time other species occur: Scaup, Ferruginous Duck, Red-crested Pochard, Pintail and Smew with, more rarely, Red-necked Grebe. Great White Egret and waders such as Snipe and Lapwing are often seen on nearby pools. The bushy areas are home to many passerines including Yellowhammer and Siskin. In winter the poplars on the island are used by roosting Cormorants, which have recently started to nest here, the first for the area.

3. *La combe de Lavaux, Gevrey-Chambertin*

Côte-d'Or (21) *IGN 37*

This combe cuts deep into the limestone escarpment that shelters the Côte-d'Or vineyards of Gevrey-Chambertin, south of Dijon. Both the valley floor and the plateau above the limestone cliffs are covered with woodland or scrub, varying greatly according to their exposure. Any of the woodland is worth exploring, especially in the breeding season. Black, Great and Lesser Spotted Woodpeckers are all resident, as are

Stock Doves, whilst four species of *Phylloscopus* warblers (Willow, Wood and Bonelli's Warblers, plus Chiffchaff) arrive to nest in summer. The few coppices of coniferous trees have Goldcrest, Coal and Crested Tits. On the plateau, areas of open scrub are always worth checking, and the clearings provide nesting sites for several pairs of Nightjar. The cliffs provide good viewpoints for scanning for Peregrine and the occasional Short-toed Eagle. In winter, a careful examination of the cliff faces may reveal the presence of a wintering Wallcreeper, though these are never easy birds to find. The whole area can be explored using a network of footpaths managed by the 'Club alpin français'.

4. Lac Kir/Dijon

CÔTE-D'OR (21) *IGN 29/37*

This is an easily visited lake on the western outskirts of Dijon, suitable for the less mobile, and accessible by public transport (bus number 18 from the city centre). The lake is most interesting during cold snaps, as it is one of the last in the area to freeze over. Pochard, Tufted Duck and Mallard occur throughout the winter, often with other commoner dabbling ducks. There are also quite a few feral species! More rarely Goldeneye, Scaup, Red-crested Pochard, Eider, sawbills, scoters or Shelduck, and even divers, may be seen. Of the grebes only Little and Great Crested are regular. There is often a Black-headed Gull roost, with other gull species occurring in smaller numbers. A few pipits and waders turn up along the shore from time to time, and both Peregrine and

WOOD WARBLER

Sparrowhawk have been seen hunting. Although not usually seen at the lake itself, there are Dippers nesting by the nearby river.

5. The Loire valley between Nevers and Neuvy-sur-Loire

NIÈVRE (58)/
CHER (18) *IGN 27/36*

This part of the Loire valley, known locally as the 'Loire des Îles', is probably the most representative section of the middle Loire as far as its diverse fauna and flora are concerned. The ever-changing water levels, especially flooding, have maintained a mosaic of habitats of extraordinary diversity: low banks often weakened by the current, mudflats, meadows and dry fields, wooded islands and river-bank forests of differing ages. Of the numerous species of animals (e.g., beaver, otter) and plants that are found here, many are rare, some threatened, and some are protected, either regionally or by European law. This exceptional diversity and abundance of species has allowed this part of the river to be classified as a Natura 2000 site, and a section of nearly 20 km is protected as the Réserve Naturelle du Val de Loire.

Access

Three sections for an initial exploration are suggested.

(1) Soulangy area (see map). The circuit here of 4 km is a good introduction not only to the islands in the Loire itself but also to the adjacent limestone plateau which includes a great variety of habitats: dry meadows, coppices, heaths and riverside forest that are also of great entomological and botanical interest. From Nevers, head north through Fourchambault, and take the D174 that follows the riverbank towards Germigny-sur-Loire. The section between the small pumping station (1) and the village of Soulangy (2) is a good area to start looking at the river itself. The banks and sandbars have nesting Little Ringed Plover and Stone Curlew, Common Sandpiper, and Little and Common Terns also breed. Kingfisher and Grey Heron occur on the river and both Hoopoe and Bee-eater breed nearby. Little Egret and Night Heron can be seen in spring and summer, and Great White Egret occurs in winter. In late summer and autumn passage waders occur (Ringed Plover, many other *Calidris* and *Tringa* species and both godwits) plus groups of Stone Curlew. Other species passing through include various dabbling ducks, Shelduck, Black Terns and Cranes. Continue to the end of the road at (3) and then on foot to the right up the hillside to a water source; follow the track on up the side of the hill as far as the buildings (4). Many passerines occur in the bushes here: check for Ortolan Bunting and Red-backed Shrike. Birds of prey use the up-currents over the slopes: Black Kite and Hobby in spring and summer, Peregrine and Merlin on passage, as well as the other commoner species. Turn to the left along a steeply sloping track and then turn left again to (5). The woodland in this area is used by Long-eared and Tawny Owls, and by Great Spotted, Lesser Spotted and Green Woodpeckers. Woodlark and Tree Pipit nest on the heaths and meadows, while Willow Warbler, Chiffchaff, Corn Bunting and Stonechat are widespread. The path continues past an area of willow scrub back to the road at (3).

(2) Réserve Naturelle du Val de Loire. Leave the A77 north of Nevers at the Pouilly-sur-Loire exit (No. 26) and stop at the bridge over the Loire, where there is a good view over the river. Colonies of Common and Little Terns with Little Ringed Plover and Stone Curlew are easily seen from the wharfs downstream and the old towpath upstream. Many

KINGFISHER

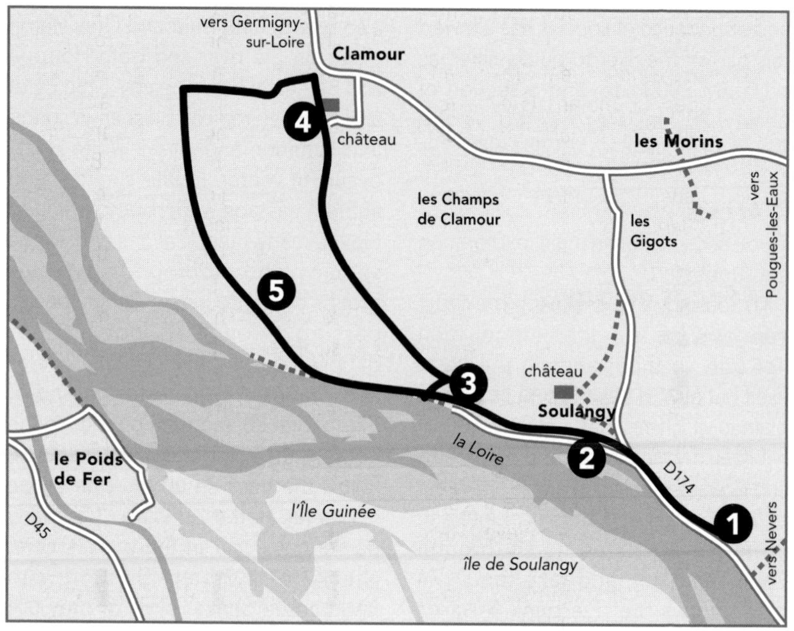

waders occur during migration. Osprey is present from April to September. The three species of marsh tern can be seen in spring and many waterfowl can be seen under good conditions in winter. The reserve interpretation centre – Pavillon du Milieu de Loire – in Pouilly-sur-Loire has information about access to the reserve. There are various marked trails, for instance at La Charité-sur-Loire and at Herry. In summer it is often easy to see terns at very close range, fishing under the Loire bridge at La Charité-sur-Loire at the southern end of the reserve.

(3) Les Brocs, at La Celle-sur-Loire. Continuing north again, beyond Cosne-sur-Loire (Exit 22 on the A77), along the N7, brings you to Myennes, La Celle-sur-Loire, and then Les Brocs. Turn left here under the railway line and take the track towards the Loire. This section is a remarkable area of dry, sandy pastures, meadows and heath, where Hen Harrier, Woodlark, Stonechat, Grasshopper Warbler and Red-backed Shrike can be found. The track continues to the bank of the Loire for more views of Little Tern and Little Ringed Plover.

Calendar

Spring: Little Egret, Black Kite, Hobby, Little Tern, Stone Curlew, Little Ringed Plover, Common Sandpiper, various waders on migration, Bee-eater, Kingfisher, Lesser Spotted Woodpecker, Hoopoe, Cuckoo, Long-eared Owl, Woodlark and Skylark, Wheatear, Grasshopper and Willow Warblers, Chiffchaff, Linnet, Corn, Cirl and Ortolan Buntings and Yellowhammer.

Summer: Little Egret, Night Heron, Hobby, Stone Curlew, Little Ringed Plover, Grey Plover, Lapwing, Dunlin, Little and Temminck's Stints, Sanderling, Curlew Sandpiper, various *Tringa* species, Snipe, Black-headed and Yellow-legged Gulls, Common and Little Terns.

Autumn and winter: Great Crested and Little Grebes, Cormorant, Grey Heron, Great White Egret, dabbling ducks, Sparrowhawk, Hen Harrier, Peregrine, Merlin, Crane, tits, Goldcrest, Firecrest, pipits and larks.

6. Étangs de Baye and Vaux

NIÈVRE (58) *IGN 36*

No shooting is allowed at this complex of lakes in the woodland north-east of Nevers, and hence they have become an important refuge. From Nevers, take the D978 and then the D958 via St.-Saulge to reach the area. During winter (except in really hard spells) it is easy to find large concentrations of Great Crested Grebe, Grey Heron, Great White Egret, and many dabbling and diving ducks including Goldeneye. The largest lake, the Étang de Vaux, is one of France's ten most important sites for wintering Goosander. Osprey and waders are commonly seen on migration, whilst Grey Heron and Black Kite breed in the area. Two marked interpretation trails have been put in place, with appropriate leaflets available. The 'Martin-pêcheur' trail starts on the dyke separating the Étang de Baye from the Grand Étang de Vaux lake (1½ km). The other, the 'Heron cendré' trail, starts from the dyke that divides the Grand Étang de Vaux. Two other sites worth checking are both about 20 km away. To the south there is a lake at Fleury-la-Tour (near Tintury), while to the east, there is a dammed reservoir, the Barrage de Pannesière. Both are worth a visit in winter.

7. Nevers

NIÈVRE (58) *IGN 36*

Just to show that even within towns good birdwatching is available, there are a couple of walking trails close to Nevers that allow some of the typical birds of the river to be seen easily, even for those with reduced mobility. Just downstream from the old bridge over the Loire in the town is a small sandy

GRASSHOPPER WARBLER

island which hosts a colony of Little and Common Terns. Both Little Ringed Plover and Common Sandpiper also nest nearby, and Black and Whiskered Terns have been seen on migration. One interpretation trail begins slightly downstream on the right bank, a two-hour walk allowing the visitor to see birds typical of the riverside woodland. There is another way-marked trail on the outskirts of Nevers, leading to the Bec d'Allier, where the River Allier joins the Loire. The tourist office in the town has full details of access. (See also site 2 in the Centre chapter.)

8. *The River Doubs at Charette-Varennes*

SAÔNE-ET-LOIRE (71)

IGN 37

In its lower reaches, before it joins the Saône, the River Doubs meanders through a wide valley, and a mosaic of habitats has been created by the changing river course: sand-bars, flooded willow-beds, large ox-bow lakes, and steep and crumbling banks. Outside the protective dykes there is a large cultivated plain, and also some areas of meadows liable to flooding. There are several lakes, many of them private, with lush surrounding vegetation, and the higher ground has some extensive woodland dominated by oak and hornbeam. The area has a rich mixture of birds associated with wetland habitats.

ACCESS

From Chalon-sur-Saône take the N73 north-east towards Dole and Besançon. After about 20 km, beyond Sermesse, fork right on the D73 towards Pierre-de-Bresse to reach Charette-Varennes. Park below the church on the side of the Doubs at a place called Bas de Charette (1). Check the river for Little Ringed Plover and Stone Curlew on the sand bars, and Night Heron and Little Egret along the river edge. Bee-eaters hunt here but nest on the other side. Kingfishers and Sand Martins can also be seen here, whilst Bluethroats occur a little further upstream. The following circuit covers about 10 km, and could well take all day, but passes through a variety of habitats.

Start, on foot, from Bas de Charette towards Lays, going as far as the small bridge. Cross and turn right immediately onto a path across the fields. About 1 km further on, cross another small bridge and continue to where four paths meet (2). Yellow Wagtails occur in the meadows here, Whinchats nest close to the water, there are Red-backed Shrikes in the hedgerows and Bluethroats along the Charetelle. The fields hold both Skylarks and Short-toed Larks whilst Curlew, Lapwing and Quail nest in the wet meadows. Turn right towards Terrans. Cross the village, passing by the church in the direction of St.-Bonnet-en-Bresse. After 1 km turn right to pass the Étang Bailly (3), which can be scanned from the embankment. Reed and Great Reed Warblers sing from the lake edge and Grey and Purple Herons, Great Crested Grebe, Gadwall and Pochard breed. The three species of harrier and Hobby hunt over the area. Another kilometre further on turn right again towards Charette-Varennes via the Bois de Vendues, the Étang de la Chênaie (4) and then via La Pommelée back to the starting point. The woodland areas are worth checking for Willow Tit and five species of woodpecker nest (Great and Lesser Spotted, Green, Grey-headed and Black).

■ Calendar

Spring and autumn: dabbling ducks, Osprey, Crane, waders and marsh terns.
Summer: Little and Great Crested Grebes, Grey, Purple and Night Herons, Cattle and Little Egrets, Gadwall, Pochard, Marsh Harrier, Hobby, Stone Curlew, Little Ringed Plover, Curlew, Common Tern, Kingfisher, Bee-eater, Short-toed Lark, Sand Martin, Blue-headed Wagtail, Bluethroat, Whinchat, Reed and Great Reed Warblers, Common and Lesser Whitethroats, Garden Warbler and Corn Bunting.
Winter: There are regularly flocks of Cormorant, Pochard, Tufted Duck, Lapwing, Black-headed Gull, Great White Egret (especially on emptied lakes and in the flood meadows), and more rarely, Greylag and Bean Geese, northern duck (Smew, Goosander, Red-breasted Merganser, Goldeneye, Eider) and Merlin. If the lakes are frozen, many birds still occur on the River Doubs itself.

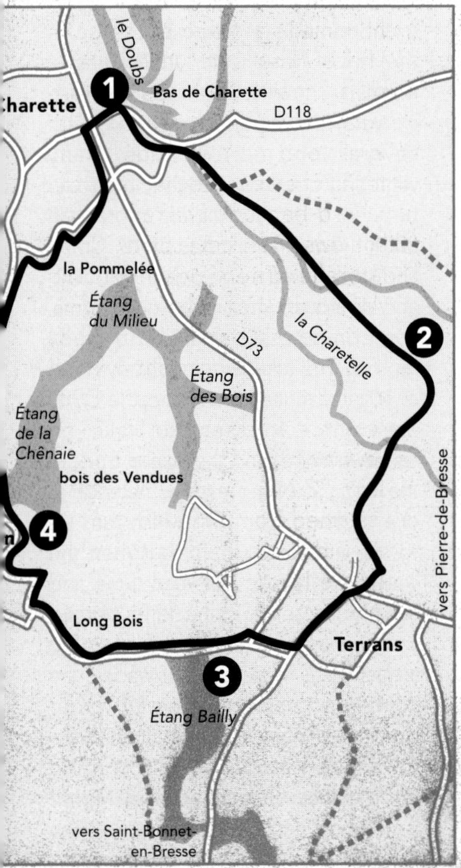

9. *The River Saône at Marnay*

Saône-et-Loire (71)
IGN 37

Marnay is a village a short distance south of Chalon-sur-Saône, where the River Grosne joins the main river. The water meadows here, on the right bank of the Saône, are often more or less completely flooded at any time between November and May, and during the rest of the year are farmed in a very traditional manner. Both the Grosne and the Frette, which also flows in here, meander between banks bordered with willows, hornbeam and alder, and the meadows between the two rivers are dotted with large mature poplars. The area is excellent for birds throughout the year. In the summer there are Great Crested Grebe, Grey Heron, Little Egret, Mute Swan, Black Kite, Hobby, Quail, Corncrake, Lapwing, Curlew, Kingfisher, Skylark, White and Yellow Wagtails, Whinchat, Fieldfare, Common and Lesser Whitethroats, Grasshopper Warbler,

Golden Oriole, Woodchat and Red-backed Shrikes, Reed and Corn Buntings. On passage the variety of birds depends on the extent of the flooding, but if there is a reasonable amount of water a wide variety of species can be expected, though the exact mix varies from year to year: waders, gulls (including Mediterranean, Little, Lesser Blackbacked, Yellow-legged and Herring), Common, Little, Whiskered, Black and White-winged Black Terns, as well as Great White Egret and White Stork. In winter, the more regular species to be seen include: Cormorant, Mute Swan, Pochard and Tufted Duck, Black-headed, Common and Yellow-legged Gulls. During periods of cold weather various northern species sometimes turn up: divers, three species of sawbills, Bewick's and Whooper Swans, various diving ducks, Greylag, White-fronted and Bean Geese, making it well worth the effort to spend some time searching through the flocks of commoner wildfowl and gulls.

■ Access

From Chalon-sur-Saône take the N6 south towards Tournus and Mâcon. After 6 km fork left on the D6 through Varennes-le-Grand, as far as Marnay. Continue through the village to stop at the small car park on the left, before the bridge over the Saône. From here, take the towpath by the Saône southwards as far as the point where the River Grosne joins the main river. Another track leads back to Marnay. Once at the D6, follow it for about 400 metres and, just after the bridge over the Grosne, take a path that crosses the meadows as far as a bridge. Cross this and follow the dyke to arrive at the Frette, and continue by this as far as the D6. After another 600 metres take the 'chemin de la Vie' footpath and then, just before the houses, take the track to the right that comes to another bridge further along the Saône. Follow the Saône southwards back to the starting point.

10. Lac de la Sorme

Saône-et-Loire (71)

IGN 36/37

This artificial lake, to the west of Chalon-sur-Saône and south of Autun, is of exceptional local interest because of the mix of open water and extensive mudflats. The lake, which is 238 hectares in extent, is roughly V-shaped, with several long narrow arms. Many wintering or migrant aquatic birds can be seen: divers, Cormorant (more than 300 in winter and it has bred), Crane and storks, swans and geese, dabbling and diving duck, sawbills, gulls, terns, sometimes even skuas, and many raptors. The lake is immediately north of Montceau-les-Mines, and the D980 from there crosses the lake on causeways. Beyond the lake, a track to the left to St.-Nizier leads to the edge of one of the longer arms which runs up to the village of Charmoy. When the water level drops between June and November, some 25 hectares of mud can be exposed here, and this is a big attraction as far as migrant waders are concerned. No less than 33 wader species (as many as 18 simultaneously) have been found here, including Pectoral, Broad-billed and Marsh Sandpipers and Lesser Yellowlegs. You can get a very good view over the

11. Lac de Bas-Rebourseaux

YONNE (89) *IGN 22/28*

CORMORANT

The LPO's Bas-Rebourseaux reserve lies in the Armançon valley, north-east of Auxerre. It was formerly a gravel-pit, dug when the nearby Paris-Lyon TGV line was being constructed, and is sandwiched between the railway and the Canal de Bourgogne, which follows the course of the nearby River Armançon very closely. The lake is of interest because the water is constantly being refreshed by the nearby river, producing an abundance of aquatic vegetation and fish. This constant flow also prevents the lake freezing over in winter. This, coupled with its being on a migration route, makes it a privileged site for observing many migrant and over-wintering birds. Access by vehicle is very much restricted; it is far better to visit the site on foot.

inlets and north of the lake from the D102 which runs west on dykes from the D980. It is also worth looking from the dam at the southern end of the lake, where many of the ducks and divers occur. Where the D102 leaves the lake turn left towards Domans. Cross another inlet and once again turn left, just after some woodland, towards Vèvre, to reach the dam in about 750 metres.

ACCESS

The nearest town is St.-Florentin, just to the north on the N77. Turn west off this along the D43 through Vergigny towards Bouilly and Mont-St.-Sulpice. On leaving Bas-Rebourseaux village take the tarmac road that leads to the Paris-Lyon-Marseille railway line (1). Once over the level-crossing turn right. Buzzard, Black (and sometimes Red) Kite, Sparrowhawk and Kestrel often hunt over the railway and surrounding fields. Continue by the railway (2), scanning the fields for Lapwing. Pass under the TGV line and go as far as the car park; the rest of the circuit has to be made on foot. Two observation

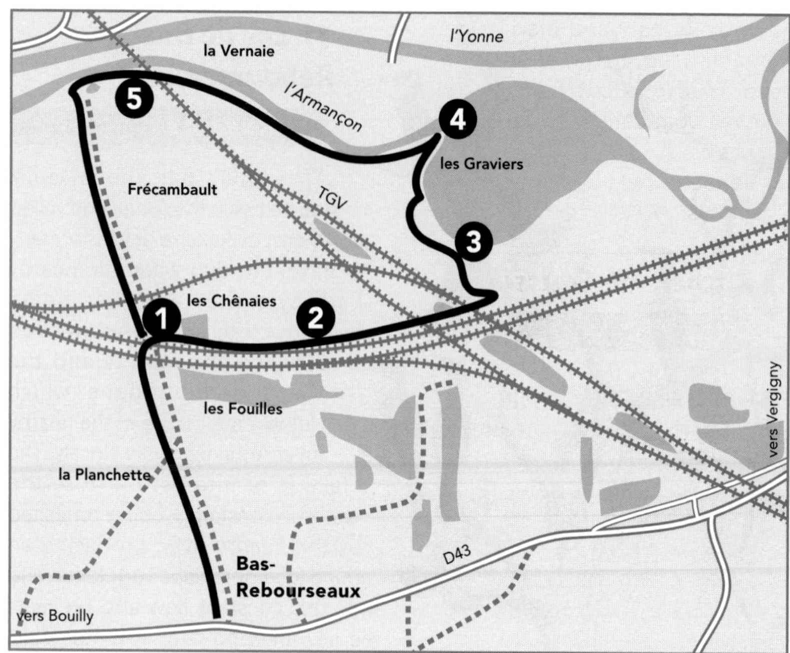

points (3) and (4) (with hides) provide views over the whole lake. From here, depending on the season, it is possible to see various grebes, ducks, waders and many other waterbirds. Continue the walk along the river (5) upstream. Kingfishers are often seen coming and going here and many passerines can be found in the riverside vegetation. Finish the visit by following the track as far as the level-crossing (1) and back to the car park.

■ Calendar

All year: Great Crested and Little Grebes, Grey Heron, Mallard, Coot, Kingfisher.
Migration periods: dabbling duck including Garganey, Osprey, waders, marsh terns.
Summer: White Stork (regular), Black Kite, Little Ringed Plover, Common Sandpiper, Common Tern, Sand Martin, many passerines.
Winter: grebes, Cormorant, many dabbling duck, Pochard and Tufted Duck, sometimes Great White Egret, Smew, Goosander, Goldeneye, Snipe and Water Pipit.

12. Yonne valley gravel pits

Yonne (89) *IGN 21*

In addition to the Bas-Rebourseaux pit (see previous site) there are many other man-made lakes along the northern part of the Yonne valley, the result of over thirty years of gravel extraction. In winter these artificial lakes attract many ducks such as Pochard, Tufted Duck, Mallard, Gadwall and Teal. There are often concentrations of Coot and Great Crested and Little Grebes. During the summer there are

Common Terns, Sand Martins and Common Sandpipers, all of which breed. The N6 follows the course of the river from Joigny to Sens. The best pits as far as birds are concerned can be found at St.-Julien-du-Sault, Villeneuve-sur-Yonne and Gron.

13. Rochers du Saussois

YONNE (89) *IGN 28*

The Rochers de Saussois are spectacular rock formations in the Yonne valley, some 30 km south of Auxerre. Take the N6, then the D100 through Mailly-la-Ville as far as Merry-sur-Yonne, where the cliffs are obvious. The main focus of interest here is the resident pair of Peregrines, easiest to see between February and late May. There is also a large colony of Jackdaws, and the nearby river holds Kingfisher, Dipper, Grey Wagtail and many common hedgerow birds. Definitely worth a stop on the way to the popular tourist town of Vézelay.

LITTLE GREBE

SITES

1. ***Réserve naturelle des Sept-Îles***
2. ***Baie de St.-Brieuc***
3. ***Cap Fréhel***
4. ***Landes de Locarn***
5. ***Sillon de Talbert***
6. ***Île d'Ouessant***
7. ***Trunvel***
8. ***Anse de Goulven***
9. ***Cap-Sizun***
10. ***Étang de Nérizelec***
11. ***Réserve des Cragous***
12. ***The Vilaine estuary***
13. ***Golfe du Morbihan***
14. ***Belle-Île***
15. ***Île d'Hoëdic***
16. ***Marais de Séné***

Brittany

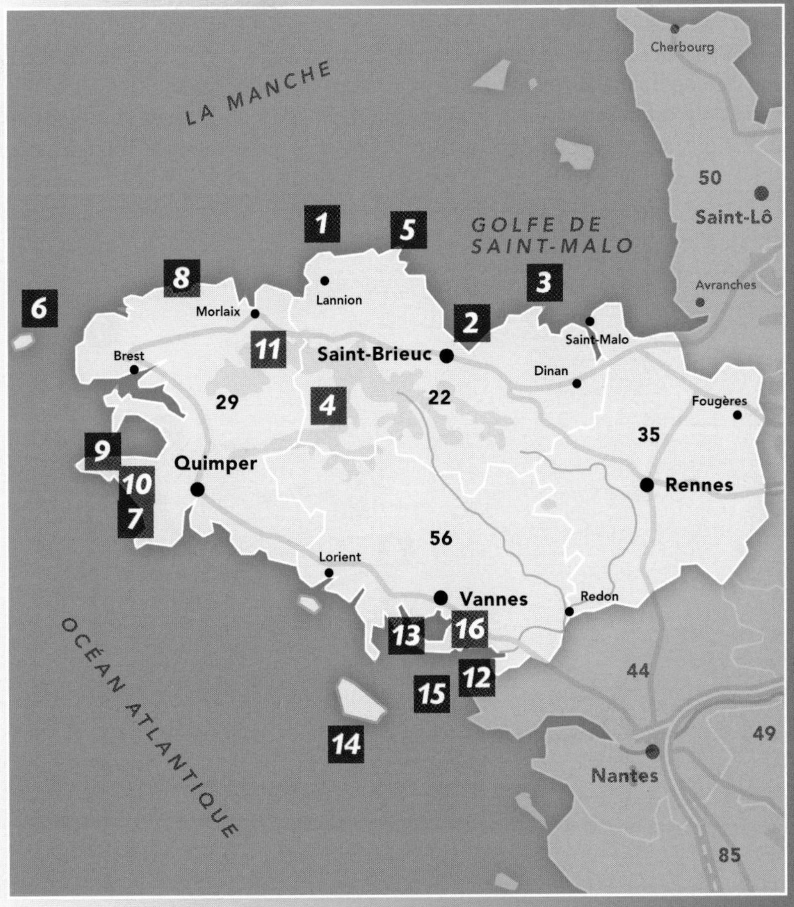

LA MANCHE
GOLFE DE SAINT-MALO
OCÉAN ATLANTIQUE
Cherbourg
50
Saint-Lô
Avranches
1
5
8
6
3
2
Lannion
Morlaix
Saint-Malo
Brest
11
Saint-Brieuc
Dinan
29
4
22
Fougères
35
9
Quimper
10
Rennes
7
56
Lorient
Vannes
Redon
13
16
12
44
15
14
49
Nantes
85

1. Réserve naturelle des Sept-Îles

Côtes-d'Armor (22)

IGN 14

The Sept-Îles reserve, a granite archipelago 5 km off the Brittany coast at Perros-Guirec, is the largest seabird colony in France, and is managed by the LPO – in fact it is their oldest reserve. It comprises five islands (Île aux Moines, Île Plate, Île de Bono, Île de Malban, Île Rouzic) and some smaller islets (Le Cerf and Costan). The most isolated, Rouzic, has the most birds: 12 species of seabird, 20,000 pairs in all, nest in spring and summer and include both Gannet and Puffin at their only breeding sites in France. Landing is strictly prohibited, except on the Île aux Moines where the lighthouse-keepers live.

Access

The only way to see the birds at close quarters is by boat from Perros-Guirec. The boats leave from the Vedettes Blanches landing-stage at the extreme left-hand end of Trestraou beach; there is a car park at the top of the beach. The trip around the Sept-Îles usually lasts about three hours and, in addition to the birds on the islands themselves, seabirds can also be seen during the crossing: Manx Shearwater and Fulmar often cross the bows and Storm Petrels are occasionally seen, although not coming ashore until after dark. The boat stops first opposite the Gannet colony (1), which is at its most impressive in late spring and summer. The next stop

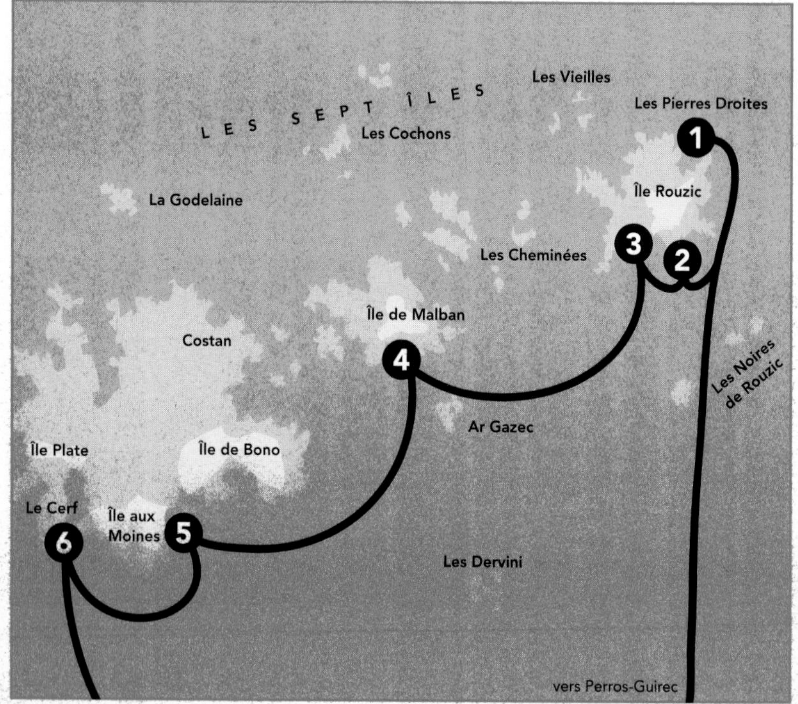

is in front of the Puffins at Rouzic (2 and 3), the island with the highest numbers. This is a good area to look at the auks on the water: in addition to the Puffins there are also Guillemots and Razorbills, and any of these species can also be seen on the rocks. The boats stop in front of the Île de Malban (4) to see the nesting Shags. Sometimes there is a half-hour stop on the Île aux Moines (5), where Rock Pipit is usually easy to find and from where it is possible to obtain distant views of Oystercatcher and Shelduck on the Île Plate. Before returning to the mainland the boats usually stop near Le Cerf (6), to look at the grey seals that sometimes haul up on the rocks here. Common Terns nest here in some years. Numerous gulls (Great Black-backed, Lesser Black-backed and Herring) nest around most of the islands, and can be seen throughout the trip. Ravens, which nest on the Île de Bono, can sometimes be seen overhead anywhere. Waders, which are quite common during spring migration, occur along the tide line around the islands. A little way to the west along the coast, beyond Trégastel, the LPO has a visitor and bird rescue centre at the Île Grande. This is a good source of information about the birds of the area, and has a video link to the Sept-Îles so that you can watch the seabirds in the warm and dry if you wish.

CALENDAR

Spring: Storm Petrel, Manx Shearwater, Fulmar, Shag, Gannet, Great Black-backed, Lesser Black-backed and Herring Gulls, Common Tern, Guillemot, Razorbill and Puffin. Other nesting species include Shelduck, Oystercatcher, Rock Pipit, Raven.

Summer: Razorbill, Guillemot and Puffin until mid-July. The Gannets remain at the colony until at least the end of September.

Autumn and winter: waders (Oystercatcher, Turnstone, Curlew, Purple Sandpiper). Grey seals are present on the reserve throughout the year.

2. *Baie de St.-Brieuc*

CÔTES-D'ARMOR (22)

IGN 14

Just east of St.-Brieuc are two bays, the Anse d'Yffiniac and the Anse de Morieux, which comprise the Réserve Naturelle de la Baie de St.-Brieuc and Yffiniac, extremely important refuges for wintering and passage waders and wildfowl. The most accessible area, with the biggest range of birds, is at Yffiniac, particularly at high tide when flocks of Knot, Dunlin, Bar-tailed Godwit and Oystercatcher can be seen feeding on the mudflats, joined in winter by Brent Geese and dabbling ducks. From the Pointe des Guettes, between the two bays, and again especially at high tide, there is the possibility to see terns, divers, Common Scoter, Balearic Shearwater and skuas offshore. The long-distance footpath, the GR34, runs along much of the shore, and provides some good viewpoints.

3. *Cap Fréhel*

CÔTES-D'ARMOR (22)

IGN 14/16

Cap Fréhel, between St.-Brieuc and St.-Malo, is within the region called the Penthièvre coast, in the eastern part of the Côtes-d'Armor. The headland is managed as a reserve by the society, Bretagne-Vivante-SEPNB (Société pour l'Étude et la Protection de la Nature en

Bretagne) and the Syndicat de Caps and contains an exceptional mixture of heath and coastal cliffs. The cliffs are used by rock-nesting House Martins, a few pairs of Black Redstarts, a pair of Ravens and also host France's most important Razorbill and Guillemot colony. A marked trail skirts the headland crossing various different habitats. The D34A runs through Sables-d'Or to the headland from the main coast road, and the GR34 footpath provides access on foot.

4. Landes de Locarn

Côtes-d'Armor (22)
IGN 14

Lying to the south-west of Guingamp, the Landes de Locarn cover several tens of hectares of heathland along a ridge of high ground. In summer, a few pairs of Nightjar occur whilst in winter the site is a roost for Hen Harriers. The D787 runs through the village of Callac from Guingamp, and just beyond here the D11 leads to Locarn. From here the D20 runs through the site to St.-Nicodème, and there is a car park close to the road between these two villages. From here, follow the marked trails for further exploration.

GANNET

5. Sillon de Talbert

Côtes-d'Armor (22)
IGN 14

Situated east of Perros-Guirec, and at the end of a wild promontory between the Jaudy and Trieux estuaries, the Sillon de Talbert is Europe's longest pebble ridge, 3 km in all. In the summer, Little and Common Terns, Ringed and Kentish Plovers breed on the shore, while in winter it is possible to see Sanderling, Bar-tailed Godwit, Curlew, Turnstone, Red-breasted Merganser, Brent Goose and Rock Pipit. In addition to the Sillon itself, both of the estuaries to the west and to the east provide good birdwatching opportunities throughout the year. From Tréguier or Lézardrieux on the D786, take the D20 north to where there is a car park near the coast. It is possible to walk along the top of the ridge, but you should be careful not to disturb the breeding birds.

6. Île d'Ouessant

Finistère (29)
IGN 13 (or 0317OT, 1:25,000)

Ouessant (sometimes called Ushant in English) is the most westerly island in France, and occupies the strategic point where the Atlantic and the English Channel join. The basic structure is of a wide plateau sloping downwards from east to west, and the whole island has a coastline of indented cliffs, ringed by a multitude of rocks and islands. There is a large bay, the Baie de Lampaul, at the western end. Because of its exceptional interest for studying bird migration (especially passerines), it has become, since 1984, France's only permanent coastal bird observatory – France's answer to the Isles of Scilly as far as vagrants are concerned! The island also has some very impressive seabird colonies.

Access

Boats for the Île d'Ouessant, and also taking in the Île de Molène en route, leave from either Brest or from Conquet, the latter being about 20 km west of Brest at the end of the D789. The crossings take two hours from Brest, one hour and a quarter from Conquet. The timetable varies according to the season: information can be obtained from the Penn ar Bed Maritime Company (Tel: 02 98 80 24 68). There is also a daily air service from Brest-Guipavas Airport although booking ahead is essential (Tel: 02 98 84 64 87). Once on the island a good way to get around is by bicycle; they can be hired at the port or in Lampaul village. There is a Bird Observatory at the western end of the island which can accept guests year-round. For more information contact the Centre Ornithologique, 29242 Île d'Ouessant (Tel: 02 98 48 82 65). There is free access on all tracks over the whole island but, as ever, please respect the environment and private property. There are too many sites to give a complete list; each small valley, section of coast or patch of heathland can be of interest at one time or another, but a few suggestions can be given, as follows, all starting from the Bird Observatory (1), following a roughly clockwise route around the island. The bushes round the Observatory itself often hold Firecrest and warblers in autumn. Sea-watching can be good from the headland of the Pointe du Creac'h (2), especially in September and October, when species that occur include petrels,

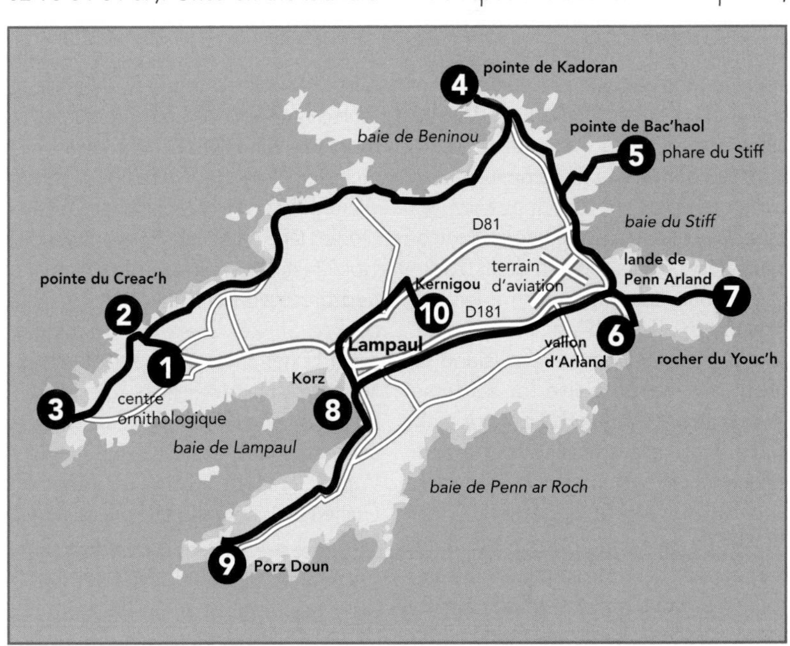

Bretagne

Gannet and shearwaters, as well as skuas and Sabine's Gull. It can be worthwhile continuing westwards as far as the Pointe de Pern (3) which is favoured by open-country passerines, including sometimes Richard's Pipit in autumn. Moving east, along the north coast, look out for the Wheatears which are common breeding birds on the heathland. At the Pointe de Kadoran (4) the bare heath is ideal for Dotterel on migration, and also for Snow and Lapland Buntings (check for these also anywhere along the north coast, e.g. at Yuzin). The point is also a good sea-watching spot. Continue to the lighthouse (Phare du Stiff, 5). Chough breed on the cliffs here, and there are other pairs dispersed around the island.

YELLOW-BROWED WARBLER

The Vallon d'Arland (6) is without doubt Ouessant's number one spot for small insectivores in autumn: warblers, Goldcrest, Firecrest, flycatchers, etc., at any time from August until October. In spring look for breeding Dartford Warbler in the gorse heath at Penn Arland (7). At the head of the Baie de Lampaul, many birds gather on the beach at Korz (8), especially during a rising tide, including Black-headed, Herring and Great Black-backed Gulls and waders such as Ringed Plover. Porz Doun (9), at the extreme south-westerly point of the island is probably the best site for waders. Oystercatcher, Ringed Plover, Redshank and other smaller species all occur, and amongst them is often a Purple Sandpiper, and during westerly gales a Grey Phalarope or even an American rarity may appear. Back at Lampaul, there are some reservoirs (10) at Kernigou, which are worth a look. Coots are resident but there are often passage duck, Whooper Swan and various waders to be seen here.

Calendar

Spring: Fulmar, Storm Petrel, Manx Shearwater, Shag, Oystercatcher, Ringed Plover, Herring, Lesser and Great Black-backed Gulls, Cuckoo, Wheatear, Dartford Warbler and Chough all nest. On passage: Gannet, Kittiwake, Razorbill, skuas, Turtle Dove, Willow Warbler, shrikes, Golden Oriole and a few rarities.

Summer and autumn: A migration hotspot, with sometimes spectacular movements of Sooty, Great, Manx, Balearic and a few Cory's Shearwaters, Storm and Leach's Petrels, Fulmar; also Sparrowhawk, Peregrine, Merlin, Dotterel, small waders, Woodcock, Grey Phalarope, Great, Arctic and Pomarine Skuas, Kittiwake, Sabine's Gull, terns, auks, Wryneck, Short-toed Lark (rare), wagtails, pipits (Richard's regular), Wheatear, Whinchat, Black and Common Redstarts, thrushes, Ring Ouzel. Many warblers including Icterine, Melodious, Lesser Whitethroat, Willow, Chiffchaff, Yellow-browed (and other rarer Siberian species), Goldcrest, Firecrest, Spotted, Pied and Red-breasted (rare) Flycatchers, Red-backed Shrike, Chaffinch, Brambling, Siskin, Linnet, Snow and Lapland Buntings. More rarely North American, Scandinavian, Siberian and North African waders and passerines, etc.

Winter: Gannet, Kittiwake, Razorbill, Guillemot; sometimes Glaucous Gull, Little Auk. During very cold spells, duck, Lapwing, Snipe, thrushes and Blackbird.

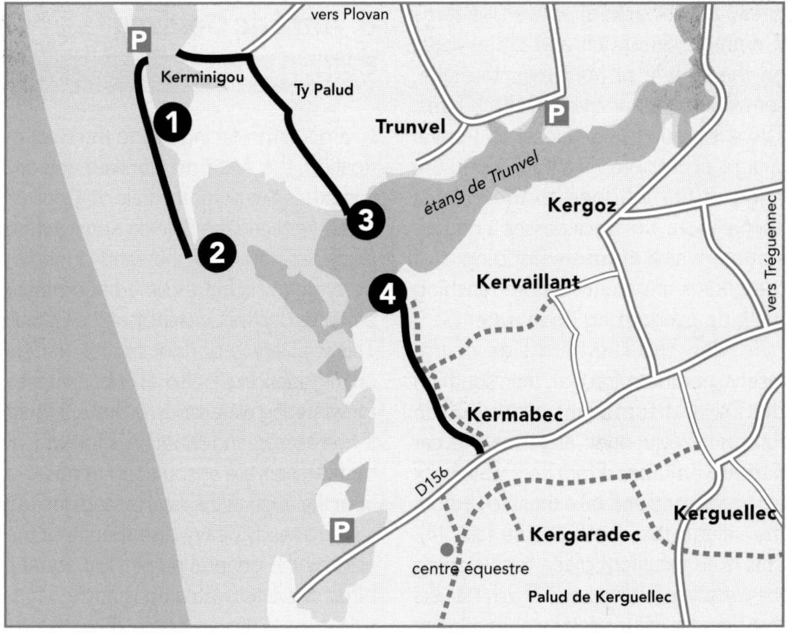

7. Trunvel

FINISTÈRE (29) *IGN 13*

At the centre, of the Baie d'Audierne, west of Quimper, this site is of international importance for nesting and migrating wetland warblers. It comprises lakes, coastal marsh, stable and moving sand-dunes in the south, reed-beds in the centre, and a large open lake inland. Gorse and blackthorn thickets as well as elm woods surround the reserve, the access to which is strictly controlled, but higher land around its limits offers excellent birdwatching. In spring many wetland passerines nest in the reedbed: Sedge, Reed, Cetti's and sometimes Savi's Warblers, Bearded Tit and Reed Bunting. Bittern is present in the reedbed throughout the year, whilst Purple Heron and Little Bittern are present from May to September. Marsh Harrier can also be seen around the lake at any time of year, and it is also a focus for migrants in both spring and autumn. Although mostly only seen when removed from a mist-net by the bird-ringers, Aquatic Warblers pass through here in regular if small numbers in autumn.

Access

From Quimper take the D785 west and then the D156 to Plonéour-Lanvern. From here the D2 runs through Tréogat and then Plovan to reach a car park near the coast at Kerminigou, a total of some 25 km from Quimper. From the car park follow the pebble beach southwards (1). Look for pipits and Wheatear here in late summer, and sometimes even Dotterel turn up on migration. Follow the edge of the reserve as far as (2). In spring it is possible to see godwits, Curlew and Sanderling in this area. Gulls (Black-headed, Little, Mediterranean, Herring, Lesser and

Great Black-backed) as well as terns (Common, Sandwich and Little) roost on the beach, or hunt over the lake, sometimes accompanied by Black Terns. There is a public hide closer to Trunvel village, accessible via a track along the edge of the reedbed to the east of Kerminigou. The track passes a ringing station, which is worth stopping at if the ringers are about, before reaching the hide overlooking open water (3).

To view the southern side of the reserve, return to Tréogat, then south on the D2 and turn right on the D156 through Tréguennec as far as the car park at Kermabec. From here walk back along the road and take the track before the village that leads to the lake (4). This is an excellent place for watching the wetland passerines and Marsh Harriers that breed in the reeds, as well as migrant and wintering species.

Calendar

Spring: Bittern, Purple Heron, Garganey, Shoveler, Kentish Plover, Lapwing, Curlew, Bar-tailed Godwit, Little and Mediterranean Gulls and Black Tern on migration, Yellow Wagtail, Reed, Sedge and Fan-tailed Warblers and Bearded Tit.
Autumn: various European waders (and North American species regularly), Meadow, Tree, Tawny and Richard's Pipits, Bluethroat, Aquatic Warbler, Snow and Lapland Bunting, many other passerines on migration.
Winter: Bittern, many duck (Pochard, Tufted Duck and sometimes Scaup, Teal, Gadwall, Shoveler, and Wigeon), Marsh and Hen Harriers, Merlin, Fan-tailed, Cetti's and Dartford Warblers, Bearded Tit.

8. Anse de Goulven

Finistère (29) *IGN 13*

A large, north-facing bay to the west of Roscoff, the Anse de Goulven actually comprises two parts: the Baie de Goulven to the west and the Baie de Kernic to the east, separated by the sand-dunes of Keremma which are owned and hence protected by the Conservatoire du Littoral. This is a very important site for waders on migration, but is also an important area for wintering waterbirds. Although there is free access, and shooting is forbidden, birdwatchers are encouraged to observe from the edge of the reserve, and not add to the already heavy disturbance of the area by the general public. For aquatic birds, the best watching is at the high-tide roosts (arrive some three hours before high tide, the higher the tide the better in general). Sea-watching from the headlands is at its best at times when strong north-westerly winds are blowing; on the other hand ducks, divers and grebes roosting on the sea are more likely to be easily located under calm conditions. In short, there are birds to be seen no matter what the weather!

Access

From Brest take the D788 to Lesneven, then the D770 north as far as Brignogan, and then fork right to the Plage du Lividic (1). Cars should be parked near the football pitch (and not on the sand-dune!). On the beach it is possible to see Sanderling, Ringed and Kentish Plovers, Turnstone and Purple Sandpiper during migration and in winter. Check the whole beach but especially its northern part. At the right season, or when there is a strong wind, it may be worth going to Brignogan signal tower (2) to do some

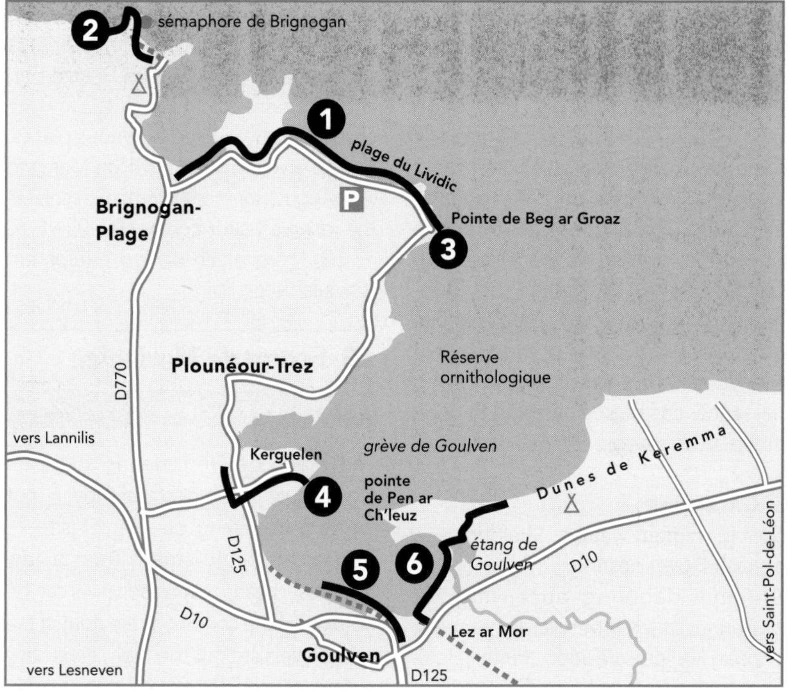

sea-watching from the point. In autumn, if you are lucky and the conditions are right, it is possible to see Storm Petrel, Gannet, shearwaters, skuas, terns (Arctic in late summer) and Sabine's Gull (in September) offshore. At the end of the Lividic beach is the Pointe de Beg ar Groaz (3), another good look-out spot. There are often wintering ducks here at their daytime roost on the sea, mainly Mallard but also divers, grebes and auks. To see the head of the bay, continue along the coast road as far as Kerguelen, where you turn left and, with caution, go as far as the sea front (4). It is possible to park in a small car park on the shore, but you should be careful not to impede any farm vehicles that may want to pass. Do not go out onto the foreshore as this may disturb the birds. On very high tides Kerguelen is a good high-tide roost for the bay's waders and it is well worth sitting down by the roadside and waiting for the birds to come nearer – the sight is rarely disappointing. The next stop is the car park at Goulven station (5). At high tide it is worth walking along the track on the disused railway line, from where it is possible to see Lapwing, Curlew and various waders on migration, out on the salt marsh. The most characteristic passerines are Meadow and Rock Pipits, but Fan-tailed Warblers can also be seen or heard. There is often a hunting Peregrine here between late August and March. The last port of call is at Lez ar Mor, where there is a car park (6). Climb onto the embankment and look left across the mudflats, one of the best areas for waders, and look right to the pool of the Étang de Goulven. In autumn and winter the full range of all the waders that feed in the bay can be seen from the embankment, together with Wigeon, Pintail and Teal. The reedbed to the east of the embankment often attracts interesting passerines on migration while during the breeding season there are Cetti's, Fan-tailed and Reed Warblers. You can continue walking along the embankment as far as the Keremma dunes where there are Golden Plover, Wheatear and Blue-headed Wagtail in autumn. At the Pointe de Pen ar Ch'leuz, to the west of the dunes, thousands of migrating passerines can be seen moving through at the same season.

■ CALENDAR

Spring: migrant waders. Shelduck and Kentish Plover nesting.
Autumn: dabbling duck, migrant passerines, often in very large numbers.
Winter: Mallard, Wigeon, Pintail, Teal, Shelduck, Dunlin, Knot, Sanderling, Purple and Common Sandpipers, Ruff, Redshank, Greenshank, Spotted Redshank, Grey, Golden, Ringed and Kentish Plovers, Snipe and Jack Snipe, Curlew, Whimbrel, Oystercatcher, Turnstone, both godwits, Lapwing.

9. Cap-Sizun

FINISTÈRE (29) *IGN 13*

To the west of Douarnenez, near Goulien, the reserve of Cap-Sizun is one of the flagship bird reserves in Brittany, renowned for its seabird colonies. During the summer the cliffs hold Fulmar, Shag, Great Black-backed Gull, Kittiwake and Guillemot. Managed by Bretagne Vivante-SEPNB, it also holds a good range of other cliff-nesting birds. Of particular note are two other species that have become hard to find in Brittany but which can still be seen here – Raven and Chough. The reserve is signposted off the D7 west of Douarnenez, and footpaths along the cliffs allow the seabirds to be viewed in various places. The reserve is open from 15th March to 31st August; for more information contact the reserve visitor centre (Tel: 02 98 70 13 53), from which optical equipment is available on loan.

10. Étang de Nérizelec

FINISTÈRE (29) *IGN 13*

The Étang de Nérizelec is a coastal lagoon just to the north of Plovan, not far from the Étang de Trunvel (site 7). Being relatively small, (just a few hectares), means that good views can be obtained if the conditions are right. If the water levels are not too high, especially in August and September, many wader, gull and tern species drop in here to feed and bathe. In winter there are grebes, dabbling and diving duck and gulls to be seen. Roads lead down to the coast both to the north and to the south of the lagoon, and in order not to disturb the birds it is best viewed from the path along the shingle-bar that separates it from the sea.

11. Réserve des Cragous

FINISTÈRE (29) *IGN 14*

The Monts d'Arrée, south of Morlaix, is an area where there still remain significant areas of the heathland which once covered much of this part of Brittany. Typical breeding birds include Montagu's and Hen Harriers, Curlew, Grasshopper and Dartford Warblers.

A good starting point is the Réserve de Cragous, near the village of Plougonven, which lies on the D9 south-east of Morlaix. It is managed by Bretagne Vivante-SEPNB (Tel: 02 98 79 71 98), from whom more details are available on access and guided visits.

12. *The Vilaine estuary*

MORBIHAN (56) *IGN 15*

The area where the River Vilaine flows into the sea, south-east of Vannes, is quite varied, with a series of contrasting habitats that make it a remarkable zone for waders, seabirds and ducks. In particular it is the most important wintering site in France for Scaup, with up to 2,000 birds present, 80% of the national total. There are three different facets to this area: the rocky coastline to the north and south, just outside the river mouth; a unique cliff of an ochre-coloured mix of clay and sand which dominates a sandy beach (the Mine d'Or) south of the estuary; and the sandy coastal strip at Bronzais, near Pénestin.

ACCESS

From Vannes, head south on the N165 and turn south at exit 21 along the D140 which leads to Damgan and the Pointe de Kervoyal headland (1). This is a good spot for a general view over the maritime part of the estuary and is useful for pinpointing groups of diving duck. In the afternoon the lighting conditions are good for watching seabirds offshore (terns, skuas, shearwaters, etc.) in the autumn. A little further east, at Cromenac'h (2), is one of the areas favoured by Scaup in some years. However, one has to bear in mind that the species moves around the estuary a lot, according to the season, the tide and the weather. From here one has to go inland to Muzillac and then back via Billiers to circumnavigate the inlet of the Étier de Billiers to reach the shore again at the Pointe de Penn Lann or the Plage des Granges (3). From the latter, one can walk along the footpath to the east, where there is a good view over the estuary from the cliff top. In winter, at high tide, this is perhaps the most regular spot for Scaup. The flood meadows next to the road attract many Lapwing, Curlew and Sacred Ibis. This last species has become naturalised in this part of France, having originated from a wildlife park at Branféré, just to the north-east. Numbers have increased year on year, and although they give an exotic tinge to the avifauna there are signs that they are already having a negative effect on the native herons and egrets in whose colonies they nest. Another viewpoint is at Moustoir (4), reached by road via Billiers. A footpath to the west by the shore gives views over what is an excellent site in winter for dabbling duck and every sort of wader. From here go inland to Arzal and cross the Vilaine on the D139. It is worth checking the area by the dam at the river crossing for terns which sometimes feed here in summer and autumn. Continue on the D34 to Pénestin and the mudflats of Bronzais (5). From August onwards this is a good area for flocks of waders and gulls, especially around high tide. In winter, disturbance from wildfowlers makes much of the area less rewarding but Brent Goose and various waders can be watched here at mid tide. The circuit can be completed at the Mine d'Or beach (6), to the west of Pénestin. This is a good spot in the morning, with the light behind you, for watching seabirds in autumn: petrels, Gannet, skuas and Sabine's Gull, mid-September being

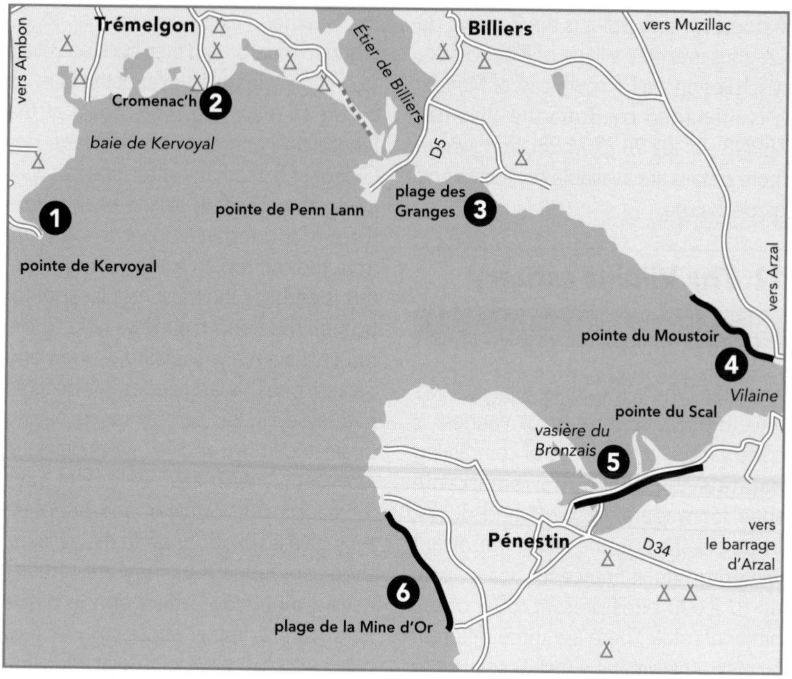

KENTISH PLOVER

the peak period. Numbers of Balearic Shearwaters sometimes gather offshore in the evening, especially at high tide, between August and early October. In winter, the main species to be seen here are Great Crested Grebe, Common Scoter and Eider, with sometimes a few divers and Scaup.

Calendar

All year: Grey Heron, Little Egret, Sacred Ibis, Shelduck, Mallard, Marsh Harrier, Oystercatcher, Redshank, Fan-tailed Warbler.

Autumn migration: Balearic Shearwater, skuas (3 species), Sabine's Gull, Sandwich Tern, Pintail, Shoveler, Teal, Eider, Common Scoter, Scaup, Avocet, Ringed Plover, Dunlin, Black-tailed Godwit, Curlew, Whimbrel and Turnstone.

13. *Golfe du Morbihan*

Morbihan (56) *IGN 15*

The Golfe du Morbihan, virtually an inland sea, is scattered with some forty islands and bordered by vast mudflats that at low tide cover 4,000 hectares, and is fringed with many abandoned salt pans. It is bounded on its southern side by the Rhuys peninsula, the coast of which alternates between rocky points and sandy bays. This vast area is an exceptional site for aquatic birds in winter (60,000 to 100,000 duck, waders and gulls in winter), for breeding waders in summer, and for migrant Spoonbills and waders in both spring and autumn. Various parts of the area are protected: there are reserves in the south-east corner (at Sarzeau and St.-Armel) and in the Séné marshes as well as the Pen En Toul marshes at Larmor-Baden.

Access

It is a complex area to visit but most of the sites mentioned below are sign-posted and easily accessible by car. The state of the tide will clearly make a difference, and tide tables are available in nearby Vannes. Starting in the north-west, the marshes at Pen En Toul (1) have various aquatic birds throughout the year, and are best at high tide when waders arrive to roost. There are guided visits in summer (Tel: 02 97 66 92 76 for more details). In the same area, during August and September, many Roseate Terns gather around the oyster beds to the north of the Île de Berder, off Larmor-Baden. Although close to the town of Vannes, the Pointe des Émigrés (2), is very good for birds in winter. Little, Great Crested and Black-necked Grebes, Goldeneye and Red-breasted Merganser can be seen diving in the channel, and good numbers of Teal occur on the small marsh there. The nearby Séné marshes (3), are covered separately (see site 16 below). East again, the Noyalo bridge (4), on the D780, is a good spot at low tide from which to see Avocets and other waders in winter, in company with Shelduck. Continuing along the D780 southwards brings you to St.-Armel-Tascon (5), a very important feeding site at mid tide during winter for any of the waders of the area, plus Brent Goose, Pintail, etc. A little further on, at the inlet near St.-Colombier (6), waders come to roost some two to three hours before high tide and can usually be seen for about the same period afterwards. In the nearby marshes Teal are the most numerous of the various ducks which come to feed here. Further on again brings us to Sarzeau, but some 500 metres before the village turn to the right towards Kerbodec, and again to the right before there to reach the shore once again (7). At mid tide this is another excellent place for watching waders, Brent Goose and dabbling duck (particularly Wigeon and Shoveler). It is worth mentioning, perhaps, that this eastern part of the Golfe du Morbihan, from (5) to (7), is the most important zone as far as wintering birds are concerned. Just to the south-east are some more areas worth exploring. The D195 leads from St.-Colombier to Le-Tour-du-Parc, just south of which lies the bay at Banastère (8), a very good place for seeing waders in winter (best one hour after high tide). It is also worth looking from the bridge for grebes and sawbills offshore. From here take the D324, then the D199 to the village of Penvins, beyond which lies the Pointe de Penvins (9). This provides a roosting site for smaller waders such as Ringed Plover, Turnstone, Dunlin and Sanderling from April/May to August/September. It is also a good sea-watching point (shearwaters, petrels, skuas) from August to October and in winter there are often various species of diving birds present offshore, most notably Slavonian Grebe. A little to the west, the marsh at Suscinio (10) is worth a visit in spring and summer for its waders, terns and especially wetland passerines which include breeding Bluethroats. There is a car park at the beach, beyond the chateau. Finally, take the D780 towards Arzon, which is at the entrance to the Golfe de Morbihan at the end of the Rhuys peninsula. Just before

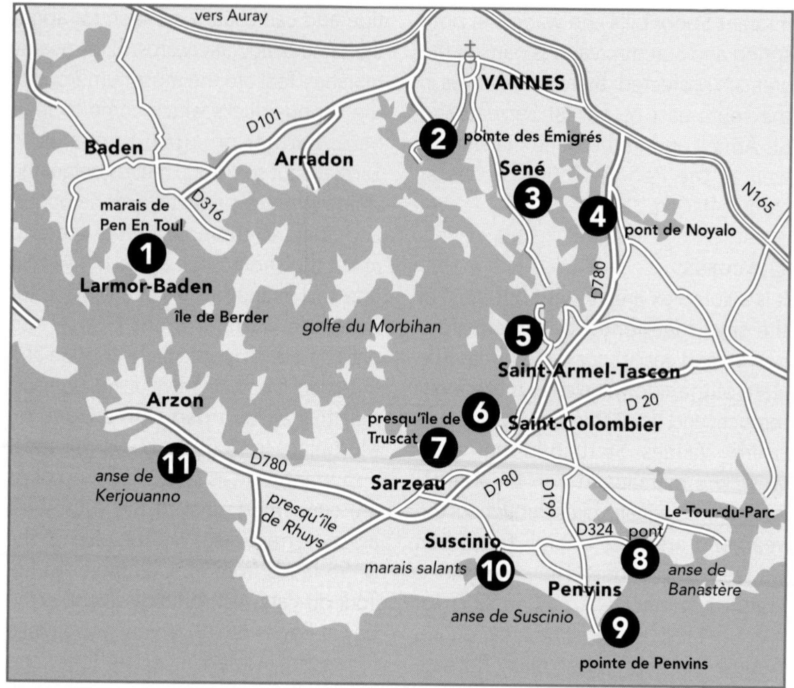

the village turn left, towards Kerjouanno (11) where the bay is a very good site in winter for divers, sawbills, Great Crested and Slavonian Grebes.

Calendar

All year: Grey Heron, Little Egret, Sacred Ibis, Marsh Harrier, Shelduck, Mute Swan, Avocet, Redshank, Kingfisher, Fan-tailed and Dartford Warblers and Bearded Tit.
Spring and autumn migration: Spoonbill (February to May), Osprey (August and September), Garganey, Bar-tailed Godwit, Curlew, various other wader species, Roseate Tern (August and September).
Breeding season: Black Kite, Black-winged Stilt, Kentish Plover, Common Tern, Blue-headed Wagtail, Bluethroat, Sedge and Reed Warblers.
Winter: Great Crested, Little, Black-necked and Slavonian Grebes, Spoonbill, Brent Goose, dabbling duck, Red-breasted Merganser, Goldeneye, Grey and Ringed Plovers, Curlew, Turnstone, Dunlin, Knot, Sanderling and Avocet.

14. Belle-Île

Morbihan (56)
IGN 15 (or 0822OT, 1:25,000)

Belle-Île lies offshore from Quiberon, and can be reached by ferry from there, the trip to the island taking about 45 minutes. In spring and summer, the whole of the unspoilt coastline on the west and south of the island is good for Shag, Lesser Black-backed, Great Black-backed and Herring Gulls, Oystercatcher, Rock Dove, Raven and Chough. The two most interesting areas are the cliffs between the Pointe de St.-Marc and the Pointe de Pouldon, in the south, and the Koh-Kastell reserve (near the Pointe de l'Apothicairerie at the northern end of the island) run by Bretagne Vivante-SEPNB. Fulmars nest at both places, joined by Kittiwakes at the latter.

15. Île d'Hoëdic

MORBIHAN (56) *IGN 15 (or 0822OT, 1:25,000)*

Another island offshore from Quiberon, but further east than Belle-Île. Although it is relatively small – 2½ km long and 800 metres wide – it has a very wide variety of habitats. In addition, the fact that it occupies a strategic position off the Vilaine estuary means that it is a magnet for a very diverse range of migrants between March and May and from August to October. Moreover, many birds winter along its coastline. Depending on the season it is possible to see divers, grebes, Gannet, shearwaters, petrels, various sea duck, birds of prey (Honey Buzzard, harriers, falcons, owls), many species of European wader with the occasional American, gulls, terns and skuas, as well as numerous species of passerine. In the autumn there may be pipits, flycatchers, redstarts, shrikes, thrushes, warblers, Goldcrests, Firecrests and various finches and buntings. This is also the time of year for rarities from farther east such as Yellow-browed and Pallas's Warblers, Red-breasted Flycatcher and Richard's Pipit. The island is accessed via the regular ferry services from the Quiberon ferry terminal (Tel: 08 20 05 60 00; http:// www.smn-navigation.fr), the boats calling in at the Île de Houat on the way to Hoëdic. It is possible to rent a cottage or book a room in the ancient fort (contact the Marie, Tel: 02 97 30 68 32 for more details). When exploring the island and looking for migrants take care to keep to the paths and not to trespass into private property or to damage the habitat in any way.

16. Marais de Séné

MORBIHAN (56) *IGN 15*

The Réserve Naturelle de Séné, covering more than 400 hectares, comprises the largest area of salt marsh and old salt pans within the Golfe du Morbihan (see also site 13 above). It lies immediately south-east of Vannes, from where it is signposted. It is an important site in winter for Spoonbill, Brent Goose, Shelduck and Avocet, and also in the breeding season, with good numbers of Avocet, Black-winged Stilt, Redshank and Bluethroat nesting. It also acts as a refuge during times of migration, when Spoonbill, Osprey, Curlew, godwits and many species of smaller wader come here to feed and roost. Some of the paths are freely open to the public throughout the year while others are only open for paying visits between February and September. For more information contact reserve-naturelle@sene.com (Tel: 02 97 66 92 76).

BRENT GOOSE

SITES

1 *Lac d'Auron*

2 *River Allier near Nevers*

3 *Marais de Contres*

4 *Écluzelles-Mézières*

5 *Vallée de la Conie*

6 *Étangs de la Brenne*

7 *Forêt de Lancosme*

8 *Val de Creuse*

9 *Lac de Rillé*

10 *Étang du Louroux*

11 *The Loire valley around Tours*

12 *The Sologne*

13 *Étang de l'Arche*

14 *The Loire valley near Orléans*

15 *La Beauce*

Centre

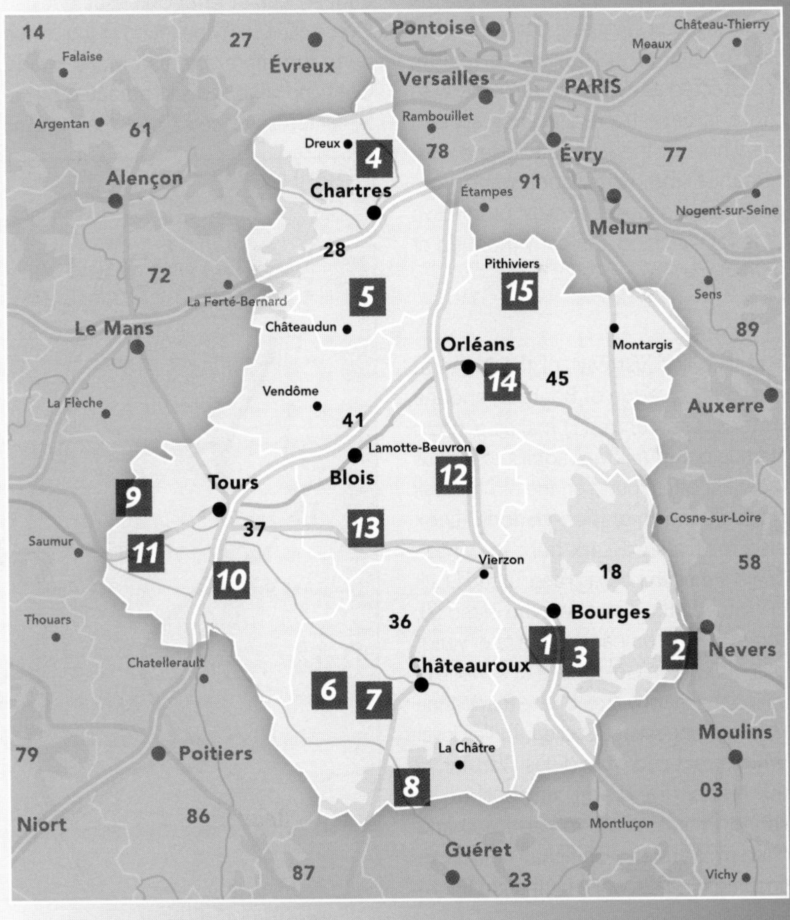

14
Falaise
27
Évreux
Pontoise
Château-Thierry
Meaux
Versailles
PARIS
Rambouillet
Argentan
61
Dreux
4
78
Évry
77
Alençon
Chartres
Étampes
91
Nogent-sur-Seine
Melun
28
Pithiviers
15
72
La Ferté-Bernard
5
Sens
Le Mans
Châteaudun
Orléans
Montargis
89
14
45
Vendôme
La Flèche
Auxerre
41
Lamotte-Beuvron
Tours
Blois
12
9
37
13
Cosne-sur-Loire
Saumur
11
Vierzon
18
58
10
Bourges
Thouars
36
1
3
2
Nevers
Chatellerault
Châteauroux
6
7
Moulins
79
Poitiers
La Châtre
8
03
Niort
86
Montluçon
Guéret
87
23
Vichy

1. Lac d'Auron

CHER (18) *IGN 35*

The Lac d'Auron, covering 82 hectares and dating from 1976, lies on the southern outskirts of Bourges where the River Auron and its tributary the Rampenne meet. The surrounding countryside is partially urbanised, the rest conserved as a green area (fields and thickets of mature trees), and there are remnants of reed-bed and marsh on the sides of the Rampenne. The lake is easy to watch, and is principally of interest during spring and autumn for migrants and for the duck that occur in variable numbers in winter. An island, on the western side, is protected as a reserve, but otherwise there is unrestricted access around the whole of the lake. Because of disturbance from water sports and from dogs running loose the most productive time for watching is in early morning or late afternoon.

Access

The lake lies just east of the N144 at the southern edge of Bourges, and the water-sports centre (1) makes a good starting point. Yellow Wagtails of various races are often found on the old football pitch during migration periods. Look also for Crested Lark here in winter. There are often Pochard and Tufted Duck in winter on the water near the island (2), sometimes accompanied by a rarer visitor such as a diver, Goldeneye or sawbill. In spring the marshy area by the Rampenne (3) is a nesting site for Cuckoo, Turtle Dove, Whitethroat and Melodious Warbler. In the reedbed and adjacent bushes, in spring, it is possible to see Reed and Garden Warblers, Chiffchaff, Blackcap and Nightingale, while Nuthatch, Short-

MEADOW PIPIT

toed Treecreeper and Rook are found in the larger trees. Many passerines also occur on migration, for instance flycatchers and various warblers which can include Icterine as well as Melodious. Reed Warblers nest in the reeds where the Auron flows into the lake at the southern end. A flock of semi-domestic Greylag Geese can usually be found at the bridge here, but there are also Mute Swans, Coot and various ducks attracted by the winter food provided. Check the shoreline

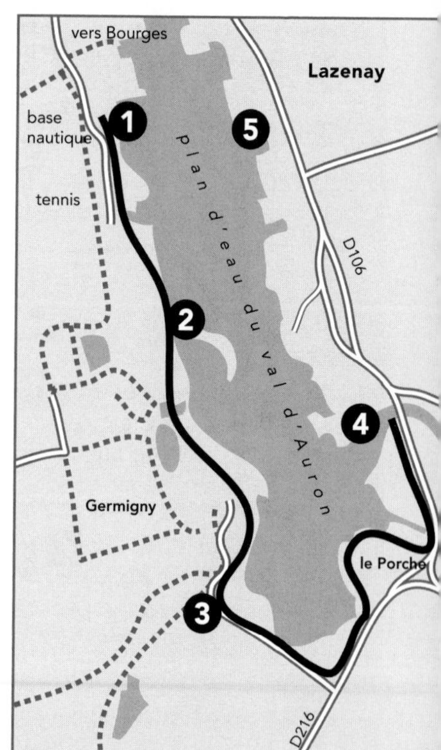

near the old football pitch (4) and wherever there are strips of sand for any migrant waders that may have dropped in. Common Sandpipers are the most frequent species but others that have been seen include Green Sandpiper, Greenshank, Spotted Redshank, Ruff, Dunlin, and sometimes Little Ringed Plover which normally outnumber Ringed Plover, this last being relatively rare. There is a large winter roost of several thousand Black-headed Gulls on the lake in front of the houses (5). During periods of hard weather or storms other species may also occur: Little and Mediterranean Gulls and more rarely Kittiwake, Common, Yellow-legged, Herring and Lesser Black-backed Gulls.

Calendar

Spring and autumn: Shoveler, Gadwall, waders regular in small numbers, Mediterranean and Little Gulls, Common, Little, Black and Whiskered Terns, the three hirundines and Yellow Wagtail (often in large flocks with various races present). Little and Great Crested Grebes, Moorhen, Mallard, Coot and Reed Warbler all breed. More occasionally: Black-necked Grebe, Pintail, Garganey, Black Kite, Kestrel, Hobby, Osprey and White Stork. Many passerines on migration include warblers and flycatchers. *Winter*: divers, Little and Great Crested Grebes, Mallard (in large numbers), Shoveler, Gadwall, Wigeon, Teal, Pochard and Tufted Duck in small numbers, occasionally Goldeneye, sawbills or scoters; Coot, Black-headed Gull, Common Gull. Very occasionally Red-necked or Slavonian Grebes, Ferruginous Duck and Scaup. Siskin and Hawfinch regularly occur in the coppices on the banks.

2. *River Allier near Nevers*

Cher (18) *IGN 36*

The River Allier, like the Loire, is a major migration route for birds, and the lowest section near Nevers (see also chapter on Bourgogne) is an area well worth exploring, both in spring and autumn and during the breeding season. Migrant birds of prey include Red and Black Kites, Osprey and Booted Eagle, all of which nest not far away. White Storks also pass through, and again there are a few pairs nesting in the area; it is a species which is steadily increasing its range in France. You should also be on the look-out for Black Stork, mostly as a migrant, although this part of France is one where they have been known to nest, usually well hidden in the forests. The river attracts a mix of waders such as Common, Green and Wood Sandpipers plus the Little Ringed Plovers that remain to breed. Little and Common Terns lay their eggs on the gravel islands, with Stone Curlew also using the same habitat. Night Herons can be seen in groups along the river when they first arrive in spring, often in the company of Little Egrets, both species nesting along the valley. It takes a lot more patience to catch a glimpse of two of the rarer mammals that occur here – European beaver and wild cat. The attractive village of Apremont-sur-Allier, just south-west of Nevers, where the départements of Cher and Nièvre join, makes a good starting point. The D45 runs alongside the river here, while the area upstream can be explored along a network of minor roads.

3. *Marais de Contres*

CHER (18) *IGN 35*

This wetland area lies about 25 km south of Bourges, in the middle of an area otherwise dominated by cereal-growing. It therefore forms a focus for a good range of species, thanks to its having a wide variety of habitats – flood meadows, pastureland, bushy thickets and reedbeds – to attract both nesting and migrant birds. In spring and summer the following breeding species can all be found: Curlew, Lapwing, Red-backed and Woodchat Shrikes, Grasshopper, Sedge, Reed and many other warblers. There are also Yellowhammers, Reed and Cirl Buntings, while Hobbies can be seen hunting overhead. It is sometimes possible to find Fan-tailed Warblers here, this being a species that often fluctuates widely in numbers from year to year. During migration periods look out for White Storks, and with luck you might also see a Black Stork, a rare nesting species in this part of France, as well as the occasional Snipe. Other migrants include Whinchat, Wheatear and Ring Ouzel, while Cranes often occur in autumn and winter. From Bourges take the N144 south to Levet, and turn left along the D28 to Dun-sur-Auron. This crosses part of the area, while the D14 back west via Contres provides alternative views.

GREAT CRESTED GREBE

4. *Écluzelles-Mézières*

EURE-ET-LOIR (28) *IGN 20*

Écluzelles and Mézières-en-Drouais are two villages in the valley of the River Eure, just south-east of Dreux. Here a disused sand and gravel pit now forms a large lake (about 75 hectares) with two small marshy areas nearby. The best wetland site in the département, it attracts many species of aquatic and hedgerow birds throughout the year. Night Herons have nested every year since 1979 in the Marais d'Écluzelles, and can be seen here from April to September. There is unrestricted access to the site, except for a few private areas. The area is however much disturbed (sailing clubs, hikers, anglers, etc.) and is thus best visited in the week, Friday evening or early in the morning during the weekends.

■ ACCESS

From Dreux, take the D929 road south-east towards Nogent-le-Roi. After about 5 km, at Écluzelles, turn left, crossing the bridge over the Eure, through the village and take the track on the left along the side of the lake, continuing on foot into the Marais d'Écluzelles (1). This is the best spot for Night Heron (from early April to early October). Kingfisher, Lesser Whitethroat, Nightingale and various other passerines breed and Siskin and Redpoll occur in winter. Another observation point on the lake-side is the car park next to the L'Aquaparc restaurant (2), which is signposted from

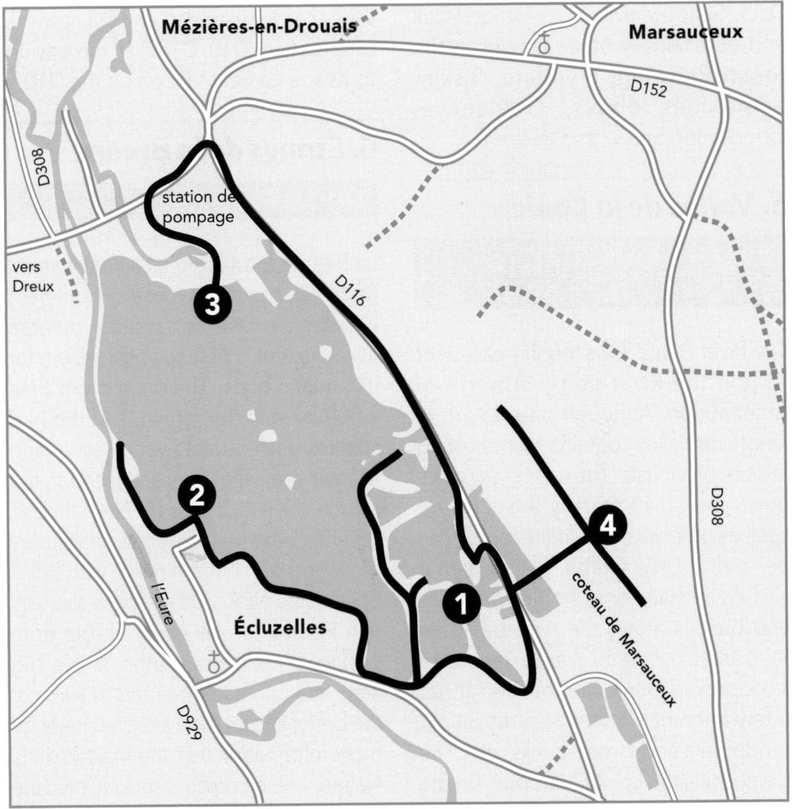

Écluzelles. In spring various terns, Swifts and hirundines hunt insects over the water and can be viewed from here. Dabbling and diving duck occur on the lake in winter and on migration (especially between October and April). Another interesting area is the Marais de Mézières at the northern end (3). For this take D116 along the east side of the lake towards Mézières-en-Drouais, turning left in the village and left again on a track after the church. Migrant and wintering Cormorant and Grey Heron can often be seen here. To the east of the lake, the hillsides near Marsauceux (4), covered in scrub, are of interest for passerines in the spring, when Cirl Bunting, Melodious Warbler and Long-eared Owl can be found, and the slopes also provide a good view over the whole of the valley. The whole route covers about 9 km.

Calendar

Spring: Great Crested Grebe, Night Heron, Garganey (passage), Shoveler, Little Ringed Plover, Common Sandpiper, Black Tern (passage), Little Owl, Swift, Kingfisher, hirundines, Nightingale, wetland warblers, Lesser Whitethroat, Willow Warbler and Chiffchaff.
Autumn: Cormorant, Grey Heron, Little and Great White Egrets, Greylag Goose, Mallard, Osprey, Black-headed Gull, warblers.
Winter: Mallard, Wigeon, Gadwall, Shoveler, Pintail, Teal, Pochard, Tufted

Duck. Sparrowhawk, Black-headed Gull and occasionally other species at the roost. Redwing, Fieldfare, Siskin. Sometimes divers, Goldeneye, Goosander, Smew and Redpoll.

5. Vallée de la Conie

EURE-ET-LOIR (28) *IGN 19/20*

The River Conie flows roughly east-west to join the River Loir just north of Châteaudun. Although only 35 km in length, its valley contains an interesting mixture of habitats. There are many reed-beds and small marshy areas where species otherwise rare in the region can be seen – Little Grebe, Marsh Harrier and Water Rail, for example. The trees and bushes along the river bank are favoured by many passerines and woodpeckers. Some stretches also attract a few migrant waders, such as Snipe, sandpipers and Greenshanks, etc. The Conie joins the Loir at Marboué, on the N10 just north of Châteaudun, and the valley can be explored along a network of lanes (e.g. D10, D132) all the way up to its source near Viabon on the D10.

6. Étangs de la Brenne

INDRE (36) *IGN 34*

La Brenne, protected as a Parc Naturel Régional, contains a mosaic of different habitats, with a remarkably diverse avifauna, but is perhaps best known for its aquatic birds. There are more than 2,000 lakes in the region, and the bird species each attracts varies according to their size, what they are used for, the season, the year, and so on. Nevertheless, several of them are reserves specifically managed with birds in mind, with hides open to the public. Others, often also very rich in birdlife, are easily visible from public roads or footpaths. It is a big area, and only a few pointers to some of the better known lakes are cited here; for more information visit the Maison de la Nature, where English is spoken, near the village of St.-Michel-en-Brenne, close to the Réserve Naturelle de Chérine.

WHISKERED TERN

ACCESS

The main routes into the area are the D925 in the east, which will bring you to Mézières-en-Brenne, in the northern part, and the N151 from Poitiers in the west, which runs through Le Blanc and along the River Creuse in the southern part. The nearest railway station is Châteauroux (45 km), but there are few public buses

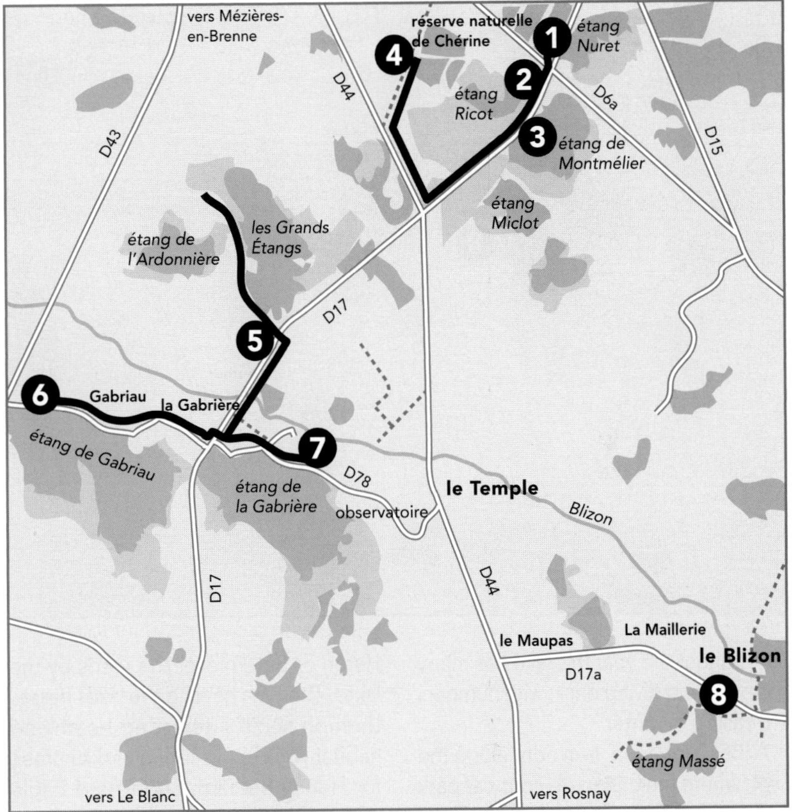

into the area. There are car parks at all the main reserves and the whole of the area can be explored along a network of quiet lanes. In addition to the lakes, there are also several forested areas which hold a good range of woodpeckers. The ideal starting point is the Maison de la Nature (Tel: 02 54 28 11 02), on the banks of the Étang Cistude (1). The visitor centre has maps, books and displays covering all aspects of the natural history of the area, and is suitable for wheelchair access. Guided visits to various parts of La Brenne can also be arranged here. The centre incorporates a public hide from which herons, gulls, waders, etc. can all be seen under ideal conditions. A short distance to the south is the Chérine reserve, which contains a representative sample of all the main habitats of La Brenne – lakes, meadows, woodland and heathland. There is a car park by the roadside, and two more public hides give excellent views over the Étang Ricot (2), with its extensive fringe of reeds. Purple Heron, Little Bittern and Bittern, all of which are under threat in France, breed in the Ricot reedbed. In addition many wetland passerines also occur here, including Cetti's, Savi's, Sedge and Fan-tailed Warblers, and birds of prey such as Marsh Harrier and Buzzard are commonly seen. A little further on along the D17 the Étang de Montmélier, which has a much larger area of open water, can be scanned from the roadside.

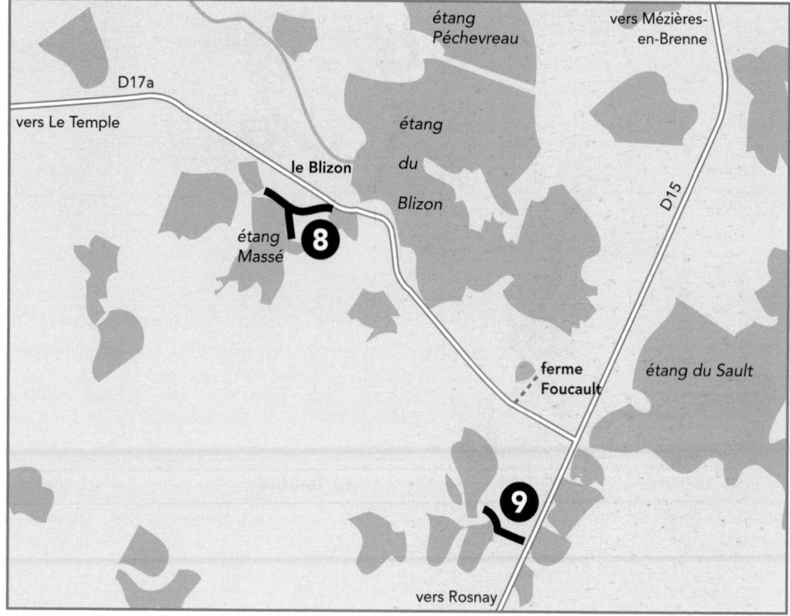

Throughout the year this lake has many dabbling and diving duck, with numbers increasing in winter.

A little further on, turn right along the D44, where there is an obvious car park on the right. From here take the public footpath northwards; after about 800 metres you come to a hide overlooking the Étang des Essarts (4). This is a particularly good area for Black-necked Grebe, Whiskered and Black Terns. Look out also for Little Ringed Plover and Little Egret among the duck and Black-headed Gulls that also breed there. Guided visits will take you to other parts of the Chérine reserve not open to the general public.

South again, the D17 passes Le Grands Étangs/Étang de Beauregard. There is limited parking by the roadside (5), with a public footpath running west along the southern side of these lakes, eventually reaching the D43, where there is a small car park. With luck you may see Purple Heron or Bittern over the reeds by the lakes. The path beyond the lakes passes through some interesting heathland habitat (look up, in spring and summer, for Honey Buzzard, Short-toed Eagle and Hobby) and meadows that have Red-backed Shrikes.

At the Gabrière crossroads turn right along the road to scan the Étang de Gabriau (6) or left to scan the Étang de la Gabrière (7). In winter they both attract many ducks, and the latter is a good spot for Black-necked Grebe and sometimes Red-crested Pochard in spring and summer.

The Étang Massé (8) lies a little further south-east. There is a roadside car park by the D17a, just before Le Blizon village. This is a private lake, whose owners have signed an agreement to protect its remarkable fauna and flora. It is best in spring and summer, when the large heron and egret colony at the far end of the reserve is active. There are also many

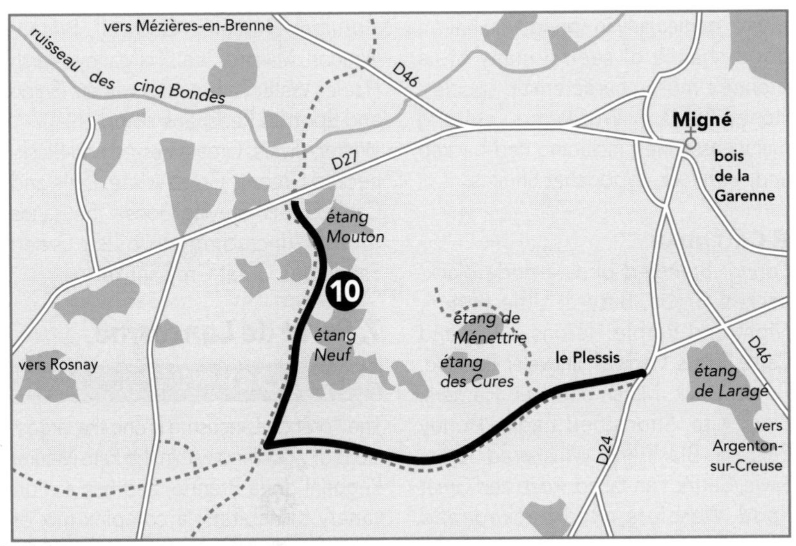

ducks, raptors and passerines here. From the car park a footpath runs through damp thickets and next to the lake for about 1 km, although you then have to retrace your steps.

There is also a hide looking down the lake to the egret colony. This is another area to which guided visits (in English if necessary), can be arranged via LPO-Brenne (Tel: 02 54 28 11 04).

East again, and south along the D15 towards Rosnay brings you to the Étangs Foucault (9), where there are two hides permanently open to the public. These can be reached either from the D17a, near the farm of Foucault, or, perhaps better if you are less mobile, from a car park on the D15. The lakes here are large and open, and provide something of a contrast to the more vegetated lakes elsewhere in La Brenne.

The final site, the Domaine du Plessis, is reached by continuing to Rosnay and then taking the D27 east towards Migné. There is a car park by this road, and a path from here leads to the Étang Mouton and the Étang Neuf (10), the latter having a public hide. The path continues round the area to reach the D24 at Le Plessis, where there is another parking spot. The route takes you through some areas

PURPLE HERON

where, particularly in spring, you have a good chance of seeing many of La Brenne's more characteristic species: Honey Buzzard, Whiskered Tern and many passerines, including Red-backed and, with luck, Woodchat Shrikes.

Calendar

Spring: Breeding birds include Black-necked Grebe, Bittern, Little Bittern, Night and Purple Herons, Little and Cattle Egrets, Gadwall, Shoveler, Pochard, Tufted Duck, Marsh and Hen Harriers, Black Kite, Short-toed Eagle, Honey Buzzard, Black and Whiskered Terns, Savi's, Cetti's, Fan-tailed, Reed and Great Reed Warblers, Red-backed and Woodchat Shrikes. Osprey, Crane and many waders are common on migration.

Autumn: Shoveler, Gadwall, Pintail, Wigeon, Mallard, Teal, Garganey, Marsh Harrier, Water Rail, various waders (Snipe and Spotted Redshank common).

Winter: divers, Great Crested and Black-necked Grebes, Great White, Little and Cattle Egrets, Greylag Goose, thousands of duck (including sawbills), Green Sandpiper, Great Grey Shrike.

7. Forêt de Lancosme

Indre (36) *IGN 34*

The Forêt de Lancosme is one the largest areas of woodland within the Parc Naturel Régonal de la Brenne, and has a wide variety of habitats: a complex mix of oaks, hornbeam, Scots, maritime and Corsican pines plus dry heather and

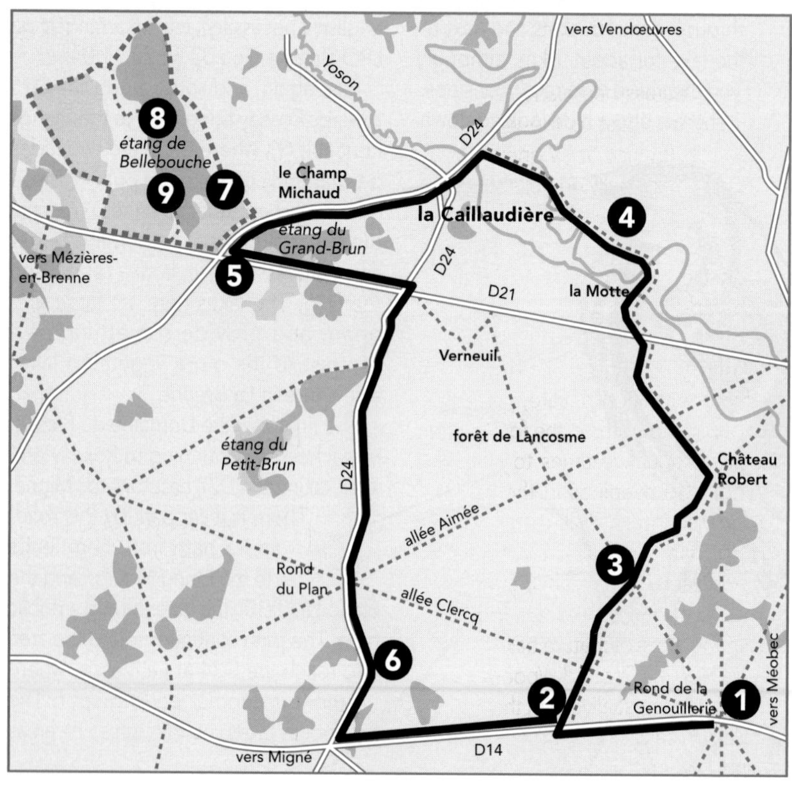

CRESTED TIT

the daytime in open areas where the woodland has been felled and in the same areas at dusk listen out for the Nightjar's reeling call. On the forest edges look for Red-backed Shrike and Stonechat. In winter mixed flocks of Crested, Coal and Blue Tits, together with the odd Goldcrest, Firecrest, Nuthatch or Short-toed Treecreeper can be seen in an otherwise quiet forest, and this is also the best time to see Woodcock.

damp moor-grass heathland. There is more heathland just to the west with several lakes (Étangs des Vigneaux, des Verdets, and especially de Bellebouche). A visit here, combined with a few days around the other lakes of La Brenne, will boost the range of species seen, with the addition of several species of raptor, woodpeckers and passerines particularly associated with mixed woodland. Although private, there are many public footpaths in the forest, and the most productive times to visit are mornings and evenings in the spring. From early spring onwards many raptors (e.g. Hen Harrier, Short-toed Eagle, Honey Buzzard) may be seen performing their aerial displays over the forested parts. In the areas of mature oak look for Black and Middle Spotted Woodpeckers that bring the forest alive with their calls, particularly in early spring. Later, between May and July, look for Tawny Pipits during

Access

The forest lies in the north-east part of La Brenne. The D925 from Châteauroux to Mézières-en-Brenne (see previous site) crosses the northern part, and the D11 from Vendœuvres on this road to Méobecq bisects it from north to south. The following are just a few suggestions of areas to explore, although a 1:25,000 map (IGN 2026E) is useful to avoid getting lost. From Méobecq, take the D14 west to the Genouillerie intersection (1), from where it is possible to make a 6 km walk to Château Robert and back, taking in a good section of the woodland. The D14 west passes through conifer plantations (2), and then one can turn north along a forest road that passes through a mixture of hardwoods and conifers (3). The route then follows what was once the embankment of a lake (the present smaller lake, the Fosse-Noire, is some 100 metres away and is a good area for watching rutting red deer in the autumn) and the area of Château Robert before crossing the D21. Next cross the Yoson stream at La Motte to reach an area where deciduous trees dominate (4). At dusk you may well hear either Tawny or Long-eared Owls calling in this area. As you emerge from the forest into the more open areas look out for species such as Whitethroat, Blackcap, Cirl Bunting and Yellowhammer. The circuit now follows the D24 road to the village of La Caillaudière, where you bear right and continue to the embankment (5) with views over the Étang de Bellebouche to the right and the Étang du Grand-Brun to the left. It is possible to walk around the Étang de Bellebouche (about 7 km), taking in three hides (7, 8 and 9) along the way to overlook the lake at different points. The area of the lake contains a very good sample of typical Brenne habitats and species, with grebes, dabbling and diving ducks to be seen through most of the year plus Purple Heron, Whiskered Tern and others in spring and summer. A little further on, turn left along the D21, close to the back of the Étang du Grand-Brun, with its many dead trees and at the crossroads turn right along the D24 to return to the forest (6). At the next crossroads, turn left along the D14 to return to the starting point. To visit the Étang de Bellebouche separately, note that there is a car park at the northern end, accessed off the D925 between Vendœuvres and Mézières-en-Brenne.

CALENDAR

Spring: Black Kite, Goshawk, Honey Buzzard, Short-toed Eagle, Hobby, Nightjar, Cuckoo, woodpeckers, Whitethroat, Blackcap, Dartford, Wood and Bonelli's Warblers, Chiffchaff and Nightingale.

Summer: Tawny Pipit, Grasshopper Warbler, Red-backed Shrike.

Winter: Buzzard, Goshawk, Sparrowhawk, Hen Harrier, Tawny Owl, Black, Great, Middle and Lesser Spotted Woodpeckers, Marsh, Crested and Blue Tits, Firecrest, Goldcrest, Hawfinch, Bullfinch.

8. *Val de Creuse*

INDRE (36) *IGN 35*

The River Creuse flows across the southern part of La Brenne, and in the section to the south-east, between Argenton-sur-Creuse and Éguzon, the river flows through a steep-sided wooded valley. By taking minor roads (e.g. D40, D48) up-river on the right bank as far as Éguzon you should have a good chance of seeing some of the typical species of this area. In spring and summer many raptors can be seen – Buzzard, Sparrowhawk, Goshawk and Kestrel – whilst throughout the year Dippers and Grey Wagtails can be seen near each bridge, mill or dam.

9. *Lac de Rillé*

INDRE-ET-LOIRE (37) *IGN 25*

The Lac de Rillé (or Retenue de Pincemaille) is an artificial reservoir dating from 1977 when the River Lathan was dammed in order to create a very large water supply (5,800,000 m^3) in order to irrigate the horticulture and market-garden areas in the Authion and Loire valleys between Saumur and Angers. About 40 hectares are used by a water-sports centre, the Complexe de Pincemaille, where the water level remains constant. The remaining 200 hectares is liable to have large fluctuations in water level which give rise to a varied shoreline, with sand-bars, meadows and mudflats. The lake is enclosed by a coniferous forest to the south and arable fields to the north. The whole forms an excellent area for birds, especially important for duck and waders. The most rewarding periods are during the autumn migration and in winter. Do not forget that outside the Pincemaille tourist centre the lake is private without public access (an inter-departmental agreement), and access is restricted. However, the roads and tracks on the edge of the lake provide for excellent watching, and two hides have been put in place by LPO-Touraine. The first is near the water treatment plant (and open to the public); the second near the Grand-Maison farm is reserved for guided visits and work carried out by the LPO.

Access

The Lac de Rillé is some 40 km to the north-west of Tours, and can be accessed by taking the N152 down the right bank of the Loire as far as Langeais then turning right on the D57 to Rillé. Here continue along the D49 towards Mouliherne and after a tourist complex (hotel and camp site on the right) turn right at a place called Le Petit Malcombe, to reach the car park (1) near the Rillé arm of the lake. Good views of the lake can be obtained from the embankment where the road crosses the lake. In autumn and winter this is a good spot from which to see Water and Meadow Pipits, White and Grey Wagtails. An LPO information board gives details of the paths, and from here a way-marked botanical trail leads, in about 500 metres, to a hide near the water treatment plant (2). This is one of the better spots from which to see Water Rails. It is possible to drive towards Petit Pin, and park at the Butte Noir crossroads (3). From here scan both the meadows and the wider section of the Rillé arm of the lake nearby. In February Greylag Geese occur here in numbers and during times of migration various waders stop to feed on the mudflats – Dunlin, stints, Snipe, Redshank, Greenshank, Curlew and Lapwing. From here walk towards La Grand-Maison, 1 km distant; note that this area is out-of-bounds to vehicles. Look to the right over the northern Channay arm of the lake (4). Grey Herons are present throughout the year, and are sometimes joined by a Spoonbill, particularly in September. Large numbers of Lapwing are present in autumn and winter, with a few Golden Plover. These, and the other waders and wildfowl, attract wintering Peregrines, and it is worth checking all the dead tree-trunks and old fence posts to see one resting between feeds. Winter is also the period when large roosts of Black-headed, Lesser Black-backed and Yellow-legged Gulls occur. Once at La Grand-Maison (5), turn right onto the old road (now partially under water) to Moque-Souris as far as the barrier that blocks it off. From here look out over the section where the two arms of the lake meet. Rafts have been provided here, and have attracted a few pairs of Common Terns to nest in summer. One can return to the car past some houses and out-buildings, and an apple orchard, scanning the Rillé arm and wooded bank opposite on the way. One can then drive towards Épronnière, crossing the Channay arm (6), and park at the nearby picnic site. Scan the Channay arm both to the south and to the north, where there are some willows and rushes. Reed and Sedge Warblers and Reed Bunting nest in the

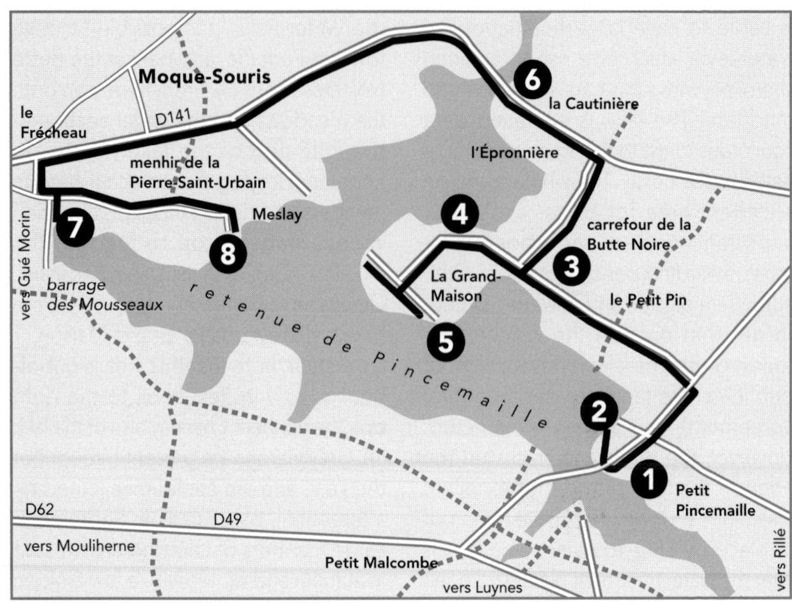

reedbed, and in some years Purple Herons also breed here. One can drive on again from here, turning left at Le Frécheau towards the dam at Mousseaux, where there is another car park (7). The dam itself make a good viewpoint and it is possible to walk the 1 km as far as Meslay (8), watching from the track as you go. The menhir at Pierre-St.-Urbain is also worth a look. From Meslay it is possible to obtain good views of dabbling and diving duck, including the occasional Goldeneye. Grebes are also often present here. The southern part of the lake can be good in June for birds of prey such as Sparrowhawk, Buzzard, Honey Buzzard and Hobby. To complete the circuit, some 8 km in all, continue to the D62 and turn left back to Rillé.

Calendar

Spring: Cormorant, Greylag Goose, Wigeon, Pintail, Gadwall, Garganey, Osprey, Marsh Harrier, various waders including Lapwing, Black-tailed Godwit, Snipe and various *Tringas*, Common Tern, Swift, three species of hirundines, Whitethroat, Stonechat.

Autumn: Great Crested, Little and Black-necked Grebes, Grey Heron, Black Stork, Spoonbill, Mallard, Teal, Pochard, Tufted Duck, Honey Buzzard, Buzzard, Hobby, Merlin, Lapwing, Golden Plover, Curlew, various small waders, wetland warblers, Chaffinch.

Winter: Cormorant, swans, Grey Heron, Great White Egret, Greylag Goose, Pochard, Tufted Duck, Goldeneye, Goosander, Hen Harrier, Peregrine, Water and Meadow Pipits, White and Grey Wagtails, Siskin, Brambling.

10. Étang du Louroux

Indre-et-Loire (37) *IGN 26*

The Étang du Louroux lies to the west of Loches, about 20 km south of Tours. In spring, Reed Bunting, Reed Warbler and Water Rail can all be seen or heard in the reedbeds, while Great Crested and Little Grebes nest commonly. On migration, Greylag Goose, Little, Common, Black and Whiskered Terns are regular. In winter all the commoner dabbling ducks occur as well as Pochard, Tufted Duck and sometimes Goosander, Smew, Goldeneye or a diver. Dependent on the season, the fields and meadows of the surrounding area hold Lapwing, Golden Plover, Skylark, a few Crested Larks, Redwing and Fieldfare. To get there, take the D760 west from Loches to Manthelan, then the D50 to Le Louroux (the road continues north towards Veigne and Tours). There is a car park in the village at the northern end of the lake, and a footpath runs along the eastern shore.

11. The Loire valley around Tours

Indre-et-Loire (37)
IGN 25/26

The Loire valley is rightly classed a UNESCO World Heritage Site, and has many worthwhile birdwatching spots throughout its entire length. The section east and west of Tours is no exception. In spring and summer Little and Common Terns use the sand bars for nesting, as does the Little Ringed Plover. Kingfishers and Sand Martins burrow into the sandy banks, and the riverside woodland has a good breeding population, including some mixed colonies of Grey Herons and Little Egrets along with a few Night Herons and Black Kites. There are some flood meadows where the River Vienne joins the Loire at Candes, home to Whinchats and a few Corncrakes. During migration periods, especially between August and September, it is possible to see many waders along the river, and Ospreys pass through in significant numbers. Some of the better birdwatching sites, from east to west, include: the section near the campsite at Mosnes, east of Amboise; Montlouis-sur-Loire, just east of Tours (park at the 'Maison de la Loire'); La Chapelle-aux-Naux, opposite Langeais; and La Chapelle-sur-Loire, downstream again.

12. The Sologne

Indre-et-Loire (41)
IGN 26/27

The Sologne, a huge area of lakes to the south of Orléans, is one of France's internationally important wetlands for its birds. The lakes were originally created during the Middle Ages, but over time they have become ecologically rich and throughout the year hold a large variety of aquatic birds. In spring there are many species to be seen – gulls, herons, ducks and grebes. In winter the area is full of a wide variety of wildfowl. However, from a birdwatching point of view, access can be rather difficult, as almost all the lakes are private, and so in general you need to watch from the roads and public footpaths. In winter the whole area is quite heavily used by the hunting fraternity, and so disturbance can be a problem. A few suggestions concerning some of the better lakes are given below.

Access

The N20 and A10 south from Orléans crosses the area, and Nouan-le-Fuzelier on the former (exit 3 on the latter) is a good starting point. From here take the D93 as far as St.-Viâtre, then the D49 towards Romarantin. The second turning to the right leads to the Étang des Brosses

(1) where there are reedbeds with Reed and Sedge Warblers singing in the summer. Another lake worth checking is the Étang de la Grande Corbois (2); for this, return towards St.-Viâtre and take the first turning on the left and continue to a small triangular area. Marsh Harrier breeds at this lake and is usually easy to see. In winter the lake often has many duck: Mallard, Teal, Pochard, Tufted Duck and a few Goldeneye and Smew, especially after spells of severe weather. To reach the Étang de Favelle (3), return to St. Viâtre and turn left just before the church square. Take the road towards Neung-sur-Beuvron, forking left on the D63 and continuing to the Château de Favelle. In autumn the muddy shore of the Étang de Favelle attracts Great White Egret, which is everywhere increasing as a wintering species in France. Breeding birds here include Pochard, Tufted Duck and Great Crested Grebe. A little further west is the Étang de Marcilly (4). Continue along the D63 and at the crossroads turn left; the lake is 50 metres further on. In spring, the lake attracts many migrant duck on their way north – Pintail, Shoveler and Garganey for instance. To reach the final lake suggested here, return to the crossroads and continue straight on. You reach the Étang des Marguilliers (5) about 200 metres further on, to the left of the road. This is a good spot in summer, particularly from March to July, as in addition to a colony of Black-headed Gulls, Great Crested, Black-necked and Little Grebes also all nest. This is one of the lakes where Whiskered Terns sometimes settle in the summer, building their floating nests on the water lilies. Breeding wildfowl include both Pochard and Gadwall.

Calendar

Spring: Great Crested and Black-necked

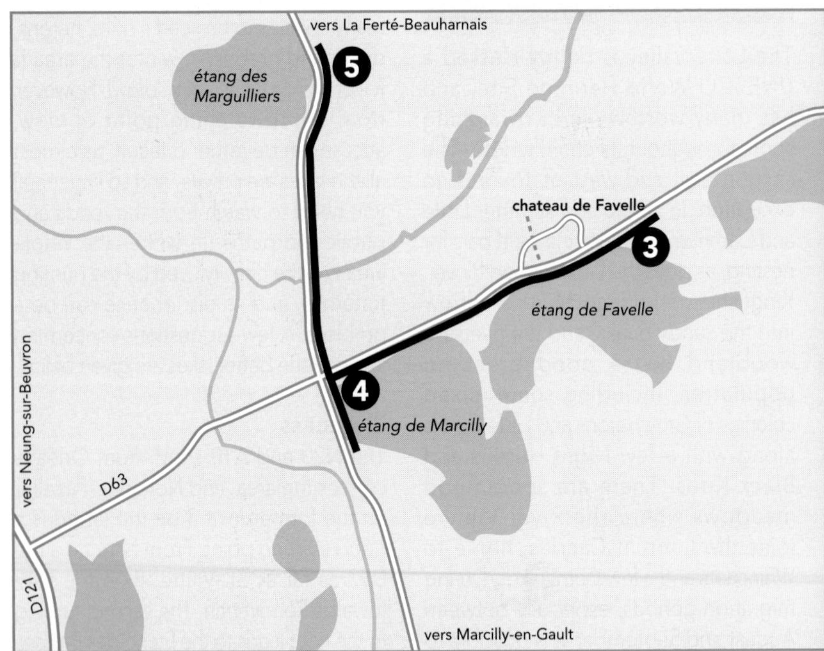

Grebes, Grey and Night Herons, Shoveler, Mallard, Gadwall, Teal, Garganey, Pochard, Tufted Duck, Marsh Harrier, Water Rail, Lapwing, Black-headed Gull, Black and Whiskered Terns, Reed, Sedge and Grasshopper Warblers.

Autumn and winter: grebes, Cormorant, Grey Heron, dabbling ducks, diving ducks, sawbills, Goldeneye, Buzzard, Hen Harrier, Osprey (September), Crane (October-November), waders, Black-headed Gull, Great White Egret.

13. Étang de l'Arche

Indre-et-Loire (41) *IGN 26*

The Étang de l'Arche lies some 30 km south of Blois, a little north of the Cher valley, at the south-west corner of the Sologne. For many years it has been the site of the Sologne's largest Black-headed Gull colony with a few pairs of Mediterranean Gulls also mixed in. From spring and into the summer seven breeding species of duck can be seen here – Mallard, Shoveler, Gadwall, Teal, Garganey, Pochard and Tufted Duck. Black-necked Grebes swimming with their young are another frequent sight here in the summer. During the migration periods, notably in April and May, Black and Whiskered Terns and Little Gull often come to feed over the lake. In October, when the water levels are low, its mudflats attract many Snipe and other waders, sometimes including a rarity, and Shelduck, Great White Egret and Water Pipit are all regular winter visitors. The numbers of wintering duck depend on the water level, disturbance by wildfowlers, and also whether it freezes over or not, but it has a history of attracting the odd unusual visitor – a diver, Goldeneye or sawbill, for instance. To reach the lake take the

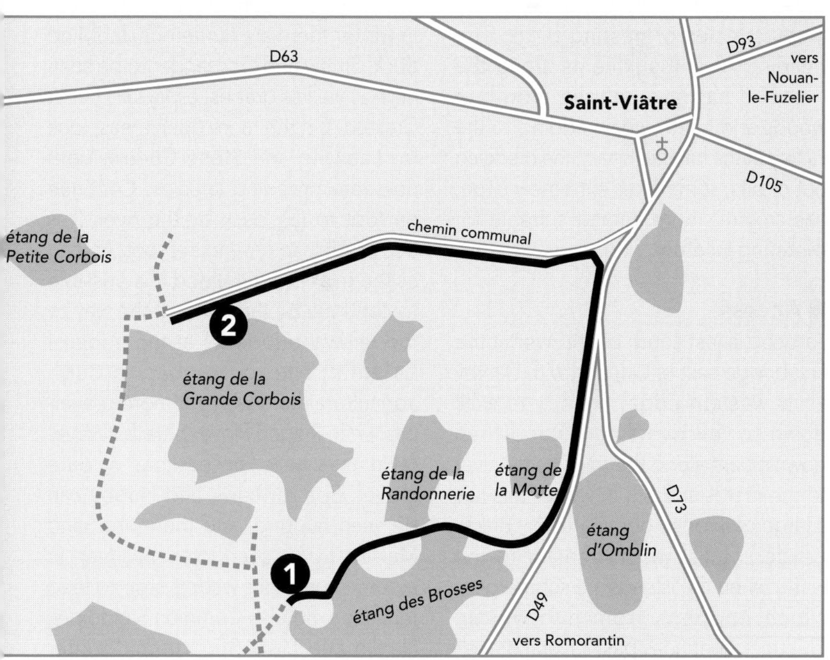

D956 south from Blois through Contres and turn left in Chémery village towards the chateau, after which take the road to the right sign-posted St.-Martin/Basse Pilaudière. Beyond the end of the surfaced road a driveable track to the right leads onto the lake's embankment, from which the water can be scanned.

14. The Loire valley near Orléans

LOIRET (45) *IGN 27*

The section of the Loire valley between Orléans and Jargeau just to the east is typical of the middle Loire, and a representative sample of the birds of the river can be seen here. Its proximity to a large city has lead to a great deal of sand and gravel extraction, which has modified the landscape in places but the sand and gravel islands – to which there is no access – have many species of nesting birds. The building of embankments along the river-bed has favoured the growth of woods and heath, again adding to the variety of the habitat. Finally, the dredging out of pits, sometimes extremely large, has created more habitat suitable for wintering wildfowl.

■ ACCESS

Jargeau is just south of the river at the first bridge east of Orléans, with Darvoy at its western edge. From here walk down to the riverside (1) and then downstream along the track by the river to the first island (2). In winter this has a large gull roost, dominated by Black-headed Gulls, which transfer to the water when the islands are submerged, which happens from mid-winter. The track continues past several gravel-pits before getting back up onto the embankment. Sand Martins build their nesting burrows in some of the artificial sand banks, and in summer there are numerous passerines typical of the vegetation to be found along the riverside: Grasshopper, Melodious and Garden Warblers, Whitethroat and Reed Bunting. Continue to (3), and look over the heathland here and across to the island near Sandillon which is specially protected with no access allowed between 1st April and 25th July. The islands, mostly bare of vegetation, are where the Common and Little Terns lay their eggs from May onwards, with many Black-headed and a few larger gulls also nesting in with them. Continue along the side of the river, on the embankment (closed to vehicles), that veers away from the river for a time and comes to an area of bushes. Stop near the flooded gravel-pits (4) a few hundred metres further on. In winter there are numerous dabbling duck, Smew and Goosander to be seen here as well as grebes, especially Great Crested. On the more open areas, look for Lapwing and Stone Curlew, both now rare breeding species. Continue on foot to (5), back by the river. It is also possible to drive to this spot. As long as the river is not in flood it is possible to continue by the Loire all the way to the railway bridge (6) at the edge of Orléans. The route goes through agricultural land with yet more gravel-pits. Little Ringed Plover breeds in several places here, on patches of bare gravel. Sparrowhawk and Hobby can be seen hunting, and there are Sand Martins to be seen over the river. In autumn numerous waders stop to feed for a time, notably Common Sandpiper, Dunlin and Little Stint. In mid-winter

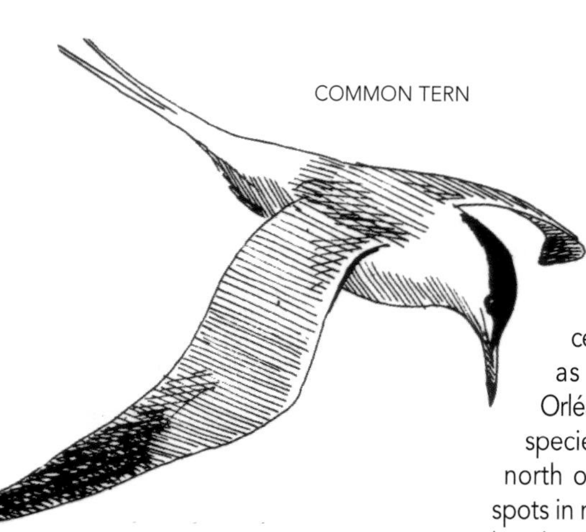

COMMON TERN

Cormorants congregate to roost at the railway bridge.

■ Calendar

Spring: Little Ringed Plover, Lapwing, Stone Curlew, Sparrowhawk, Hobby, Common and Little Terns, Black-headed and Mediterranean Gulls, with a few pairs of Yellow-legged and the occasional Common Gull, Sand Martin.
Autumn: Osprey, Greenshank and other waders, Snipe.
Winter: Cormorant, Mallard, Teal, Goosander and Smew, Black-headed and Common Gulls.

15. La Beauce

Loiret (45) *IGN 20*

Notwithstanding its uniform appearance, and intensive cereal production, the area known as La Beauce, to the north of Orléans, still retains some interesting species in places. The area west and north of Pithiviers is one of the few spots in northern France where one still has the chance to see Short-toed Larks, which (from May to August) nest on sugar-beet storage areas colonised by mayweed – Moncharville (Marsainvilliers), Ézerville (Engenville), Charmont-en-Beauce, Châtillon-le-Roi and Bazoches-les-Gallerandes are known sites – but they also occur at the Pithiviers-le-Vieil dried-out sugar-beet decantation beds (at the factory and at the flying-club). During migration periods the same areas attract Ortolan Buntings and a few waders. Pithiviers lies on the N152 north-east from Orléans.

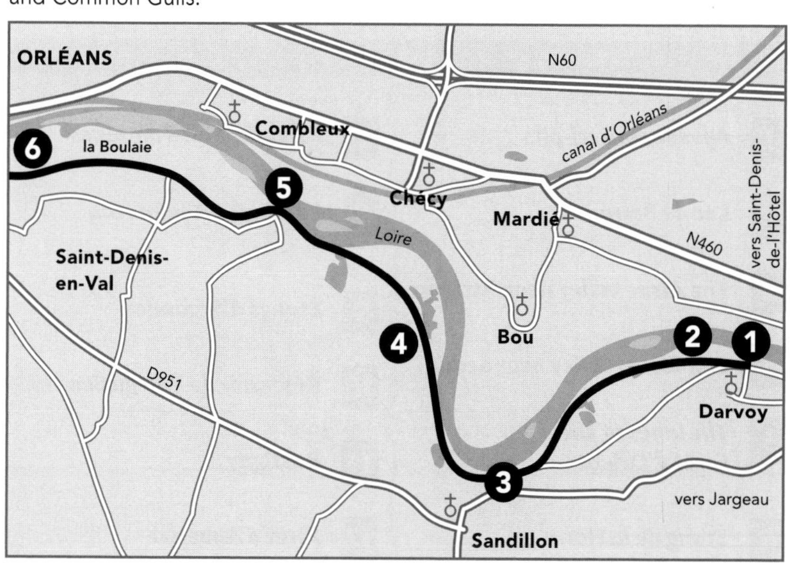

SITES

1. *Ayvelles gravel-pits*
2. *Lac de Bairon*
3. *The Aisne valley near Attigny*
4. *The Chiers valley near Sedan*
5. *The lakes of the Forêt d'Orient*
6. *Étang de la Horre*
7. *Forêt de Trois-Fontaines*
8. *Lac du Der-Chantecoq*
9. *Étangs d'Argonne*
10. *Réservoir de Villegusien*
11. *Bassigny*
12. *Forêt d'Auberive*

Champagne-Ardenne

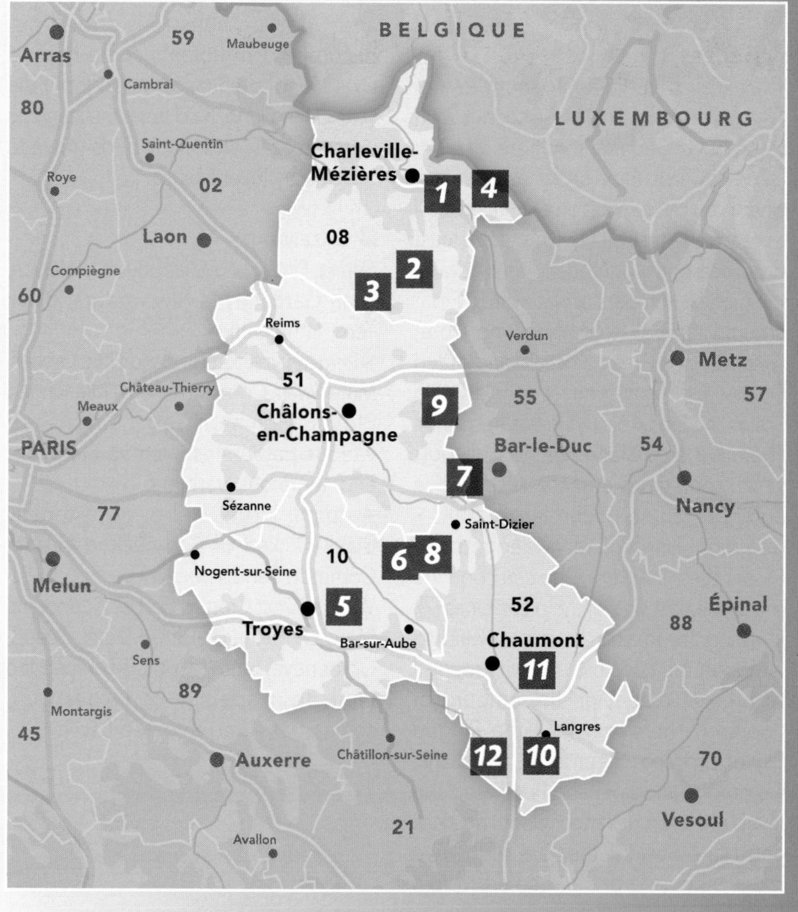

1. Ayvelles gravel-pits

Ardennes (08) *IGN 05*

This complex of ballast excavations lies in the Meuse valley between Charleville-Mézières and Sedan. Although unfortunately often disturbed by human activities (hunting, angling, hiking, sailing) because of the open access, the site is nevertheless of great interest for the birdwatcher, especially in winter and during migration. The nearby meadows together with several areas of scrub and the presence of open water has led to a diversified and interesting list of birds.

Access

The excavations lie to the south-east of Charleville-Mézières, close to exit 7 on the A203 to Sedan. From here take the D764 towards Flize as far as Ayvelles, where you can turn left on a surfaced road to reach the first pit (1). This is the least disturbed one in winter and thus attracts the highest numbers of waterbirds. From autumn through to early spring Coot, Great Crested Grebe, Pochard and Tufted Duck are the commonest species, with Scaup and Smew occurring less frequently. There is a large Black-headed Gull roost which sometimes attracts, and in large numbers, some of the larger gulls – Common, Herring, Yellow-legged and Lesser Black-backed. One can continue round the east side of the pit as far as (2). In spring this area can be quite rewarding although the species seen will depend to a great extent on the amount of flooding. There may be Little Ringed Plover, Lapwing, Greenshank, Redshank, Common Sandpiper and Fieldfare if the levels are low, but various dabbling duck and Mute Swan if they are high. Two lakes either side of the road are visible from (3): Great Crested Grebe, Coot and Moorhen all breed, as do many passerines in the surrounding bushes. The two largest lakes (4 and 5) are of most interest during both spring and autumn migration as well as in the summer. Visits in the spring especially can produce Pintail, Shoveler, Gadwall, Wigeon, Teal, Garganey, Black Tern and Little Gull, the numbers varying from one year to the next. Great Crested Grebe and Coot are the most obvious breeding species but there are also Mallard, Moorhen, Little Grebe, Mute Swan, Little Ringed Plover and two or three pairs of Common Tern. In winter, Great Crested Grebe and Coot are numerous and, if not disturbed, Cormorants come here to roost. Kingfishers occur throughout the year. During long, hard frosts the standing water freezes, and many birds move to the nearby River Meuse.

Calendar

Spring: Pintail, Shoveler, Gadwall, Wigeon, Teal, Garganey, a few waders, Black Tern, Little Gull.

Summer: Great Crested and Little Grebes, Mute Swan, Coot, Moorhen, Little Ringed Plover, Common Tern, Kingfisher; various passerines such as Fieldfare, and numerous warblers.

Autumn: Little Grebe, occasionally Black-necked or Red-necked Grebe, Common Sandpiper.

Winter: Great Crested Grebe, Cormorant, Mallard, Pochard, Tufted Duck, Scaup, Goldeneye, Smew, Coot, Black-headed Gull, four species of larger gull, sometimes a Red-throated Diver.

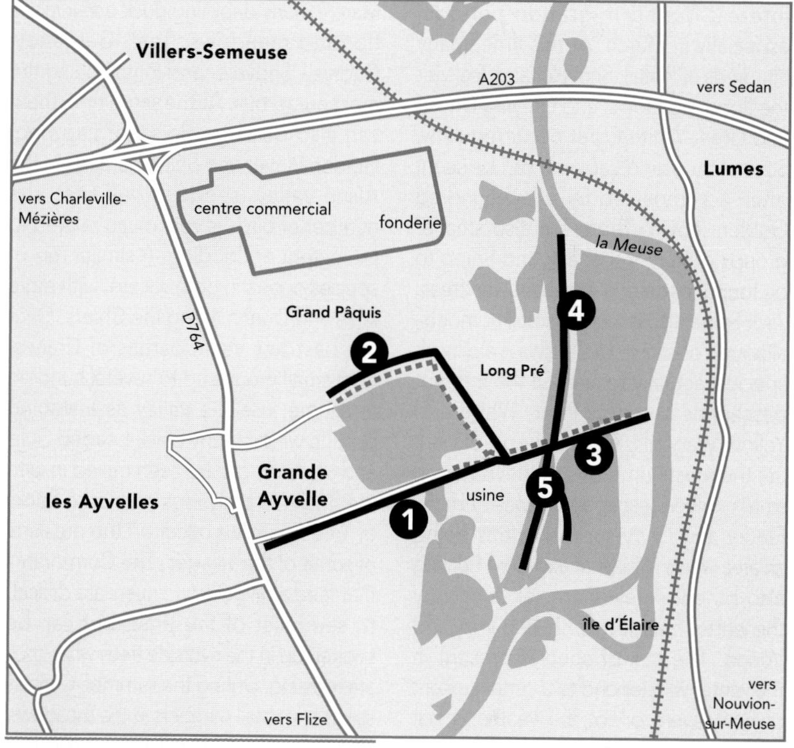

2. *Lac de Bairon*

ARDENNES (08) *IGN 10*

Situated about 25 km south of Sedan, the Lac de Bairon is the largest body of water in the Ardennes département. The western part has an extensive reedbed whereas the eastern part is used for leisure activities. It is a site to visit in winter, between November and March, when dabbling and diving ducks (sometimes sawbills), divers, Bittern and a few Water Pipit occur. In spring, especially April and May, various raptors hunt over the area: Black and Red Kites, Marsh Harrier and Hobby. Other less common species such as Purple Heron and Black Stork also occur. Breeding species include Savi's, Grasshopper and Reed Warblers, Reed Bunting, Kingfisher and Grey Wagtail, with small numbers of Water Rail, Moorhen, Great Crested Grebe and Coot as well as, for the past few years, Little Bittern. In autumn Osprey, Common Sandpiper, Black Tern and Little Gull often pass through on migration. The lake is just north of Le Chesne, on the D977 from Sedan to Vouziers, and it can be viewed from minor roads that run next to and across it.

3. *The Aisne valley near Attigny*

ARDENNES (08) *IGN 10*

The valley of the River Aisne from Vouziers through Attigny to Rethel, taking in places like Voncq, Givry-sur-Aisne, Ambly-Fleury and Amagne can be of great interest during migration periods, especially in March. At this time, many hundreds of Pintail, Shoveler and Teal visit the flood meadows, and Greylag Goose and Great White Egret occur regularly. Several thousand Lapwing can be seen, often accompanied by a few hundred Golden Plover. There are also smaller groups of Ruff, Redshank and Snipe to be found feeding in the shallower areas. Jack Snipe also occurs in small numbers, although of course this is always a difficult species actually to see. Of the migrant passerines Meadow Pipit, White and Yellow Wagtails, Fieldfare and Skylark are the most numerous. Curlews nest in small numbers, especially between Ambly-Fleury and Givry-sur-Aisne, this being an area where Whinchat and Corn Bunting also breed. A few Corncrakes occupy the wetter meadows between Vrizy and Voncq. The mix of species present in the winter will depend to a certain extent on how severe, or not, the weather is, but species to be expected include Lapwing, Golden Plover, Hen Harrier and Fieldfare.

4. The Chiers valley near Sedan

ARDENNES (08) *IGN 10*

The confluence of the Rivers Chiers and Meuse lies just to the east of Sedan, and the section of the Chiers valley upstream from Remilly-Aillicourt to La Ferté-sur-Chiers is often flooded in late winter and in to the spring. During the spring migration (especially in March) many dabbling duck occur in the flooded meadows, Teal, Garganey, Gadwall, Shoveler and Pintail being the most numerous. At the same time there can also be large flocks of Lapwing, Golden Plover and Snipe here. As in the Aisne valley (see previous site), the number of birds is very much related to the extent of flooding. A similar mix of species occurs in both valleys, with more larks and Dunlin along the Chiers. Over the past few years parties of Cranes, from small groups up to several hundred at a time, use the valley as a staging post. In winter many Black-headed Gulls and Starlings can be seen mixed in with the flocks of Lapwings and large flocks of Tree Sparrows occur on the outskirts of some of the villages. The Cormorants that feed along the two rivers are difficult to see most of the time, but can be spotted up in the riverside trees when they are roosting. During the summer, Curlews still nest in small numbers in the meadows, and there is a good population of Whinchats. However, it seems that the Corncrakes have now ceased to breed here. The N43 east from Sedan runs along the north side of the Chiers valley through Carignan to Margut and provides a general overview. Quieter minor roads run through the meadows and villages on the left bank of the river from La Ferté-sur-Chiers to Remilly-Aillicourt for closer inspection of the area.

LAPWING

5. The lakes of the Forêt d'Orient

AUBE (10) *IGN 22*

Just to the east of Troyes lies a huge complex of forest and lakes known as the Parc Naturel Régional de la Forêt d'Orient. The area is bordered by the Barrois hills to the east and the extensive Champagne chalk plains to the west. The woodland contains three very large artificial reservoirs, built not so much for water storage as to alleviate flooding downstream, and because of this the water levels vary considerably from one season to another. One, the Lac d'Orient, covering 2,300 hectares, was built to regulate the flow on the River Seine, which passes just to the south-west. The other two, the Lac Temple (1,500 hectares) and Lac Amance (500 hectares) regulate the flow of the River Aube which passes to the north. The general area is known as the 'Champagne humide', the damp ground contrasting with the dryer plains to the west, and supporting rich forests and various smaller wetlands. As the area lies on an important migration route, the lakes attract a multitude of birds, especially during the autumn migration when the water levels tend to be low, exposing extensive mudflats and flood meadows. But, being such a rich and varied area, the lakes and forest can provide good birdwatching opportunities whatever the time of year, especially as the park is a hunting-free zone. Although parts of the area are classified as 'réserve ornithologique', where access is forbidden, there is no problem in finding places to watch birds in such an extensive area, and the circuit suggested below is just a starting point.

Access

The proposed circuit starts at the Mesnil-St.-Père, a village at the southern end of the Lac d'Orient, some 15 km to the east of Troyes and easily reached from there (and exit 32 on the A26) along the N19. Have a good look in the port (1) where there is a gull roost in autumn and winter, Great Crested Grebe throughout the year and in winter the possibility of divers, Velvet Scoter or Eider. Next take the D43, north-east along the side of the lake, stopping at bays (2) and (3) that can be veiwed from the side of the road, where there are lay-bys. Various species of duck can be seen in winter and when water levels are low there are often waders (Dunlin, stints, Snipe, Greenshank, Spotted Redshank, Lapwing and various plovers, etc.). In late winter there are sometimes Bewick's Swans at the lake while in late summer Little and Great White Egrets appear. Check the dead trees carefully as a Peregrine, and occasionally a White-tailed Eagle, may be seen perched on one of them. The Maison du Parc, where you join the D79, is worth visiting for up-to-date information on access. Turn left here to reach the hide (4) that overlooks the bird reserve area, but do not venture out beyond the hide to avoid disturbing the birds. From the hide it is possible to see between 10,000 and 20,000 ducks in late summer and early autumn, Pochard being the most numerous. In winter Greylag Geese, Goldeneye and Peregrine can be seen, while in the summer there are nesting Yellow-legged Gulls. Both Common and Black Terns occur on passage. Continue along the same road as far as the beach at Géraudot (5). In winter this is the best area for Bean Geese, often accompanied by Greylag and White-fronted Geese. From here return towards the Maison du Parc but take the first road to the left, the D50, which runs along the embankment of the Lac Temple. Stop near the blue access gates (6) and look out over the lake. At the end of the summer this is a good area for watching waders, with the chance of Purple Heron and Black Stork on occasion. Black Kites can be seen throughout the summer months and Garganey appear in early spring. Farther on (7) is another good area for waders in late summer and early autumn and between August and October this is often the best spot for Osprey. Goosander and Smew can be seen on the water in winter, in addition to Crane and Greylag Goose on the islets and peninsula. The posts provide a roosting site for the Cormorants. Just as you enter the village of Brévonnes, take the first small road to the right, towards the wood yard with its tall brick chimney. In autumn a Crane roost can be seen from the embankment (8) on the far shore in front of the forest beyond. In winter, when the water levels are low, the point opposite is a favoured spot on which to see a Peregrine or White-tailed Eagle. Return through Brévonnes to the D11 and turn right towards Dienville and Brienne-le-Château, to the village of L'Étape. From the embankment (9), at a place called La Bosse de l'Étape, it is often possible to watch birds moving from one lake to another (e.g., raptors and geese in winter; Wigeon, Gadwall, Shoveler, Pintail, Garganey and Cranes in the spring). This is another good spot for waders during both migration periods. Continue on the D11 towards Radonvilliers and here take the first small road to the right (by a pump and water fountain) to reach a blue gate (10) on the embankment at the northern end of the Lac Amance. Here, in late autumn and winter it is possible to see Bewick's Swan, Shelduck, Dunlin, Little Stint, Snipe, Golden Plover and Curlew on the mudflats. In winter there may be divers (three species), Velvet Scoter, Goosander or Smew.

Continue as far as the hide (11) for closer views of the wildfowl and to check through the waders, which may well include a rarity in late summer and early autumn. Other species seen in this north-western part of the lake include

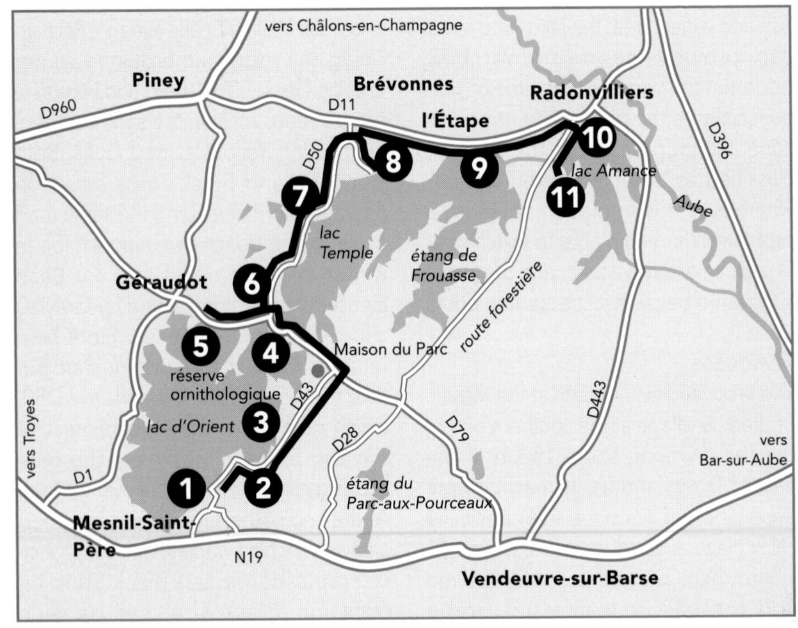

White-tailed Eagle or Peregrine in winter, and Little Gull, Common, Black and Whiskered Terns in spring and late summer. To complete the circuit, return to the D11 and turn right past the port at Dienville and continue down the east side of the forest on the D443 and N19. It is also possible to take the track which continues south-west from the hide (11) through the forest closer to the east side of the lake to reach the D79 not far from the Maison du Parc. This circuit is quite long (30–35 km) and, depending on what's about, may take the whole day.

Calendar

Spring: Black-necked Grebe, geese, various ducks, Osprey, Crane, Little Gull, Common Tern, Black and Whiskered Terns.
Breeding season: Great Crested Grebe, Goshawk, Sparrowhawk, Black Kite, Black, Grey-headed and Middle Spotted Woodpeckers.
Late summer and early autumn: Great Crested and Little Grebes, Grey and Purple Herons, Great White and Little Egrets, Black Stork, Gadwall, Shoveler, Pintail, Garganey and Teal, Red-crested Pochard, Pochard, Tufted Duck, Black and Red Kites, Osprey, Crane, Grey, Golden, Ringed and Little Ringed Plovers, Dunlin, Little Stint and many other waders, Yellow-legged Gull, Black Tern, three hirundine species and various passerines.
Winter: Small numbers of divers, Cormorant, Bewick's Swan, Greylag, Bean and White-fronted Geese, Shelduck, Wigeon, Velvet Scoter, Eider, Goldeneye, Goosander, Smew, occasionally White-tailed Eagle, Peregrine, Crane, Curlew, Common Gull.

PEREGRINE

6. Étang de la Horre

Aube (10)/Haute-Marne (52) *IGN 22*

A few kilometres south-west of the Lac du Der (see site 8 below), the Étang de la Horre is one of the most beautiful lakes in France. Protected as a réserve naturelle since 2000, it is a shallow lake covering some 330 hectares, with extensive reedbeds and is surrounded by extensive woodland. Breeding birds include Bittern, Little Bittern, Marsh Harrier, Hobby and many wetland passerines. It is a traditional breeding site for a few pairs of Purple Herons, here at the northerly edge of their range in France. It is also worth watching during migration periods (February to May and August to October) when many ducks, raptors, including Osprey and Peregrine, herons, etc. can be seen. It is one of the more reliable sites for seeing Great White Egret in autumn and winter. Take the D173 west from Montier-en-Der via Puellemontier, then the D62 towards Lentilles. The D62 crosses the southern end of the lake, with good views from the roadside here.

7. Forêt de Trois-Fontaines

Marne (51) *IGN 22/23*

This is one of several large deciduous

forests in the 'Champagne humide', and mainly comprises beech, mixed oak and hornbeam woodland with ash, maple and alder in the many damp hollows. It includes some areas that were once cultivated but which are now regenerating naturally, with the creation of many interesting bushy areas. The woodland holds a typical selection of the woodland birds to be expected in this part of France, including both Middle Spotted and Black Woodpeckers. Short-toed Treecreeper, Nuthatch, and Goldcrest and Firecrest all breed and often occur in mixed tit flocks in winter. Sparrowhawk and Goshawk are two resident raptors, though not easy to see, and they are joined in summer by Honey Buzzards. Look for the latter between May and August, especially around any of the cleared areas in the forest. The damper areas attract Redpoll and Siskin in winter. Although many of the forestry roads are closed to cars, there is unrestricted access on foot, except to the newly-planted areas.

Access

From St.-Dizier (8 km to the south) take the D157/D16 as far as the village of Trois-Fontaines-l'Abbaye. It is possible to park here (1). Take the small road uphill past the church, and look across at the two small lakes (2). The track enters the forest to reach La Neuve-Grange; turn left here onto a surfaced road which can then be followed back to the starting point, taking in clearings as well as continuous woodland. Woodpeckers are more often found in areas with mature trees and are most active in April and May, as well as September. Look for warblers such as Chiffchaff, Willow and Wood Warblers in areas with taller trees, but note that by July these species stop singing and become harder to locate. For further exploration there are plenty of alternatives. The loop to the east starts by passing just to the south of the two pools mentioned above and takes in an attractive valley near the source of the River Bruxenelle (3).

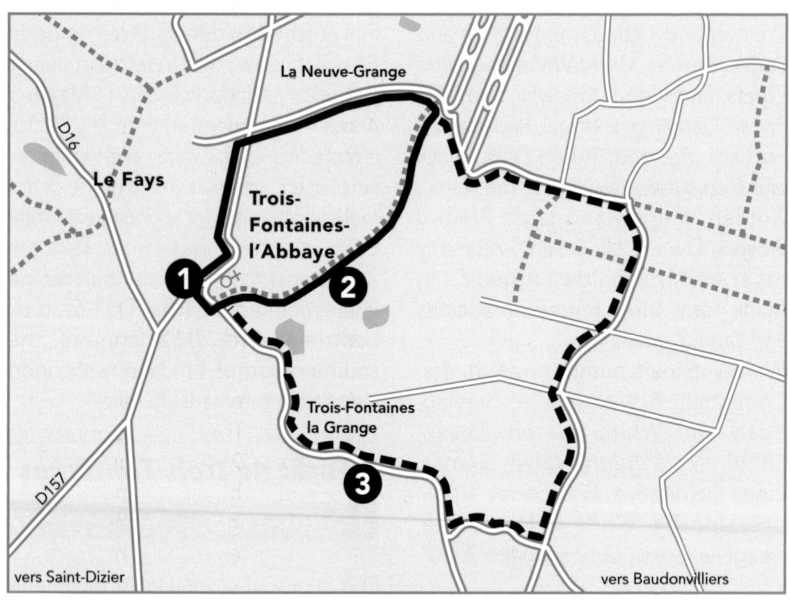

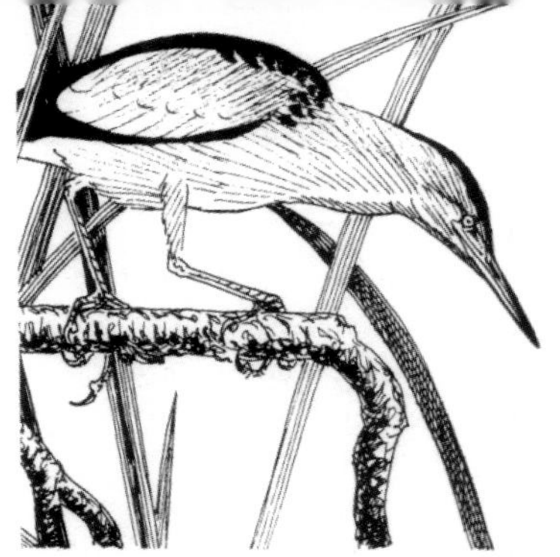

LITTLE BITTERN

Calendar

All year: Sparrowhawk, Goshawk; woodpeckers (five species, including Black and Middle Spotted), tits, Nuthatch, Short-toed Treecreeper and Hawfinch. *Spring and summer*: Honey Buzzard, Wood and Willow Warblers, Chiffchaff. Near to the lakes: Water Rail, wetland warblers, Stonechat, Whinchat, Red-backed Shrike and sometimes Wryneck. *Winter*: various migrant and wintering passerines such as Fieldfare, Redwing, Siskin and Redpoll.

8. *Lac du Der-Chantecoq*

MARNE (51) *IGN 22*

The Lac du Der-Chantecoq, south-west of St.-Dizier, is the largest man-made body of water in France (4,800 hectares) and was constructed to regulate the flow of the River Marne. The whole area, including the outlying lagoons of the Étangs des Landres, du Grand Coulon and de la Forêt, is a protected area, with no shooting allowed. Because of its function as a flood-control reservoir, water levels vary greatly according to season, the lake progressively dropping between July and November to start filling again in December. The shoreline is varied, and there are several large islands which act as important refuges, especially for roosting birds. There are areas of willow scrub of different ages, reedbeds and flood meadows. The western part of the lake is bordered by an embankment which separates it from the typical Champenois countryside of hedgerows, meadows, arable fields, woods and lakes, while much of the surrounding land is wooded. All this adds to the richness of the habitat and it has rapidly become one of the best-known birding sites in northern France, particularly from autumn through to the spring when spectacular numbers of Cranes can be seen, along with several White-tailed Eagles and a wide variety of wildfowl, including good numbers of Bean, Greylag and White-fronted Geese.

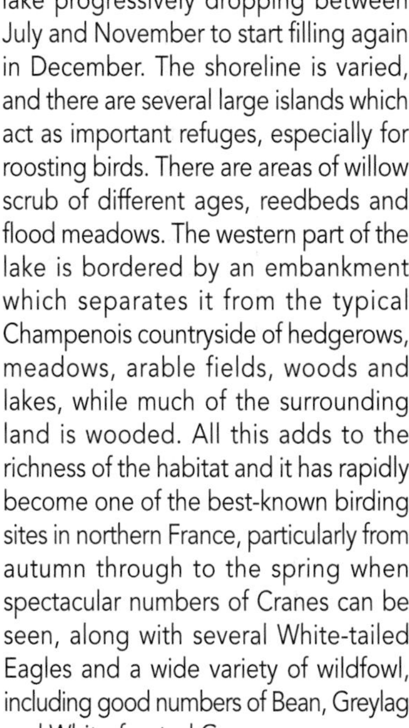

Access

There are many places all round the lake from which it can be viewed, and a more detailed map showing tracks and footpaths is a great help. The route suggested below is just an initial introduction. The lake itself is well-signposted from the nearby towns of Vitry-le-François, St.-Dizier and Brienne-le-Château. The most substantial village on the southern side of the lake is Giffaumont-Champaubert, and it is possible to reach the embankment of the lake here and walk east to the Port de Giffaumont or west towards the Port de Chantecoq. The latter is accessible by road, the D13, and from here it is possible to walk north along length of the embankment. Alternatively, continue along the D13 and drive up onto

POCHARD

the embankment at (1). From here one can either walk north, or drive south along the embankment, stopping to scan as you go. The first section is one of the best places in autumn and winter from which to watch the Cranes flighting in at dusk to roost at the lake. They mostly spend the day feeding out in the arable fields to the west of the lake. There are patches of willows and reeds along the lake shore here (2), breeding habitat for various wetland warblers in summer, and favoured by dabbling ducks in winter. The large oak tree ('le gros chêne') on the island out from here is a favoured perching spot for Cormorants, Peregrine and White-tailed Eagle. The road drops down from the embankment but then rejoins it at (3). This is another good spot and often provides good views of geese, Great White Egret and waders. Between (3) and (4) rafts have been provided as nesting platforms for Common Terns and Black-headed Gulls, which are occupied in spring and summer. This is also a good section for waders in August and September. The embankment at the Port de Chantecoq (4) is another vantage point for scanning the central part of the lake. From the nearby roundabout, one can visit the Maison de l'Oiseau et du Poisson visitor centre (5), in a converted half-timbered barn. This is a good spot to stock up on information about the area, and to get up-to-date information on what has been seen. A footpath (often wet and muddy) leads down a slope to three lakes in the woodland just to the west of the main reservoir enclosure. At the bottom of the slope a path to the right leads to a hide overlooking the Étang des Landres (6). A way-marked trail leads through woodland and clearings, sometimes on boardwalks, to other hides that overlook the Étang du Grand Coulon

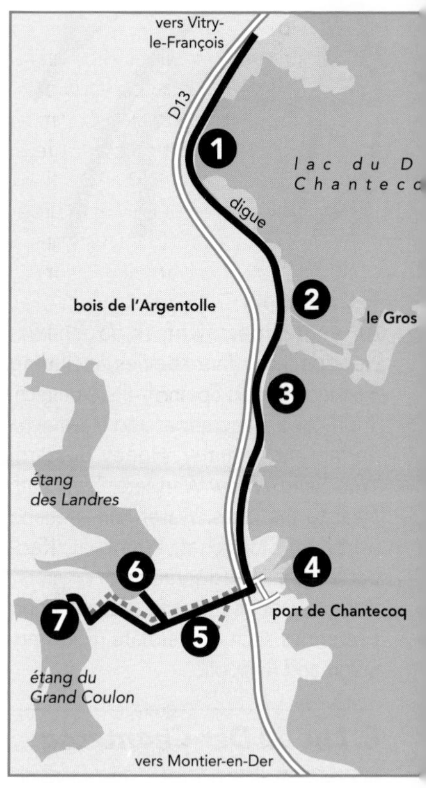

(7). These sheltered lakes are a refuge for various wildfowl, but also attract Cranes, herons and egrets (including Great White in winter). The woodland and hedges have an interesting breeding population, including Lesser Spotted Woodpecker and Red-backed Shrike. There are plenty of other places around the lake from which birds can be seen, including the wooded peninsulas of La Cornée du Der and the Presqu'île de Nemours on the northern side of the lake. To see Cranes feeding during the day, there is a visitor centre and hide overlooking specially managed stubble fields at the Ferme aux Grues, located at St.-Rémy-en-Bouzement, a short distance away to the north-west, off the route to Vitry-le-François.

■ **Calendar**

Spring: Little Bittern, Night and Purple Herons, Little Egret, Black Kite, Marsh Harrier, Little and Common Gulls, Common and Black Terns, wetland warblers (including Savi's Warbler), Reed Bunting.
Summer and autumn: Little Bittern, Purple and Night Herons, Little Egret, Garganey, Pochard, Marsh Harrier, Osprey, Ringed and Little Ringed Plovers, Curlew Sandpiper, Ruff, Snipe, Curlew, Spotted Redshank, Greenshank, Lesser Black-backed and Yellow-legged Gulls, Black Tern.
Autumn and winter: Great White Egret, swans (3 species), Greylag, Bean and White-fronted Geese, Shelduck, Wigeon, Goldeneye, Goosander, Smew, Red Kite, White-tailed Eagle, Hen Harrier, Peregrine, Crane, Grey and Golden Plovers, Lapwing, Dunlin, Curlew, Water Pipit.

9. Étangs d'Argonne

Marne (51) *IGN 10*

About 40 km north of St.-Dizier is an area dotted with lakes, many of which are of interest for their birds. In winter, so long as the lakes are not frozen, it is possible to see White-tailed Eagle (often wanderers from the Lac du Der-Chantecoq), Smew, Goosander, Goldeneye, and Whooper and Bewick's Swans on passage. Small numbers of Greylag Geese winter in the area, and Great White Egrets have steadily increased as a winter visitor. Cranes pass through the area in both spring and autumn, and there is a small roost in the maize stubble near Éclaires. Other migrants include Osprey and Red Kite in the spring and Black Kites that remain to nest (but in declining numbers). Both Bittern and Great Crested Grebe breed, and many wetland warblers can be seen in the strips of reeds surrounding the lakes. The surrounding hedgerows and fields attract Red-backed Shrike, Stonechat and Yellowhammer as breeding species. As summer turns to autumn, many duck congregate on the lakes and the muddy margins attract migrant waders such as Common Sandpiper, Greenshank and Lapwing. The lakes can be found on the eastern side (mostly) of the D982 north from Vitry-le-François through Givry-en-Argonne to Ste.-Ménéhould. The majority of the lakes are private and so have to be watched from the minor roads that run through the area. The area bounded by Givry-en-Argonne, Belval-en-Argonne, Villers-en-Argonne and Epense makes a good starting point.

10. Réservoir de Villegusien

Haute-Marne (52) *IGN 29*

The Réservoir de Villegusien (or de la Vingeanne after the river that flows into it) is a feeder reservoir for the Marne to Saône Canal, and lies to the south of Langres, on the route to Dijon, in a still relatively unspoilt countryside of meadows, woods and thickets. There are two marshy bays, the Baie de Percey and the Baie de Vêvres, the latter being crossed by the N74 on a causeway and its edges are well wooded. Being at the foot of the Langres plateau on the Marne-Rhône-Saône corridor, the site is best known for the autumn migration of waders and duck and to a lesser extent for wintering wildfowl. Numbers are never high but this is compensated for by the fact that one can obtain good views at close range. Some of the more interesting species that can be seen include marsh terns and Little Gull during April and May, August and

September. Both Red and Black Kites and Osprey come to feed over or around the lake, primarily on migration, but can also be seen during the summer. It is also a good place for roosting or feeding duck in spring and especially in autumn; species to be expected are Teal, Shoveler, Pochard, Tufted Duck, sometimes Goosander, Smew, Eider, Common or Velvet Scoter. The range of breeding species is limited, but includes Kingfisher, and Great Crested Grebe. In addition many common warblers and Reed Buntings occur in the lakeside vegetation, and Fieldfares breed not far away. There is unrestricted access but the site is also used for fishing, bathing and sailing, and there is a certain amount of shooting.

Access

From Langres take the N74 south to Longeau, then the D67 south-east towards Besançon to reach Percey-le-Pautel. Just beyond here turn right on the D128 towards Villegusien to reach the bank of the reservoir, where there is a recently constructed hide (1). This area is favoured by waders when bare mud is exposed (e.g., August to October), and wagtails and Meadow and Water Pipits occur on the shore during migration. From here you can take the track leading northwards, but be careful not to enter the reserve area at the back of the Baie de Percey, or to go onto the shoreline, especially during the hunting period (August to February), as this is an area where shooting is forbidden, and hence is a valuable refuge for ducks and waders at this time. There is a car park a little further on (2), and Common Sandpiper can be seen on the banks here during migration periods. From here, walk north to the hide or south to the dam (3), where you will get a good view over the whole reservoir. In spring there are often many hirundines and Swifts feeding over the water, and there is a large Black-headed Gull roost in winter. The lake can also be viewed in both directions from the N74, although you need to take care because of the traffic. This gives you a view into the Baie de Vêvres.

Calendar

Spring: Grebes, Cormorant; many species of duck, Hobby, Red and Black Kites, Golden Oriole, *Acrocephalus* warblers, Reed Bunting. Shelduck, scoters, sawbills, and marsh terns occur on passage.

Late summer and autumn: Mallard, Shoveler, Teal, Pochard, Tufted Duck,

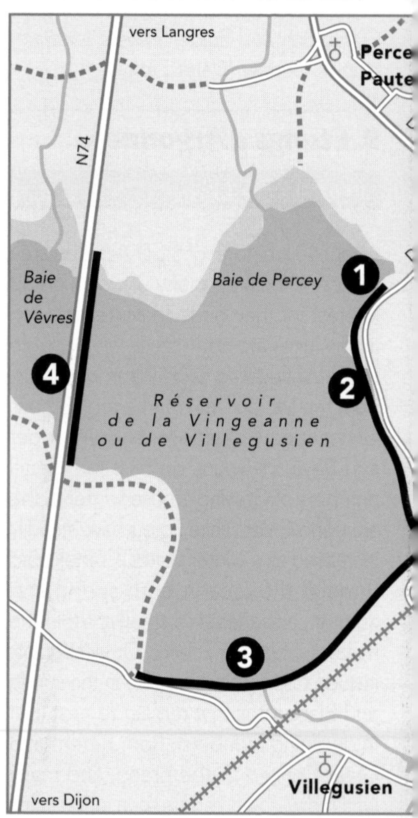

Red and Black Kites, Osprey, Lapwing, Little Ringed Plover and other small waders, Spotted Redshank, Redshank, Common Sandpiper, Black-headed Gull. *Winter*: Grey Heron, Mallard, Coot.

11. Bassigny

HAUTE-MARNE (52) *IGN 29*

The countryside of Bassigny, which extends from Langres north-east to Neufchâteau is dominated by expanses of grassland primarily devoted to cattle rearing. A few fine mixed woods of oak, beech and hornbeam grow on hillocks or in the damp depressions. The area is drained by the River Meuse, which has its source here and flows northwards through the Bassigny. Several notable breeding species are associated with the river valley such as Curlew and Great Grey Shrike. The villages and surrounding orchards are worth exploring for two more localised birds – Hoopoe and Woodchat Shrike – which arrive in summer. Both Black and Red Kites can be seen circling overhead, searching for food, along with the more common species of raptor such as Buzzard and Kestrel. The woodlands are also of interest, as six species occur in this area, including Black and Middle Spotted. Grey-headed Woodpeckers occur mainly in the riverside woodland of the smaller valleys. Collared Flycatcher is another localised summer visitor. Parts of the river are liable to flooding, and in the spring these flooded areas attract a variety of migrants, such as ducks, waders, Crane and both Black and White Storks. The D74 runs along the Meuse valley, the section from Clefmont to Bourmont being one of the more interesting sections, with plenty of minor roads for further access.

GREAT GREY SHRIKE

12. Forêt d'Auberive

HAUTE-MARNE (52) *IGN 29*

Situated about 20 km to the south-west of Langres, this beautiful beech and oak forest on the Langrois plateau has a rich and varied bird population, including Sparrowhawk, Goshawk, Honey Buzzard in summer, many woodpeckers (including Grey-headed and Black) and Wood Warbler. Hazel Grouse and Tengmalm's Owl are two sought-after species here, but they are both extremely difficult to locate. The forest edges and more open bushy areas have Woodlark, Great Grey and Red-backed Shrike, among other passerines. There are regular sightings of Black Storks on migration, particularly in March and September. The D48 from just south of Langres runs through the middle of the forest before reaching Auberive village, and forestry tracks can be used for further exploration.

SITES

1 **Bonifacio**

2 **Col de Bavella**

3 **The River Liamone**

4 **Forêt d'Aitone**

5 **Barcaggio**

6 **Réserve naturelle de Scandola**

7 **Vallée de la Tassineta, Asco**

8 **Vallée du Varghello, Venaco**

9 **Étang de Biguglia**

10 **Vallée du Fango**

Corsica

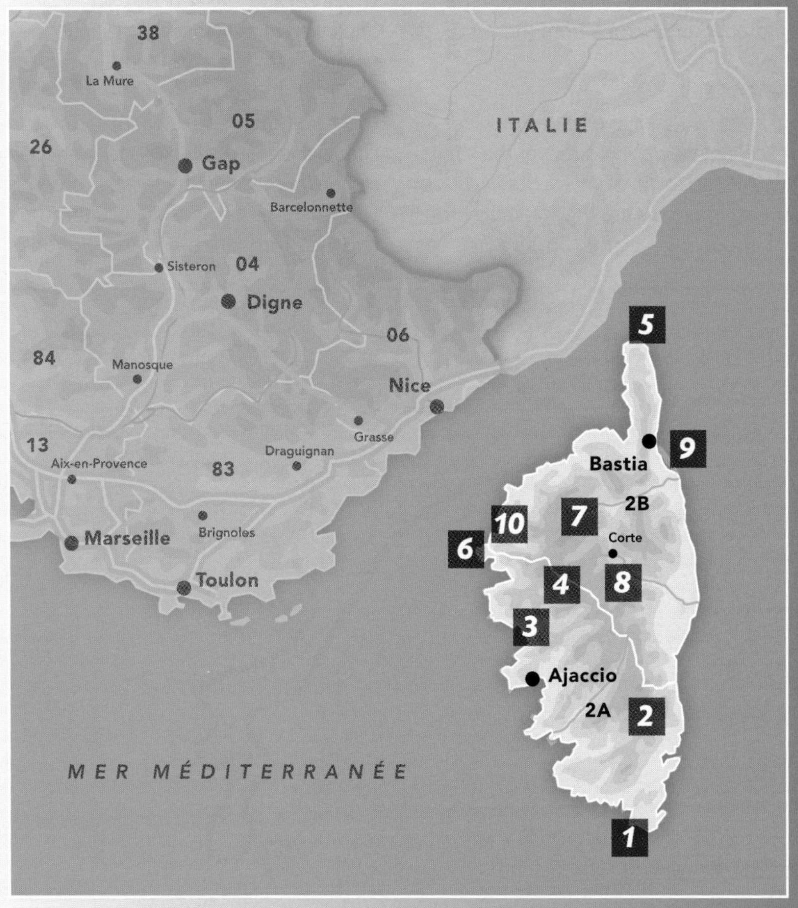

38
La Mure
05
26
Gap
ITALIE
Barcelonnette
Sisteron
04
Digne
06
84
Manosque
Nice
5
Grasse
13
Draguignan
Aix-en-Provence
83
9
Bastia
2B
7
10
Marseille
Brignoles
Corte
6
Toulon
4
8
3
Ajaccio
2A
2
MER MÉDITERRANÉE
1

1. Bonifacio

Corse-du-Sud (2A) *IGN 74*

The attractive and historic town of Bonifacio, perched on a limestone cliff close to the southernmost point of Corsica, looks across the straits to Sardinia. The plateau to the south-east, between the town and the signal-station and lighthouse at Capo Pertusato, is covered with low maquis, the typical Mediterranean scrubby vegetation favoured by several species of *Sylvia* warblers. There are also small valleys and old-established gardens surrounded by high walls, protecting the crops from the wind.

Access

In Bonifacio itself, the citadel provides an excellent viewpoint out over the straits. Within the town, Spotless Starlings and Italian Sparrows are the standard forms of these two common species, as everywhere in Corsica, the latter usually being classified as a subspecies of House Sparrow. The situation is complicated by the fact that in Bonifacio they sometimes hybridise with Spanish Sparrows, which breed widely on Sardinia. Although pure Spanish Sparrows are sometimes also recorded here, the simplest way to see the real thing is to take a day-trip to Sardinia on the ferry, a good way also to see shearwaters at close range from the boat. Just offshore, Grain-de-Sable island (1) can be viewed from the foot of a flight of steps that leads down to the base of the cliffs. In the evening, listen out for Cory's Shearwaters calling as they fly in to their nesting burrows on the island. To explore the plateau to the south-east, take the footpath that starts from the citadel and follows the cliffs to the signal-station (2). In spring the maquis resounds to the songs of Sardinian, Marmora's and Dartford Warblers. Cirl Buntings

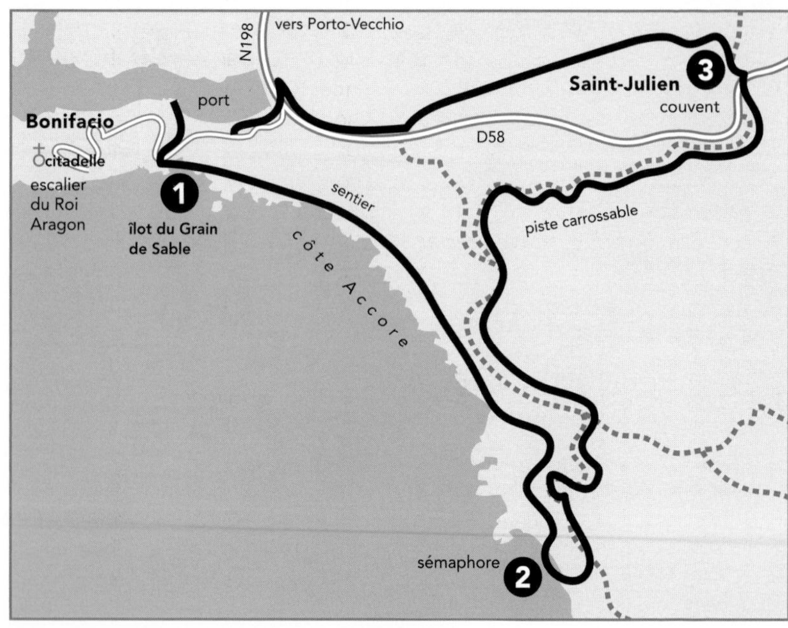

MARMORA'S WARBLER

and Corsican Citril Finches also occur in the same area. The Mediterranean race of Shag can be seen just offshore, and Yelkouan Shearwaters also occur. In summer both Pallid and Alpine Swifts chase each other along the cliffs. From the signal-station one can either walk to the lighthouse, or return to Bonifacio along the roads via the convent of St.-Julien (3), checking the fields and bushes along the way, the full circuit covering about 6 km.

CALENDAR

Spring: Cory's and Yelkouan Shearwaters, Shag (Mediterranean race), raptors, Yellow-legged Gull, Pallid and Alpine Swifts, hirundines, Tawny Pipit, Sardinian, Marmora's and Dartford Warblers, Spotless Starling, Corsican Citril Finch, Italian Sparrow, Cirl Bunting. *Winter*: Gannet, Yelkouan Shearwater, Shag.

2. Col de Bavella

CORSE-DU-SUD (2A) IGN 74

At 1,243 metres, the Col de Bavella, in the south-east of the island, is a magnificent spot from which to view the mountainsides and pine forests which host some of the island's most sought-after birds. Among the pines, look for Corsican Nuthatch, Crossbill, Corsican Citril Finch and Coal Tit, while at night Scops Owls can be heard calling. The more open areas have Woodlark and Water Pipit, while the spectacular peaks of the Aiguilles de Bavella are always worth scanning for Golden Eagle and Lammergeier. Alpine Accentors also breed in the higher sections of the surrounding mountains. The Col de Bavella lies on the D268 between Zonza (accessed from Sartène to the south-west or Porto-Vecchio to the south-east) and Solenzara on the east coast. Long-distance footpaths start from the pass for further exploration (IGN 4253ET/OT and 4253ET/OT, 1:25,000 may be useful).

3. The River Liamone

CORSE-DU-SUD (2A) IGN 74

This point where the River Liamone flows into the sea about 30 km north of Ajaccio is always worth a stop, as the mix of habitats here – small fields, reedbeds, maquis, sandbanks and scattered trees – holds a good variety of species associated with the coast and lower ground. Near the mouth of the river the following may well be seen: Turtle Dove, Tawny Pipit, Short-toed Lark, Red-backed and Woodchat Shrikes, Blue Rock Thrush, Sardinian and Marmora's Warblers, Cirl and Corn Buntings. Along the river look for Water Rail, Little Ringed Plover, Kingfisher, Reed, Great Reed and Cetti's Warblers. There are several colonies of Bee-eaters nearby and Alpine Swifts can be seen overhead. Ospreys breed not far away, and may be seen offshore. Red-rumped Swallows have nested under the bridge in the past, and Shags can be seen on the offshore islands.

4. *Forêt d'Aitone*

CORSE-DU-SUD (2A) *IGN 73*

The Forêt d'Aitone, towards the north of the island, is one of the more reliable spots to see the much sought-after Corsican Nuthatch, endemic to the island, and associated with the ancient stands of Corsican pine. Other residents include Goshawk, Sparrowhawk, Great Spotted Woodpecker, Coal Tit, Crossbill and Jay and a few Siskins breed on an irregular basis. Common Treecreepers can also be found here; note that Short-toed is just an extremely rare vagrant to the island. The D84 from Porto runs up through the sweet chestnut woods around Évisa and then through the forest to reach the Col de Vergio pass. The Forêt de Valdo Niello around Poppaghia on the far side of the pass is also worth exploring as the nuthatch also occurs here.

5. *Barcaggio*

HAUTE-CORSE (2B) *IGN 73*

Barcaggio, at the northern tip of Cap Corse, is a strategic spot for watching migrants, particularly between March and June. A small stream, the Acqua Tignese, runs into the sea here, adding to the variety of the habitat by forming a small delta with a willow-bed, a lagoon and dunes covered in juniper woodland. Nearly 250 species have been identified here so far, including such rarities as Pallid Harrier, Booted Eagle, Trumpeter Finch and White-rumped Swift. Hirundines (Red-rumped Swallow included) pass through in numbers, as do Common, Pallid and Alpine Swifts. Red-throated Pipits are seen annually on spring migration here along with the various races of Yellow Wagtail, the most numerous being *cinereocapilla*, the one that breeds in Italy. A little way back from the coast, where the ground is higher, migrant birds of prey gather in spring before heading north over the sea: Honey Buzzard, Lesser Kestrel, Red-footed Falcon, Marsh and Montagu's Harriers all occur. At other times of year it is less special, although it is known as a wintering site for Wallcreeper.

■ ACCESS

From Bastia take the D80 coast road north to where it turns inland to reach Ersa, a drive of some 59 km. From here the D253 will bring you to Barcaggio. Just before the village, it is possible to park on the right, opposite a chapel, close to the river (1). Walk upstream to where a ford and a footbridge allow access to the far side, passing some willows where, at night, it is possible to hear Scops Owl. The path leads to a lagoon (2), which should be checked for Garganey, waders (especially Common and Wood Sandpipers) and Red-throated Pipit. Both Little and Spotted Crakes have been noted in the reedbeds in April. One can follow the dunes as far as the old tower at the Punta di Agnello (3). Ringed and Little Ringed Plovers can be found along the shore, while near the tower check for Blue Rock Thrush and Peregrine. This is a favoured spot for Wallcreeper in winter. Gannet, Cory's Shearwater and Audouin's Gull can all be seen offshore, particularly around the island of Giraglia.

■ CALENDAR

Spring: Cory's and Yelkouan Shearwaters, Gannet (even in winter), Shag, White and Black Storks, Grey, Squacco and Night Herons, Little Egret, Little Bittern, Little and Spotted Crakes, waders, Scops

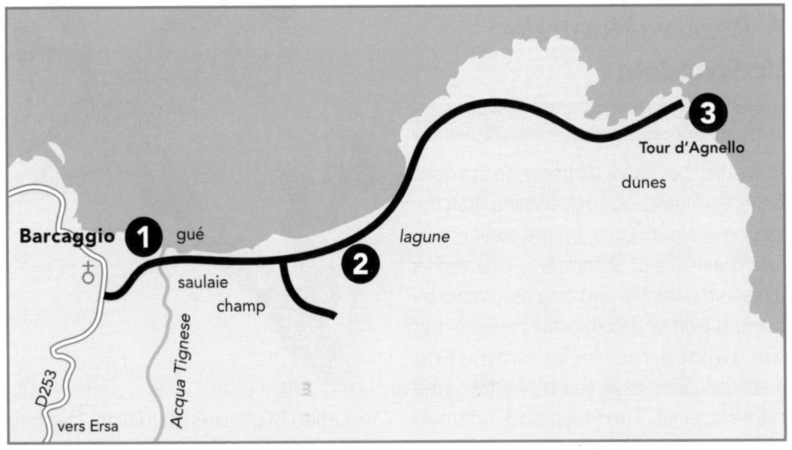

Owl, Nightjar, Cuckoo, Bee-eater, Roller, Red-rumped Swallow, House and Sand Martins, Red-throated Pipit, Robin, Bluethroat, Redstart, Sedge, Grasshopper, Reed, Great Reed, Icterine, Willow, Wood and Garden Warblers, Chiffchaff, Whitethroat and Pied Flycatcher.

NIGHT HERON

6. *Réserve Naturelle de Scandola*

HAUTE-CORSE (2B) *IGN 73*

It would be hard to imagine a more beautiful area to go birdwatching than the region around Porto, on the west coast. The peninsula of Scandola, protected as a réserve naturelle and only accessible by boat, is part of a collapsed volcano and the twisted red rocks contrasting with the clear blue sea make this area rather special. The steep and indented coastline is used by nesting seabirds, rock-dwelling species and the symbol of conservation of the Corsican coast, the Osprey. These nest on the cliffs and fish out over the sea. The cliffs also provide nesting sites for Shag, Peregrine, Blue Rock Thrush, Rock Dove, Crag Martin, Pallid and Alpine Swifts. The interior of the peninsula is covered with mixed maquis, home to a wide range of birds, including Marmora's, Sardinian, Dartford and Subalpine Warblers.

CIRL BUNTING

■ ACCESS

The best starting point is Porto, although some boat trips are organised from Ajaccio, Calvi and Sartène. In Porto, boat trips are advertised in the hotels and bars, some of which sell tickets, or you can enquire at the tourist office. The trip lasts two or three hours with the possibility

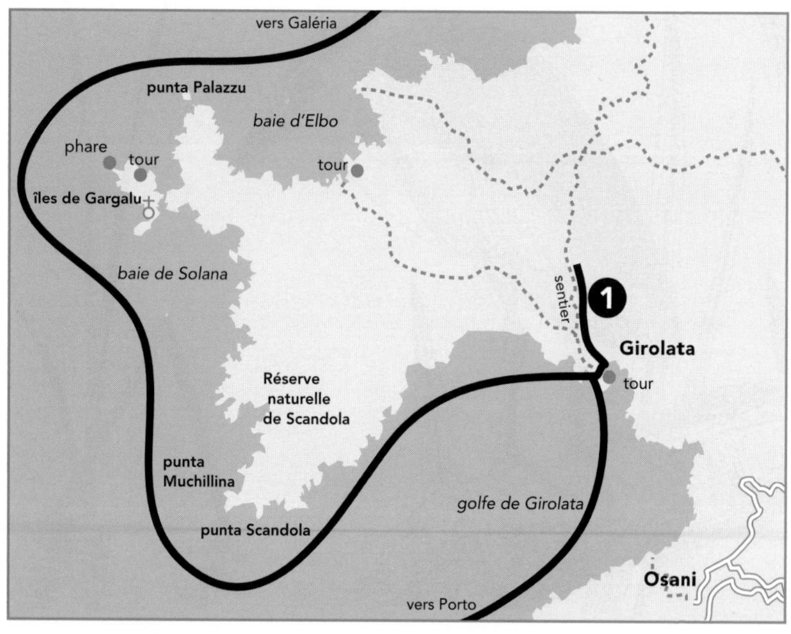

of a halt at the village of Girolata, which is only accessible by boat. A path leaves the village north-westwards (1) into the scrub where *Sylvia* warblers hide. The main boat trip follows the coast west and north to Punta Palazzu and then returns to Porto. The boatmen will know where the Ospreys are nesting – they can be difficult to see from the sea. Other breeding birds of the cliffs and feeding shearwaters can also be seen from the boat. Although the reserve is only accessible this way, the coast road north and south of Porto passes through plenty of maquis where the various warblers can be found, and where Corsican Citril Finches also occur, even down to sea-level.

Calendar

Spring and summer: Shag (Mediterranean race), Osprey, Kestrel, Peregrine, Yellow-legged Gull, Rock Dove, Pallid and Alpine Swifts, Crag Martin, Blue Rock Thrush; Marmora's, Sardinian, Dartford and Subalpine Warblers, Spotted Flycatcher.

7. Vallée de la Tassineta, Asco

Haute-Corse (2B) *IGN 73*

This site is an offshoot of the beautiful Asco valley, with its succession of impressive granite gorges, hemmed in by craggy ridges and forests of Corsican pine. The main valley is bounded on its southern side by Monte Cinto, the highest point of the island, and it is one of the prime areas to find the endemic Corsican Nuthatch. The path along the Tassineta valley runs by the stream where clear torrents cascade over small waterfalls, the effect being remarkably beautiful. Higher up, the landscape is closed by cliffs and the mountains to the north. Apart from the nuthatch, other small birds in the woodland include Coal Tit, Common Treecreeper, and both Goldcrest and Firecrest. It is an outstanding area for birds of prey, with Lammergeier and Golden Eagle breeding in the mountains and Goshawk and Sparrowhawk in the forests. Ravens and Alpine Choughs breed on the cliffs (Red-billed Chough is only a rare vagrant to the island), and can often be seen soaring along the ridges. The more open rocky areas beyond the woodland, at higher levels, are the best areas to find species such as Alpine Accentor, Water Pipit and Blue Rock Thrush which all breed here.

CORSICAN NUTHATCH

Access

The Asco valley and gorges lie to the north of Corte, and the D47 runs the length of the valley. Continue through Asco village for 8½ km towards the Haut Asco ski resort. There is a small car park near the Refuge Giunte, 100 metres before the old footbridge (1). Cross the River Stranciacone by the ford and take the right bank of the Tassineta (2). Fork left once near the Bergerie de la Tassineta sheep-fold (3) which is 3 km further on. In the woodland, listen for the distinctive, harsh calls given by Corsican Nuthatch. Also scan the

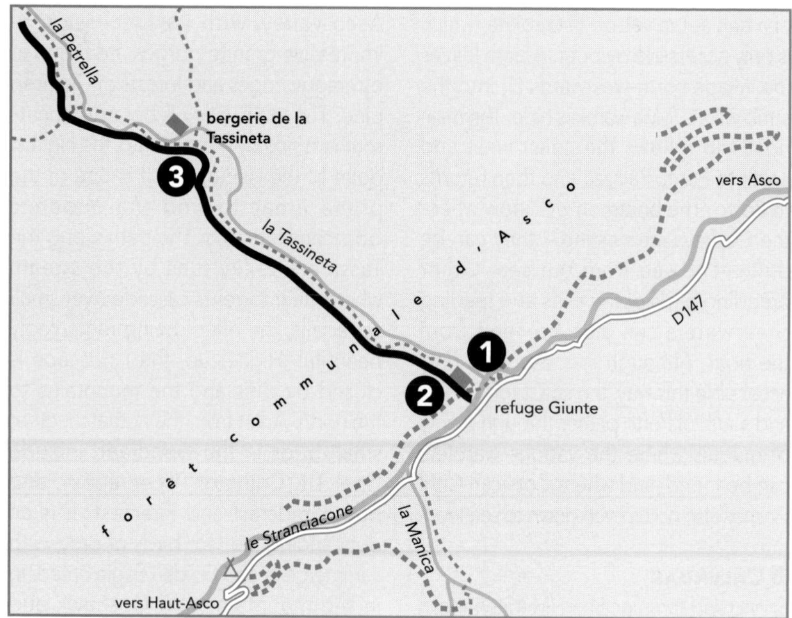

hillsides for Lammergeier and Golden Eagle soaring overhead, along with the Alpine Choughs and Ravens. The more detailed map, IGN 4250OT, 1:25,000 will be helpful here.

■ Calendar

Spring, summer and autumn: Lammergeier, Golden Eagle, Goshawk, Sparrowhawk, Water Pipit, Blue Rock Thrush, Goldcrest, Firecrest, Spotted Flycatcher, Coal Tit, Corsican Nuthatch, Common Treecreeper, Alpine Chough, Raven.

8. Vallée du Varghello, Venaco

Haute-Corse (2B) *IGN 73*

Corte is a good starting point for exploring the valleys and high mountains of the central part of the island. The Restonica, west of Corte, is just one of several valleys that provide spectacular background scenery to some high-level specialities, most notably Lammergeier and Golden Eagle. The Vallée du Varghello, a little further south, is surrounded by the high peaks of Monte Cardo, Monte Rotondo and Monte d'Oro and allows you to see three well-defined vegetation zones: high Mediterranean, montane, and sub-alpine. This diversity produces an excellent range of species, as Mediterranean birds can be seen side-by-side with mountain and forest species.

■ Access

Leave Corte on the N193 southwards and, after 17 km, beyond Venaco, you reach the entrance to the valley (1), just before the Vecchio bridge. Although it is possible to drive part of the way up the valley on the D723, it is better to leave your car at the start and explore on foot. In the valley bottom there is a good mixture of typical maquis plants such as holm-oak, heather, strawberry tree, juniper and rockrose, ideal habitat for Marmora's Warblers, which can be heard singing from as early as March. Sardinian Warblers and Cirl Buntings are also typical of this section. The track continues past Piferini to reach the Vacchereccio bridge after 4 km. Great Spotted Woodpecker is a characteristic bird here, but the Corsican pine forests beyond the bridge also hold Corsican Nuthatch. The track winds its way onwards through more open country to reach the pass of the Col de Tribali (3), 10 km from the starting point, and at a height of 1,590 metres. Throughout this section scan above the higher crags to the north of the trail for Lammergeier or Golden Eagle. Look for Corsican Citril Finch in the same area, particularly around the Col de Tribali.

CORY'S SHEARWATER

The 1:25,000 IGN map 4251OT covers this area in more detail.

Calendar

Spring: Lammergeier, Golden Eagle, Peregrine, Sparrowhawk, Alpine Swift, Great Spotted Woodpecker, Mistle Thrush, Water Pipit, Alpine Accentor, Marmora's and Sardinian Warblers, Great, Coal and Long-tailed Tits, Corsican Nuthatch, Common Treecreeper, Wallcreeper, Spotted Flycatcher, Crossbill, Corsican Citril Finch, Cirl Bunting.
Autumn: Migrant Dotterel are sometimes seen on the high ridges.

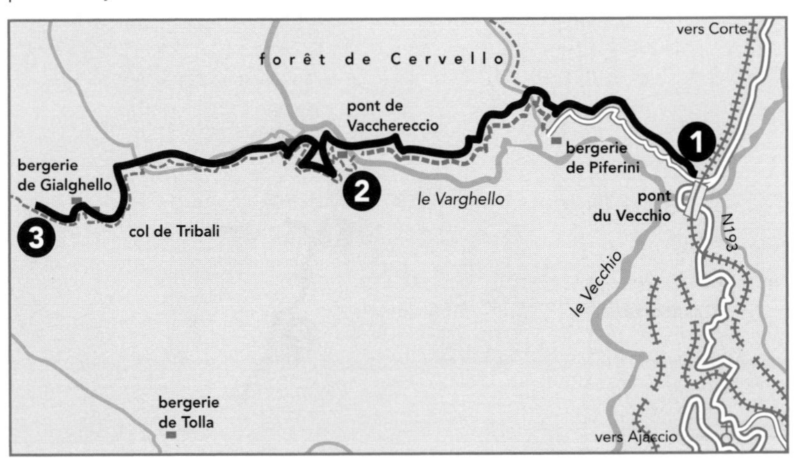

9. Étang de Biguglia

HAUTE-CORSE (2B) *IGN 73*

The coastal lagoon of the Étang de Biguglia is the largest wetland in Corsica, covering 1,450 hectares, and is situated just south of Bastia. It occupies one of several low-lying sections of coast on the east side of the island, and provides a strong contrast to the mountains and rocks found almost everywhere else. Although some of the interest of the site has been affected negatively during the last thirty years due to agricultural and urban development, it is still an attractive wetland for wintering and migrant birds, with more than 250 species recorded. The lagoon is classified as a réserve naturelle, and hence gains a certain amount of protection. Historically it was a breeding site for White-headed Duck (up until 1966) and White-tailed Eagle. A reintroduction programme for the former has been instigated and is already showing signs of success. The mudflats are used by migrants for resting and feeding, especially by waders, of which about forty species have occurred including Marsh and Terek Sandpipers and Red-necked Phalarope. Great White Egret and Greater Flamingo are among the other species that have been seen.

ACCESS

From Bastia head southward along the N193 as far as the Furiani roundabout and then turn left on the D107 coast road. After 2 km, park opposite the beach (1). Check all the ancient fishing piles opposite the Genoese fort carefully as they are used as perches by many species: Cormorant (September to February), Grey Heron, Little Egret, Osprey, Black-headed, Yellow-legged and Audouin's (February and March) Gulls and Sandwich Tern. A sign-

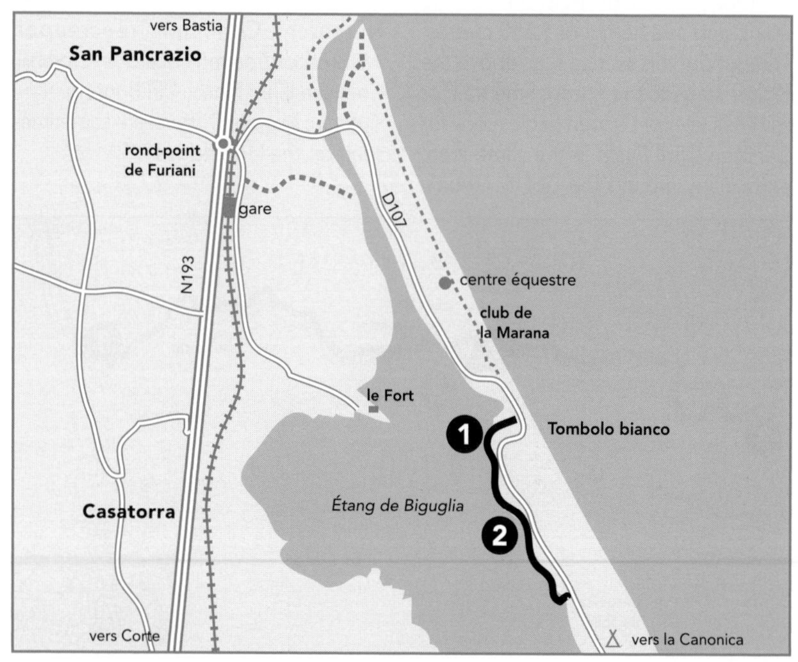

posted interpretation trail continues along the shore as far as a hide (2) overlooking the mudflats. Typical migrant waders include Curlew and Wood Sandpipers, Dunlin and Little Stint, as well as Black-winged Stilt and Black-tailed Godwit.

Calendar

Spring and autumn: Grey, Squacco and Night Herons, Little Egret, Spoonbill, Ferruginous Duck, Osprey, Marsh Harrier, Red-footed Falcon, Collared Pratincole, Oystercatcher, Black-winged Stilt, Grey Plover, Dunlin, stints and other small waders, Black-tailed Godwit, Curlew, Whimbrel, Turnstone, Audouin's Gull, Black and White-winged Black Terns.
Breeding season: Great Crested and Little Grebes, Purple Heron, Little Bittern, Red-crested Pochard, Hobby, Marsh Harrier, Bee-eater, Hoopoe, Cetti's, Fan-tailed, Reed and Great Reed Warblers.
Winter: Black-necked Grebe, Cormorant, Cattle, Little and Great White Egrets, Greater Flamingo, Pochard, Tufted Duck, Pintail, Shoveler, Wigeon, Teal, Coot, Sandwich Tern, Kingfisher, Moustached Warbler, Chiffchaff, Penduline Tit and Reed Bunting.

10. Vallée du Fango

HAUTE-CORSE (2B) *IGN 73*

Lying to the north of the Scandola reserve (site 6), the valley of the River Fango is one of the more isolated sections of Corsica. The area around the river mouth, near Galeria, owned by the Conservatoire de l'Espace Littoral and hence a protected site, is particularly well wooded with alder. Breeding species here include Sparrowhawk, Nightjar, Scop's Owl, Spotted Flycatcher and Corsican Citril Finch while Ospreys nesting on the coast regularly fish near the river's mouth. Further up the valley is the Forêt de Pirio (a UNESCO world heritage site), considered to be one of the best mature holm-oak woodlands on the island. Here are such woodland species as Goshawk, Scops Owl, Great Spotted Woodpecker, Blackcap and Robin. The winding D81 between Porto and Calvi crosses the River Fango near Galeria, and the D351 runs alongside much of the river. Turn downstream to Galeria and the coastal section, and head inland to Manso and beyond to explore the forests and hillsides further upstream, almost as far as the river's source.

BLACK TERN

SITES

1 *The Mont-d'Or*	**7** *Baume-les-Messieurs*
2 *Réserve Naturelle de Frasne*	**8** *Sablières de Desnes*
3 *Lac de Bouverans*	**9** *Lac de Vaivre-Vesoul*
4 *Roches de Pont-de-Roide*	**10** *Saône valley near Vesoul*
5 *Lower valley of the River Doubs*	**11** *The Ognon valley*
6 *Massif de la Serre*	**12** *Sundgau*

Franche-Comté

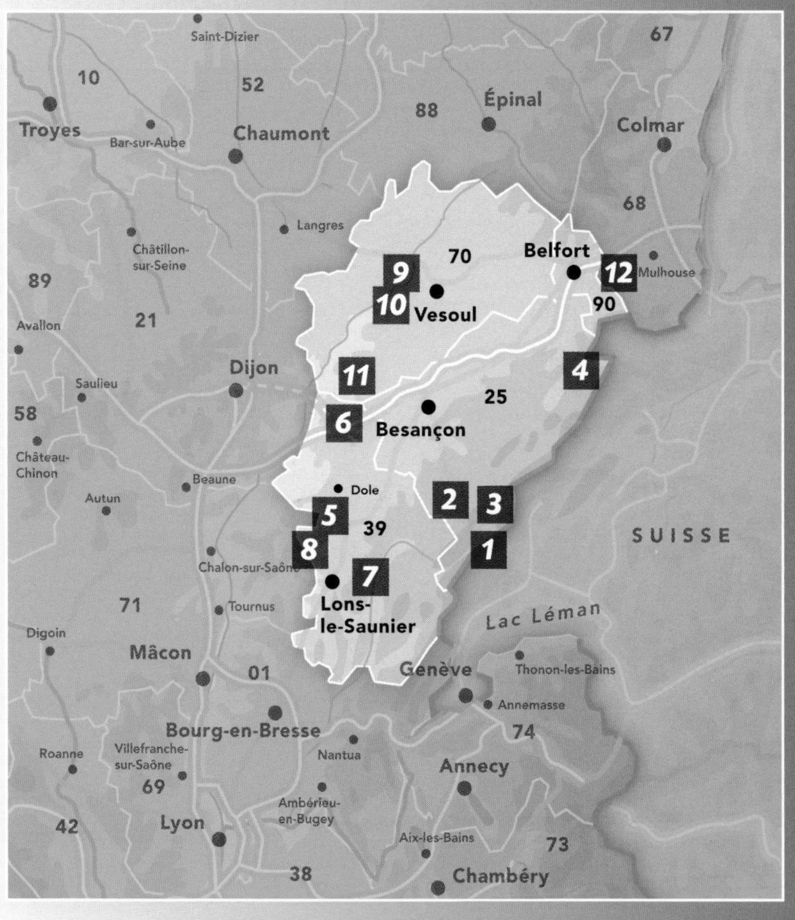

1. The Mont-d'Or

Doubs (25) *IGN 38*

One of the highest points in the Jura region, the Mont d'Or rises to 1,463 metres. On its western slopes, beech and fir forests alternate with more open habitats – meadows, thickets and open woodland) up to 1,400 metres. An alpine meadow type habitat then starts with climate and vegetation typical of the sub-alpine zone. To the east, there is a stretch of more than a kilometre of cliffs (200 metres to 250 metres in height) at the bottom of which is a large area of rocky scree. The whole area is remarkable for the range of montane and sub-alpine birds that nest here. There is free access at all times but note that some of the roads may well be blocked with snow for periods in winter.

Access

The nearest large town is Pontarlier, to the north. From here take the N57 south towards Vallorbe (in Switzerland) as far as Les Hôpitaux-Neufs. From here turn right on the D9 and then the D45 towards Mouthe. Having passed Les Longevilles-Mont-d'Or turn left towards the Mont-d'Or; there is a car park (1) at the end of the road. Two possible walks are suggested (IGN 3426OT, 1:25,000

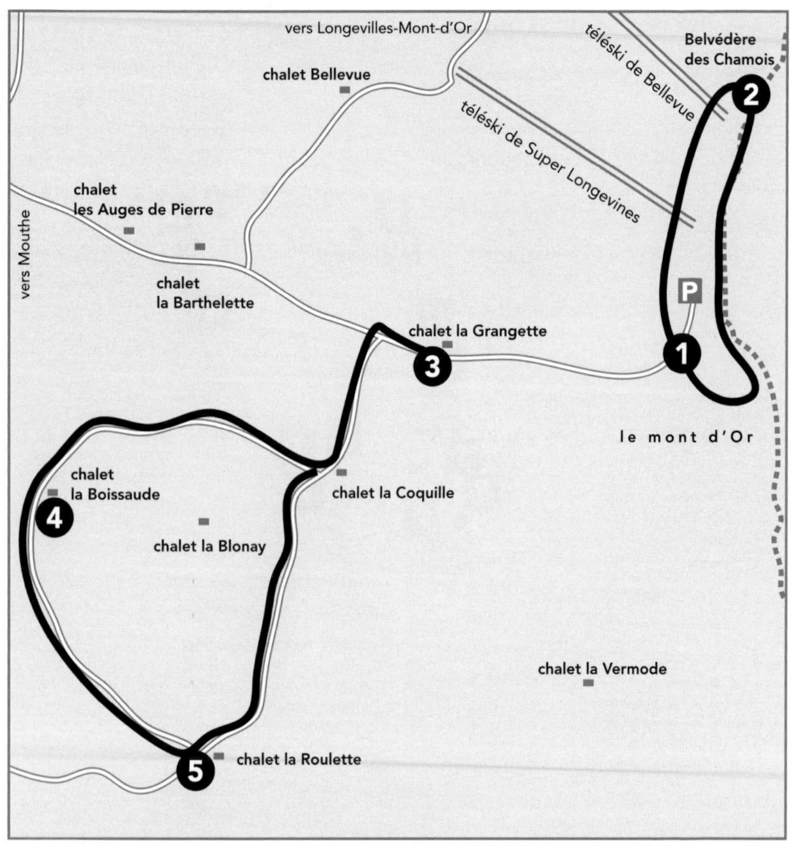

TENGMALM'S OWL

may be useful). For the first, head to the highest point of the Mont d'Or and then follow the ridge northwards as far as the Belvédère des Chamois viewpoint (2). From late August to late September the short vegetation on the slopes here is a stop-off point for migrant Dotterel. Peregrine, Kestrel, Crag Martin and Raven all nest on the nearby cliffs. Although Wallcreepers are present throughout the year in the Mont d'Or area, they are difficult to locate in summer. The best time to look for them is in the autumn, especially in the area around this viewpoint. In winter and spring Alpine Accentors should be looked for on the flatter areas around the cliffs, and Ring Ouzels can also be found here at this time. From here return along the ridge back to the car park. Water Pipit and Skylark both nest here and Wheatears can be seen perched on walls or piles of stones.

For the second walk, go down the road for about 1 km as far as the chalet of La Grangette (3). From here walk along the road leading to another chalet, La Boissaude (4). This is an area where Tengmalm's Owl can be found breeding; they are best located by call between March and May. Other breeding species of the forest include Black Woodpecker, Crossbill, Common Treecreeper and Siskin. Another sought-after breeding species is the Nutcracker, also not very easy to see, especially when they are actually nesting, from mid-March onwards. The route continues to the chalet of La Roulette (5). In this part of the forest both Hazel Grouse and Capercaillie breed, but once again these are difficult species to find, and seeing them is often a matter of luck to some extent! One can continue along the road to the starting point. Various species such as Citril Finch, Ring Ouzel and Fieldfare all nest on the forest edge or in cleared woodland, and are not quite so difficult to see.

Calendar

Summer: raptors include Goshawk, Sparrowhawk, Kestrel and Peregrine. Hazel Grouse, Capercaillie, Woodcock, Tengmalm's Owl, Black Woodpecker, Crag Martin, Water Pipit, Wheatear, Ring Ouzel, Fieldfare, Wood and Bonelli's Warblers, Spotted Flycatcher, Wallcreeper, Common Treecreeper, Citril Finch, Crossbill, Siskin, Nutcracker, Raven.
Autumn: a well known site for migrant Dotterel.
Winter and early spring: a regular site for Alpine Accentor.

2. Réserve Naturelle de Frasne

Doubs (25) *IGN 38*

The Réserve Naturelle de Frasne, south-west of Pontarlier, was created to protect a remarkable acid peat-bog with a diversity of evolving habitats (floating and raised bogs), and also includes some birch and mountain pine woodland. The peat-bog is of most interest for birds during the breeding season, and for its beautiful landscape. To its west are two lakes, the Étangs de Frasne. The larger one is used for water sports and is hence more disturbed but the smaller one is a migratory stop-over for duck, gulls, terns and waders. It is a very shallow lake (rarely more than one metre deep), which was created in 1960 when a marshy depression was flooded. The aquatic and marshland vegetation is well developed and many small islands have been formed. The banks are open, with only a few willows growing on the eastern bank. Surrounded by water-meadows, the lake is filled from the south-west by the outflow from the larger lake. Access in general is unrestricted, apart from onto the reserve itself, although way-marked tracks allow entry to the most interesting areas.

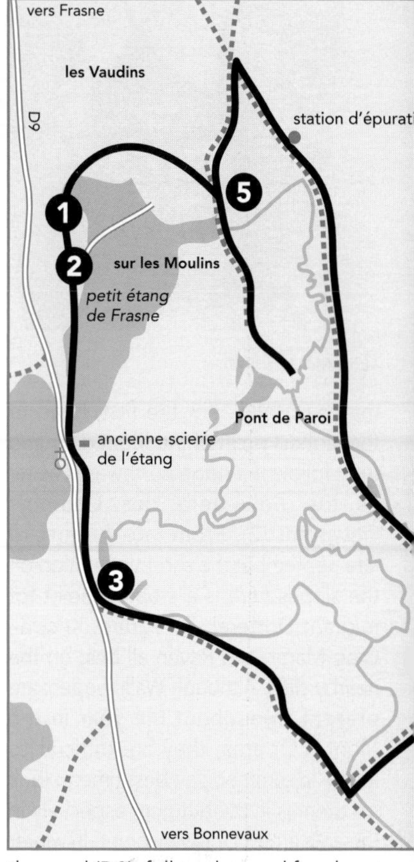

ACCESS

From Pontarlier, 9 km to the north-east, take the D72 and then the D471 towards Champagnole as far as Frasne (also accessible by rail, including by TGV). From here take the D9 towards Bonnevaux: the smaller lake can be seen on the left of the road on leaving Frasne. Park on the side of the road near the wooden hut (1) to the north-west of the lake, and view from here. In spring the islands often attract various species of wader. From the hillock (2) to the west of the lake Great Crested Grebe, Coot and Mute Swan (two breeding pairs) can be seen throughout the year. In spring various duck occur – Shoveler, Gadwall, Teal, Garganey, Pochard, Tufted Duck and Red-crested Pochard, for instance. During May it is a good site for Hobby and Red-footed Falcon is sometimes seen. From here continue on foot along the western side of the lake as far as the road (D9), follow the road for about 800 metres to reach the picnic site (3) on the left; way-marked trails lead to the peat-bog from here. Although luck is needed, this is an area where Hazel Grouse can be seen. Walk through the forest as far as the surfaced track (4). Crossbills occur in the coniferous forest throughout the year. It is also possible to hear or see a Woodcock along one of the forest rides, especially on evenings in spring. At the track (4) turn left and walk as far as the lake's outflow. Look for Marsh Warbler wherever there is angelica growing; the Reed Warblers are much more limited to the few areas of reedbed. Redpoll breeds in the silver birches on

GREAT CRESTED GREBE

the edge of the bog. Continue as far as the spruce plantation on the east side of the lake (5). Both Spotted Flycatcher and Fieldfare nest in the plantations, while Red and Black Kites, Hobby, Hen and Marsh Harriers regularly occur along the lakeshore and over the meadows. Meadow Pipit nests along the lakeside and Wheatear and Yellow Wagtail occur regularly on passage. During the autumn migration the lakeside willows are much used by various other passerines, such as Sedge, Grasshopper and various other warblers, Spotted and Pied Flycatchers, Bluethroat and Penduline Tit.

Then return to the outflow the way you came, and complete the circuit (about 6 km) to the wooden hut in the meadow.

■ **Calendar**

Spring: various grebes and duck (Shoveler, Teal, Garganey, Pochard, Tufted Duck, Red-crested Pochard), raptors (harriers, Hobby, Red-footed Falcon, Osprey, Black and Red Kites), Black, White-winged Black and Whiskered Terns, Little Gull, many waders including Curlew, Whimbrel, Black-tailed Godwit, Lapwing and Snipe, the three commoner hirundines, Blue-headed Wagtail, Meadow Pipit, Wheatear.

Summer: Great Crested Grebe, Mute Swan, Pochard, Tufted Duck, Curlew, Lapwing, Reed and Marsh Warblers, Spotted Flycatcher and Fieldfare.

Autumn (especially August and September): the same species as in the spring plus White and Black Storks, Merlin, Dunlin, Curlew Sandpiper, Little and Temminck's Stints, Ringed and Little Ringed Plovers and Penduline Tit.

3. Lac de Bouverans

Doubs (25) *IGN 38*

The Lac de Bouverans (or Lac de l'Entonnoir) lies about 3½ km to the south-east of the previous site, Frasne. During the breeding season Great Crested Grebe, Garganey, Pochard and Tufted Duck nest on the lake. The wet meadow and marsh to the north-west are home to Spotted Crake, Curlew, Lapwing and Snipe, and Hobbies often hunt over the area. There is also a colony of Fieldfares and a pair Great Grey Shrikes. The mixed beech and fir wood on the south-eastern side of the lake has a Grey Heron colony, and the woodland also holds breeding Raven and Black and Red Kites. Other birds of the mixed forest include both Black Woodpecker and Tengmalm's Owl. At times of migration it is possible to see Great White Egret, Purple Heron, Black Stork, ducks, gulls and various waders. In autumn, hunting activities make the site less attractive, but in spring the lake has up to 1,000 waterfowl, mainly Pochard and Tufted Duck. The D47 from Bonnevaux to Bouverans runs past the lake, which can be viewed in several places: from a small car park on the side of the D47 road; from the extreme eastern corner of the lake; and from the disused station and railway tracks at the end of the road on the north-east side of the lake. Yet more wetland habitat, similar to that of the Étangs de Frasne and de Bouverans can be found further to the south-east again, at the Lac de Remoray-Bougeons. From Bonnevaux take the D9 for about 12 km to reach the village of Labergement-Sainte-Marie. The lake is maintained as a reserve, and there is a visitor centre ('maison de la réserve') in the village from where details of access can be obtained. Both the marshy area near the lake and the woodland of the Forêt de la Grande-Côte are worth exploring if you have time to spend in the area.

4. Roches de Pont-de-Roide

DOUBS (25) *IGN 31/38*

Some 14 km to the south of Montbéliard, the Roches de Pont-de-Roide is one of the best places for watching autumn migration in the Franche-Comté region. Birds moving south from the plains of Alsace are either channelled via Switzerland or, as here, along the first foothills of the Jura. Birds of prey are the big attraction, but they are not the only species involved. From late July right through to late November many birds can be seen on the move: Osprey, Honey Buzzard, Red and Black Kites, Sparrowhawk, Goshawk, Buzzard, harriers (three species), Kestrel, Hobby and Merlin. In addition, look out for Great White Egret, Grey and Purple Herons, Black and White Storks, Woodpigeon, Stock Dove, various crows, as well as many passerines, the latter particularly later in the season when many pipits, finches and larks pass through. The heaviest visible passage occurs during overcast days with a moderate westerly wind. On the other hand, very few birds are seen on fine days with an easterly wind. From Montbéliard take the D437 south to Pont-de-Roide, where the road crosses the River Doubs. From here follow signs for Porrentruy for about 300 metres and then take the D124 to the right towards the Roches de Pont-de-Roide and the 'parcours sportif'. Continue along this winding road for a few kilometres until you reach an old fort. It is possible to park in the sports-centre car park, and from here walk to the fort from where there is a good lookout point.

OSPREY

5. Lower valley of the River Doubs

JURA (39) *IGN 37*

The lower valley of the River Doubs, downstream from Dole, is a wide alluvial plain where crops such as cereals and sugar-beet are interspersed with extensive meadows. Here the Doubs takes a meandering course between tree-lined banks, the meanders, ox-bow lakes and sand and gravel banks, forming a series of different habitats, each with their own attraction for birds. A good example of these habitats can be found near the village of Petit-Noir, where an ancient meander of the Doubs, cut off from the main river, has now turned into a large reedbed. In the same area, the sandy banks of the river can be miniature cliffs two or three metres high, ideal habitat for species like Sand Martin and Bee-eater. This is an important area for nesting species (e.g., herons, warblers) as well as those on migration (gulls, marsh terns, waders).

Access

From Dole (to the north-east), take the N73 towards Chalon-sur-Saône for about 20 km, as far as the village of Beauchemin. Here, turn left towards Petit-Noir. On entering the village turn immediately right and keep going straight ahead towards Saulçois. After a sharp right-hand bend, take the first track to the left and park on the embankment (1) on the side of what was the old river, now an ox-bow lake. In July and August there is a hirundine and Starling roost in the reedbed here, where Purple Heron and Marsh Harrier nest. Little Egret and Night Heron are regularly present in the summer months, although neither appears to breed here. One can walk south-west along the embankment for about 1 km, with good views over the wet meadows, favoured hunting grounds for Montagu's and Marsh Harriers. Take a farm track to the right as far as the bank of the River Doubs (2) where there is a high sand bank. Kingfisher nest in the sand cliff, and there is also a colony of Bee-eaters and Sand Martins. Follow the bank as far as the ruined buildings (3). Common Sandpiper, Little Ringed Plover, Stone Curlew and Common Tern all breed on the gravel islands in the river. Continue along the track to rejoin the embankment and follow this to the southern end of the ox-bow lake. On the left and right are numerous ponds and patches of bushy vegetation. Species breeding in the bushes and embankment reeds here include Reed, Great Reed, Grasshopper

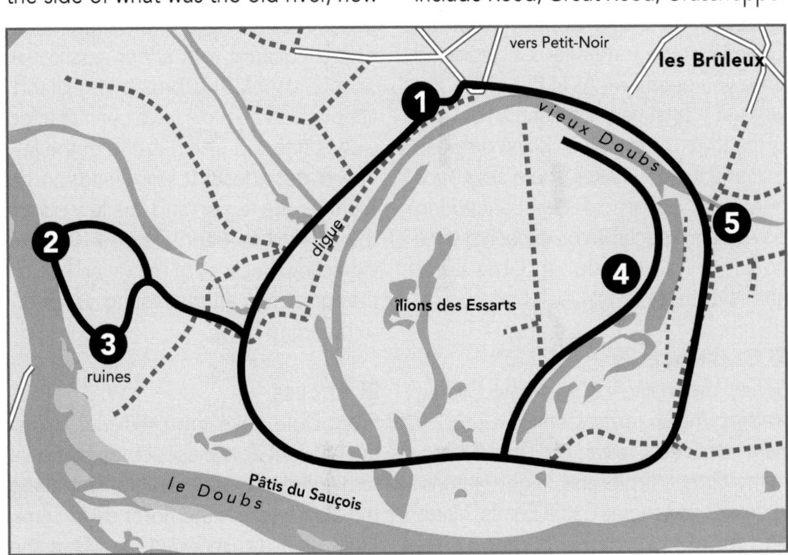

and Melodious Warblers, Nightingale and Bluethroat. It is possible to view the ox-bow lake by taking a raised track to (4), although one then has to retrace one's steps. Both Lesser Spotted Woodpecker and Wryneck can be found in the large trees near the ox-bow, and Golden Orioles can be heard calling in the same area. Continue along the embankment to the south-east point of the ox-bow lake and then take a track to the left leading north. Stonechat, Red-backed Shrike, Corn Bunting and Blue-headed Wagtail all breed in the flood meadows here. After having crossed a small canal (5), follow the side of the ox-bow lake back to the starting point. Although in general there is unrestricted access to this area, please avoid entering any of the meadows or going onto any of the islands, so as not to disturb nesting birds. The full circuit covers about 7½ km.

Another area with similar habitat, also with reserve status, can be found about 15 km upstream, at Gevry, just to the south-west of Dole. The village lies on the N5, just to the south of that road's junction with the N73, and the Île du Girard réserve naturelle is signposted once you get there. As at Petit-Noir, the wetland habitat here lies along an old arm of the River Doubs, on an island between that and the main river. There are notice boards which give details concerning access, and species to be expected once again include Bluethroat, Little Egret and Night Heron.

Calendar

Spring (especially April and May): Osprey, waders, marsh terns, Common Tern.
Summer: Great Crested and Little Grebes, many Grey, Purple and Night Herons, Little and sometimes Cattle Egrets, Marsh and Montagu's Harriers, Black Kite, Hobby, Kestrel, Buzzard, Quail, Red-legged and Grey Partridges, Pheasant, Water Rail, Curlew, Little Ringed Plover, Stone Curlew, Common Sandpiper, Barn, Long-eared and Little Owls, Cuckoo, Hoopoe, a colony of Bee-eaters, Turtle Dove, Lesser Spotted Woodpecker, Wryneck, colony of Sand Martins, Blue-headed Wagtail, Nightingale, Bluethroat, Stonechat, Red-backed Shrike, Common and Lesser Whitethroats, Grasshopper, Reed, Great Reed, Sedge and Melodious Warblers, Corn and Cirl Buntings.
Autumn (especially August): the same species as in spring plus a large hirundine, Starling and White Wagtail roost in the reeds.

6. Massif de la Serre

Jura (39) *IGN 37*

The Massif de la Serre (altitude 400 m) is one of the rare granite outcrops of Franche-Comté. It dominates the valleys of the River Ognon to the north and the River Doubs to the south. Most of it is covered with either sessile oak or mixed oak and beech woodland, although some plots have been planted with conifers. It also has one of the few fine sweet chestnut woodlands to be found in the region and in a few places the forest has been cleared for sand extraction. Because of the varied habitat the forest has an interesting assembly of breeding birds.

Access

From Dole, take the D475 north past the A36 (exit 2), and about 8 km from here turn right in the village of Moissey along the D37 towards the Forêt de la Serre. There is a disused sand-pit (1) at the entrance to the forest. Melodious Warbler and Cirl Bunting occur in the bushes around the sand-pit, and this is a good area for Golden Oriole. Check the wooden huts for the resident Little Owls. From here, continue over the ridge and turn left on the Chemin de la Poste, following this road for about 1 km. Mistle and Song Thrushes, Blackbird and Dunnock are typical species of this part of the forest, while Coal and Crested Tits occur wherever there are conifers. Park on the right-hand side of the road at (2). Here a botanical interpretation trail, 400 metres long and presenting some 50 locally occurring species, goes as far as the Grotte de l'Hermitage and a spring (3). Return to the road and continue for about another 400 metres north-east until you come to another forest track, where you can turn right. After about 700 metres the road drops down into a valley and turns to the right and eventually rejoins the surfaced road. There are Goshawks nesting in this area and Sparrowhawks in the conifer plantations. Other woodland breeding birds include Stock Dove and Great Spotted Woodpecker in the beech forest. Check the larger trees for the nest holes of Black Woodpeckers, which also tend to favour the beeches. Middle Spotted Woodpeckers also occur in the area, and are best searched for in the tops of any of the older oak trees. Continue back along the road as far as some more sand-pits (4). At dusk this is a good spot to listen out for the churring calls of Nightjars, which breed nearby. Look out for Tree Pipits in any of the more sparsely wooded areas, and Grey Wagtails along the stream.

CALENDAR

Breeding season: raptors (Honey Buzzard, Goshawk, Black and Red Kites), Tawny Owl, Nightjar, Woodpigeon, Stock Dove; Black, Green, Great Spotted

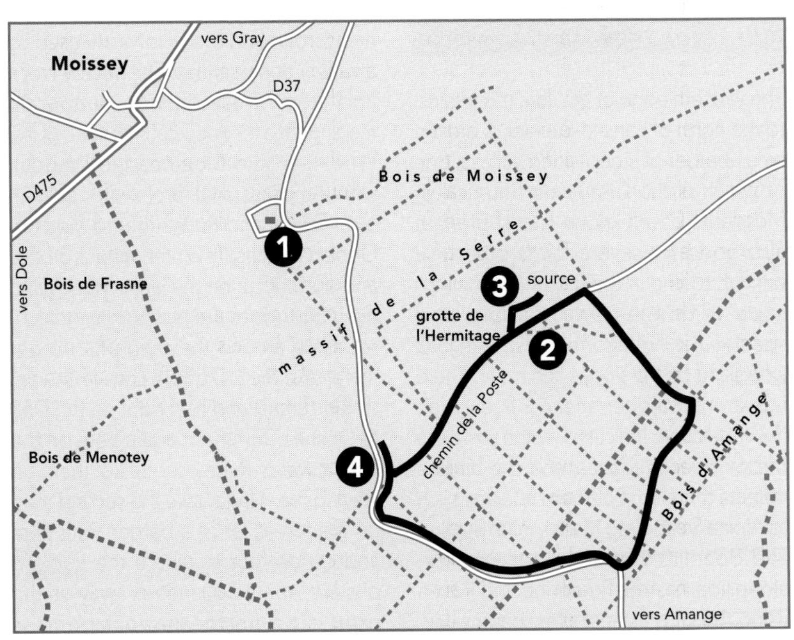

GOLDEN ORIOLE

and Middle Spotted Woodpeckers, Tree Pipit, Spotted Flycatcher, Wood and Melodious Warblers, all the forest tits, Golden Oriole.

7. Baume-les-Messieurs

JURA (39) *IGN 37*

The western edge of the Jura mountains, to the north of Lons-le-Saunier, is broken by a number of steep-sided valleys, one of which is the Cirque de Baume-les-Messieurs, a well-known tourist site, but also good for several birds otherwise difficult to find in the region. The landscape is dominated by steep and spectacular limestone cliffs, with oak woodland on the slopes and scree. There is a strong Mediterranean influence on the vegetation, indicated by the presence of box trees in places, and the birdlife reflects this also. Southern species such as Alpine Swift, Crag Martin, Rock Bunting and Bonelli's Warbler all occur here, alongside Kestrel, Peregrine and Raven using the cliffs as nest sites. Baume-les-Messieurs is about 8 km east of Lons-le-Saunier, just to the left of the D471 towards Champagnole. Either view from the foot of the cliffs or take any of the minor roads and footpaths (very steep!) that go to the village itself.

8. Sablières de Desnes

JURA (39) *IGN 37*

Some 15 km north-west of Lons-le-Saunier is an area of old sand extraction works in the agricultural plain around the villages of Bletterans and Desnes. The site is mainly of interest to the birdwatcher during migration periods when a variety of species stop off on their way north or south. The wet areas attract such species as Purple and Night Herons, Osprey, various species of wader, gulls and marsh terns, while the hedgerows and the willows are used by a variety of passerines. The nearby crops and stony areas provide temporary feeding sites for open-country species like Wheatear and Blue-headed Wagtail, with the occasional rarer visitor as well, e.g., Tawny and Red-throated Pipits or Ortolan Bunting. In winter, various grebes and duck occur on the larger ponds and Grey Partridges are resident in areas of set-aside around the sand-pits. To get there, take the D470 from Lons-le-Saunier to Bletterans, and turn right on the D58 to Desnes. Turn right again here on the D38 towards Ruffey-sur-Seille, then, on leaving the village, take the second road on the left as far as a barrier. Park here and go on foot to where the flooded pits are, about 300 metres away on the right. The northern-most pond is surrounded by a wire fence, and hunting is forbidden here, but the water can be scanned from the higher ground outside the enclosure.

9. *Lac de Vaivre-Vesoul*

HAUTE-SAÔNE (70)

IGN 29/30

This 90 hectare lake on the western outskirts of Vesoul was built in the late 1970s and is bounded on its northern side by the embankment of the River Durgeon with its flood-plain beyond. Urban sprawl and leisure complexes (camp site and sailing club) fringe the east, south and west sides, but the northern part of the lake (including a small island) is protected as a reserve with no hunting or fishing allowed. In addition, leisure activities on the lake are prohibited during the winter months. A footpath, open throughout the year, goes around the lake, and this can easily be used by the less mobile. The lake is a migratory stop-over point for many aquatic species (e.g., duck, waders, gulls) while the nearby flood-plain is also of interest during the breeding season. Because of disturbance, the most productive time for a visit is in the mornings.

ACCESS

From the southern edge of Vesoul, take the D13 west towards Vaivre, and follow the signs to 'Lac and Camping'. There is a car park near the camp site (1). From here, walk towards the lake via the camp site, cross the wooden bridge (2) and walk on along the path by the lakeside. Access to the damp areas between the lake and the River Durgeon is prohibited, but it is easily visible from the raised embankment (3). Passerines nesting here include Blue-headed Wagtail, Whinchat, Sedge Warbler and Reed Bunting. Grey Herons nest on the island (4) in the lake, this also acting as a secure refuge for waders and ducks, while gulls and terns can often be seen perched on the buoys and posts around the island. On the water itself, wintering wildfowl include dabbling duck (e.g., Teal, Gadwall, Wigeon) and diving duck (e.g., scoters, Goldeneye, sawbills) while grebes and divers sometimes also occur. Continue along the path as far as the sailing club (5); from here you can look over the plain to the north of the lake. Waders such as Greenshank, Lapwing, Curlew and Snipe often stop here at migration times but in winter only Lapwing and Curlew are regular. A migrant Osprey may come to the lake to fish (April and August are the best months), and often perch in the trees beyond here to feed on their catch undisturbed. Return by the same route. For the less mobile it is possible to watch birds from the car park (7) near the flats to the south of the

CURLEW

lake or from the road that runs along the western bank (8).

In order to watch birds on the floodplain to the north of the lake (6), return to Vesoul and take the dual-carriageway north-west towards Pusey. Leave this at the second exit (the Clinique St.-Martin/Parc des Haberges exit), and immediately turn left to pass back over the main road. Park where the road forks towards the farm of Montoilotte, and then continue on foot on farm tracks. The wetland area is a protected site but the footpaths are open to the public; however, take care not to disturb nesting birds, which include Lapwing and Snipe.

Calendar

Spring: Black-necked Grebe, Cormorant, Garganey and particularly waders, gulls and terns; Greenshank, Spotted Redshank, sandpipers, Curlew, Whimbrel, Black-tailed Godwit, Lapwing, marsh terns, Common Tern, Little Gull. A stop-over site for Osprey (April), Black and Red Kites.

Summer: Black Kite, Hobby, Corncrake, Curlew, Lapwing, Snipe, Blue-headed Wagtail, Sedge Warbler, Whinchat, Reed and Corn Buntings.

Autumn: Cormorant, ducks, Greylag Goose, Osprey, Crane, flocks of Lapwing and Golden Plover, Dunlin.

Winter: dabbling duck (all the European species but especially Teal) and more rarely diving duck (Pochard, Tufted Duck, scoters, Goldeneye, sawbills), Black and Red-throated Divers, grebes (Great Crested, Red-necked, Slavonian), Shelduck, Greylag Goose, Lapwing and Curlew. A Black-headed Gull roost often contains Little or Common Gulls and sometimes other gull species.

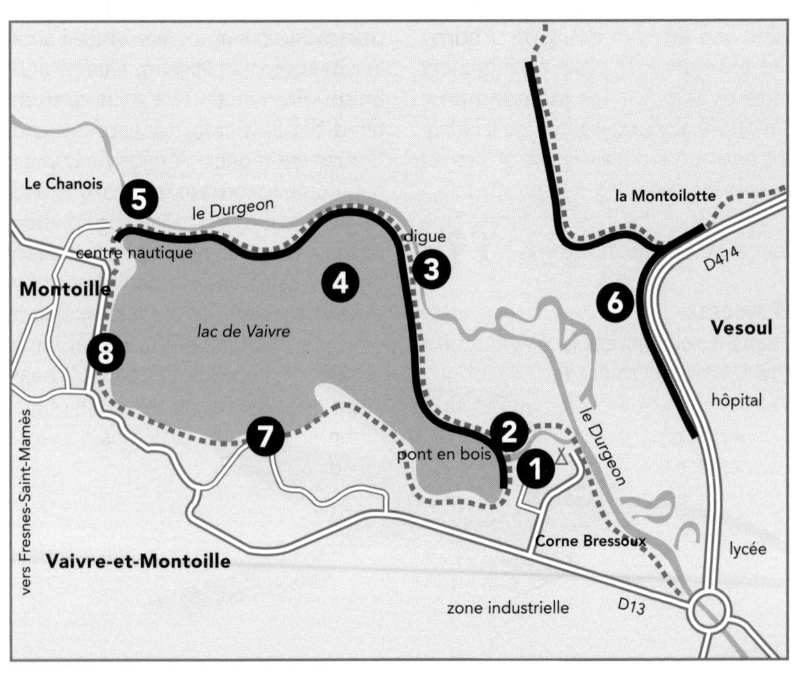

10. Saône valley near Vesoul

Haute-Saône (70) *IGN 29/30*

Thanks to its north-east/south-west orientation, the Saône valley to the west of Vesoul is a natural corridor for many migrating species. To explore the area take the N19 west to cross the river at Port-sur-Saône and take any of the minor roads down-river towards Gray. The section to Membrey is particularly wide and, therefore, very attractive to migrants. Most of the area is taken up by meadows and a few crops, but there is also a certain amount of marshland. Crane, Greylag Goose and Osprey are seen in spring and autumn, with Bean Goose and Whooper Swan recorded more rarely. Waders are frequently noted, including Lapwing, Golden Plover, Black-tailed Godwit and Ruff. Curlew, Montagu's and Hen Harriers and Corncrake all occur during the breeding season.

11. The Ognon valley

Haute-Saône (70) *IGN 37*

The valley of the River Ognon, west of Besançon has a wide flood-plain of alternating meadows and marshland. It is of particular interest during times of migration and also in winter. Many species of wader can be seen – Curlew, Black-tailed Godwit, Jack Snipe, Lapwing, Golden Plover, etc. – as well as Cormorant, Crane and Greylag and Bean Geese. Osprey and all three harriers are also regular on migration. In places there are reedbeds along the side of the river, and these have also formed wherever the river has been straightened and ox-bow lakes have been left on its previous course. These attract breeding birds such as Water Rail, Sedge, Reed, Great Reed, Savi's and Grasshopper Warblers. The D67 between Besançon and Gray crosses the river at Marnay, the area upstream from here being the most productive.

12. Sundgau

Territoire de Belfort (90) *IGN 31*

The Sundgau, south-east of Belfort, is a continuation of the Alsace plain further north and consists mainly of alluvial deposits, which have resulted in an undulating countryside with many lakes scattered through woodland dominated by oak trees. In spring and autumn, Common and Black Terns, various sandpipers, Greenshanks and small waders are all frequent visitors and Ospreys pass through between the end of March and the end of April. Black Storks occur regularly and could well nest in the neighbourhood. Among the more interesting breeding species to be found are Garganey and Teal, Hobby, Curlew, Little Ringed Plover, Lapwing, and both Grey-headed and Middle Spotted Woodpeckers. To explore the area, take the N19 south-east from Belfort as far as Delle, and then work north-eastwards on minor roads north of Faverois.

SITES

1 **Bois de Boulogne**

2 **Bois de Vincennes**

3 **Parc de Bagatelle**

4 **The Seine and Yonne valleys near Monterau**

5 **Plaine de Chanfroy and Forêt des Trois-Pignons**

6 **The Loing valley**

7 **Forêt de Fontainebleau**

8 **Jablines**

9 **The Seine valley at Moisson**

10 **Lakes of the Forêt de Rambouillet**

11 **Réserve naturelle de St.-Quentin-en-Yvelines**

12 **Seine valley at Guernes**

13 **Île Aumône at Mantes-la-Jolie**

14 **Étang-Vieux de Saclay**

15 **Bruyères-le-Châtel reservoir**

16 **The River Seine between Grigny and Vigneux**

17 **Saulx-les-Chartreux**

18 **Parc de Sceaux**

19 **Parc de La Courneuve**

20 **Lac de Créteil**

21 **Valenton**

22 **Étangs de Cergy-Neuville**

Île-de-France

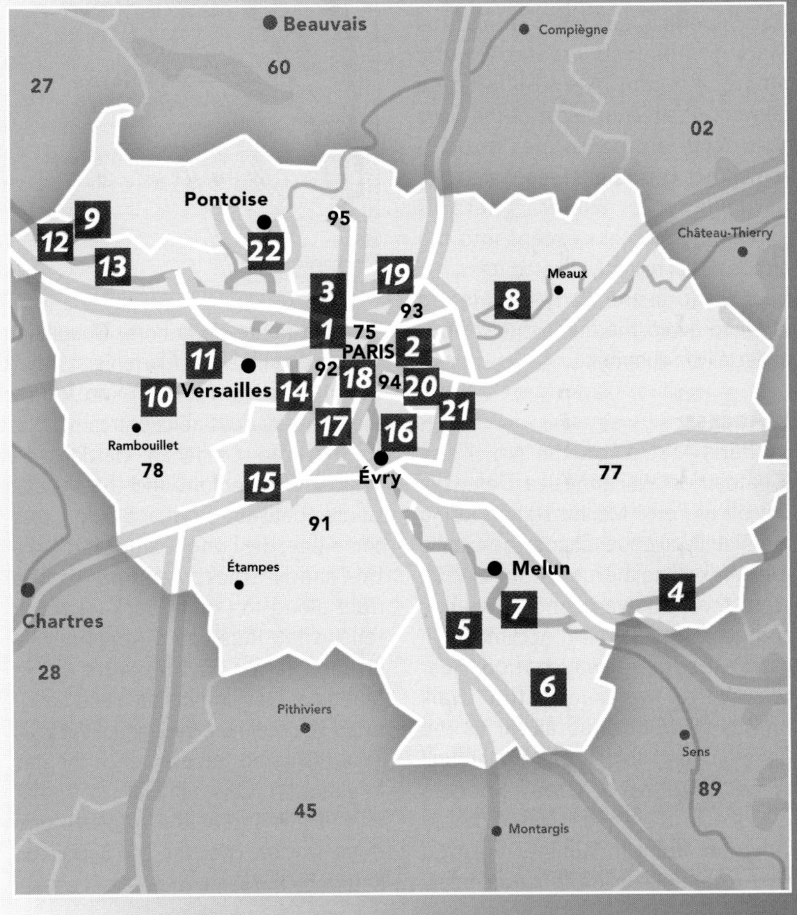

1. Bois de Boulogne

VILLE DE PARIS (75)

IGN 90

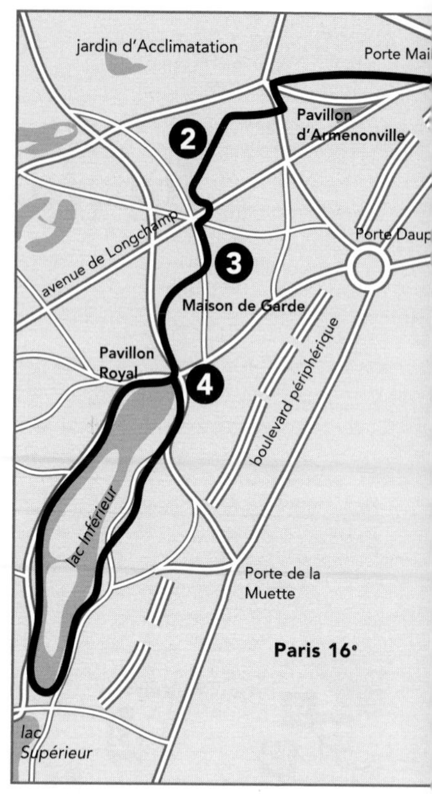

The Bois de Boulogne, on the west side of the city, is the last vestige of the Forêt de Rouvray, which surrounded Paris on its northern and western sides two thousand years ago. The 1999 storm devastated much of the ancient oak forest. Some areas have been replanted while others are being managed as more or less open spaces, increasing the area's interest. There are three principal water bodies (Lac Supérieur, Lac Inférieur and the Mare St.-James), created in the nineteenth century and filled by a network of streams. Most of the birds that occur are passerines but it is sometimes possible to see waterfowl, particularly in winter. There is unrestricted access except into the enclosures of recently-planted trees. It is best to go in the early morning in order to avoid the numerous visitors, especially in summer.

■ ACCESS

By Paris Metro, on the No. I line (Château de Vincennes-La Défense), get off at Porte Maillot station (using the Neuilly-avenue Charles-de-Gaulle exit). Walk along the rue J.-et-M.-Hackin, cross the Boulevard André-Maurois and go to the Jardin d'Acclimatation narrow-gauge railway station, near to where the suggested walk begins (1). Continue as far as the Carrefour des Sablons, passing through some pine trees. Great Spotted Woodpecker is often seen here, especially in winter while in summer Spotted Flycatchers occur in the larger trees. Turn left (route de la Porte Dauphine) then right (allée des Marroniers). After 200 metres turn left (2) and follow the Ruisseau des Sablons stream. Look for Blackcap, Chiffchaff, Garden and Willow Warblers around the Île des Cedres between April and July. Cross the Allée de Longchamp and take the sandy track, keeping to the right along the cycle track (3) which follows the Ruisseau d'Armenonville stream as far as the route de la Muette at Neuilly. Nuthatch and Long-tailed Tit occur here throughout the year. Take the same track to reach the Lac Inférieur (4). One can walk to the far end of this and at the southern end obtain a view over the Lac Supérieur. Return by the same route.

■ **CALENDAR**

All year: Sparrowhawk (has returned since the late 1990s), Tawny Owl, Green, Great Spotted and Lesser Spotted Woodpeckers, Nuthatch, Short-toed Treecreeper, tits (seven species), Goldcrest, Bullfinch and Crossbill.

Spring: Swallow, House Martin, Nightingale, Chiffchaff, Blackcap, Whitethroat, Willow, Melodious and Garden Warblers, and Spotted Flycatcher all nest. Cuckoo, Golden Oriole, Redstart and Pied Flycatcher all occur on passage.

Winter: Pochard, Black-headed Gull, northern passerines (Redwing, Fieldfare, Siskin, Brambling).

BULLFINCH

2. *Bois de Vincennes*

VILLE DE PARIS (75)

IGN 90

The Bois de Vincennes, on the east side of the city, and which also suffered from the 1999 storm, is in many ways similar to the Bois de Boulogne, at least as far as birds are concerned. Again, passerines are the main group to be seen here, including Stonechat, Nightingale and Cirl Bunting. It also has duck in winter (particularly Pochard and Tufted Duck). An artificial pond has recently been created, adding more interest to the site. Like the Bois de Boulogne it is best to go early in the morning in order to avoid the general public. The park is just outside the périphérique (Porte de Vincennes exit).

3. *Parc de Bagatelle*

VILLE DE PARIS (75)

IGN 90

This park is adjacent to the Bois de Boulogne, and as an access fee is payable, and because no dogs or cyclists are allowed, it tends to be rather more tranquil than the other parks. The birds can be very tame and easy to see, even Green, Great Spotted and Lesser Spotted Woodpeckers. Tits, Nuthatch and Robin approach without fear, providing ideal watching conditions for the novice bird-watcher. Being watched quite intensively, the park's list of species is quite long, and even includes some rarer species that have stopped briefly on migration. There is a belvedere which provides a good all-round view, useful for watching birds moving through. Access as for the Bois de Boulogne.

4. The Seine and Yonne valleys near Montereau

SEINE-ET-MARNE (77)

IGN 21

The area where the Rivers Seine and Yonne join near Montereau, to the south-east of Paris, is a good place for observing aquatic birds throughout the year and for watching migrants in spring and autumn. There are lakes which in winter are used by a few hundred duck, while farther upstream, the large number of flooded gravel-pits are ideal areas for waders and gulls, especially in spring and summer. The area also has an important population of breeding Common Terns (200 to 300 pairs, depending on the year) and France's only inland colony of Little Terns north of the Loire. In the past few years a small breeding population of Red-crested Pochards has been established, and about 50 pairs of Tufted Duck also nest in the area.

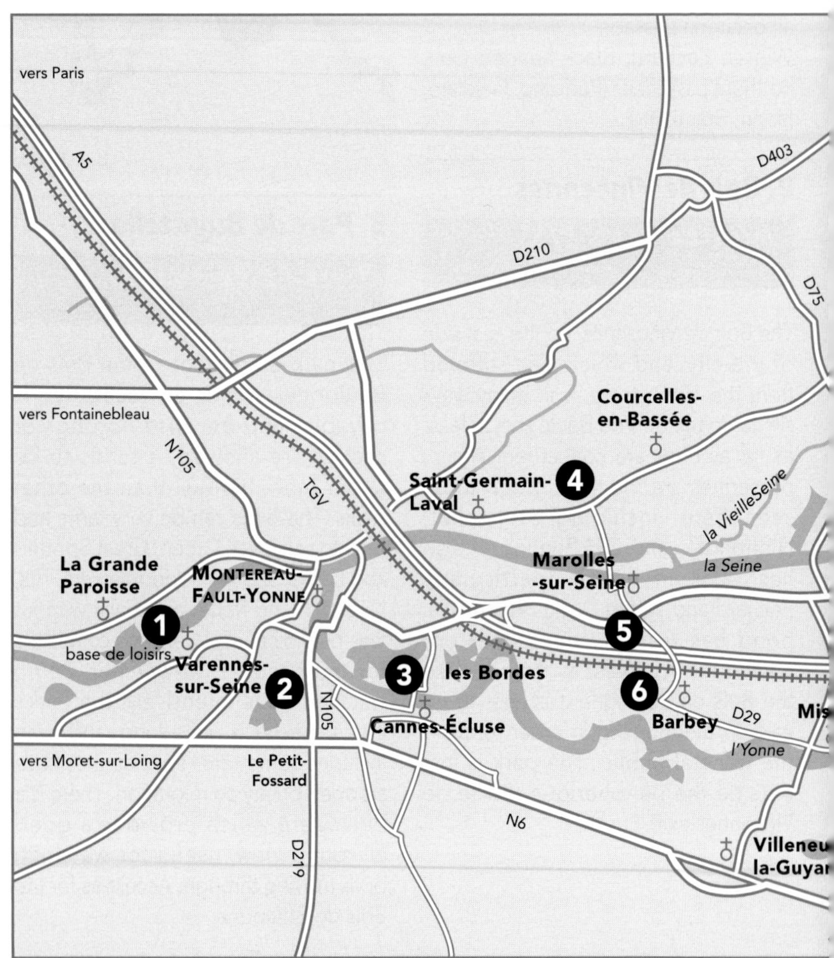

■ Access

Montereau is close to the A5, exits 17 and 18, and is also accessible by rail. A selection of possible sites is given here. Just south-west of Montereau are the lakes at Grande-Paroisse and Varennes-sur-Seine (1). They are just to the north of the N6 and can be watched from the roadside. However, it is better to take the tracks that leave from near the Varennes leisure centre. At the time of writing there is a project underway to create a nature trail and to erect a hide here. There is something of interest to see at all times of the year, but in summer the site has one of France's largest Black-headed Gull colonies (nearly 1,500 pairs), usually with a few pairs of Mediterranean Gulls as well. Here also is one of the area's largest Common Tern colonies, and one of its few regular Little Tern sites. A little to the east is the Petit-Fossard bird reserve (2). This is a recently created site, so there are few records to go on at present, but there is

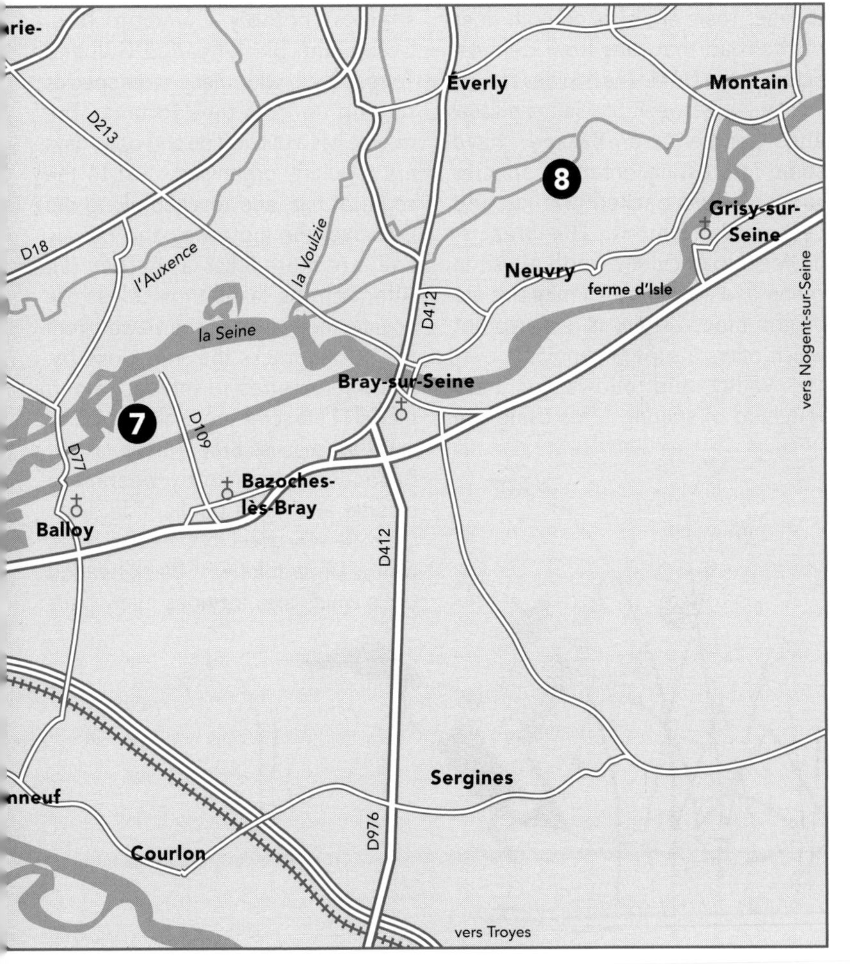

no reason to believe that it will not be a good spot for birds. The lake is viewable from the track to its west, accessible from Varennes, and guided visits are regularly organised by the local naturalists association. There are more lakes at Cannes-Écluse (3). In winter these lakes attract several hundred wild-fowl, especially diving ducks. It is a good spot for grebes, with Slavonian and Red-necked seen most years. Cormorants are often present and rarer species such as divers, sawbills, Eider and scoters are seen from time to time. There are lakes on both sides of the road that runs from Cannes-Écluse to the D411. The hillsides around Tréchy (4), between St.-Germain-Laval and Courcelles-en-Bassée, have some interesting breeding species such as Red-backed Shrike and Lesser Whitethroat. The area is, however, particularly worth a visit in spring and autumn when migrants are on the move. There is a viewpoint which offers a superb panorama over the valley and allows for easy watching of soaring birds using the thermals created by the hillside or which are following the course of the River Seine below. It is not uncommon, on good days, to see at least ten species of birds of prey, and in November and March Cranes are often seen. Access to the site is via the D29 that crosses the Seine at Marolles-sur-Seine. Access to the slopes generally is limited, but the viewpoint is open to the public. Down in the valley, at Marolles-sur-Seine is another bird reserve (5), close to exit 18 on the A5. Created some ten years ago, the site has numerous breeding species, notably Common Tern, Cormorant, Black-headed Gull and Tufted Duck, with many rarer species turning up from time to time. The reserve has a public hide and open days are regularly organised. Just to the south of this, and reached along the D29 over the motorway and railway line, are more lakes at Barbey (6). Although the lakes themselves are private, they can easily be viewed from the public tracks that run close by. A few kilometres to the east along the D411 are some more lakes at Balloy and Bazoches-les-Bray (7). The lake at Bazoches has recently become a reserve and has a public hide. Both lakes are very good for breeding birds, with a large colony of Black-headed Gulls which also includes many pairs

SHOVELER

of Mediterranean Gulls, plus nesting Common Terns and Tufted Ducks. They are also good for migrants and wintering species, attracting more than 5,000 ducks at a time between late October and early March. Finally we come to the Réserve Naturelle de la Bassée (8), which covers some 850 hectares of riverside forest, flood meadows and reedbeds in the Seine valley just upstream from Bray-sur-Seine. It is the last stronghold of the Great Grey Shrike in the region, with a few breeding pairs of this declining species still hanging on. Other interesting species such as Red-backed Shrike and Hobby can also be seen. Although most of the land is private, it is possible to see much of the area from the public footpaths that cross the reserve. It is also worth visiting the ponds to the south of the reserve, near the Ferme d'Isle at Grisy-sur-Seine, which can partially be seen from the road that runs between the villages of Neuvry and Port-Montain. Although the whole area is of interest at any time of year, spring is a particularly good period when, for instance, large flocks of duck can be seen – up to 300 Pintail, for example.

5. Plaine de Chanfroy and Forêt des Trois-Pignons

SEINE-ET-MARNE (77)

IGN 21

Lying immediately west of the Forêt de Fontainebleau (see site 7 below), this area comprises a stony and sandy plain, dotted here and there with thorn bushes and broom, rather steppe-like in appearance. There are a few permanent pools of water in some of the hollows. This sort of habitat is rare elsewhere in this region of France, and hence is a good place to see certain birds otherwise difficult to locate without travelling much further. In addition, because there is quite a diversity of habitats in such a small area, the range of species to be seen is a large one, although passerines are the main group of most interest. The best conditions for watching occur in the very early morning, when it is not too hot, and the disturbance caused by walkers, sometimes numerous at weekends, is at its lowest.

Access

From Fontainebleau, take the D409 west as far as Arbonne-la-Forêt. Here turn left on the D64 towards Achères-la-Forêt, but about 800 metres along this road, immediately after the Corne-Biche equestrian centre, turn left along a forest track to reach a car park at the end of this road (1). Leave the car here (but beware of break-ins!) and continue east along the main track towards the plain, passing through wooded areas where Chiffchaff and Willow, Wood and Bonelli's Warblers can be heard and seen in spring. The whole area can be explored along the various tracks that cross the area, but note that some areas are fenced off in order to protect the plants growing there from being trampled. Turning to the right, before the plain itself, is a track that runs through an interesting wooded area (2). Not far away are some heathland areas where Dartford Warblers are resident, although it is never easy to see this skulking species. The route passes several ponds (3) which should be checked carefully, as they hold Reed Warblers in the breeding season. A speciality of the

Plaine de Chanfroy is the Woodlark, which can be heard giving its beautiful song overhead in the early part of the year. Ring Ouzels regularly occur as a migrant in April; other migrants include Stonechat, Whinchat or Wheatear, often to be seen perched on fence posts, and Tawny Pipit out on the plain in May or September. Continue eastwards across the plain along the Allée des Fusillés forest track. After 750 metres, turn left (4), then left again 300 metres further on, and return on this track to the car park. The open parts of the plain are a hunting ground for Buzzard, Sparrowhawk and, in summer, Honey Buzzard. With a little luck Woodcock and Nightjar can also be found here if you visit at dusk.

■ Calendar

Spring and autumn: migrants include Hoopoe (rare), Cuckoo, pipits, Redstart, chats, Ring Ouzel; breeding species include raptors, Nightjar, Woodlark, Dartford Warbler and Red-backed Shrike.

6. The Loing valley

Seine-et-Marne (77)

IGN 21

Although less well known than the Seine and Marne valleys, the River Loing valley, to the south-east of Fontainbleau, can also be a very good area for birdwatching. It has a wide variety of habitats – marshes, meadows, limestone hillsides and lakes – with a diverse bird population. It is of most interest in the spring when Golden Orioles can be heard singing from the poplars and Red-backed Shrike, Stonechat and Kingfisher are breeding.

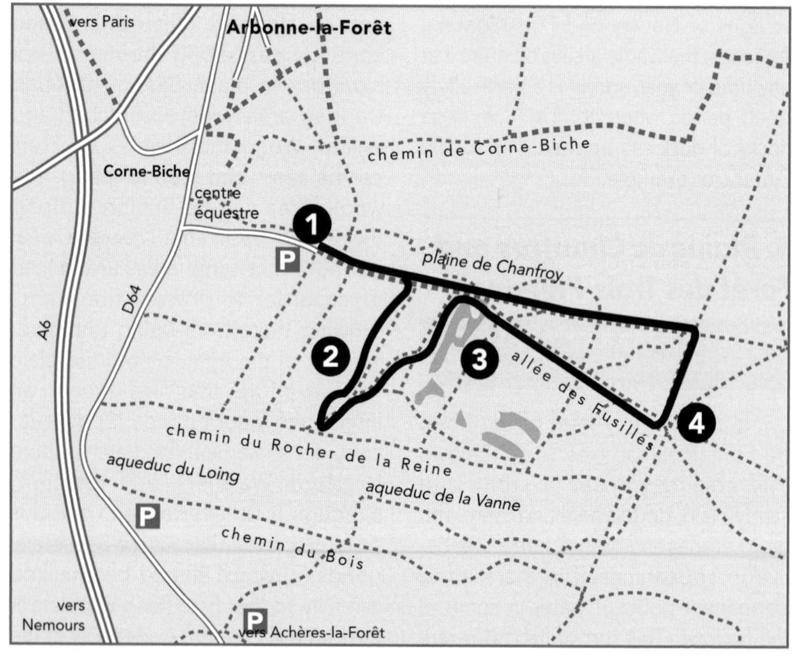

HONEY BUZZARD

Access

From Fontainbleau take the N6 east as far as the river at Moret-sur-Loing, then turn right along the riverside to reach Sorques (1).There is an area of old gravel-pits, ancient woodland, scrub and natural meadows here which is of particular interest in spring and autumn. Black-headed Gull, Common Tern, Cormorant, Grey Heron and Little Ringed Plover all nest, and five species of woodpecker are often seen (Green, Black and Great, Middle and Lesser Spotted). In winter a variety of duck occurs, including Pochard, Tufted Duck, Mallard, Gadwall and Teal. The site has a public nature trail that crosses the different habitats, including the banks of the Loing, and there are two hides and provision for car parking. To the east, a foot and cycle path leads to Moret-sur-Loing across land owned by the Conservatoire Régional des Espaces Naturels. From here, cross the river and turn right along the D40 towards Nemours. At the edge of the village of Épisy is an area (2) which was previously a peat bog, although most of the original habitat was destroyed due to peat extraction during the 1970s. After a great deal of restoration work, aimed at conserving as much as possible of the original peat bog vegetation, the area is now a reserve which also includes a lake with many small islands. A nature trail will shortly be open to the public. The area is of most interest in the spring when Grasshopper and Sedge Warblers, Reed Bunting and Red-backed Shrike all breed. Continuing upstream brings us to some lakes at Montcourt-Fromonville (3), these being old gravel-pits which attract many wintering and nesting waterbirds. Mute Swans are abundant and most of the commoner duck can be found in winter. In spring, when birds are on the move and the chance of finding something of interest is more likely, it is worthwhile leaving the major footpaths to follow the lakesides. It is better to avoid the summer months and sunny Sundays when there are many visitors about and disturbance levels quite high. From here, cross the river to Grez-sur-Loing and then minor roads south-west to Larchant, just north of which is a marshy area (4) in a lower-lying area cut into the Beauce agricultural plain to the south-west. This marsh of some 100 hectares is home to some interesting species – Marsh Harrier, Hobby, herons, wetland warblers and Bee-eater, for instance. The mix of species very much depends on the water levels that vary depending on whether there have been several years of flooding or whether there has been a period of drought. Although the site itself is private with no public access, it can be viewed from the roads and paths which run along its edges.

Apart from these specific listed sites, the whole Loing valley from its confluence with the Seine at Moret-sur-Loing right up through Nemours to Dordives is worth exploring via the numerous tracks, paths and roads by the river. As well as the river itself, there is a good mix of habitats on both sides – marshes, meadows and riverside woodland – although some are, of course, on private land. The valleys of the Orvanne and Lunain, two smaller tributaries near Moret-sur-Loing and Nemours, are worth a detour and can also have some interesting birds. Finally, one way to appreciate this beautiful river and its birds is by canoe. These are easily hired, particularly at Moret-sur-Loing; contact the tourist office for further information.

7. Forêt de Fontainebleau

SEINE-ET-MARNE (77)

IGN 21

The Forêt de Fontainebleau, some 60 km south-east of Paris, is a real paradise for the naturalist and particularly the birdwatcher. A spring visit may well produce Green, Black, Great, Middle and Lesser Spotted Woodpeckers, Redstart and Pied Flycatcher, this last being rare elsewhere in the Île-de-France but which nests here in good numbers. Buzzard, Honey Buzzard, Sparrowhawk and Hobby also all nest in the forest, together with all the passerines typical of the woodlands of northern France. Fontainebleau lies on the N6 and N7 main roads, and is also well served

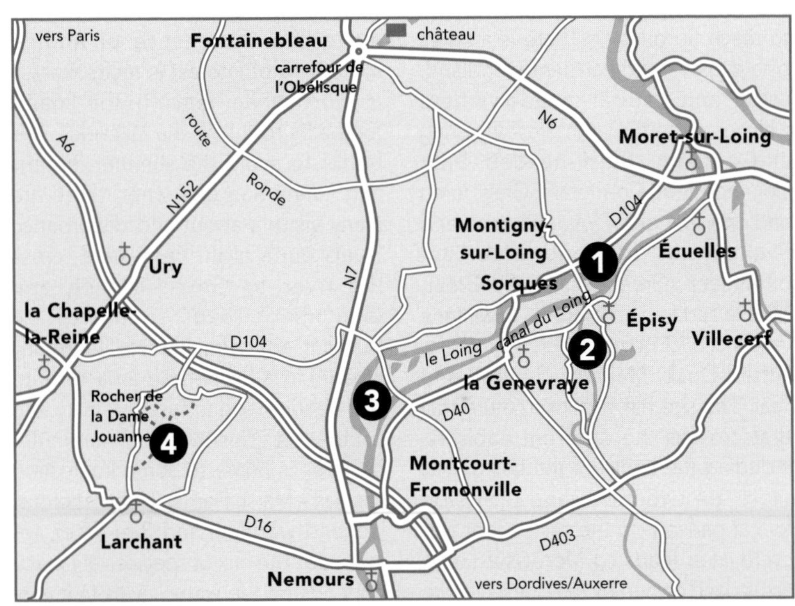

by public transport. There are birds to be found throughout this huge area, and one needs to explore as many habitats as possible to find them all. Black and Middle Spotted Woodpeckers, two sought-after species, are both associated with older trees. The two nature reserves of La Tillaie and Le Gros-Fouteau in the Hauteurs de la Solle and Gorges d'Apremont areas to the north-west of Fontainebleau are good places to start. (See also site 5 above.)

8. Jablines

SEINE-ET-MARNE (77)

IGN 90

The lakes of the leisure centre at Jablines, situated within one of the River Marne's many meanders as it approaches Paris from the east, has become a focus for many waterbirds, and hence for birdwatchers. There are two main lakes, the largest one having an active sailing centre, and the other used for water-skiing. Despite the disturbance these lakes are both worth watching, and in addition there are two other smaller lakes nearby also worthy of attention. The site is of most interest from late autumn to spring for wintering and migrant waterbirds. In winter up to 1,000 diving duck occur with small numbers of divers, all the grebes, sawbills, Goldeneye, scoters and Ruddy Duck. Bittern also regularly occur in winter, as does Common Sandpiper. In the evening an immense gull roost (30,000 birds) forms on the largest lake, the one with the sailing centre. The main species are Black-headed and Herring Gulls, with smaller numbers of Yellow-legged and Common Gulls and a few of the increasingly regular Great Black-backed Gull. Caspian Gulls have also started to be identified here in recent years. Note that the best views will usually be obtained from the western side of the lake, between the Marne and the sailing centre, with the light behind you. Provided that the lakes do not freeze completely, the lakes are worth a visit during periods of severe weather when wildfowl from elsewhere come to the area, and are concentrated on any patches of ice-free water. Spring is the best time for seeing Black-necked Grebe, Garganey, Mediterranean Gull (which has bred), marsh terns, flocks of hirundines and Yellow Wagtail. In the autumn the first dabbling duck start to arrive and passage birds include Osprey, Hobby and sometimes a few waders.

■ ACCESS

From Paris take the N3 east towards Meaux. This crosses the A104 (exit 6) and then passes round Claye-Souilly. Just beyond here, turn south on the D404 to Annet-sur-Marne. Both Jablines and the leisure centre are signposted as you approach the area. Cross the river on the D45 at Annet-sur-Marne, to reach the centre, which is well supplied with car parks. These are free between 1st November and 31st March, thereafter there is a charge at weekends during April, May, September and October and every day from June to August. Note that the site is closed between 19.00pm and 08.30am, so take care not to get locked in. Once at the site, footpaths round the lakes make for easy exploration.

STONE CURLEW

9. *The Seine valley at Moisson*

YVELINES (78) *IGN 90*

Some 50 km downstream from Paris, between Mantes-la-Jolie and Vernon, the River Seine makes two large meanders, which result in sections of countryside which are to a certain extent by-passed by traffic, and hence of more interest for the birdwatcher (see also sites 12 and 13 below). The loop at Moisson contains an interesting and contrasting mix of habitats. First is the Mousseaux-Moisson leisure centre (also known as the Lac de Lavacourt). This is an old gravel-pit lying close to the left bank of the Seine, and covers about 300 hectares. For more than twenty-five years it has been an important site for wintering duck, among which are Mallard, Shoveler, Teal, Pochard, Tufted Duck, Goldeneye and Common and Velvet Scoters. During migration periods or spells of hard weather, the range of species to be seen is much wider and has included White-fronted Goose, Spoonbill, Little Gull, and all three species of diver, sometimes even all on the same day! The lake attracts a gull roost dominated by Black-headed Gulls but it is also one of the largest and most regularly used roosting sites for Herring Gulls in the Île-de-France with up to 2,000 birds sometimes present. Mixed in with these are other species, numbered in the hundreds, including Common, Lesser Black-backed, Yellow-legged, and sometimes Caspian and Great Black-backed among the others. The second section, the Forêt de Moisson, contains two more interesting habitats. There is the woodland itself, and its clearings and immediate surrounds. Here there are more than sixty species of breeding birds in the summer. These include not only Tree Pipit, Garden and Willow Warblers but also Hawfinch, Spotted Flycatcher, Willow Tit and Wood Warbler. Other interesting species to be found are

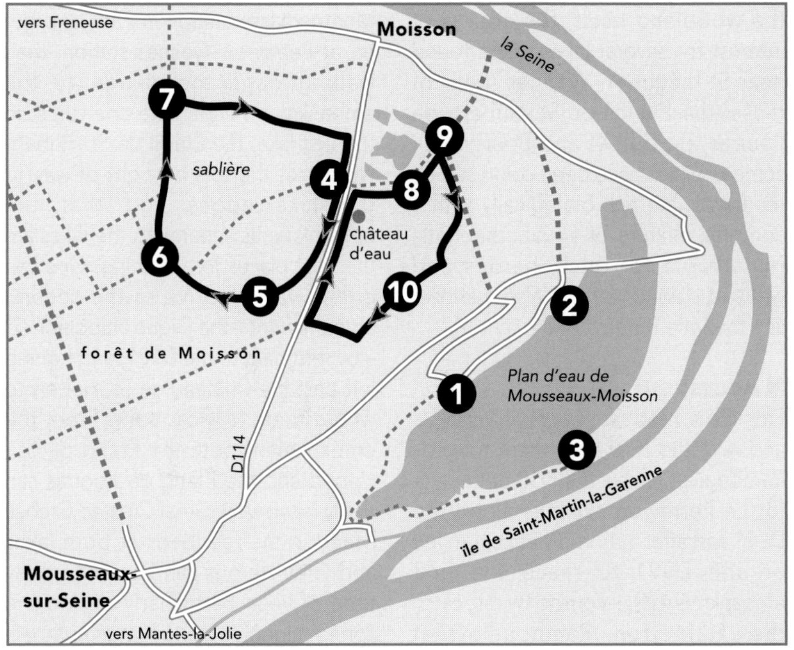

Wryneck, Nightjar in the clearings and good numbers of both Buzzard and Honey Buzzard. Just to the east of the forest itself is an extensive area dominated by heather, formerly used for sand extraction, and which is now protected from further development. This fragile habitat is one of the strongholds of the Stone Curlew in the Île-de-France, and is also a breeding site for Woodlark.

Access

From Paris take the A13 west as far as Mantes-la-Jolie (exits 11 or 12), then follow the N13 near the river towards Bonnières. Turn right at Rolleboise towards Freneuse and the Mousseaux-Moisson leisure centre, where there is car parking available. In winter there is no entrance fee and it is possible to walk the whole way round the lake. The best places for watching are at (1), (2) and (3), the latter being one of the better spots from which to see the diving ducks. For the Forêt de Moisson, return towards Mousseaux-sur-Seine, but turn right before there along the D114 towards Moisson. Stop near the water-tower (4). The western part can be toured by making the circuit from (4) through (5), (6) and (7) and back to the road. The eastern part can be viewed from point (8), and also by continuing along a path round the circuit via points (9) and (10), once again back to the starting point. The two circuits allow a full exploration, with no need to stray from the marked paths.

10. Lakes of the Forêt de Rambouillet

Yvelines (78) *IGN 90*

South-west of Versailles is the extensive Forêt de Rambouillet. In addition to the woodland itself, the area is of interest for several lakes to be found near St.-Léger-en-Yvelines. Four of these (the Étangs de St.-Hubert, de Pourras, de Corbet and Bourgneuf), some of which have been colonised by reedbeds, are rich biologically with a complex mixture of aquatic habitats, remarkable for duck, herons and wetland passerines. It is also a known site for Little Bittern.

■ Access

From Paris, head south-west via Versailles and take the N10 from there towards Rambouillet. Leave the N10 at the exit for Le Perrey-en-Yvelines along the D191 and after a short distance turn left on the D991 to reach the first embankment (1). If coming by rail, catch the train for Rambouillet at Montparnasse station in Paris and get off at Perray-en-Yvelines station, then walk through the village to the embankment. From here one can scan the first lake, the Étang de St.-Hubert. Note that there is no right-of-way to the lake edges and that the embankments separating the lakes are the best places for watching. One can either walk or drive to the second embankment – the Digue Napoléon (2) – by returning to the D191, and turning left past the Château de St.-Hubert to where there is a car park. From the embankment both the Étang de St.-Hubert and the Étang de Pourras can easily be viewed. Great Crested Grebes breed in the reedbeds at both lakes and Grey Herons can be seen at any time of year. Particularly during the spring migration period large numbers

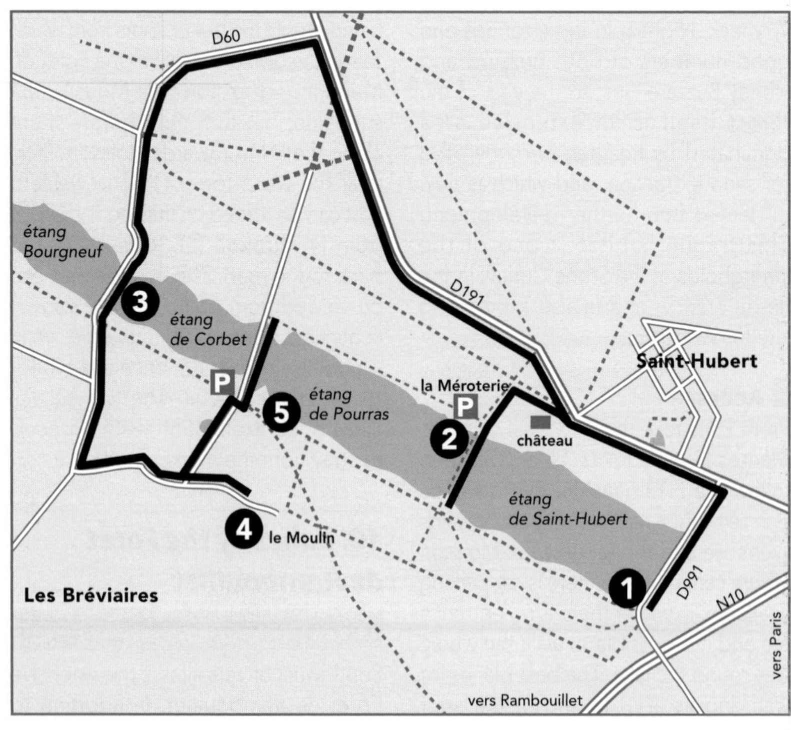

of Sand Martins, Swallows and Swifts can sometimes be seen hunting over the water while in the autumn Ospreys are regularly seen from early September to mid-October. In spring and autumn large numbers of Mallard, Shoveler, Teal, Pochard and Tufted Duck may congregate here. From here, return to the D191 and continue to the D60 where one should turn left towards Bréviaires. After crossing the bridge (3), between the Étangs de Corbet and Bourgneuf, take the first track on the left, then left again onto the Chemin de la Canarderie. One can park near the bridge (5). The embankment here between the Étangs de Pourras and de Corbet is the best place for seeing a Little Bittern, most often as one flies from one reedbed to another. There is a large Black-headed Gull colony on both sides of this embankment. Do not forget to look on the posts in the water for Cormorant, Common Tern and marsh terns during the spring and autumn. From here it is not far to walk or drive to the open country near the Ferme du Moulin (4). In autumn and winter Lapwing and Golden Plover can often be seen on plain here, a favoured hunting ground for Hen Harrier in winter.

Calendar

Spring: Breeding birds include Great Crested and Little Grebes, Little Bittern, Hobby, Black-headed Gull, Cetti's, Reed and Sedge Warblers. Black Tern, hirundines and Swift occur on migration.
Autumn: Cormorant, Grey Heron, Greylag Goose and Osprey.
Winter: Cormorant, Teal, Shoveler, Pochard and Tufted Duck.

11. Réserve naturelle de St.-Quentin-en-Yvelines

Yvelines (78) IGN 90

Close to Versailles, and in fact resulting from the work carried out there by Louis XIV, is the Étang de St.-Quentin-en-Yvelines, the shallowest part of which, on the western side, is protected as a réserve naturelle. Covering some 90 hectares, the lake and its adjoining settling beds, where the water levels fluctuate throughout the year, is a remarkably rich wetland habitat, especially being so close to the capital, studded with areas of bulrush and reed, and providing a refuge for over-wintering duck and for significant number of waders on migration. In spring the reedbeds resonate to the sound of nesting Black-headed Gulls and there is a large roost of the same species in winter. Mallard, Shoveler, Pochard and Tufted Duck can be seen on the lake from October to April. During times of migration the settling beds and mudflats often have Redshank, Common Sandpiper, Dunlin, Little Stint or Snipe. The bushes around the settling beds provide nesting sites for Blackcap, Garden Warbler and Common and Lesser Whitethroats. In autumn and winter the blackthorn bushes shelter Chaffinch, Greenfinch, Goldfinch, Linnet and Bullfinch.

Access

From Paris, take the A13 (autoroute de l'Ouest) as far as the Rocquencourt interchange, then the A12 and the N10 (towards Rambouillet) as far as the traffic-lights at Trappes. Turn right on the D912 as far as the golf-course entrance, where there is a fee-paying

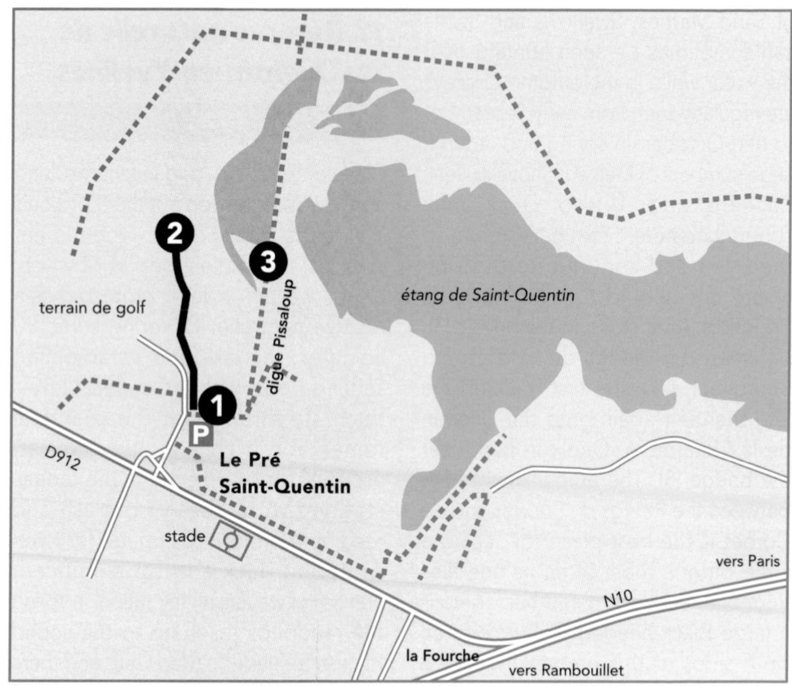

car park and the entrance to the reserve (1). If coming by train, from the Montparnasse mainline station in Paris, take a train going to Rambouillet and get off at Trappes. If using the RER C7 urban service, get off at St.-Quentin-en-Yvelines station. Then take the 463 bus. Access to the reserve is strictly controlled, and there are thus two main ways to visit the site. First, it is possible to see at least part of the reserve from its periphery along a way-marked trail (2) north from the car park. Alternatively it is possible to arrange a guided visit for small groups into the reserve itself (3) along a 1½ km path with access to several hides. There are guided and unaccompanied visits once a month for small groups, but advance reservation is necessary (Tel: 01 30 62 20 12).

Calendar

Spring: Great Crested Grebe, Greylag Goose, many duck, Black-headed and Mediterranean Gulls, Black Tern, Swift, hirundines. More irregularly: Marsh Harrier, Common Sandpiper, Black-tailed Godwit and Grasshopper Warbler.
Autumn: Grey Heron, Cormorant, small waders (particularly *Tringa* species) and wetland warblers.
Winter: Mallard, Gadwall, Shoveler, Teal, Pochard and Tufted Duck. Large Black-headed Gull roost.

12. Seine valley at Guernes

Yvelines (78) *IGN 90*

Lying some 50 km to the west of Paris, the meander in the River Seine at Guernes, to the north-west of Mantes-la-Jolie, encloses a series of interesting habitats.

There has been much gravel and sand extraction in the area, resulting in a series of lakes close to the river. Part of the area is being restored and currently is not fully open to the public, but there is a hide from which birds can be watched undisturbed. The meander lies within the Parc Naturel Régional du Vexin Français, and hence has an increased level of protection. (See also site 9 above and 13 below.)

ACCESS

From Paris take the A13 west as far as Mantes-la-Jolie (exits 11 or 12), then take the bridge over the Seine, towards Limay, immediately then turning along the D147 towards Dennemont. Here turn left onto the D148 to Guernes and turn right in the village towards Sandrancourt (1) and the first of the pits. Typical birds on the water are Great Crested Grebes throughout the year, with numbers of duck increasing in winter. Returning along the road and turning right brings you to (2), where there is a hide, well-placed for watching aquatic birds in winter. The road continues to the Port de l'Ilon (3) and more open water. Note that when water-sports activities are taking place the birds move around the pits to find the least disturbed spots. A visit at dusk in summer can often be worthwhile as Stone Curlews can be heard calling and sometimes a Long-eared Owl will put in an appearance.

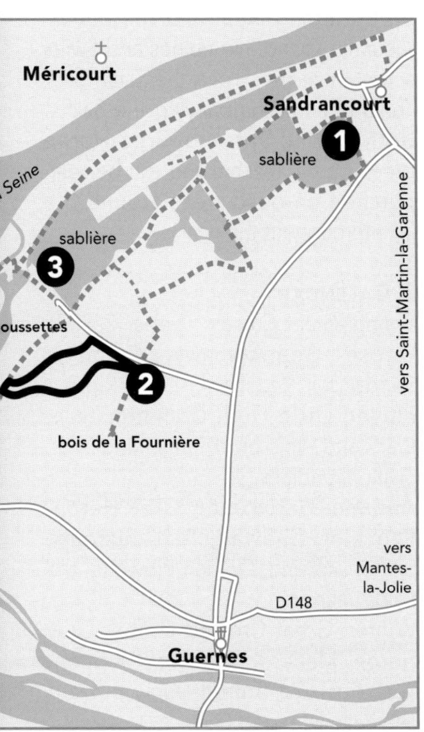

CALENDAR

Spring and autumn: Osprey, Marsh Harrier, marsh and Common Terns attracted by the abundance of small fish. Waders also occur: Redshank, Greenshank, Green, Wood and Common Sandpipers, occasionally Avocet, Black-winged Stilt or Black-tailed Godwit.
Summer: Pochard and Tufted Duck, Stone Curlew, Sand Martin nesting colony, Hobby. Little Egret regularly occurs in August.
Winter: most of the commoner ducks, Black-headed Gull, Grey Heron and Cormorant.

13. Île Aumône at Mantes-la-Jolie

YVELINES (78) *IGN 90*

The Île Aumône bird reserve in the River Seine close to the previous site is of recent origin and is managed by the local authorities. At the moment the site is mainly of interest for passerines, attracted by the berry-bearing hedgerows that provide food and safe nesting sites. A few Grey Herons have started to visit the recently created ponds but are often disturbed by uncontrolled dogs. As the site is still being developed the vegetation has not yet fully re-grown on certain parts of the island and hence does not yet attract as many birds as hopefully it will in future. From Paris take the A13 motorway as far as Mantes-la-Jolie, exit 11. Cross the bridge over the Seine on the N183 towards Limay, exit to the right onto the island, then turn immediately right again, towards a metal bridge, and drive as far as the car park. Then walk to the hide.

---

14. Étang-Vieux de Saclay

ESSONNE (91) *IGN 90*

The lakes at Saclay, like those of St.-Quentin and St.-Hubert, were built in the 17th century as part of the water supply for the château of Versailles, which lies not far away to the north-west. They have been much studied by Parisian ornithologists ever since they became a reserve in the 1950s, but it was not until August 1980 that the Étang-Vieux (the west lake) became fully classified as a réserve naturelle (the first in the Île-de-France). The land still belongs to the Ministry of Defence, so that access is very restricted, but it is possible to birdwatch from the road that separates the Étang-Vieux from the Étang-Neuf.

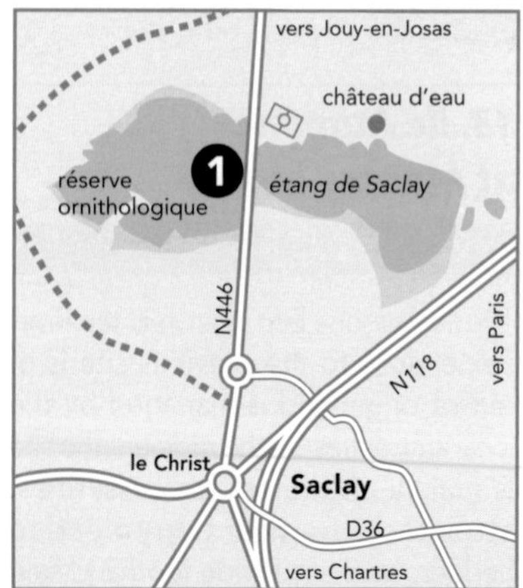

ACCESS

Saclay is at exit 8 on the N118 from Paris towards Chartres. The N446 north from Christ-de-Saclay to Jouy-en-Josas runs between the two lakes, and it is easy to stop the car on the roadside and birdwatch from a small promontory at (1). Access to the rest of the lake is forbidden. At all times, but especially during autumn and winter, this a good place to come and learn how to identify grebes, herons, geese and ducks. The Great Crested Grebe, visible throughout the year is a common breeder, both on the Étang-Neuf and the Étang-Vieux. In spring, hirundines and Swifts actively hunt insects over the water, Black Terns often accompanying the Swifts. Both Cormorant and Grey Heron breed on the reserve and can be seen perched on dead trees around the lake throughout the year.

CALENDAR

Spring: Great Crested Grebe, Canada Goose, Sparrowhawk, Common Sandpiper, Redshank, Little Ringed Plover, Little Gull, Common Tern, Black and Whiskered Terns, Kingfisher, Swift, hirundines.
Autumn: Cormorant, Grey Heron, Shoveler, Gadwall, Teal, Buzzard, Snipe, Lapwing, Golden Plover (in the fields nearby).
Winter: Great Crested Grebe, Grey Heron, Mallard, Shoveler, Wigeon, Teal, Pochard, Tufted Duck, Buzzard and Yellow-legged Gull.

15. Bruyères-le-Châtel reservoir

ESSONNE (91) *IGN 90*

This reservoir (28 hectares, and also known as the Basin de Trévoix) is on the Orge river, near Bruyères-le-Châtel, about 30 km south-west of Paris. To get there, take the N20 towards Étampes as far as Arpajon, then the D97 and D116 to Bruyères. At the church turn left on the D82, the reservoir being about 2 km from the centre of Bruyères, between the Rivers Rémarde and Orge. A footpath round the lake makes for easy viewing. At all times of the year it is possible to see Great Crested Grebe, Grey Heron, Mute Swan, Mallard, Coot and Black-headed Gull here. In winter various duck occur (e.g., Wigeon, Teal, Pochard and Tufted Duck) and, in the autumn or spring, a few waders and many migrant passerines can be seen.

BLACK TERN

16. The River Seine between Grigny and Vigneux

ESSONNE (91) *IGN 90*

Lying just south-east of Paris-Orly airport, are a series of ancient sand-pits ('fouilles') on both banks of the River Seine between Grigny to the south and Vigneux to the north. Most date back to sand extraction carried out at the time when the Paris metro was first built. Inevitably they subsequently filled with water through canals linking them with the nearby River Seine. In all there are eight small lakes along the riverside, mostly open to the public. They vary in interest as far as birds are concerned; the Fosse aux Carpes (or Fouille des Sablières), for instance, has a large Cormorant roost in winter as well as many duck that can also be seen on the leisure activities lake, the Port aux Cerises. Farther north, nearer to Vigneux there is an interesting area of scrub and crops, between Fosse Montalbot and the Seine, where Kingfisher, Little Ringed Plover, Marsh Warbler and Lesser Whitethroat all nest.

17. Saulx-les-Chartreux

ESSONNE (91) *IGN 90*

The nature reserve of Saulx-les-Chartreux (35 hectares), to the south-west of Paris-Orly airport, comprises a reservoir (varying in extent from 7-10 hectares depending on the water-level) primarily used for the regulation of flooding by the River Yvette, and small islands surrounded by arms of the river which form the actual reserve. The Île-aux-Oiseaux in the centre of the reservoir was declared a nature reserve in 1988. Throughout the year there are

Great Crested Grebe, Little Grebe, Grey Heron, Mallard, Coot and Black-headed Gull as well as migrant passerines. In winter it is possible to see various species of duck, especially Pochard and Tufted Duck, and in autumn small numbers of waders may pass through (Greenshank, various sandpipers, Ringed Plovers), depending on the water level. From Paris, take the N20 south and leave at the Saulx-les-Chartreux exit. Turn right towards Villebon-Champlan on the D118. The first road on the right, Route de Champlan, leads to the main car park. A tour of the site is made easy by the presence of a raised path (a 'parcours de santé' – a health circuit) from which the whole area where birds are likely to be seen can be surveyed. Guided visits can be organised by the association NaturEssonne.

18. Parc de Sceaux

HAUTS-DE-SEINE (92)

IGN 90

This large and varied park in south-west Paris is worth a visit if you are staying in that part of the city. Passerines are numerous, especially in spring and autumn. In winter there are Fieldfare, Redwing, Siskin and sometimes Redpoll. During migration (spring and autumn) many passerines pass through the park and various ducks and grebes occur on its large lake.

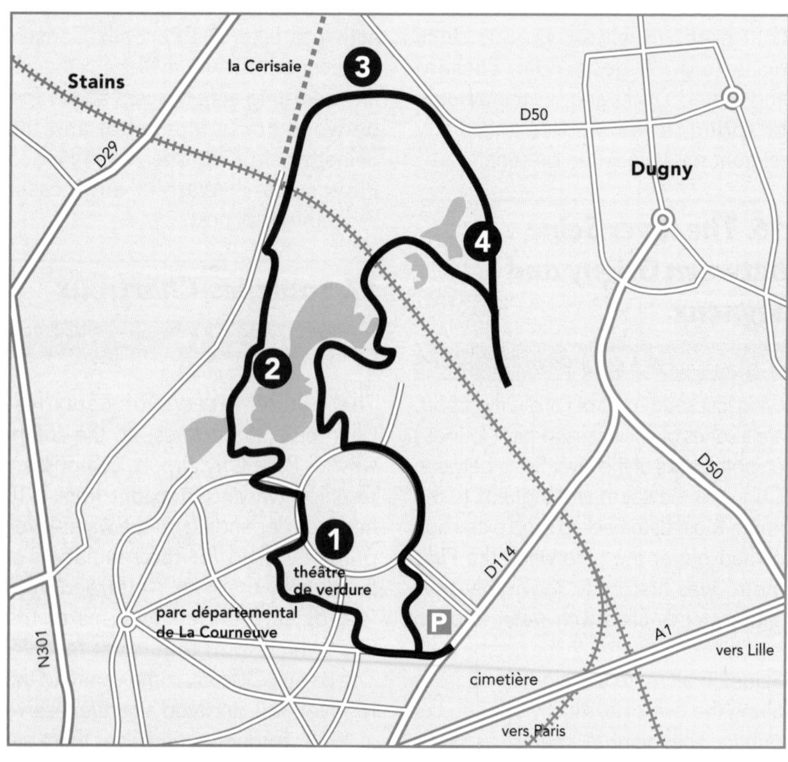

19. Parc de La Courneuve

SEINE-SAINT-DENIS (93)

IGN 90

This is a park in northern Paris, whose undulating landscape covering 400 hectares encompasses a remarkable variety of habitats (woods, lakes, reedbeds, lawns, grassy and bushy scrub). The park is surrounded by some heavily-urbanised areas, both housing and industrial, and it makes a kind of oasis of verdure in an otherwise sterile area as far as birds are concerned. The Paris-Le Bourget airport lies just to the north-east, the open grassland of which also tending to be a magnet for birds moving through the area.

ACCESS

From Paris take the Metro (line 7) as far as Aubervilliers-Pantin, then the 249 bus towards Dugny-centre-ville as far as the 'Cimetière' stop; alternatively take the RER (line B) as far as Aubervilliers-La Corneuve station, and then the 249 bus to the same stop. By car there are various possibilities via the A1, A86 or the N301 roads; there is a car park 'Tapis vert' on Avenue Waldeck-Rochet at La Courneuve (NB: the park closes at sunset). The proposed circuit is about a three-hour walk, starting from the 'Tapis vert' car park and passing through most of the available habitats. Wooded areas (1) have Green, Great Spotted and Lesser Spotted Woodpeckers. Long-eared Owls can be seen where there are coniferous plantations year-round, while flocks of Crested and Coal Tits, Goldcrest and Firecrest occur in the same woods in winter. Great Crested and Little Grebes and Moorhen nest on the Grand Lac (2) where Grey Herons often come to feed. The grass and bushy plateau (3) is an area favoured by Little Ringed Plover (which may sometimes nest), Skylark and Meadow Pipit and Whinchat and Wheatear sometimes make an appearance. The Étang des Brouillards and the 'vallon écologique' reedbeds (4) have breeding Reed Warbler and Little Bittern, and Water Rail and Spotted Crake have been seen here. Many Swifts and hirundines come to feed over the lakes, and on certain days in autumn it is possible to watch active passerine migration overhead.

CALENDAR

Spring: Great Crested and Little Grebes, sandpipers and Greenshank, Stonechat, Wheatear, Willow Warbler; and, less frequently, Garganey, Black Kite, Woodcock, Ring Ouzel, Penduline Tit, Redpoll.
Breeding season: Little Bittern, Great Crested Grebe, Little Grebe, Moorhen, Little Ringed Plover, Reed and Marsh Warblers, Skylark, Meadow Pipit, Common and Lesser Whitethroats. Three species of raptor nest: Long-eared Owl, Kestrel and Sparrowhawk.
Autumn: Bittern, Water Rail, large flocks of passerines (Redwing, Fieldfare, Linnet, Serin, Greenfinch, Goldfinch, buntings).
Winter: Grey Heron, Cormorant, Mallard, Pochard, Black-headed Gull, Coot, Reed Bunting; also, more rarely, Long-eared Owl (roost), Brambling, Goldcrest and Firecrest, Coal Tit and Hawfinch.

20. Lac de Créteil

VAL-DE-MARNE (94) *IGN 90*

About 10 km to the south-east of Paris, between the Rivers Marne and Seine, and situated on an alluvial plain, the Lac de Créteil originated as an old sand-pit, and is now situated in the middle of an otherwise urban area. However, the lake is visited by quite a few aquatic birds particularly in autumn during the migration period, and in winter when there can be quite large numbers of duck. The lake is heavily used as a recreation zone, with leisure activities taking priority over conservation considerations, and so there is a lot of disturbance from the public, this disturbance only decreasing in winter, and even then disturbance from water sports activities occurs, such events being common most weekends of the year. However, like several of the sites considered in this section, it is of interest to birdwatchers either living in Paris or staying in the city for a few days for other reasons.

ACCESS

The lake lies close to the N186 (route de Choisy) in Créteil and also the D60 (route de la Pompadour), and it is possible to park in several places nearby. You can also come by bus (392, stop 'Lac') or on the Metro (station Crétail-Préfecture). A public footpath goes right round the lake. One starting point is the car park in the Rue Jean-Gabin (1). From here follow the track that passes in front of the Maison de la Nature visitor centre. Mallard are very tame and come to collect bread out of visitors' hands. Duck (especially Pochard) are found in front of the Préfecture in winter. A few hundred Coot pass the winter on the lake. To make a complete tour, pass by the Préfecture by going up the Boulevard du Général-de-Gaulle (2). Open grass or bushy areas attract migrant passerines (wagtails, warblers, etc.). There are some small reedbeds which have breeding Reed Warbler and even Little Bittern probably nests sometimes. Finally, Crested Lark can be seen along the 'quai Offenbach' in winter.

CALENDAR

Spring: Great Crested Grebe, Mallard, Coot, Swift and hirundines, warblers on migration, Reed Warbler nesting.

Autumn and winter: Great Crested Grebe, Mallard, Pochard, Tufted Duck, sometimes Ferruginous Duck and Scaup, Common and Velvet Scoters; also Goldeneye, Goosander and Smew (in cold winters), Coot, Common Sandpiper and Black-headed Gull.

21. Valenton

VAL-DE-MARNE (94) *IGN 90*

Just 1 km (as the crow flies) south from the Lac de Créteil, is the Plage Bleue leisure centre, in Valenton, a wetland area resulting from the rehabilitation of an ancient sand and gravel extraction site. It comprises a $1\frac{1}{2}$ hectare lake with channels between several small islands, the lake being surrounded by a public footpath, lawns and copses. The site is less frequented than the Lac de Créteil (and has no water-sports facilities) and has thus become a popular refuge for wintering and migrant birds, particularly when the

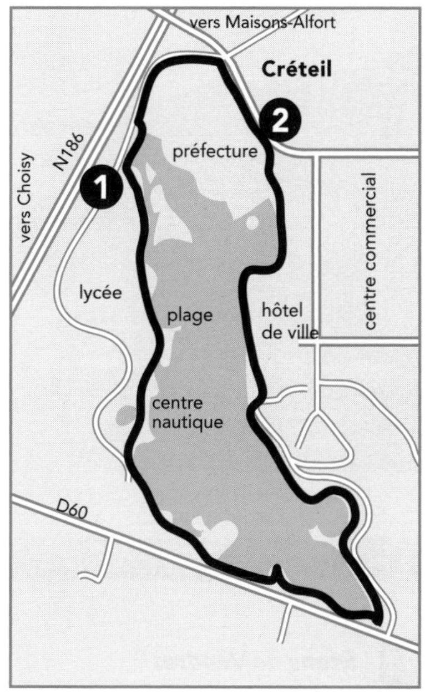

previous site is disturbed. Pochard and Tufted Duck often occur and occasional rare visitors such as Velvet Scoter have been seen. Little Ringed Plovers have nested on more than one occasion.

22. *Étangs de Cergy-Neuville*

VAL-D'OISE (95) *IGN 90*

The Étangs de Cergy-Neuville occupy a meander of the River Oise river, some 27 km north-west of Paris, near Pontoise. They are in fact flooded, disused sand-pits that are now used as a leisure centre, and cover a total area of 250 hectares. Many birds (migrant, wintering or breeding) are attracted here, especially as the area is close to both the Rivers Seine and Oise, both migration flyways. In winter it is sometimes possible to see the three species of diver, Shelduck and various diving ducks, which can include scoters, Goldeneye and sawbills. There is a roost of a few thousand Black-headed Gulls which always has a few of the larger gulls mixed in. Among the passerines that winter, Siskins are regularly recorded here. The breeding waterbird population is limited to just the commoner aquatic species – Great Crested Grebe, Coot and Moorhen. To reach the site from Paris, take the A15 as far as Cergy-Préfecture and follow signs to the Cergy-Neuville leisure centre ('base de loisirs'). Entry is free of charge in winter.

SITES

1 *Gruissan and the Étang de Campignol*

2 *Port-la-Nouvelle*

3 *Gorges de l'Orbieu*

4 *Leucate*

5 *Étang de Pissevaches*

6 *Causse de Blandas and Cirque de Navacelles*

7 *Étang du Scamandre*

8 *River Arre at Le Vigan*

9 *Étang du Bagnas*

10 *Étang du Grec and Étang du Prévost*

11 *Causse d'Aumelas*

12 *Étang de Vendres*

13 *Étang de Vic-la-Gardiole*

14 *Minerve*

15 *Parc National des Cévennes near Le Rozier*

16 *The River Tarn*

17 *Causse Méjean*

18 *Étang de Canet*

19 *Villeneuve-de-la-Raho*

20 *Eyne*

21 *Montescot/Corneilla del Verco*

Languedoc-Roussillon

1. Gruissan and the Étang de Campignol

AUDE (11) *IGN 72*

Gruissan is a small town to the south-east of Narbonne, surrounded by lagoons and salt-pans, close to the sea. To the north is the high ground of the Montagne de la Clape; to the south is the Île St.-Martin, with its Mediterranean rocky landscape of vineyards and bushy garrigue. South again is the Étang de l'Ayrolle, separated from the sea by a strip of sand and fringed by lagoons and salt-pans. The Étang de Campagnol is an offshoot of this to the north, a brackish lake receiving fresh water from the north, and sea water from the south. To the west and north-east it is edged by reedbeds and 'sansouire' (a low Mediterranean saltmarsh-like vegetation) with a few tamarisks. Protected as a reserve and with restricted access, it is a remarkable area for duck, herons, raptors and marshland passerines. Lastly, the Roc de Conilhac, to the north of this lake, is a small hillock rising from the marsh, an ideal migration watch point.

ACCESS

Gruissan can be reached from Narbonne along the D32 which crosses the A9 at exit 37. Continue through the town and over the canal to the Île St.-Martin side, turning left and continuing along the side of the salt-pans for about 1 km. This will bring you to the Étang de l'Ayrolle where there is a collection of fishermen's huts (1). Black-headed, Mediterranean and Yellow-legged Gulls and terns can be seen here. Both lagoon and salt-pans provide feeding grounds for waders (e.g., Grey Plover, Dunlin, stints, etc. on migration) and have an interesting selection of breeding birds, including Avocet and Kentish Plover. From here, return towards Gruissan, but then turn left towards Château-Bel-Évêque, to reach a car park (2) next to a couple of lagoons between the road and the main étang. These lagoons attract waders, terns and gulls (including Slender-billed) and in spring both Great Spotted Cuckoo and Hoopoe occur in the adjacent garrigue. The rocky ground and vineyards nearby are good places to look for Dartford, Sardinian and Subalpine Warblers, Black-eared Wheatear and Southern Grey Shrike. From here return to Gruissan but before the canal turn left towards Mandirac, to reach an area of open marsh and lagoons (3), a good spot to look for Grey and Purple Herons

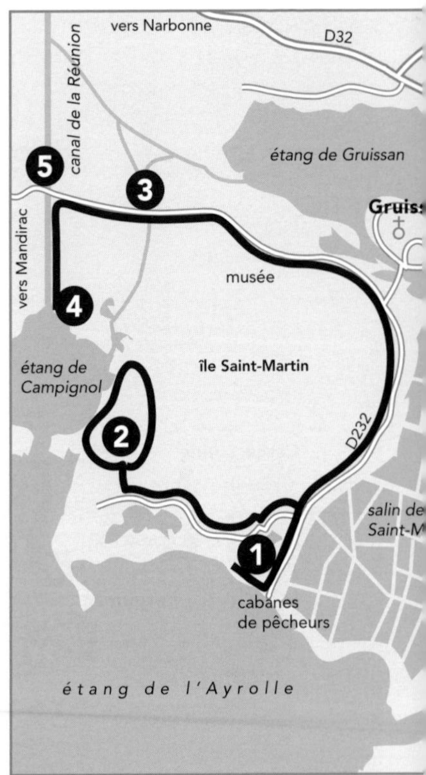

GREATER FLAMINGO

and Greater Flamingo. The road crosses another canal further on (5), where the LPO has a birdwatching centre in a small white building by the roadside. Park here and walk south by the canal to reach the Étang de Campignol (4). The reedbeds host numerous breeding or migrant passerines, including Bearded and Penduline Tits, Moustached and other wetland warblers. Next to the LPO building, the low outcrop of the Roc de Conilhac is an exceptionally good migration watch point, between March and May, August and November, when a wide variety of birds can be seen moving through – birds of prey, storks, swifts, Bee-eater, hirundines, etc.

Calendar

Spring and autumn: Black and White Storks, Red-crested Pochard, Honey Buzzard, Short-toed Eagle, Osprey, Hobby, Kestrel, Merlin, Eleonora's Falcon, Black-winged Stilt, Avocet, Ringed Plover, waders, warblers, finches.

Breeding season: Great Spotted Cuckoo, Black-eared Wheatear, Short-toed Lark, Southern Grey and Woodchat Shrikes, Mediterranean warblers.

Winter: Greater Flamingo, herons, Mallard, Shoveler, Wigeon, Pintail, Teal, Coot, Marsh Harrier, Bearded and Penduline Tits, buntings.

2. Port-la-Nouvelle

AUDE (11) *IGN 72*

The jetty at Port-la-Nouvelle, south of Gruissan, is one of the best places for watching seabirds in Languedoc-Roussillon, both during passage periods and in winter. Almost anything can turn up – grebes, divers (mainly Black-throated), Gannets, shearwaters, gulls and terns, Red-breasted Merganser, scoters (winter), skuas (spring) and auks, primarily Razorbill (winter). From Narbonne, take the N9 or A9 (exit 39) south to Sigean, then the N139 to Port-la-Nouvelle. Follow the quayside as far as the jetty; the best place is next to the beacon at the far end. Visits during the week, between 15.00 and 17.00, are often productive, when the fishing boats are returning to port.

3. Gorges de l'Orbieu

AUDE (11) *IGN 72*

Situated in the hills of the Corbières, these deep gorges provide nesting sites for a variety of cliff-dwelling species, such as Golden Eagle, Peregrine and Raven. In spring and summer Short-toed and Booted Eagles, Hobby, Red-backed Shrike and Woodlark may also be seen. In winter look for Wallcreeper and Alpine Accentor on rocky outcrops. The main access route is via the D613 which runs from Couiza on the D118 Carcassonne/Limoux/Quillan road across to the N113 just west of Narbonne. To reach the gorges, take the D212 which heads north from the D613 between Albières and Mouthoumet, and runs along the gorges via Lanet and Montjoi. It is also worth taking the D70 up onto the open plateau around Bouisse, where there are oaks and birches as opposed to the garrigue and holm oaks further east.

4. Leucate

AUDE (11) *IGN 72*

At Leucate, on the coast north of Perpignan, the coastline alters direction from north to north-east, the limestone plateau of Cap Leucate forming a kink in the otherwise fairly straight low-lying shoreline. This makes it a spot where migrants moving along the coast tend to become concentrated, particularly in the spring. Raptors moving through are perhaps the most conspicuous species – kites, Honey Buzzard, Short-toed Eagle, harriers, falcons, etc. – but other species include White and Black Storks, Grey,

WALLCREEPER

Purple and Night Herons, Little and Cattle Egrets, Woodpigeon, Bee-eater, Hoopoe, swifts, hirundines (including Red-rumped Swallow), wagtails, Serin, Linnet and Chaffinch. On the plateau it is possible to see Great Spotted Cuckoo, Rock and Blue Rock Thrushes, Crested Lark, Tawny Pipit, Ortolan Bunting and Bonelli's, Orphean, Spectacled, Subalpine, Dartford and Sardinian Warblers, some of which remain to breed in the area. In winter, on the sea, or on the Étang de Leucate just to the south, look for Black-throated Diver, Crested and Black-necked Grebes, Cormorant, Shag, Gannet, Teal and Wigeon. Leucate village is accessed along the D327 from the N9 or A9 (exit 40) between Perpignan and Narbonne. Continue past the village to Leucate-Plage and climb up to the lighthouse on the plateau. There is open access along the coast, with views out to sea and over the small fields just inland.

5. Étang de Pissevaches

AUDE (11) *IGN 72*

The Étang de Pissevaches is one of a series of lagoons set in saltmarshes, mudflats, salt-pans and reedbeds on the coast south of Béziers where the River Aude flows into the sea. Nearly 220 bird species have been seen, including some good rarities, making it one of the Aude's best birding sites. In spring and autumn Shelduck, Little Gull, marsh terns and other gulls and terns feed around the salt-pans or roost on the mudflats or embankments. Depending on the water levels, waders can be seen either on the mudflats or around the settling beds. A spring migrant speciality is the Red-throated Pipit, seen in early May, though it helps to know the call to locate one. During the summer, the areas of salt marsh provide breeding habitat for Kentish Plover, Short-toed Lark and Tawny Pipit. From Gruissan, take the coast road north to St.-Pierre-sur-Mer and turn left just before the Pissevaches camp site. Continue past the Domaine de l'Oustalet on the left. The road finishes near the coast, and there are tracks into and around the edges of the wetland area to the north.

6. Causse de Blandas and Cirque de Navacelles

GARD (30) *IGN 65*

The 'causses' are the open stony limestone plateaux of central France, the southern end of the Massif Central, vegetated with meadows, arable fields, grassland, heathland and patches of conifer plantations. It is a good area for shrikes, harriers and various warblers. It is also very rich botanically, with many species of orchid. The Causse de Blandas is one of the most southerly, and thus one of the first to be reached when coming up from the Mediterranean. The Cirque de Navacelles is a spectacular valley where the River Vis cuts through the plateau in a series of winding loops, with some fine cliffs and cedar and pine woodland. The river is on a raptor and passerine migration route, both in spring and autumn, as well as having several specialised breeding species.

■ ACCESS

The Causse de Blandas is west of Ganges where the D999 west from Nîmes and the D986 north from Montpellier meet. The D999 continues to Le Vigan, where one can turn left on the D48 through Avèze and Montdardier. Beyond the latter, stop at the 'lavogne' at Flouirac (1) (a lavogne is a local word for a watering place for sheep) near the D413 turning for Blandas and Barral. Quite a few warblers breed in the area, including Orphean, and there are also Nightingales to be heard. Red-backed and Woodchat Shrikes breed here, along with a few Southern Grey Shrikes. Tawny Pipit is another bird of these open areas. Both Montagu's and Hen Harriers breed, but only in small numbers. At times of migration various warblers, Chaffinch, Brambling, Greenfinch and Linnet can all be found on the causses. Continue south along the D48; there is a parking place on the left at (2), another good place to scan from. Look for Rock Thrush on the electricity pylons. Among the corvids in the fields, look out for the Choughs which can be seen throughout the year. The village of Rogues is an excellent place for seeing migrant birds of prey in spring – Black and Red Kites, Honey

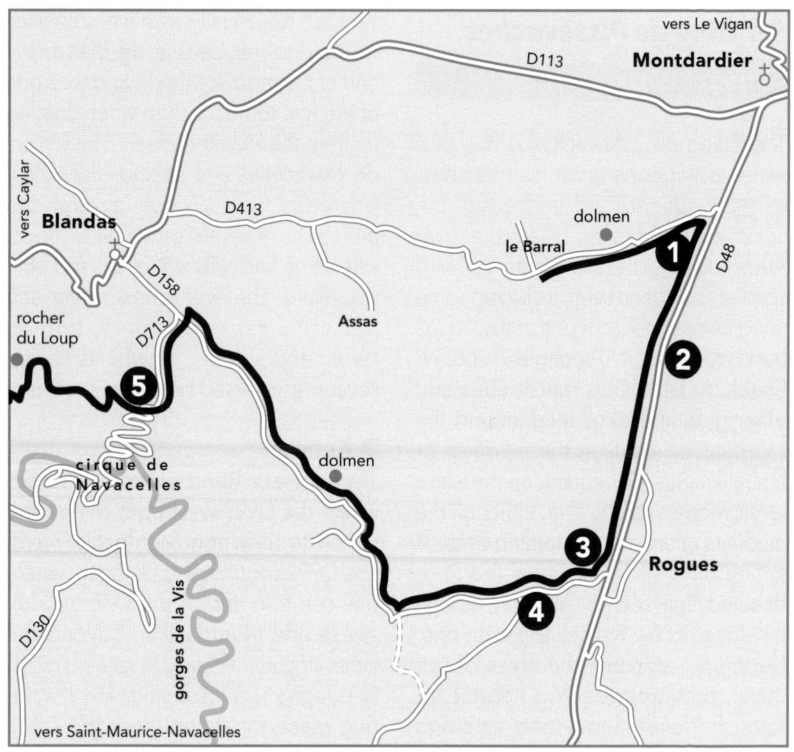

Buzzard, Short-toed Eagle, Marsh Harrier and various falcons. Beyond the village of Rogues, turn right on the D158, and stop at the Rogues lavogne (3), another good spot for a walk. Quail can be heard here in spring. Then another 1½ km further on stop at the turning for Jurade (4). Scops Owl often breeds in this part of the causse, as does Hoopoe. Continue on the D158 towards Blandas, but turn left just before the village onto the D713 towards the Cirque de Navacelles. Along here look for Rock Thrush, Woodlark, Tawny Pipit, Wheatear and Black-eared Wheatear (rare), Whitethroat and Ortolan Bunting, all of which breed not far away. There is a car park near the cirque (5). Either scan from the top, or take one of the footpaths which run through the garrigue and woodland, breeding habitat for Sardinian and Subalpine Warblers, among others. Around the cirque itself look for Crag Martins flying along the rock faces. Blue Rock Thrush and Alpine Swift are other species that can be found breeding here. In winter, this is a regular site for Wallcreeper and Alpine Accentor. Although for most species the best time for watching is the early morning, the most productive conditions at times of migration is when there are northerly winds blowing.

Calendar

Spring and autumn: Black and Red Kites, harriers, Short-toed Eagle, Honey Buzzard, larks, wagtails, chats, Chaffinch, Brambling, Linnet, buntings.

Breeding season: Alpine Swift, Tawny Pipit, Mediterranean warblers, Blue Rock and Rock Thrushes, Red-backed,

Woodchat and Southern Grey Shrikes, buntings (including Ortolan), Chough. Also Little, Scops and Long-eared Owls. *Winter*: thrushes and Blackbird, Chaffinch, Brambling, Wallcreeper, Alpine Accentor.

7. Étang du Scamandre

GARD (30) *IGN 66*

The Étang du Scamandre is part of the 'Petite Camargue', in the north-western part of the Rhône delta, and is protected as a nature reserve. It mostly comprises open water with extensive reedbeds, but there are also some grazed water meadows. This is an area worth a visit at any time of year. In summer the reserve is a good place to have a reasonable chance of seeing several species that are often considered difficult to find elsewhere, such as Little Bittern, Bittern, Collared Pratincole and Moustached Warbler. Purple Heron and Black-winged Stilt also breed. In winter, birds to be seen include Grey Heron, Cattle, Little and Great White Egrets, Bittern, many species of duck, Marsh Harrier, Water Rail, Golden Plover, Snipe, Bearded and Penduline Tits. During both spring and autumn migration periods the range of species is even wider: herons, godwits, *Tringa* waders including Marsh Sandpiper, other smaller waders including Temminck's Stint, the three species of marsh terns, Great Spotted Cuckoo, Hoopoe, Roller, hirundines, various warblers, chats and flycatchers. The Étang du Scamandre is roughly half-way between Montpellier and Arles. From Montpellier, along a route that is also good for birds, take the D62 towards Aigues-Mortes, then the D58 towards Saintes-Maries-de-la-Mer. At Montcalm turn left on the D179 and after 7 km one arrives at the Scamandre reserve visitor centre. The road continues north to join the N572 near Gallician, for access from Nîmes or Arles. Guided visits are available. See also site 16, etc. in the Provence-Alpes-Côte d'Azur chapter.

8. River Arre at Le Vigan

GARD (30) *IGN 65*

The footpath running along the River Arre, between Avèze and Le Vigan (for access see site 6 above), is a perfect place for watching Dipper, Kingfisher, Short-toed Treecreeper, Tree Sparrow and for hearing Cetti's Warbler, throughout

LITTLE EGRET

the year. In winter, the riverside woods are full of Chaffinches and Greenfinches, while in some years, Siskin, Citril Finch and Brambling also occur. Woodpeckers and tits are present throughout the year.

9. Étang du Bagnas

HÉRAULT (34) *IGN 65*

The Étang du Bagnas, close to the coast at Agde, is a 375 hectare lake, 100 hectares of which is a dense reedbed. It is one of the best birdwatching wetlands in Languedoc-Roussillon, and since 1983 has been protected as part of the Réserve Naturelle de Bagnas.

ACCESS

From Agde take the N112 east towards Sète, and at the turning for Marseillan-Plage, turn left on the D51E towards Marseillan. After crossing the railway, take the first track on the right past Les Onglous, where there is a lagoon on the left, and continue to where the road ends at the southern end of the Bassin de Thau. Typical birds here include Grey Heron, Little Egret and Greater Flamingo. Return to the D51E and look at the settling beds on the left of the road (2). In April and May this is a good area for Little Gull and marsh terns. Further along on the right (3) is good at migration times, particularly spring, for Avocet, Black-winged Stilt, Ringed Plover and Redshank. Migrant hirundines feeding here may include a Red-rumped Swallow. Further on again brings you to a parking area (4) from which the main Étang du Bagnas can be viewed. There is a notice giving details concerning the reserve (for more information contact the Mas du Grand Clavelet to the south of the site, Tel: 04 67 01 60 23). Apart from by prior

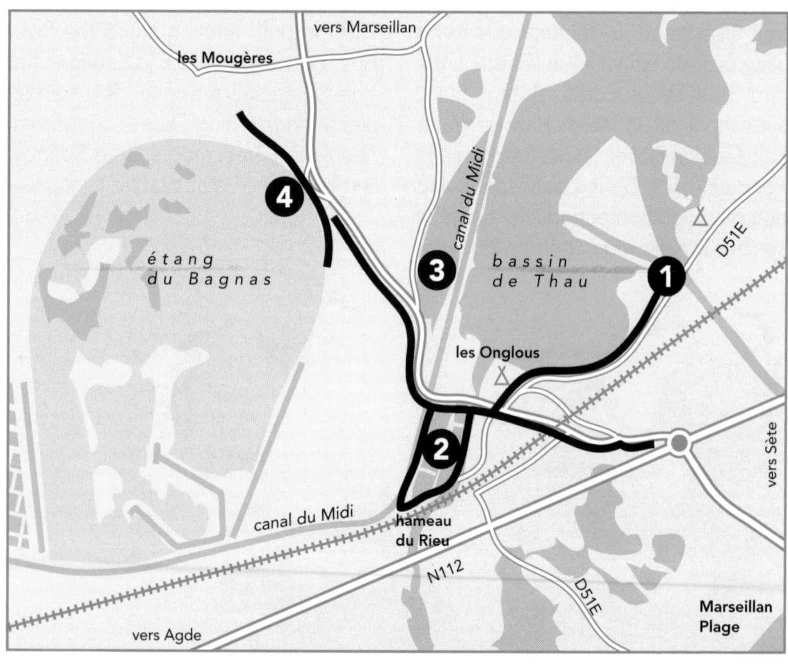

arrangement, this is the only place from which the lake can be viewed, and a telescope is useful. In winter large flocks of duck – Mallard, Shoveler, Pintail, Pochard, Tufted Duck, Red-crested Pochard – can be seen. The reedbeds are home to many wetland passerines – Reed, Great Reed and Moustached Warblers – while Savi's, Grasshopper and Aquatic Warblers occur on migration. Marsh Harrier is present throughout the year.

Calendar

Autumn and spring: Greater Flamingo, many duck including Red-crested Pochard, Osprey, Black-winged Stilt, marsh terns, swifts, Hoopoe, Bee-eater, Roller, Reed, Great Reed, Sedge, Aquatic, Savi's and Grasshopper Warblers, hirundines sometimes include Red-rumped Swallow.

Winter: Great Crested and Black-necked Grebes, Greater Flamingo, Cormorant, Great White and Little Egrets, Shoveler, Pintail, Mallard, Wigeon, Teal, Marsh Harrier, Buzzard, Reed Bunting, Bearded and Penduline Tits.

10. Étang du Grec and Étang du Prévost

Hérault (34) *IGN 66*

These two lagoons are part of a series strung out along the coast near Montpellier. The Étang du Grec is a shallow lagoon with saltmarsh, mudflats and small islands, separated from the Étang du Méjean to the north-west by the Rhône-Sète canal, and from the sea to the south-east by the Carnon-Palavas road. It is a protected site: interpretation trails and hides are in place. The Étang du Prévost, which was open to the sea until recently is now almost completely cut off by a line of sand-dunes. There is an area of 'sansouire' saltmarsh vegetation at its south-western end.

Access

From Montpellier, head towards Carnon-Plage and turn off onto the D21 towards Palavas-les-Flots. There is a car park at the Cabanes de Carnon (1) from which the east end of the lagoon can be scanned. Avocet and Black-winged Stilt occur here in spring and summer. Take the towpath on foot as far as the hide (2). Greater Flamingos can be seen feeding on the Étang du Grec throughout the year. From the hide terns (including Caspian) are often visible especially in the spring, as are gulls (including Mediterranean and Slender-billed). Return to (1) and continue along the D62 to Palavas-les-Flots. The road can be busy, but there some places to stop. The Étang du Prévost is best accessed from its southern end, which means taking the D986/D185 to Villeneuve-les-Maguelone and then out to the coast and Maguelone abbey, where there is a car park. From here on access is only on foot. An island (3) sometimes appears in the lagoon, a good spot in spring for various waders and terns as well as, from time to time, Slender-billed Gull. Both the sea and the lagoon can be scanned from the dunes (4), and in winter there are concentrations of Great Crested and Black-necked Grebes to be seen. The saltmarsh (5) provides nesting sites for Kentish Plover, Oystercatcher and Avocet.

Calendar

Spring: Greater Flamingo, Little Egret, Oystercatcher, Grey Plover, godwits, small waders; Mediterranean and Slender-billed Gulls, Caspian, Sandwich, Common and Little Terns, Yellow Wagtail,

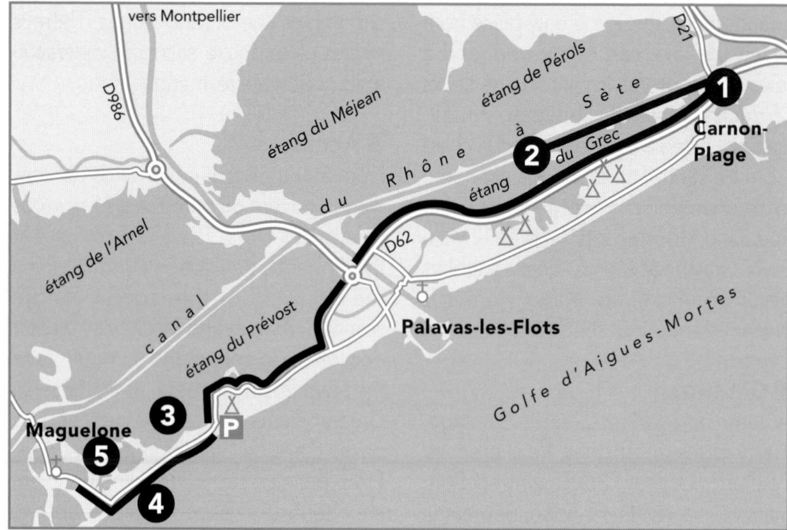

Fan-tailed Warbler, Crested Lark.
Autumn: herons, Marsh Harrier, Osprey, Black-winged Stilt, Dunlin, Black-headed and Mediterranean Gulls, terns, wagtails, chats and flycatchers.
Winter: Black-throated and Red-throated Divers, Great Crested and Black-necked Grebes, Cormorant, Greater Flamingo, Shelduck, Red-breasted Merganser, Avocet, Yellow-legged and Lesser Black-backed Gulls.

11. Causse d'Aumelas

HÉRAULT (34) *IGN 65*

The Causse d'Aumelas, west of Montpellier, is a large area of open garrigue with rocky outcrops, and meadows, scattered bushes, holm-oaks and burnt patches – typical Mediterranean scrubland with the characteristic bird species of such areas. In winter the resident species are joined by visitors from further north: Hen Harrier, Golden Eagle (occasionally Bonelli's Eagle), owls, thrushes, Sardinian Warbler, Southern Grey Shrike, and various finches. On migration it is possible to see Black Kite, Short-toed Eagle, Montagu's Harrier, Sparrowhawk, Hobby, Red-footed and Eleonora's Falcons. In summer, the breeding population includes Eagle and Scops Owls, Red-rumped Swallow, Bee-eater, Roller, Blue Rock and Rock Thrushes, Sardinian, Subalpine, Dartford, Orphean and Spectacled Warblers, Black-eared Wheatear, Tawny Pipit, Southern Grey and Woodchat Shrikes, Cirl and Ortolan Buntings and Rock Sparrow. From Montpellier, take the D5 south-west as far as Cournonterral. From here follow the D114 north-west towards Gignac, then turn left on the D114E which crosses the causse all the way to Cabrials, stopping at various places along the way.

12. Étang de Vendres

HÉRAULT (34)/AUDE (11) *IGN 65/72*

The Étang de Vendres, south of Béziers, covers an area of more than 1,800

NIGHT HERON

hectares of salt marsh, sansouire and reedbeds. The lake is on an important migration route and is one of the best places to watch visible migration in the Hérault. In winter there are Great White Egret, Bittern, many ducks, Hen Harrier and Merlin, and Spotted Eagle has been seen. There are also many waders and Bearded and Penduline Tits. In spring and in autumn migrants include Black and White Storks, Glossy Ibis, Purple, Squacco and Night Herons, Osprey, both kites, Honey Buzzard, various falcons (including Eleonora's), Black-winged Stilt, various *Tringa* waders, all three marsh terns, Little Gull, Great Spotted Cuckoo and various migrant insectivorous passerines. In summer breeding birds include Bittern and Little Bittern, Red-crested Pochard, Roller, Bee-eater, Scops Owl, Moustached and Great Reed Warblers. To get there, take the D64 from Béziers, crossing the A9 at exit 36, and follow signs to the village of Vendres. A track leads from the village to the eastern side of the lagoon and the remains of the Temple of Venus. The reeds and part of the lagoon can be viewed from a track that runs along this side of the lagoon as far as the sea; elsewhere views tend to be more distant.

13. Étang de Vic-la-Gardiole

HÉRAULT (34) *IGN 65*

This is another of the lagoons along the coast south of Montpellier. It is brackish and shallow and is separated from the sea by a line of sand-dunes and the Rhône-Sète canal. The most interesting part is near the village of Vic-la-Gardiole, where no shooting is allowed. In winter, among other species to be seen, are Greater Flamingo, Grey Heron, Little Egret, Shoveler, Pintail, Teal, Shelduck, Marsh Harrier and Water Pipit. In spring and autumn many migrants occur – herons, egrets, Cormorant, Redshank, Greenshank and Spotted Redshank, godwits, plovers, small waders, swifts, hirundines, wagtails and pipits. Finally, Avocet, Black-winged Stilt, Kentish Plover, Shelduck and Little Tern all breed. Vic-la-Gardiole is on the D114, off the N112 about halfway between Montpellier and Sète. The road continues to the coast, and the D116 to Villeneuve-les-Maguelone (see also site10 above) runs along the northern side of the lagoon.

14. Minerve

HÉRAULT (34) *IGN 65*

Minerve is a mediaeval Cathar town in the hilly country inland from Narbonne. It stands on a rocky promontory, with a river winding round it and is surrounded by splendid garrigue. Blue Rock Thrush, Rock Sparrow, Crag Martin, Red-rumped

Swallow, Raven and Alpine Swift all nest on the cliffs around the town, and in winter this is a known site for Alpine Accentor and Wallcreeper. In the spring migrant raptors such as Black Kite and Honey Buzzard move through the area, and Montagu's Harrier and Short-toed Eagle both breed nearby, along with the resident Sparrowhawk and Golden Eagle. Other breeding birds include Red-legged Partridge, Woodlark, Tawny Pipit, Stonechat, Black-eared Wheatear, Nightingale, Orphean, Sardinian, Dartford and Subalpine Warblers, Whitethroat, Cirl and Ortolan Buntings, and Southern Grey, Woodchat and Red-backed Shrikes. Minerve can be reached along minor roads north from the D5, halfway between Béziers and Carcassonne. Having walked round the town, take the D147 into the hills around Boisset, where the vegetation becomes taller, changing from low garrigue to high garrigue with oaks.

DARTFORD WARBLER

15. Parc National des Cévennes near Le Rozier

LOZÈRE (48) *IGN 58/59*

The Cévennes are the southernmost part of the Massif Central, dominated by wide open limestone plateaux, with an exceptionally rich flora (see also sites 6 and 8 above). To the north-east of Millau the Rivers Tarn and Jonte have cut into the limestone to form long winding gorges, providing secure nesting sites for many birds, raptors in particular. The gorges have provided one of the big conservation success stories of recent years with the reintroduction of Griffon and Black Vultures. For walkers the 1:25,000 IGN map 2640OT will be useful.

Access

From Millau take the N9 north to Aguessac, then the D908 to the village of Le Rozier, where the Tarn and Jonte gorges join. This is a good spot to leave the car (1) and start walking. From the village take the way-marked track that goes up onto the high ground between the two gorges, passing via the Rocher de Capluc, to the Rocher de Cinglegros (2). The path continues via La Bourgarie, onto the plateau via Volcegur, Cassagnes (3) and back to Le Rozier again. It is a strenuous route but all the viewpoints provide good opportunities for watching raptors drift along the cliff tops. Short-cuts are available at points (2) and (3) if you do not want to complete the full 16 km circuit. Griffon Vultures are omnipresent in good numbers, well over 200 these days, but you should have a reasonable chance of also seeing Black Vulture, as the number of pairs is now into double

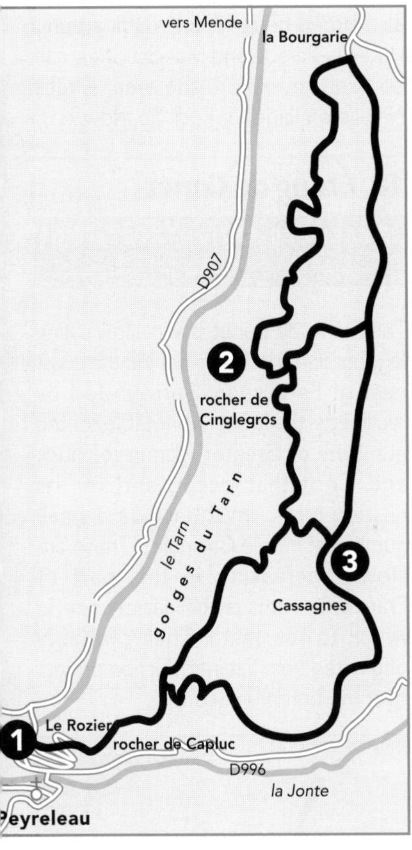

figures. Look out also for Egyptian Vulture, of which a few pairs have now re-established themselves 'naturally'. A good source of information is the Belvédère des Vautours veiwpoint and visitor centre (Tel: 05 65 62 69 69 / www.elvederedesvautours.fr), which is well-signposted and can be found a few kilometres east of Le Rozier by the D996. There is a lot more to the area than the vultures, of course. Golden Eagles also hunt along the gorges and over the adjacent causses, as do Honey Buzzard, Black and Red Kites and Montagu's Harrier. Choughs and Raven can be seen gliding in front of the cliffs. A visit at dusk in early spring may produce the sound of an Eagle Owl calling – several pairs nest along both the Jonte and Tarn gorges. Among passerines, typical Mediterranean species such as Blue Rock Thrush and Subalpine Warbler can be found along the tops of the cliffs, while birds of the open causse include Rock Thrush, Rock Sparrow and Ortolan Bunting. Hoopoes often use the old sheep-pens as nesting sites. Alpine Swifts and Crag Martin nest along the Tarn gorges, and in winter the cliffs are used by Wallcreeper and Alpine Accentor. (See also sites 3 and 4 in the chapter on Midi-Pyrénées.)

Calendar

All year: Griffon and Black Vultures, Golden Eagle, Goshawk, Sparrowhawk, Buzzard, Red Kite, Peregrine, Kestrel, Red-legged Partridge; Tawny, Barn, Eagle and Little Owls, Stock Dove, Raven, Chough and Jackdaw.

Spring: Egyptian Vulture, Short-toed Eagle, Black Kite, Osprey, Honey Buzzard, Montagu's Harrier, Peregrine, Scops Owl, Blue Rock and Rock Thrushes, Ring Ouzel, Subalpine Warbler.

Winter: Hen Harrier, Alpine Accentor, Wallcreeper and sometimes Snow Finch.

16. The River Tarn

Lozère (48) *IGN 58*

A good way of seeing the Gorges du Tarn, is to take the footpath that runs along the side of the Tarn from Les Vignes, to the north of Le Rozier (see previous site) through La Malène to Ste.-Enimie. In addition to the species mentioned above there are some waterside species, notably Dipper, Kingfisher, Grey Heron and Common Sandpiper, that breed here.

17. Causse Méjean

LOZÈRE (48) *IGN 58*

The Causse Méjean, between the Jonte and Tarn gorges, is a typical area of limestone plateau, with grassland, scattered bushes and conifer plantations, where most of the steppe-type birds can be found. Starting from the Belvédère des Vautours (see site 15 above), go east on the D996 to Le Truel, then turn left up onto the plateau at St.-Pierre-des-Tripiers and east to La Parade. The area here is more wooded, but birds like Bonelli's Warbler and Woodlark can be found. East of La Parade the landscape is more open, and favoured by species such as Stone Curlew, Tawny Pipit, Short-toed Lark, Skylark, Wheatear, Black-eared Wheatear (now rare), Rock Thrush, Rock Sparrow and Ortolan Bunting. Scop's Owl and Hoopoe also breed here. Minor roads around Hures-la-Parade and Mas-St.-Chély can be used to explore the area. Check Nivoliers village for Rock Sparrow.

18. Étang de Canet

PYRÉNÉES-ORIENTALES (66) *IGN 72*

The Étang de Canet is a shallow saline lagoon of 480 hectares behind the coast east of Perpignan. Surrounded by reedbeds, the lagoon is notable for the numbers of Greater Flamingo, duck and Coot that occur, and for its nesting birds, which include a small number of Purple Gallinules. These are slowly increasing in this part of France, but this is the easiest site in which to see them. They probably originated from a reintroduction project over the border in Spain

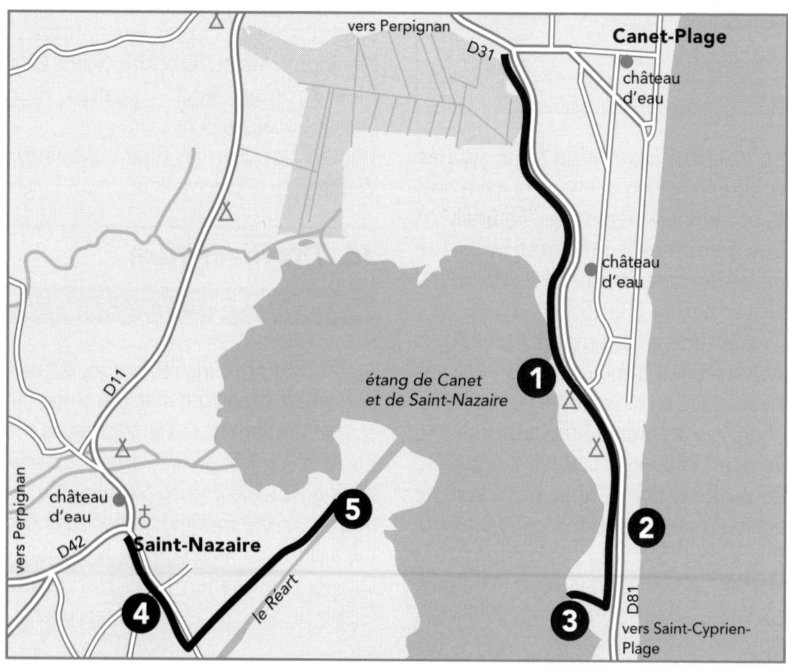

Access

From Perpignan, take the D611 towards Canet-en-Roussillon, then south along the D81 coast road towards St.-Cyprien-Plage. The road runs close to the lagoon, and it is possible to park (1), near the camp site. Greater Flamingos can be seen here for most of the year, with peak numbers at the end of the breeding season when they disperse from the Camargue and the Ebro delta. The reedbeds provide breeding sites for Reed, Savi's, Moustached and Sedge Warblers plus Penduline and Bearded Tits. Scan the shoreline opposite to locate Purple Gallinules along the edge of the reeds. Continue south for about 1 km (2). This is a good spot for looking out to sea. Mediterranean and Little Gulls and terns can be seen on migration, while Gannet, Balearic Shearwater and Razorbill occur in winter. 1 km further south, take a small track on the right (3). This is a good spot in winter to find Red-breasted Merganser, as well as Coot and grebes. Either via Alénya to the south or back via Canet-en-Roussillon to the north, take the D11 on the western side of the lagoon to reach the village of St.-Nazaire. South of the village, beyond the petrol station, take a surfaced track on the left (4). Continue on foot into the reserve area along the River Réart (5). Grey and Purple Herons, Little and Cattle Egrets can all be seen along the river. In spring, wader species sometimes include Marsh Sandpiper and Collared Pratincole is also seen regularly. Other spring migrants include larks, pipits (including Red-throated) and Blue-headed Wagtails. Note that the northern part is private, with no entry allowed.

Calendar

All year: Great Crested Grebe, Grey Heron, Little Egret, Bittern, Marsh Harrier, Greater Flamingo, Purple Gallinule, Coot and Water Rail.

Spring and autumn: Osprey, various waders including Sanderling, Knot, Curlew Sandpiper, Dunlin, Little Stint, Ruff, Curlew, Whimbrel, Redshank, Spotted Redshank, Greenshank, sometimes Collared Pratincole. Many passerines including Red-throated Pipit (April and May).

Summer: Purple Heron, Little Crake, Black-winged Stilt and Little Tern.

Winter: Black-necked Grebe, Great White and Cattle Egrets, Pintail, Mallard, Wigeon, Shoveler, Pochard, Tufted Duck, Red-breasted Merganser, Moustached Warbler, Bearded and Penduline Tits.

19. Villeneuve-de-la-Raho

Pyrénées-Orientales (66)
IGN 72

Lying to the south of Perpignan, this is an artificial reservoir split into three parts and is partially used for water sports. The most interesting, and the smallest, lies at the southern end of the site. This is the only section with woodland on the shore, and is an important roost site in winter for Cormorant and Cattle Egret. Although numbers have declined in recent years, the reservoir still attracts a large number of ducks in winter, Black-necked Grebe is regular at this time, and Black-throated Divers sometimes come in from the coast. In spring both Great Crested Grebe and Little Bittern breed here. Small waders, especially *Tringa* species, occur on the mudflats on the reserve during both autumn (July to October) and spring (April and May) migrations.

Access

Villeneuve-de-la-Raho lies south of Perpignan, off the N114. From the village follow the northern shore of the lake on the D39. Beyond the car park serving the water sports centre, take the first surfaced road to the left and continue to the 'réserve écologique' where there is a car park (1). Continue on foot to the embankment (2), just 1 km away, separating the main lake from the smaller reserve area. This is the best spot to watch from in the evenings when birds are coming in to roost, and also from where you have the best chance of seeing Little Bittern.

Calendar

Spring and autumn: herons, duck, kites, Honey Buzzard, harriers, falcons, Common and Wood Sandpipers, Ringed Plover, Hoopoe, Bee-eater, swifts, shrikes, leaf warblers and flycatchers.

Winter: Great Crested and Black-necked Grebes, Pintail, Shoveler, Teal, Red-crested Pochard, Pochard, Tufted Duck, Ferruginous Duck (rare).

20. Eyne

Pyrénées-Orientales (66)
IGN 71

Although less well-known than the

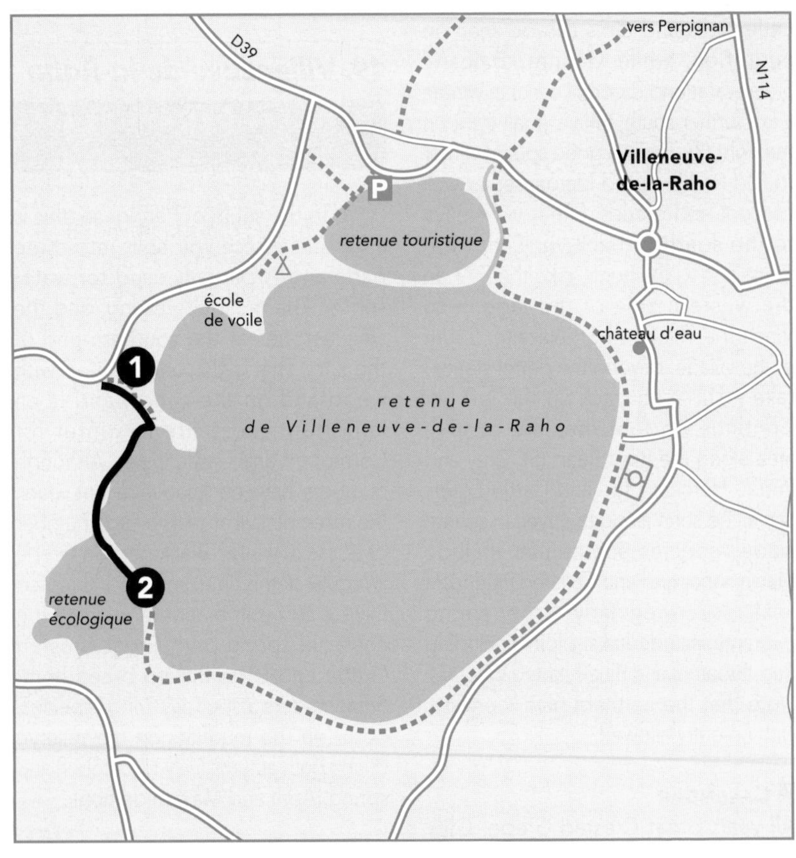

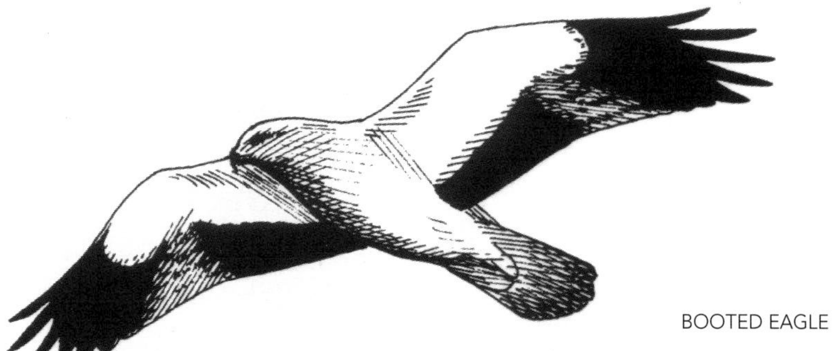
BOOTED EAGLE

migration watchpoints at the western end of the Pyrenees (see site 15 in the chapter on Aquitaine), the valley of the River Têt also channels large numbers of post-breeding migrants towards gaps in the chain, as at Eyne. The best time of year is August and September when the total numbers of birds passing through may be as high as 20,000. These include Black and White Storks, Black Kite, Sparrowhawk, falcons and three species of harrier. Honey Buzzard is usually the most numerous species, but it is also a significant site for seeing Short-toed Eagles, as the bulk of their population in France is in the east. Similarly, it is an excellent site in autumn for seeing flocks of Bee-eaters heading south. From Perpignan head west to Prades, then take the N116 through Montlouis towards Saillagouse. Before here, at the Col de la Perche pass, turn left on the D33 towards Eyne. Once here, turn right on the D29, the observation station being about 2 km beyond the village, on a low hillside, looking back towards the Têt valley to the north-east, the direction from which most birds come. To the south-west is a picturesque plateau with alternating meadows, cultivated fields, pine woods and poplar- and birch-lined streams. As well as looking for migrants overhead, this area is worth a walk, as Dotterel, another of the specialities of the area, sometimes stop in the meadows here.

21. Montescot/Corneilla del Vercol

PYRÉNÉES-ORIENTALES (66) *IGN 72*

The villages of Montescot and Corneilla del Vercol lie just to the south-east of Villeneuve-de-la-Raho (see site 19 above) and between them is a slightly saline depression, and meadowland. It is an important halt for migrants, either before or after crossing the Pyrenees. Species that can be expected to occur in spring or autumn include White Stork, Crane, Booted Eagle and Red Kite. In the summer, birds of the area include Stock Dove, Roller, and both Little and Scops Owls. In winter the fields attract various herons, Lapwing, Golden Plover, with Kingfisher along the streams and ditches. Corneilla del Vercol is on the N114 just north of Elne, and Montescot can be reached along the D80 which runs between the two villages. Either watch from the road or walk by the river that runs through the area, the Agouille de la Mar.

SITES

1 ***Tourbière du Longéroux***

2 ***Gorges de la Dordogne***

3 ***Étang des Landes***

4 ***Tourbière des Dauges***

Limousin

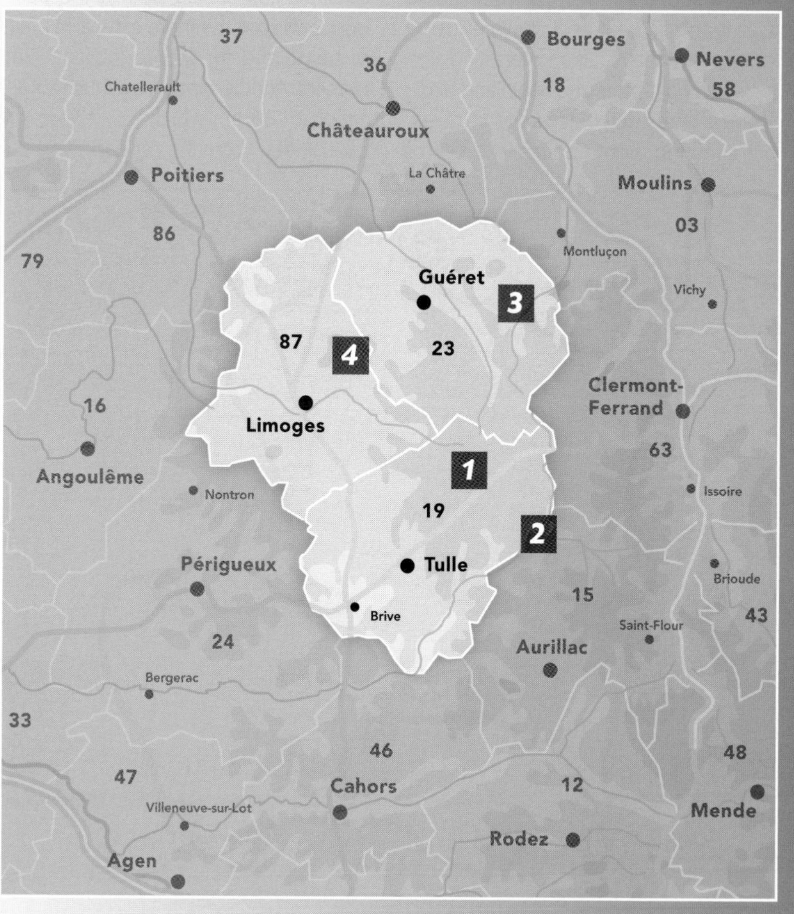

37
36
Bourges
Nevers
18
58
Chatellerault
Châteauroux
Poitiers
La Châtre
Moulins
86
03
79
Montluçon
Guéret
3
Vichy
87
4
23
Clermont-
Ferrand
16
Limoges
63
Angoulême
1
Nontron
Issoire
19
2
Périgueux
Tulle
Brioude
15
Brive
43
Saint-Flour
24
Aurillac
Bergerac
33
46
48
47
Cahors
12
Villeneuve-sur-Lot
Mende
Rodez
Agen

1. Tourbière du Longéroux

CORRÈZE (19) IGN 41/48

This site at Longéroux, protected by law, is a vast 255 hectare peat-bog on the southern edge of the Millevaches plateau, at an average altitude of 900 metres, with an underlying bedrock of granite. The surrounding granite hills, which were once covered by extensive areas of sheep-grazed heathland, are now largely planted with conifers. Nevertheless, numerous patches of heather-dominated moorland still persist, interspersed with a few meadows and crops. The reserve itself is an acid peat-bog, slowly evolving into a peaty heath. It is an interesting area for watching raptors and heathland birds. There is unrestricted access to the area, but camping, lighting fires, the use of vehicles off-road, and parking away from official car parks is forbidden.

ACCESS

The nearest autoroute to the area is the A89, running north-east from Tulle. If one leaves this at exit 23, one needs to take the D979 north-west towards Limoges through Meymac. About 9 km after this turn right towards Celle on the D109. A short way beyond this village one comes to a car park (1). From here there are various possibilities. The first is a 5 km round walk as far as Les Cent Pierres (2). Look for Whinchats in grassy areas on the side of the peat-bog, and scan the more extensive areas of heathland for Montagu's and Hen Harriers. Another option is a much longer circuit of 16 km which, if walked, will take all day. From the car park, take the

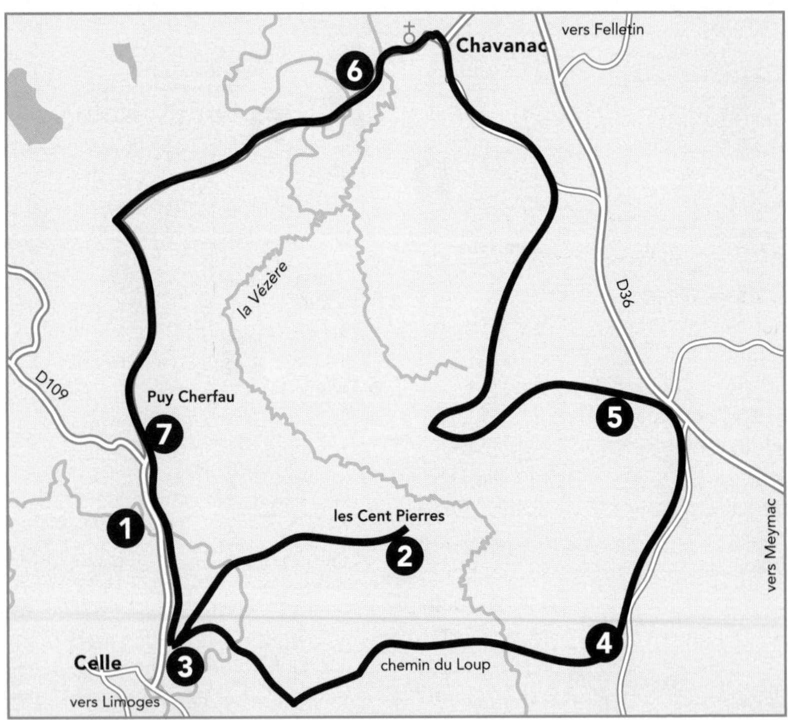

NIGHTJAR

forest track (3) which joins the Chemin du Loup, a forest road to the east side of the bog (4). Nightjars can often be heard giving their churring song at dusk, especially where there are clearings, while the conifers have Crested and Coal Tits, Goldcrest and sometimes Crossbill. The route now goes northwards for a few kilometres before joining the D36. Continue north-westwards on this for a little less than 1 km before taking the track (5) to the left towards Chavanac. Along the way it is possible to see Snipe, wherever there are wetter patches. At Chavanac village take the path that crosses the River Vézère (6). Look out for Dipper by the stream. The route then continues south-west to the D109 and back to the start of the circuit. Look out also for birds of prey circling over the higher ground of the Puy Cherfeau (7), especially on days when the breeze or the sun creates up-currents. Quail can sometimes be heard to the north of the car park and Tree Pipits are common in all the drier areas.

Calendar

Spring and early summer: Buzzard, Honey Buzzard, Goshawk, Sparrowhawk, Short-toed Eagle, Red Kite, Hen and Montagu's Harriers, Meadow and Tree Pipits, Whinchat, Linnet, Yellowhammer, Rock Bunting.

2. Gorges de la Dordogne

Corrèze (19) IGN 42/49

To the south of Bort-les-Orgues, the River Dordogne flows through a series of gorges, deeply enclosed, with slopes covered with hardwood and coniferous forest. Here and there are a few rocky slopes and patches of wooded heathland. The whole of the valley here, the boundary between the Limousin and Auvergne regions, is remarkably rich in birds (see also site 6 in the chapter on the Auvergne). There is a wide range of raptors to be found – Buzzard, Honey Buzzard, Red and Black Kites, Hen Harrier, Short-toed Eagle, Booted Eagle, Peregrine, Kestrel, Goshawk and Sparrowhawk; all breed in the area or not far away. There are also many passerines, including Rock Bunting, Dipper, House and Crag Martins and Redstart. Three sites are worthy of particular mention. First, there is an excellent viewpoint over both the Gorges de la Dordogne and those of the Diège at St.-Nazaire, perfect for raptors as well as heathland species. From Bort-les-Orges this site is accessible along minor roads west through Sarroux and St.-Julien-près-Bort. Second is the observation point further downstream at Gratte-Bruyère (see site 6 in chapter on Auvergne for details), another excellent site for raptors and also with a fine view over the valley. Finally, the Barrage de l'Aigle dam, further downstream again, near the village of Chalvignac, is another good site for watching raptors such as Red and Black Kites and Peregrine, while both House and Crag Martins nest on the dam itself.

ROCK BUNTING

3. *Étang des Landes*

CREUSE (23) *IGN 41/42*

The Étang des Landes is to be found in the north-east of the département of the Creuse, south-west of Montluçon, and lies in a hollow dating back to the Tertiary era. At an altitude of about 400 metres, this largely sand and clay sedimentary depression is characterised by its oceanic-type climate, modified by a continental influence which makes it less wet than might otherwise be expected (less than 800 mm of rainfall per year). Due to its geographical position the lake is important as a stopover site for migrant duck and waders. It also has some interesting breeding aquatic species. There are also some interesting mammals, including otter and wild cat, amphibians such as the great crested newt and the parsley frog, and some forty species of dragonfly.

In public ownership since 1995, this 120 hectare lake has recently become a Natura 2000 site, and should soon be classified as a réserve naturelle. Fishing is allowed in the northern part (it causes little disturbance), whereas hunting is totally banned.

Access

The nearest main road is the N145 between Guéret to the west and Montluçon to the north-east. Turn off this at Gouzon along the D915 east towards Lussat. After about 5 km, take the first road on the right signposted 'Genévrier' and 'Observatoire de l'Étang des Landes'. There is a car park near the lake, from which one can walk along the promontory put in place by 'Espaces Naturels du Limousin' and watch from the end (1). In March many ducks on migration can be seen out in the middle of the lake and the nearby meadows often have Crane, Lapwing and Blue-headed Wagtail at the same time, also feeding up on their way north. In the autumn and winter you have a good chance of seeing a Great White Egret, which is steadily increasing in much of France. The embankment on the far side of the lake, nearly 4 km away, can also be a good spot to watch from. Go back north to the D915 and turn right towards Lussat, continuing through the village and taking the first road on the right towards the lake (follow signs for 'Étang des Landes'). There is another car park here (2), and one can watch from the tracks which run both north and south from here. Various wetland warblers breed in large numbers wherever there are reedbeds and Marsh Harriers can be seen hunting throughout the year. The site is still under development as a reserve, and it may be that in future there will be other parts of the lake made accessible to visitors.

Calendar

Spring: Black-necked Grebe, Black Stork, Crane, Osprey, Marsh Harrier, Lapwing, Ruff, various other waders,

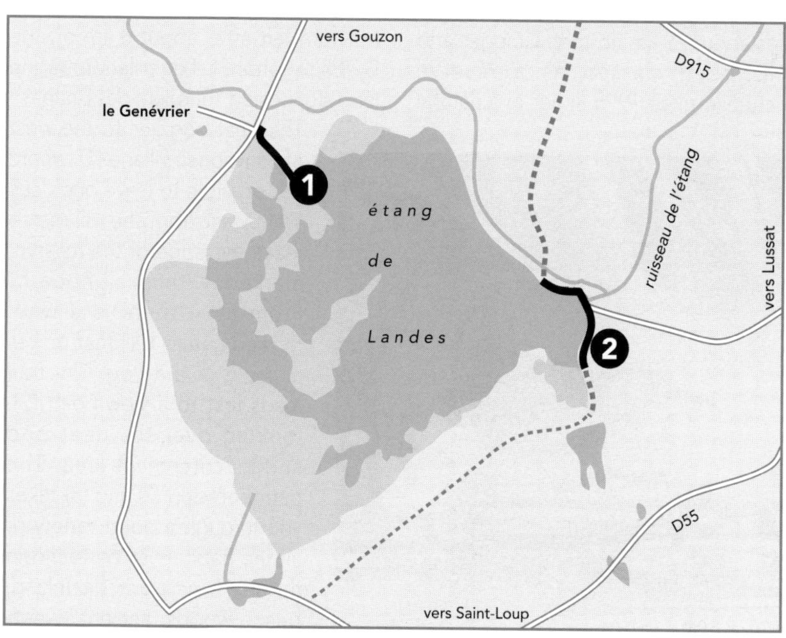

gulls (Black-headed and Yellow-legged), Common, Black and Whiskered Terns, Blue-headed Wagtail.

Breeding season: Little Grebe, Grey, Purple and Night Herons, Little Egret, Garganey, Teal, Gadwall, Shoveler, Pochard, Marsh Harrier, Water Rail, Lapwing, Black-headed Gull, Kingfisher, Grasshopper, Sedge and Reed Warblers and Reed Bunting.

Autumn and winter: Grebes (including Red-necked), Great White Egret, Shelduck, Mallard, Shoveler, Gadwall, Wigeon, Teal, Pochard, Tufted Duck, sometimes Eider, Velvet Scoter, Ferruginous Duck, Scaup or Goldeneye, Greylag Goose, Hen Harrier (sometimes in mixed roost with Marsh Harrier), Peregrine, Water Pipit and Reed Bunting.

4. Tourbière des Dauges

HAUTE-VIENNE (87) *IGN 41*

The Tourbière (or peat-bog) des Dauges lies about 25 km north of Limoges and has been classed as a réserve naturelle since 1998. It lies in a natural amphitheatre, flat at the bottom and is surrounded by rounded hills dominated by granite. Although nominally a peat-bog, the central area is quite small, and even that contains a hillock (the Puy Rond), which has scattered trees and some restored heathland. The slopes around the peat-bog itself are wooded, with a high proportion of deciduous trees, interspersed with some meadows and heathland. Because of this it is a good site for woodland species as well as for those associated with damper and heathland habitats. Access is unrestricted, but fires, camping and the use of vehicles (except those used locally for agriculture or forestry) is strictly forbidden.

WATER RAIL

■ ACCESS

From Limoges take the A20 north as far as exit 26, and then the D5 to Ambazac. From here turn left on the D914 towards La Jonchère and Laurière, but turn left after about 6 km on the D28A towards St.-Léger-la-Montagne (also signposted Tourbière des Dauges).

The peat-bog lies to the west of Sauvagnac village (1), where it is possible to leave one's car. Walk west from the village to reach the edge of the reserve, marked with a signboard. From here there is a way-marked nature trail that makes a circuit of the bog. The trail leads first to a view-point (2), looking over the peat-bog and its catchment area. The path between (2) and (3) takes you through a good variety of all the habitats to be found in the area – meadows, heathland, beech woods, ancient sweet-chestnut woods – each with its own specific species. Look out particularly for Black Woodpecker and Bonelli's Warbler in the wooded areas. From (3) you get a good view of the peat-bog habitat itself, and of the Puy Rond hill out in the middle. Continue towards (4), across the main catchment area of the reserve, close to the underlying peat, where waterproof footwear may well be needed. Either return the same way, or continue if suitably shod. This is a good area for Tree Pipits and Linnets. At the Bois du Rocher (5) it is possible to make a circular detour through the woodland, dominated by beech trees, and a good spot for Wood Warbler and Song Thrush. The main trail then continues in a circuit back to the starting point, about 4 km in all.

Calendar

Spring and summer: Buzzard, Honey Buzzard, Goshawk, Sparrowhawk, Woodcock, Nightjar, Black Woodpecker; Tree and Meadow Pipits, Stonechat, Willow, Wood and Bonelli's Warblers, Chiffchaff, Linnet, Bullfinch, Rock Bunting, Yellowhammer.
Winter: Snipe, Fieldfare, Redwing, Reed Bunting.

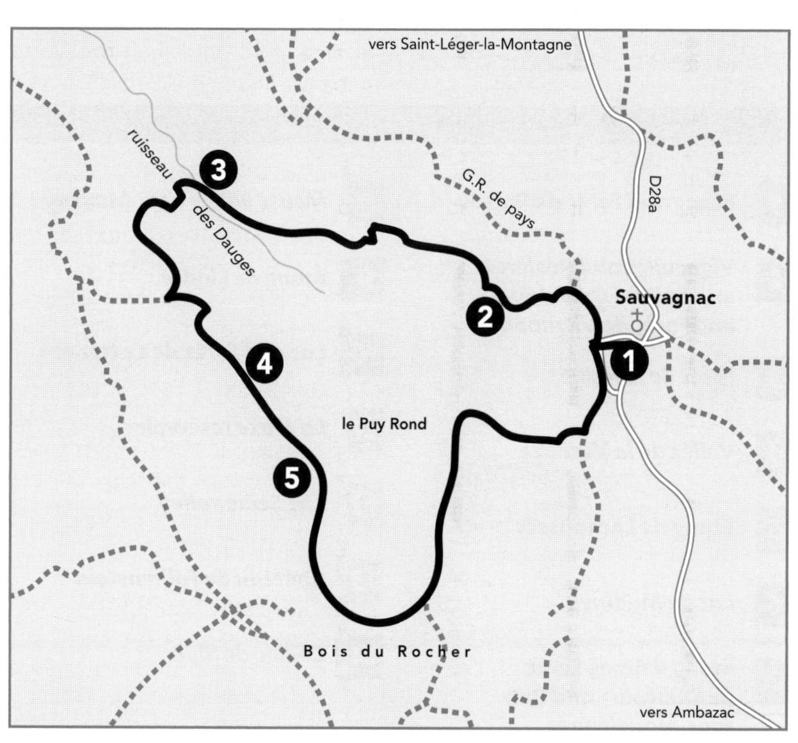

SITES

1. Étang and Forêt de Parroy
2. Vigneulles and Rosières-aux-Salines gravel-pits and Forêt de Vitrimont
3. Forêt de la Reine
4. Vallée de la Vezouze
5. Étang de Lachaussée
6. Lac de Madine
7. Étang d'Amel, Forêt de Spincourt and Billy-sous-Mangiennes
8. Meuse valley near Mouzay
9. Étang de Lindre
10. Lac and Forêt de Cattenom
11. La Maxe reservoir
12. The Seille valley
13. Château de Falkenstein
14. Colline de Sion

Lorraine

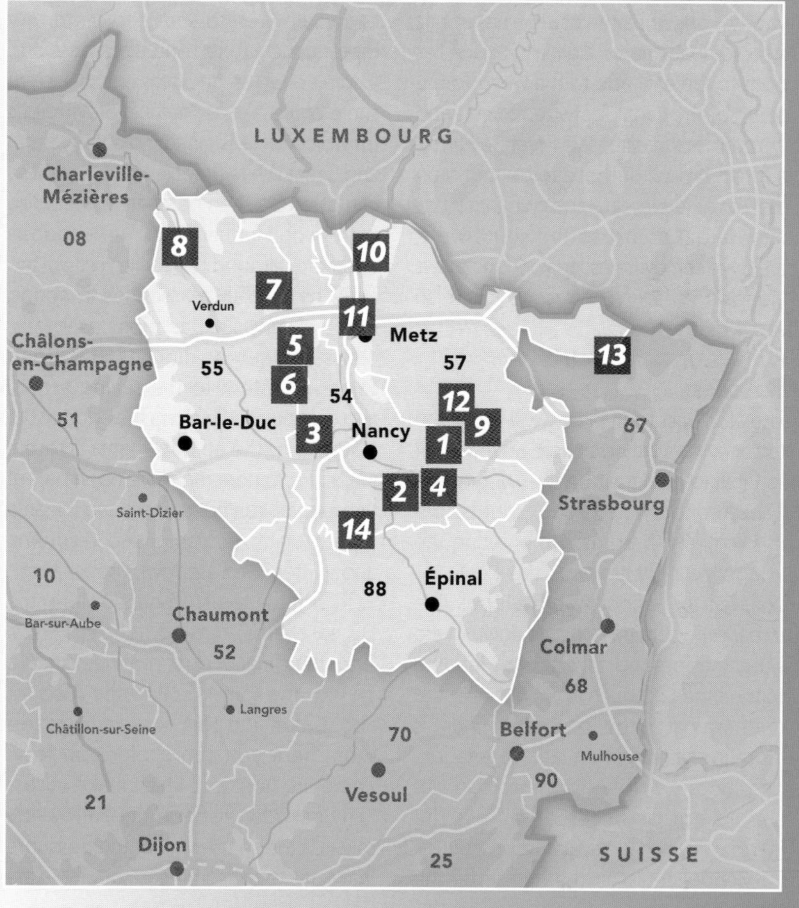

LUXEMBOURG
Charleville-Mézières
08
8
10
7
Verdun
11
Metz
Châlons-en-Champagne
5
55
57
13
6
54
12
51
Bar-le-Duc
3
Nancy
9
67
1
2
4
Strasbourg
Saint-Dizier
14
10
Épinal
88
Bar-sur-Aube
Chaumont
Colmar
52
68
Langres
Châtillon-sur-Seine
70
Belfort
Mulhouse
90
21
Vesoul
Dijon
25
SUISSE

1. Étang and Forêt de Parroy

MEURTHE-ET-MOSELLE (54)
IGN 11

Both the lake and the forest are found on the Lorraine plateau, 25 km to the east of Nancy and just to the north-east of Lunéville. The lake is a reservoir for the Marne-Rhine canal which runs between it and the forest, and which has been widened where it passes the lake. The reservoir's water level is often very low in summer. The northern part of the lake has been invaded by aquatic vegetation, while the southern part has steep embankments. Agricultural land lies both to the east and to the west. To the south of the canal, between Sânon and Vezouze, is the extensive Forêt de Parroy, a forest typical of those to be found on the Lorraine plateau, and dominated by mature oaks. Just to the south-west, there are some interesting flood meadows alongside the River Vezouze (see also site 4 below).

ACCESS

The N33 east from Nancy will bring you to Lunéville. Turn north here on the D914 to Einville then east on the D2 through Bauzemont towards Parroy, but before this turn left to Bures. On entering the village go right towards the École de Voile (sailing school) where it is possible to park (1). Continue on foot down to the water's edge and take a path leading to the hide (2), which looks out over the northern part of the lake where there is more in the way of aquatic vegetation. The hide is visible from the road but should not be accessed across the meadow, which is private property. Look for Penduline Tit in the hedge by the path to the hide in April, and for thrushes and Blackbird in October. Great Reed, Reed and Sedge Warblers are found in the reedbeds in spring, with Marsh Warbler in the drier vegetation towards the back of the inlets. Little Bittern and Marsh Harrier breed each year, and rarer visitors include Purple Heron and Bittern. At the end of summer, when the water level drops and extensive areas of mud are exposed, this is a good spot for checking through the waders which stop off on passage. The pools that have been created in the reedbeds, close to the hide, attract Garganey, Teal, Spotted Crake, Water Rail, Snipe and Kingfisher, especially in late summer. Migratory raptors, such as Red and Black Kites and Osprey, often use the trees on the eastern shore of the lake as perches. Grey Herons (of which there is a nesting colony here) and Great White Egret (an autumn visitor) can often be seen perched at the edge of the wood further north. The meadows and fields around the sailing school are used by migrant passerines in spring and autumn, such as pipits, wagtails, chats, Wheatear, finches and Reed Bunting. Return to the sailing school and continue south along the edge of the reservoir to the embankment (3) to the south. From here the more open part of the reservoir can be scanned, and this area is particularly recommended in autumn and winter, for waterfowl, grebes, etc.

To visit the forest, continue along the D2 eastwards, turning right in Parroy. After the canal bridge, continue straight on into the forest. Follow the road for about 2 km and park near a crossroads. From here you can explore on foot. There are rides cut which make access fairly easy, for instance the Parroy ride towards the south-west or the Bossupré that goes to the south-east, but there are other forest tracks throughout (take care not to get lost – IGN 3515O, 1:25,000 may be useful). Six species of woodpecker nest in the woodland, including Black, Middle Spotted and Grey-headed, and are best looked for early in the year. This is also the best time for Goshawk – look for them displaying above the forest during the first fine days of late winter (late February and March). Both species of treecreeper are resident, allowing for useful comparison of their songs and calls. Among summer visitors, Collared Flycatcher can be found in areas of mature oaks, between late April and late June. Honey Buzzard breeds and can be seen from May to August. It is an area where Black Storks have been seen in summer, but locating them is never easy.

Calendar

Spring migration: Black-necked Grebe, Purple Heron, Red Kite, Osprey, Crane, Redshank, Ruff, Little Gull, Common, Black and Whiskered (rare) Terns, Whinchat, Penduline Tit.

Breeding season: Great Crested Grebe, Little Bittern, Black Stork (rare), Gadwall, Honey Buzzard, Goshawk, Marsh and Montagu's Harriers, Black Kite, Hobby, Water Rail, Corncrake (rare), Lapwing, Curlew, woodpeckers (six species), Wryneck, Meadow Pipit, Stonechat, Whinchat, Grasshopper, Savi's (rare), Great Reed, Reed, Marsh and Sedge Warblers, Lesser Whitethroat, Collared Flycatcher, Common and Short-toed Treecreepers, Red-backed Shrike and Golden Oriole.

Late summer and autumn: Red Kite, Osprey, Peregrine, Merlin, Crane, Lapwing, Ringed, Grey and Golden Plovers, small waders including Snipe and Jack Snipe. Black Tern, Skylark, Meadow and Water Pipits, Blue-headed Wagtail, thrushes, Wheatear and Penduline Tit.

Winter: Great Crested and Red-necked (rare) Grebes, Mallard, Teal, Tufted Duck and Pochard, Goldeneye, Goosander and Hen Harrier.

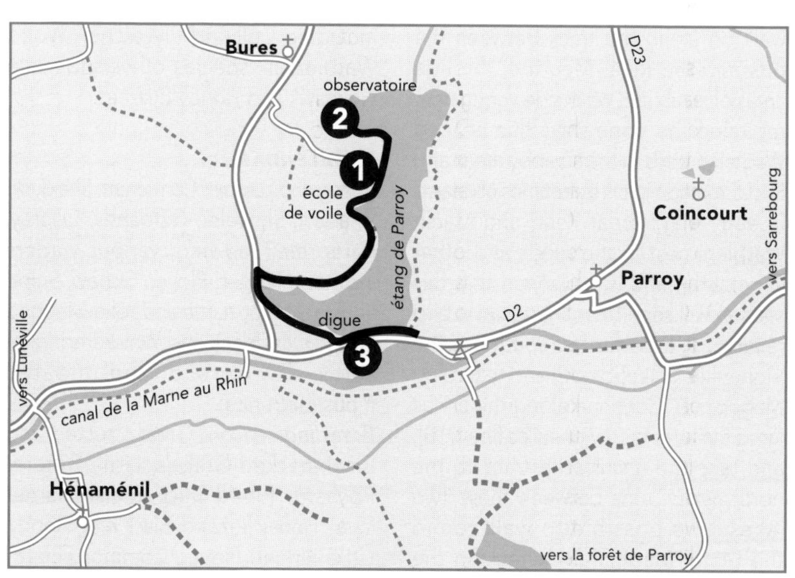

2. *Vigneulles and Rosières-aux-Salines gravel-pits and Forêt de Vitrimont*

MEURTHE-ET-MOSELLE (54)
IGN 11/23

Lying in the Meurthe valley between Lunéville and Nancy are a series of gravel-pits, some old, some new, and despite constant changes of habitat they are always of interest for birds. Across the river is the Forêt de Vitrimont, which adds some contrast to the day's birdwatching.

ACCESS

From Nancy, take the A33 towards Lunéville and leave at exit 5 to join the D1 at Rosières-aux-Salines in the direction of Damelevières. A track off the D1 will bring you to the Rosières gravel-pit (1); take care as the gravel workings are still active. Take this track as far as the River Meurthe and follow its bank for about 250 metres to where it is possible to park just beyond an overhead inflow pipe to the pits. One can walk on along the track between the pits and the River Meurthe, through areas of scrub and waterside vegetation, returning the same way. Blue-headed Wagtail breeds in the scrubby areas and Red-throated Pipit is sometimes observed in early May. Great Reed and Marsh Warblers nest in the reeds and other vegetation, and it is planned that this section will soon be managed as a bird reserve. A little further south are the Vigneulles gravel-pits (2) and the Étang Maginal (3). Continue along the D1 as far as the turning to Vigneulles (the D1B), and take the unsurfaced track to the north, which runs between these two lakes. It is possible to walk round the Étang Maginal (3), checking the small islands for Little Bittern, which breed on them. The Vigneulles pit (2) is the largest one and is the best one for duck in winter, and for gulls and terns in spring. Marsh, Great Reed and sometimes Savi's Warblers breed here, as does Penduline Tit. During migration periods any of the pits or the flooded meadows in the area are worth checking for waders. The settling beds area (4) has Curlew throughout the year (up to 150 roosting together) and a Black-headed Gull colony, with a few Mediterranean and Common Gulls and Common Tern. Access onto this private part of the industrial site is strictly prohibited, but the birds can usually also be seen on the accessible lakes or in the surrounding meadows.

The nearby Forêt de Vitrimont (5) is on the opposite side of the River Meurthe. To get there, continue on the D1 to Damelevières and turn left on the D1D (Route des Sables) across the river towards Dombasle-sur-Meuthe. Various tracks run from this road into the forest, which has similar species to those of the Forêt de Parroy (previous site), including Collared Flycatcher, Wood Warbler, six species of woodpecker, Goshawk and Honey Buzzard.

CALENDAR

Spring and autumn: Cormorant, Shelduck, Wigeon, Shoveler, Garganey, Osprey, Peregrine, Lapwing, various waders including Ringed Plover, Curlew, Snipe and Jack Snipe, Little and Yellow-legged (rare) Gulls, Black and Whiskered (rare) Terns, Tawny and Red-throated Pipits (both rare).

Breeding season: Great Crested and Black-necked Grebes, Little Bittern, Pochard, Tufted Duck, Marsh Harrier (rare), Honey Buzzard, Black Kite, Hobby, Little Ringed Plover, Common, Black-

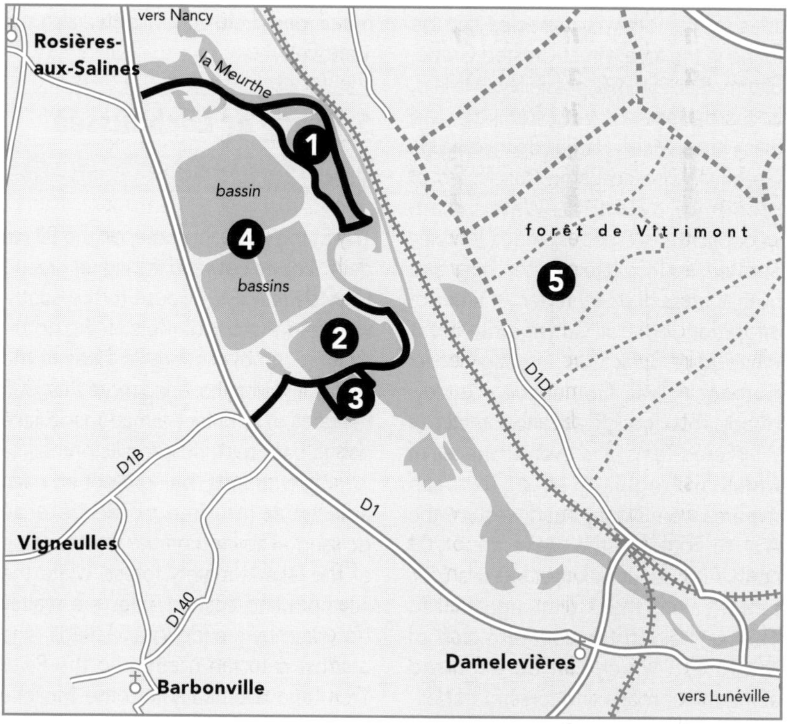

GREAT REED WARBLER

headed and Mediterranean (rare) Gulls, Common Tern, six species of woodpecker, Blue-headed Wagtail, Great Reed, Marsh, Grasshopper and Savi's (rare) Warblers, Collared Flycatcher, Penduline Tit.
Winter: Goosander, Smew, Goldeneye, Curlew.

3. Forêt de la Reine

MEURTHE-ET-MOSELLE (54)
IGN 11

The Forêt de la Reine is situated on the southern part of the Plaine de la Woëvre, some 15 km north-west of Toul, and, together with a series of adjoining forests, forms a large woodland area, dominated by oaks, and still used actively for forestry purposes. The forest contains a good number of lakes, around 15 in all, which are used for fish-farming, of which the Étang Romé is the largest. In addition to the woodland and water, the surrounding farmland consists of both arable fields and grazed meadows, and this mixture of habitats is very attractive for a wide variety of birds, particularly raptors. During the breeding season the following species can be found in the area: Great Crested Grebe, Bittern, Black Stork (a possibility), Mallard, Pochard, Honey Buzzard, Red (rare) and Black Kites, Marsh Harrier, Sparrowhawk, Goshawk, Booted Eagle (suspected of breeding), Hobby, Water Rail, woodpeckers (six species), Wood Warbler, Spotted and Collared Flycatchers and both species of treecreeper. At times of migration look for Cormorant, Great White Egret, Black Stork, Greylag Goose, Garganey, Teal, Goldeneye, Osprey, Hobby, Woodcock, Black and sometimes Whiskered Terns, and even Crane, all of which are regularly seen. To reach the area from Nancy head west on the A31 to Toul and then take the D904 north. After about 13 km, at Ménil-la-Tour, turn left along the D10 through Sanzey. This runs along the southern side of the forest, which can be explored along minor roads and forestry tracks.

4. *Vallée de la Vezouze*

MEURTHE-ET-MOSELLE (54) *IGN 23*

The River Vezouze is a tributary of the Meuthe which it joins at Lunéville, and the section immediately upstream from there as far as Marainviller is of particular interest. The best spots for birdwatching are between Jolivet and Chanteheux, between Chanteheux cemetery and Croismare, and at Marainviller. The most characteristic breeding species is the Curlew, but the Corncrake breeds occasionally, and both Marsh Warbler and Whinchat breed commonly. During the spring floods, in March and April, Redshank and Ruff occur in the meadows, often accompanied by rarer species. Explore the area along minor roads from Lunéville (see also site 1 above).

5. *Étang de Lachaussée*

MEUSE (55) *IGN 11*

The Étang de Lachaussée, on the Plaine de la Woëvre between the higher ground towards the River Meuse to the south-west and the city of Metz to the north-east, is one of the largest lakes in the Lorraine region, covering more than 300 hectares. It is in fact a man-made lake dating back centuries, and its prime use is for fish-farming, being emptied each autumn at the time of the 'fête du poisson'. The land on the western side of the lake is mainly forest, while the northern and eastern sides are mainly occupied by meadows and fields. The outflow is to the north, into the River Yron, and eventually into the Moselle to the north of Metz. Currently the site does not benefit from any measure of protection and is used for wildfowling in the autumn and winter. In addition, because of the fishing, forest and farming activities of the area, access is to a certain extent restricted.

■ ACCESS

The A4 between Metz and Verdun runs to the north of the area. From exit 32, take the D908 to Fresne-en-Woëvre then the D904 for about 19 km as far as St.-Benoît-en-Woëvre. Turn left here on the D901, and after about 3 km left again on the D131 through Haumont as far as Lachaussée. The D904 north from Toul or the D903/D952 from Metz will also bring you to the area. In Lachaussée, park near the church and walk to the 'Vieux Moulin' estate (private but access is allowed). You can get an overview of the site from the lake's embankment (1), and a hide here is useful in bad weather. This is the best place for watching aquatic birds, especially in spring. It is also possible to walk from the village along the northern side of the lake as far as the forest (2), a 3 km walk there and back. For further exploration of the forest, return via St.-Benoît-en-Woëvre to the D904 and drive north to a maison forestière (forester's house) (3). From here one can walk east along a forestry track as far as the farm at Francheville (4), though access beyond here is not allowed. It is about a 7 km walk there and back. The lake can be observed from just before the farm, and woodland birds looked for from the track. May is the best month for seeing such summer visitors to the forest as Collared Flycatcher or Golden Oriole whereas a visit earlier in the spring will be better for the two species of treecreeper, or for any of the woodpeckers.

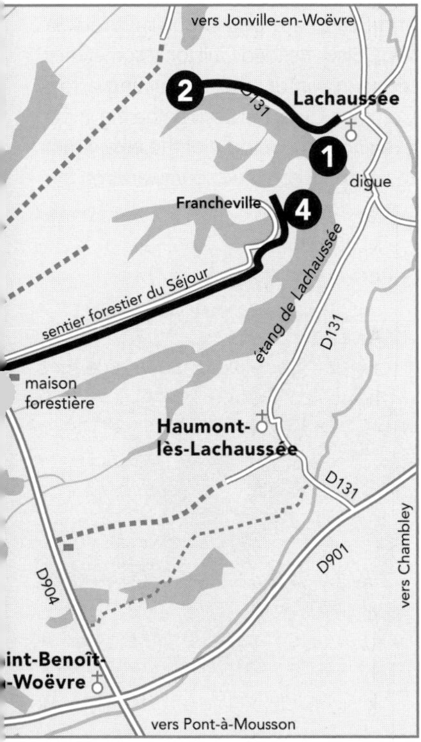

Calendar

Spring: Red Kite, Osprey, Crane, Black Tern, Blue-headed Wagtail, Red-throated Pipit (rare).
Breeding season: Bittern (best site in Lorraine), Little Bittern, Purple Heron, White (occasionally) and Black (rare) Storks, Garganey, Honey Buzzard, Black Kite, Goshawk, Marsh Harrier, Hobby, Crane (rare), Spotted and Little Crakes (both rare), Middle Spotted Woodpecker, Kingfisher, Grey Wagtail, Sedge and Savi's (rare) Warblers, Collared Flycatcher, Common and Short-toed Treecreepers, Golden Oriole.
Autumn (especially whilst the lake is emptied): Cormorant, Great White Egret, Grey Heron, Bewick's Swan, Greylag Goose, Pintail, Red Kite, White-tailed Eagle (rare), Goshawk, Merlin, Peregrine, Crane (roost of hundreds), Lapwing (thousands), Snipe, various waders including Grey and Golden Plovers, Black-headed Gull (hundreds), Woodpigeon, Fieldfare, Redwing, Siskin.
Winter: Bittern, Goldeneye, Goosander, Smew, Hen Harrier, Crane (hundreds), Water Pipit, Great Grey Shrike.

6. Lac de Madine

Meuse/ (55)
Meurthe-et-Moselle (54)
IGN 11

The Lac de Madine is a recently-built reservoir, created by damming a tributary of the Rupt de Mad river, in order to provide water for the city of Metz. It is situated on the Plaine de la Woëvre at the foot of the higher ground sheltering the Meuse valley to the west. It lies at an altitude of 227 metres and with more than 40 km of shoreline it is the biggest lake in Lorraine. When it was built it flooded a region of farmland and forests, some of which still border most of the southern shore. It has embankments on its northern side, whilst there are some large open fields and meadows on the western side, with higher wooded ground to the west again. The lake has two islands: the smaller Île Verte, opposite Heudicourt, and the larger Île du Bois Gerard in the centre. It is a very important site for water birds, particularly as shooting is not allowed at the lake. It is also of tourist importance, with two leisure centres, one at Heudicourt to the west and the other at Nonsard to the east. A public cycle track goes around the whole lake, making it very accessible to all.

Access

The Lac de Madine lies some 20 km to the west of Pont-à-Mousson, which is halfway between Metz and Nancy. From there take the D958 as far as Flirey, then right along the D904 as far as Pannes. Turn left here along the D133 through Nonsard to get to Heudicourt. In the centre of the village take what was the old road to Nonsard and which now goes to the lake. At the first intersection, turn right and park in the car park on the lakeside. From here one can walk to a small lake (1) where, in spring and autumn, waders, marsh terns and gulls can be watched from the embankment. To view the main lake, walk to the end of the Pointe aux Chênes peninsula (2), the best spot site from which to scan the northern and central part of the water surface, although a telescope is essential. In winter there are large flocks of dabbling duck to be seen, along with Pochard, Tufted Duck, Goldeneye, Goosander and Smew. Both Velvet Scoter and Scaup are also regular visitors. A large Black-headed Gull roost sometimes forms in winter, also containing a few Common Gulls, the birds gathering in the evening in the middle of the lake. From the car park continue southwards on the

HEN HARRIER

embankment to a second smaller lagoon (3) which is also worth checking. In August and September, when the water level drops to expose bare mud, many different waders can be seen here. Check also for Water Rail and Spotted Crake, and even the rare Little Crake has been recorded. The path skirts the forest for a time before reaching a third lagoon (4). In spring, Great Reed, Reed and Sedge Warblers are easy to find here. Listen out in summer for Penduline Tit, often located by their characteristic call. Cross the embankment and walk into the woodland of the Bois de la Sorbière – areas of mature oak here attract Collared Flycatcher in May and June, whilst Middle Spotted Woodpeckers are resident. After crossing through the wood the path arrives at the fourth embankment which cuts off the inlet of Nouettes (5). Depending on how energetic you are feeling, you can continue as far as the Madine inlet (6) and then out north-eastwards along a peninsula to look across at the southern end of the large island (7) of Bois Gérard.

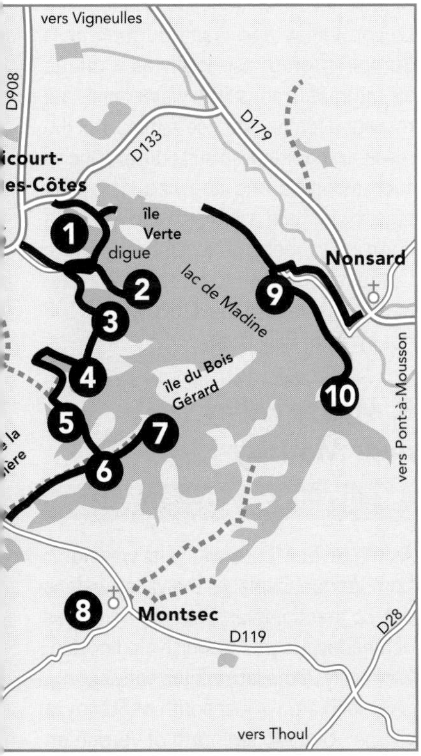

It is also worth visiting the Butte du Montsec (8), where there is a large war memorial, with plenty of parking, on a hilltop from which you get a wonderful view over the lake and the whole of the surrounding area. From Nonsard village one can drive to the port (9) and the Marmont embankment (10), near the outlet, this part of the lake being a good area for divers, grebes and diving duck, as well as being another viewpoint from which to look across at the Île du Bois Gérard. In winter the island is a favourite haunt of flocks of Greylag Geese, sometimes accompanied by a few Bean Geese. The isolated poplar wood in the centre of the island is a favourite resting spot for White-tailed Eagle, another occasional winter visitor.

Calendar

Spring: Wigeon, Shoveler, Pintail, Garganey, Crane, Common, Black (occasionally White-winged Black or Whiskered) Terns, Little Gull, Blue-headed Wagtail.

Breeding season: Grey Heron, Gadwall, Goldeneye (rare), Black Kite, Goshawk, Sparrowhawk, Marsh Harrier, Hobby, Water Rail, Black, Lesser Spotted and Middle Spotted Woodpeckers, Great Reed, Sedge and Grasshopper Warblers, Lesser Whitethroat, Collared Flycatcher and Penduline Tit.

Late summer and autumn: Great White Egret, Osprey, Peregrine, Spotted and Little (rare) Crakes, Crane, various small waders, Penduline Tit.

Winter: Great Crested Grebe, sometimes Slavonian and Red-necked Grebes, divers, Greylag Goose, many dabbling and diving duck, Goosander, Smew, White-tailed Eagle (rare), Hen Harrier, Crane, Common and Black-headed Gulls, Great Grey Shrike.

7. Étang d'Amel, Forêt de Spincourt and Billy-sous-Mangiennes

MEUSE (55) *IGN 11*

WHITE-TAILED EAGLE

These three sites lie close together in the northern part of the Plaine de la Woëvre some 15 km to the north-east of Verdun, and are well worth a visit. To reach the area from Verdun take the N3 for 20 km east to Etain then the N18 north for 7 km and then left through the village of Senon to reach the Étang d'Amel. This has recently been purchased by a conservation body (Conservatoire des Sites Lorrains) whose management plans include non-intensive fish-farming. Although the embankment is closed to the public, there is a public hide on the western side of the lake. The following species occur in the breeding season: Bittern, White Stork, Greylag Goose (rare), Teal, Gadwall, Marsh Harrier, Crane (rare), Water Rail and Great Reed and Marsh Warblers while during migration periods look out for Great White Egret, Black Stork, Osprey, Hen Harrier, Merlin, Snipe and Jack Snipe. The Forêt de Spincourt lies just north and west of the lake, and is a site for Middle Spotted Woodpecker (resident) and Collared Flycatcher (May to August), amongst other woodland birds. North again, the site at Billy-sous-Mangiennes is on agricultural land in the Loison valley and was bought with a European grant especially as a refuge for migrant Cranes. The water levels are managed for this purpose in mind, but the resulting habitat also suits other species such as Snipe and Lapwing. The best time to visit here is in March and April and again in October and November when the Cranes are on the move. There is a hide at the west end of the site, by the D105 not far from Billy itself.

8. Meuse valley near Mouzay

MEUSE (55) *IGN 10*

As the River Meuse winds its way north from Verdun, in places the valley widens out, so that the river flows through areas of meadows, some of which are flooded, especially in the late winter/early spring. One such area is just south of Stenay, a village about 45 km north of Verdun on the D964 to Sedan. The most productive part is the area known as the 'Grande Prairie', lying between the River Meuse and the canal de Mouzay to the north, and the village of Sassey-sur-Meuse to the south. The latter is accessible from the D964 via the D30. During the breeding season many species typical of low-lying hay meadows can be found here, such as Lapwing, Curlew, Quail, Corncrake, Meadow Pipit, Blue-headed Wagtail, Whinchat and Corn Bunting. There are some sand-pits near the river where Great Grey Shrike has been seen. As the valley lies on a north-south axis, it is an important corridor for migrants. There can be some spectacular concentrations of migrants here in February and March, and again in October and November, especially when the Meuse is in flood – look for Great White Egret, Black and White Storks, Greylag Goose, Wigeon, Pintail, Shoveler, Garganey, Osprey, Lapwing (thousands), Crane (hundreds), Golden Plover, Ruff, Black-tailed Godwit and other waders at such times. Unfortunately the area is unprotected, and intensively shot over during the hunting season, so that migrants are often disturbed, and also the chances of species such as Curlew establishing themselves as breeding species have been reduced.

9. *Étang de Lindre*

MOSELLE (57) *IGN 12*

The Étang de Lindre is a long-established lake, dating back to the Middle Ages, that was created by damming the River Seille near Dieuze, which is about 40 km north-east of Nancy. It is just one of a myriad of lakes in the woodland that lies on the Lorraine plateau (altitude 210 metres), protected as part of the Parc Naturel Régional de Lorraine. In fact it is the second largest body of water in Lorraine, and probably (and justifiably) the best known for birds. The lake is used for fish-farming, which involves its being emptied for two months in late autumn, the resulting mudflats providing excellent feeding habitat for waders before the lake fills up again for the winter. It is enclosed by two national forests – St.-Jean to the west and Romersberg to the east, adding to the variety of birds to be found, and the whole area is very much being developed with green tourism in mind.

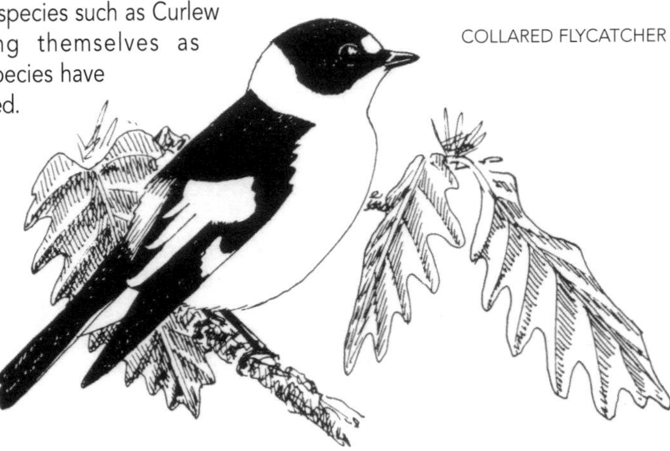

COLLARED FLYCATCHER

■ ACCESS

The lake is about 45 minutes by road from Nancy, taking first the N74 to Moyenvic and then the D38 as far as Dieuze. Once at the lake, there are many options available. If time is limited, the north-west corner of the lake is a good place to start. From Dieuze take the D999 south, and then turn left on the DI99E to Lindre-Basse. Continue through the village to the edge of the lake, where it is possible to park. Continue on foot to the lake's embankment (1), from which you get a good general view. There are some captive White Storks in this area, part of a breeding and rescue project, but there are also truly wild birds to be seen as well. Look for Kingfishers along the lakeside, and near the fish-farm. In autumn scan the shore for Great White Egrets, while once the lake starts to refill this is a good spot from which to look for divers, grebes and diving ducks in winter. Continue along the embankment and then a track, skirting the fish-farm, to reach a hide (2). If you have time, the track continues all the way to Tarquimpol village (3). A new hide (4) is planned to enable the north side of the lake to be scanned more easily. To explore the south-west part of the area, leave Dieuze southwards on the D999 towards Gelucourt. The road passes through the Forêt de St.-Jean, where both Collared Flycatcher and Middle Spotted Woodpecker breed. Forestry tracks allow access to the woodland here. On leaving the forest turn left towards Tarquimpol, which occupies the foot of a peninsula sticking out into the middle of the lake. Leave the car here (3), and continue on foot along a track that does a circuit of the peninsula, giving excellent views over much of the water surface, including the 'arms' that run up to Assenoncourt and Guermange to the east. White Storks nest in and around the village itself (please respect private property when watching) and the peninsula is used by Cranes on migration and sometimes as

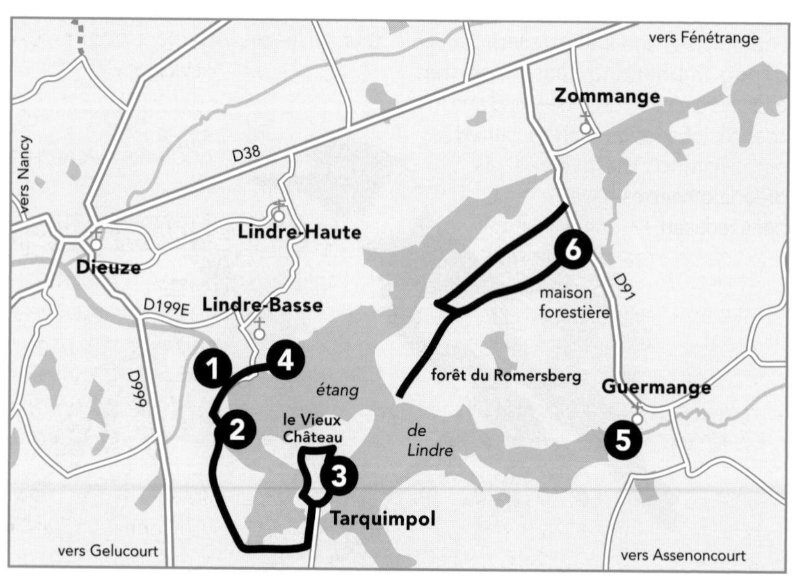

a feeding site by Bean Geese. To explore the eastern side, leave Dieuze eastwards on the D38, and after about 5 km turn right towards Guermange, from where one can walk to the lakeside. A new hide (5) should be in place shortly, to replace its predecessor destroyed by the December 1999 gales. This inlet is a good spot during the breeding season, as it is well supplied with reedbeds, the home of birds such as Bittern, Purple Heron, Little Bittern, Black-necked Grebe, Garganey, Pochard, Marsh Harrier and Savi's Warbler. To investigate the Forêt du Romersberg, drive back north from Guermange on the D91 and park by a barrier (6) at the start of one of the forestry tracks, the Tranchée du Milieu. One can walk west along this and return along one of the other tracks. In this mature forest it is possible to find Black Kite, Honey Buzzard, Goshawk, Short-toed Treecreeper, Middle Spotted, Grey-headed and Black Woodpeckers and Collared Flycatcher, all breeding. Those with more time can go to the end of the central track as far as the lake itself, with views across to the Tarquimpol peninsula. However, this part is best avoided in autumn or winter, so as not to disturb the birds unduly.

Calendar

Spring migration: large variety of duck in March and April. In May: marsh terns (including Whiskered and White-winged Black), Little Gull, often large numbers of hirundines and Swift, wagtails and pipits (including Red-throated).
Breeding season: Great Crested and Black-necked Grebes, Cormorant, Purple Heron, Little Bittern, Bittern, Black (rare) and White Storks, Mute Swan, Gadwall, Garganey, Pochard, Red-crested Pochard, Marsh Harrier, Black and Red (very rare) Kites, Goshawk, Hobby, Spotted and Little (occasional) Crakes, woodpeckers (six species), Fieldfare, Grasshopper, Savi's (rare), Reed, Great Reed, Marsh and Sedge Warblers, Collared Flycatcher (late April to late June), both treecreepers and Golden Oriole.
Late summer and autumn: large concentrations of Pochard (sometimes more than 5,000 birds), later many Shoveler. When the lake is emptied in the autumn: Cormorant (hundreds), Great White Egret and Grey Heron (many), hundreds of duck (Mallard, Teal, Shoveler), Peregrine, thousands of waders (mainly Lapwing, but also *Tringa* sandpipers, Greenshank, Snipe, Curlew, plovers, etc.), Black-headed Gull (thousands), hundreds of Woodpigeons in the forests. During November and December: Bewick's Swan, Greylag Goose, hundreds (sometimes thousands) of Cranes, White-tailed Eagle (rare), Redwing.
Winter: Whooper Swan, Bean Goose, Wigeon, Goldeneye, Smew and Goosander (many), Hen Harrier, Peregrine, Great Grey Shrike, Siskin. If the lake freezes over (a frequent occurrence), then most wildfowl will leave.

10. Lac and Forêt de Cattenom

Moselle (57) *IGN 11*

The River Moselle flows north through Metz and Thionville, and then past Cattenom nuclear power station, whose lake attracts many aquatic birds (grebes, Cormorant, Wigeon, Black-headed and Common Gulls), especially during protracted periods of hard weather as the warm water outflow from the power station stops ice from forming. To reach the area take the D1 north-east from

Thionville for about 7 km to Cattenom, and turn left on the D56 towards the power plant. The lake is viewable from the car park next to the power plant or from the embankment at the southern end of the lake. A small flock of Bean Geese comes to this area, moving between the lake, the Moselle valley and the fields between here and the Luxembourg border; they can often be seen in crops to the south of the lake. A pair of Peregrines breeds on an artificial ledge on one of the cooling towers, and can be seen throughout the winter. The extensive Forêts de Garche and de Cattenom are worth exploring – the woodland here is a breeding site for the localised Pied Flycatcher. The low-lying area around Sentzich, just downstream from Cattenom, with its ponds and marshes, can be productive during migration periods when Mute and Whooper Swans, dabbling duck, waders and various passerines (Blue-headed Wagtail, Penduline Tit, buntings) can all be seen.

11. La Maxe reservoir

Moselle (57) *IGN 11*

This artificial reservoir is another lake associated with a power station, this time the one at La Maxe, immediately north of Metz and again in the Moselle valley. As with the previous site, the lake also receives warm water from the power station, which keeps it ice-free and also attracts many waterfowl in winter. To get there, leave the A31 at exit 34 to reach the power station, which lies between the motorway and the river. A narrow peninsula separates the lake from the Moselle to the east, while to the west there is some arable land. The lake can be viewed from a track running along its western bank, the track continuing along the banks of the Moselle, which can also be of interest. It is also possible to get near to the lake by car from La Maxe village, just north of the power station. The area is of most interest in winter, especially when the other lakes of the Lorraine region are frozen. The lake may then have hundreds if not thousands of water birds of at least 15 different species: divers (rare), grebes, Cormorant, Velvet Scoter, Scaup, Red-crested Pochard, Goosander, Smew, Goldeneye, Common and Yellow-legged Gulls can be found among the more regular, Pochard, Tufted Duck, Coot and Black-headed Gulls. Bean Geese and Peregrine sometimes occur in the fields not far away.

12. The Seille valley

Moselle (57) *IGN 11/12*

The Étang de Lindre has been covered in detail above (see site 9), but there are other lakes and wetland areas in the valley of the River Seille that are also worth exploring. A few kilometres back along the D38 from Dieuze, beyond Mulcey, near the turning to St.-Médard, take a small road off to the left towards the river. One can walk along various tracks here as far as a bridge over the Seille and also walk along the river's left bank. Both Curlew and Lapwing breed regularly in the damp meadows here, arriving in March. Corncrake and Great Grey Shrike also occur occasionally and both Montagu's and Marsh Harriers hunt over the area. Passerines typical of these damp meadows are Meadow Pipit, Whinchat, Stonechat, Reed and Corn Buntings and Blue-headed Wagtail. They also attract migrant waders – Lapwing (hundreds), Golden Plover, Ruff, Snipe and Jack Snipe – and a Merlin

WHINCHAT

can sometimes be seen hunting the area. Other lakes near the Étang de Lindre worth checking are those at Zommange just to the east, and several near Gelucourt just to the south – the Étangs d'Axin, de Videlange and de Gelucourt.

13. Château de Falkenstein

VOSGES (88)/MOSELLE (57) *IGN 12*

The Château de Falkenstein occupies an impressive sandstone peak in the Parc Naturel Régional des Vosges du Nord, almost on the border with Germany. From the top of the château there is a magnificent panoramic view over the hills, a typical northern Vosges landscape. The site lies just north of the N62 between Bitche and Haguenau, near Philippsbourg, from which it is signposted, and where there is a car park. Some 500 metres after the car park, the trail skirts an old beech-grove which has Pied Flycatcher, Black and Grey-headed Woodpeckers and Common Treecreeper. Continue your walk by going into the Rothenbruch, a large pine wood about a kilometre beyond the car park. There are good populations of Pied Flycatcher, Crossbill and Crested Tit in this area, but it is best visited when the birds are singing (April to July), preferably in the early morning. Other species breeding in the vicinity include Goshawk, Woodcock, Tengmalm's Owl (very rare), and Peregrine. There are various trails through the woodland, indicated on a board near the château, and the nearby Étang de Hanau is also worth a visit, although often quite disturbed by the general public.

14. Colline de Sion

VOSGES/ (88) MEURTHE-ET-MOSELLE (54) *IGN 23*

Some 30 km south of Nancy and 10 km north of Mirecourt, the hilltop by the village of Sion is a good spot to look out over the other villages of the surrounding countryside, which still retains plenty of ancient orchards, primarily dedicated to growing Mirabelle plums. From a birdwatching point of view this area is home to one of the largest populations of Woodchat Shrikes and Hoopoes in Lorraine, two species that have suffered badly as such old orchards have disappeared over so much of their former range in Europe. Sion itself lies just west of the D913 between Mirecourt and Nancy, but is just one of a group of similar villages, although its hill is worth checking, not just for the view, but also because it is a breeding site for Woodlark. Other birds of the orchards include Wryneck, Little Owl and Redstart. The best places to look are the grazed orchards on the outskirts of villages with a southern exposure.

SITES

1 Vicdessos
2 Lac de Montbel
3 Gorges de la Dourbie
4 The Causse Rouge
5 Étangs de Ségala
6 Lac de Pareloup
7 Lac du Moulin de Bannac
8 Forêt de la Cardeilhac
9 Forêt de Bouconne
10 Néouvielle
11 Cirque de Gavarnie
12 Lac de Puydarrieux
13 Forêt de Grésigne
14 Gorges de l'Aveyron
15 Cambounet-sur-le-Sor
16 The River Garonne at St.-Nicolas-de-la-Grave

Midi-Pyrénées

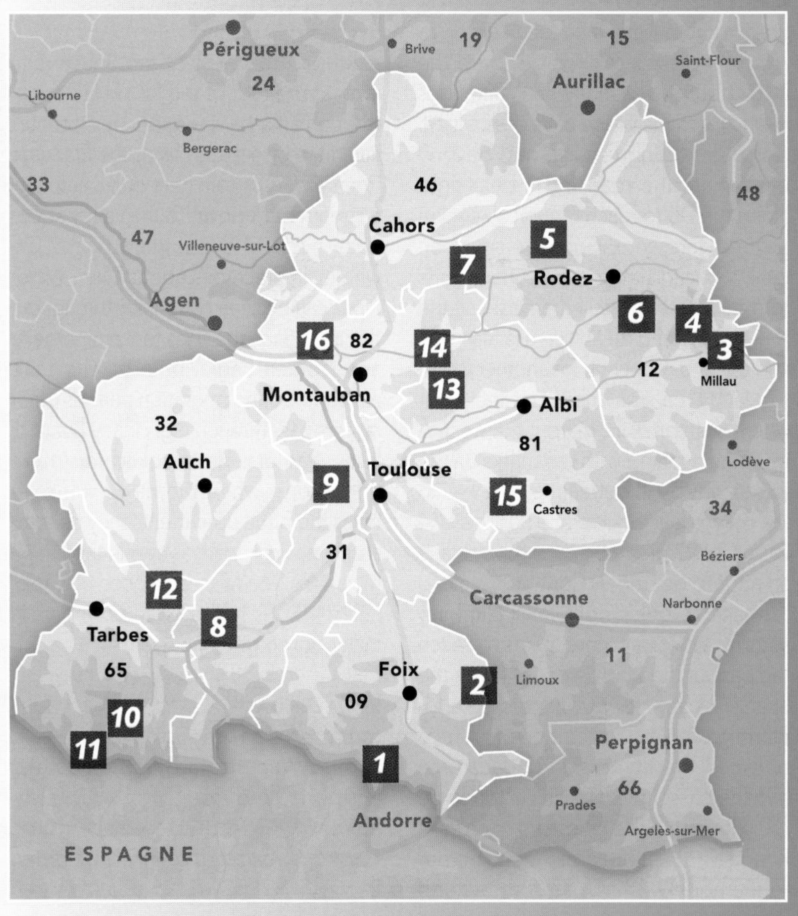

1. Vicdessos

ARIÈGE (09) *IGN 71*

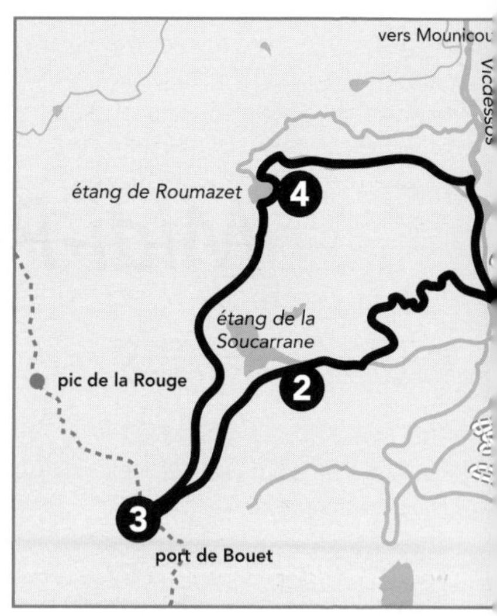

Vicdessos is a Pyrenean village, in a valley that runs up into the mountains on the border with both Spain and Andorra. The area is accessible between June and November without special equipment and comprises a typical mixture of rocky outcrops, high peaks, alpine meadows and mountain lakes, and has a good selection of the special birds of the Pyrenees.

ACCESS

Starting from Foix, take the N20 for 16 km to Tarascon-sur-Ariège, then the D108 south-west along the Vicdessos river to reach the village of Vicdessos itself. Continue through Auzat, and beyond this, where the road forks, bear right along the D8 to reach Mounicou (24 km beyond Tarascon). Continue south on the D108, and although the surface starts to deteriorate it is still driveable all the way to the Étang de Soulcem (a reservoir) and beyond. Continue for another 2½ km to reach (1) a small house at the point where a stream runs in from the west. A footpath, marked with red marks on the rocks, runs by this stream all the way to the Étang de la Soucarrane (2). This lake lies at 2,292 metres, and it should take an hour to get there. Continue, leaving the lake to one's right, and climbing south-west for another 2 km to reach the pass of the Port de Bouet (3) on the Spanish border at 2,509 metres. Look for Ptarmigan on the scree slopes anywhere between the Étang de la Soucarrane and the pass. Rock Thrush can often be found on the flanks of the Pic de la Rouge (2,909 metres), along the border to the north-west. A path to the north passes to the west of the Soucarrane lake, at the foot of the Pic de la Rouge, through an area where Alpine Accentor can often be seen, as far as the Étang de Roumazet (4). From here one can follow a stream back down to the valley about 1 km north of the starting point. The whole circuit covers about 7 km. Water Pipits can be seen commonly throughout this area. Scan the skies for Lammergeier and Golden Eagle, both of which are resident. During migration periods other raptors pass through e.g. Honey Buzzard, kites, harriers, best looked for in the afternoons, when the rising warm air gives them the up-currents they need to soar. One final point: as ever in these high mountains, you will need a good map (e.g. IGN 2148OT, 1:25,000) and compass in order not to get lost.

CALENDAR

Summer: Ptarmigan, Water Pipit, Alpine Accentor, Black Redstart, Dipper, Wheatear, Rock Thrush, Raven, Red-billed and Alpine Choughs; Lammergeier and Golden Eagle.

Autumn (August to September): wandering birds or migrants may include Griffon Vulture, Black Kite, Honey Buzzard, Montagu's Harrier, Wryneck, and passerines such as Ortolan Bunting and Tree Pipit.

GRIFFON VULTURE

2. *Lac de Montbel*

ARIÈGE (09) *IGN 71*

This large lake of around 600 hectares lies 25 km to the east of Foix. In spring and autumn it attracts a good variety of migrant waders, including Ringed and Little Ringed Plovers, Black-winged Stilt, *Tringa* sandpipers, and other small waders as well as marsh terns. Both Great Northern and Black-throated Divers are regular visitors, while Cormorant, Great White Egret and ducks (Red-crested Pochard regular in late summer) can be seen in autumn and winter. At this time there are many finches (especially Chaffinch and Brambling) and good flocks of Rock Sparrow to be found near the lake and this is the best time to look for Black Woodpecker in the nearby woodland. As with any such lake there are often surprise visitors (both White-tailed and Bonelli's Eagles have been seen here), and the lake's species list has already passed the 200 mark. To reach the area take the D117 east from Foix as far as Lavelanet, then north through Laroque-d'Olmes and east to Léran. From here minor roads lead down to the shore, and the lake is crossed by a causeway at its eastern end.

3. *Gorges de la Dourbie*

AVEYRON (12) *IGN 58*

The Gorges de la Dourbie, immediately east of Millau, are similar to the Jonte and Tarn gorges a short way to the north. The river has cut deeply into the limestone plateaux of the Causse Noir to the north and the Causse du Larzac to the south, to form spectacular cliffs, up to 400 metres in height, much used by large raptors. In addition the open stony plateaux also have their own special birds. (See also sites 15, 16 and 17 in the chapter on Languedoc-Roussillon.) Griffon and Black Vultures can be seen throughout the year, drifting over from the nearby Jonte and Tarn gorges, and Egyptian Vulture is sometimes also present in spring. Both Raven and Chough breed on the cliffs, which in winter are favoured by Wallcreepers. During the summer, from late April onwards, listen out for Scops Owl at dusk.

■ ACCESS

From Millau, cross to the east side of the River Tarn, and then take the D991 which runs by the River Dourbie all the way to Nant, 32 km away. The most spectacular cliffs are along the first part of the route, and can be viewed from various pull-ins by the side of the road. However the section further upstream

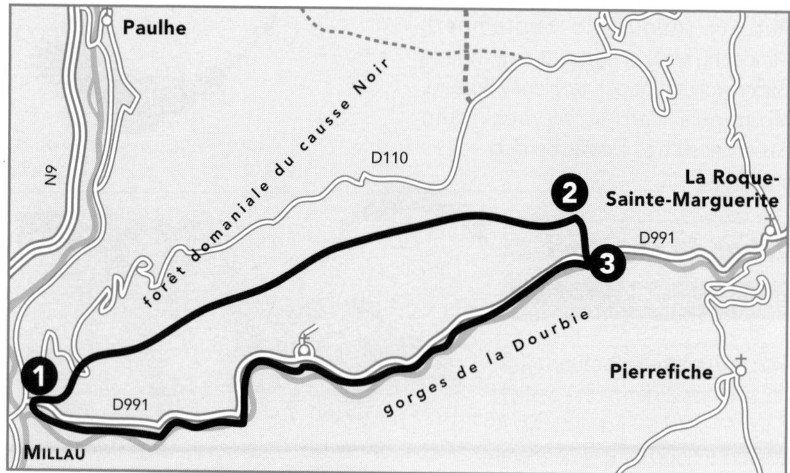

should not be ignored as the more open bushy slopes hold good numbers of warblers and other passerines. To explore the area on foot, one possibility is to take the long-distance footpath, the GR 62 (the 1:25,000 map IGN 2641OT will be useful), which starts from Millau and first climbs up onto the Causse Noir plateau at Cureplats (1). This section of the causse has been planted with conifers, so that species like Woodlark and Crested Tit should be looked for, but there are also some clearings where Stone Curlews can be found. Continue along the footpath as far as Caoussou (2) from where you can either return by the same route or drop down the Dourbie valley via the Valat Nègre ravine (3) and return to Millau along the D991.

Calendar

Spring: Short-toed Eagle, Black Kite, Honey Buzzard, Egyptian Vulture, Hobby, Scops Owl, Alpine Swift, Black Woodpecker, Crag Martin, Dartford Warbler, Raven and Chough. On the plateau, Stone Curlew and Nightjar.
Autumn: White and Black Storks, Osprey, Ring Ouzel.
Winter: Golden Eagle, Griffon and Black Vultures, Peregrine, Merlin, Eagle Owl, Red Kite, Water Pipit, Alpine Accentor, Wallcreeper and Citril Finch.

4. The Causse Rouge

Aveyron (12) *IGN 58*

Although the most spectacular scenery of the Tarn gorges is to be found to the north-east of Millau, the area downstream should not be neglected either. The D41 runs by the right bank of the river down to the village of Candas, and from this road various minor roads lead up onto the Causse Rouge, which has a distinctive Mediterranean feel to it, with birds such as Short-toed Eagle, Scops Owl, Short-toed Lark, Dartford, Orphean and Subalpine Warblers, Rock Bunting and Rock Sparrow all to be found in this area.

5. Étangs du Ségala

Aveyron (12) *IGN 57/58*

These lakes, now part of the Natura 2000 network, are important sites as far

MOORHEN

as the département of Aveyron is concerned, as it is an area poor in wetland habitats. They attract a great variety of aquatic birds, albeit only in small numbers. In summer the following breeding species can be found: Great Crested and Little Grebes, Grey Heron, Mallard, Black Kite, Hobby and Kingfisher. The best birdwatching opportunities are during the spring migration period, when ducks such as Garganey, Shoveler and Pochard, a wide range of waders, Night and Purple Herons, Great White and Little Egrets can be seen. In winter a few dabbling and diving duck come to join the resident Little and Great Crested Grebes, Coots and Moorhens. The lakes lie between Rodez and Villefranche-de-Rouergue. Starting from Rodez, take the D994 west for 26 km to Rignac, then turn right on the D43 then D53 to Bournazel. Before reaching this village the road crosses the embankment of the first of the lakes, the Étang de Bournazel, without doubt the best one, 25 hectares in extent, with a good growth of water-lilies. There are two Grey Heron colonies nearby, and the lake can be viewed from the roadside. The other group of three lakes is situated to the south-west, near the village of Privezac. To get to these, continue to Bournazel, then west on the D658 to Roussennac and the D994 as far as the D5. Turn left here for about 5 km to the D1, and continue straight on along the D26 towards the village of Privezac. The three lakes can be found just to the east of the village, by the D48 and D156.

6. *Lac de Pareloup*

AVEYRON (12) *IGN 58*

This large reservoir is situated about half-way between Rodez and Millau. It covers 1,239 hectares and has 107 km of heavily indented shoreline, and is a significant wintering site for wildfowl. Mallard, Gadwall, Shoveler, Pintail, Wigeon, Pochard and Teal all occur, with the occasional Shelduck. The sheltered bays are favoured by Great Crested Grebes, which are occasionally joined by a Black-throated or Great Northern Diver. The D993 from the Rodez/Millau road just east of Pont-de-Salars runs along the eastern side of the lake to Salles-Curan, and other minor roads approach the shore in many places, though it takes a long time to view the whole water surface properly. Just north of the dam at the western end is the smaller Lac de la Gourde where the same species can be seen, along with waders such as Lapwing and Snipe.

7. *Lac du Moulin de Bannac*

AVEYRON (12) *IGN 57*

Situated 5 km west of Villefranche-de-Rouergue, this 20 hectare artificial lake is used mainly for tourist activities, although some 6 hectares have been set aside as a reserve. In winter the lake is used by dabbling duck such as Mallard and Teal, joined sometimes by other species such as Cormorant. Snipe and Water Rail feed along the shoreline, and sometimes a Great White Egret will stop for a time. Various wintering passerines can be found, most notably thrushes, Water Pipit and Reed Bunting, and the concentration of prey will tempt Peregrine to hunt over the area. The widest range of species occurs between March and May, when migration is in full swing. Dabbling ducks and various waders can be seen, as can Purple and Night Herons, Little Egret, Black and White Storks, Spotted Crake and Black and Whiskered Terns. Osprey is another regular migrant. Golden Oriole, Hoopoe, Middle Spotted Woodpecker, Red-backed Shrike and sometimes Woodchat Shrike all breed in the area and there is a Grey Heron colony close by. The autumn migration period is another good time to look for waders, plus sometimes Greylag Goose and Crane. To access the lake, take the D911 west from Villefranche-de-Rouergue for about 14 km and a little after Marroule turn left on the road to the small village of Loupiac, then follow signs to the Mas de Benoy. Park by the road near the reserve, which is indicated by a noticeboard, and walk along a footpath to a hide overlooking the best area.

WATER PIPIT

8. Forêt de la Cardeilhac

Haute-Garonne (31)

IGN 70

The Forêt de la Cardeilhac, about 1,000 hectares in size, lies on the eastern part of the Lannemezan plateau. The woodland in this area is a mixture of local native trees – principally oak and sweet chestnut – growing together with various introduced species, both deciduous and coniferous. The forest incorporates an interesting arboretum, comprising many unusual tree species, well worth a visit in its own right. Although woodland birds are the prime attraction, the surrounding farmland also adds a few species to the day's birding.

Access

The nearest large town is St.-Gaudens to the south (exit 18 on the A64). From here head north on the D9 via St.-Ignan to Lodes, and here turn left towards Cassagne on the D69. About 1 km beyond here turn right (1) on the D69E to a small car park on the left (2), opposite the entrance to the arboretum. There is a board at the car park indicating the various way-marked trails. The following is just one of several options that could be devised for a walk. The circuit through the arboretum and the woodland to the east is the best area for forest species such as Mistle Thrush, Nuthatch, Short-toed

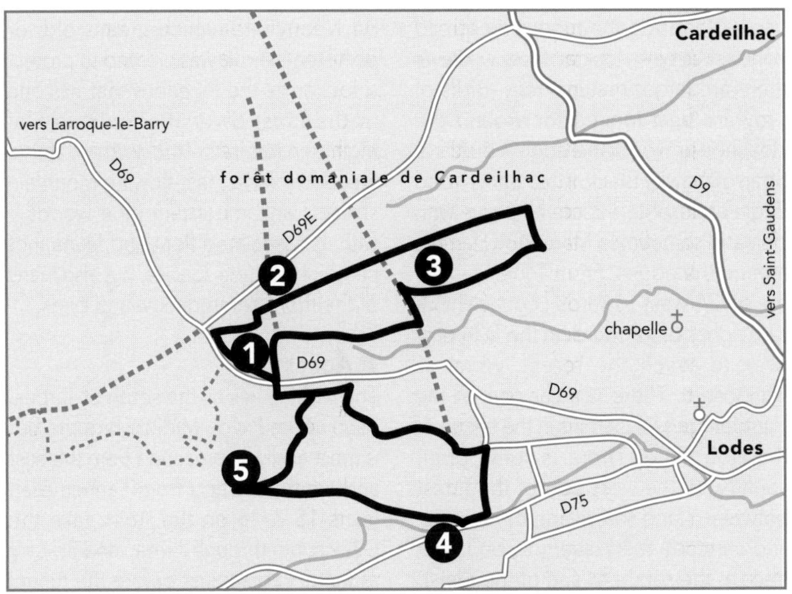

Treecreeper and Crested Tit. Having walked east from (2), one can return on a parallel path to (3), turn left and right along the wide firebreak, before regaining the road at (1). Turn left here for a short distance along the road, then take the next path on the right, through the woodland and out to the edge of the fields at (4). This damp part of the forest is a breeding area for Sparrowhawk, joined by Hobby in spring. Next, turn right and take the next track on the right and follow this for about 3½ km. This section looks south over farmland towards the Pyrenees, and these forest edges are favoured hunting areas for Black Kite, Honey Buzzard and Hen Harrier. A visit at dusk on a warm June evening may well produce the sound and sight of a Nightjar. Turn right into the forest at (5) to return to the road and complete the circuit. It is worth checking open clearings in the area for Red-backed Shrike and Tree Pipits, a few pairs of which breed here.

Calendar

Spring and summer: Buzzard, Honey Buzzard, Black Kite, Sparrowhawk, Hen Harrier, Hobby, Nightjar, Great Spotted, Lesser Spotted and Green Woodpeckers, Woodlark, Tree Pipit, Mistle Thrush, Melodious Warbler, Marsh, Coal and Crested Tits, Cirl Bunting.

9. Forêt de Bouconne

Haute-Garonne (31)
IGN 64

Lying 15 km to the west of Toulouse, this large oak and pine wood (2,300 hectares), in a region almost devoid of forest or hedgerow, is a good spot to see some woodland birds. The best time to come is in spring, when the summer visitors have arrived and the birds are singing. Look for Nightjar in the newly felled areas, this also being the habitat favoured by Dartford and Melodious Warblers. A few pairs of Wood Warbler occur, alongside the more widespread Bonelli's Warbler – look for these wherever there are larger mature trees. Birds of prey are best looked for around the clearings or woodland edge – Buzzard, Sparrowhawk, Black Kite, Short-toed Eagle and Booted Eagle all occur, with Hen and sometimes Montagu's Harriers around the edges. From Toulouse take the N124 west towards Léguevin, but turn right before there on the D24 past Brax to reach the forest, which is signposted. There is a car park at the Carrefour des 4 Chemins in the centre of the woodland. There is some open country on the west side of the forest between it and the village of Lasserre, and currently there seem to be larger trees at the southern end of the forest.

10. Néouvielle

Hautes-Pyrénées (65)

IGN 70

Dating from 1935, the Réserve Naturelle de Néouvielle (which means old, or persistent, snow) was created to protect a section of the Pyrenees that has one of the most diversified mixtures of mountain habitats – rocky scree, alpine meadows, lakes, fast-flowing mountain streams and mountain pine woods – with its associated flora and fauna, not only high-altitude species, but also many of the more common lowland birds.

Access

The reserve lies to the south of Tarbes, beyond the Pic du Midi de Bigorre, but is most easily approached from the east and south. Starting from Lannemezan (exits 15 & 16 on the A64), take the D929 south through Arreau and St.-Lary as far as Fabian, just before the tunnel to Bielsa. Still on the D929 bear to the right, and onto the Lac d'Orédon. Keep right again here and continue to the car park at the Lac d'Aumar (1). The circular hike proposed here will take between four and six hours, and covers an altitude range between 1,800 and 2,381 metres.

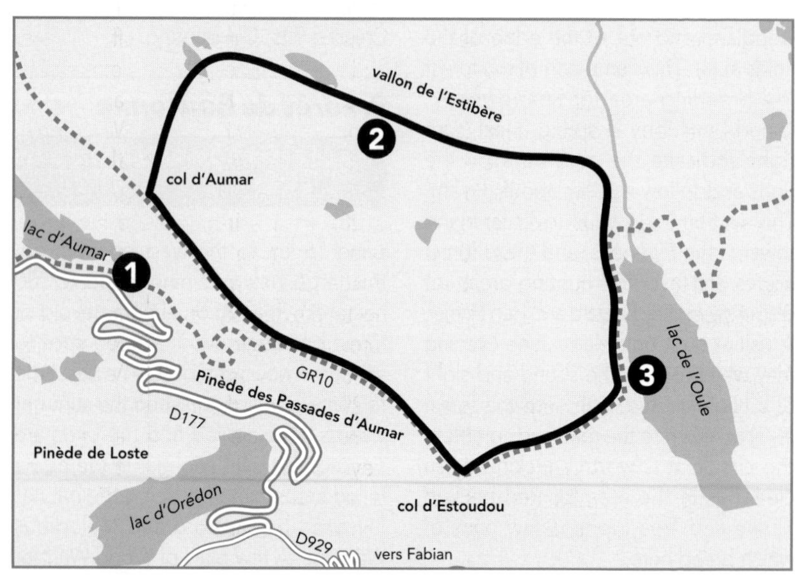

SPARROWHAWK

As ever in the mountains, you will need a detailed map (e.g. IGN 1748ET, 1:25,000) and a compass. From the car park, head towards the Col d'Aumar pass (2,381 metres) through some mountain pine woods; here there are often Ring Ouzel, Siskin, Citril Finch, Coal and Crested Tits, Common Treecreeper and Crossbill. Beyond the pass, drop back down into the rocks and alpine meadows of the Estibère valley (2), where it is possible to find, Alpine Accentor, sometimes Snow Finch (rare) as well as Water Pipit, Wheatear and Black Redstart. Continue walking among the various lakes and streams, eventually reaching the forests around the Lac de l'Oule (3). Black Woodpeckers occur in the pine woodland here, as do Capercaillie, though neither species is ever easy to see. Continue down the western side of the lake before turning right on the long-distance trail, GR10, up and over the Col d'Estoudou and back to the starting point.

Calendar

Spring and summer: Lammergeier, Golden Eagle, Griffon Vulture, Capercaillie, Black Woodpecker, Grey Wagtail, Water Pipit, Ring Ouzel, Wheatear, Black Redstart, Alpine Accentor, Dunnock, Dipper, Goldcrest, Coal and Crested Tits, Common Treecreeper, Citril Finch, Snow Finch (rare) and Crossbill.

11. Cirque de Gavarnie

Hautes-Pyrénées (65)
IGN 70

There can be few places more spectacular to watch birds than the Cirque de Gavarnie. It lies on the Spanish border at the end of the D921 south from Tarbes, via Lourdes, Luz-St.-Sauveur and Gèdre. Most members of the high-mountain fauna can be found here: large raptors including Golden Eagle, Griffon Vulture and Lammergeier, and passerines such as Citril Finch, Red-billed and Alpine Choughs, Snow Finch and Wallcreeper. It is popular with walkers, so disturbance is relatively high, and much of the area is inaccessible in winter, unless you take to your skis. From the village of Gavarnie there are footpaths up to the foot of the cirque, but it is also worth exploring the Ossoue valley which runs west towards Vignemale (3,298 metres), the highest peak on the French side of the mountains, and the road beyond the ski station to the Col de Boucharo, on the border at 2,270 metres. The 1:25,000 map IGN 1748OT covers the area.

12. Lac de Puydarrieux

Hautes-Pyrénées (65)

IGN 70

The 200 hectare reservoir, Lac de Puydarrieux, lies in rolling countryside due north of Lannemezan. It has some extensive mature oak forest on its steep eastern side, with more in the way of pines to the north. On the western side is a more open area of farmland, with large areas of maize, but also some interesting damp meadows, riverside woodland and copses. The southern end benefits from a local protection order, and is less disturbed than the areas nearer the dam. It is one of the most important sites for migrant and wintering birds in the Midi-Pyrénées region – Cormorant, Greylag Goose (20 to 40 birds), Great White Egrets (one and twos in winter), ducks (especially surface-feeders such as 200-300 Wigeon and 400-500 Teal) and raptors such as Peregrine and Merlin (on passage and in winter). If the water levels drop, large areas of mud are exposed at the southern end, attracting waders such as Lapwing, Dunlin, Ruff, Greenshank and Curlew, among others. Other migrants include Black and White Storks, Spoonbill, Osprey and Red Kite. It is a stop-over for Cranes in both spring and autumn, with usually 100 or so over-wintering. Both Black Kite and Grey Heron breed in the woodland near the lake, and good numbers of finches and other woodland passerines can be found in the oak forests in the winter. To get there, take the D929 north from Lannemezan for about 22 km, then the D632 west through Castelnau-Magnoac towards Trie-sur-Baïse. The road passes through the Forêt de Campuzan, just north of the lake. A minor road to Puydarrieux at the far edge of the woodland leads left to a parking area at the west end of the dam, from which the northern part can be viewed. Minor lanes lead on through the farmland to the west of the lake and round to the more interesting southern end where the River Léoup flows in. There is a small information hut at the south-east corner with good views over the shallows here, just west of Campuzan village.

13. Forêt de Grésigne

Tarn (81) *IGN 57/64*

The Forêt de Grésigne, between Montauban and Albi, is a mature sessile oak forest with an undergrowth of hornbeam, and with stands of beech on its northern and western slopes. It occupies a large natural basin, with high ground along its northern edge so that a large part faces to the south. It is noted for the diversity and abundance of its woodland birds, especially in the spring.

Access

From Gaillac, the nearest large town to

HAWFINCH

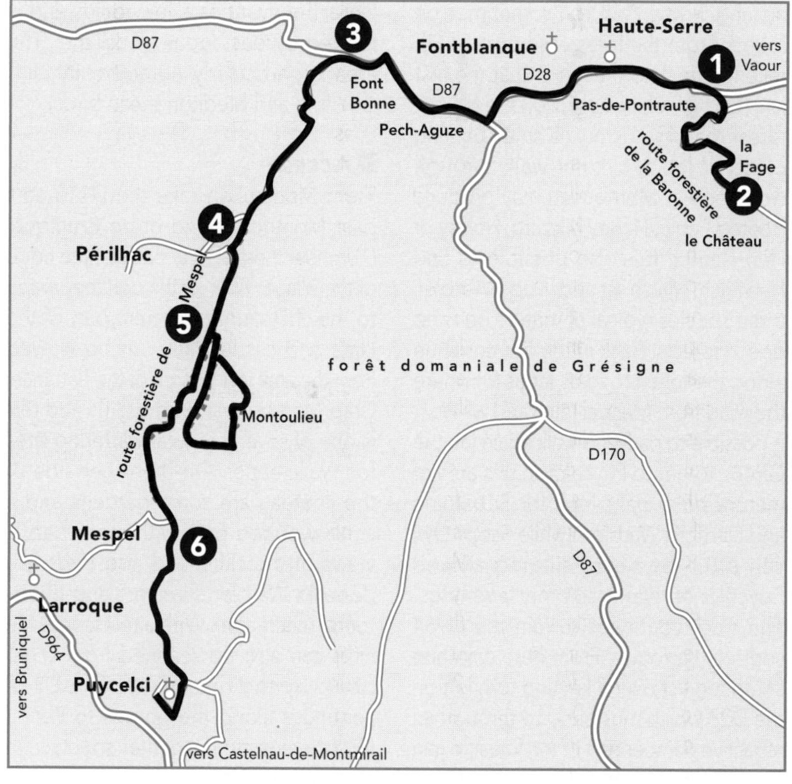

the south, take the D964 towards Castelnau-de-Montmiral, forking right before then on the D15 towards Vaour. About 1½ km before Vaour turn left on the D28 and left again at the first junction (about 500 metres farther on) to reach Pas-de-Pontraute, where there is a large car park at the entrance to the forest (1). A trail through the woodland leads to a spot below the Château de la Fage with an excellent view out over the forest to the south (2). This a good place in spring to watch displaying birds of prey such as Buzzard, Short-toed and Booted Eagles, Sparrowhawk and Goshawk. Return to the Pas-de-Pontraute, then take the D28 west as far as Haute-Serre. Along this section is the 'Mur de Grésigne' boundary wall, part of which has a footpath running alongside it, so you can either do this section on foot or in parallel along the road. After Haute-Serre turn right along the road that leads to Fontblanque, and at the first bend to the right, continue straight on, still following the Mur de Grésigne, as far as Pech-Aguze, the highest point in the forest at 494 metres. The south-facing slopes of the ridge here have some fine mature woodland with Middle Spotted Woodpecker and Woodcock, whilst the scrub on north-facing slopes over the ridge have Bonelli's Warbler and Red-backed Shrike. Continue as far as the Font Bonne holiday centre (3), then take the D87 road for about 800 metres, then the first road to the left. On the limestone plateau, between Font Bonne and Périlhac (4), nesting Tawny Pipit can sometimes be found. From the forester's house at (4), take the track to the left and at the first junction turn left again. Follow the Mespel forest road for 1 km to a small parking place at (5). A circular walk through woodland at Montoulieu may produce Booted Eagle, Honey Buzzard, Hobby or Hen Harrier. It is also possible to find Hawfinch, Marsh Tit and Wood Warbler, three species typical of mature oak and beech forests. Back in the car, continue along the forest road as far as (6) where the road from Mespel joins and where it is possible to park and walk again (on the GR46), to get to Puycelci. In this area of mature holm oaks look for Subalpine and Dartford Warblers, while Scops Owl can often be heard singing around Puycelci on warm summer evenings. The track continues to join the D964 south of Larroque. From here continue south for just over 2 km and turn left on the D28 which runs back up through an attractive damper part of the forest to join the D87 at La Grande Baraque, where there is another parking place.

Calendar

Spring: Buzzard, Goshawk, Sparrowhawk, Booted and Short-toed Eagles, Woodcock, Middle Spotted Woodpecker, Wood Warbler, Marsh Tit and Hawfinch.

14. Gorges de l'Aveyron

Tarn (81)/Tarn-et-Garonne (82) *IGN 57*

About 40 km east of Montauban, the River Aveyron flows through a series of spectacular limestone gorges, about 12 km long, with cliffs 150 to 200 metres high. The cliffs, as well as the adjacent plateau, have a sub-Mediterranean flora, while the river has a few rapids and is fringed by deciduous woodland. The area is particularly noted for its cliff-dwelling and Mediterranean birds.

Access

From Montauban take the D115 east past Montricoux and on to Bruniquel (1), where there are car parks at the edge of the village. Walk up through the village to the château, from where part of the cliffs and castle walls can be viewed from the area just to right of the entrance. Crag Martins nest on the cliffs and this is one of several regular wintering sites for Wallcreeper. On the other side of the château are some gardens and a small wooded park with more partial views of the cliffs, and also birds like Bonelli's Warbler, Firecrest and Short-toed Treecreeper. With a telescope, the cliffs can also be scanned from D115 down by the river itself. The D115 continues along the gorges to Penne (2), where there is another spectacular château, another Wallcreeper wintering site. It is possible to walk around the foot of the château in the village, although some of the footpaths are rather dangerous. Again, scanning from a distance with a telescope can be productive (e.g. near the La Terrace restaurant). From Penne either continue along the D115, or cross the river and take the quieter D173 to Couyrac (3), from where there are particularly good views. The road continues to join the D958, where there is another viewpoint and good habitat for birds like Subalpine and Bonelli's Warblers, and on to St.-Antonin-Noble-Val. In spring and summer any of the cliffs at Bruniquel, Penne and Couyrac have Alpine Swift and Crag Martin, whilst Raven can be seen throughout the year.

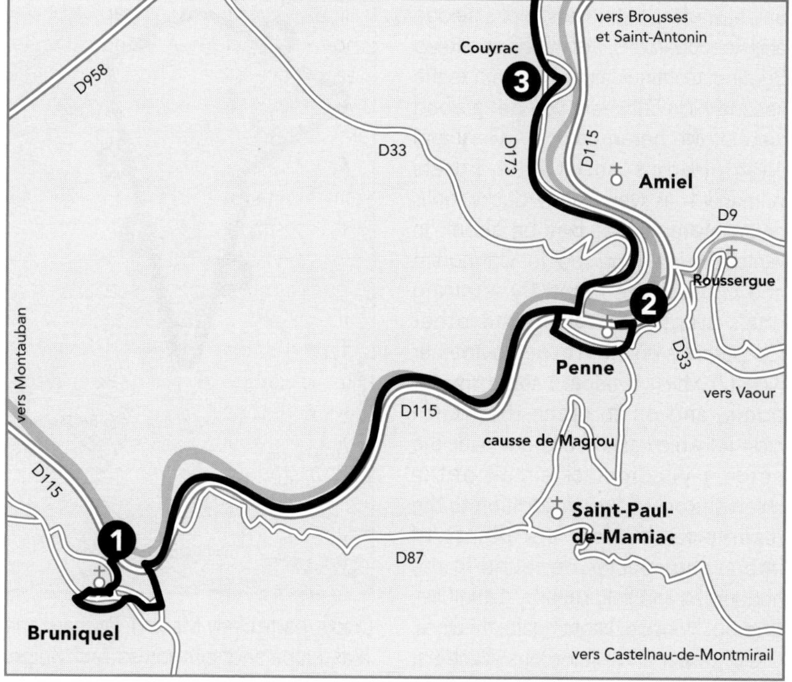

Calendar

Spring: Breeding species include Black Kite, Short-toed Eagle, Hobby, Peregrine, Kestrel, Stock Dove, Lesser Spotted Woodpecker, Eagle Owl, Alpine Swift, Crag Martin, Dipper, Subalpine and Bonelli's Warblers, Red-backed Shrike, Golden Oriole, Raven and Jackdaw.
Winter: Wallcreeper (regular from December to April).

15. Cambounet-sur-le-Sor

Tarn (81) *IGN 64*

The réserve naturelle of Cambounet-sur-le-Sor, about 10 km west of Castres, has been formed out of a series of old gravel-pits in the valley of the River Agout. The reserve has two water bodies: one colonised by reedmace, the other with banks covered with willow and poplar. In addition there is a boating lake and leisure complex adjacent to the reserve area. The major ornithological interest here is a large mixed heron colony (several hundred pairs) between April and August, but is worth a visit at any time of year.

Access

From Castres, take the N126 west towards Toulouse for about 10 km as far as the roundabout just before Soual. Turn right here on the D14 towards Cambounet-sur-le-Sor, then right again and follow signs to the reserve. Maps and leaflets giving details of access are available here. The first hide (1) is reached by taking the disused railway line along the east side of the reserve, with the leisure-centre to the right. From here look for Little Grebe, Grey Heron, Little Ringed Plover, Snipe, sometimes Jack

Snipe, waders, hirundines, pipits, Sedge and Reed Warblers, flycatchers and Reed Bunting. Continue along the path to the second hide (2) where you get a good view of the heron colony – Grey and Night Herons and Cattle Egrets primarily – as well as any ducks, gulls or marsh terns that may be about. In winter this is a good spot for Cormorant and Great White Egret. By retracing one's steps and taking the other footpath it is possible to get to another hide (3) which overlooks some smaller pools, and on to reach the fourth hide (4) which also looks out over the heronry. A complete circuit of the reserve is only 2 km. In addition to the reserve itself there are plenty of interesting species be found in the hedgerows and fields nearby: Little Owl, Cuckoo, Hoopoe, Nightingale, thrushes, Grasshopper and Melodious Warblers, Penduline Tit, Short-toed Treecreeper, Golden Oriole and buntings, depending on the time of year.

Calendar

Spring: Little and Cattle Egrets, Night, Grey, Purple and sometimes Squacco Herons, Garganey, Shoveler, Black Kite, Booted Eagle, Hobby, Little Ringed Plover, Ruff, Black-winged Stilt, Common and Green Sandpipers, Yellow-legged and Black-headed Gulls, Black and Whiskered Terns, Cuckoo, Bee-eater, Kingfisher, hirundines, Blue-headed Wagtail, Sedge, Reed, Great Reed, Garden and Willow Warblers and Penduline Tit.

Autumn: Black-necked Grebe, Great White Egret, Osprey, Marsh Harrier, Hobby, waders, Water Pipit, Pied Flycatcher and Reed Bunting.

Winter: mixed roost of Cormorant, Cattle and Little Egrets, Night and Grey Herons.

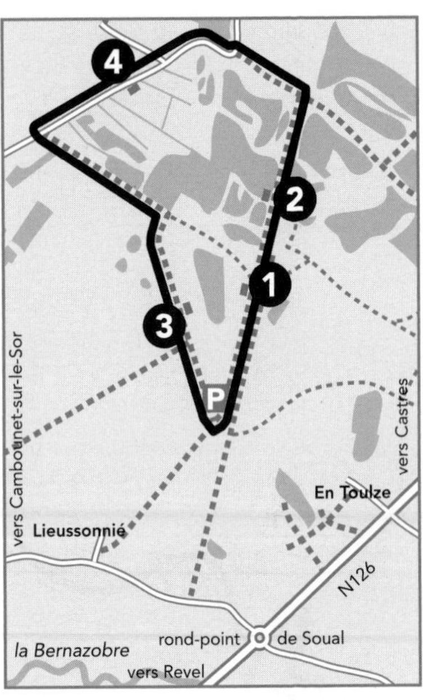

Ducks, particularly Mallard, Pochard and Teal, Snipe and sometimes Jack Snipe.

16. The River Garonne at St.-Nicolas-de-la-Grave

Tarn-et-Garonne (82) *IGN 57*

About 25 km west of Montauban, the River Garonne has been dammed just downstream from where it is joined by the River Tarn, to form a 400 hectare lake. There is a leisure centre on the northern part of the lake, but the southern part of the Garonne upstream is less disturbed and is therefore suitable as a refuge for duck and waders. During the winter there are always Shoveler, Teal, Tufted Duck and Pochard on the water along with the resident Coots and Great Crested Grebes. From time to time the latter are joined by a wintering Black-throated or Red-throated Diver for a few days. The islands provide a secure winter roosting site for an impressive number of Cormorants, with Cattle Egrets also arriving in the evening. There is also a large gull roost, with sometimes nearly a thousand Yellow-legged and Black-headed Gulls while Lesser Black-backed and Common Gulls occur regularly in small numbers. In spring, waders often occur for a short while, as early as February for Black-tailed Godwit, April for most of the sandpipers and Greenshanks. Black Terns and Little Gull pass through, and Ospreys can be seen from time to time. The installation of nesting rafts has allowed a Common Tern colony to become established. Kingfisher and Purple Heron are to be found in the flooded woods beyond the reservoir. Typical birds of the more wooded and damp areas along the shore include Cetti's Warbler, Chiffchaff, Blackcap and Marsh Tits, whilst Hobbies hunt overhead during the summer.

Access

From Moissac, take the N113 west and then turn south on the D15 towards St.-Nicolas-de-la-Grave. Shortly after crossing the Garonne, turn left into the leisure centre to arrive at the car park by the water's edge (1). The reservoir is well-signposted as 'Plan d'eau de la Tarn'. There is unrestricted access to the lakeside on foot, and at least part of the track is suitable for wheelchairs. The lake can be viewed from the track, and there is a hide (2) in one place. The tern nesting platforms can also be seen from the bank. The more open area, favoured by hirundines and terns, is at the western end of the reservoir, where the Tarn flows in. The river is fringed with brambles and rough ground in places, but the path also passes through some orchards and poplar plantations. The further on one goes (it is about 5 km to point (3) and back), the more chance there is of woodland species. It is always worth scanning the islands offshore and the more overgrown far bank for birds like Little Egret, Grey Heron, Black Kite, Osprey and Night Heron. There is a large heronry on the far side in this further section.

Calendar

Spring: Pintail, Black-tailed Godwit, Spotted Redshank, Greenshank, Wood Sandpiper, Black Tern.
Breeding season: Grey, Purple and Night Herons, Little Egret, Mallard, Yellow-legged Gull, Common Tern.
Autumn: Little Grebe, Greylag Goose, Osprey, Lapwing, Golden Plover, Kingfisher.
Winter: Great Crested Grebe, Cormorant, Gadwall, Shoveler, Teal, Tufted Duck, Pochard, sometimes Ferruginous Duck and Red-crested Pochard.

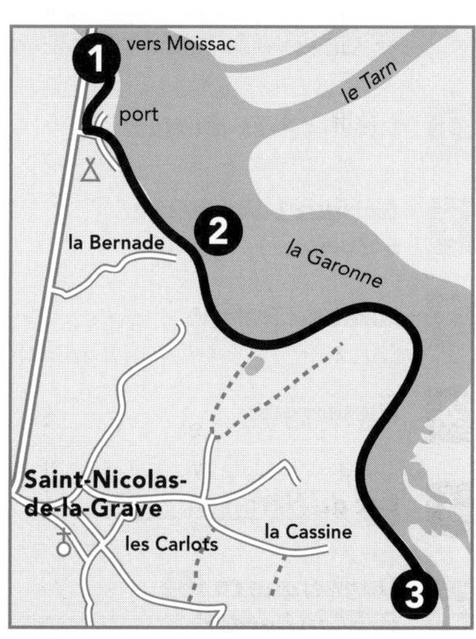

SITES

1 *Lac des Prés-du-Hem*

2 *Goriaux Lake (Mare à Goriaux)*

3 *Forêt de Trélon*

4 *Dunkerque*

5 *Lac du Héron*

6 *Dunkerque to the Belgian border*

7 *Cap Gris-Nez and Cap Blanc-Nez*

8 *Étang de Rumaucourt*

9 *Platier d'Oye*

10 *Réserve Naturelle du Romelaere*

11 *Baie de Canche*

Nord-Pas-de-Calais

1. Lac des Prés-du-Hem

Nord (59) *IGN 02*

An artificial lake in the suburbs of Armentières, the Prés-du-Hem leisure centre lies within an ancient meander of the River Lys. Once a flood zone, the meadows have been replaced by a reservoir, providing water for Lille, which is a short distance away to the south-east. Filled by the river, covering about 45 hectares and around 3 metres deep, the lake is very suitable for aquatic birds, especially in winter when there are large flocks of duck during the day and a gull roost forms in the evening. Two small islands provide safe refuges for birds throughout the year. There is a protected sector to the north of the lake which acts as a bird reserve, especially important for migrant and breeding species. The north-east/south-west orientation of the Lys valley, lying on a migration route on the French/Belgian border, leads to a large variety of migrants being seen here, on their way between the Dutch polders and the Picardy estuaries.

Access

From the centre of Armentières take the road north towards Ypres and Prés-du-Hem to reach the main entrance of the leisure centre (1). One can park outside the centre and walk towards the river port and the south of the lake (2). Throughout the year there are Coot and Moorhen along the River Lys. From October to March Tufted Duck and Pochard can be seen on the lake, along with Shoveler, Gadwall, Wigeon and Pintail. The Grey Heron colony on the wooded island is visible from the lakeside, the same island hosting a Cormorant roost in winter. Follow the trail along the top of the embankment to reach the bird reserve area, where there are hides (3), though those with reduced mobility need to make advance arrangements to use them. Grey Heron and Cormorant can often be seen from the first hide, sometimes joined by a Spoonbill in September. Gulls occur by the thousand in winter, and various terns pass through on spring passage. It is also a good site for hirundines on migration, when flocks of hundreds of Sand Martins, Swallows and House Martins can be seen over the lake in April and September, with Swifts joining them in May. Continue the circuit along the lakeside (4), passing by the beach and the poplar wood, this being a good area for both Green and Great Spotted Woodpeckers. The far end of the lake has waders in spring and autumn, particularly *Tringa* species and Snipe. Access is free except during the three summer months when a fee is charged. Note that the site is closed at night.

Calendar

Spring: waders (many *Tringa* species in small numbers). Large groups of Swifts and hirundines in April. Regular passage of Common, Little and Black Terns and Little Gull.

Breeding season: Grey Heron, Shelduck, Shoveler, Tufted Duck, Hobby, sometimes Avocet, Green Woodpecker, Cuckoo, wetland warblers.

Autumn: Cormorant, Spoonbill, Greylag Goose, dabbling and diving duck, Osprey, Marsh Harrier, Water Rail, numerous waders (from as early as August: *Tringa* species, Ringed and Little Ringed Plovers, Snipe, Ruff, Avocet, Lapwing), Kingfisher and passerines.

GOLDENEYE

Winter: Great Crested and Little Grebes, many dabbling duck (Shelduck, Pintail, Gadwall, Shoveler, Wigeon, Teal and Garganey) and Pochard and Tufted Duck. During periods of hard weather there may be Goldeneye, Smew, Goosander or Red-breasted Merganser; occasionally Scaup or Long-tailed Duck. Buzzard and Sparrowhawk are regular in winter. Roosting gulls, Cormorants and Jackdaws.

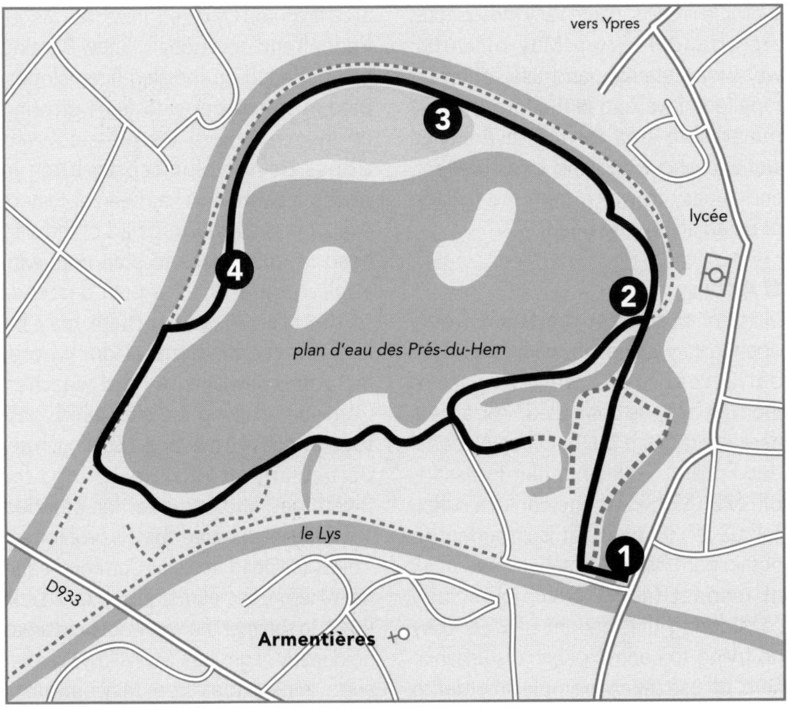

vers Ypres
3
lycée
4
2
plan d'eau des Prés-du-Hem
le Lys
1
D933
Armentières

2. *Goriaux Lake (Mare à Goriaux)*

NORD (59) *IGN 02/04*

Situated in the Parc Naturel Régional de Scarpe-Escaut near Valenciennes, with large areas of woodland to the north, this large forest lake was formed by mining subsidence (the Wallers-Arenberg pithead can be seen at the south of the site). Settling, which is still occurring, has brought about a decrease in the area of reedbed, which now only grows in the south-west (where muddy water arrives from the mine). Along the whole of the south side, slag from the mine has been dumped. Around the lake there is degraded humid woodland (birch) or plantations (pines), but the bird life is extraordinary thanks to the amount of food available (insects, particularly mosquitoes, are abundant from May onwards; wear long sleeves and use an insect repellent if walking in the forest). It is a remarkable area for the diversity of wetland and woodland birds present, and is easy to watch from the flat top of an adjacent slag heap.

Access

Most of the forest roads are freely open to cars (signposts mark otherwise), but access to the western part of the slag heap is controlled. For access here contact the ONF (Office National des Forêts, 3 place Jehan-Froissart, BP 422, 59322 Valenciennes Cedex; Tel: 03 27 30 35 70). It is important to obtain permission beforehand as a mark of respect to the ONF, especially considering the amount of work they do trying to control public disturbance here; please set an example. In order to watch the birds under good conditions, avoid Sundays and public holidays and try to go first thing in the morning.

When coming from Lille or Valenciennes on the A23 motorway, take the Raismes-Parc Naturel de St.-Amand turn-off (exit 6), which is close to the car park (1). The site is also accessible by bus from Valenciennes (from the coach station in Valenciennes, place du Hainaut). From the car park take the path that leads to the flat top of the slag heap. From the summit (2) there is a splendid view over the whole subsidence area and the forested area north to St.-Amand, with its magnificent baroque tower, part of an ancient abbey, visible 6 km away. In good weather, the Monts de Tournai (30 km away) can also be seen. This sector of the lake suffers too much disturbance from fishing for there to be many birds to be seen, but at quieter times this is the area favoured by divers in winter. Siskin, Redpoll and occasionally Snow Bunting can be found on the slag heap slopes, bare in places but with trees growing on them in others, the grass-covered slopes being colonised by birch in places. If permission has been obtained, continue to the western part of the slag heap. A good place to scan from with a telescope is where a path descends to the lake. In winter there may be large concentrations of duck here, including sawbills in hard weather. Continue on along the track which passes the edge of a reedbed. Listen out here, particularly at dusk in spring, for Bluethroat, and in winter for Bearded Tit. Entry into the reedbed is prohibited. Check the dead trees for Cormorant and Grey Heron, sometimes joined by a Little Egret. In summer the wet woodland areas hold many Nightingales, Willow Warbler and... mosquitoes (from May onwards).

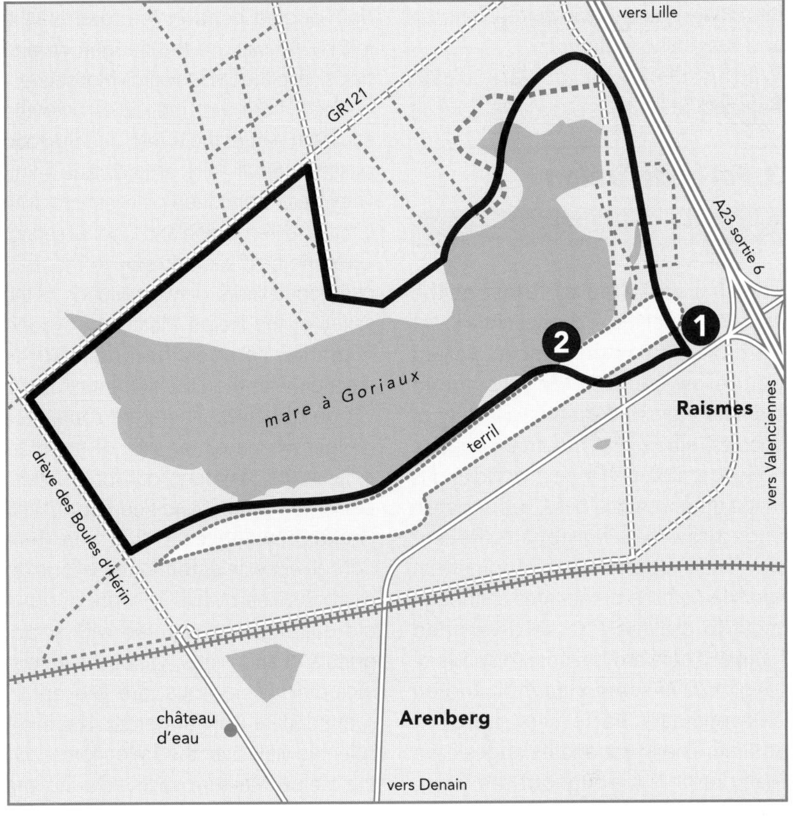

Woodcock can be heard roding here in March. After walking along the base of the slag heap for about 100 metres, cross a bridge over the stream that feeds into the lake and follow the path that leads to the Drève des Boules d'Hérin, a badly-paved sector of road, used as part of the Paris-Roubaix cycle racecourse. Turn right along this for about 400 metres and at the junction with a gravelled forest track turn right again. The large trees in the wood here are used by hole-nesting passerines (e.g., tits, Short-toed Treecreeper and Nuthatch). Birds of prey can be seen displaying above the forest between February and June, including Buzzard, Honey Buzzard, Sparrowhawk and Hobby. Great Spotted, Black and Green Woodpeckers are quite common. After 1 km at another junction, turn right on a track that goes towards the pond. At the end, turn left along a winding path that follows the northern bank of the pond (in winter, in the evening, a large Black-headed Gull roost forms here) and leads back to the slag heap and car park.

Calendar

Spring: Great Crested Grebe; raptors (Buzzard, Honey Buzzard, Hobby, Osprey on passage); Bluethroat.

Spring and autumn: spectacular movements of Swift (spring), and

hirundines; geese, Lapwing, Chaffinch and Brambling (autumn).
Winter: ducks (particularly Teal); Bearded Tit.

3. Forêt de Trélon

NORD (59) *IGN 05*

This is a vast area of forest at the western end of the Ardennes. At a lower altitude and with a more varied hedgerow countryside and humid habitats there is a greater diversity of species, albeit that mountain species no longer occur. The best woodland is made up of very old oaks, with a dense undergrowth of hornbeam. Recent plantations of conifers have somewhat spoilt large parts of the forest, although they do provide a more diversified habitat. There are beautiful displays of foxgloves in some clearings and an extraordinary variety of fungi in autumn. The forest and its edges have many raptors (throughout the year), wetland birds (on migration and in winter) and passerines (especially in spring and summer).

Access

From Maubeuge, take the N2 south for about 20 km to Avesnes, then turn east on the D951 through Sains-du-Nord to reach Trélon, the best areas for birds being in this area, in the southern and eastern parts of the forest. (The Val-Joly area to the north is best given a wide berth in summer when it is invaded by a mass of visitors.) From here continue on the D951 for another 3 km, then turn left to the village of Wallers-Trélon. There is a parking site for a few cars about 100 metres after the last house in the village, on the road to Moustier-en-Fagne, at a right-angled bend in the road on the left (1). To explore the hedgerows and fields, take the D83 towards Moustier-en-Fagne. There are fine views over the southern part of the forest, and the road passes a small lake after about 1 km. Grey Herons are often present here, with Great Crested Grebe and Coot in spring. Over the next kilometre or so the road offers good views, between woods, of the valley of the Helpe Majeure – a good migration corridor. Turn right at the junction with the D283 (2) towards the village of Baives. There are some nice hedgerows on either side of the road as far as the cemetery; look for Fieldfare, Lesser Whitethroat and Red-backed and Great Grey Shrikes in this area. Turn right directly on entering the village, to climb the nearby hill (3), a site of some old quarries now covered with scrub, grassland and pines. Various warblers, including Melodious, are present in summer (late April onwards). There is a splendid view over the Trélon forest and the Helpe Majeure valley. During the first fine days of January or February birds of prey can be seen displaying anywhere over the woods, notably Buzzard, Sparrowhawk and Goshawk. To arrive back at the car, take the first road on the right in Wallers-Trélon village, which contains some fine stone-built houses, just before the church. A small detour can be made in order to follow a pretty river for 500 metres by taking the little road on the left just after the church to (4). It is usually easy to find either Dipper or Grey Wagtail along the river here. For a longer (9 km) forest walk, take the dirt-track that goes towards the forest. Note that access within private parts of the forest is restricted to the tracks. Follow the track straight on to the Carrefour du Prince-Philippe junction.

Turn left taking the winding forest track as far as the Carrefour de Blois junction (5). Take the third forest track on the left, which after nearly 1.5 km without a bend, joins a forest road. Turn left, following the Réserve de la Folie (no access) fence to get to the forest road that leads back to the starting point. There is no public access to the Étang de la Folie lake (which is a reserve of the Nord hunters federation). During this circuit you should have a better chance of seeing some of the forest birds. Honey Buzzards display along the forest edge in spring, Hawfinches occur in areas of mature trees with little undergrowth. The Great Grey Shrike nests in cleared areas of the forest, and Grasshopper Warblers occur in the same general area. Ancient stands of large trees have Middle and Lesser Spotted Woodpeckers, as well as Black. The conifer plantations have Goldcrest, Firecrest, Crested and Coal Tits, and a visit at dusk on a spring evening may well produce a sighting of a Woodcock 'roding' over the forest.

CALENDAR

Spring: Lesser Spotted, Middle Spotted and Black Woodpeckers, Fieldfare, Lesser Whitethroat, Wood Warbler, Hawfinch, Great Grey and Red-backed Shrikes. Lapwing nests.
Spring and autumn: interesting wetland species (Black Stork) in the wetter parts.
Winter: raptors (Buzzard, Goshawk, Sparrowhawk), Whooper Swan (irregular).

4. Dunkerque

NORD (59) *IGN 01*

The port of Dunkerque (or Dunkirk in English), economically the third most

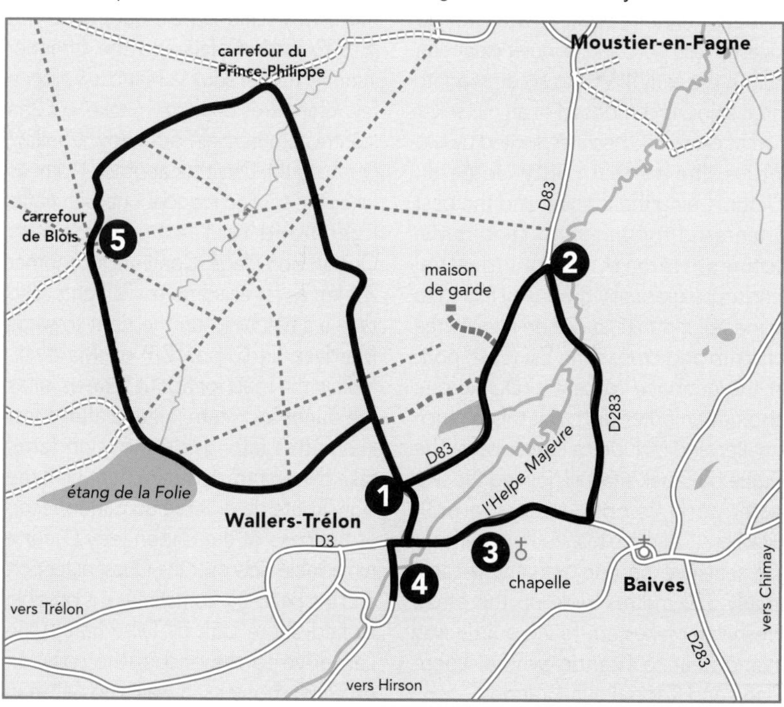

LITTLE TERN

important in France, is an immense complex covering more than 8,000 hectares, along 17 km of coast between the towns of Gravelines and Dunkerque itself. It is separated into two distinct parts, the Ouest and the Est ports, linked by a long sea wall (the digue du Braek), with a maritime canal used by sea-going vessels, running parallel with it. The Ouest (West) port, and an outer extension built in the early 1970s to accommodate large ships, is composed of an oil tanker port of nearly 500 hectares, limited by two jetties, the northern jetty (Jetée du Clipon) being the longest and the best orientated for watching seabirds in autumn. Here, this very industrial landscape gradually gives way inland to some relict dunes and then a vast area of scrub and crops. The Est (East) port, at the entrance to central Dunkerque also has an outer port, but this is much smaller, and includes a leisure port. The Digue du Braek seawall, joining the two outer ports, is open to cars in both directions. For more than 6 km it overlooks the seashore on one side and a canal nearly 300 metres wide on the other. Freshwater lakes are found a little way inland near to Grande-Synthe, Loon-Plage and Cappelle-la-Grande.

Access

The starting point is the best sea-watching site in the region, the Jetée du Clipon (especially well known for seabird passage in autumn). From this point, a circuit of nearly 30 km takes in a tour of the ten most interesting sites of the area.

If coming from Lille on the A25 motorway (Lille-Dunkerque), take the A16 towards Calais and the Channel Tunnel (Tunnel sous la Manche). After a few kilometres on the A16 take exit 25a (centre commercial/FortMardyck/Sollac/Dunkerque). Drive for another 1½ km as far as the second roundabout (with traffic lights) and turn left towards Port Ouest/Loon-Plage. Continue for another 2¼ km as far as some traffic lights, and take a small road on the right towards Mardyck/Le Clipon/ZIP de Mardyck. Follow the road for about 5 km as far as the dunes lock, turn left and after a few kilometres (alongside the wind farm) take the first track on the right with the sign 'Route de la Jetée du Clipon'. Stop at the base of the Clipon jetty (1) for a remarkable view over the Ouest outer port and the beaches. Sometimes it is possible to find Shore Lark or Twite here. One can drive to the end of the jetty, an excellent spot for sea-watching between

August and November, with the passage of various shearwaters (Sooty, Manx and Balearic), Storm Petrel, Gannet, dabbling and diving ducks, waders, terns, skuas, gulls and auks. Some rarer species occur regularly in small numbers, e.g., Grey Phalarope, Long-tailed Skua, Sabine's Gull and Little Auk can all occur with suitable weather conditions (a front moving from the north with north-westerly winds). During October and November large flocks of Brent Geese pass the jetty (10 to 15 thousand each year).

The Plaine du Clipon (2), behind the dune on the side facing the port, is good for passerines, birds of prey and waders at times of migration, mainly on the rubble in the centre of the open area. On the beach to the east of the Jetée du Clipon there is quite a large colony of Little Terns; Ringed and Kentish Plovers also breed here.

Parallel with the dune or wind farm road, the 6 km Canal des Dunes (3) between the quay to the west and the dunes lock to the east, is well worth checking in winter for diving duck. Continuing on from here, the Digue du Braek (4) offers, along its 6 km length, good views over the sea on one side and the canal on the other. In winter on the canal side can be found divers, grebes (5 species), Red-breasted Merganser, and sometimes common seal; on the sea side there are hundreds of gulls in winter (including Caspian and Glaucous) as well as Sanderling and Snow Bunting, with terns in spring and summer.

Diving duck are often visible from the very eastern end of the Digue du Braek, the western jetty of the old Dunkerque port (5). This jetty, a few hundred metres long, offers an alternative to using Clipon for sea-watching when conditions are too bad at that extremely exposed spot. Return by the same route as far as the dunes lock, at the very western end of the Digue du Braek. Here the two canals join at a wider stretch of water called the Bassin de Mardyck (6). Pass the dunes lock again and follow the signs 'Toutes Directions'. Less than 2 km farther on, on the side of the road there is a long stand of poplars, called the 'Haie de Mardyck' (7). This is probably the best site for migrant passerines in autumn, and warrants more coverage than it usually receives. On the right less than 500 metres farther on take the small road that enters Mardyck village and leads to an area of cereals (8) much hunted over by birds of prey, particularly harriers.

Continue on to the main N1 road and turn right towards Port Ouest/ Pondereux/Loon-Plage/Gravelines. After some 4½ km pull off onto the verge (be very careful, it's a busy road). The Étang du Petit Denna (9) lake lies to the left of the road, but is well hidden. Many dabbling duck use it in winter and a wide selection of waders in spring and autumn; it is also the best site in the area for Spoonbill (usually in August) and for Bewick's Swan in winter. The track, the 'Vieux Chemin de Bourbourg' winds through the fields to the south of the lake and is useful for searching for birds of prey in winter – Hen Harrier, Peregrine or Short-eared Owl.

Then continue along the N1 as far as the next traffic lights and turn right towards ZIP des dunes/Port Pétrolier. At the roundabout follow signs to the Institut Pasteur. Continue for 2½ km as far as a spot which affords views over the western part of the Ouest outer port (10), the most sheltered and interesting part of the port complex. From here you get the best views over the oil-tanker port;

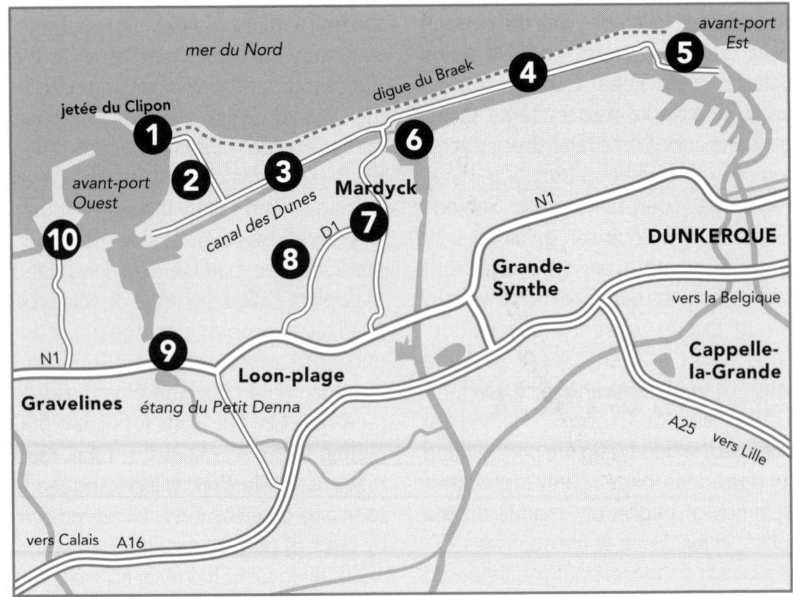

in winter look for divers, smaller grebes (usually several Black-necked and Slavonian pass the winter, often in groups), diving duck (Red-breasted Merganser, Common Scoter, Goldeneye). It is also one of the best sites for seeing grey and common seals. The landing stages are sometimes used by Shag and at low tide the small beach that is uncovered is often occupied by various waders and gulls.

Calendar

Spring: grebes (5 species), harriers (3 species), Osprey (rare), wader passage (*Tringa* species, godwits, Curlew), terns, Pied Wagtail (as opposed to White – in March), Yellow Wagtail (April and May), Ring Ouzel.
Summer: Marsh Harrier, Montagu's Harrier (regularly summers), Ringed, Little Ringed and Kentish Plovers, Yellow-legged Gull, Little Tern.
Autumn: good passage of divers, grebes, shearwaters, storm-petrels, Gannet, ducks, waders, skuas, gulls, terns, auks and passerines.
Winter: divers (3 species), grebes (5 species), diving duck (Eider, scoters, Goldeneye, Red-breasted Merganser), Sanderling, gulls, Guillemot, Razorbill, Snow Bunting, Shore Lark.

5. Lac du Héron

Nord (59) *IGN 02*

The Lac du Héron lies in Villeneuve-d'Ascq, on the eastern edge of Lille. Despite its urban setting and much human disturbance all round, some 235 species of bird have been seen here and local interest has led to the creation of a reserve at the eastern end of the lake. There is a wide mosaic of different habitats at the site, comprising a lake, river and ditches, flood meadows, crops, scrub and woodland. In winter, and especially during both migration seasons, many grebes and ducks occur. From September to February thousands of gulls come to roost each evening. Breeding species include Kingfisher, a good population of Marsh Warblers and a small population of Little Owls. Grey Herons are always present and various birds of prey breed nearby.

6. Dunkerque to the Belgian border

NORD (59) *IGN 01/02*

The distance between central Dunkerque (Dunkirk) and the Belgian border is about 15 km, and much of the coast is occupied by the seaside resorts of Malo-les-Bains, Leffrinckoucke, Zuydcoote and Bray-Dunes. However, interspersed among these urban areas are a few unspoilt stretches of dune and a few green sites, refuges which attract migrant passerines in both spring and autumn, the latter season being notable for the appearance of a few Siberian rarities every year. The D60 runs parallel to the coast the whole way, and is the initial access route.

When leaving Dunkerque Port Est, next to the outlet canal look for the Musée d'Art Contemporain – it is well sign-posted. This museum has a small park with a few hedges and isolated copses, easy to look through for insectivorous passerines in autumn, among which Yellow-browed Warbler is just one of the possibilities in October. A grassy hillock overlooks the museum and offers a fine view both towards the sea and inland, an ideal spot for watching daytime passage in autumn of species such as herons, birds of prey and various passerines.

Following the D60 eastwards, check the hockey fields in Malo-les-Bains; being situated just behind the coastal dunes their associated hedges provide shelter for many insectivorous migrants, which stop to feed here for a day or two. Yellow-browed and Pallas's Warblers and Siberian Chiffchaff are among the species which have been found here in the past few years.

The Fort de Dunes park is a little farther on, in Leffrinckoucke. This comprises an extensive area of dunes, part of which is accessible on foot, although part is a military camp, closed to the public. From the top of the high Leffrinckoucke dunes you can get a very good view north-eastwards – this is another good spot for watching visible passage in spring and autumn, the same mix of species as mentioned before. Behind the line of dunes, the large military camp remains quite wild and in spring provides a secure breeding site for many insectivorous species, including Icterine Warbler, Lesser Whitethroat, Golden Oriole and, mostly recently, Bee-eater. Sheltered from the wind, in autumn the park is another oasis for many passerines, including rarities from Siberia.

Continuing east again brings us to Zuydcoote, where there is a small park next to the camp site of L'Estran. This park has several way-marked walks and is another focal point for passerines in autumn.

Finally, continuing to the Belgian border, the Dune Marchand at Bray-Dunes is a vast area of dunes where one or two pairs of Bee-eaters have been present in summer for the last few years.

7. Cap Gris-Nez and Cap Blanc-Nez

PAS-DE-CALAIS (62) *IGN 01*

These two headlands, between Calais and Boulogne, form a remarkable peninsula which marks the boundary between the Channel to the west and the North Sea to the east. Cap Gris-Nez is the closest point to Britain in France, the Straits of Dover being only 28 km wide here. The coastline takes the form of a large bay, with the town of Wissant at its centre, backed by a line of sand-dunes, terminated at each end by a rocky headland. Gris-Nez (Jurassic rock) to the west rises some 50 metres above the sea. To the east, the chalk cliffs of Blanc-Nez are more than 100 metres high and extend for several kilometres. The low-lying ground behind the dunes is occupied in part by a large marsh. The countryside inland from Cap Blanc-Nez, the Artois, is made up of open fields, whereas that at Gris-Nez, the Boulonnais, is more of a mosaic of habitats with hedgerows.

This is considered by many as the best place in northern France to observe migration, and one of the best in Europe. Hundreds of thousands of seabirds, waders and passerines pass this strategic point each year. There is unrestricted access onto the cliff tops of both headlands, and no hunting is allowed along this stretch of coast.

ACCESS

From Boulogne take the D940 northwards towards Wimereux, then through Ambleteuse and Audresselles to Audinghen. From Calais, to the east, take the A16 motorway towards Boulogne and leave at exit 7 for Marquise, then take the D191 towards Audinghen. There is a TGV station at Calais-Fréthun and a main line station at Boulogne with direct trains from Lille, Dunkirk or Paris; in the summer there is a bus service between Calais and Boulogne which stops in the villages in the area concerned. There are large car parks at each headland.

Cap Gris-Nez: The D191 leads from Audinghen to the car park at the foot of the lighthouse (1); from here walk to the top of the cliff a little farther north (2), looking towards the English coast, the best spot from which to watch visible migration. It is worth bringing a folding chair if you are thinking of doing some prolonged watching, as well as water- and wind-proof clothing, as strong, cold winds are frequent. During the autumn there can be large numbers of a wide variety of birds moving past offshore: divers, grebes, Brent Goose, duck, waders (especially in August and September), Kittiwake, Little Gull (mainly October and November), sometimes Sabine's Gull (in October), and various species of larger gulls (Great Black-backed, Lesser Black-backed, Herring and Common). Further out, look for Gannet, Manx and Sooty Shearwaters (especially in October), and sometimes Leach's Petrel. Terns (especially Common and Arctic) fish over the shallows along the coast and these attract skuas (Arctic, Pomarine, Great and occasionally Long-tailed).

In addition to the static pursuit of sea-watching, various walks along the coast are possible from Cap Gris-Nez. The circuit proposed here runs along the cliffs eastwards, across dunes, arriving at a beach and then Tardinghen marsh,

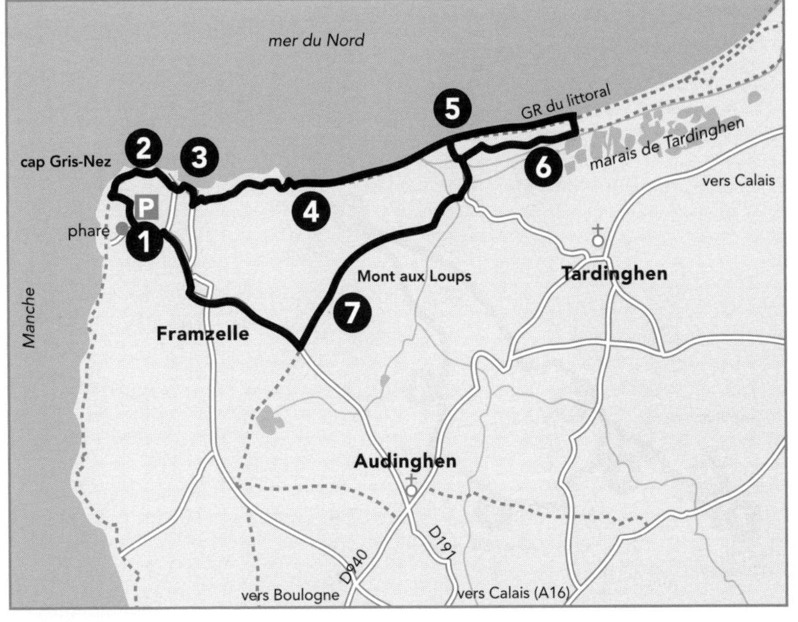

coming back to the headland via the fields. It thus covers most of the habitats, and birds, of the area. Out at sea (3) there are Gannet and Eider throughout the year; in autumn and winter there are Common and Velvet Scoters, Red-breasted Merganser, Guillemot, grebes and divers; and between March and October many terns that sometimes attract skuas. The dunes (4) are attractive to insect-eating passerines in autumn. Many gulls and waders occur on the Tardinghen-Wissant beach (5), for instance Oystercatcher and godwits on migration. Look for Marsh Harrier, Bluethroat and Bearded Tit in the wetland habitat of the Marais de Tardinghen (6). Return along the track that passes via the Mont aux Loups and through arable fields (7) before reaching the village of Framzelle. Look for pipits (Tree, Meadow and Tawny) on any area of meadow and ploughed land in autumn. In summer, look out for Yellow Wagtails (*flavissima*) which breed in small numbers in cultivated areas. The various copses are used as roosts by finches (Greenfinch, Brambling, Chaffinch, Goldfinch) and by thrushes and Blackbird, from October to December. Curlew and more rarely Dotterel occur on open cultivated ground, especially in autumn, and Lapland Buntings are seen regularly.

Cap Blanc-Nez: From Audinghen, continue north on the 940 through Wissant to Escalles, and then on to the car park at the foot of the obelisk (1). From here, walk across the heathland and short grass that covers the top of the limestone cliffs (2), but take care because of the risk of landslips. Visible migration can be watched from the car park both in spring, and also in autumn, the latter being the season with the largest number of birds. In spring look for Stonechat and Grasshopper Warbler, while Short-

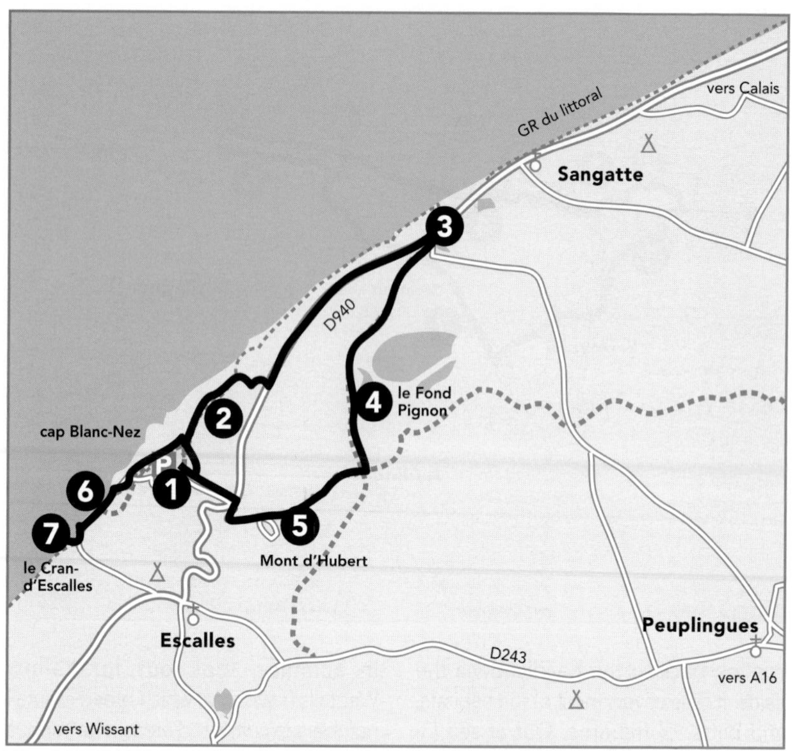

eared Owl often hunts over the meadows from mid October onwards.

Follow the track as far as the Latham monument and take the D940 towards Sangatte. At the junction with the road to Peuplingues (3), take the small dirt track near the cross that climbs towards Le Fond Pignon (4), where there is a small lake. Although access to the lake itself is forbidden, it is possible to scan it from the path. In spring Avocet and Stone Curlew nest in this area and in late summer migrant birds of prey are quite often present. Ducks, Coot and gulls all occur in winter.

Follow the track, through the blackthorn as far as the Mont d'Hubert (5). In spring the surrounding fields have Wheatear and Ring Ouzel, and it is another good area for birds of prey. Then continue downhill back to the Cap Blanc-Nez car park.

Just to the south, the Escalles beach (6) is worth a visit to see the colony of seabirds (Kittiwake, Herring Gull, Fulmar) present from April to October. From the Cran-d'Escalles (7) it is possible to get down to the base of the cliffs.

The Marais de Tardinghen: There are two car parks by the D940 a short distance south of Wissant, at a place called the 'Carrière du Phare'. There is a nature trail here which runs through the different habitats of the marsh and around the quarry, where Red-throated Diver is regular in winter. Species to be seen on the marsh include Grey Heron, Bittern, Teal, Marsh Harrier

SHORT-EARED OWL

and Cetti's Warbler. There are several hides along the trail.

Calendar

Spring: divers, grebes, Gannet, Cormorants, duck, waders, terns, Guillemot and Razorbill.
Autumn: divers (three species), Great Crested and Red-necked Grebes, Gannet, Sooty, Balearic and Manx Shearwaters, Cormorant, Spoonbill, Grey Heron, geese, Shelduck, Goldeneye, sawbills, Common and Velvet Scoters, skuas (4 species), Mediterranean and Sabine's (rare) Gulls, terns, Guillemot, Razorbill, numerous migrant passerines.
Winter: divers, grebes, sea-duck, Razorbill, Guillemot.

8. Étang de Rumaucourt

Pas-de-Calais (62) *IGN 04*

Situated in the triangle formed by Douai, Arras and Cambrai are a series of marshes and lagoons near the villages of Rumaucourt, Écourt-St.-Quentin and Oisy-le-Verger. Two rivers, the Hirondelle and the Sensée, flow through the valley depositing peat. Peat-digging has lead to the creation of a series of lakes of which the largest considered here is the Étang de Rumaucourt (20 hectares of open water and 13 hectares of reed-bed). Three-quarters of the banks are in a natural state with a good belt of reeds, areas of mixed willow and alder, and in places some oak woods. Clear water and abundant and varied vegetation mean that there is a diversity of animal life at all seasons. The lakes and marshes are leased for shooting and fishing, and public access is limited to the paths, but nevertheless this is perfectly adequate. Although shooting from hides and fishing from boats means that the number of duck is not high, there are good numbers of other birds to be seen here.

Access

The village of Baralle lies on the N939, about 20 km from Arras and 10 km from Cambrai. From here take the D19 northwards to get to the village of Rumaucourt. Continue north towards Écourt-St.-Quentin; the entrance to the site lies between these two villages, and it is possible to park near the football pitch, about 200 metres from the road.

From the car park (1), walk along the side of the lake as far as its northern end (2). One can scan the whole surface from this section. Coot and Moorhen are numerous and, like Great Crested and Little Grebes, are present throughout the year. Marsh, Reed and Great Reed Warblers breed in the reedbeds. Among passage migrants, Common Sandpipers can be seen in May and Snipe occur in spring and autumn.

From here it is possible to turn right,

cross a stream and follow a path between a wood and some fields that goes as far as a spring (3), from where the lake is again visible. Little Bittern can often be seen in late May or early June flying over the reeds while various warblers and Nightingale are present in the bushes along the lakeside in spring and early summer. Three species of hirundine, Swift and Black Tern come to hunt over the lake in May.

Follow the tarmac track as far as the poplars, and just after this take a dirt-track to the right that leads back to the car park. Marsh Harrier can often be seen gliding over the reeds from late March onwards.

As an extension to this circuit, it is possible to continue from (2) alongside some other small lakes, where Savi's Warbler and Bluethroat both breed in the more overgrown parts of the marsh. Walk for about 100 metres along a tarmac road, turning off to the left just after the camp site; this route passes between some wooded marshland and the Étang Béquerel, where Great Crested and Little Grebe also occur throughout the year.

Beyond a metal bridge (4), the path runs alongside a ditch and leads to another road by an old brick bridge (5). From here one can continue to rejoin the original route, either directly or by making a circuit through the meadows to the south. Hen Harriers can be seen hunting over the fields and they come to roost in the reedbed in the evening. Check also for Willow Tit, best identified by call, which occurs in the willows and wooded marsh.

There are other lakes and marshes at Palluel, Arleux, Écourt-St.-Quentin and Lécluse, where the same mix of species occurs. The GR121 long-

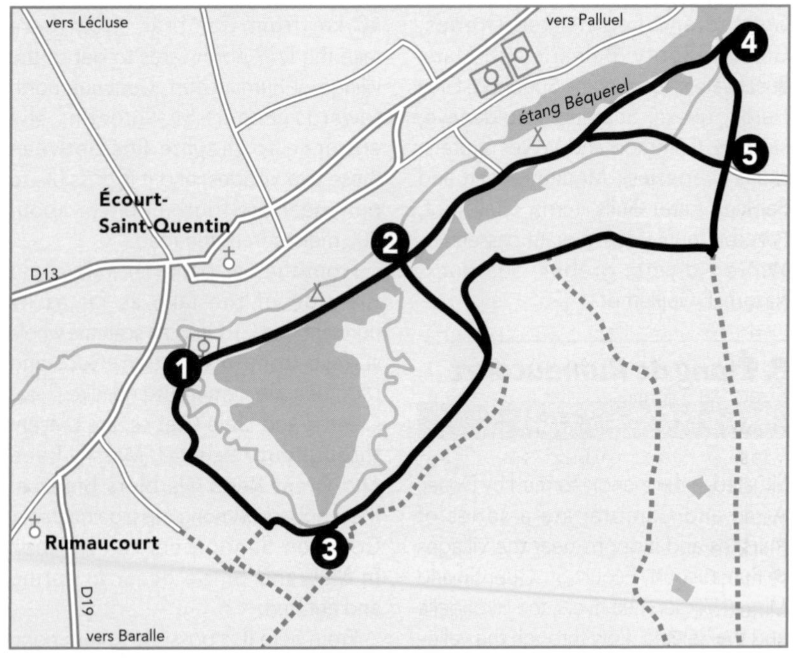

HEN HARRIER

distance footpath runs through the area and makes a convenient access route.

CALENDAR

Spring: (especially as soon as the hunting season is closed at the end of February) groups of duck (Wigeon, Gadwall, Pintail, Shoveler, Teal and Garganey, Pochard and Tufted Duck), Osprey, Black Tern, hirundines, Swift.
Breeding season: Great Crested and Little Grebes, Little Bittern, Marsh Harrier, Hobby, Moorhen, Coot, Bluethroat, Nightingale, wetland warblers, Golden Oriole. It is one of the last sites in the region for Great Reed Warbler.
Autumn: Greylag Goose, Osprey, Hobby, Black Tern.
Winter: Great Crested and Little Grebes, Mute Swan, Grey Heron, Coot, Moorhen and Water Rail. Buzzard, Sparrowhawk, Kestrel and Merlin (the least common), Hen Harrier and Kingfisher.

9. *Platier d'Oye*

PAS-DE-CALAIS (62) *IGN 01*

The Réserve Naturelle du Platier d'Oye lies to the east of Calais and is one of the few sections of this coast that has been spared from industrial development. The reserve dates from 1987 and contains all the habitats typical of this low-lying littoral of northern France: sandy beaches, mudflats and salt marsh, dunes, meadows, marshes and lagoons. The site is managed by a local consortium, 'Eden-62'. Access to the main part of the reserve is controlled, but a nature trail and hides allow for all habitats to be viewed well. Access to the seashore itself is unrestricted, but dogs should be kept on the lead, and care needs to be taken not to disturb ground-nesting birds, which include Ringed Plovers and one of France's largest Sandwich Tern colonies. There is also a large Black-headed Gull colony which includes significant numbers of Mediterranean Gulls as well. A word of warning: this area is shot over in the hunting season, and there have been several confrontations between wildfowlers and conservationists here.

ACCESS

The village of Oye-Plage lies on the D940 between Calais and Gravelines, and can be accessed from exit 21 on the A16 motorway east of Calais. From Oye-Plage go north towards the coast, following signs to the reserve, to reach the Plage du Casino (1). One can park at the reserve car park near the 'L'Abri Côtier' café. Scan the salt marsh and dunes in front of the car park for migrant passerines in winter; species such as Skylark, Shore Lark, Linnet, Twite and Snow Bunting can be seen here. There is a high-tide wader roost here (outside the hunting season) and Kentish Plover nests.

From here one can walk along the coast using the coastal footpath, and in fact make a complete circuit of the reserve (about 7 km). Alternatively, one can drive on the landward side to reach a car park, with a hide (2) not very far away. From here one gets a good view over the central part of the reserve, an area of flood meadows and lagoons. Among breeding species are Black-headed Gull, Avocet, Oystercatcher, Ringed and Little Ringed Plovers. Migrants include a wide range of waders, plus Spoonbill and Little Egret, and over-wintering species include waders, ducks and sometimes geese.

It is possible to go farther on foot by taking the marked trail which leaves from the Platier hide, going via the Les Écardines and returning via the dunes and beach. There is another hide by the roadside at Les Écardines and others along the trail on the seaward side at (4), (5) and (6). In addition to the species mentioned above, and the gull and tern colonies, other breeding species include a few pairs of Herring Gulls, Redshank and Greylag Geese.

To the north-east of the area (6), the path runs alongside an area of mudflats and dunes where numerous shooting butts can be seen (these are the

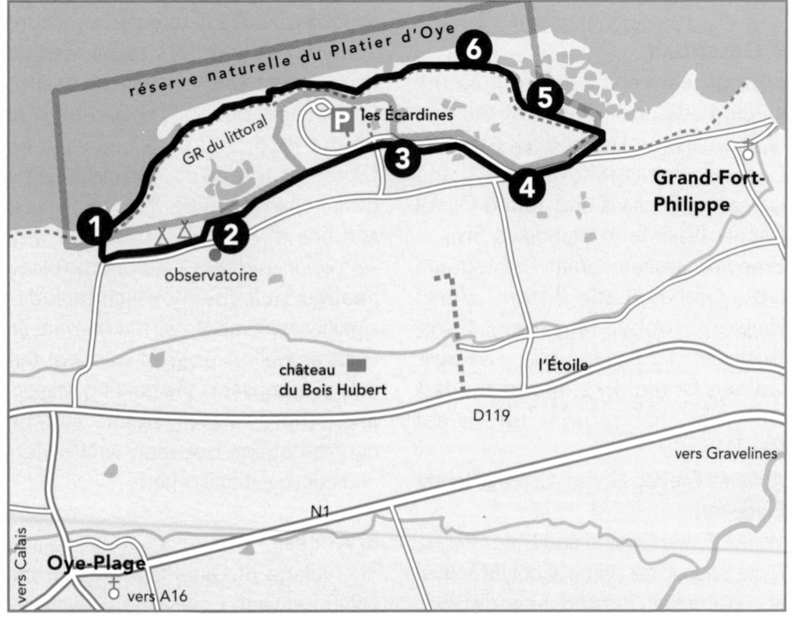

ones that, despite the area's status as a reserve, are still sometimes used by wildfowlers). This is a good area, well worth a visit during spring and summer, as it attracts both migrant and nesting waders and passerines.

Calendar

Spring: depending on the date, many migrants pass or make a brief halt. Little Egret, Spoonbill, many duck, various small waders (including Temminck's Stint – regular in May and July to September), phalaropes, gulls and many passerines. Many rare species have been found, including American Wigeon, Broad-billed, Pectoral, Marsh, Terek and Baird's Sandpipers, Lesser Yellowlegs, Rose-coloured Starling.

REDSHANK

Breeding season: Little and Black-necked Grebes, Greylag Goose, Shelduck, Shoveler, Teal, Garganey, Pochard, Tufted Duck, Oystercatcher, Avocet, Ringed, Little Ringed and Kentish Plovers, Lapwing, Redshank, sometimes Black-winged Stilt, Black-headed, Mediterranean and Herring Gulls, Sandwich and sometimes Common and Little Terns, numerous passerines including Marsh and Icterine Warblers and Golden Oriole.
Winter: Shelduck, dabbling duck (especially Wigeon and Teal), a few waders, Shore Lark, Snow Bunting.

10. Réserve Naturelle du Romelaere

Pas-de-Calais (62)
IGN 01/02

Le Romelaere is a network of large lakes, the end result of peat extraction in the 19th century, each one of which is separated from the next by earth embankments and surrounded by reedbeds, wet meadows and small woods on peat soil. Lying not far from St.-Omer, it is an island of calm and of great biological interest within a 3,600 hectare marsh which has elsewhere been heavily influenced by agricultural and leisure activities. It is an important staging point for migrant duck in spring and acts as a wildfowl refuge in winter. Bittern also occurs here in winter. During the breeding season it is one of the last wetlands in the Pas-de-Calais that is suitable for wetland warblers, Little Bittern and Marsh Harrier. A Cormorant nesting colony has also become established since 1992.

Access

From St.-Omer take the D209 north-east to Clairmarais, from where the réserve naturelle is signposted. There is a car park at the Grange-Nature visitor centre (1) for the reserve, open every weekend and every day in the summer; there are slide shows about the birds of the marshes, information for walkers, and a natural history exhibition.

At the site three different walks are possible:

The lakes walk, a 3 km round trip via point (6), and for which there is an explanatory leaflet available at the centre.

The nature trail, a 4 km walk there and back, which leads to a hide (5) opposite the Cormorant colony, this being a route adapted for the less mobile.

The following species are easily observed on both of these first two circuits: Great Crested Grebe, migrant duck, as well as Black Tern, hirundines (3), Mute Swan, Marsh Harrier (2), Moorhen and Turtle Dove. In the reedbeds and bushes at (4) look out for Bluethroat, Nightingale, Mistle Thrush, Cetti's, Savi's, Reed and Marsh Warblers, Whitethroat, *Phylloscopus* warblers, flycatchers, tits, Short-toed Treecreeper, Reed Bunting, and with a little luck and patience Little Bittern.

The water meadows circuit, a 3 km walk, leads to an observation point (7), overlooking the water meadows to the east of the reserve. During times of migration this is a good area for Sparrowhawk, Snipe, Lapwings and *Tringa* waders.

The circuits going to (5) and (6) are open from 08.00 am to 20.00 pm in the summer (March to September), 08.00 am to 18.00 pm in the winter

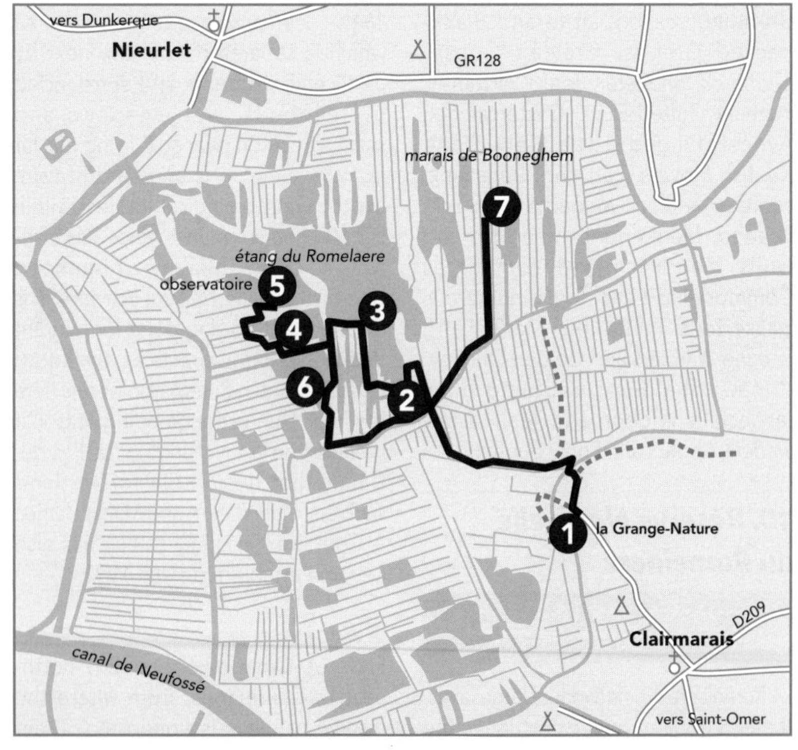

RINGED PLOVER

(October to December). The reserve is closed between 15th December and 15th March. The most productive visits are usually early morning or in the evening during the summer.

Calendar

All year: Great Crested Grebe, Cormorant, Grey Heron, Mute Swan, Mallard, Moorhen, Coot, Black-headed Gull, Long-eared Owl, Kingfisher, various tits.
Spring and summer: Little Bittern, Marsh Harrier, Swift, hirundines (3 species), various woodland passerines and wetland warblers (Reed, Marsh, Sedge, Grasshopper and Savi's Warblers, Bluethroat, Reed Bunting). Duck on migration, especially during March and April (Teal, Garganey, Wigeon, Pintail, Shoveler, Pochard).
Autumn: visitors include Snipe, Lapwing, many passerines (thrushes, Siskin).
Migration: Cattle and Little Egrets, Shelduck, Pintail, Buzzard, Osprey, Common Sandpiper, Common and Black Terns.
Winter: Bittern, Mallard, Shoveler, Wigeon, Gadwall, Teal, Pochard, Tufted Duck, Water Rail, Hen Harrier, Sparrowhawk, Long-eared Owl.

11. Baie de Canche

PAS-DE-CALAIS (62)
IGN 01

The Canche is a small river which flows into the sea about 30 km south of Boulogne, its mouth being the first estuary of any significance on the Picardy coast for birds arriving from the north. It is not as well known as the Baie de Somme estuary further south but it is nevertheless not without interest. All of Picardy's estuarine habitats are found here – sea, shore, dunes, buckthorn, etc. Some areas are part of a reserve whilst others are shot over on a regular basis. For those who like gulls, a close look at the many gulls in the afternoon in late autumn or winter can be well worth the effort, when tens of thousands of birds can be present, including thousands of Great Black-backed Gulls, and sometimes rarer species.

The southern side of the estuary can be viewed from the northern edge of Le Touquet, although a telescope is essential for good views of the various waders, Shelduck, etc. The reserve area is on the northen side. Drive via Étaples north along the D940 towards Camiers. At the British cemetery there is a car park, from where a footpath leads through the reserve, passing various hides and viewpoints. The drier parts of the dunes shelter a variety of small birds, including Lesser Whitethroat in the bushier areas, and Green Woodpecker in the woodland. The area attracts raptors in winter; these have included Rough-legged Buzzard and even White-tailed Eagle.

SITES

1 *The Baie d'Orne*

2 *Falaises du Bessin*

3 *Marais de la Dives*

4 *Baie du Mont-St.-Michel*

5 *La Hague*

6 *St.-Vaast-la-Hougue*

7 *Regnéville-sur-Mer*

8 *Marais de Réthoville*

9 *Parc Naturel des Marais du Cotentin et du Bessin*

10 *Phare de Gatteville*

11 *Réserve naturelle de Beauguillot*

Basse-Normandie

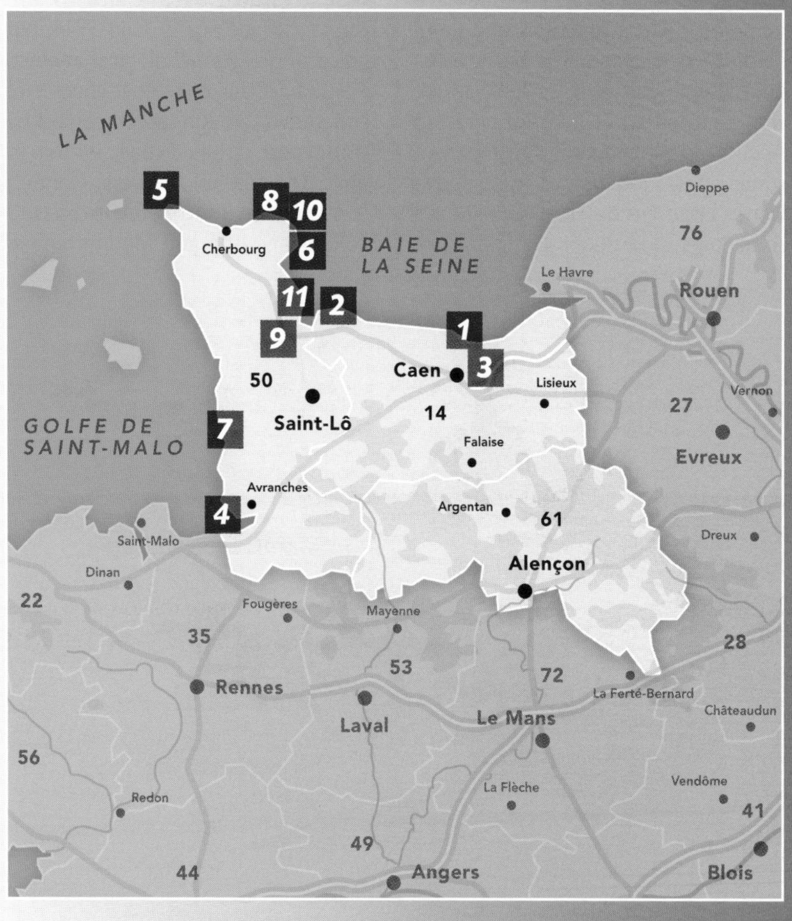

1. Baie d'Orne

CALVADOS (14) *IGN 07*

The River Orne flows into the sea at Ouistreham, the cross-channel ferry port north of Caen, and the wide shallow bay here has a good cross-section of estuarine habitats, plus an area of coastal dunes, pines and scrub. Great Crested Grebe, gulls and Eider can be seen on the sea throughout the year, whilst the vast tidal sand-flats and the Pointe de Merville are important roosting sites for migrant waders. In the spring Redshank, Ringed Plover, Turnstone and Avocet are numerous, whilst Shelduck and Little Ringed Plover breed. The bushy areas hold Nightingale and Cetti's Warbler, with Long-eared Owl in the pines. In August and September, it is an important staging post for terns and skuas, and in winter Little Grebe, Teal, Dunlin and sometimes Snow Bunting or Shore Lark add interest. There is a visitor centre at Sallenelles, which is on the D514 coast road east of the river, which has details concerning the natural history of and access to the area. There are way-marked trails and several hides at the Réserve du Gros-Banc, accessed a little further on along the D514 before Merville.

2. Falaises du Bessin

CALVADOS (14) *IGN 06*

The stretch of coast north-west of Caen is best known as the site of the Normandy landings in June 1944, but is also of great ornithological interest. In autumn Black and other species of terns move through, accompanied by Arctic and Great Skuas, whilst in winter the sea holds divers, Gannet, Cormorant, Shag, Red-breasted Merganser, Little and Mediterranean

WIGEON

Gulls, Razorbill and Guillemot. Cap Manvieux, north-east of Bayeux, is a good look-out spot, as is the Blockhaus du Chaos a little to the west. Further west again, at the Pointe du Hoc, is a reserve managed by the Groupe Ornithologique Normand. France's largest Kittiwake colony is sited on the cliffs here, and other nesting species include Fulmar, Cormorant, Lesser Black-backed and Herring Gulls, Stock Dove, Grasshopper and Dartford Warblers.

3. *Marais de la Dives*

CALVADOS (14) *IGN 07/18*

The River Dives winds its way through meadows, arable crops and fields bordered by hedgerows typical of this part of Normandy, to reach the sea at Cabourg, east of Caen. Among the breeding species can be found Cuckoo, Blue-headed and White Wagtails, Whinchat, Stonechat, Redstart, Grasshopper, Sedge, Marsh and Fan-tailed Warblers, Common and Lesser Whitethroats, Golden Oriole, Red-backed and occasionally Great Grey Shrikes, Reed, Corn and Cirl Buntings and Yellowhammer. Two species mostly heard rather than seen include Quail and Corncrake. Various waders occur on migration, as do White Stork and Grey Heron. The area is also interesting for birds of prey: Buzzard, Honey Buzzard, Kestrel, Hobby, Short-eared and Long-eared Owls (the latter at a winter roost), Barn and Little Owls. The A13 crosses the river east of Caen. To the north the area around Bricqueville and Robehomme are worth exploring along the minor lanes, and the area to the south around Brocottes and Hotot-en-Auge is also of interest.

4. *Baie du Mont-St.-Michel*

MANCHE (50) *IGN 16*

At the extreme western end of Normandy, the Baie du Mont-St.-Michel is of European renown, and is of interest throughout the year. Its vast expanses of mudflats and sand extend from Cancale in the west to Carolles on the west-facing Cotentin coast to the north. There are two islands in the bay: the Mont-St.-Michel itself and Tombelaine, the latter protected as a reserve. The vast extent of marine vegetation, its variety and the extraordinary amplitude of the tides in the area means that a very wide diversity of estuarine habitats occurs. The bay is of international importance for several bird species, both migrant and wintering, duck and waders particularly. It is also of great interest in spring and summer: various species breed in the estuarine vegetation and there is a seabird colony at Tombelaine (no access between March and July). To the north the cliffs at Carolles, which mark the limit of the bay, reach 60 metres in height and are backed by heathland. Their geographical position at the south-west end of the Cotentin peninsula makes them a migration crossroads for birds from the north and east and several hundreds of thousands of passerines migrate through the area each year between late August and November.

ACCESS

One initial point to note: the great extent of the inter-tidal zone makes watching difficult at low tide and it can be very dangerous here during an incoming tide, so great care needs to be taken throughout this area. Mont-St.-Michel itself (1) is well-signposted.

Interesting species to be seen here include Peregrine, Brent Goose, Shelduck, gulls and terns. Starting from here and heading south along the causeway, turn left on the D275 towards Bas-Courtils, and fork left towards Roche Torin; the road follows the shore, and the grazing meadows are of interest in winter for birds such as Brent Goose, raptors and Lapland Bunting. It is possible, on minor roads, to follow the coast and cross the river south of Avranches. From here head towards Granville but turn left at Pont-Gilbert towards Genêts on the D911. At the Vains bridge, turn left towards le Rivage on the D591, then left again to Village-du-Rivage. Grouin du Sud (2) provides an excellent observation spot. On the shore look for Grey Heron, Cormorant, waders and Shelduck but beware of the presence of Chilean Flamingos, escapees from captivity. Continue on the coast road northwards, stopping at Pointe du Mont-Manet (3) where a coastal footpath towards Genêts passes a reedbed where Bluethroat and Bearded Tit are possibilities. On arriving at Genêts (4), stop at the 'Maison de la Baie' (behind the town hall); on the shore, check for Brent Goose, Shelduck, Little Egret, Marsh Harrier, Peregrine and Merlin. Continue to the 'Bec d'Andaine'

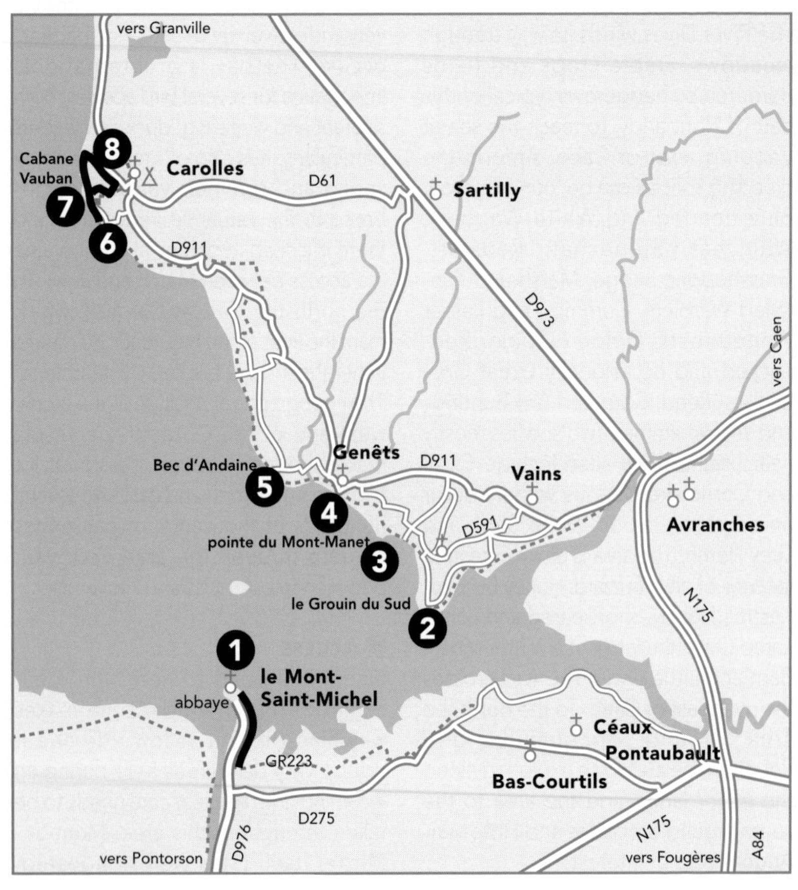

(5), and scan the beach and dunes for birds of prey, waders, gulls, and terns, especially in August and September.

The D911 coast road continues northwards to Carolles. On arriving in the village, turn left just after a small bridge, following signs towards the Cabane Vauban and after 750 metres along a narrow, winding road, park in the car park (6).Take the footpath to the left towards the sea, then right to reach the Cabane Vauban (7), a shelter overlooking the cliffs. This is a good spot for looking for birds on the sea (flocks of scoters, Balearic Shearwater, Gannet, Cormorant, Shag, terns, Little Gull, Guillemot, Razorbill) and there are Ravens on the cliffs. It is also the best place for watching the autumn migration of passerines moving along the coast. In spring, it is worth following the path northwards and descending into the Lude valley (8), then walk upstream for about 300 metres before turning right onto a trail leading back to the Cabane Vauban. This is a good area for heathland species such as Dartford and Melodious Warblers, Lesser Whitethroat, Cirl Bunting and Yellowhammer).

The area to the west of Mont-St.Michel, just over the regional border in Brittany, should not be ignored either. The GR34 long-distance footpath runs between salt marsh on one side and arable fields on the other, as far as La Chapelle-Sainte-Anne. From here to St.-Benoît-les-Ondes, the vast mudflats can easily be scanned from the road. The slightly higher patches formed by the accumulation of sea-shells provide both nesting sites and high-tide refuges for waders. The Pointe du Grouin which closes the bay beyond Cancale is another strategic spot from which to watch for passing seabirds, particularly under gale conditions.

MALLARD AND TEAL

Calendar

Spring: very many waders on migration and various duck. Hobby breed, also Quail, Kentish and Little Ringed Plovers, Skylark, Meadow Pipit, Blue-headed Wagtail and Reed Bunting. Raven nest on the cliffs, Dartford Warbler and Lesser Whitethroat on the heaths.

Summer: on the sea, numerous Common Scoter, many Balearic Shearwater, Razorbills and Guillemots.

Autumn and winter: Many migrating passerines at Carolles. Gannet, Cormorant and Shag, grey geese, Brent Goose (with a few pale-bellied birds), Mallard, Wigeon, Teal, Peregrine, Merlin, Marsh and Hen Harriers, Oystercatcher, Dunlin, Knot, Black-tailed and Bar-tailed Godwits, five species of large gull, Little Gull, terns, Short-eared Owl, Snow and Lapland Buntings.

5. La Hague

Manche (50) *IGN 06*

The Cap de la Hague lies at the far north-west corner of the Cotentin peninsula. The north-facing coast is low and rocky with many reefs in the sea and the tide-races, among some of the strongest in Europe, discourage seabirds from lingering offshore. Moving southwards, the coast rises and we come to an area of high granite and gneiss cliffs, often an impressive 100 metres high with sheer faces of some tens of metres. On the spray- and wind-covered slopes, there are good areas of thrift-covered grassland and gorse heath before we arrive at the headland of the Nez-de-Jobourg. Access to the reserve here is prohibited, but the nearby Nez-de-Voidries is an accessible watchpoint.

Access

From Cherbourg, take the D901 past Beaumont-Hague, and after passing the Hague nuclear-waste treatment plant turn left on the D401 to Nez-de-Jobourg. At Dannery, turn right on the D202 which, after 3 km leads to a car park (1). Take the track towards the signal-station, then turn left towards the sea to reach the Nez-de-Voidries headland (2). Shags, which nest here, can be seen throughout the year. The Nez-de-Jobourg reserve (3) lies to the south, where Great Black-backed and Herring Gulls nest, with the Îlots des Bréquets (4) beyond. From January to July, Fulmars can be seen gliding along the cliffs, and sometimes perched (especially at Nez-de-Voidries).

For the Cap de la Hague, you can follow the 'sentier des douaniers' footpath (GR 223) northwards as far as Goury, where there is a small harbour with a life-boat station. The walk of 6 km will take about an hour, but can be dangerous in high winds. Alternatively drive on the D202 as far as Jobourg where it joins the

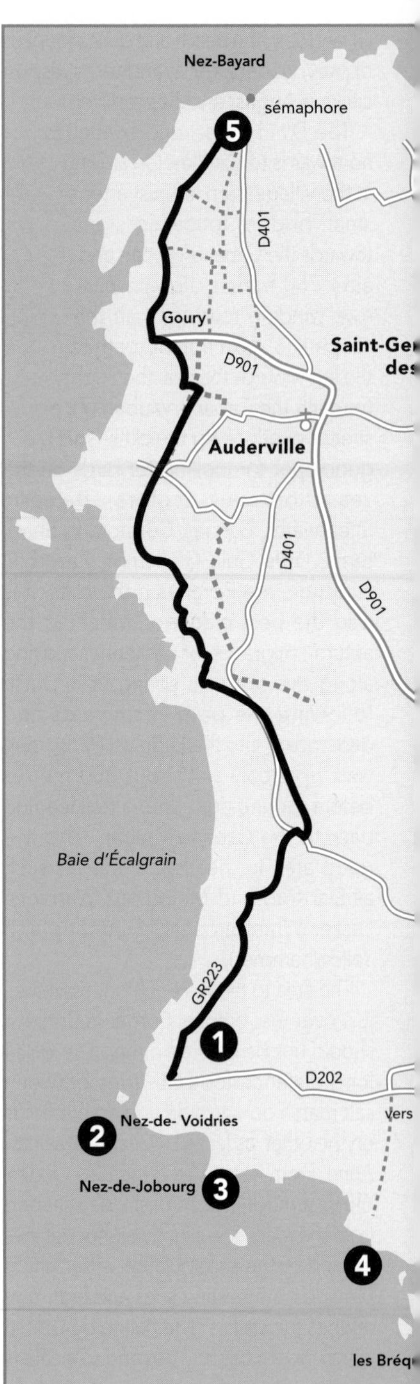

D901, continue to Auderville and then Goury; from here follow the coast to the blockhouse before the signal-station (5), the best spot for watching migrants. Migrant seabirds (July to December and March to May) include divers, Gannets and terns (especially Sandwich). Snow Buntings occur on the tideline in autumn and winter. Purple Sandpipers, quite a rare wintering species in France, occur here, and are best looked for on the rocky shore at high tide, from August to early May, but are often very well camouflaged against the rocks.

Calendar

Spring and autumn: depending on the weather there may be good seabird passage, the most numerous species being the Gannet (with some tens of thousands of birds). Also Mediterranean Gull and Purple Sandpiper. Some migrant passerines may be seen: of note are Snow Bunting and sometimes Lapland Bunting.

Summer: there are nesting seabirds on the cliffs: Fulmar, Shag (the largest mainland colony in France, outside of Brittany), Great Black-backed and Herring Gulls, Oystercatcher, Kestrel, Rock Pipit (rare), Jackdaw and Raven. On the heathland: Dartford and Grasshopper Warblers and Stonechat breed. Some migrant landbirds may be seen: Merlin, Wheatear and Ring Ouzel.

6. St.-Vaast-la-Hougue

Manche (50) *IGN 06*

St.-Vaast-la-Hougue forms the northern limit of the low sandy coast on the east side of the Cotentin peninsula. The River Saire flows into the sea here, whilst to the north is the granite headland of the Pointe de Barfleur. The area is of importance as the bio-geographical boundary between northern and Atlantic invertebrates, which led to the establishment of a biological research station of great renown in the nineteenth century. For birds also, the shallow coast here is an area of contact, with species from the North Sea meeting those from the Atlantic, Iceland or even North America. The variety of habitats increases its attractiveness to birds. Perhaps of greatest interest are the exceptional numbers of fish-eating birds that occur between September and March.

Access

St.-Vaast-la-Hougue lies some 30 km south-east of Cherbourg, accessed via Valognes along the D902, and then the D1 from Quettehou. Park at the port (1), where it is often worthwhile searching through the gulls for one of the rarer species. Then walk southward towards the Fort de la Hougue, which is signposted. At the tennis courts (2) there are often many waders feeding on the nearby mudflats: Curlew, Redshank, Grey and Ringed Plovers, Dunlin, with Oystercatcher, Turnstone and Purple Sandpiper in the rockier areas. Take the path along the side of the Cul-de-Loup bay, where Shelduck and Brent Goose feed on the mudflats, and continue on a signposted trail to the fort. Along the length of the walk there is easy birdwatching, but the area is of most interest at high tide. Sea duck (scoters and Red-breasted Merganser from September to April) are often out at sea, and there are also grebes and divers from October to March or April: Great Crested, Slavonian and Black-necked Grebes and Red-throated Diver;

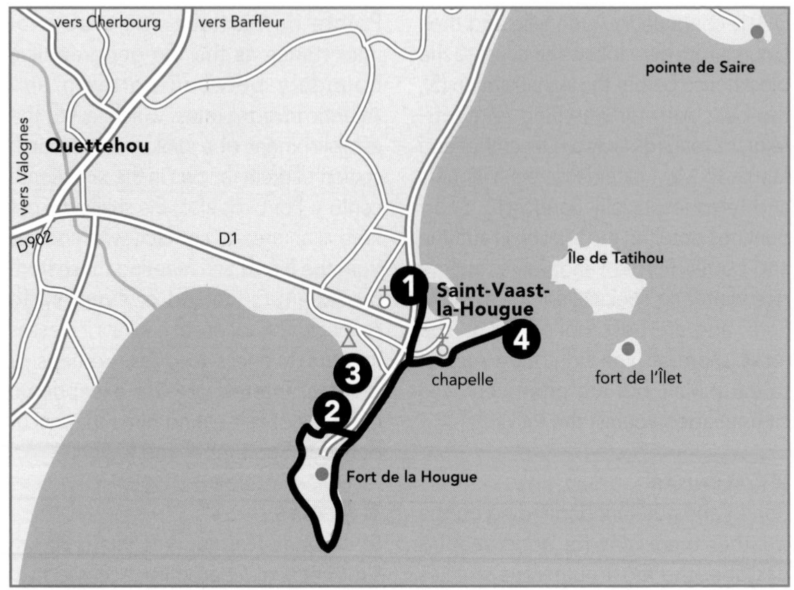

irregularly Red-necked Grebe, Black-throated or Great Northern Divers. Be patient, these diving birds can be hard to find, and spend long periods underwater. From July to April Gannet, terns, Cormorant, Shag, Guillemot and Razorbill can all be seen here, and Eiders are present throughout the year. To return to the port, follow the beach (3), checking the high-tide line for passerines such as White Wagtail, Rock and Meadow Pipits, Black Redstart, Greenfinch, Linnet and Snow Bunting. From the chapel walk to the very end of the dike (4), an excellent viewpoint over sea and towards the Île de Tatihou.

Calendar

Summer: Gannet, waders, marsh terns, terns, and skuas. Breeding species include Great Black-backed, Lesser Black-backed and Herring Gulls; Shelduck and Oystercatcher.

Autumn and winter: divers occur regularly (in order of frequency: Red-throated, Black-throated and Great Northern), grebes, particularly Great Crested, Slavonian and Black-necked (Little and Red-necked are rarer). Also Gannet, Shag, Cormorant, Red-breasted Merganser, Brent Goose, Shelduck, Eider and Common Scoter, and in smaller numbers Velvet Scoter, waders (Curlew, Grey Plover, Ringed Plover, Oystercatcher, Turnstone and Purple Sandpiper), numerous gulls, with sometimes Glaucous, Iceland, Yellow-legged and Caspian, a few late migrant or wintering Sandwich Terns, Razorbill and Guillemot. More rarely, Merlin and Peregrine. Lastly, many passerines: Meadow and Rock Pipits, White Wagtail, Black Redstart, Greenfinch, Linnet and Snow Bunting. In the bushy areas, warblers are abundant during times of migration.

SMALL WADERS

7. Regnéville-sur-Mer

MANCHE (50) *IGN 06*

Some 11 km to the west of Coutances, on the west coast of the Cotentin peninsula, the River Sienne flows into the sea at Regnéville-sur-Mer. The river bends round to the south before reaching the open sea, and is sheltered by the dunes of Agon-Coutainville on its western side. In winter the village of Regnéville-sur-Mer is an excellent spot to watch a wide variety of waders, particularly on a rising tide: Shelduck, Grey Plover, Bar-tailed Godwit, Curlew, Redshank and Dunlin. At the end of the day the estuary also holds good numbers of roosting gulls. The area is particularly well known for being the only regular wintering site for Light-bellied Brent Goose in France. This sub-species with almost white underparts comes from Greenland and Canada with between 300 and 400 birds passing the winter here. The most favoured section for these birds is around the salt marshes and sheep-grazed meadows to the north of Regnéville, in the area of the Marais and La Trancardière, and December and January are the best months for finding them. They can also be seen along the banks of the Sienne a bit further upstream, near Incleville. In autumn, the Agon-Coutainville dunes, across the river, can be interesting for migrant passerines (such as pipits, wagtails and chats) and sometimes, in September, a Dotterel will stop here.

8. Marais de Réthoville

MANCHE (50) *IGN 06*

On the north coast of the Cotentin at Réthoville, a line of dunes forms the boundary between the sea on one side and low-lying ground with ponds and wet meadows, flooded in winter, on the other. A marshy area has been formed, with some interesting breeding birds including Lapwing, Blue-headed Wagtail, Fan-tailed Warbler and Bearded Tit. Many migrants can be seen in autumn, particularly waders and passerines on the marsh, including Dotterel on the meadows. Other species include

SMALL WADERS

Spoonbill, Garganey, Marsh Harrier, Hobby and Avocet. Snow and Lapland Buntings can be seen in winter, and sometimes Shore Lark. Réthoville is on the D116 between Cherbourg and the Pointe de Barfleur, and a road from the centre of the village leads to the shore. It is possible to view the marsh from the coastal footpath that runs to the west. The same footpath runs in the opposite direction to the Pointe de Néville, for further exploration.

9. Parc Naturel des Marais du Cotentin et du Bessin

MANCHE (50) *IGN 06*

The Parc Naturel des Marais du Cotentin et du Bessin covers a large section of the southern part of the Cotentin peninsula, protecting many wetland sites as well as the typical 'bocage' countryside of hedgerows and small fields. The best place to start is the Ponts d'Ouve visitor centre, which is just north of Carentan, off the road to St.-Côme-du-Mont, and is well-signposted. Not only can you pick up information about other sites in the area, but the wetland next to the centre is well worth a visit, and the entrance fee that is required. The site is open every day from Easter to the end of September; from the 1st to 15th October at weekends; from 15th October to Easter, every day except Monday; it is closed during the Christmas school holidays. It covers some 100 hectares, with a circular walk passing a series of hides overlooking lagoons, reeds and wet meadows. In the spring and summer White Stork, Blue-headed Wagtail, Whinchat, Bluethroat, wetland warblers and Reed Bunting all breed. During migration there can be various waders and marsh terns. It is of particular interest for duck in winter and for Snipe. At this time of year there is usually a Bittern or Great White Egret, a Peregrine or Merlin to be seen.

10. Phare de Gatteville

MANCHE (50) *IGN 06*

Situated at the north-eastern tip of the Cotentin peninsula, Gatteville lighthouse is an excellent place for sea-watching. It is best when a strong north-easterly is blowing, particularly between September and December. Species passing offshore include divers (3 species), Gannet, Sooty, Balearic and Manx Shearwaters, skuas (four species), Kittiwake, Little and Sabine's Gulls, terns and auks. In addition, various migrant passerines occur in the bushes and fields in the area in the autumn, whilst Purple Sandpipers can be found on the rocks in winter. The lighthouse lies at the end of a minor road out to the Pointe de Barfleur, and makes a good shelter when a strong wind is blowing. The coastal footpath to the south passes Crabec bay, where the offshore islets host a gull roost, among which in winter there are often large numbers of Mediterranean Gulls. Taking the footpath west brings you to the dunes around the Étang de Gattemare, a good area in winter for Lapland and Snow Buntings and Shore Lark.

11. Réserve naturel de Beauguillot

MANCHE (50) *IGN 06*

This reserve, part of the Parc Naturel des Marais du Cotentin et du Bessin, occupies the southern end of Utah Beach, at the foot of the eastern side of the Cotentin peninsula. Immediately to the south are the vast mudflats of the Baie des Veys, part of which are included in the reserve, the landward part of which comprises ancient salt marsh, meadows and lagoons, all reclaimed from the sea in the past. In winter the most numerous species out on the shore is the Dunlin, with up to 8,000 birds sometimes present, but there are also plenty of Oystercatchers, Curlew and Grey Plover. From November to April there are good numbers of wildfowl here, including White-fronted, Greylag and, more rarely, Bean Geese, as well as Teal, Pintail and Wigeon. Other species to be expected at this time include Little Egret, Spoonbill, Marsh and Hen Harriers, Peregrine and Merlin. The reserve is accessed via the D913 which runs from Carentan to the Utah Beach. Although the reserve itself is private, the D329 south from the museum runs alongside it, and there are several hides overlooking the wet meadows. A track continues along t he southern side of the reserve towards the sea, providing views over the salt marsh.

SNOW BUNTING

LAPLAND BUNTING

SITES

1. ***River Seine at Poses***
2. ***Les Andelys***
3. ***Seine valley forests near Rouen***
4. ***Fécamp and the Côte d'Albâtre***
5. ***The Seine estuary***
6. ***The Seine valley flood meadows near Rouen***

Haute-Normandie

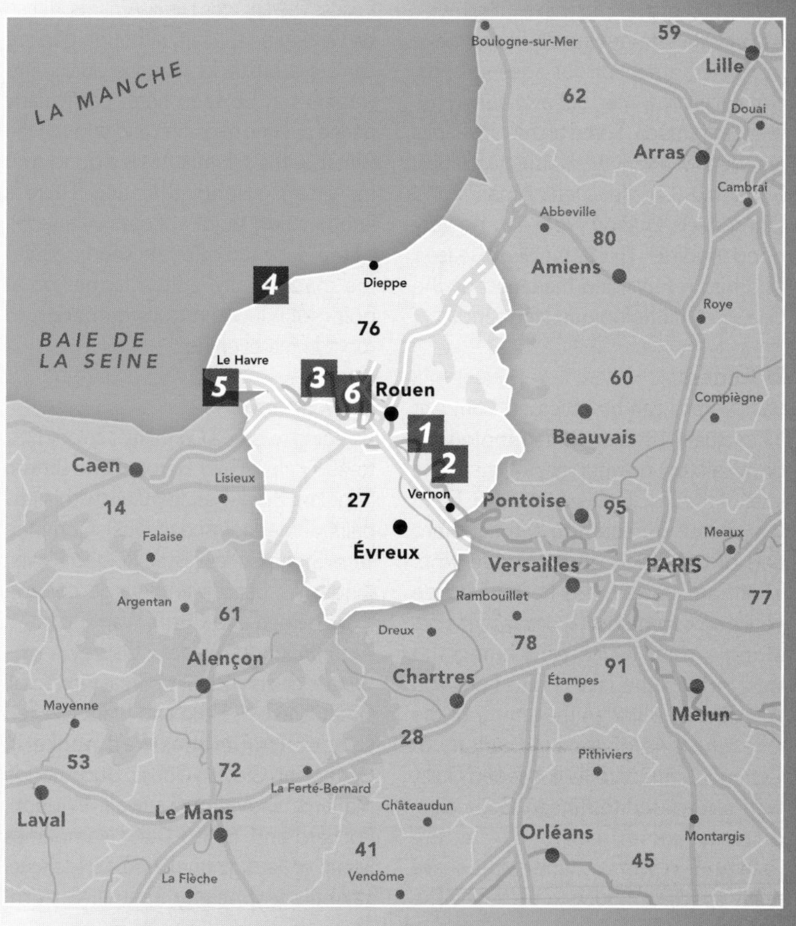

1. River Seine at Poses

EURE (27) *IGN 08*

The lower course of the River Seine is marked by a series of large meanders, several of which have important habitats for birds. To the south-east of Rouen, near Val-de-Reuil, the meander (or 'boucle') at Poses has long been a site of gravel extraction and as a consequence very little now remains of the original meadows and grasslands on sandy soil, a remarkable habitat which once sheltered many rare plant species. On the other hand, the gravel-pits have filled with water, and have rapidly become a significant attraction for aquatic birds, particularly in winter, but also during the breeding season. Some of the gravel-pits are used for a variety of leisure activities, but some (Lac des Deux-Amants and Étang de la Grande Noë) can be very good for birds. This latter lake is leased as a bird reserve and managed by the Groupe Ornithologique Normand.

■ ACCESS

Val-de-Reuil can be accessed from exit 19 of the A13 Paris-Rouen motorway, or by rail (the gravel-pits are just to the east of the SNCF railway station). From the station go south to the southern end of the Étang de la Grande Noë. There are three hides here with free public access, the first (1) being 50 metres along a road which runs along the west side of the lake. From here you can view an island in the centre of the lake which holds a mixed colony of Common Terns and Black-headed Gulls, with a few Mediterranean Gulls also. Bitterns sometimes occur in the reedbed in winter, when there are many species of duck to be seen. The next hide (2), the one closest to the road, is some 300 metres farther north, and there is a car park here. This is a good spot to view the Cormorant colony, and again is good for wildfowl. The third hide (3) is reached via a path north from here; as the three hides face in different directions it is sometimes worth moving from one to the other to get better lighting conditions when the sun is shining. Other pits further north in the same area are also worth checking. One can drive north towards the prison but before that turn right on a new road (not marked on older maps) towards Poses. The Lac des Deux-Amants (4) can be viewed on the left, although parking can be a bit tricky. Various ducks and waders can be seen here, particularly during autumn migration and through the winter. In the summer this is a good spot for watching Hobbies hunting. There is another view-point at Poses village (5), where duck can often be seen close to the road. Finally, a little farther on at point (6), view the gulls gathering to roost in the evening.

■ CALENDAR

Breeding season: a Cormorant colony (300 to 400 pairs), Grey Heron, Little Bittern (regular), Black-headed Gull (with a few pairs of Mediterranean Gull), Common Tern, Stone Curlew, Little Ringed Plover, Kingfisher, Sand Martin (large colony), Marsh, Reed and Cetti's Warbler.

Autumn: ducks, waders, Osprey.

Winter: divers (including Great Northern), Great Crested, Little and Black-necked Grebes (sometimes Red-necked), Cormorant, Greylag Goose. Duck include Mallard, Shoveler, Gadwall, Wigeon, Pochard and Tufted Duck (sometimes Scaup or Ferruginous Duck), Goldeneye, sawbills (especially Smew). Bittern,

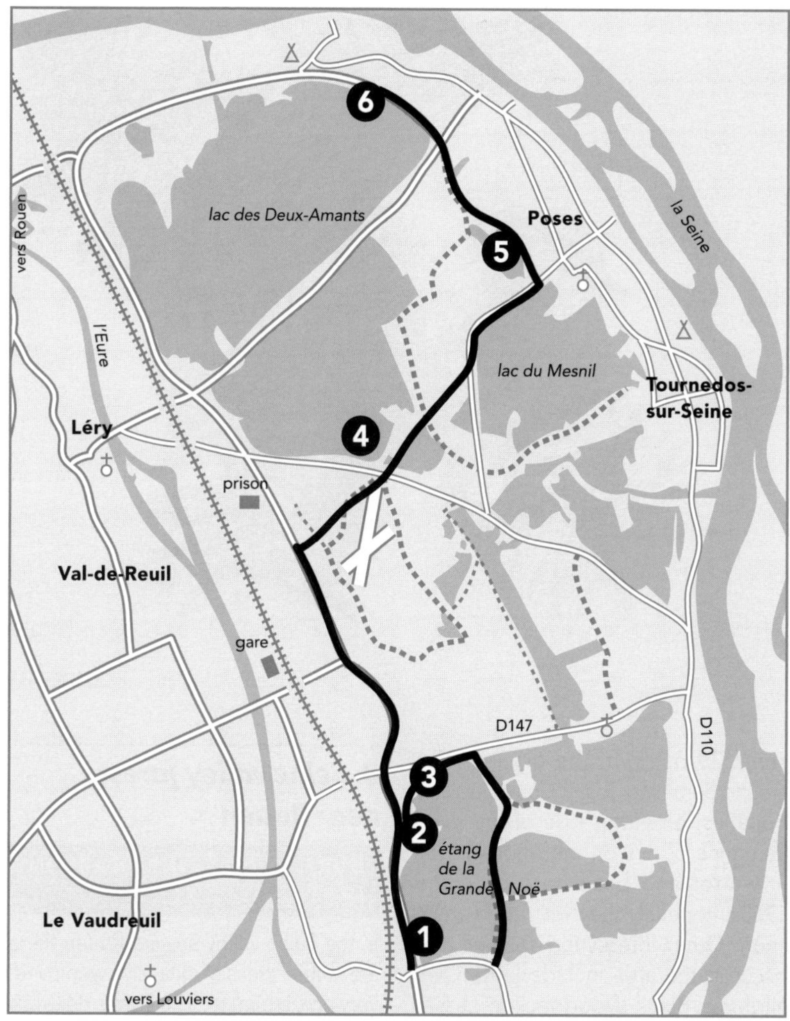

scoters, Eider and Ruddy Duck all occur regularly. Black-headed and other gulls (particularly Yellow-legged).

2. *Les Andelys*

EURE (27) *IGN 08*

A little further up-river from the previous site the Seine makes another wide meander near the town of Les Andelys. The northern part of the valley here is occupied by dry grassland and heath with scattered gravel-pits and dry quarries. In the southern part there is a mixture of forest, cultivated fields and a few strips of orchard. The cliffs on the right bank near Château-Gaillard dominate the surrounding countryside. Perhaps the most interesting species here is Stone Curlew. The whole of the Haute-Normandie population occurs here,

GOLDCREST

some 25 pairs, in the dry quarries around Bernières, Tosny, Courcelles and Bouafles, on either side of the river. Peregrine occurs on the Andelys cliffs in winter and bred here until the 1960s; hopefully they will return again soon. Other interesting species that occur in the area include Little Owl, Nightjar, Black Woodpecker, Lesser Whitethroat, Yellow-legged Gull and Red-backed Shrike (the only breeding site in Haute-Normandie). There are high densities of Turtle Dove, Green Woodpecker, Nightingale and Melodious Warbler and both Hobby and Honey Buzzard are seen regularly. The D135 which crosses the Seine at Les Andelys runs through the main part of the meander, and there are also other minor roads off the D313 on the eastern bank which allow access to this area.

3. *Seine valley forests near Rouen*

Eure (27)/Seine-Maritime (76) *IGN 03/07/08*

In the Seine valley around Rouen there are several areas of extensive woodland, very rich in birdlife. The Forêts de Lyons and de Brotonne have vast areas of beech, whilst the Forêts de la Londe and de Roumare have extensive stands of oak. All are very good for birds. Among birds of prey, Buzzard, Honey Buzzard, Hobby and Sparrowhawk are all common, although Goshawks disappeared in the middle of the last century. There are high densities of Middle Spotted Woodpecker wherever there are ancient oaks, with several hundred pairs to be looked for in the area. Black

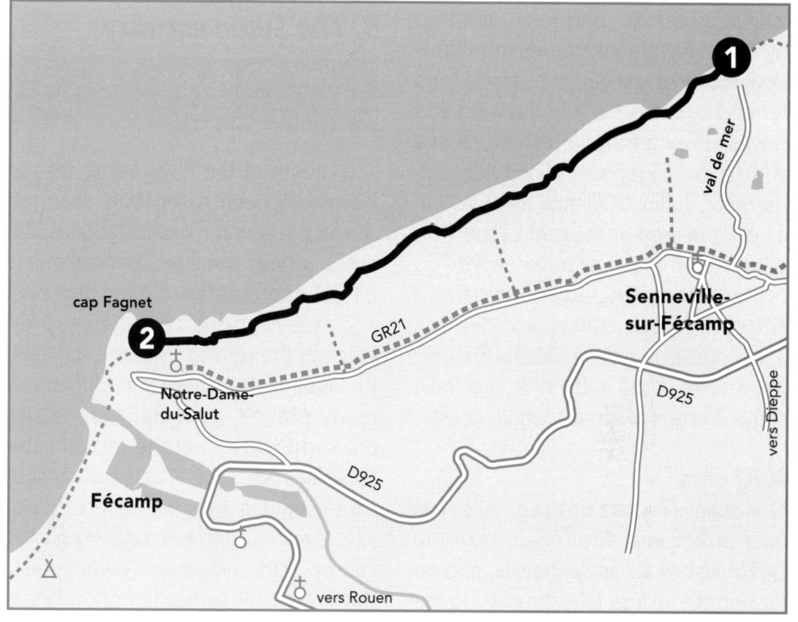

Woodpeckers, a fairly recent arrival, are now widespread. Nightjar occurs wherever clearings have been opened up in the woodland, and there are also a few breeding Woodcock. Both species are best looked for at dusk, of course. Hawfinch, Goldcrest and Firecrest are all common, and all the usual tits can be found, although Willow is quite rare. Of the two treecreepers, Short-toed is the commonest but it is interesting to know that Common Treecreeper also occurs here, a relict from pre-glaciation times. Here (only about 50 pairs) it still occurs at low altitude, far from the mountains and northern forests that are its main habitat, in areas of ancient beeches, where there is an under-storey of holly, and should be looked (or listened) for in the Forêts de Lyons, La Londe and Brotonne. The Forêt de Lyons lies to the east of Rouen, between the N31 and N14. The Forêt de la Londe is immediately south-west of Rouen (near Exit 34 on the A13), with the Forêt de Roumare immediately to the north on the other side of the river. The Forêt de Brotonne is in the Seine valley west of Rouen, and the D913 runs along its eastern edge. All the forests can be explored along minor roads and forestry paths.

4. Fécamp and the Côte d'Albâtre

SEINE-MARITIME (76)
IGN 07

The chalk cliffs along the north Normandy coast – the Côte d'Albâtre – are one of the most remarkable habitats of the Haute-Normandie region. They stretch for 140 km between the Seine estuary at Le Havre and the Somme estuary near Le Tréport, and in places can reach a height of nearly 100 metres. The chalk was created under the sea some 80 million years ago, and then raised up by earth movement, something that is slowly continuing today, to be eroded and formed by the actions of the wind and waves. They are home to several sea and cliff-dwelling species of bird. Although Razorbill, Puffin, Guillemot and Chough all disappeared at the end of the 19th century, others that have arrived to replace them include Fulmar and Kittiwake. Peregrines have recently made a welcome return, re-establishing themselves in the mid 1990s, with now some 20 pairs along the whole coast.

Access

One rewarding section of coast lies just east of Fécamp. From here take the D925 east as far as Senneville, and on leaving the village take the road to the Val de Mer. Steps lead down to the shore (1) from the end of this road. From here it is possible to walk the 4 km to Cap Fagnet (2), where there is a Kittiwake colony, along the foot of the cliffs, looking at the cliffs and out to sea along the way. However, the shore is covered at high-tide, so the walk is best done when the tide is still falling to ensure you have time to get there and back without getting cut off! It is worth checking any Rock Pipits, particularly in spring, as the *littoralis* sub-species from Scandinavia has been recorded here on more than one occasion.

Calendar

Breeding season: Fulmar, Cormorant (about 500 pairs), Peregrine, Herring Gull (also a few Lesser Black-backed and Great Black-backed Gulls), Kittiwake, Stock Dove, Black Redstart, Jackdaw.
Autumn and early spring: divers, scoters, Eider, Mediterranean Gull, terns, auks, Rock Pipit.

5. The Seine estuary

Seine-Maritime (76)
IGN 07

The mouth of the River Seine near Le Havre has been extensively changed due to the creation of port facilities; the river has been canalised, embankments have been created around the port and heavy industry has occupied much of the former estuarine habitats. Because of this, access is difficult in many places, especially since the creation and extension of the container port. The area is heavily shot over in winter, and the hunters do not always respect the laws concerning what can be shot and when. Nevertheless, there are still some natural habitats remaining, and birds to be seen, and being close to a ferry port it can be worth spending some time here while waiting for the boats to leave. The area on the north shore of the river between the Pont de Normandie and Pont de Tancarville is protected as a réserve naturelle, with mudflats, reedbeds, salt marsh and wet meadows holding a good mix of birds. It is an important breeding site for Bitterns, and the reedbeds also hold Marsh Harrier, Bluethroat, Savi's Warbler and Bearded Tit. The meadows still shelter a few Corncrakes in summer, and Black-tailed Godwit, Lapwing and Spoonbill on migration, particularly in the spring (March). The mudflats attract large numbers of waders both on migration and during the winter, and Short-eared Owl is a regular winter visitor. The Pont de Normandie has a car park and restaurant at its northern end, and the footpath over the bridge gives a good overview of the whole area.

SHELDUCK

6. The Seine valley flood meadows near Rouen

Seine-Maritime (76)
IGN 07

In several places downstream from Rouen, the Seine winds its meandering way through a series of flood meadows, still used for hay or grazing, and separated by lines of pollarded willows. In places there are still a few orchards to add variety to the landscape, as at Jumièges. The most characteristic species of the hay meadows is the Corncrake, although this species is declining with only a few birds still present, despite there being between 25 and 30 pairs in the mid 1990s. The hay meadows also hold a few Whinchats in summer and Lapwings breed in the grazed areas. The hedgerows of pollarded willows have a good population of Redstarts, some Little Owls and the only Tree Sparrows to be found in the region. Common species include Hobby, Turtle Dove, Sand Martin, Blue-headed and Yellow Wagtails, Grasshopper and Cetti's Warblers and Nightingale. White Storks breed near Anneville and the meadows here are good for migrants including Crane, Spotted Crake, Snipe and Red-backed Shrike. Both Reed and Marsh Warblers breed in the reeds and bushes lining the ditches. The most interesting areas are the meanders at Jumièges and Anneville, between the Forêt de Roumare and the Forêt de Brotonne (see site 3 above), west of Rouen.

SITES

1 *Marais de Guérande*

2 *The Loire estuary*

3 *Forêt du Gâvre*

4 *Marais de Grée*

5 *Basses Vallées Angevines*

6 *Lac de Maine at Angers*

7 *Lac du Verdon*

8 *Mont des Avaloirs*

9 *Étang de la Rincerie*

10 *Étang du Gué-de-Selle*

11 *Forêt de Bellebranche and the Étang de Curécy*

12 *Parcé-sur-Sarthe*

13 *Forêt de Bercé*

14 *Lac de la Monnerie*

15 *Baie de l'Aiguillon*

16 *Baie de Bourgneuf*

17 *Poiré-sur-Velluire*

18 *Étangs des Boucheries/ Cité des Oiseaux*

19 *Lagune de la Belle-Henriette*

20 *Marais d'Olonne*

21 *Marais de Müllembourg / Île de Noirmoutier*

22 *St.-Denis-du-Payré*

23 *Beauvoir-sur-Mer*

Pays de la Loire

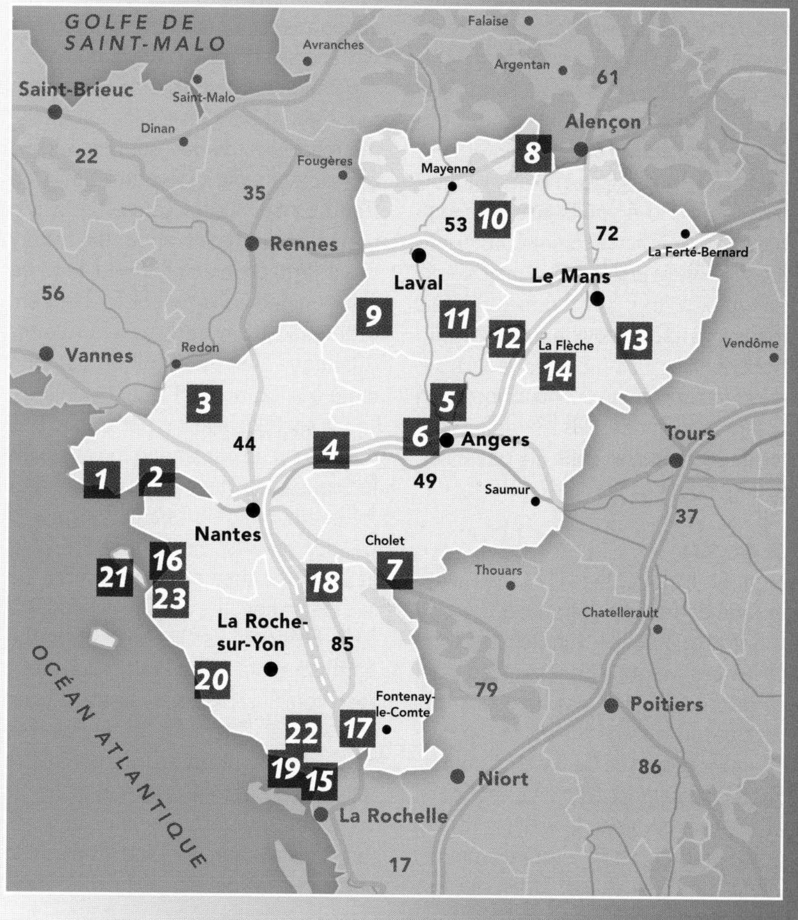

1. Marais de Guérande

Loire-Atlantique (44)
IGN 32

This complex of mudflats and salt marshes lies to the west of the mouth of the River Loire at St.-Nazaire, and is dominated by a still-active salt extraction industry. The area can be delimited by several well-marked features: to the north-west by the La Turballe-Pen-Bron sand-bar, to the north-east by the higher ground around Guérande, to the south-east by the holiday resort and magnificent beaches of La Baule, and to the south-west by the rocky coast of Croisic, Batz-sur-Mer and Le Pouliguen. There is good birding to be enjoyed here at every season. There are gulls and waders throughout the year, ducks and grebes in winter, and Common Tern, Avocet, Black-winged Stilt, Kentish Plover and Bluethroat among breeding birds in the summer. Entry into the salt-pans is prohibited as they are still being exploited, but the many public roads and tracks provide good viewing opportunities. For the gulls, waders and ducks it is best to go during an incoming tide or at high tide; this is true for both the mudflats and salt-pans. For passerines, spring mornings are ideal.

Access

From St.-Nazaire, the N171 leads west to Guérande; from here take the D99 towards La Turballe. Turn left at Clis as far as Les Maisons-Brûlées, then right to get to Lergat. From here take the road to the left which leads to the Pen-Bron Marine Rescue Centre (1). Common Scoter (sometimes with a Velvet Scoter or two) are common in winter offshore from Pen-Bron, and a few birds summer along the coast. A few Eider can also be seen throughout the year (though fewer than before the *Erika* oil-spill disaster of 1999). Great Northern and Red-throated Divers are regular species in winter off this section of coast. From the car park in the centre of Pen-Bron, a footpath allows access to the jetty and the beach, looking across to Le Croisic on the far side of the channel. From here you can get a good view along the shore, much favoured by waders. The harbour entrance and the smaller of the two channels (Le Petit Traict) behind the sand-bar are where you are most likely to see a Black-necked Grebe, which winters here in small numbers. Spoonbills can be seen in the Petit Traict bay and salt marsh in early autumn.

Having returned towards Guérande, turn right at Maisons-Brûlées and take the road towards Batz-sur-Mer and Le Croisic. At Pradel it is worth visiting the 'Terre de Sel' visitor centre (2), which provides information about the history of salt extraction and the wildlife to be seen; guided walks to look for birds are organised from here by LPO Loire-Atlantique (Tel: 02 40 62 08 80), and there is a log-book of recent sightings. To the south of here it is possible to turn right and wind out among the salt-pans to Sissable (3). The point is a good spot for seeing waders (many *Tringa* and *Calidris* species) throughout the year; at high-tide they can be seen on the salt marsh from the car. Grey Heron and Little Egret are usually present on the northern shore of the Petit Traict, easily seen from Sissable, as are Oystercatcher and Avocet. There are small colonies of Common Terns on islands in the salt-pans close to the road (stay in the car so as not to disturb them). Bluethroats (singing actively in April and May) can be seen in the low scrub in this area, along with Reed Bunting, Fan-tailed Warbler and Stonechat. There is a Black-headed and Common Gull roost in summer and autumn on the salt-pans.

From here, return to the road and continue south to Batz-sur-Mer (4). Throughout this area it is worth taking one's time and making frequent stops, as the route can be difficult and there are always plenty of birds to be seen from the car. You can also leave the car on the side of the road and go by foot on the many paths into the marsh.

At Batz-sur-Mer take the road west to Le Croisic, and stop for a time at the port (5). From here there is a good view of the mudflats, the entrance channel, and the breakwater. In addition, continue to the end of the Tréhic jetty (6) which sticks out into the Pen-Bron shallows. From this point, as at Pen-Bron opposite, it is possible to see either Slavonian or, more rarely, Red-necked Grebe in winter. Here, on an incoming tide there are large concentrations of gulls: Black-headed (with a few Mediterranean), Great Black-backed, Lesser Black-backed, Herring, Common and sometimes Yellow-legged, as well as Common and Sandwich Terns.

To visit the rocky coastline at the Pointe du Croisic (7) continue along the D45 coast road westwards. From the tip of the point, mainly in August and September, it is possible to see Great, Arctic and Pomarine Skuas, Balearic Shearwaters (with sometimes Manx, and occasionally Sooty Shearwaters), and

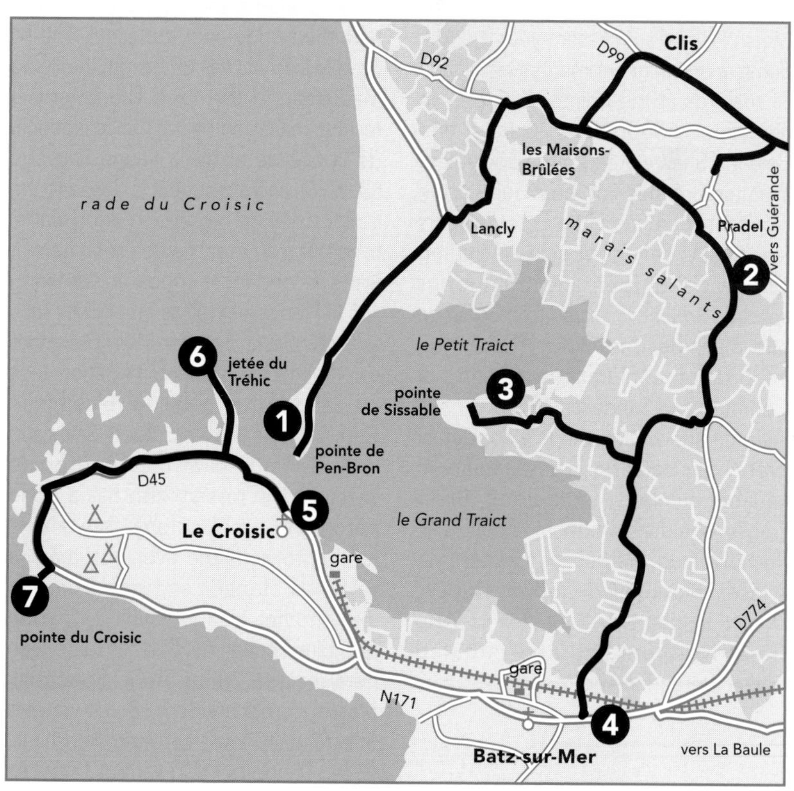

many Gannets. Also at this time Sabine's Gull might be seen, especially when a strong westerly wind has been blowing. During September and October small flocks of Brent Geese and Common and Velvet Scoters follow the coast to get to wintering sites further south and can be seen from the point.

■ Calendar

Spring: waders on passage, such as Grey Plover, Bar-tailed Godwit, Dunlin, Knot, Little Stint, Redshank (which breeds), Spotted Redshank, Greenshank, Green Sandpiper and sometimes Wood Sandpiper.
Breeding season: Little Egret, Black-winged Stilt, Avocet, a high density of nesting Bluethroats, more than 100 pairs of Common Terns; Kestrel and Marsh Harrier are present year-round.
Summer and autumn: impressive passage of seabirds at the Pointe du Croisic in August and September: Gannet and Balearic Shearwaters, three species of skua, sometimes Sabine's Gull. In the salt-pans there are Little Egret, waders (especially *Calidris* species including Curlew Sandpiper, and *Charadrius* species), Spoonbill, Sacred Ibis, Common and Black-headed Gulls. There is an important pre-migration gathering of Common and Sandwich Terns.
Autumn and winter: the five species of grebe can be seen in the estuary in variable numbers, Little Egret, Brent Goose, Shelduck, Wigeon, Pintail, Teal, Red-breasted Merganser, Goldeneye, Avocet, Black-tailed Godwit, Curlew, Dunlin, Ringed and Grey Plovers. Also Great Northern and Red-throated Divers, Peregrine and Merlin.

2. *The Loire estuary*

Loire-Atlantique (44)
IGN 32

The River Loire is an important river for birds, and its estuary, despite industrial development, is no exception. It can be viewed in several places along its southern side between Nantes and the St.-Nazaire bridge. One place to start is Frossay, about halfway between these two points. From here the D78 runs north to the village of Migron, on the banks of the Canal de la Martinière. Coot and Great Crested Grebe can be seen here, while Blackcaps can be heard singing in the spring.

From the campsite at Migron, turn left and, after a short distance, right to take the bridge over the canal. The Île de la Maréchale lies to the left, the Île du Massereau to the right. The latter is a reserve managed by the Office National de la Chasse et de la Faune Sauvage (ONCFS), and although it is closed to the public, they do organise guided walks. In winter many Teal can be seen here (it is the second most important wintering site in France) as well as other duck such as Gadwall and Shoveler. Many passerines use the reedbeds during migration: look for Sand Martin, Swallow, Bluethroat, Cetti's, Sedge, Aquatic, Reed, Savi's and Willow Warblers at the appropriate seasons. The reserve also has a good heron and egret colony. By walking further, towards the river, you reach a vast area of reeds and meadows and into another area in which it is worth spending some time. Species to be seen here include White Stork, Spoonbill, Marsh Harrier, Avocet, Black-winged Stilt, Ringed Plover, Lapwing, Redshank, Green Sandpiper and various terns. As at any migration spot, one never knows what may turn up, and there are plenty of opportunities for discovery.

Returning to the D723 and continuing west through Paimboeuf, there are wide mudflats at Corsept, and there are places where one can look out to the Banc de Bilho in the middle of the river where extensive mudflats are also exposed at low tide. This area attracts many thousands of birds in winter and during migration.

Finally, it is worth stopping at the bottom of the St.-Nazaire bridge, on the northern side, to check the mudflats here; even among the large ships vagrants are always a possibility along with the commoner species.

3. Forêt du Gâvre

Loire-Atlantique (44)
IGN 24

The Forêt du Gâvre, a vast mature beech wood some 45 km to the north-west of Nantes, has a diverse breeding bird population. As ever in woodland areas, spring is the best time for birdwatching, especially once the summer visitors have arrived. Buzzard, Sparrowhawk and Goshawk can be seen displaying over the woodland on mild sunny days in February and March, with Hen Harriers over the replanted and more open areas. Of the other birds of prey, the Black Kite does not arrive until mid-March, Hobby not until mid-April and Honey Buzzard in May last of all. There are the five species of woodpecker (Great, Middle and Lesser Spotted, Green and Black), both Black and Middle Spotted being relatively common here. Golden Orioles can be heard singing, usually hidden in the foliage. Smaller birds are also present: Marsh, Crested and Coal Tits, Bonelli's and Wood Warblers, Redstart, Spotted Flycatcher, plus Whitethroat, Garden and Dartford Warblers, Yellowhammer and Cirl Bunting. In the evening it is possible to hear Nightjar and Long-eared and Tawny Owls.

From Nantes, take the N137 north and then the D164 west to Blain. From here the D15 leads to the Carrefour de la Belle-Étoile in the centre of the forest, which can be explored along other forestry roads and tracks.

4. Marais de Grée

Loire-Atlantique (44)
IGN 24

The Marais de Grée, one of a complex of wetlands in the Loire floodplain, lies just east of Ancenis, halfway between Angers and Nantes. The whole area is criss-crossed with sedge-lined canals, with a few ponds and in periods of flood they can cover 400 hectares. The marshes are most rewarding in spring, as they are an important stop-over site for migrants at this time. Both the numbers and variety of ducks (at least ten species, with hundreds of birds) increase. Waders arrive in number as early as February: Black-tailed Godwit, Ruff, Golden Plover in particular, with Curlew, Ringed Plover and Dunlin in smaller numbers. They are followed in April and May by Redshank, Greenshank and Little Ringed Plover; Ruff may stay into early May (with males in breeding plumage). Hobby, marsh terns, hirundines, pipits and wagtails can also be seen at this time. Breeding species include Great Crested and Little Grebes, Garganey, Shoveler, more rarely Pochard and occasionally Pintail, Lapwing, Coot, Blue-headed

BLACK-TAILED GODWIT

Wagtail and Whinchat. On spring evenings it is possible to hear Corncrake or Spotted Crake, and sometimes Water Rail. The nearby open hillsides provide breeding sites for Stone Curlew, along with Red-legged and Grey Partridges and Little Owl. In winter, unless shooting activity causes too much disturbance, many thousands of Lapwing occur along with Golden Plover. The Wigeon is the most numerous duck, followed by Shoveler and Pintail. Greylag Goose and Snipe occur regularly. During hard weather, Bewick's and Whooper Swans may join the Mute Swans, and rarities like Smew may also occur.

The wetland area lies immediately east of Ancenis, and although the whole area is private and has to be watched from a distance to avoid disturbing the birds or the livestock, it can be viewed from the roads that encircle it. These are the D923 on the western side, and the D19 on the east, linked by a minor road at the north and the N23 at the south. Scan from the roadside anywhere where there is a good view.

5. Basses Vallées Angevines

Maine-et-Loire (49)
IGN 25

The Rivers Loir, Sarthe and Mayenne all join just to the north of Angers, before running through that city to join the River Loire itself. The flood plain for several kilometres north of Angers – the Basses Vallées Angevines – is a spring stop-over of major European (even international) importance for many ducks and geese as well as waders, and in the breeding period there are many interesting and rare wetland species, most notably Corncrake. The water-meadows are still farmed in a traditional manner, with conservationists and farmers working closely together to this end; the hay is cut in July in a 'Corncrake-friendly' manner, with the re-growth grazed by cattle. There is a network of drainage ditches and scattered willows, plus several areas of poplar plantations which it is hoped will not be allowed to extend further at the expense of the meadows. Periodic flooding almost completely covers the meadows between October and May. Wildfowling in winter causes much disturbance, but the birds move in again once the season is over.

Access

From Angers, take the D107 northwards towards Cantenay-Épinard. At the entrance to the village, turn right in the direction of Châtillon and Vieux-Cantenay (1), and then round via Vaux (2). The lanes are lined with willows and taller trees, there are many ditches, and it is possible to scan the meadows from the roadside. Any patch of wetter ground is worth checking for migrant waders: from mid-February to March Black-tailed Godwit pass through in large numbers on their way to the Netherlands, and Ruff and Golden Plover also occur.

From Vaux, return to the D107 and continue north towards Noyant village; here, take the track which runs out into the centre of the Baillie meadows (3) and which eventually reaches the bank of the River Sarthe. In spring (February and March) many dabbling duck and Greylag Geese stop in the flooded fields here. You can get an excellent view over the whole area from the track, although if groups of birds are close, it is better to stay in the car in order not to frighten them. During the summer (especially May and June), Corncrakes can be heard in the late afternoon and at night calling in the meadows. Various tracks run through the fields which can be used to explore the area, although you should not enter the crops themselves. Corncrakes are notoriously difficult to see, but with luck one will eventually cross one of the tracks and allow itself to be seen. Whinchats are numerous, and Sedge Warblers occupy the wetter areas of meadow, where a few reeds can grow. During April, the *flavissima* race of the Yellow Wagtail is a regular migrant, with Water and Meadow Pipits also passing through.

Return to Noyant, and turn north towards Soulaire-et-Bourg as far as the hamlet of Les Chapelles, then turn right on the DI09 towards Briollay, where the road eventually crosses the Sarthe. Stop at various spots (4, 5, 6) along this road to scan the meadows either side. In April there are often plenty of hirundines on migration. The meadows south of Briollay are also worth checking along the farm tracks. One word of warning: at times of flooding (when the level of the Maine at Angers is 3.5 metres or more), many of the access roads indicated here may be under water and therefore impassable.

Calendar

Spring: principally between mid-February and April when the meadows are still partially flooded, there can be large numbers of migrants, such as dabbling duck (mainly Pintail), Greylag Goose (February and March), Lapwing, Golden Plover, Ringed Plover, Dunlin, Ruff, Black-tailed Godwit by the thousand (late February to mid-March), Curlew, Snipe, *Tringa* waders, Black-headed, Common and Lesser Black-backed Gulls, marsh terns and numerous passerines including hirundines, pipits and Blue-headed Wagtail.

Summer: from May to July, Grey Heron, Garganey, Quail, Corncrake, Spotted

Crake, Lapwing, Curlew, Kingfisher, Blue-headed Wagtail, Whinchat, Fan-tailed, Grasshopper, Sedge and Reed Warblers, Reed and Corn Buntings.
Winter: (depending on water-level) Cormorant, a variety of dabbling duck, Lapwing, Golden Plover, Snipe, Skylark, Meadow and Water Pipits, Reed Bunting.

6. *Lac de Maine at Angers*

MAINE-ET-LOIRE (49)
IGN 25

This 90 hectare lake, a municipal leisure park in Angers, lies in the southern part of the city, close to the River Maine. In winter, the lake is used by thousands of

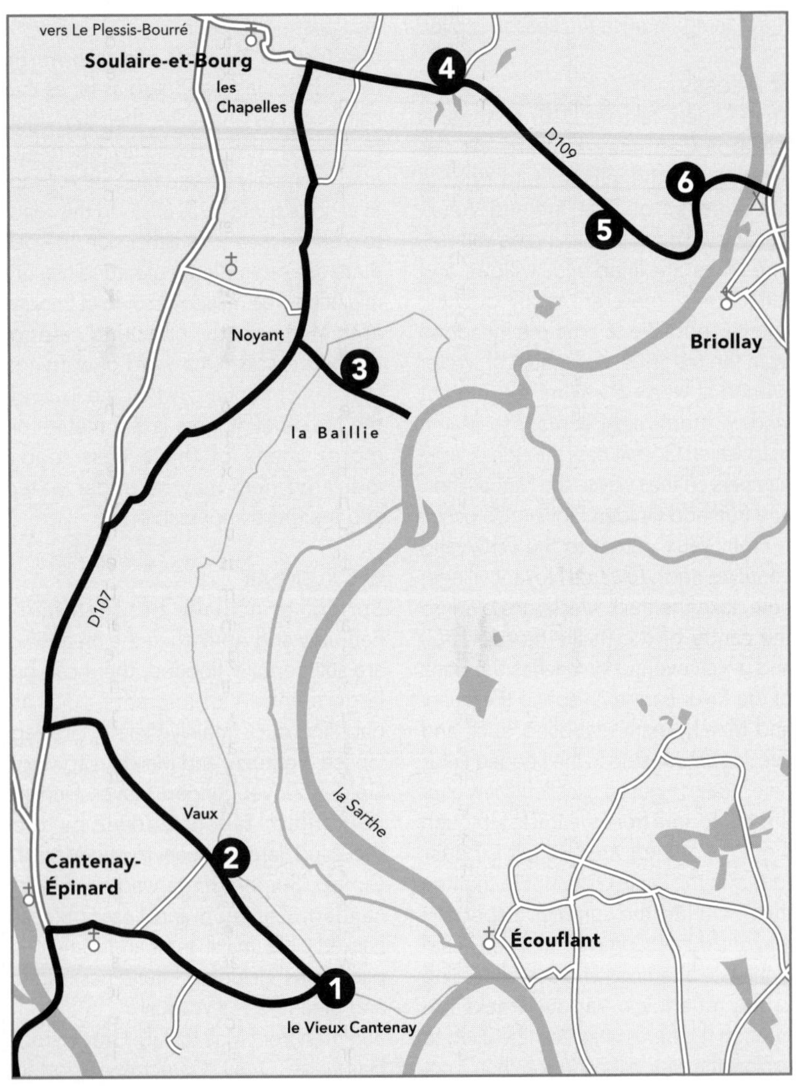

gulls and both dabbling and diving duck whilst the willow beds host an impressive roost of Cormorants, Stock Doves and corvids. During the spring Little and sometimes Cattle Egrets also join the roost. In the breeding season there is a Grey Heron and Little Egret colony here. To the south are some more flood meadows with Water Rail, Blue-headed Wagtail, Reed Bunting and where one or two Corncrakes can be heard calling. Greylag Goose, Lapwing and Black-tailed Godwit move through the area on spring migration, and are sometimes seen here.

The lake lies close to the D111 road from Angers to Bouchemaine. The 'Base de Loisirs' is well signposted, and there is a car park and Maison de l'Environnement information centre here. Footpaths run right round the lake, the part between the lake and the river being the most productive. The path continues south along the river bank to reach the meadows near Bouchemaine, and a footbridge at Pruniers allows you to cross to the other side.

7. Lac du Verdon

MAINE-ET-LOIRE (49) *IGN 33*

Dating from late 1979 and covering about 240 hectares, the Lac du Verdon reservoir was built to provide drinking water for Cholet and regulate the flow of the River Moine. In winter it is possible to see Greylag Goose (sometimes White-fronted or Bean), various dabbling and diving ducks, gulls (several thousand Lesser Black-backs come to roost) and Short-eared Owl. About one third of the lake's surrounds are grass-covered and flat and are grazed by Wigeon and Coot. There are a few sections of shore where mud is exposed when the water levels are low, and these flats are used by small numbers of migrant waders in both spring and autumn. Other passage migrants at both seasons include Little Gull, Common, Little, Whiskered and Black Terns, which all occur on a regular basis.

To reach the site, take the D20 south-east from Cholet towards Maulévrier, but after 1½ km turn right onto a road that crosses a disused railway line and follow signs to 'Barrage du Verdon'. A footpath round the lake starts at the 'Auberge du Verdon' and there is a hide to the south of the reservoir, open to the public every Sunday in winter.

8. Mont des Avaloirs

MAYENNE (53) *IGN 18*

The Mont des Avaloirs, in the Forêt de Multonne about 30 km west of Alençon, is the highest point (417 metres) in this part of France. The woodland is set in undulating countryside, and contains both deciduous and coniferous trees, as well as remnants of the former heather moorland, bilberry and bracken. It is a breeding site for several species otherwise rare in the region and is also a good place for seeing migrants. Many footpaths wind their way through the area, allowing for good views of the birds.

■ Access

From Alençon take the N12 west to Pré-en-Pail, and then the D144 southwards towards St.-Pierre-des-Nids. After 3 km turn left again to reach the Mont des Avaloirs in another 2½ km, following signs to the 'Belvédère' (1). There is a car

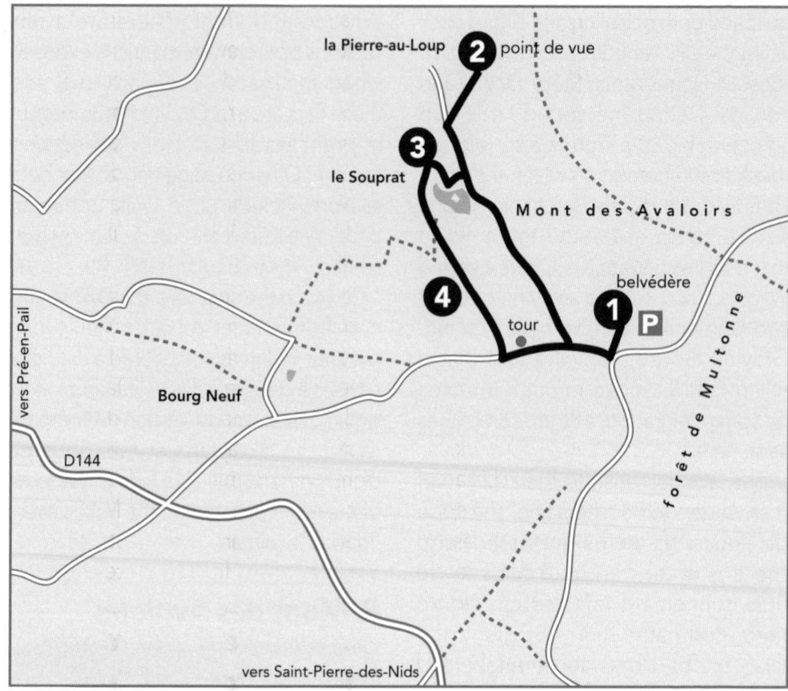

park here, and several panels explaining the local geology. Climb to the top of the lookout tower, for excellent views over the surrounding countryside. This is also a good spot to watch for soaring birds of prey, which include Buzzard, Hen Harrier and Honey Buzzard, especially in spring and early summer when they are displaying. Walk back to the road, turn right, and after a short distance right again on a signposted path that leads to the Pierre-au-Loup viewpoint (2), although in summer the trees obscure much of the view. Both Wood and Willow Warblers can be heard singing here, and the woodland holds Short-toed Treecreeper, Marsh, Willow and Crested Tit, and the commoner warblers. Woodpeckers can also be seen here. One can return via the farm of Le Souprat (3) along a surfaced road (barriered for cars), through more open woodland, and some meadows and remnant heathland (4). Species to be looked for here include Grasshopper and Dartford Warblers, Whitethroat, Stonechat and Linnet as well as open-country species such as Wheatear and Tree Pipit.

There are other footpaths through the woodland to the east, and the farmland to the south holds species such as Red-backed Shrike and Cirl Bunting.

Calendar

Spring: Hen Harrier, Honey Buzzard, Nightjar, Dartford, Wood and Grasshopper Warblers, Hawfinch. Also many species on spring migration, including raptors, passerines, Ring Ouzel.
Winter: Woodcock, Jack Snipe, Coal and Willow Tits, Redpoll and Crossbill.

9. Étang de la Rincerie

MAYENNE (53) *IGN 17/24*

Although the site of an ancient lagoon, this lake about 40 km south-west of Laval was only refilled in 1987, and access made easy for visitors. It is an excellent site for aquatic birds in winter and during migration, and the western end is maintained as a réserve naturelle. This is the section which attracts the majority of the migrant waders – Dunlin, *Tringa* sandpipers, godwits, Ringed and Little Ringed Plovers, Lapwing, Golden Plover, etc. Marsh and sea terns, Marsh Harrier and Osprey are also all regular visitors at this time. Among the more interesting rarities that have been seen here are Spotted Crake, Temminck's Stint, Caspian and Whiskered Terns, and Snow and Lapland Buntings. Good numbers of duck and other waterfowl occur in winter and there is a gull roost containing between 3,000 and 6,000 Black-headed Gulls, plus smaller numbers of other species. The surrounding meadows and farmland attract Golden Plover and Lapwing, Curlew and Greylag Geese, and wintering raptors include Merlin, Short-eared Owl and Hen Harrier.

From Laval take the N171 south-west to Craon, then the D25 west to Ballots. The lake lies just to the south, beyond the Forêt de Craon.

10. Étang du Gué-de-Selle

MAYENNE (53) *IGN 17*

This recreational lake, about 20 km south-east of Mayenne is owned by the local authority and has been part of a protected area since 1963. It is one of several lakes in the area, and plays an important role as a refuge when shooting causes disturbance elsewhere. Its main interest is for the many duck which can be seen here in winter, their numbers and variety swelled in hard weather when Goldeneye, sawbills or divers may appear. There is a large Black-headed and Lesser Black-backed Gull roost and both Common and marsh terns pass through on migration in spring and autumn. In summer the surrounding reedbeds provide shelter for various breeding warblers (Reed, Marsh, Cetti's and Sedge). The lake is next to the D7 south-east of Mayenne, beyond the well-signposted Roman remains at Jublains, but before the village of Mézangers. There is a car park, and a footpath round the lake makes for easy access.

11. Forêt de Bellebranche and the Étang de Curécy

MAYENNE (53) *IGN 17/25*

This area of woodland, about 10 km north-west of Sablé-sur-Sarthe, has a good mixture of mature deciduous trees – oak, hornbeam and beech, and is easily of accessible. Immediately adjacent is the Étang de Curécy wetland, which adds variety to the birds to be seen here. Among the breeding woodpeckers are Lesser and Middle Spotted while other species include Tawny and Long-eared Owls, Tree Pipit, Wood Warbler and Golden Oriole. In addition to the usual Buzzard and Sparrowhawk, other breeding birds of prey have included Hen Harrier, Hobby, Honey Buzzard and Black Kite at various times in the past. Among migrants, Marsh Harriers often make protracted stays, Ospreys occur regularly and Peregrines are an annual visitor to the area. On the more open and heathland areas can be found Nightjar, Melodious, Garden and Willow Warblers, Whitethroat and Red-backed Shrike, while Great Grey Shrike sometimes occurs in winter. The lake has attracted many aquatic species, both as breeding birds and in winter. These include grebes, Grey Heron, egrets, Spoonbill, all the commoner dabbling and diving duck, Coot and occasionally Bittern. The surrounding shore provides feeding habitat for Lapwing, Snipe and plovers, while species seen on passage include Wheatear, Whinchat, Blue-headed Wagtail and Water Pipit.

From Sablé-sur-Sarthe, take the D21 towards Laval, and turn left on the D235 about 2 km beyond St.-Loup-du-Dorat. The road passes the eastern end of the lake, which can easily be viewed from the roadside here. A little further on is a parking area with details of access to the forest and to the hide that overlooks the southern side of the lake.

12. *Parcé-sur-Sarthe*

SARTHE (72) *IGN 25*

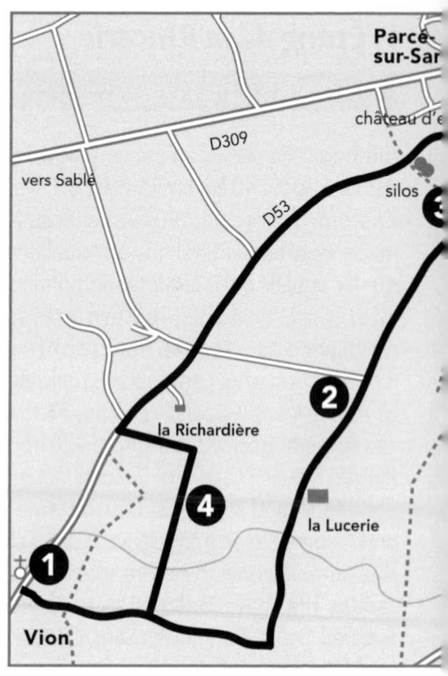

This area of farmland lies just south of the winding wooded valley of the River Sarthe, between Sablé-sur-Sarthe and La Flèche. The stony limestone-dominated plateau is now mostly used for growing cereals (maize, wheat, barley, oil-seed rape and sunflowers), but nevertheless it remains an important wintering and stop-over site for migrants, with over 100 species recorded to date. At times of migration and in winter it is possible to see Lapwing, Golden Plover, Dunlin, Ruff, various *Tringa* waders, Ringed and Little Ringed Plovers, Black-tailed Godwit and Dotterel here. It is also a good area for birds of prey: Merlin and Peregrine, Black Kite, Marsh, Hen and Montagu's Harriers, Sparrowhawk, Kestrel and Buzzard have all been seen, with, in summer, Hobby and Honey Buzzard. Barn and Long-eared, and sometimes Short-eared Owls, also hunt over the area. There are often good numbers of passerines in the stubble or ploughed fields in winter, including Reed and Lapland Buntings. Corn Bunting breeds and is present in winter. Stone Curlew, Lapwing, both partridges and Quail breed on the plain and Little Bustard has been seen in the past. During migration look for Wheatear, Stonechat and Whinchat as well as various pipits and wagtails. Blue-headed Wagtails nest in the pea fields.

ACCESS

From Sablé-sur-Sarthe take the D306 south-east towards La Flèche. Just before

Louailles, turn left on the D53 to Vion, reached in about 3½ km. It is possible to park at Vion church (1). Take the road opposite the church and then, at the first surfaced road left, pass the farm of La Lucerie to reach the water tower and here turn left along the D53. Just after the farm of La Richardière take the track to the left which cuts across a corner of the plain, before completing the circuit back to Vion. It is often worthwhile stopping at points (2), (3) and (4) and scanning for any raptors and waders that may be present. After periods of heavy rain, a temporary pond develops next to the house 'Les Périaults', just north of Vion on the road to Parcé. Spoonbill, Shelduck, Avocet, Temminck's Stint and Black Tern have all been seen there. As with many migration spots, watching in the early morning or the evening is often the most productive time.

Calendar

Spring: White Stork, Hen and Montagu's Harriers, Hobby, Black Kite, Lapwing, Quail, Stone Curlew, Grey and Red-legged Partridges, sometimes Little Bustard, Blue-headed Wagtail.
Migration: Lapwing, Golden Plover, Dotterel (a very good site during spring migration), Ruff, Ringed and Little Ringed Plovers, Curlew, Snipe, Dunlin, Black-tailed Godwit and various *Tringa* waders. Various passerines (Tawny Pipit – rare, Blue-headed, Yellow and Pied Wagtails, Wheatear and Whinchat), also Greylag Goose and Black and Red Kites.
Winter: Merlin, Peregrine, Marsh Harrier, sometimes Short-eared Owl. Large numbers of Lapwing and Golden Plover and gulls (notably Black-headed and Lesser Black-backed). Stock Dove and large flocks of passerines, including Lapland Bunting.

13. Forêt de Bercé

SARTHE (72) *IGN 25*

This is a splendid forest of mature sessile oaks nearly 300 years old, mixed with areas of beech and sweet chestnut. It is 5,415 hectares in extent and lies on a plateau about 30 km south-east of Le Mans. The site holds a remarkable number of species and is best visited in the spring (April or May), when there is the best chance of locating displaying raptors. Birds of prey to be expected include Goshawk, Sparrowhawk, Hobby, Kestrel, Buzzard, Honey Buzzard and Hen Harrier. The woodland is also well-supplied with woodpeckers – Middle, Great and Lesser Spotted, Green, Grey-headed and Black all occur – although a visit earlier in the year (February and March) will be more likely to find them drumming and calling, and hence easier to locate. Also present in the more wooded areas are Stock Dove, Redstart, the four species of *Phylloscopus* warblers, Goldcrest and Firecrest as well as both of the treecreepers. When the spruce cones are in seed, Crossbills may occur, although this species is prone to strong population fluctuations everywhere. In the more open areas look for Woodcock, Nightjar, Long-eared Owl, Tree Pipit, Grasshopper, Garden and Dartford Warblers and Blackcap.

The N138 south from Le Mans cuts through the western end of the forest, which can be explored along the many forestry tracks and roads both to the east and to the west.

14. Lac de la Monnerie

SARTHE (72) *IGN 25*

This artificial lake in the valley of the River Loir at La Flèche was created from gravel workings as a leisure centre for the town. Currently it is 21 hectares in extent but may well soon be increased to cover 53 hectares as more pits become available. The site attracts birds both on migration and in winter. An exploration of the adjoining river valley, where there are flood meadows and more gravel pits, scrub and hedgerows, as well as the river itself, will extend the number of species encountered. In the breeding season look for Coot, Moorhen, Little Ringed Plover, Common Tern, Crested Lark, Sand Martin, Reed, Sedge and Cetti's Warblers and Reed Bunting. On migration species seen include Black-necked, Little and Great Crested Grebes, Shelduck, Wigeon, Pintail, Shoveler, Gadwall, Mallard, Pochard and Tufted Duck plus on occasion Velvet Scoter, Goosander and Red-breasted Merganser. Osprey, a variety of waders, gulls, Whiskered and Black Terns also occur on migration.

The site, actually labelled as 'Lacs de la Monnerie' is well signposted from La Flèche town centre, and lies a short distance east of the town, by the N23 towards Le Mans. There is plenty of parking, and notice boards give details of access, both to the main lake itself and to the adjacent riverside. A footpath runs round the lake, and other footpaths provide access through a 'zone écologique' to the banks of the River Loir. Being a leisure centre, the site is popular with the public, and so visits in the early morning or in the evening are more likely to be productive.

15. Baie de l'Aiguillon

VENDÉE (85) *IGN 39*

This 6,500-hectare bay lies on the borders of two départements, Charente-Maritime and Vendée, where the Sèvre Niortaise flows into the sea just north of La Rochelle. The larger northern part, where hunting has been banned since 1973, became a réserve naturelle in 1996, the reserve being extended in 1999 to include the southern half of the bay. The reserve is jointly managed by the ONCFS (Office National de la Chasse et de la Faune Sauvage) and the LPO. At low tide, the bay comprises a vast series of mudflats which provide feeding opportunities for many birds, and is one of the most important sites in France for wintering and migrant waders. In winter large flocks of duck can be seen, along with small groups of Cranes, which are increasingly staying to winter in France rather than continuing to Spain. The bay is surrounded by polders that provide good hunting habitat for birds of prey, both diurnal and nocturnal. The Pointe de l'Aiguillon, at the entrance to the bay, is an important passerine migration watch-point in autumn (with camps organised by LPO Vendée from September to November), counts having been carried out here for more than ten years already.

ACCESS

From L'Aiguillon-sur-Mer, take the D46 towards the Pointe de l'Aiguillon as far as 'Les Caves', and stop by the road just before a small jetty (1). On a rising tide, look through the small groups of waders feeding on the mudflats sheltered behind the Pointe d'Arçay opposite; in the past these have included the odd rarity (e.g.,

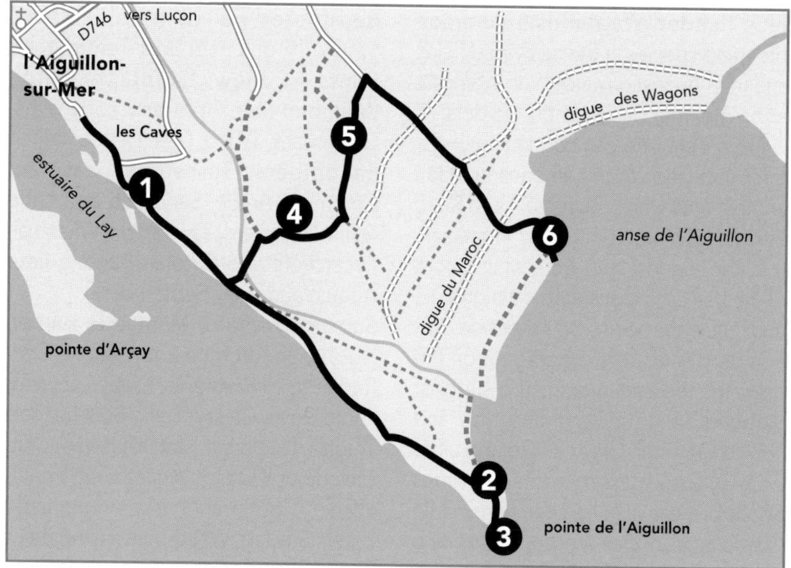

Marsh Sandpiper in the autumn). In addition, this part of the bay (the estuary of the River Lay) is sometimes favoured by Caspian Tern. Continuing towards the point, look for Hen and Marsh Harriers on the polders, especially in autumn and winter. From late April onwards the Montagu's Harrier arrives to breed in the same habitat. Arriving at the car park at the point (2), scan the fish and oyster beds; Ospreys regularly fish here in the autumn, various terns use the posts as perches, and a few sawbills or Goldeneye can be present in winter. Next, walk towards the point itself (3) and look out over the bay, the dunes, the wet depressions and the beach. Bluethroats nest in the areas of low vegetation at the upper edge of the mudflats (schorres), while there are a few Tawny Pipits and Short-toed Larks in the dunes. Black-headed, Lesser Black-backed, Great Black-backed, Yellow-legged, Herring and Common Gulls come here to roost at high tide, with Sandwich, Common, Little, Caspian and sometimes Arctic Terns in late summer and autumn. A good number of waders and Shelduck feed on the mudflats here as well. In autumn various migrant raptors occur - Black and Red Kites, Honey Buzzard and harriers, along with tens of thousands of migrant Linnets, Goldfinches, Blue-headed Wagtails and hirundines, and many other species. A few Great and Arctic Skuas and Balearic Shearwaters can also be seen passing offshore. Both Merlin and Peregrine can be seen in autumn and winter.

Next drive back along the coast road for about 5 km before turning right for the La Dive cliffs (4). Kestrels nest in this area, and it is possible, even during the day, to see both Little and Barn Owls hunting. In the autumn and winter a few Short-eared Owl also hunt over the surrounding cultivated polders. Continue along the road for another 2 km to (5), a good spot in autumn to search for migrant passerines, often numerous in the hedgerows. This is an area which in October may turn up a Siberian rarity.

Blue-headed Wagtail is a common breeding species in the cultivated fields and from August onwards both Whinchat and Wheatear occur on the polders.

From here one can continue along a track that leads to the embankment (6), another area where Bluethroat and Reed Bunting both breed in the low vegetation. It is also a good spot from which more of the bay can be scanned. At high tide, and during the hour or so either side, vast numbers of waders congregate on the edge of the salt marsh, the biggest numbers being in April and May and July to October. Great White and Little Egrets, Grey Heron, and sometimes Spoonbill, can also be seen here, while Cormorants dry their wings while standing on the posts out in the bay. Between October and March the salt marshes attract various geese whilst during the same period large flocks of Shelduck, Avocet and dabbling duck occur out in the bay. In winter, in late afternoon, watch for the Cranes returning to roost in the bay, having spent the day feeding on the the polders and inland marshes.

Two spots on the east shore from which the bay can be watched are the Port-du-Pavé at Charron, and the Pointe St.-Clément at Esnandes, both of which offer a good view over a wide area of mudflats.

Warning: It is ill-advised to venture out onto the salt marshes or mudflats in the winter, but rather remain on solid ground and watch from the surrounding embankments. High-tide visits are always more productive, and a telescope is essential for good views.

Calendar

Spring and autumn: A wide variety of migrants, including Spoonbill, Black Stork, Black and Red Kites, Sparrowhawk, Red-footed Falcon (rare), Osprey, Sanderling, Little and Temminck's Stints, Curlew Sandpiper, Ruff, Whimbrel (late April and early May), Greenshank, Wood, Green and Common Sandpipers, Turnstone, Caspian, Common, Arctic, Sandwich and Little Terns, hirundines, Tawny Pipit, Wheatear, flycatchers and Ortolan Bunting (late August and early September).

Summer: Mallard, Montagu's Harrier, Hobby, sometimes Short-eared Owl, Red-legged Partridge, Quail, Lapwing, Turtle Dove, Crested Lark, Blue-headed Wagtail, Bluethroat, Stonechat, Whinchat, Melodious Warbler, Whitethroat, Linnet.

Winter: Cormorant, Grey Heron, Little Egret, Greylag, White-fronted and Brent Geese, Barnacle Goose (in small numbers), Shelduck, dabbling duck (Wigeon, Mallard, Pintail, Shoveler and Teal), Eider, Common Scoter, Crane, Marsh and Hen Harriers, Kestrel, Merlin, Peregrine, Oystercatcher, Avocet, Ringed and Grey Plovers, Dunlin, Knot, Black-tailed and Bar-tailed Godwits, Redshank, Spotted Redshank, Great Black-backed, Lesser Black-backed, Herring, Common and Black-headed Gulls, Barn and Short-eared Owls, Skylark, Meadow and Water Pipits, Reed and Corn Buntings, sometimes Snow and Lapland Buntings.

16. Baie de Bourgneuf

Vendée (85) *IGN 32*

This vast bay, about 20 km to the south of the Loire estuary, is a shallow sheltered area lying between the mainland and the Île de Noirmoutier (see also site 21 below). The deposits of marine mud laid down over centuries are exposed at low tide to provide food and sanctuary for thousands of waders and ducks.

Protected by an embankment, the polders at the head of the bay are used for agriculture and oyster-farming, but also serve as a high-tide refuge and breeding ground for many birds. (See also site 23 below.)

BLUETHROAT

ACCESS

From La-Roche-sur-Yonne take the D948 west via Challans to reach Beauvoir-sur-Mer. From here continue towards the coast on the D51 to reach the Port du Bec (1) where it is possible to park. The 'Mord'eau' café is a good place to meet local fishermen and find out about guided natural history outings that may be available. Note that the time and coefficient of the tides influence the movements of the birds, and that for the best views, two hours before or after high tide is the time to come.Walk towards the sea by taking the left bank (south) of the port (2). There are good views over mudflats here, beyond the remains of former embankments. Continue along these southwards to (3), beyond which stretch yet more mudflats, home to hundreds of waders, including Curlew and Bar-tailed Godwit, Grey Plover and Oystercatcher. Avocet also occur here and all the waders may rise up if a wintering Peregrine should pass over. Other regular species include Teal, Wigeon, Shoveler and Pintail, sometimes difficult to see on the salt marsh, and Brent Goose and Mallard.

Return to the port and follow the track on the embankment on the other side of the inlet to reach the navigation light (4). In spring it is worth checking the bean and oil-seed rape fields, roadsides and embankments, for the various passerines that can be seen here – wagtails, Bluethroat, Fan-tailed Warbler, Whitethroat, Linnet, Corn and Reed Buntings. One can continue along the embankment, always checking the shore for waders that are forever moving with the tide. After about 5 km, at the spot where there is a bend in the embankment (5), take the steps up to the top, moving very quietly so as not to disturb the birds, to look over the top at the Lagune de Bouin just behind the seawall. You may have already noted birds moving between the lagoon and the shore. More than 100,000 waders can be concentrated here at high tide, and it is important not to disturb them. Among them will be Grey Plover, Bar-tailed Godwit, Dunlin and Knot with Shelduck and Brent Goose on the shores of the lagoon, the peak period for the latter being between December and April. Marsh and Montagu's Harriers and Kestrel hunt over the polders, and Merlin can be seen chasing passerines here in winter. In spring there is a very large Black-

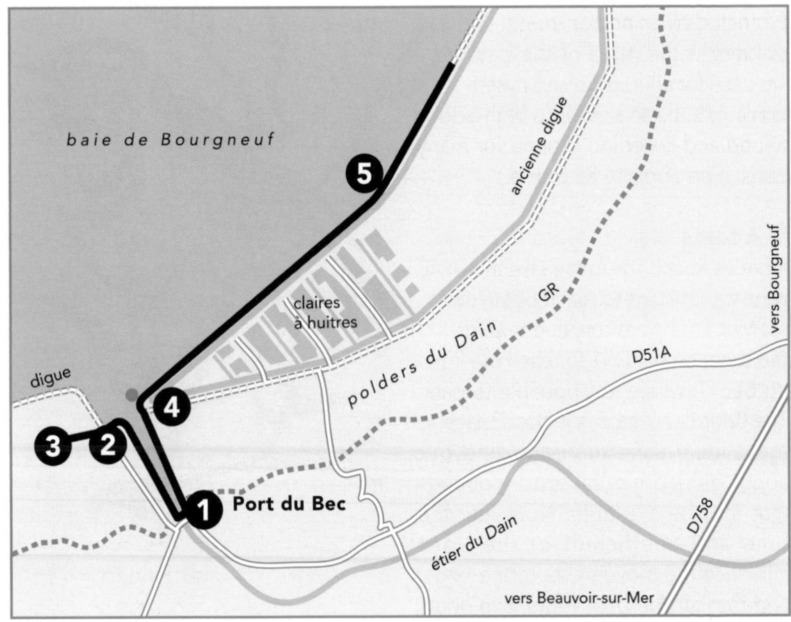

headed Gull, Common Tern and Avocet colony. Access to the lagoon is strictly forbidden – you must not go beyond the embankment.

Calendar

Spring: hundreds of Knot, Bar-tailed Godwit, Redshank, Whimbrel, Ringed Plover, Yellow and Blue-headed Wagtail on the polders, Wheatear.
Summer: Avocet, Black-headed and Mediterranean (irregular) Gulls, Common and Sandwich Terns, Montagu's and Marsh Harriers, Kestrel and Bluethroat.
Autumn and winter: Avocet, Oystercatcher, Grey Plover, Dunlin and Curlew. Cormorant, Brent Goose, Shelduck, dabbling duck (Pintail, Shoveler, Wigeon, Teal). Hen and Marsh Harriers, Merlin, Peregrine, Lapwing, Golden Plover and passerines (pipits, larks, buntings).

17. Poiré-sur-Velluire

Vendée (85) *IGN 39*

Situated in the north-eastern part of the Marais Poitevin, the local community of the village of Poiré-sur-Velluire has created a réserve naturelle covering about 250 hectares of its communal grazing meadows. Between October and March spectacular numbers of Lapwing can be seen in the fields, along with many Golden Plover, and at times of flooding good numbers of dabbling duck are also drawn in. Inevitably, both Peregrine and Merlin are attracted to this wealth of prey. Black-tailed Godwit and Greylag Goose occur in early spring, sometimes in large numbers, and Whimbrel pass through in early May; Garganey, along with other ducks and a wider range of waders occur during migration when surface water remains on the meadows. Night and Purple Herons feed along the ditches bordering the reserve in the summer, and Little Bustard has been known to stay during the winter.

Poiré-sur-Velluire lies about 8 km south-west of Fontenay-le-Compte. Access is via the D938 to Nizeau and then the D68. The reserve can be viewed from the roadside which runs alongside the meadows, and there is a public hide near the village of L'Anglée. An annual fête takes place during the last weekend of April when the cattle are let out into the grazing meadows for the summer. (See also site 22 below, also in the Marais Poitevin).

18. Étangs des Boucheries/ Cité des Oiseaux

VENDÉE (85) *IGN 33*

These lakes, to the south-west of Cholet and now owned by the Vendée département, have been managed as a bird reserve since 1988. They attract, principally in winter and spring, many diving and dabbling duck, with Smew and Goosander during hard weather. Waders are mainly seen on migration. Great Crested and Little Grebes, Mallard, Garganey, Teal and Tufted Duck all breed. From Cholet take the D753 west towards Montaigu for about 18 km, then turn left in Tiffauges on the D37 to Les Landes-Genusson. The reserve, to the west, is well sign-posted as 'La Cité des Oiseaux'. There is a car park, visitor centre and hide, and there is good access for the less mobile.

19. Lagune de la Belle-Henriette

VENDÉE (85) *IGN 39*

This coastal lagoon lies a little to the north-west of the Baie de l'Aiguillon (see site 15 above). In spring the lagoon comes to life with the start of the breeding season and the return of the Bluethroats and Reed Buntings. Savi's Warbler, Bearded Tit and Little Bittern all occasionally breed, although they are all rare in the Vendée. Tawny Pipits can be found in the dunes. Nevertheless, late summer and early autumn are without doubt the best times for birds; if water levels are favourable there may be many waders here: Kentish, Ringed and Little Ringed Plovers, Dunlin, Little Stint, Knot, Curlew Sandpiper, Snipe, Bar-tailed and Black-tailed Godwits and the various *Tringa* species. There have also been several rarities. Other regular migrants include Spoonbill, various dabbling ducks and Black Tern. It is also worth checking the edges of the reeds for Spotted Crake, although Water Rail is the common species here, of course. From late August onwards passerine migration gets under way: Sedge and Reed Warblers feed in the reeds, accompanied on occasion by Aquatic and Grasshopper Warblers. A Sand Martin roost usually forms, variable in size from one year to another, but thousands of birds can accumulate. Little Gulls can be seen right through the winter (also on spring and autumn passage), and other wintering species may include both Bearded and Penduline Tits in small numbers, although usually well hidden in the reeds.

From l'Aiguillon-sur-Mer, take the D46 west through La Faute-sur-Mer. The lagoon is situated between the D46 and the sea just to the west, and can be viewed from the roadside. The habitat is easily damaged, so please keep to the paths.

20. Marais d'Olonne

VENDÉE (85) IGN 32

These marshes extend over some 10 km from Les Sables-d'Olonne north to Brétignolles-sur-Mer. They attract many breeding birds - Avocet, Black-winged Stilt, Redshank, Lapwing, Common Tern, Great Black-backed, Lesser Black-backed, Yellow-legged, Herring, Black-headed and Mediterranean Gulls. In autumn, there are many waders on migration, and in winter dabbling duck. Access is rather limited, but there is a bird observatory (signposted) just south of Île d'Olonne, where minor roads cross through the wetland areas, from which guided walks, in the summer only, can be arranged. The dunes between the sea and the marshes are good for migrant passerines in autumn.

In Les Sables-d'Olonne itself, the La Chaume lighthouse and the Corniche de Sion-sur-l'Océan to the south of the town are both excellent spots for watching seabird passage, especially in August and September. There is sometimes a spectacular concentration of several thousand Balearic Shearwaters offshore here; other species include Cory's Shearwater, more rarely Great or Sooty Shearwaters, and Storm Petrel, Fulmar, skuas, terns and auks. In winter, a small flock of Purple Sandpipers can usually be found on rocky parts of the same stretch of shoreline; the best sites are the small jetty at Sables-d'Olonne port, the breakwater at La Chaume and the Cinq Pineaux, to the north of St.-Gilles-Croix-de-Vie. High-tide visits are usually the most productive.

21. Marais de Müllembourg / Île de Noirmoutier

VENDÉE (85) IGN 32

The Île de Noirmoutier, accessed by roadbridge and/or casuseway from the mainland at the Baie de Bourgneuf (see site 16 above), is another good sea-watching site in autumn, but also has a rich breeding and wintering bird population. The LPO manages a reserve at the Marais de Müllembourg, next to the Jetée Jacobsen causeway which runs east from the town of Noirmoutier-en-l'Île. On one side is the port's entrance channel, while the reserve occupies an area of old salt pans, some still in use, on the other. Viewing is easy from the surfaced road, and the less mobile should encounter few problems. In spring and summer breeding species to be seen here include Shelduck, Avocet, Black-winged Stilt, Redshank, Black-headed Gull, Common Tern and Bluethroat. Many migrant waders and terns use the site as a roost at high tide during the autumn while in winter there are flocks Brent Geese, Shelduck and Avocet to be seen. When strong westerly winds are blowing, the best sea-watching spot is usually the Pointe de l'Herbaudière, at the north-west corner of the island, when any of the skuas, terns, shearwaters and other seabirds that move along this coast in spring and autumn may be expected. At other times, especially in the summer, the salt-pans to the south of here, between L'Herbaudière and L'Epine are worth exploring. In addition to Black-winged Stilt and Avocet as at Müllembourg, both

Marsh and Montagu's Harrier can be found here, although both species range quite widely on the island

22. St.-Denis-du-Payré

VENDÉE (85) *IGN 39*

Situated in the north-western part of the Marais Poitevin, the Réserve Naturelle de St.-Denis-du-Payré is managed by the Association de Défense de l'Environnement en Vendée (ADEV) to protect a large area of wet meadows, often flooded in winter. At this time the reserve attracts thousands of dabbling duck, including Pintail, Wigeon, Shoveler, Mallard, Gadwall and Teal. Also present are Greylag and White-fronted Geese, plus many Lapwing and Golden Plover while Marsh Harrier, Buzzard, Peregrine and Merlin all hunt over the area. In spring other species occur, such as Garganey, Black-tailed Godwit, Ruff and Black Tern, this last sometimes nesting here. A good variety of raptors visit the reserve and the surrounding countryside in summer - Marsh and Montagu's Harriers, Short-toed Eagle, Black Kite, Buzzard, Hobby and Kestrel. In summer and autumn, many species of wader can be seen, along with both White and Black Storks and Spoonbill.

St.-Denis-de-Payré lies between l'Aiguillon-sur-Mer (see sites 15 and 19 above), and Luçon to the north. Visits start from the Maison de la Réserve visitor centre in the village, with slide shows, exhibitions and a permanent observation point that affords a good view over the marsh. From here the reserve is reached via a raised boardwalk, 400 metres long, which leads to the hide. There are telescopes at the site and it is accessible to the less mobile. The reserve and visitor centre are open during all school holidays, and an entrance fee is charged. Group visits can be arranged in advance (Tel: 02 51 27 23 92).

23. Beauvoir-sur-Mer

VENDÉE (85) *IGN 32*

To the south of the village of Beauvoir-sur-Mer, a little way back from the Baie de Bourgneuf (see also site 16 above) is an area of abandoned salt pans and natural grazing meadows, with ponds and freshwater depressions, bounded by ditches filled with water from the sea. This is one of the more interesting parts of the Breton-Vendée marshes, especially for waders and duck, and particularly between April and July. Breeding species of the meadows and salt-pans include Lapwing, Redshank, Black-tailed Godwit, Snipe, Avocet, Black-winged Stilt, Mallard, Garganey and Shoveler. Ruff, Whimbrel and various other waders occur on spring and autumn migration. In spring the tamarisk, blackthorn and bramble hedges offer shelter to a large number of passerines, including Nightingale, Bluethroat, Cetti's and Sedge Warblers. It is also of interest during late summer and early autumn when migrants are on the move. Short-toed Eagle is seen quite frequently, Spoonbill is also a regular visitor, whilst Osprey and Black Stork are other passage birds often recorded here.

From La-Roche-sur-Yonne take the D948 west via Challans to reach Beauvoir-sur-Mer. From here go south on the D22 to where the road crosses a tidal channel. View from the road, or explore on foot along minor roads in the area.

SITES

1 *Plan d'eau de l'Ailette*

2 *Marais d'Isle de St.-Quentin*

3 *Forêt de Compiègne*

4 *Marais de Sacy-le-Grand*

5 *River Oise south of Compiègne*

6 *River Oise north of Noyon*

7 *Bas-Champs de Cayeux*

8 *Baie de Somme*

9 *Falaises d'Ault-Onival*

10 *Forêt de Crécy-en-Ponthieu*

11 *The Somme valley near Amiens*

Picardie

MER DU NORD
Dunkerque
Calais
59
Boulogne-sur-Mer
Lille
62
Douai
Arras
Valenciennes
Maubeuge
Cambrai
7
8
10
9
Abbeville
80
11
2
Amiens
Saint-Quentin
Dieppe
Roye
02
76
Charleville-Mézières
6
Laon
Rouen
60
08
1
Compiègne
4
Beauvais
5
3
Reims
Vernon
27
Pontoise
95
Château-Thierry
Meaux
51
Évreux
Versailles
PARIS
Châlons-en-Champagne
Rambouillet
77
Dreux
78
Evry
Sézanne
91
Chartres
Étampes
Nogent-sur-Seine
Melun
10
28
Troyes
Pithiviers
Bar-sur-Aube
Sens

1. Plan d'eau de l'Ailette

Aisne (02) *IGN 09*

This artificial lake, some 12 km to the south of Laon, is 160 hectares in extent and was constructed in 1983 by damming the River Ailette. It now forms part of a larger leisure centre where hunting is forbidden, and angling controlled so that birds can find calm conditions here throughout the year. The various habitats (open water, reedbeds, willow and alder beds, water-meadows, mudflats) attract many birds, the areas to the north and the east where the water flows in being particularly good. It is noted as a good site for ducks and waders (October to March/April) and for Osprey (April to October).

Access

From Laon, take the D967 south for about 13 km to reach the village of Chamouille, and continue south to cross the western end of the lake. There is free entrance to the park from the start of October to the end of March. The embankment (1) is a good spot from which to scan the largest section of open water. In winter there are good numbers of Pochard, Tufted Duck, Mallard and Mute Swan to be seen here. Return to Chamouille and take the D19 eastwards towards Neuville-sur-Ailette. Stop again at the point (2) where a stream runs into the lake. Great Crested Grebe, Mallard, Tufted Duck and Coot all nest in this area. Continue for another 600 metres, turn right towards the camp site, and turn right again towards the water-sports centre (3), another spot from which it is possible

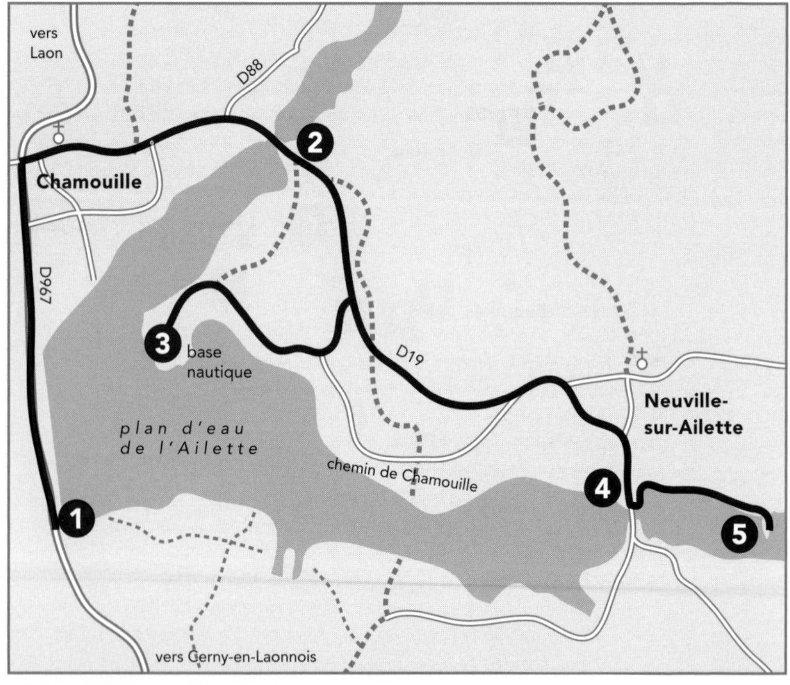

to scan the lake. In winter there may be sawbills, scoters or divers offshore here. At times of migration, in both spring and autumn, there are often large numbers of Swifts and hirundines feeding over the lake, sometimes accompanied by Black Terns. Waders should be looked for anywhere along the shoreline. There are often Lapwing to be seen (they sometimes breed), and Little Ringed Plover, among other species. Continue on the D19 towards Neuville-sur-Ailette, but some 200 metres before the village turn right and stop near the eastern arm of the lake (4). This is another place from which the main part of the lake to the west can be scanned. In addition, you can walk east along the part of the lake used by anglers to get to an embankment (5) from where, in winter, the Cormorant roost is easily visible and, in summer, a Black-headed Gull colony can be viewed. Two floating rafts have been set in place here since spring 2003, to provide nesting sites for Common Terns. Reed Bunting and Cetti's Warbler breed in the reeds at the back of the lake.

■ Calendar

Spring and autumn: Osprey, Crane, gulls, marsh terns, Swifts, hirundines and wagtails (three species).
Summer: Great Crested and Little Grebes, Coot, Mallard, Black-headed Gull, Reed and Cetti's Warblers and Reed Bunting. Mute Swan and a few pairs of Tufted Duck nest. Common Tern occurs regularly.
Winter: thousands of duck (Mallard, Pintail, Shoveler, Gadwall, Teal, Tufted Duck and Pochard). Also grebes, Cormorant, Grey Heron, Great White Egret, sawbills, Black-headed Gull, Snipe, Lapwing, Green Sandpiper, Meadow Pipit, Brambling and Tree Sparrow.

2. Marais d'Isle de St.-Quentin

Aisne (02) *IGN 04*

This 50 hectare réserve naturelle, in the Somme valley, despite being actually within the middle of the town of St.-Quentin, is a natural oasis for flora and fauna alike. Numerous channels of water flow through damp woodland, creating a variety of habitats – ponds, reedbeds and wooded islands – and the reserve is noted for several rare plants, as well as many species of bird. Breeding species include Great Crested Grebe, Grey Heron, Mallard, Coot and Reed Warbler, and Little Bittern, Bluethroat and Marsh Harrier have all been noted. Migrants include various geese, ducks and gulls. There is a Maison de la Nature visitor centre in the Avenue Léo-Lagrange which can organise guided visits for groups. In addition, there is an interpretation trail along the edges of the reserve from which it can be viewed by those visiting independently.

3. Forêt de Compiègne

Oise (60) *IGN 09*

This forest, to the south of the town whose name it carries, is the largest (15,000 hectares) in Picardie and certainly the one with the most varied bird population. It has, among other species, nationally important numbers of Middle Spotted Woodpecker, Wryneck and Pied Flycatcher.

The D332 runs south through the centre of the woodland, with other roads and forest tracks to facilitate exploration. The best time of year is, of course, the spring, especially May and June when all the migrants have arrived. Among the more interesting breeding species are Honey Buzzard, Hobby (rare), Woodcock, Stock Dove, Black (common) and Middle Spotted Woodpeckers, Wryneck (localised), Redstart, Wood, Grasshopper and Melodious Warblers, Pied Flycatcher, Red-backed Shrike and Hawfinch. There are a few pairs of Common Treecreepers (rare in lowland France) in the Beaux-Monts/Chapelle Sainte-Corneille area, immediately east of Compiègne. For Middle Spotted Woodpecker, Pied Flycatcher and Wood Warbler, take the D973 from the 'Carrefour Napoléon' (the large roundabout on the outskirts of Compiègne where the D332 and D973 meet) and continue for about 5 km to the Parquet de Bois and Mares St.-Louis intersections. The area of damp oak forest to the right of the road here is worth exploring for any of these species. For birds of more open habitats, it is worth visiting the clear-felled areas at the 'Carrefour Antoine', about 2 km south from the 'Carrefour Napoléon' along the D332 towards Crépy-en-Valois. In addition, near this felled area is a mature beech wood, a good area for Stock Dove, Black Woodpecker and Redstart.

4. Marais de Sacy-le-Grand

OISE (60) *IGN 09*

This marsh, about 20 km south-west of Compiègne, is the result of peat extraction in the past, and has attracted the attention of local birdwatchers for many years. However, its future is in a certain amount of doubt, as it has increasingly become colonised by scrub, suffers from the attentions of hunters, and currently is not afforded any measure of protection. Nevertheless, some good birds can still be seen here, particularly in the breeding season. There is a good population of Savi's Warblers, in addition to the very numerous Sedge and Reed Warblers. Other summer birds include Hobby, Water Rail, Bluethroat, Lesser Whitethroat and Marsh Warbler, while, although very difficult to see, both Bittern and Little Bittern can be heard calling from the dense cover. Migration times always offer the chance of a surprise, Osprey and Great White Egret being just two visitors seen in the past.

From Compiègne, take the N31 west as far as Catenoy, then turn left on the D10 to Sacy-le-Grand. The D75 from here south to Cinqueux crosses from one side of the marsh to the other, providing views from the road, particularly from the small bridge in the middle.

5. River Oise south of Compiègne

OISE (60) *IGN 09*

Downstream from Compiègne, as far as Creil, are a series of gravel-pits some of which are good for birds, others less so. None of them is protected, but the area is nonetheless an important wintering site for aquatic birds, especially for Pochard and Tufted Duck. There are also good numbers of Great Crested Grebe, Cormorant and Coot, but few dabbling duck. Rarer species sometimes occur, such as divers, grebes, sawbills, Scaup or Ferruginous Duck. During spring migration it is possible to see Black-necked Grebe, Little Gull, Black Tern and hirundines.

From Compiègne take the D200 or

D932A to Verberie, and then the D123 west. At Moru, just after passing under the A1 motorway, turn right. The road then runs between a series of gravel-pits, usually the most productive ones. The large fenced-off lake to the left of the road can be good for birds as can the one to the right and farther from the road, towards Pont-Sainte-Maxence (used for windsurfing). Every winter there are Goldeneye to be seen and a gull roost (including a few of the larger species) forms here. Jack Snipe occurs in winter and there is a small colony of Common Terns, which manages to survive, despite disturbance. The Remises d'Herneuse gravel-pits, between the D932A and the river, to the north of Verberie before you reach Lacroix-St.-Ouen, are sometimes also worth checking.

BLACK WOODPECKER

An area which attracts waders during spring and autumn migration is the sugar-beet factory settling-beds near Houdancourt. Spotted Crake, Buff-breasted Sandpiper and Temminck's Stint have all been seen here. From Verberie, take the D155 north to Chevrières, then west on the D13 as far as Houdancourt. Turn left here in front of the church and continue southwards to cross the railway line. The settling-beds are on the left at the end of this no-through-road. The site itself is closed to the public and potentially dangerous, and should only be viewed through the fence.

6. River Oise north of Noyon

Oise (60)/Aisne (02)
IGN 04/09

Near Noyon, about 20 km north-east of Compiègne, and also in the Oise valley, is an area of flood meadows traditionally used by livestock and regularly inundated in late winter. Despite the planting of stands of poplars, the modernisation of agricultural practices, and, even worse, the changes of landscape wrought by gravel extraction, the flood plain here is still of ornithological interest. The Conservatoire des Sites Naturels de Picardie maintains a policy of acquiring land whenever possible and collaborating with farmers to protect the habitat. The valley still holds a few pairs of Corncrake, a species everywhere threatened by agricultural changes. The flood meadows are also the last stronghold of Whinchat in Picardie. Other reasonably widespread breeding species include Hobby, Bluethroat, Lesser Whitethroat, Grasshopper and Marsh Warblers, Willow Tit, Red-backed Shrike and Golden Oriole. White Storks often occur on spring migration.

From Noyon, take the D87 east via Morlincourt to Varesnes. There is a gravel-pit here ('La Fosse Cochue') which can be of interest. From here minor roads wind east through the valley, the area between Brétigny, Quierzy and Manicamp being one of the best sections. During spring migration, in February and March, the valley is used by Greylag Geese and dabbling duck, with large numbers of Pintail of particular note; one of the best sites at this time of year is the 'Fief d'Arblincourt', to the right of the D6 east of Manicamp on the way to Marizelle. The valley beyond Chauny is also worth a visit – a few pairs of Curlew still breed around Beautor, and the water-sports centre in an old gravel-pit at Tergnier can also attract birds.

South-east of this part of the valley is the Forêt de St.-Gobain, worth a visit for woodland species. Birds of prey include Goshawk and Honey Buzzard and there are also Middle Spotted and Black Woodpeckers and a variety of passerines – Pied Flycatcher, Redstart and Wood Warbler, among others. A network of minor roads facilitates exploration. Although the village of St.-Gobain is in the eastern part of the forest, the woodland extends as far west as Varesnes, and the whole area is worthy of investigation.

7. Bas-Champs de Cayeux

SOMME (80) *IGN 01/03*

The Bas-Champs de Cayeux lies on the Channel coast to the south of the Somme estuary. The site comprises a series of ponds and lakes within an area of extensive meadows and pebble beaches, all protected from the sea by a long sea-wall. The largest of the lakes, the Hâble d'Ault is an ancient coastal lagoon separated from the sea, surrounded by reedbeds, quite extensive in places. Technically wildfowling is not allowed here, nor in the nearby marshes, but the law has proved difficult to enforce. Farther south is another collection of ponds, also open to the public and of interest to the bird watcher, but much of this section is certainly heavily shot over during the hunting season (September to January).

■ Access

From Abbeville take the D40 west, then turn left on the D940 past the town of St.-Valery-sur-Somme, and continue on the D3 to Cayeux-sur-Mer. From the village take the coast road southwards as far as the coastal beacon of l'Amer (1). From here turn left and then right (2), and on as far as a barrier (3), where it is possible to park. A track continues southwards near the Hâble d'Ault itself, passing several hides on the way. Bearded Tit, Bluethroat and a variety of wetland warblers all breed in the extensive reedbeds that you pass on the way and Wheatear breeds in the dunes. During April and May many hirundines and Swifts hunt over the wetland areas.

Alternatively, from (1), continue south by the pebble embankment on the track to reach another car park. From here it

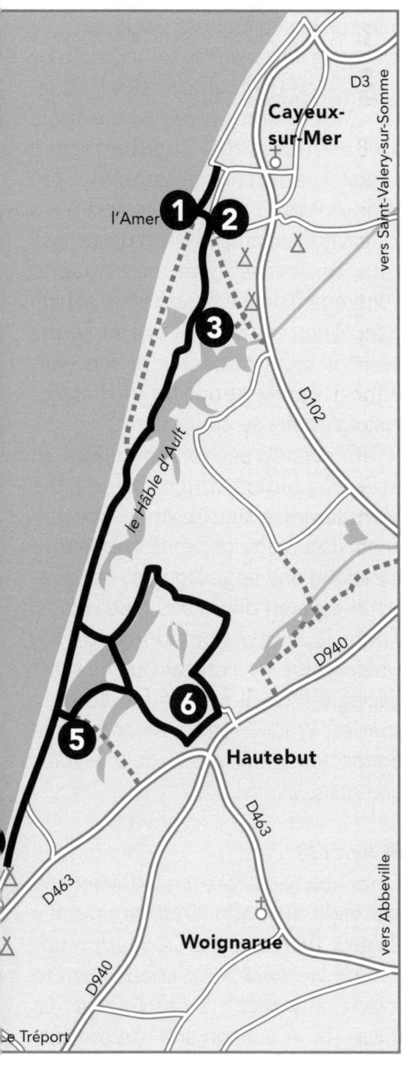

is possible to look out over the meadows, expanses of pebble and ponds and also to climb up onto the pebbles to look out to sea. Ringed, Little Ringed and Kentish Plovers all breed along this section of coast, so check all the plovers carefully. In winter and early spring look for Snow Bunting, Shore Lark and the occasional Lapland Bunting along the embankment, and out to sea you may find divers, grebes, Gannet, scoters and Eider as well as gulls and terns at migration times.

Either way, continue along the embankment as far as the small lake (4) at the southern end of the area, near the village of Ault. Various species of wader occur on the ponds during April, May, August and September. On the way back, turn right at (5) to pass between two of the lakes and keep right along the track straight ahead as far as Hautebut (on the D463/D940). Keep scanning the meadows and ponds all the time. Lapwing breed in the meadows and crops while in winter some of the ponds attract divers, grebes, Cormorant and diving duck (including sawbills). In recent years there have been several records of Red-crested Pochards, possibly of wild origin, possibly feral, breeding successfully in this area. It may well be that a new population is in the process of establishing itself along this stretch of coast, so it is worth checking all the wildfowl carefully. The track continues (6) in a loop back to Cayeux-sur-Mer.

Note that site 9 (below) is not far away to the south, and that beyond Cayeux to the north the D102 leads on along the coast to the point of Le Hourdel, at the southern entrance to the Somme estuary, a good spot for scanning the mudflats for gulls and waders (see site 8 for more details of this area).

■ Calendar

Spring: large numbers of waterfowl during March and April (Greylag Goose, dabbling duck, especially Shoveler) and, in May, waders (*Tringa* species, Ringed Plover, godwits, Curlew, Whimbrel, Avocet and Temminck's Stint regularly), Purple Heron, Black and (sometimes)

Whiskered Terns, Little and Mediterranean Gulls, a few birds of prey, harriers (all three species), Hobby, Merlin, Kestrel, Peregrine and various passerines including pipits and wagtails.
Summer: Bittern, Shelduck, Shoveler, Garganey, Pochard, Tufted Duck, Avocet, Ringed, Little Ringed and Kentish Plovers, Lapwing, Bluethroat, Bearded Tit, Wheatear.
Autumn: during August and September: waders, terns and various other migrants; Sparrowhawk, Buzzard, falcons, passerines including pipits. Various ducks, waders, gulls and terns passing offshore.
Winter: divers, grebes, Bittern, diving duck (Pochard, Tufted Duck, Scaup, Goldeneye and sometimes sawbills), Coot, Bearded Tit. Short-eared Owl, Rough-legged Buzzard (rare). On the pebble beaches and other areas devoid of vegetation: Shore Lark and Snow Bunting. On the sea: divers, grebes, Red-breasted Merganser and other sea duck.

8. Baie de Somme

SOMME (80) *IGN 01*

A large part of the Somme estuary – 3,000 hectares of the north-western third out of 7,000 hectares in all – is protected as a réserve naturelle. The area can be considered as comprising two different landscapes, each with its own specialities. The first, an extensive area open to the sea – the bay itself – consists of large mud and sand flats, the estuary of a small river (the Maye) with its mudflats and salt marsh, and a dune system. The dunes range from a simple embankment of sand which protects the Marquenterre bird reserve immediately to its eastern side, to more extensive white dunes to the south by the Banc de l'Ilette. The reserve includes the Anse Bidard, a bay where there are various small reedbeds and sedge-lined ponds. Throughout the year, ducks, waders, gulls and terns (often by the thousand) use this inter-tidal zone for feeding and roosting, and congregate on the Banc d'Ilette at high tide. When the bay is covered by the sea it is usually possible to see seals either swimming not far offshore or resting on the sandbanks.

The second section comprises an area of polders which include the Marquenterre bird reserve. The site contains a range of habitats: extensive meadows and large lagoons, marshes, scrub-covered dunes and pine woods. There is always something to see, whatever the time of year, but the site is especially well known for aquatic species: White Stork, Little and Cattle Egrets, Spoonbill, geese, duck, waders and gulls.

ACCESS

From Abbeville, take the D40 west and turn right along the D940 to reach Le Crotoy. Then take the D4 which winds its way westwards for about 2 km to eventually reach a car park at La Maye (1). In autumn and winter many passerines – Linnet, Twite, Reed Bunting, Rock Pipit – occur in the low vegetation around the Maye estuary. In August and September an Osprey can often be seen fishing over the river or, at high tide, over the sea. A way-marked trail, indicated on the reserve notice board, goes north-eastwards. Cross the salt marsh (called 'mollières' locally), taking care not to fall into any of the deep water-filled dikes and follow the embankment as far as the channel at Férolles (2). As early as March Lapwings can be seen displaying over the wet meadows. Cross the channel and continue along the sand embankments (3), which look over many of the ditches in the Marquenterre bird reserve; there are strategically placed hides in places. From these it is possible to see dabbling and diving duck and Coot throughout the year. During autumn and winter Greylag Geese occur on the meadows, sometimes accompanied by Lapwing and Golden Plover, and numbers of all the ducks increase. From here follow the outside of the reserve boundary to arrive at the Pointe de St.-Quentin (5). Offshore is a semi-circular sandbar – the Banc de l'Ilette (4) – used as a roost by waders during very high tides. It is in this area that the largest concentrations of birds occur, although one should stay on the dunes in order to see them without disturbing them. In addition, the tide comes in very quickly here, and it is easy to get stuck in the mud or cut off if you venture away from the shore. Oystercatcher, Curlew, Dunlin, Bar-tailed Godwit, Grey Plover and Ringed Plover concentrate by the thousand here at high-tide, often with gulls and terns. In autumn, particularly October and November, large numbers of passerines and birds of prey migrate through the area. Check the sandbanks for a resting Peregrine in winter. Continue northwards around the sandbank as far as the Anse Bidard (6). In winter, Shore Lark and Snow Bunting are regularly seen on the beach here, feeding along the high-tide line. In winter there is a gull roost on the incoming tide, and in autumn (July to September) passage terns also come to roost in some numbers, often attracting Arctic Skuas. Return by the same route. There is free access to the whole of this area, providing the reserve rules are respected and directions on the various panels are followed. Dogs are not allowed and camping, taking plants or animals, using motorised vehicles and disturbing the wildlife are all forbidden.

The Parc Ornithologique du Marquenterre reserve itself is well signposted along lanes to the north of Le Crotoy. The reserve is open throughout the year, with a fee payable to enter, although it is closed on some days during the winter (Tel: 03 22 25 68 99 or see www.marcanterra.fr for further details). It is well supplied with hides, trails and other visitor facilities.

Calendar

Spring: many migrants, duck, Spoonbill, White Stork, Greylag Goose, Brent Goose, waders of many species) and raptors.
Summer: many species in Marquenterre bird reserve: Grey Heron, Little and Cattle Egrets, White Stork, Spoonbill, Shelduck, Avocet, Oystercatcher, Mediterranean Gull, passerines (wetland warblers, Stonechat). In the bay: Kentish Plover, wetland warblers, Fan-tailed Warbler.
Autumn: many migrants, Spoonbill, Black Stork, geese, ducks, waders, terns (Arctic, Common, Sandwich and Little), accompanied by skuas, raptors (Osprey), important numbers of passerines (mid-August to mid-November) especially visible around the Banc de l'Ilette (pipits, finches, larks, thrushes and Blackbird) accompanied by birds of prey (Buzzard, harriers, Sparrowhawk, Merlin).
Winter: in the bird reserve and from the hides outside, egrets, a few geese,

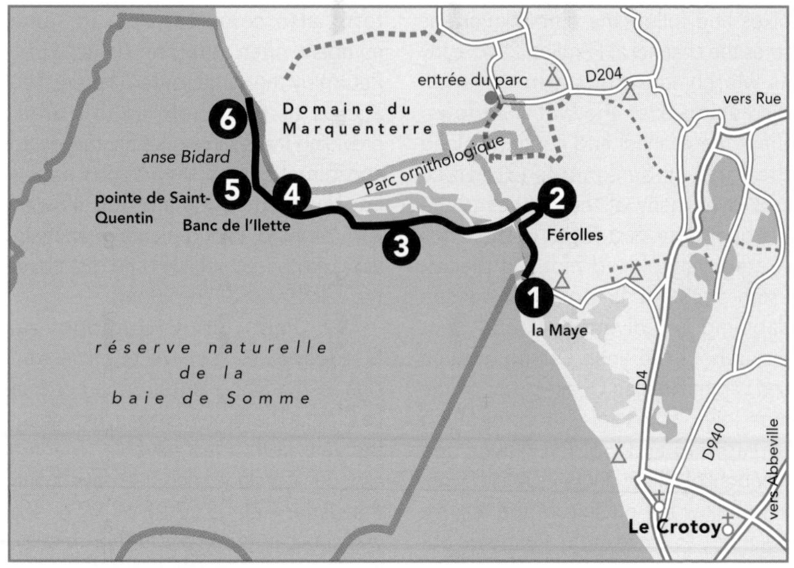

thousands of dabbling duck (Pintail, Wigeon, Mallard, Shoveler, Teal), some diving duck (e.g., Pochard, Tufted Duck, Goldeneye and sawbills) and various waders (e.g., Redshank, Snipe). On the inter-tidal mudflats: many thousands of duck (e.g., Shelduck, Pintail) and waders such as Oystercatcher, Curlew and Dunlin. Along the beach, on the high-tide line, Shore Lark and Snow Bunting are regular. The salt marshes (the Maye estuary) shelter Twite (rare) and other passerines (pipits, larks, buntings). On the sea (off the Anse Bidard): divers, grebes, auks, sea duck (Eider and scoters). Various birds of prey occur throughout the area, notably Peregrine that can be seen almost anywhere.

9. Falaises d'Ault-Onival

Somme (80) *IGN 01/03*

Just to the south of Bas-Champs de Cayeux (see site 7 above) is a line of chalk cliffs stretching for about 7 km from Ault-Onival as far as Mers-les-Bains. They vary in height between 60 and 80 metres and in the winter and during migration periods they provide an excellent vantage point for sea-watching. Various divers, grebes, scoters, Eider, Red-breasted Merganser and auks can all be seen. During the breeding season the cliffs provide nest sites for several species, notably Fulmar, Peregrine, Kestrel, Herring Gull, Jackdaw, Stock Dove, House Martin and Starling. From the D940 north of Le Tréport, take the turning that leads to the coastal viewpoint at Le Bois-de-Cise (the wood is worth a look for woodland species such as Short-toed Treecreeper). The cliffs in Ault itself also provide a good viewpoint. There are paths down to the beach at the foot of the cliffs in both places, and at Mers-les-Bains to the south, to view the cliffs themselves – take care not to get cut off by the tide.

OYSTERCATCHER

10. Forêt de Crécy-en-Ponthieu

SOMME (80) *IGN 01*

This forest, some 15 km to the north of Abbeville and covering about 4,300 hectares, is a beech wood with some stands of pines, rich in birds and mammals (e.g., roe deer, wild boar). It is a breeding site for both raptors (Buzzard, Honey Buzzard, Sparrowhawk) and for many other species, including Stock Dove (in areas of mature trees), Black, Great Spotted, Lesser Spotted and Green Woodpeckers, Redstart, Wood Warbler, Nuthatch and Hawfinch. In the clearings and areas of re-growth look for Melodious and Grasshopper Warblers, Tree Pipit and Hen Harrier. In winter, there are sometimes large flocks of Chaffinches, accompanied in some years by good numbers of Bramblings. Also in winter, Long-eared Owls regularly roost in the conifer plantations and Woodpigeons are particularly plentiful at this time. From Abbeville take the N1 north for 11 km to Nouvion-en-Ponthieu, and then the D111 into the forest. Explore along the many forestry roads and tracks.

11. The Somme valley near Amiens

SOMME (80) *IGN 03*

About 15 km west of Amiens is a complex of wetland areas in the Somme valley. They are mostly the result of former peat extraction which has created a series of relatively large ponds, separated one from another by reedbeds, clumps of willow and meadows. The area is of most interest during the breeding season, from March to July, when wetland species to be looked for here include Bittern, Little Bittern, Marsh Harrier, Hobby, Bluethroat, Cetti's, Savi's, and both Reed and Marsh Warblers. It is also on the migration route of birds such as Greylag Goose, various ducks, Osprey and Black Tern.

From Amiens take the N235 west to Picquigny. From the centre of the village follow signs for the 'marais communal/camping', cross the railway and view from paths on the far side. The valley can also be viewed from Belloy-sur-Somme on the opposite side of the river. Here walk south past the stadium ('stade') and again explore along footpaths near the river. A little further upstream, at La Chaussée-Tirancourt, there are other tracks to the riverside near 'Samara'.

SITES

1 **Barrages de Lavaud and Mas-Chaban**

2 **Forêt de la Braconne**

3 **The Touvre valley**

4 **Fier d'Ars and Lilleau des Niges (Île de Ré)**

5 **Marais de Moëze-Oléron**

6 **Marais d'Yves**

7 **Baie de Bonne Anse**

8 **Île d'Oléron**

9 **La Lasse / Loix-en-Ré (Île de Ré)**

10 **Marais de Brouage**

11 **Phare des Baleines (Île de Ré)**

12 **Station de Lagunage at Rochefort**

13 **Lac du Cébron**

14 **Bois de l'Hôpiteau**

15 **Landes de Chevais**

16 **Niort**

17 **Thouars**

18 **Forêt de Moulière and Réserve Naturelle du Pinail**

19 **Étang de Combourg**

20 **Mirebeau**

21 **Plan d'eau de St.-Cyr**

Poitou-Charentes

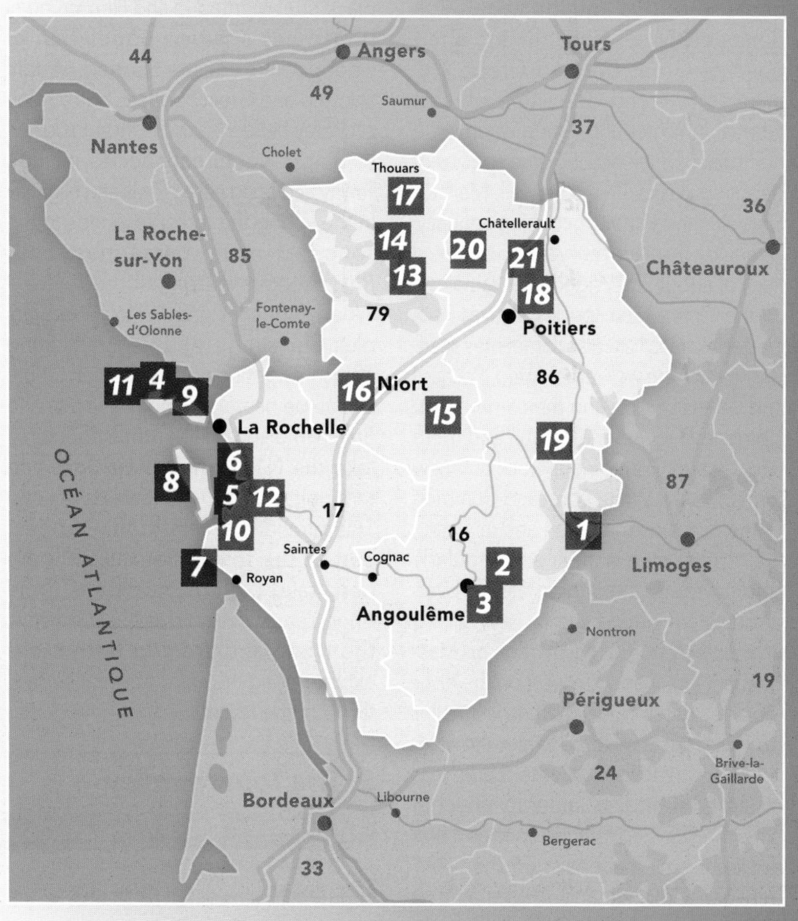

1. Barrages de Lavaud and Mas-Chaban

CHARENTE (16) *IGN 40*

Situated between Chabanais and Massignac, 45 km north-east of Angoulême, are two large reservoirs, the Barrage de Lavaud and the Barrage de Mas-Chaban. The former, on the River Charente, covers 225 hectares and dates from 1988, and was built as a backup source of water for the region in summer. In some hot and dry years the lake's level can drop by more than 10 metres and because of this aquatic vegetation does not thrive. Nevertheless a few pairs of Great Crested Grebe still manage to breed. The site is of most interest in winter and spring when large numbers of duck occur. Some species of dabbling duck – Teal, Gadwall, Mallard, Shoveler and Pintail - occurring annually, while for the last ten years or more a flock of about 200 Wigeon has remained for the winter. Rarer species, such as Red-crested Pochard are also sometimes seen. Diving duck are well represented, Pochard and Tufted Duck being the commonest; Goldeneye sometimes occur, and more rarely Scaup, Ferruginous Duck or Smew turn up. Great White Egret and Common Crane occur on migration and in winter, the latter being annual and regularly landing rather than just passing over. Ospreys are often seen in early spring on their way north.The Barrage de Mas-Chaban, less than 4 km west on the River Moulde, dates from 2000. It is smaller (180 hectares), and is used to regulate water levels on the River Charente. Being less disturbed it attracts larger numbers of birds than Lavaud, but the species mix is similar. From Chabanais, on the N141 between Limoges and Angoulême, a network of minor roads leads to both reservoirs, which can be viewed from the roadside in several places.

2. Forêt de la Braconne

CHARENTE (16) *IGN 40*

This large woodland, 4,000 hectares in extent, is situated 15 km to the north-east of Angoulême. Beech, oak and hornbeam of various ages are mixed together. There are many nesting raptors in the area – Short-toed Eagle, Honey Buzzard, Goshawk, Sparrowhawk, Buzzard, Hobby, Black Kite, Montagu's and Hen Harriers. It also has a varied population of woodpeckers – Lesser Spotted, Middle Spotted and Great Spotted, both Green and Grey-headed, plus the recent addition of Black. Nocturnal species include Tawny and Long-eared Owls and Nightjar. In the spring the forest resounds to the songs of many passerines. Four *Phylloscopus* warblers breed here – Wood, Bonelli's and Willow Warblers plus Chiffchaff – and Redstart, Song Thrush, Nightingale and Golden Oriole can all be heard singing. Hawfinch and Bullfinch also occur. From Angoulême take the N141 towards Limoges and turn right on the D110 towards Bunzac. This provides access to the southern part of the forest. For the northern part, take the D12 north-east from Angoulême. This crosses the D88 within the woodland area. In both cases explore along the many tracks and roads through the forest.

3. The Touvre valley

CHARENTE (16) *IGN 40*

Situated 10 km east of Angoulême, the

River Touvre emerges from underground before flowing on to join the Charente (it is the second most important such 'source' in France, after the Fontaine-de-Vaucluse). Three natural ducts bring water from two other rivers (the Bandiat and the Tardoire) to the surface here, to form a river that is very clear, well oxygenated and of an almost constant temperature, winter and summer alike. This explains why, despite heavy urbanisation nearby, the valley is important for birds in winter, providing an abundant and varied food supply. There are usually plenty of Little Grebes and Moorhens to be seen, and it is a reliable site for Water Pipit. Other species occurring in small numbers include wagtails, *Phylloscopus* warblers, Black Redstart, Stonechat, Blackcap, Siskin, Hawfinch, as well as Teal, Pochard, Tufted Duck, Grey Heron, Snipe, Water Rail, Lapwing, Black-headed Gull, Kingfisher, Cetti's Warbler, Reed Bunting and Redpoll.

In spring large numbers of Little Grebe remain to breed and it is the only nesting site of Common Sandpiper in west-central France. Golden Oriole, Lesser Spotted Woodpecker, Reed and Sedge Warblers are all relatively easy to see in the summer, while Water Rail, quite common in the valley, can be seen throughout the year. Ruelle-sur-Touvre lies just to the east of Angoulême, and from here the 'Souces de la Touvre' is well signposted, and there is a car park near the lake when you arrive.

4. Fier d'Ars and Lilleau des Niges (Île de Ré)

CHARENTE-MARITIME (17)
IGN 39

The Île de Ré, immediately west of La Rochelle, and now connected to the mainland by a roadbridge, contains several areas which are good for birds

COOT

(see also sites 9 and 11 below). Towards the western end the habitat is particularly varied, this being responsible for the great diversity of birds to be found there, more than 300 species having been identified. Wind-blown beaches, lines of dunes, public forests, crops and an inter-tidal rocky shore can all be found here while at the Fier d'Ars, a large area of salt-marsh and salt-pans, some used, others not, encircles a nearly closed-off bay, 800 hectares in extent, with extensive mudflats and salt marsh exposed at low tide. There are two reserves where birds are free from disturbance: the Réserve Naturelle de Lilleau des Niges, to the south of Portes-en-Ré, managed by the LPO and the Fier d'Ars maritime reserve. Because of the changes in the habitats across the island, particularly marked in the past couple of decades, the birdlife has also experienced changes. Species that have increased include Grey Heron, Herring Gull, Buzzard and Mute Swan, all of which are widespread now. On the other hand species that have declined or disappeared completely as breeding species include Kittiwake, Quail, Montagu's Harrier and Ortolan Bunting. For some of these, of course, climatic changes and habitat changes in mainland France more generally will have had an effect, always more marked in a spot like this right on the very edge of the continent. However, it is important to keep track of such changes, and the LPO coordinates a team of observers which make regular counts of winter ducks, geese and waders, as well as carrying out census work on the breeding species. Many of the waders have been colour-ringed, and sightings of marked birds are always welcome. The wildlife of the island has become an important feature of the economy of the island, and locals are encouraged to become involved in surveys of easily recognised species such as Hoopoe, House Martin and the various owls.

Access

The itinerary suggested here will vary according to the state of the tide. Les Portes-en-Ré lies near the western end of the island. From here follow signs to Trousse-Chemise and turn left towards Trousse-Chemise beach. Park in the car park and walk to the sea (1). In winter this is a good area for seeing divers or grebes. On a rising tide, especially in autumn, look through the gulls and the terns, Common and Sandwich primarily, that roost on the sand bars. Return on the same track, then drive to the Patache car park, at the southernmost point of this part of the island (2). In the narrows offshore, in winter from November to March, many birds can be seen here at close quarters: Black-necked and Great Crested Grebes, Brent Goose, Red-breasted Merganser and Goldeneye.

On foot take the one-way track (the wrong way!) which runs along the beach as far as the golf course and large a disused building (3). From October to March large numbers of waterfowl (Brent Goose, Shelduck, dabbling ducks) and waders gather on the Fier d'Ars. A rising tide induces thousands of birds to leave the mudflats in spectacular flocks to go to roost in the reserve.

From here there are two possibilities for exploring the area to the west: either continue along the embankment on foot, or return to the car park and drive back towards Les Portes-en-Ré, but, before the village, take the road to the left, opposite a supermarket, that leads to Vieux-Port. Follow the signs for 'réserve naturelle' as far as a large black building (4). This old salt warehouse, now the Maison du Fier visitor centre (Tel: 05 46 29 50 74) is managed by the LPO and is an excellent source of information.

Park here and continue on foot along the cycle track (5) or on the track to the left of the reserve sign-board, towards the embankment (6) from La Patache. In spring and summer, Black-winged Stilts breed in the disused salt-pans, along with Avocet and Redshank, and the tamarisk bushes provide song-posts for Bluethroats. In winter, with a rising tide and at high tide, flocks of Brent Goose, Mallard, Pintail and Shoveler can be seen on the reserve's pans. Spoonbills also come to feed and rest here, as do Grey Herons and Little Egrets.

In order not to disturb the birds, it is very important that visitors stay on the paths and respect private land. The best times for watching are two or three hours either side of high tide. Tide tables and the IGN Île-de-Ré 1:25,000 map (1329OT) which covers the island in more detail, both well worth having, are on sale in most local shops.

Calendar

Spring: waders and gulls on passage (March to late May).
Summer: Little Grebe, Grey Heron, Little Egret, Shelduck, Mallard, Marsh Harrier, Black Kite, Hobby, Coot, Avocet, Black-winged Stilt, Lapwing, Kentish Plover, Little Ringed Plover, Redshank, Great Black-backed, Lesser Black-backed, Herring, Yellow-legged and Black-headed Gulls, Common Tern, Long-eared Owl, Hoopoe, Meadow and Rock Pipits, Blue-headed Wagtail, Bluethroat, Fan-tailed

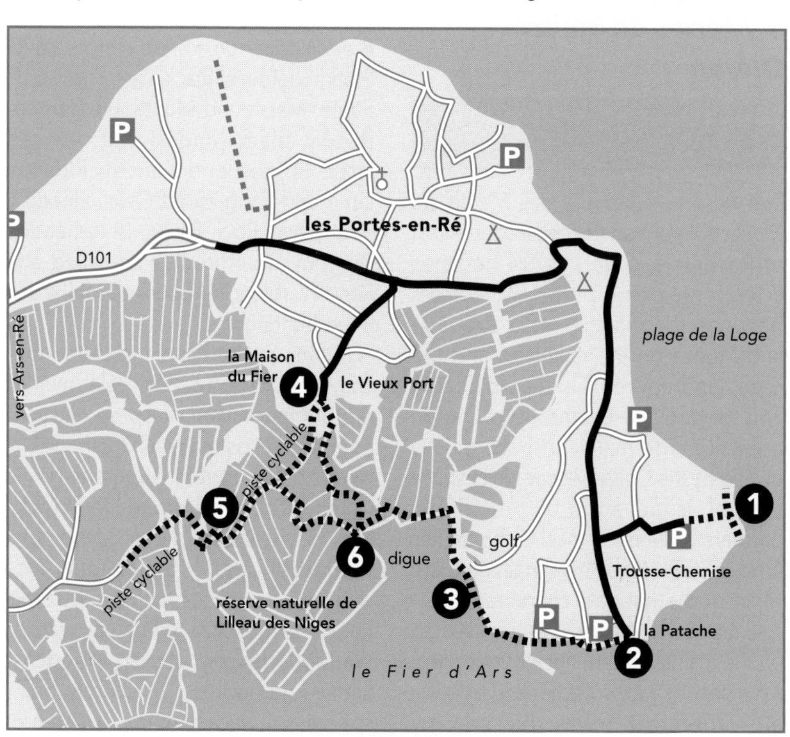

Warbler and Whitethroat.

Autumn: Spoonbill, Greylag Goose, birds of prey (Osprey and Peregrine are fairly regular), waders (more than 30 species), gulls and migrant passerines. Sometimes rare vagrants.

Winter: divers (three species), grebes (five species), Cormorant, Grey Heron, Little Egret, Spoonbill, Brent Goose, Shelduck, Mallard, Shoveler, Pintail, Wigeon, Teal, Red-breasted Merganser, Goldeneye, Avocet, Oystercatcher, Grey and Ringed Plovers, Dunlin, Sanderling, Purple Sandpiper, Curlew, Bar-tailed and Black-tailed Godwits, Snipe, Redshank, Spotted Redshank, Turnstone, Yellow-legged, Lesser Black-backed, Great Black-backed, Common, Mediterranean and Black-headed Gulls, Sandwich Tern, Kingfisher and Fan-tailed Warbler.

5. Marais de Moëze-Oléron

CHARENTE-MARITIME (17)
IGN 39

The Réserve Naturelle des Marais de Moëze-Oléron, on the coast south-west of Rochefort, covers 6,714 hectares (6,500 of which are maritime) and stretches between the marshes near Brouage and Moëze on the mainland and the coastline between Château-d'Oléron and Boyardville on the Île d'Oléron opposite. The mainland part, mostly owned by the Conservatoire de l'Espace Littoral, is managed by the LPO in partnership with the local communities (that of St.-Froult being a main partner). Most of the habitats characteristic of Atlantic coastal marshes are represented on the mainland part: ancient salt-pans, salt marsh meadows, ditches and lagoons, all protected from the sea by embankments. The maritime area is more dynamic due to the tides and moving sandbanks but has, especially on Oléron, a patchwork of salt marsh meadows, dunes, sand spits, lines of scrub, embankments, oyster beds and an extensive area of mudflats, exposed at high tide.

CALENDAR

Spring: an important stopover for many migrant estuarine birds between February and May: many Spoonbills, hundreds or even thousands of Greylag Geese (February) and ducks until April (Pintail, Shoveler and Garganey), thousands of waders in breeding plumage (April and May) including Knot, Whimbrel, six species of *Tringa* waders; various passerines on visible migration including Swift, Sand Martin, pipits, Wheatear and Ring Ouzel.

Breeding season: Purple Heron, White Stork, Shelduck, Black Kite, Short-toed Eagle, Marsh and Montagu's Harriers, Hobby, Black-winged Stilt, Avocet, Little Ringed and Kentish Plovers, Little and Long-eared Owls, Hoopoe, Tawny and Rock Pipits, Blue-headed Wagtail, Bluethroat, Fan-tailed and Reed Warblers, Red-backed Shrike and Reed Bunting.

Autumn: on the mainland, Spoonbill, Greylag Goose, Pintail, Shoveler, migrant raptors (particularly Osprey and Red Kite), Crane, as many as 30 species of wader between mid August and mid October including Dotterel, Temminck's Stint, Curlew Sandpiper, Jack Snipe, Whimbrel, Marsh Sandpiper; also Wryneck, passerines such as Tree Pipit, Redstart, Whinchat, Wheatear, Garden Warbler, Pied Flycatcher, Woodchat Shrike and finches. On Oléron: many species of wader, many species of passerines in the scrub and buckthorn on the dunes.

Winter: on the mainland, Cattle and Little Egrets, Greylag and White-fronted Geese, Shelduck, six species of dabbling duck, Marsh and Hen Harriers, Merlin, Peregrine, Lapwing, Golden Plover, Ruff, Little Stint, Snipe and Jack Snipe (uncommon), thousands of coastal waders at high tide (Dunlin, Black-tailed Godwit, Curlew, Spotted Redshank), Short-eared Owl (irregular), Kingfisher, Meadow and Rock Pipits, Dartford Warbler. On Oléron: Cormorant, Little Egret, Brent Goose, Shelduck, dabbling duck, Marsh Harrier, Peregrine, tens of thousands of coastal waders at roost at high tide, also visible on the mudflats at low tide, especially Oystercatcher, Avocet, Ringed and Grey Plovers, Bar-tailed Godwit, Curlew, Redshank, Knot, Sanderling and Turnstone.

GREYLAG GOOSE

Access

Mainland part: From Marennes, before the bridge to the Île d'Oléron, take the D3 north through Brouage towards Moëze, and turn left on a minor road to the car park at Plaisance (1), following signs to the reserve. This is just one of four car parks in the area. It is essential that visitors do not disturb the birds and by keeping to the public rights of way and the observation points open to the public. There is no access to the body of the mainland part of the reserve, apart from on one of the guided walks organised by the LPO. NB. At any season the best time to see coastal waders is during the three hours before high tide with a coefficient of at least 70.

Firstly, one can continue northwards to the Sables de Plaisance (2), a walk of 3 km there and back. Look out over the mudflats from the dunes – in spring this is an ideal place for seeing waders and passerines on migration. Both Bluethroat and Tawny Pipit breed in the area.

Secondly, the 'Sentier des Polders' interpretation trail (1½ km, open from 1st February to 31st August) runs through the salt-pans to a hide overlooking the reserve. Herons, egrets, coastal waders and passerines can all be seen from the trail. The hide is a good place from which to watch ducks, geese, coastal and breeding waders (the latter including Avocet and Black-winged Stilt), depending on the season.

Thirdly, there is the footpath to La Tanne Ronde (4), a walk of 6 km there and back. A multitude of species can be found here, the mix varying with the season. On the meadows there are Cattle Egret, Greylag and White-fronted Geese, harriers, Peregrine, Hobby, Merlin, Golden Plover and Black-tailed Godwit. In the old salt-pans there are Wigeon, Teal, Garganey, Greylag and White-fronted Geese, Little and Temminck's Stints and Curlew Sandpiper. On the nearby fields

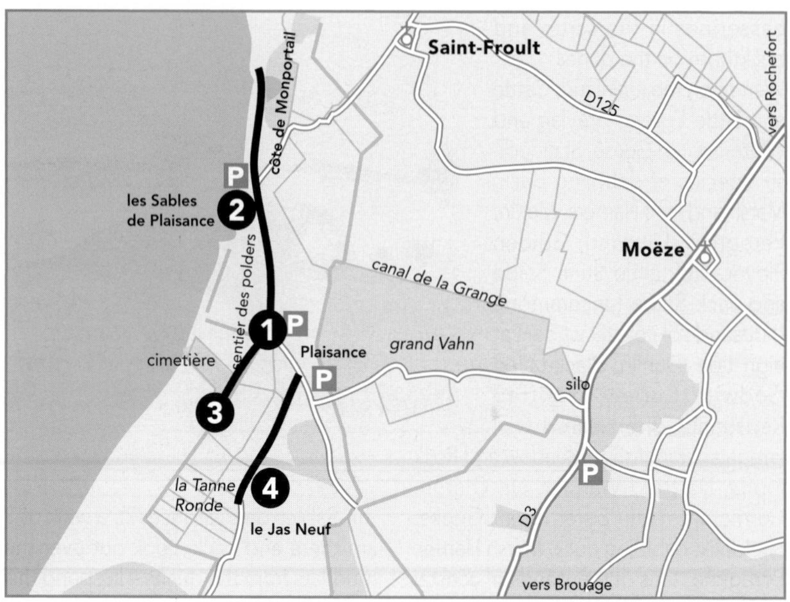

look for pipits, larks and Dotterel, and in the hedgerows and ditch reedbeds check for Red-backed Shrike, migrant passerines and Penduline Tit. The salt marsh along the Brouage maritime canal is a breeding site for Bluethroat, Reed Bunting and Blue-headed Wagtail.

The Île d'Oléron part: (See also site 8 below) From Marennes, cross the bridge to the island and take the first turning right on the D734 towards the Château d'Oléron, and skirt the town to join the 'route des huîtres' and eventually arrive at the edge of the reserve. Follow the coast and park on the right on a small open spot after crossing the first canal bridge, at the 'Pointe des Doux' (1), a pebble bank going far out to sea. This is a good site for seeing Brent Goose in winter as well as coastal waders at pre-roost gatherings, two hours before high tide.

Continuing farther north, still on the 'route des huîtres', there are several small parking spaces on the roadside that allow for watching over the mudflats. On arriving at La Baudissière (2), park in the car park on the right. From here it is easy to see Brent Goose, as well as various waders, feeding at low tide in winter (Grey Plover, Curlew, Bar-tailed Godwit, Dunlin, etc.).

Still continuing northwards, turn right after a large green warehouse onto a road which runs alongside the Arceau oyster-beds as far as the Pointe d'Arceau (3). An observation platform gives a good view of the end of the Bellevue sand spit to the left and a winter high tide wader roost, the one most favoured by Oléron's Curlew and Redshank. Dunlin, Knot, Bar-tailed Godwit and Brent Goose also occur here in large numbers.

Northwards again, turn right round a large bend towards Bellevue (4), where at the end of the road there is a car park. An unstable line of dunes has been formed here, and in an area sheltered by the sand spit, a salt marsh has formed. This is a good site for Bluethroat, Blue-headed Wagtail, Fan-tailed Warbler and

SWALLOW

Reed Bunting in spring and summer.

From here, return to the 'route des huîtres' and, in Les Allards, turn right to get to Boyardville, reached after 6 km. Just before the bridge to the town, turn right towards Fort-Royer. On arriving at the oyster-beds the first track on the left provides access to an area of mudflats next to the sand spit of La Perrotine (5). In winter this sand spit is another of the major high-tide wader roosts (up to 40,000 birds). Once the roosting birds have settled it is important not to go to the end of the spit so as not to disturb them. However, if a Marsh Harrier, Peregrine or Great Black-backed Gull passes too close the resulting movement of birds can be spectacular! In spring the salt marsh to the left of the sand spit is a breeding site for Kentish Plover, Tawny Pipit, Bluethroat and Blue-headed Wagtail.

In this part of the reserve there is open access, provided visitors respect shell-fishing activities on the inter-tidal zone, and take care not to damage or interfere with the oyster-farming which dominates this part of the world. In addition take care not to disturb the birds unnecessarily, particularly during the hunting season, as the area outside the reserve is quite heavily shot over.

6. *Marais d'Yves*

CHARENTE-MARITIME (17)
IGN 39

This réserve naturelle, between La Rochelle and Rochefort, comprises a shallow ancient coastal lagoon, fringed to the west by dunes. To the north there is a sandy area overgrown with willows, with ponds from old sand workings which have been invaded by bulrushes and reeds. It is of particular interest in winter and spring for the number of duck and waders that occur, but there is something of interest to see throughout the year.

■ Access

The reserve lies between the N137 dual-carriageway and the sea, but the reserve's visitor centre (1) can only be reached by road from the north, from the La Rochelle direction, at the Marouillet service area (2). If coming from Rochefort, you need to continue to the Trois Canons interchange and cross over to the other lane and come back south again. The visitor centre (1) is open every day between 09.30 am and 12.00 noon, 15.00 pm and 19.00 pm in July and August, and on Wednesday and Sunday afternoons at other times of year (see http://marais.yves.reserves-naturelles.org for more details). The reserve is managed by the LPO which organises guided visits to the hides within the reserve itself, although there are good views from the visitor centre. If the centre is closed, parts of the reserve can be viewed from the car park (2), and it is possible to walk out to the beach and on to L'Oasis (3). From the beach one can look both into the reserve and out into the bay offshore. Various species including Brent Goose, Shelduck, ducks and coastal waders, can be seen on the seaward side on a rising tide. During autumn migration the dunes attract Whinchat and Wheatear and Tawny Pipit and Short-eared Owl are sometimes seen here.

It is also possible to approach the northern end of the reserve by taking the road towards Les Boucholeurs from the Trois Canons interchange. Just after the railway, turn left at (4) past an area of reeds as well as oyster-beds (5), the whole area being worth checking. Bearded Tit and Penduline Tit can be seen in the

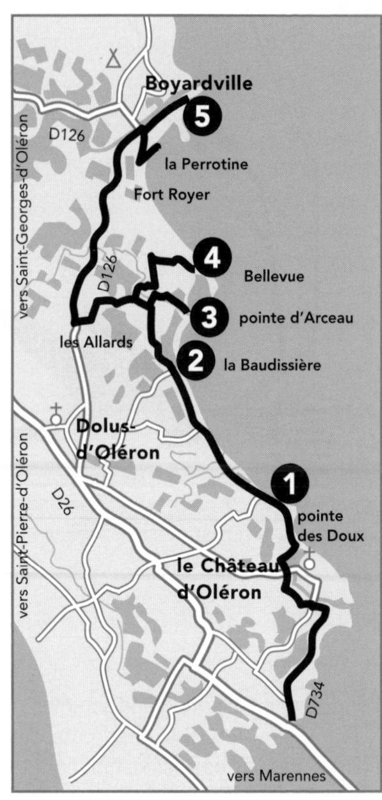

reeds in winter as well as various migrant passerines in the autumn. In spring look in the same habitat for Savi's, Reed, Great Reed and Sedge Warblers. Grey Heron and Little Egret are present throughout the year, and White Storks arrive in early spring to nest on the platforms erected for them by the LPO. Snipe, Ringed Plovers and a variety of other small waders can be seen on the lagoon, especially at hide tide, and waterfowl include Little Grebe, Pochard and Tufted Duck. Marsh Harriers are a frequent sight over the reserve and surrounding fields throughout the year.

■ Calendar

Spring: dabbling duck (including Garganey), hirundines and Swift.

Summer: White Stork, Marsh Harrier
Autumn: same species with many migrant waders.
Winter: Greylag and Brent Geese, many Pintail and Shoveler, Oystercatcher, Grey Plover, Dunlin, Knot, Black-tailed and Bar-tailed Godwits and Curlew. Also Penduline and Bearded Tits.

7. Baie de Bonne Anse

Charente-Maritime (17)
IGN 39/46

The bay of Bonne Anse lies on the coast north-west of Royan, beyond the entrance to the Gironde estuary, and is almost entirely closed off from the open sea by a long curved sand spit. It is a very good site for numerous waders (on migration and in winter) as well as for geese and duck. It is also good for sea-watching (Gannet, skuas, gulls and terns), particularly with an on-shore wind blowing. Kentish Plover and Tawny Pipit have both bred in the area, both rather localised species in this part of France, and in autumn it attracts a share of the passerine migrants moving down the coast.

8. Île d'Oléron

Charente-Maritime (17)
IGN 39

Although probably less well known than the Île de Ré, the Île d'Oléron is nonetheless well worth visiting for birds (IGN 1330OT, 1:25,000 covers the island in more detail). On the eastern coast, the mudflats between Château d'Oléron and Boyardville, between October and April, provide good feeding sites for Brent Geese (see site 5 above). To the north of Boyardville, the Anse de Maleconche bay shelters, during the winter, flocks of Common Scoter, usually with a few Velvet Scoter mixed in. Red-throated Diver is also a regular visitor in late winter (February and March). The Pointe de Chassiron at the northern end of the island is a good spot for watching for various sea and shore birds. Gannet and Sandwich Tern can be seen most of the year, Balearic and Cory's Shearwaters pass in summer and early autumn, whilst Common Tern, skuas and Little Gull are more likely as the season progresses. In the winter it is the turn of various grebes (Great Crested, Black-necked and sometimes Slavonian), Cormorant, Red-breasted Merganser and Mediterranean Gull to be seen here. The western coastline has many areas of rocky shore (e.g., Pointe de Chaucre,

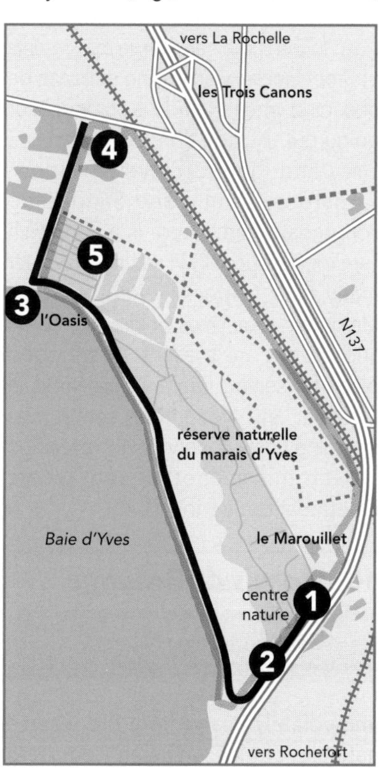

Poitou-Charentes

Pointe de Chardonnière, la Menounière) which are good places, on a rising tide in winter, to look for Purple Sandpiper, Sanderling, Turnstone and Oystercatcher. A little further south, the harbour at la Cotinière always has a good mixture of gulls and during stormy weather it is not unusual to find Guillemot, Razorbill or Kittiwake here.

9. La Lasse / Loix-en-Ré (Île de Ré)

CHARENTE-MARITIME (17)
IGN 39

On the Île de Ré, the Pointe de la Lasse, west of Loix-en-Ré and immediately opposite La Patache (see site 4 above for access), is another good spot for waders and wildfowl, with birds often coming very close to the shore here. Large movements of Brent Geese, waders and gulls can be observed when the tide is coming in or going out. At high tide, Oystercatcher, Grey and Ringed Plovers, Curlew, Turnstone, Dunlin and Sanderling congregate here; there is a Sandwich Tern roost, especially in autumn; in winter many duck (especially Red-breasted Merganser, sometimes Goldeneye), divers and grebes are present. It is a good place for seeing migrant passerines in October and November, sometimes including Snow Bunting. In the breeding season this is another spot where Bluethroat can be found.

10. Marais de Brouage

CHARENTE-MARITIME (17)
IGN 39

Immediately inland from the réserve naturelle of Moëze-Oléron (see site 5 above for access) is a large area, 10,000 hectares in all, of freshwater and salt marsh with its typical landscape of ancient salt-pans, wet meadows and ditches plus some wooded areas around the edges, and 1,000 hectares of crops. The 'Conservatoire de l'Espace Littoral' which owns nearly 900 hectares here, has initiated water and grazing management practices to favour the area's fauna and flora, in conjunction with the local wildfowlers. Although disturbed by shooting in the winter, from February to early September this a very good place to see migrants such as Spoonbill, waders and various birds of prey and it also has a good mix of breeding species, including Purple Heron, Cattle and Little Egrets, Marsh Harrier, Black Kite, Little Owl, Avocet, Black-winged Stilt, and various wetland warblers. The area concerned is centred on the village of Hiers, and stretches from Brouage to the D123. It can be viewed from the minor roads through the area.

11. Phare des Baleines (Île de Ré)

CHARENTE-MARITIME (17)
IGN 39

At the extreme north-west tip of the Île de Ré (see also sites 4 and 9 above), this lighthouse is strategically placed for sea-watching, and is at its best in autumn and winter. Gannets can be seen fishing offshore at almost any time, while Common Scoter, skuas (three species), gulls and terns all pass in front of the point, principally between August and November but also in spring during April and May. With westerly winds it is often possible to see Balearic Shearwater, Storm Petrel, Grey Phalarope,

Kittiwake, Little and Sabine's Gulls and Arctic Tern. In general high tide visits tend to be better, with birds passing rather closer inshore. Winter can be a good time for seeing divers, grebes, Red-breasted Merganser and Purple Sandpiper and sometimes Eider, Razorbill or Guillemot. It is also a good place for migrant birds of prey and passerines in late summer and autumn, with many insectivorous species attracted to the bushes around the lighthouse.

12. Station de Lagunage at Rochefort

CHARENTE-MARITIME (17) *IGN 39*

This sewage works and settling lagoons on the outskirts of Rochefort, close to the River Charente, as well as still performing its primary function, is also managed as a bird reserve by the LPO. It attracts a wide range of wetland species, and has turned up some rarities such as Pectoral and Buff-breasted Sandpiper. In winter dabbling ducks (especially Shoveler), diving ducks and grebes (notably Black-necked) are regular visitors. Little Gull and marsh terns (including White-winged) turn up on migration. In the reedbeds along the nearby River Charente breeding species include Bluethroat and Sedge, Savi's and Great Reed Warblers. In late summer and autumn migrants passing through include Night Heron, Spotted Crake and almost any of the usual inland wader species, including the odd Temminck's Stint or Marsh Sandpiper. In Rochefort, head towards the D733 that crosses the Charente, but instead of taking the bridge, turn off just before, and follow signs to the 'station de lagunage'. The site is still being developed for visitors, and the best views will always be on a guided tour organised by the LPO (Tel: 05 46 82 12 44), but a reasonable amount can be seen from the paths around the edges and by the river.

13. Lac du Cébron

DEUX-SEVRES (79) *IGN 33*

This reservoir, about 15 km north of Parthenay dates from 1982. As soon as it was flooded, the lake attracted many birds. In order to ensure that it would continue to be used by birds protection was put in place, with leisure and sports activities (angling, sail-boards, hiking, etc.) being strictly controlled and shooting forbidden at the lake itself. In late winter and spring many wildfowl gather at the lake, with Mallard, Gadwall, Pintail, Wigeon, Shoveler, Garganey and Teal as well as Pochard and Tufted Duck the most regular. In February and March Greylag Geese sometimes stop here during their migration between Spain and their more northerly breeding grounds. Breeding species of the surrounding hedgerows include Nightingale, Melodious and Garden Warblers, Whitethroat, Blackcap, Red-backed and Woodchat Shrikes, Yellowhammer and Cirl Bunting. Stock Dove, Little Owl and Hoopoe also all breed in the vicinity of the lake and several species of raptor may be seen hunting not far away, including Buzzard, Honey Buzzard, Black Kite, Sparrowhawk, Hen Harrier, Kestrel and Hobby. In the autumn a good number of migrant passerines may be seen passing through, e.g., Blue-headed Wagtail, Wheatear, Whinchat, Redstart, Spotted and Pied Flycatchers, Chiffchaff and Willow Warbler.

At the same time, especially if the lake's level has dropped significantly, small numbers of a wide range of wader species stop off on their way south. Later, as autumn turns to winter, it is possible to find such species as Meadow and Water Pipits, Dunnock, Stonechat, Black Redstart and a variety of buntings in the surrounding countryside.

Access

From Parthenay, take the D938 north towards Thouars and Saumur for 15 km, then turn right on the D46 towards St.-Loup-sur-Thouet and then right again to reach the dam ('barrage de la retenue'). There is a car park at the northern end (1) and another 500 metres further on, beyond the dam (2). This is the best point for watching the northern part of the lake, but do not go beyond the fence and follow any instructions regarding access that are displayed. One can continue along a minor road eastwards to view a little more of the reservior or return to the D938 towards Parthenay. After about 1 km turn left, towards Orfeuille, then immedately right to reach Les Jinchères and another point (3) from which the narrower southern section of the lake can be scanned.

Calendar

Spring: grebes, Greylag Goose (February and March), wide range of dabbling and diving ducks, waders, gulls and marsh terns.

Summer: Great Crested Grebe, Mallard, Coot, Lapwing, Little Ringed Plover. Common Tern nesting on rafts.

Autumn: herons, egrets, Black Stork, dabbling duck, Osprey, waders, Black Tern and quite often Peregrine.

Winter: Cormorant, Mallard, Gadwall, Wigeon, Shoveler, Teal, Pochard, Tufted Duck, Coot, Lapwing, Golden Plover, Green Sandpiper, Curlew, Snipe, Lesser Black-backed, Yellow-legged and Black-headed Gulls; in some years White-tailed Eagle has been seen.

14. Bois de l'Hôpiteau

DEUX-SEVRES (79) *IGN 33*

Situated about 8 km west of the previous site, this area of woodland, heather and gorse, also encompassing a small lake, is one of the few remnants of the original habitat of this part of France, the Haut-Poitou. The Conservatoire Régional d'Espaces Naturels, the Groupe Ornithologique des Deux-Sèvres, local hunters and the local authorities have combined to maintain the integrity of the habitat, notable for its breeding Dartford Warblers and for its large winter Hen Harrier roost. In the spring, particularly around the edges of the woodland and adjacent heathland it is possible to hear the song of Chiffchaff and Willow, Wood and Bonelli's Warblers, the churring of a Nightjar or the distant call of the Black Woodpecker. More unusual visitors have included Short-toed Eagle, Osprey and Purple Heron. The N149 from Parthenay to Bressuire runs past the woodland, as does the D143 north-east to l'Hôpiteau. The lake is just south of the village, and at least some of the area can be seen from nearby tracks and minor roads.

15. Landes de Chevais

DEUX-SEVRES (79) *IGN 40*

About 40 km east of Niort is an area of heathland and an associated lake, with an interesting mixture of breeding species. Chevais is a village just to the east of the

D45 which runs south from Lezay to Clussais-la-Pommeraie (from Niort take the D948 east to Melle, then the D950 and D14 north-east to reach Lezay). The area is the most important breeding site for Curlew in the region and also has many breeding Red-backed Shrikes as well as Honey Buzzard. The lake attracts several species of duck during migration, such as Shoveler, Wigeon, Gadwall, Pintail, Teal, Garganey, Pochard, and sometimes Shelduck, as well as various waders. The wet meadows that are scattered from Lezay through Chevais south to Mairé-l'Evescault have a rich orchid flora, as well as providing hunting opportunities for Goshawk, Hobby and occasionally Peregrine or Short-toed Eagle as well as the three species of harrier. In addition, the surrounding plains have nesting Little Bustard and Stone Curlew (which are responsible for the site having a Natura 2000 designation) and Lapwing.

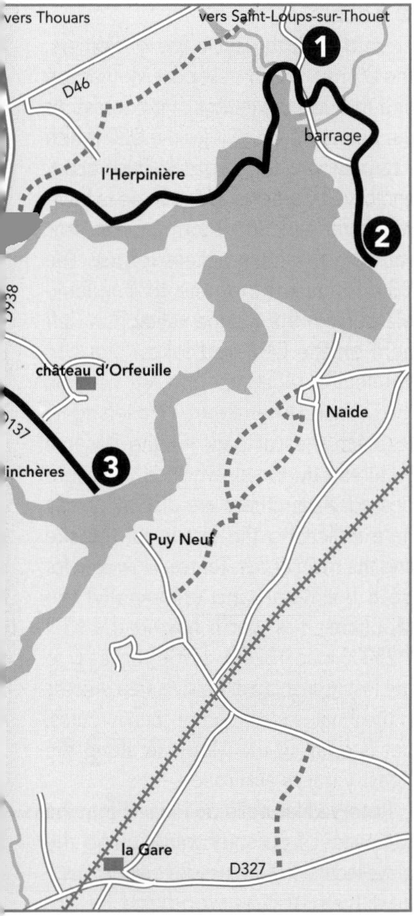

16. Niort

DEUX-SÈVRES (79)

IGN 33/40

The plains both to the north and the south of Niort, although mostly used for arable crops, still provide breeding sites for Stone Curlew, Hen and Montagu's Harriers, and Little Bustard. However, this last species is under serious threat everywhere in northern France, being particularly sensitive to agricultural change, and nowhere easy to see. Little Owl occurs around many of the villages and at night you have the chance to hear Scops Owl in the southern part of the area. In recent years there have been a few sightings of Bluethroats in oil-seed rape fields here; elsewhere in France they are normally associated with coastal marshes. In winter, flocks of Skylarks and finches feed in the fields, along with Lapwing and Golden Plover, attracting the attention of raptors such as Merlin and Peregrine. During years when vole numbers are high, Hen Harriers and Long-eared and Short-eared Owls sometimes stay all winter as well. From Niort, take the D744 to the north-west or the D740 to the south-east, and explore the area along the many minor roads through the fields and villages.

17. Thouars

DEUX-SÈVRES (79) IGN 33/34

In a similar way to the previous site, the agricultural plains to the south-east of Thouars provide breeding sites for Stone Curlew, Marsh, Montagu's and Hen Harriers, Crested Lark, Tawny Pipit and Wheatear. There is also the chance of Little Bustard, although numbers are low. From autumn through to the spring Merlins hunt the passerines wintering here, and Peregrines are also seen on occasion. Lapwing and Golden Plover spend the winter in large numbers, while variety is added by the dabbling and diving duck that can be found along the valleys of the nearby Rivers Thouet and Dive. The D37 from Thouars towards St.-Jouin-de-Marnes and on towards Mirebeau (see site 20 below) crosses the plains, and again there are many minor roads along which to explore the area.

18. Forêt de Moulière and Réserve Naturelle du Pinail

VIENNE (86) IGN 34

This area lies some 20 km north-east of Poitiers and comprises two distinct habitats, each with its own special birds. The Forêt de Moulière is a huge woodland area, 4,000 hectares in all, replanted with conifers in many places but also containing plenty of mature sessile oaks and beeches with large clearings adding to the variety of the habitat. The woodland has a wide range of woodpeckers, raptors and passerines typical of this part of France.

The Réserve Naturelle du Pinail occupies a plateau immediately to the north of the forest and is an open area of heather-dominated heathland ('brande de Poitou'). The area was a source of millstones for centuries, resulting in a landscape pitted with shallow depressions, which now form gradually a patchwork of peat-bogs of great botanical interest, including insectivorous plants such as sundew. It is an important site for breeding harriers, both Hen and Montagu's occurring in good numbers, and has a healthy population of Dartford Warblers.

ACCESS

From the north-east edge of Poitiers, the D3 runs north-east past Montamisé and through the centre of the forest. At the point where it crosses the D20 (which runs between St.-Georges-lès-Baillargeaux and Lavoux) there is a Maison de la Forêt with a car park and information boards showing the main access routes. The D3 continues from here to Bonneuil-Matours, in the Vienne valley. Turn left here on the D82 and follow signs to Vouneuil-sur-Vienne. Turn left here on the D15 and after about 1 km left again to reach the car park for the Réserve Naturelle du Pinail, which is well sign-posted. Again there are display panels here indicating the history of the site and the main access routes. However, for both the Pinail and (especially) the Moulière, it is worth having the IGN 1:25000 map 1826O, as it is very easy to get lost in such an extensive area. Access in the Pinail is restricted to certain routes, but is open in the Moulière along the forestry tracks and roads.

Réserve Naturelle du Pinail. From the car park (1), go southwards along the gravelled track ('Chemin des Gendarmes'), next to a strip of woodland before

TAWNY PIPIT

reaching the open heathland which extends to right and left. Typical breeding passerines of the heathland are Stonechat, Grasshopper and Dartford Warblers, Linnet and Reed Bunting, the latter especially near the ponds. Among the birds of prey that hunt over the open country, Hobby, Short-toed Eagle and Honey Buzzard can be seen at any time from April to September, while Buzzard and Sparrowhawk occur throughout the year joined by Merlin in winter. The star species are perhaps the harriers, with both Montagu's (ca. 15 pairs) and Hen Harrier (ca. 10 pairs) breeding here and in the adjacent forest. During periods of migration the heathland attracts Whinchat, Wheatear, Ring Ouzel and Willow Warbler, as well as Crane in the spring (early March) and autumn (early November). At the south-west corner of the reserve (2), one can take either of two routes which both lead back to the car park. The route to the right runs through the western heather-dominated area (3), and returns via an old track (4) overlooking a small valley running away to the north. Alternatively, by turning left (a 6km circuit), the path follows the edge of the conifers, then crosses the valley of the Rivau (5), the only stream in the forest. This is a good area to hear both Meadow and Tree Pipits singing in flight in the spring. The path then goes northwards through an area where pines for early harvest are planted (6). This section is particularly favoured by the harriers; note that Hen Harriers are present all year whereas Montagu's are purely a summer visitor. The ponds (7) and wetter patches provide feeding opportunities for Grey Herons, Snipe and Jack Snipe while Lapwing can be seen on any patch of newly cleared heath. The route continues by skirting the heath and forest edge to the north of the reserve area proper; listen for Nightjar on warm evenings in spring and summer.

Forêt de la Moulière. Starting from the 'Maison de la Forêt', the road leads south-east to another parking area at

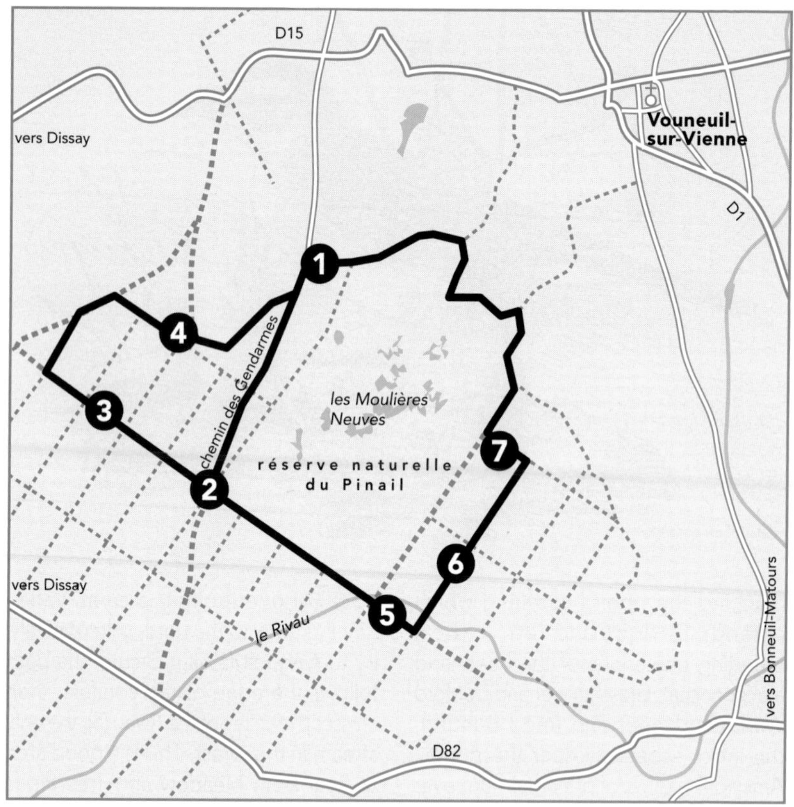

'Le Grand Recoin' (8). From here take a path that runs south with woodland to the left and a meadow in the Meurs valley on the right. At the edge of the forest (9), turn right and cross the valley (a short section with no path, but not too difficult). You now have to cross a ditch to re-enter the forest, into a section which contains some of the best mature oak woodland in the forest. Once within the forest there are many paths for exploration, laid out in a grid-like pattern between clearly numbered plots. Some of the main rides also have names. The route suggested is a little way to the left, taking the ride between plots 268 and 269. Continue as far as the first main cross-ride (the 'Sommière des Meurs') (10), and turn left. Turn left again at (11), between plots 270 and 271 to reach another track at the edge of the forest (12). Turn right here and follow the track as far as the ride between plots 272 and 273, where you again turn right to regain the 'Sommière des Meurs'. Turn right and continue along this all the way back to the edge of the Meurs valley (13). The path continues along the edge of the woodland to rejoin the road, the whole circuit being about 6 km. This route is just one of many that could be designed, but it does run through a mixture of habitats ranging from mature deciduous woodland to conifers. The species seen will depend on the habitat. Look for Crested and

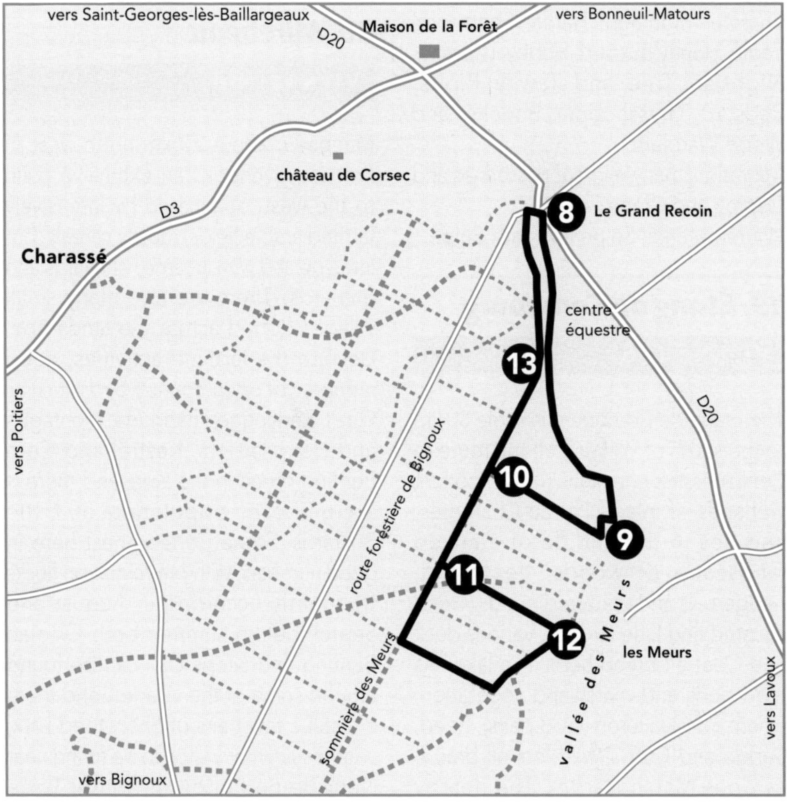

Coal Tits, Goldcrest and Bonelli's Warbler in the pines, and Nightjar in the open mature forest or recently felled areas. Nuthatch, Short-toed Treecreeper and Long-tailed Tit can be seen almost anywhere. Look for Redstarts in the more open mature forest, and along the edges of clearings. The more open areas are also those favoured by raptors such as Buzzard and Honey Buzzard. Wood Warblers prefer mature areas of woodland with little undergrowth, and Stock Doves need mature trees to provide suitable nest sites. Views of Hawfinches are usually fleeting at best, and nocturnal birds like Tawny and Long-eared Owls are more likely to be heard rather than seen. There is a good mix of woodpeckers to be found – Black, Green, Great Spotted, Middle Spotted and Lesser Spotted. The area around (8) and (13) is worth checking, as all five species have been seen in the mature deciduous and coniferous trees here.

Calendar

All year: Grey Heron, Mallard, Buzzard, Goshawk, Sparrowhawk, Hen Harrier, Kestrel, Woodcock, Tawny and Long-eared Owls, Black, Middle Spotted, Great Spotted, Lesser Spotted and Green Woodpeckers, Woodlark, Meadow Pipit, Dartford Warbler, Crested Tit, Short-toed Treecreeper, Nuthatch, Hawfinch and Reed Bunting.

Summer: Montagu's Harrier, Short-toed Eagle, Honey Buzzard, Hobby, Lapwing, Nightjar, Tree and Tawny Pipits, Redstart, Grasshopper, Bonelli's and Wood Warblers.
Migration: many migrant passerines and Osprey and Crane.
Winter: Merlin, Snipe and Jack Snipe.

19. Étang de Combourg

VIENNE (86) *IGN 40*

The Étang de Combourg is some 80 km to the south of Poitiers, off the route to Confolens. It is one of the most important wetlands of inland Poitou-Charentes, and lies in the middle of a mixed landscape of woods, heathland, hedgerows and scattered ponds. Great Crested and Litle Grebes, various duck and Coot all breed here. The lake has reed-beds and marshland vegetation, where Purple Heron (ca. 3 pairs), Reed, Sedge and Cetti's Warblers all breed, as does Marsh Harrier. The nearby woods hold a colony of Grey Herons, as well as all the common passerines to be expected in central France. The area is also of interest during migration periods, with Night Heron, most of the ducks, many waders, gulls and terns passing through, and it is a regular staging post for Crane, Osprey and Greylag Geese.

From Confolens, take the D148 north to Pressac, then north to the village of Combourg. A path west from near the château leads past the northern end of the lake, and continues on into the surrounding woodland.

20. Mirebeau

VIENNE (86) *IGN 33/34*

Mirebeau, about 20 km north-west of Poitiers, overlooks an extensive plain to the west, dominated by intensively farmed arable fields, mostly cereals, but interspersed with lucerne, vineyards and orchards. There are also many small villages dotted across the landscape. Despite the farming activities, good numbers of open-country birds such as Quail, Red-legged Partridge, Montagu's and Hen Harriers, Kestrel and Corn Bunting breed in the area, and there is a significant population of Little Bustards. Stone Curlews nest here in good numbers, with pre-migration flocks frequently occurring in August and September. In summer both Ortolan Bunting and Scops Owl can be found around some of the villages, and there are still a few pairs of Short-toed Lark, another summer visitor, to be found near Neuville-de-Poitou. In winter large flocks of Lapwing, Golden Plover and Rooks gather on the bare fields, and Merlin occurs regularly at this time. The N147 from Poitiers runs north-west through Mirebeau towards Loudun, with a network of roads through the villages to the west providing viewpoints for scanning the fields. The area between Neuville-de-Poitou and Mirebeau west to Thézenay is probably the most productive, but similar habitat stretches away to the north-west as far as Thouars (see site 17 above).

21. Plan d'eau de St.-Cyr

VIENNE (86) *IGN 34*

This 80 hectare lake, next to the River

Clain about halfway between Poitiers and Châtellerault, is a former gravel-pit. Much of the site is used for leisure activities but the northern part has been set aside for birdwatching. It is of most interest at times of migration and in winter. At these times it shelters the largest number of aquatic birds anywhere in the department: Great Crested Grebe, Cormorant, Grey Heron, Mallard, Pochard, Tufted Duck, Teal, Coot, Moorhen and Black-headed Gull are the most numerous species but there may also be Shelduck, Wigeon, Shoveler, Gadwall, Pintail or Common Sandpiper. Rarer visitors have included Great Northern and Black-throated Divers, Greylag Goose, Velvet Scoter, Ferruginous Duck and Avocet. A variety of waders, gulls and terns also passes through and Osprey is an annual visitor in both spring and autumn.

From Poitiers take the N10 north as far as Beaumont and turn right to cross the river to St.-Cyr. The 'parc de loisirs' is signposted just north of the village, and there is a hide, erected by the LPO, at the north-eastern corner of the lake. There are two car parks near the lake, and it is possible to make a complete circuit on foot. Note that the Réserve Naturelle du Pinail is not far away to the south-east (see site 18 above).

LONG-TAILED TIT

SITES

1 *Lac de l'Escale*

2 *Espinouse*

3 *Gorges du Verdon*

4 *Plateau de Valensole*

5 *Parc National des Écrins*

6 *Parc Naturel Régional du Queyras: North-west*

7 *Col du Lautaret*

8 *Lac de Mison*

9 *Marais de Manteyer*

10 *Parc Naturel Régional du Queyras: East and south*

11 *Bois des Ayes*

12 *The Var estuary*

13 *Caussols*

14 *Fort de la Revère*

15 *Le Boréon*

16 *The Camargue: The Réserve Naturelle*

17 *Étang de Berre*

18 *Plaine de la Crau*

19 *Réservoir du Réaltor*

20 *The Durance valley near Puy-Sainte-Réparade*

21 *The Camargue: Marais du Vigueirat*

22 *The Camargue: Saintes-Maries-de-la-Mer*

23 *The Camargue: Salin-de-Giraud*

24 *Salins d'Hyères*

25 *Vinon-sur-Verdon aerodrome*

26 *Étangs de Villepey*

27 *Îles d'Hyères*

28 *Massif des Maures*

29 *Dentelles de Montmirail*

30 *Petit Luberon*

31 *Gorges de la Nesque / Sault*

Provence-Alpes-Côte d'Azur

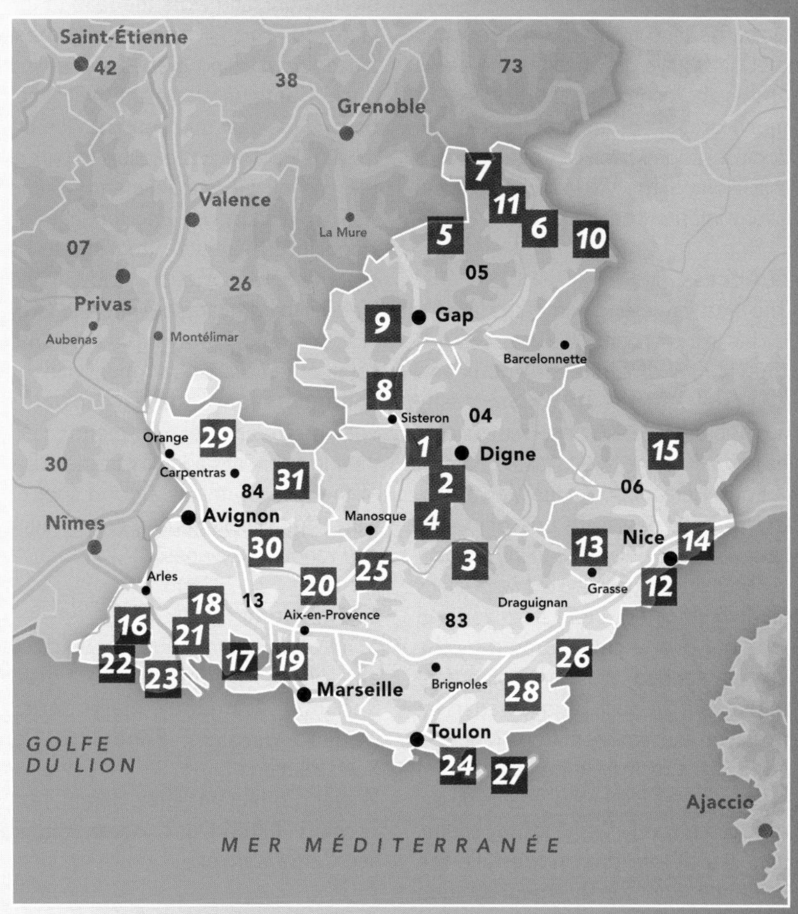

1. Lac de l'Escale

Alpes-de-Haute Provence (04) *IGN 60*

Formed by damming the River Durance 15 km south of Sisteron, the Lac de l'Escale was constructed to generate electricity as part of a hydro-electric scheme. A large reservoir was created behind the dam, and quickly became a water-sports centre. However, as time has passed, and with the erosion caused upstream by the Durance and its tributaries, large quantities of sediment have been washed down into the lake, slowly settling as mud. Consequently reedbeds have grown along the banks and in the centre, to create a site of much greater biological interest. In addition, its geographical position means that it is much used by many migrant and over-wintering species.

Access

The most interesting part of the lake for birds is that just north of the dam, between the villages of Château-Arnoux and L'Escale, and the banks are easily accessible in several places. From Sisteron head south on the N85 as far as Château-Arnoux. Here, opposite the Mairie, take the track that passes the post office and goes under the railway line to the lakeside; continue straight on to the old water-sports landing stage (1). From here you can look out over a creek formed by the central reedbed; there are Snipe here throughout the year, various waders on migration and families of Coot, Moorhen and Great Crested Grebe can be seen in late summer. Follow the 'chemin du lac' on foot south as far as the railway bridge, and just before the bridge take the cemetery road (2). The rough ground on the left is favoured by birds such as Stonechat, Sardinian Warbler, leaf warblers and Serin. Skirt round the right of the cemetery to arrive at a spot that overlooks the end of the central reedbed. Here it is possible to see herons and egrets, Cormorant, gulls, as well as marsh terns, Greylag Goose, Shelduck and various ducks, depending on the season. On the left, below the track, be careful not to disturb the Night Herons that often roost there. Return the same way and from Château-Arnoux take the N85 south again towards Digne-les-Bains. Park just before the bridge (3), on the right, and cross the road to the lakeside. This is probably the best place for watching grebes and diving duck. Continue along the N85 and, beyond the dam, turn left onto the D4 towards Volonne. It is possible to park at the end of the embankment (4), and walk for a short way into the lakeside woodland. There are often Teal to be seen here, with Wigeon, Gadwall and Pintail in hard weather. White and Grey Wagtails and Water Pipit are quite common on the embankment. Finally, continue along the D4 towards Volonne for another 700 metres, and then fork left into a lay-by at the edge of the lake (5), this is a good spot to watch for Marsh Harrier, diving duck and various passerines.

Calendar

Spring and autumn: Purple, Squacco and Night Herons, Cattle Egret, Spoonbill, Garganey, marsh terns, wetland warblers, Penduline Tit, Reed Bunting.
Winter: Cormorant, Grey Heron, Teal, Pochard, Tufted Duck, White Wagtail and Cetti's Warbler.

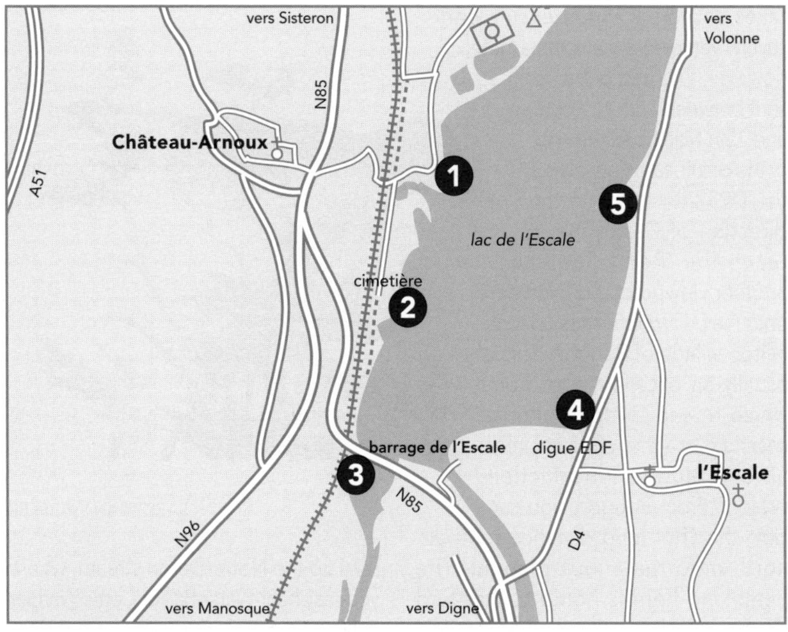

2. *Espinouse*

Alpes-de-Haute Provence (04) *IGN 60*

This site has an interesting mixture of species in spring and summer, with several Mediterranean specialties to be seen: Rock and Cirl Buntings, Sardinian, Subalpine, Dartford and Orphean Warblers, Red-backed, Southern Grey and Woodchat Shrikes, Turtle Dove and Quail are all quite common. From Château-Arnoux, take the N85 south towards Digne-les-Bains. Turn right in Malijai on the road to Mées but after crossing the bridge over the River Bléone, take the D8 east towards Chaffaut. The road follows the Bléone for 5 km and then forks right towards Espinouse. The area beyond the village is particularly good for Mediterranean warblers. Continue as far as the viewpoint at the 838 marker. From here it is best to proceed on foot; there are various tracks in this area from which the surrounding fields, meadows and ravines can be explored.

3. *Gorges du Verdon*

Alpes-de-Haute Provence (04) *IGN 61/68*

The Verdon gorges are a spectacular area, situated between Digne-les-Bains to the north and Draguignan to the south-east. The 'Grand Canyon du Verdon' is home to many typical cliff-dwelling species: Golden Eagle, Griffon and Egyptian Vultures, Peregrine, Alpine Swift, Blue Rock Thrush and Chough in summer; Wallcreeper and Alpine Accentor in winter. The D71 runs along the southern side of the area, with the D952 along the northern side. Starting from the village of La Palud-sur-Verdon on the D952, the D23 'route des crêtes' takes you on a 15 km circuit with several vertiginous viewpoints (note, however, that part of the road is shut between 15th November and 15th March). At the end of the circuit, turn right along the D952 for 8 km, in the direction of Castellane, to reach the 'Point Sublime', another viewpoint. Fork left here onto the D17 which leads up to the hilltop village of Rougon. This is usually an excellent spot from which to see Griffon Vultures soaring past – they originate from an on-going re-introduction project. From Rougon, you can take the GR4 long-distance footpath north onto the Suech plateau. The heathland here is home to Dartford Warbler, Rock Bunting and Short-toed Eagle and other birds include Blue Rock Thrush, Ortolan Bunting and Tawny Pipit. Beyond the plateau, the path descends through an oak wood to the small village of Chasteuil.

SARDINIAN WARBLER

4. Plateau de Valensole

ALPES-DE-HAUTE PROVENCE (04) *IGN 60*

Situated to the west of the previous site, the Valensole plateau is a vast patchwork of cereal and lavender fields and copses, punctuated by wooded valleys. From Manosque, in the Durance valley, cross the river and then take the D6 eastwards for about 15 km to reach Valensole and continue to the far side of the village (in the direction of Riez). Just beyond the village, park near the football pitch. From here the different habitats can be visited on foot along the various tracks around the village. One of these runs up the Notre-Dame stream, where you may hear Water Rail or Cetti's Warbler calling from the riverside vegetation. The hedgerows provide cover for the common passerines of the area. Check all the exposed perches and wires for Roller. The more open meadowland areas are where you are more likely to find birds such as Hoopoe, Stonechat, Sardinian Warbler, Woodchat or Southern Grey Shrikes and Cirl Bunting. Once up onto the higher ground of the plateau, among the arable crops, look for Stone Curlew and Tawny Pipit in the short vegetation (Little Bustard if you are lucky). There are Spectacled Warblers in the less intensively farmed areas of lavender and Ortolan and Corn Buntings can be heard singing from the wires and bushes. Quail and Skylark also occur in the farmland. Keep a lookout for passing birds of prey – Hen or Montagu's Harriers, Short-toed Eagle, Black Kite and Hobby can all be seen here at different times.

5. Parc National des Écrins

Hautes-Alpes (05) *IGN 54*

The Écrins national park covers a vast area of alpine habitat, and is situated north-east of Gap and south-east of Grenoble. A good succession of habitats can be found in the area between the Séveraisse valley at La Chapelle-en-Valgaudémar (at 1,100 metres) and the granite ridge at the Pic Pétarel (at 2,618 metres). Three vegetation layers can be identified: there is the north-facing mountain forest, mainly of beech, birch and fir; then a band of subalpine heathland and scree, covered in a mixture of juniper and rhododendrons; and finally, the landscape of the Cirque des Lacs de Pétarel, dominated by rocks but interspersed with alpine meadows and scattered Arolla pines. By spending time in each of the habitats one has a good chance of encountering the majority of the mountain birds typical of the western Alps.

Access

Starting from Gap (accessible by rail), take the N85 north to St.-Firmin, then turn right on the D985A to reach La Chapelle-en-Valgaudémar after about 18 km. From Gap it is also possible to get here by bus, changing at St.-Firmin. In La Chapelle-en-Valgaudémar, it is worth looking at the national park visitor centre (see also www.les-ecrins-parc-national.fr for information, and details of access). For walking in the mountains a detailed map (IGN 3437OT, 1:25,000) is essential. Start by taking the minor road which goes up to a car park (1) just before the small village of Les Portes (1,280 metres). Above the village it is usually quite easy to see (or at least hear) Bonelli's Warbler in the mountain forest. The path onward, the Sentier de Pétarel, is signposted from the middle of the village and, once the snows have melted (from mid-April),

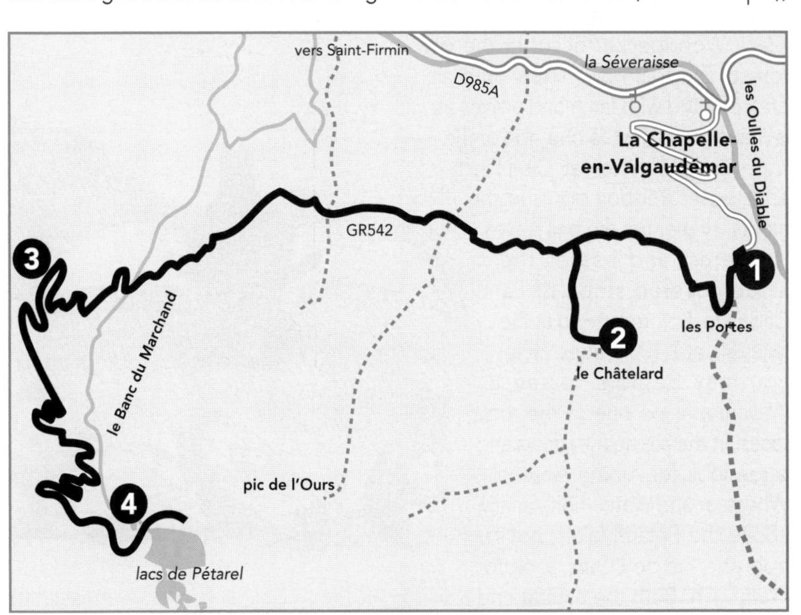

the first part is accessible fairly easily. A deviation to the Belvédère du Châtelard (2) at 1,572 metres is also worth taking. The fascinating courtship of male Black Grouse (with many interrupted hissings and cooing) can be seen in April and May from birds displaying on snow fields hardened by overnight frosts. In addition, and always harder to see than to hear, is the Rock Partridge which seemingly never stop giving their staccato calls to each other as they creep about, hidden in rocky alpine meadows and creeping shrubs of the Clôt des Portes. The trail climbs above the pine forest and crosses the Pétarel stream via a ford. Look for Marsh and Coal Tits and Goldcrest in the beech and fir woods. Spring migrants, such as Rock Thrush, gradually move up with the retreating snow line. On the Banc du Marchand, the Nutcracker may be seen hiding seeds as early as August. The Ring Ouzel's song carries far in the spring air. Look out for a passing Golden Eagle, often seen using the thermals. Crossbill, Common Treecreeper and Black Woodpecker occur in the yew forest. The trail now climbs onto an area planted with larch and arrives at a viewpoint (3) just to one side of the trail. Lesser Whitethroat, Citril Finch and Lesser Redpoll occur in the alders. Higher up, the trail leaves the forest and passes the scree-covered slope of La Casinière, before arriving at the lakes (4), at 2,100 metres. Here, you may be able to see a Wallcreeper on one of the rock faces. In the alpine meadows and scree look for Alpine Accentor, Wheatear and Water Pipit. Finally, above the Pétarel lakes, not far from the Pic de l'Ours, look for Ptarmigan. Both the habitat and the populations of several species are quite fragile. Although protected within the central part of the park, some of the gamebirds such as Rock Partridge and Black Grouse are hunted not far away, and should certainly not be disturbed unnecessarily. Do not approach too close, particularly when they are displaying, and avoid taking photographs of any of the birds at the nest.

Calendar

Spring and summer: Golden Eagle, Black Grouse, Ptarmigan, Rock Partridge, Black and Great Spotted Woodpeckers, Water Pipit, Alpine Accentor, Wheatear, Black Redstart, Rock Thrush, Ring Ouzel, Mistle Thrush, Lesser Whitethroat, Blackcap, Garden and Bonelli's Warblers, Chiffchaff, Goldcrest, Coal and Willow Tits, Common Treecreeper, Nutcracker, Lesser Redpoll, Crossbill and Citril Finch, all of which nest.

PTARMIGAN

6. Parc Naturel Régional du Queyras: North-west

Hautes-Alpes (05) *IGN 54*

The Parc Naturel Régionel du Queyras, another alpine park, lies to the south-east of Briançon. The part considered here (but see also site 10 below), to the south of the Col d'Izoard, lies in an old glacial valley, drained by a mountain stream, the Rivière. The lowest part of the circuit is at 1,800 metres in a deep-sided valley, cut into the limestone. A dense mountain pine wood with a few larch trees grows on the scree and on the moraines. Higher up (2,000 metres) there are three glacial constrictions flanked by cliffs which form successive plateaux, originally lakes but as they slowly filled with sediment, they became hay meadows, now abandoned and surrounded by alpine chalets. Above this (2,300-2,500 metres), the valley opens out into a landscape where each hollow in the turf has become a small peat-bog. However, the north and south of the valley are bordered by large limestone outcrops.

Access

From Briançon head south on the D902 to the Col d'Izoard pass, and on in the direction of Guillestre as far as the small village of Brunissard, which lies at the foot of the pass, on its southern side. From here it is possible to drive as far as the campsite of Le Planet and park. The walk suggested here covers 12 km with a total change in altitude of some 700 metres, and is likely to take the whole day. It is essential to have a detailed map (IGN 3537ET, 1:25,000) before setting out. On the way up, the track is marked in red and white (the GR 5) as far as the fork to the Col des Ayes, then in yellow. The start of the trail is along a track (forbidden to tourist vehicles) which climbs through a wood to the Pré des Vaches (1). As early as February Crossbills may be nesting among the pines here. Other birds to be looked for include Coal, Crested and Willow Tits, Goldcrest, Bullfinch and Serin. There are also Siskin and Citril Finch in the area, but they are usually less easy to find. Look also for signs of woodpecker activity in the form of damaged stumps and branches. Continue through an area strewn with large rocks to reach the plateau of Pra-Premier (2) at 2,000 metres. This is a good spot to stop and scan the surroundings. Mistle Thrush and Ring Ouzel feed in the semi-open habitat of alpine meadows with scattered larches. A Dipper can usually be seen feeding near the waterfall at the bottom of the meadow. Take the winding track below the cliffs (3). House Martins nest on the lower cliffs, a few Crag Martins occurring higher up, with Alpine Swifts nesting towards the top. The cliffs also provide nesting sites for Alpine and Red-billed Choughs, Raven and Kestrel. If you are lucky you may see a Wallcreeper on the cliffs, but sometimes they venture onto the rocks lower down or even come to feed on the chalet walls. In general these cliffs are at their best in the morning when the sun is shining on them. At the end of the track (4) look for Black Redstart, Wheatear and Whinchat. Cross the stream, keeping to the trail marked in yellow. This leads through some attractive meadows as far as the peat-bogs at the lakes of Cogour and Marion (5) and then the Col de Néal pass. Take care not to trample the fragile vegetation, particularly in the wetter areas. Common and Green Sandpipers are sometimes seen here, but only as

ALPINE CHOUGH

Clapeyto. It is in this high landscape of snow and boulder scree on north-facing slopes that Ptarmigan can be found. Often, however, all that can be found are its droppings; it is a declining species very susceptible to disturbance.

passage birds. The alpine meadows mixed with rocky ledges, slabs and scree are the haunt of Alpine Accentor and Snow Finch, though they are never as easy to see as the omnipresent Water Pipits. To return, either retrace your steps or continue to follow the yellow marked trail. This route, along a ridge, passes via Lac de la Favière and then drops down to the left (to the north-east) through an area of boulders (6) to get back to Clapeyto (4). Alternatively one can return via Le Collet (7), avoiding

■ Calendar

Spring and summer (May to mid-August): Ptarmigan (June and July), Common and Green Sandpipers (on migration), Alpine Swift, Crag and House Martins, Water Pipit, Alpine Accentor, Whinchat, Wheatear, Ring Ouzel, Mistle Thrush, Coal, Crested and Willow Tits, Siskin, Citril Finch, Serin, Wallcreeper and Snow Finch.

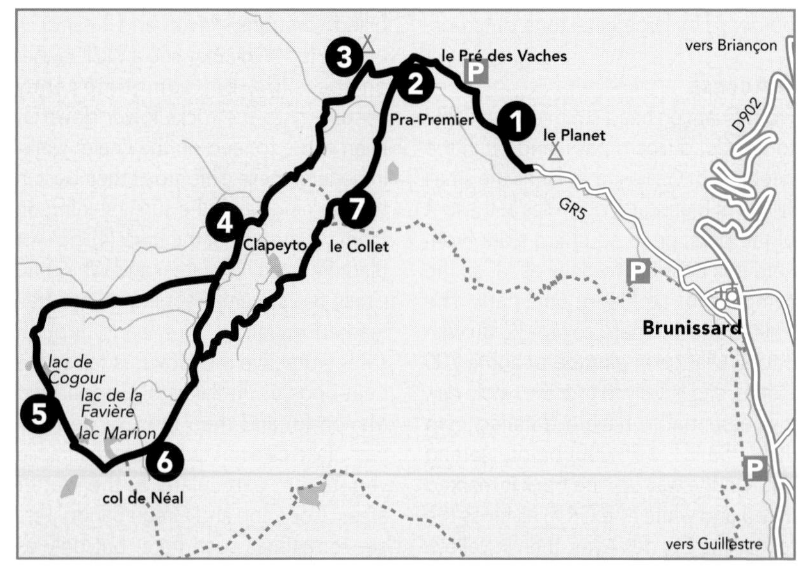

7. Col du Lautaret

HAUTES-ALPES (05)
IGN 53/54

This pass is a high point on the main N91 road that runs north-west across the northern edge of the Écrins national park (see site 5 above). It is worth stopping at Les Sestrières, below the Marionnaise avalanche-protection tunnel about 1½ km east of the pass. The altitude here is 1,970 metres, and a walk along the old road, now a footpath, which leads towards the Col du Galiber to the north can be productive. The track passes through an area of alpine meadows, traversed by streams and lined with stands of green alder; this is a good area for seeing Alpine Chough, Red-billed Chough, Alpine Accentor, Snow Finch, Water Pipit and Whinchat. The slopes on both sides the main road are the hunting ground of Golden Eagles, which have a healthy population in the area. There is an information centre about the park at the Col du Lautaret, and the Sentier des Crevasses which starts from near here leads through an area of alders where, remarkably, Marsh Warbler has been found. Check any of the areas of scree and rock faces for Rock Thrush and Wallcreeper, both of which breed in the area.

8. Lac de Mison

HAUTES-ALPES (05)
IGN 60

This small artificial lake (20 hectares) lies at a height of 630 metres between the villages of Upaix and Mison, between Gap to the north and Sisteron to the south. It is also roughly equidistant from the valleys of the Rivers Buëch and Durance. It is an area of interest throughout the year due to its strategic position and the varied habitat – the lake itself, a reedbed in the north-west corner and a zone of deciduous woodland, hedges, meadows and crops around it. Great Crested and Little Grebes, Little Bittern, Black Kite, Hobby, Water Rail, Scops and Little Owls, Reed and Great Reed Warblers are all present in the breeding season. During spring and autumn migration and/or in winter it is possible to find Marsh and Hen Harriers, Sand Martin and Swallow, Reed Bunting and Yellowhammer all using it as a roosting site. Other species that have been recorded here include Great White Egret, Bittern, White and Black Storks, Red-breasted Merganser, Merlin, Crane, Curlew, Short-eared Owl and Savi's Warbler. From Sisteron, take the D75 north-west to reach Mison, then the D324 which runs past the lake (it becomes the D622 on the far side which is in a different département).

9. Marais de Manteyer

HAUTES-ALPES (05)
IGN 54/60

This 40 hectare marsh, at an altitude of 950 metres, is located between Manteyer and La Roche-des-Arnauds, some 11 km west of Gap. Take the D944 west from Gap to reach the area. The marsh has a large reedbed, and a small lake, with conifer forests, streams and open hillsides in the area adding to its interest. Even in winter there can be something to see. Access is along a variety of farm tracks between the two villages. The following species can be found in spring and early summer: Little Bittern, Honey Buzzard, Montagu's Harrier, Hobby, Tawny and

Little Owls, Reed, Marsh and Bonelli's Warblers, Chiffchaff, Red-backed Shrike, Reed, Cirl, Ortolan and Corn Buntings and Yellowhammer. During the autumn migration a Swallow and Sand Martin roost forms in the reedbed. Other species recorded during migration periods have included Bittern, Purple Heron, Black and White Storks, Red Kite, Hen Harrier, Curlew, Eagle Owl, Sedge, Wood and Willow Warblers.

10. Parc Naturel Régional du Queyras: East and south

HAUTES-ALPES (05)

IGN 54

The eastern part of this park, close to the Italian border contains some magnificent scenery, especially in the area of Ristolas. This is reached from the Col d'Izoard (see site 6 above) by taking the D902 southwards to join the D947, and turning east through Château-Queyras for 15 km. On the gentle western slopes, which were once cultivated, it is possible to see Rock Partridge and Rock Thrush, as well as lots of marmots. The latter are the favoured target for the Golden Eagles which inhabit the area in good numbers. The steep eastern slopes are covered in dense mature forests of larch and Arolla pine, some areas having some remarkably fine trees. Here are Nutcracker (easily seen in August), Black Grouse, Goshawk, Sparrowhawk, Ring Ouzel, Crossbill and Common Treecreeper. In winter the calls of Pygmy and Tengmalm's Owls, and sometimes even Eagle Owl, can be heard from the cross-country ski trails along the River Guil. Roe deer and chamois are abundant, mouflon, alpine ibex and a few red deer also occur, providing prey for a few wolves that first reappeared in the area in 1997. Lammergeiers have also recently arrived here, probably originating from reintroduction schemes elsewhere in the Alps. The area can be explored along the many footpaths and long-distance trails, and the park authorities publish a variety of leaflets about the local flora and fauna.

11. Bois des Ayes

HAUTES-ALPES (05)

IGN 54

The Bois des Ayes, just to the south of Briançon, is one of the finest Arolla pine forests in France and has been classed a biological forest reserve because of its outstanding biodiversity – flora, animals and birds alike. From Briançon take the D94 south but almost immediately turn left towards Villard-St.-Pancrace. A little after entering the village follow directions to Ayes (intersection on the left). Where the road forks, just beyond a chapel, turn right, still following signs for Ayes, taking the unsurfaced forest track labelled as the long-distance footpath GR5 (don't take the shortest road – the D236T – to the left as it is narrow and dangerous!). Continue for about 2 km through the small village of Les Chalets de Ayes. A surfaced road leads to the 'Plan du Peyron'. Cross the Orceyrette stream via a small bridge to the left of the road to reach a picnic site (at 1,860 metres) where it is possible to park. Note that the road is often impassable in winter, even as late as late May or early June. There is a panel showing access at the picnic site and it is possible to make a circuit of the reserve on foot, starting along a track to the left from here. The 1:25,000 map IGN 3536OT will help you not get lost in what is quite an extensive area of mountain woodland. Look for Nutcrackers among the larches and Arolla pines. Lower down, it is possible to hear Black Grouse giving their cooing calls during their spring displays. Listen out also for the brief repeated whistles that indicate the presence of Pygmy Owl; being semi-diurnal is not quite so difficult to locate as, say, Tengmalm's. Higher up over the open ground a soaring Golden Eagle or a flock of Alpine Choughs can often be seen. At the 'de Vers le Col' chalets, at 2,200 metres look for Black Redstart, Water Pipit and Wheatear. The more adventurous might want to continue along the GR5 to the 'Col des Ayes' at 2,477 metres, which leads on into the Queyras park, though the track is steep. Part of the area is hunted over from September onwards and it is advisable not to venture into the mountains in bad weather.

12. *The Var estuary*

Alpes-Maritimes (06)

IGN 68

The mouth of the River Var is bounded on one side by Nice airport, immediately to the east, and by a commercial centre to the west. Nevertheless, and despite its small size, the area is of remarkable interest for birds, with up to 260 species noted each year. The western bank of the river mouth is covered with a reedbed that grows upriver as far as the Napoléon III bridge, varying in density from one place to another. Patches of willow, alder and bramble often mixed with clematis grow on both banks. There are gravel bars along the length of the river. Those nearest to the sea change position each year with variations of water flowing down the river and of course the birds to be seen vary according to the state of the tide.

Access

Whether coming from Nice (to the east) or Cannes (to the west), take either the A8 motorway (exit 49, St.-Laurent-du-Var), the N7 or the N98 coast road. From St.-Laurent-du-Var head for the Cap 3000 commercial centre, whose southern car park is the best placed for the river mouth. It is possible to get to the Cap 3000 site by bus and train. At the mouth of the estuary there is an information board, with details of access. From point (1) you get a good view over the estuary and its small islands to the airport opposite. Various herons occur in the riverside woodland – Night, Purple and Squacco Herons (during April and May) and Grey Heron throughout the year. Several species of duck occur – Teal (in winter), Gadwall, Shoveler, Mallard and Pochard (migration and winter), as well as Coot, Spotted Crake (March and April) and sometimes Water Rail. Many of the commoner waders occur (mid-March to mid-May and August and September). It is also worth looking offshore for seabirds. To get to the beach, take the causeway by the sewage farm as far as (2); divers and grebes can be seen on the sea in winter, and Yelkouan Shearwater, gulls and terns in spring. Return to the starting point, and continue for another 150 metres upstream to where there is a projection into the river (3). From here you get another view over the river mouth and a reedbed where many passerines breed or stop off on migration: chats (on migration), Nightingale (breeds), Cetti's, Reed, Great Reed and various other warblers, shrikes, flycatchers. Look out also for the naturalised Indian Silverbill, at least a thousand of which are now resident in the Nice area, having escaped as a cage-bird in the 1980s. Continue up-river, stopping to search the bushes, trees and gravel banks (4) for passerines (pipits and wagtails on migration). Go as far as the Napoleon III bridge (5), looking at the gravel banks and small islands where there is a small colony of Common Terns and a few pairs of Little Ringed Plover breed. There is strictly no access to the islands and river banks – everything can be seen from the embankment without causing unnecessary disturbance.

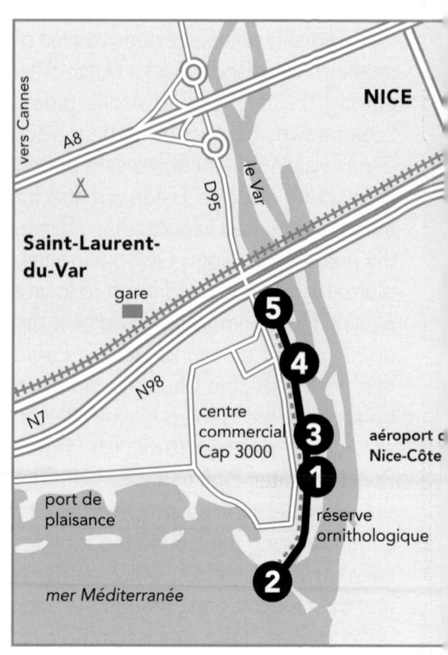

■ Calendar

Spring: the best period for a large variety of species: Purple and Night Herons, Garganey, Spotted Crake, numerous species of wader, Little Gull, all three marsh terns, other terns and passerines such as hirundines (including Red-rumped Swallow), chats, Icterine, Melodious and other species of warbler, flycatchers and Woodchat Shrike. A resident population of Indian Silverbills has become established.

Winter: Cormorant, Grey Heron, duck (particularly Teal), Coot, Moorhen, a few waders, Sandwich Tern, Sardinian Warbler, Penduline Tit and Marsh Harrier.

13. Caussols

Alpes-Maritimes (06)
IGN 68

The open countryside north of Grasse is worth exploring, for a typical mix of Mediterranean species. One starting point is the village of Caussols, accessed from Grasse west on the N85 to St.-Vallier-de-Thiey, then north on the D12 for about 10 km to reach the village. The meadows around the village itself can be quite good in winter for species such as Meadow and Water Pipits, Hawfinch, Crossbill, Raven, and Brambling. In spring, a short walk from Caussols village as far as the Plateau de Calern to the north, using the GR4 long-distance footpath could produce sightings of Short-toed Eagle, Chough or Wheatear, with Sardinian Warbler, Blackcap and Whitethroat all to be heard singing from the undergrowth. Once on the plateau itself look for Rock Thrush, Red-backed Shrike and Tawny Pipit, all of which are breeding species here. The path continues across the plateau as far as the village of Cipières. To the south, the GR4 crosses the Plateau de Caussols and eventually leads to Grasse. Other birds of the area include Red-legged Partridge, Hoopoe and Wryneck, Subalpine and Dartford Warblers, Ortolan, Corn, Rock and Cirl Buntings. The D12 continues east from Caussols, and the CERGA astronomical observatory is also accessible by road, but exploration on foot is usually more productive.

14. Fort de la Revère

ALPES-MARITIMES (06)

IGN 68

The Fort de la Revère, just to the north-east of Nice, has recently received a lot of attention from migration watchers, particularly in the autumn. Its position at 700 metres on a hilltop yet only 2 km from the sea means that it is well-placed for observing birds moving westwards along the coast. September is the best month for seeing large numbers of raptors, with up to 18 species regularly noted here. These include Short-toed Eagle, Osprey, Honey Buzzard, Marsh Harrier, Black and Red Kites, Sparrowhawk, Hobby and occasionally Eleanora's Falcon. Black and White Storks pass at the same time, as do large numbers of Bee-eaters, nearly 2,500 being counted in a fortnight recently. As the autumn moves on, other species such as Common, Pallid and Alpine Swifts, hirundines (including Crag Martins), Tree, Meadow and Water Pipits, White Wagtails, Starling and various larks and finches also pass overhead, along with vast numbers of Woodpigeons. Outside the migration period the area has Dartford and Sardinian Warblers, Rock and Cirl Buntings as breeding species, with the chance of Alpine Accentor and Wallcreeper in winter. The Fort de la Revère is halfway between Nice and La Turbie, off the D2564 near the Col d'Eze. The Col de l'Arme and Mont Gros east of La Turbie are alternative viewpoints.

15. Le Boréon

ALPES-MARITIMES (06)

IGN 61

Le Boréon is a ski-station in the northern part of the Parc National du Mercantour, on the Italian border to the north of Nice. From here take the D202 and then the D2565 to St.-Martin-Vésubie, and then the D89 to Le Boréon. There are many footpaths on which to explore the various mountain habitats (the IGN 3741OT, 1:25,000 map is essential). The streams and lakes have Grey and White Wagtails, plus Dipper. A walk through the larch, pine and spruce forests of the higher slopes will give you the chance to locate some of the breeding species of the woodland – Goshawk, Black and Great Spotted Woodpeckers, Song and Mistle Thrushes, Firecrest and Goldcrest, Coal, Crested and Willow Tits, Crossbill, Bullfinch and Siskin. Higher up again in the Arolla pines Nutcrackers are widespread. Once above the tree-line look for Golden Eagle and Alpine Chough and there is always the chance of seeing Lammergeier soaring overhead. Both Tengmalm's and Pygmy Owl are resident here, but unless you come in the early part of the year when they are calling most frequently they are difficult to locate.

16. The Camargue: The Réserve Naturelle

BOUCHES-DU-RHÔNE (13)

IGN 66

The Camargue, the vast area formed by the Rhône delta, provides many exciting birdwatching opportunities (see also other sites below, plus site 7 in the Languedoc-Roussillon chapter). Different parts of the delta benefit from various levels of protection. A section covering 13,117 hectares, centred on the Étang du Vaccarès, is classified as a réserve naturelle, and although access is restricted to the roads and tracks, the open nature of the terrain means that there is plenty to be seen throughout the year. As one moves from south to north one passes through a series of different habitats. First there are the coastal beaches and dunes next to the Mediterranean. Then comes the Digue à la Mer embankment which protects the main body of the Camargue from the sea. Behind this are the 'sansouires', one of the most typical of Camargue landscapes, a salty steppe with glasswort, a habitat much favoured by waders and duck when flooded in the winter. In the middle of this, on an east-west aligned area of ancient dunes, are a group of bush-covered islands, the Bois des Rièges. North again is the huge Étang du Vaccarès, a refuge for diving duck and grebes, together with its fringe of reedbeds.There are also major changes of habitat depending on the time of year. With the coming of the winter rains the whole area is transformed into an immense wetland, gradually drying out in the summer between March and September. Only a few of the lagoons retain water throughout the year, Vaccarès, Le Lion and La Dame being the most important. Elsewhere, wherever the surface is slightly higher, it becomes a dry and salty desert due to evaporation. The annual deficit of rainfall, due in a large part to the violent north-west winds coming down the Rhône valley (the famous Mistral), is to a certain extent compensated for artificially by water from the surrounding rice fields.

RED-CRESTED POCHARD

Access

Starting from Arles take the D570 towards Saintes-Maries-de-la-Mer, and then after 15 km turn left at Albaron on the D37 towards Salin-de-Giraud. After 4½ km, you reach the Marais de Basse-Méjanes (1), a wetland area to the north of the road. In the spring and early summer this is a good spot for Cattle and Little Egrets, Grey, Purple and Squacco Herons. There is a good chance of hearing a Bittern 'booming' from the reedbeds, or flying a short distance across the top of the reeds. Look out also for Gull-billed Tern which usually breed in this section of the Camargue. In winter there are many duck to be seen, especially Wigeon, Gadwall, Mallard and Teal, and Bewick's Swan can also be seen (up to 100 birds winter in the Camargue). Great White Egret also occurs in winter, and Glossy Ibis is also occasionally seen at this time. Continue along the D37 road for another 2 km to where there is a hide (2), just before the junction with the road to the Mas d'Agon on the left. This is a good spot from which to scan the northern part of the Étang du Vaccarès, for wildfowl and raptors. From here, take the Mas d'Agon road north for a short distance to another area of marshes (3) which can be viewed from the roadside. This is another area in spring for Grey, Purple and Squacco Herons, Cattle and Little Egrets, and Bittern can be heard from the reedbeds. There are usually Black-winged Stilts nesting here, and sometimes Collared Pratincole can be seen. To get to the eastern side of the Étang du Vaccarès, return to the D37 and continue to Villeneuve and turn right in the village, following signs towards the 'Réserve Nationale de Camargue' and Salin de Badon. There are several places worth stopping at by the side of the lake (4 and 5), both before and after the reserve's information centre at La Capelière (6). In winter, the waters of the Étang du Vaccarès can be thronged with wildfowl – grebes, dabbling duck, Red-crested Pochard, Pochard, Tufted Duck, Ferruginous Duck, Goldeneye and Eider. A 1½ km interpretation trail with hides starts from the La Capelière information centre. Various saltmarsh species may be seen, with Penduline Tit in winter and on migration. There are often quite a few duck (Teal, diving duck) in front of the hide by the small lake next to the trail. If you wish to visit the Salin de Badon reserve which lies to the south you need to make the arrangements here in advance. From La Capelière continue southwards. At Mas de Fiélouse turn left and after about 1 km you reach the Marais de Grenouillet (7). This is a good area for Bee-eaters while Whiskered and Black Terns (sometimes White-winged Black) occur over the marsh in May. Always check any horses or cattle, as they often have Cattle Egrets feeding nearby. Return to the D36 and continue south as far as the Bois de la Ville. Just beyond the wood (8) is a good spot for scanning both sides of the road as in winter this is one of the more likely places to locate one of the Spotted Eagles that often roost near here. Then, after the road turns sharp right, go straight on for another 4 km, following the northern edge of the Étang du Fangassier salt-pan (9). This is the site of France's only Greater Flamingo breeding colony, with usually well over 10,000 pairs. The colony can only be seen from a distance, but feeding birds can often be seen in many other parts of the area. Then continue on to La Comtesse, where there is a car park. The road passes through an area where

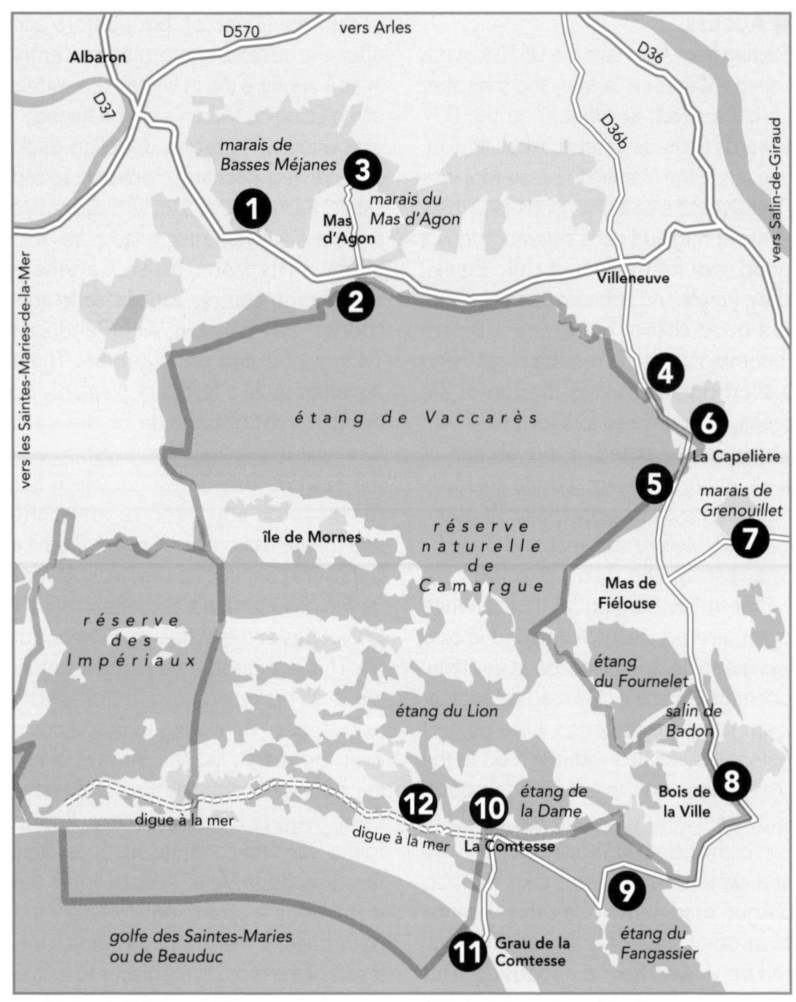

Avocets and Slender-billed Gulls breed, Shelduck can be seen throughout the year and there are many wildfowl in winter. From here there are two possibilities, both on foot. To the south the track leads to the Grau de la Comtesse (11) where you can look out to sea. During the winter and spring, scan the sea for divers (especially Black-throated), grebes, scoters and Razorbill while during migration periods shearwaters, Gannet, skuas (including Long-tailed), and terns can be seen. Alternatively, take the 'Digue à la Mer' (12) which runs to the west through extensive areas of glasswort, the favoured habitat of Spectacled Warbler which breeds here from March to September, and is occasionally seen in winter. Greater Flamingos can often be seen from the causeway and waders are numerous. In the spring passerine migration can be impressive, with many birds making their first landfall after crossing the Mediterranean.

CASPIAN TERN

Autumn and winter: grebes, Grey Heron, Bittern, Great White, Little and Cattle Egrets, Glossy Ibis (rare), dabbling duck, Red-crested Pochard, Pochard, Tufted Duck, Goldeneye, Marsh Harrier, Spotted Eagle (annual), Peregrine, waders, Black-headed, Little and Yellow-legged Gulls, marsh terns, Bearded and Penduline Tits, many migrant passerines.

Calendar

Spring and summer: breeding colonies of Greater Flamingo, many heron species, Black-headed, Mediterranean and Slender-billed Gulls, Sandwich, Common, Little and Gull-billed Terns, raptors, waders (Black-winged Stilt, Avocet, Kentish Plover), Collared Pratincole, Bee-eater, Roller, Hoopoe, hirundines (sometimes Red-rumped Swallow on spring passage), Blue-headed Wagtail, *Acrocephalus* warblers, Moustached and Spectacled Warblers, many migrant passerines (March-May).

17. Étang de Berre

Bouches-du-Rhône (13)
IGN 66/67

The Étang de Berre is a vast Mediterranean lagoon (15,500 hectares) with various other wetlands nearby and bordered by the limestone cliffs so typical of this part of the Mediterranean. Over the centuries the quality and nature of the water in the lagoon has seen many changes, and at present, the water is becoming gradually more

GREATER FLAMINGO

saline and is now similar to seawater. With both Marseille and Aix-en-Provence not far away to the east, the lagoon has long been at the centre of much economic development associated with these conurbations. However, despite unrestricted construction along its banks, pollution and a rapidly increasing human population, the area still boasts a rich and varied natural history.

Access

From a birdwatching point of view, the Étang de Berre can be viewed from a variety of places, but they are well spaced apart. Much of the 80 km of its shoreline is accessible to the public, although parts are restricted or closed; take note of any notices displayed, particularly near the more industrial sections. The circuit suggested here starts at Marignane, at the south-east corner of the étang. From the embankment here one can look out over the Étang de Bolmon (1) which has a variety of habitats similar to those of the Camargue, such as reedbeds, sansouire, lagoons, marshes and tamarisk thickets. It is some 800 hectares in extent and is protected by belonging to the Conservatoire du Littoral. More than 220 species of bird have been seen here, regular visitors including Osprey, Garganey, the three species of marsh tern, Little Gull, Great Spotted Cuckoo and various waders on migration; each year both Gadwall and Red-crested Pochard breed in the nearby Marais des Paluns-Barlatier. There is a nature trail just to the south, with two hides that usually provide views of a wide range of aquatic species, including breeding Night and Squacco Herons and Little Bittern. Access is via the Châteauneuf-les-Martigues rubbish tip ('déchetterie'), or the Marignane sewage works ('station d'épuration'), both on the side of the Canal du Rove. Opposite, on the northern part of the site, is the line of dunes of Le Jaï (2), which separates the Étang de Berre from the Étang de Bolmon. In winter this can be a productive spot from which to scan the main lagoon for species such as Great Northern and Black-throated Divers, Eider, Common and Velvet Scoters, Red-breasted Merganser, Slavonian Grebe and Lesser Black-backed Gull. A short distance north from here, between the airport and the A7 motorway, are the remnants of some ancient salt-pans, the Salins du Lion (3) at Vitrolles. These are of interest throughout the year, the following species being typical: grebes, Greater Flamingo, Cormorant, Mute Swan, Teal, Mallard and Shoveler, diving ducks and Coot, in winter, with various *Acrocephalus* warblers in summer. The access to the site is indicated at the entrance to Marseille-Provence airport. A little farther on, on the other side of the Étang de Vaïné, are the Salins de Berre (4), to the west of the town of Berre-l'Étang, sign-posted from the town centre. This is the only remaining site used for salt production and is an excellent

BLACK-WINGED STILT

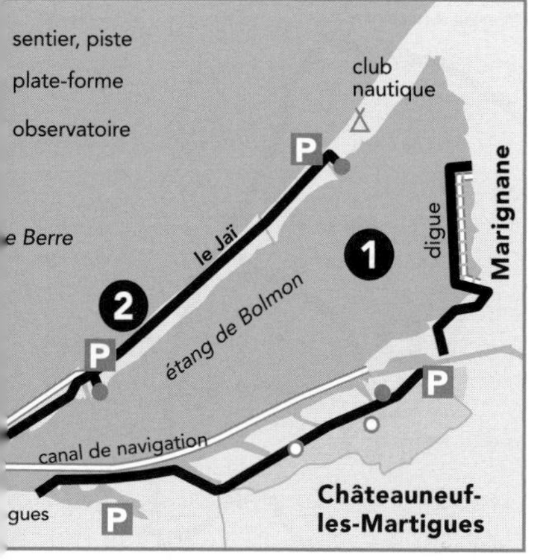

area for migrants, waders, gulls and terns; regular species here include Shelduck, Avocet, Black-winged Stilt, Collared Pratincole, Ringed, Little Ringed and Kentish Plovers, plus various other waders including Marsh Sandpiper, Curlew and Whimbrel, Sandwich, Caspian, Common and Little Terns. In 1999 a pair of Spotless Starlings bred here, and as this species is increasing its range it is worth double-checking to see if the event is repeated. Beyond the salt-pans is the Port de la Pointe (5), a harbour for the oil and chemical industries used in winter by sea duck and other northern diving birds. Continuing on around the lagoon to the northern side,

BLACK-NECKED AND SLAVONIAN GREBES

along the D10 at the foot of the higher ground west of Calissane, it is worth stopping near the St.-Chamas hydro-electric power station (6), which channels water from the River Durance into the Étang de Berre. Goldeneye often occur in winter, and there are often large concentrations of Black-necked Grebes sometimes over 5,000 birds gathered here at what is France's most important wintering site for this species. A few hundred metres farther on, there is a footpath below the road that runs along the edge of the lake. This leads to the Palous de St.-Chamas (7), also called the 'Petit Camargue', another area owned by the Conservatoire du Littoral and offering good birdwatching throughout the year. Species found here include Little Grebe, Greater Flamingo, Great White Egret, Marsh Harrier, Little and Spotted Crakes, Water Rail, Coot, Kingfisher, various wetland warblers, most notably Moustached Warbler, and Bearded Tit. The final protected area includes the lagoons to the west of the étang, in the section between Istres, Martigues and Fos-sur-Mer. This group of small lagoons also results from former salt extraction activities. The ancient, disused salt- pans at Rassuen (8) have small colonies of Black-winged Stilt, Shelduck and Grey Heron in spring. Situated on the outskirts of Istres, take the D52 towards the St.-Blaise archaeological site ('fouilles archéologiques') which passes the old salt- pans. Continuing south along the same road brings you to the Étang de Citis and then the Étang de Pourra (9), between St.-Mitre-les-Remparts and Port-de-Bouc. Here the disused salt-pans have been submerged and have developed into lakes surrounded with wide reedbeds. They shelter a good

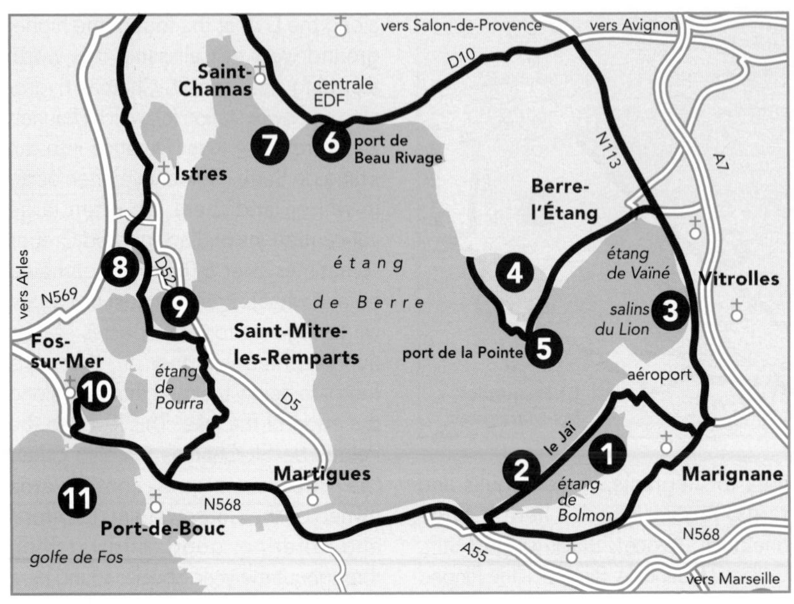

variety of birds – grebes, Greater Flamingo, various members of the heron family, including Bittern, Little Bittern and Purple Heron, Marsh Harrier, Black Kite, flocks of diving duck in winter, Great Reed and Reed Warblers, etc. The salt-pans at Fos-sur-Mer (10), just to the east of this ancient town, provide a breeding site for various waders, terns and gulls: Shelduck, Oystercatcher, Avocet, Black-winged Stilt, Little Ringed Plover, Mediterranean Gull, and Common and Little Terns. On the seaward side, reached by crossing the N568 to the Cavaou beach, the sheltered bay of the Golfe de Fos (11) usually holds a few seabirds in winter, including the odd rarity. Typical visitors include Gannet, Eider, scoters, sawbills and Razorbill. The surrounding hills also include some prime birdwatching areas. East of Vitrolles is the Plateau de l'Arbos; east of St.-Chamas is the high ground between Calissane and Lançon; there is more high ground between St.-Mitre-les-Ramparts and the Étang de Berre; and to the south is the high ground of the Chaîne de l'Estaque. Southern species are well represented, with several Mediterranean specialities to be seen, including Bonelli's and Short-toed Eagles, Little and Scops Owls, Nightjar, Roller, Spectacled, Sardinian, Dartford and Subalpine Warblers.

MOUSTACHED WARBLER

18. Plaine de la Crau

BOUCHES-DU-RHÔNE (13)

IGN 66/67

The plain of La Crau, immediately to the east of the Camargue, is the site of the ancient delta of the River Durance. The characteristic habitat is called 'coussous', a flat expanse of stones covered with herbaceous plants. The traditional human activity here was sheep rearing. The coussous once covered the whole of the Crau plain, some 50,000 hectares, but started to be partially transformed into irrigated meadows from the 16th century, and in the 20th century has suffered from industrial development and the expansion of fruit-growing. Happily, the remaining coussous (11,500 hectares) has been classified as a SPA, and 7,500 hectares have been designated as a réserve naturelle. In addition to the traditional landscape, which in summer is dry and steppe-like, the irrigated fields with hedgerows in the northern part of the plain are always green, and have their own distinct birds.

PIN-TAILED SANDGROUSE

ACCESS

Although it is possible to see a certain amount from the roadsides, quite a lot of La Crau is fenced off by military and industrial development. It is therefore well worth heading for the reserve area of Peau-de-Meau. From Arles, take the N113 east towards Salon-de-Provence, stopping first in St.-Martin-de-Crau to visit the Écomusée de la Crau. This is situated near the church, with free entry, and is open every day. Your can purchase a permit to visit the reserve from here. From the écomusée, take the D24 south-west towards Mas Thibert-La Dynamite, then turn left and continue past the Étang des Aulnes for several kilometres to reach the car park at Peau-de-Meau (1). From here follow the track by the Canal de Vergière south-westwards, and then turn left towards the sheep-fold ('bergerie') of Peau-de-Meau. Check the trees to the north of here for Roller and Lesser Grey Shrike, and look for Hoopoe and Little Owl on the piles of stones that are scattered across the landscape as well as checking the sheepfold (2) itself, at the end of the track. There is an observation platform here, a good place for scanning across the open landscape for Pin-tailed Sandgrouse. This is the only area in France where this species can be found, a little over 100 pairs in all. They are usually located by call as they fly over, very fast, from one part of the plain to another. It is also possible to see Little Bustard from here, another breeding bird of these stony steppes. The best time to look is in April, May and June, when males can be seen giving their strange grunting display calls. Stone Curlew also breed here, and become more active towards the evening, when

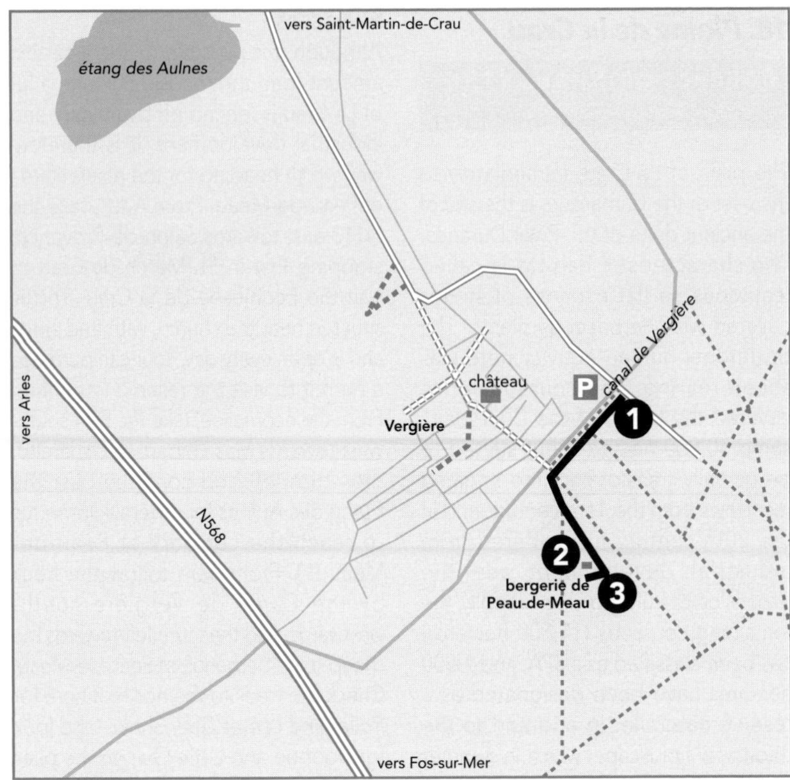

again their eerie calls attract attention. Among passerines, there are plenty of Short-toed and Skylarks to be heard singing overhead, while both Tawny Pipit and Crested Lark also occur in smaller numbers. Of the birds of prey, Black Kite is usually easy enough to see, and with luck you may also encounter an Egyptian Vulture. A pair or two nests up in the nearby hills and they wander quite widely in search of food. The rubbish tip near the Étang d'Entressen to the north-east is a big attraction for both of these scavenging species. The star raptor here, however, is the Lesser Kestrel, for which the reserve is managed specifically, with artificial nest sites in place in and around the sheep-fold. About 50 pairs of this insect-eating summer visitor breed in the area and birds can often be seen hunting over the coussous. Other specialities of the area, not necessarily to be seen at the Peau-de-Meau itself but not far away, are a few Calandra Larks and Southern Grey Shrikes. Spring is the best time for a visit as this is when most birds are active, calling and displaying. Later in the year the area can be extremely hot, and birds hard to see except early in the morning and in the evening.

Calendar

Spring: Lesser Kestrel (in the western part of the Crau), Little Bustard, Stone Curlew, Pin-tailed Sandgrouse, Little Owl, Hoopoe, Southern Grey Shrike, Skylark, Short-toed Lark, Calandra

Lark (rare), Tawny Pipit. Red-footed Falcon on migration (May).

Summer: best time for seeing Roller on the edge of the coussous and the hay meadows. In July, young Kestrels and Lesser Kestrels can be found over the coussous, hunting the now abundant grasshoppers.

Autumn and winter: Little Bustard and Pin-tailed Sandgrouse flock together, but their erratic movements make them hard to find. Winter visitors include Red Kite, Bonelli's Eagle, Hen Harrier, Peregrine, Merlin, Lapwing, Golden Plover and Corn Bunting.

19. Réservoir du Réaltor

BOUCHES-DU-RHÔNE (13)
IGN 67

This reservoir is situated next to the D9 about half-way between Aix-en-Provence and Vitrolles on the Étang de Berre. It is of particular interest during the winter when up to 8,500 Pochard and 6,000 Tufted Duck may gather here. Both Scaup and Ferruginous Duck have been seen several times, although one always needs to be aware of the possibility of 'look-alike' hybrids. Rarities such as Ruddy Duck and Long-tailed Duck turn up on occasion while Bittern, Great White Egret, Red-crested Pochard, Teal and Garganey are also regularly seen. There is quite a large Cormorant roost from September onwards. Wintering passerines include both Bearded and Penduline Tits and Reed Bunting. Osprey, Garganey and the various marsh terns pass through on migration, particularly in the spring. Breeding species include Great Crested and Little Grebes while the reedbeds hold Great Reed, Reed and Moustached Warblers as well as, unusually for this species, a colony of Grey Herons.

20. The Durance valley near Puy-Sainte-Réparade

BOUCHES-DU-RHÔNE (13)
IGN 67

The valley of the River Durance between Pertuis and Mérindol, north of Aix-en-Provence, although modified by gravel-extraction and other developments, has several sites of interest at any time of year, with over 250 species of bird recorded in the area. Summer birds include Little Bittern, Purple Heron, Squacco Heron (regular), Garganey (rare), Reed, Great Reed and Moustached Warblers, Great Crested and Little Grebes, Spotted Crake (rare) and Egyptian Vulture (regular). The riverside trees have a heron colony (including Night), Black Kite, Honey Buzzard, Hobby, Melodious Warbler and Golden Oriole. Both Common Tern and Little Ringed Plover breed along the Durance. Look also for Red-rumped Swallow which breeds in the surrounding area. On migration it is possible to see Osprey, Spotted and Little Crakes, Black-winged Stilt, many small waders (including Temminck's Stint and Marsh Sandpiper) and Sedge Warbler. In winter look for Bittern, Great White Egret, Snipe and Jack Snipe, Penduline Tit and Reed Bunting. Exit 15 on the A51 north of Aix is one point of access. The gravel-pits by the river between here and the village of Puy-Sainte-Réparade are one area worth exploring. A little further west along the D561, just beyond the village of St.-Estève-Janson, is a wetland reserve between the road and the river to the right, accessible on foot. From here cross the river to Cadenet and continue west on the D973 to Mérindol. Follow signs to the left towards the 'observatoire ornithologique', crossing the railway to reach a hide overlooking more areas of wetland habitat. See also site 30 below.

21. The Camargue: Marais du Vigueirat

Bouches-du-Rhône (13)
IGN 66

An exceptional site in the eastern Camargue of some 1,000 hectares, the Marais de Vigueirat comprises a whole mosaic of different habitats – lakes, reedbeds, woodland and sansouire. In autumn and winter as many as 35,000 waterfowl (Greylag Goose, many species of duck, Coot) may congregate here, with birds of prey that can include Peregrine (regular), Spotted Eagle or even Lanner. Many waders and passerines are also present at this time. During spring and summer all the typical herons of the Camargue breed here, as does White Stork. Other interesting breeding or migrant species include Savi's and Moustached Warblers and Bearded Tit (the last two in good numbers). There is an important Bee-eater colony plus a few pairs of Roller. Egyptian Vulture, Lesser Kestrel and Pin-tailed Sandgrouse may also occur at this time as wanderers from the nearby plains of La Crau. From Arles take the D35 towards Port-St.-Louis-du-Rhône, as far as Mas-Thibert, then turn left on the D24 and immediately right. The reserve is signposted and is reached after about another 2 km. From the site entrance follow signs to the visitor centre. Access is strictly controlled, with guided visits possible on foot or by horse-drawn wagon. For these it is essential to book in advance (Tel: 04 90 98 70 91). There is an interpretation trail along a 2½ km boardwalk, open to the public between 09.00 and 17.00 for those who wish to visit independently.

22. The Camargue: Saintes-Maries-de-la-Mer

Bouches-du-Rhône (13)
IGN 66

The town of Saintes-Maries-de-la-Mer, famous for its gypsy festivals, is on the coast right in the centre of the Camargue, at the end of the D570 from Arles. A short walk west will bring you to the mouth of the Petit Rhône, a good spot to look out to sea. In winter one can see Gannet, Eider, Razorbill and scoters offshore while at migration times various terns pass along the coast and inland here while both Slavonian and Black-necked Grebes can be seen in summer plumage before they move off to their breeding grounds. Alternatively, to the east is the causeway of the Digue à la Mer (see also site 16 above) from which the herons, terns, waders and other species typical of the Camargue wetlands can be seen.

23. The Camargue: Salin-de-Giraud

Bouches-du-Rhône (13)
IGN 66

Salin-de-Giraud is another site within the Camargue, this time in the south-east near the mouth of the Grand Rhône and is reached from Arles along the D36. Continue through the town on the D36D to the beach (the 'Plage d'Arles') in another 11 km. Scan the sea from the Grau de Piémanson. In winter this is another spot from which to see the various divers, grebes, scoters and Razorbills which winter offshore, with shearwaters, Gannet, skuas and gulls passing through on migration. On the return towards Salin-de-Giraud check the salt-pans to the west of the road. In spring and autumn this is a good area for passage waders, among them often a rarity; recent examples include Broad-billed Sandpiper and Red-necked Phalarope, while Audouin's Gull has also been seen here.

24. Salins d'Hyères

VAR (83) *IGN 68*

Hyères lies to east of Toulon, and to the south are a series of salt-pans, bought by the Conservatoire du Littoral in 2001 following the end of commercial salt production in order to protect the area from urban development. There are two areas of salt-pans at Hyères, some 6 km apart, the Salins des Pesquiers (550 hectares) on the Giens peninsula, and the Vieux Salins (350 hectares) to the east of Hyères. The Giens peninsula is composed of a double 'tombolo' (a raised line of pebbles or sand that links an island to the mainland) which goes 7 km out to sea. The mix of habitats – sansouire, coastal pine woods, lakes and mudflats – of varying salinity has created a complex ecological system which is favourable for migrant, wintering and breeding birds. Thus, in spring and summer, there are many species typical of the warm lagoons of the Mediterranean, replaced in autumn and winter with a different set of species from farther north.

Access

In order not to disturb birds there is controlled access, with guided visits to the site organised by LPO PACA (Tel:04 94 57 01 98) which take visitors right into the heart of the salt-pans. Nonetheless, it is quite feasible to see the birds of the Pesquiers salt pans from the roadside. Starting from Almanarre (1) walk south along the beach. The pans at (2) often have terns and Greater Flamingos on them, this being an important non-breeding site

YELLOW-LEGGED GULL

for birds nesting in the Camargue away to the west. Continue southwards to reach a hide (3) which overlooks the division between the two separate parts of the Étang des Pesquiers. Duck often occur on the northern lake whereas the mudflats of the southern part are much used by waders, Shelduck and Greater Flamingos. The Marais des Estagnets (4), which can be viewed from the beach, often holds good numbers of duck and the sheltered Golfe de Giens to the west is a wintering site for divers. Continuing to the eastern side of the peninsula, the salt-pans opposite the village of La Capte (5) are also worth a look. North again brings you to the Marais Rodon (6), an area favoured by breeding species such as Avocet, Black-winged Stilt, and Little and Common Terns. The Vieux Salins site is not so easy to see from the exterior, although it is possible to take the coastal footpath east from Salins village along the edge of the pans. Away from the saline areas, the fringes of the airport are worth a look, especially during spring migration and in the summer. To visit the site, park near the exercise circuit (CRAPA) (7) and follow the track that leads to the small Roubard river. A path follows this all the way to the sea, through some riverside woodland (8), meadowland and past the airport (9). There are some reedbeds by the river which provide cover for herons, rails and passerines and birds of prey can be seen over the more open areas.

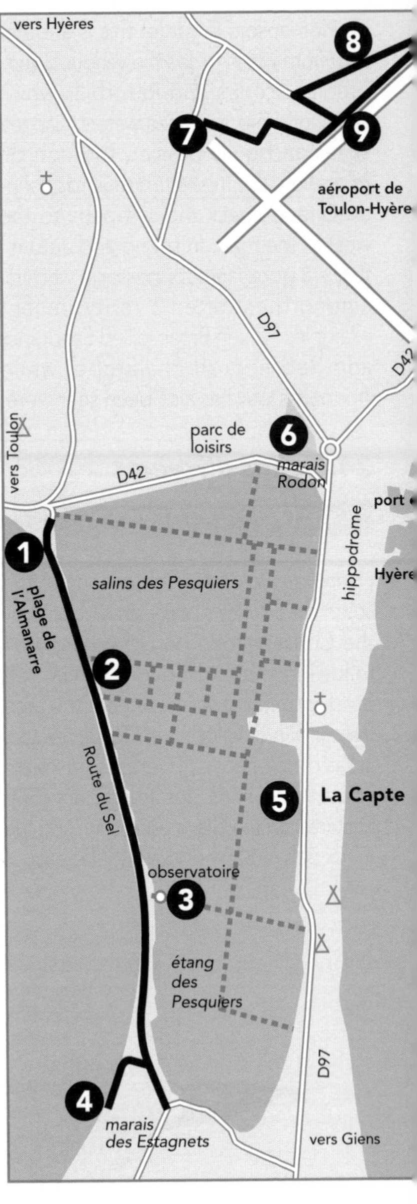

■ Calendar

Spring: Ruff, Wood, Common and Marsh Sandpipers, Redshank, Spotted Redshank, Whiskered, Black and White-winged Black Terns.

Summer: Avocet, Black-winged Stilt, Little and Common Terns.

Autumn: Turnstone, Knot, Temminck's Stint, Red-necked Phalarope; also many Greater Flamingos.

Winter: various waders such as Ringed, Kentish and Grey Plovers, Dunlin, Little

Stint, Curlew; and also divers, Cattle Egret (roost), Greater Flamingo, Shelduck and other duck (especially Red-breasted Merganser).

25. Vinon-sur-Verdon aerodrome

VAR (83) *IGN 68*

The major interest of the site, an aerodrome to the north-east of Aix-en-Provence where the Rivers Durance and Verdon join, comes from its steppe-like vegetation that attracts some rare and declining breeding species. Little Bustard, Stone Curlew, Woodlark, Skylark, Crested Lark and a few Short-toed Larks can all be found here. It is also the site of one of France's last remaining populations of Calandra Lark, with five or six pairs of this seriously threatened species still hanging on. Black Kites nest in the riverside trees not far away, and Montagu's Harrier, Quail, Tawny Pipit, Fan-tailed and Melodious Warblers and Corn Bunting can all be found in the area. On migration regular species include Honey Buzzard, Short-toed Eagle, Marsh, Montagu's and Hen Harriers, Red-footed Falcon (annual in spring), Golden Plover and Whimbrel. In winter there are flocks of finches and buntings which attract the attention of both Peregrine and Merlin. Vinon-sur-Verdon is 6 km east of exit 17 on the A51 north-east from Aix. From here cross the River Verdon on the D4 towards Manosque. The aerodrome is sign-posted less than a kilometre after leaving the village.

26. Étangs de Villepey

VAR (83) *IGN 68*

The coastal lagoons of the Étangs de Villepey lie just to the south of Fréjus, on the right bank of the River Argens just before it reaches the sea and form part of a wider alluvial floodplain. Habitats include riverside woodland, dunes, reedbeds, sansouires and sea-lavender meadows, and so a wide variety of birds can be seen here at different times of year. Breeding species associated with the damper areas include Little Bittern, Bee-eater and Kingfisher, while the riverside woodland has the usual passerines. Greater Flamingos, and a good range of wildfowl, can be seen throughout the year, and at migration times waders, Black, Whiskered, Common and Little Terns are attracted to the lagoons and their surrounds. From Fréjus take the N98 south towards Villepey and St.-Aygulf, the road crossing the River Argens and then

FAN-TAILED WARBLER

RED-LEGGED PARTRIDGE

passing close to the end of the first of the lagoons, visible from the road. At the edge of Villepey turn right and follow the D7 towards Roquebrune-sur-Argens. Near the bus-stop at 'Le Pas des Vaches', there is an information board. A track to the right runs through a pine wood and marshy area with a walkway to a hide overlooking the marsh. Depending on water levels, it is also possible to walk further around the site.

27. Îles d' Hyères

VAR (83) *IGN 68*

Lying offshore from the Giens peninsula (see site 24 above) are a series of islands – Porquerolles, Port-Cros and Lavant – running roughly east-west parallel to the coast. These are the Îles d'Hyères, strategically situated for watching migrant passerines. The second half of April is the peak period, with good numbers of species such as Pied and Spotted Flycatchers, Redstart, Willow and Bonelli's Warblers, Woodchat Shrike, Wheatear and Whinchat passing through, as well as Bee-eater, Turtle Dove and Subalpine and Spectacled Warblers. A few pairs of Peregrines breed on the islands and it is also worth looking for Eleanora's Falcon which is a regular passage migrant here in late summer and early autumn. Yelkouan and Cory's Shearwaters breed, and can be seen offshore or gathering on the sea towards evening. Scops Owls can be heard at night; it is a common nesting bird on the islands and over-winters on the Île de Port-Cros. This is protected as a national park and is the easiest of access, with ferries from Hyères-Plage throughout the year. Maps are available on the island, which can be explored along various way-marked footpaths. Sites to be visited on Port-Cros include the dam, the manor house, La Vigie, any of the higher ridges and the beach at La Palud. On the Île de Porquerolles, Plaine de la Courtade, the high ground and cliffs on the south coast, the woods, the lagoon and the Conservatoire's orchards are all worth investigation. Note that access to forested areas may be restricted at times when there is a high fire risk.

28. *Massif des Maures*

VAR (83) *IGN 68*

The Massif des Maures is a huge and rugged area north-east of Hyères as far as Fréjus, and contains a variety of habitats: dry heath and grassland, conifer and deciduous forests, temporary and permanent water courses, rocky outcrops, etc. Of particular interest is the northern central area close to the valley of the River Argens at Le Cannet-des-Maures. From the A57/A8 intersection here take the D558 south-east towards Garde-Freinet. After 5 km the road crosses the River Aille at La Basse Verrerie. About 700 metres beyond here take a forest track south-east which leads to the Lac des Escarcets, about 1½ km further on, to the left of the track. The lake's breeding species include Little Bittern, Kingfisher and Roller. Check the more open habitats such as heathland with scattered trees and extensively grazed areas for species such as Southern Grey and Red-backed Shrikes, Tawny Pipit and Ortolan Bunting. At dusk listen in such places for Nightjar. The valley of St.-Daumas, in which the lake is situated, is a good place for finding many of the typical warblers and other birds of the Mediterranean. To the north, the woodland of the valleys of the River Aille towards Vidauban, and the River Argens on eastwards to Roquebrune-sur-Argens provide breeding sites for Night Heron, Lesser Spotted Woodpecker, Bee-eater and Red-rumped Swallow. This area is best visited in spring and early summer when the majority of migrants have arrived.

29. *Dentelles de Montmirail*

VAUCLUSE (84) *IGN 59/60*

The Dentelles de Montmirail is a typical Provençal range of hills, lying about 20 km east of Orange. It is bounded on the north and west by the Ouvèze valley, to the east by the lower ground around Malaucène, and drops down sharply into the plains south of Beaumes-de-Venise. Its 'lace-like' wooded slopes give the Dentelles their name. The garrigue/maquis on the southern slopes provides habitat for several of the Mediterranean warblers while the cliffs are home to an interesting range of species in both summer and winter.

ACCESS

Three suggested points of access are given below. In addition to the surfaced roads there are forestry tracks, although these are best explored on foot. From Carpentras to the south take the D7 to Aubignan and then the D90 via Beaumes-de-Venise towards Lafare. After 2½ km take the small tarmac road to the left (often in a bad state of repair), which, after crossing the Salette, climbs up towards the Grand-Montmirail cliffs (1). From the car park, explore the surrounding area on foot. Birds to be seen include Hoopoe, Scops Owl, Subalpine and Orphean Warblers (all four from April to August), with Sardinian and Dartford Warblers, Blue Rock Thrush and Southern Grey Shrike present throughout the year. The resident Eagle Owls are most easily heard when calling from December to March. The Egyptian Vulture occurs from mid-March to August, and both Alpine Swift and Crag Martin breed here. In winter Wallcreepers occur, birds moving out of their alpine breeding haunts to the east. Another good area is a little further north, near Gigondas. From here take the minor road through the hamlet of Florets to the pass at the Col du Cayron (2); park here and explore on foot, with good views over the central Dentelles. A forest road skirts the cliffs to the west; a second, to the east, leads to Lafare and the D90 north to Suzette. The woodland holds Nuthatch throughout the year, and Ravens are also resident, breeding on the cliffs. Bonelli's Warblers can be heard singing in the summer (April to July). There is a good chance of seeing a Short-toed Eagle soaring overhead, again in the summer, while both Wallcreeper and Alpine Accentor occur in winter. The third area worth checking is Mont St.-Amand (3). From Suzette take the minor road west to Château-Neuf-Redortier, but note that the road is narrow and it is not always easy to park. Continue a little past a farm before leaving the car, then continue on foot

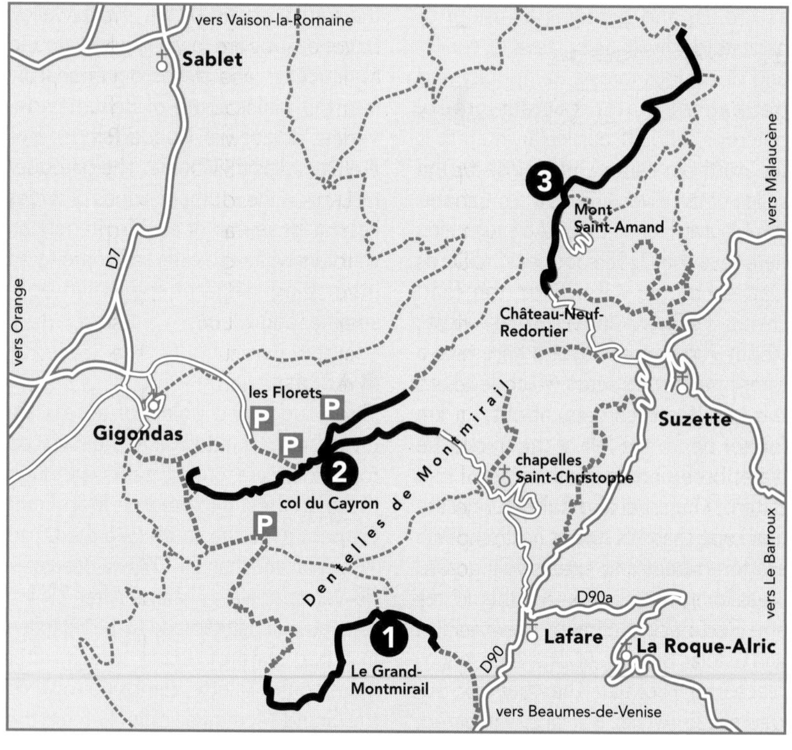

to get to the northern slope of the Crête de St.-Amand. There are way-marked trails that enable you to make a circuit round the hills or to access the summit. In the breeding season look for Woodlark, Tree and Tawny Pipits, Bonelli's Warbler and Firecrest. In winter, both Snow Finch (irregular) and Alpine Accentor occur here.

Calendar

Spring and summer: Egyptian Vulture, Short-toed Eagle, Alpine Swift, Hoopoe, Bee-eater, Scops and Eagle Owls, Nightjar, Tawny and Tree Pipits, Crag Martin, Blue Rock Thrush, Subalpine, Dartford, Sardinian, Orphean and Bonelli's Warblers, Southern Grey Shrike, Raven. *Winter*: Kestrel, Eagle Owl, Alpine Accentor, Sardinian and Dartford Warblers, Wallcreeper, Snow Finch, Raven.

30. Petit Luberon

Vaucluse (84) IGN 60/67

The Montagne de Luberon is a typical expanse of Mediterranean hill habitat, 40 km east of Avignon, and much of it can only be explored on foot. The D973 runs along the southern side, east from Cavaillon, and from the village of Mérindol (see also site 20 above), 16 km south-east of here, a minor road runs north up to the Font-de-l'Orme arboretum, where there is a car park. From here the GR6 long-distance footpath crosses all of the principal habitats of the Petit Luberon. The best time to visit is in the spring and early summer, from late March to late June, when birds to be seen here include Bonelli's Eagle (nowadays a rare breeding bird in France with fewer than 30 pairs remaining), Egyptian Vulture, Short-toed Eagle, Red-legged Partridge, Nightjar, Alpine Swift, Tawny Pipit, Black-eared Wheatear, Orphean, Dartford and Sardinian Warblers, Ortolan Bunting and Raven. The Gorge du Régalon just to the west is also worth a visit.

31. Gorges de la Nesque / Sault

Vaucluse (84) IGN 60

These spectacular gorges lie on the Sault plateau, east of Carpentras and with the high ground of Mont Ventoux to the north. From Carpentras the D942 runs east to Villes-sur-Auzon, and then winds its way through the gorges eventually to reach Monieux and then Sault. The rocky cliffs are home to Golden Eagle, Egyptian Vulture, Peregrine, Alpine Swift, Alpine Accentor and Raven, depending on the season. Beyond the gorges themselves, in the agricultural areas between Sault and Monieux it is possible to find Stone Curlew, Little Owl, Wryneck, Red-backed and Woodchat Shrikes, with the chance of Little Bustard. At Monieux, a small lake at the entrance to Nesque gorges is one of the highest sites in France to have breeding Little Bittern and Great Reed Warbler. Look out also for Rock Sparrow, particularly in the area near Aurel, to the north of Sault.

SITES

1 *La Dombes*

2 *Ceyzériat*

3 *Défilé de l'Écluse*

4 *Marais de Cormaranche-en-Bugey*

5 *Marais de l'Étournel*

6 *Val de Saône flood meadows*

7 *Col de l'Escrinet*

8 *Vogüé*

9 *Massif du Tanargue*

10 *Plateau de Jastre*

11 *Forêt de Saou*

12 *Rémuzat*

13 *Chamrousse*

14 *Barrage de Saint-Égrève*

15 *Défilé de la Malsanne*

16 *Étang de Haute-Jarrie*

17 *Charmant Som*

18 *Écopôle du Forez*

19 *Monts du Forez*

20 *Étangs du Forez*

21 *Gorges of the upper Loire valley*

22 *Le Pilat*

23 *Roanne*

24 *Miribel-Jonage and Le Grand Large at Lyons*

25 *Landes de Montagny*

26 *Forêt de Bellevaux*

27 *Golfe de Coudrée on Lac Léman*

28 *Alpage de Doran/Sallanches*

29 *Le Hucel*

Rhône-Alpes

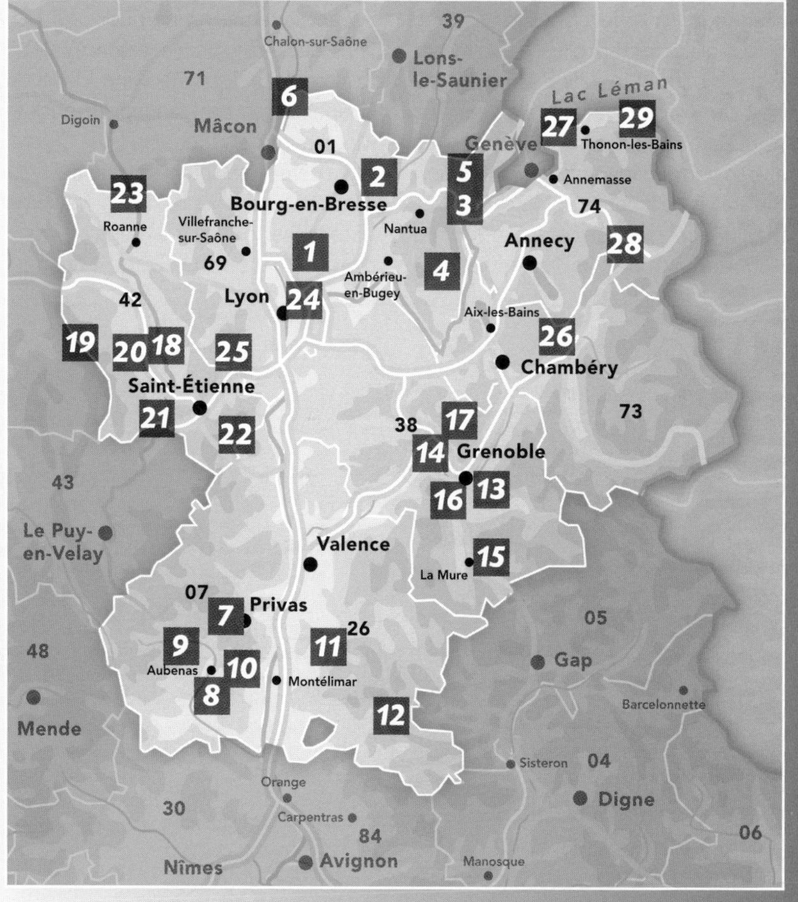

39
Chalon-sur-Saône
Lons-le-Saunier
71
Lac Léman
6
27
29
Thonon-les-Bains
Digoin
Mâcon
01
Genève
2
5
Annemasse
23
74
Bourg-en-Bresse
3
Roanne
Villefranche-sur-Saône
Nantua
Annecy
28
69
1
4
Ambérieu-en-Bugey
42
Lyon
24
Aix-les-Bains
19
20
18
25
26
Chambéry
Saint-Étienne
21
22
38
17
73
14
Grenoble
43
16
13
Le Puy-en-Velay
Valence
15
La Mure
07
Privas
7
05
9
11
26
48
Aubenas
10
Gap
Montélimar
8
Barcelonnette
12
Mende
Sisteron
04
Orange
Digne
30
Carpentras
84
06
Nîmes
Avignon
Manosque

1. La Dombes

AIN (01) *IGN 44*

La Dombes is the name given to the extensive plateau (about 100,000 hectares in all) between Lyon and Bourg-en-Bresse to the north-east, and on which there are about 1,000 lakes. The whole area has been completely modified by man, and changes according to the season (many of the lakes are emptied annually, usually in October and November) and over the years, as the empty lakes are cultivated, generally at one- to three-year intervals. These activities lead to a continuous change in water levels, which is often favourable to migrant birds. It also means that it is difficult to define which are the best areas for birds at any one time. The whole area is quite heavily shot over, and so from a birdwatching point of view the area is best between March and late May for waders and ducks and in July and August for waders, crakes and herons.

ACCESS

Villars-les-Dombes is a good starting point, on the N83 about halfway between Lyon and Bourg-en-Bresse. There is a Parc des Oiseaux just to the south of the town, and from the car park the Étang Turlet (1) can be viewed easily. No shooting is allowed here, and it is therefore a refuge for flocks of duck in winter, roosting gulls and Greylag Geese. The Parc holds many captive birds, but there are also about 20 pairs of wild White Storks breeding. From here take the D904 east towards Versailleux, and then the small dead-end road to the right to Bochères (2); look here for Squacco Heron, diving duck or marsh terns, depending on the season. Continue to Versailleux (3), where the Étang du Chapelier can be scanned for duck in winter and a few breeding Little Bittern. From here head south-west on the D2D as far as Birieux via the D2D. The large lakes to the north of the village are worth checking, then the Grand Étang de

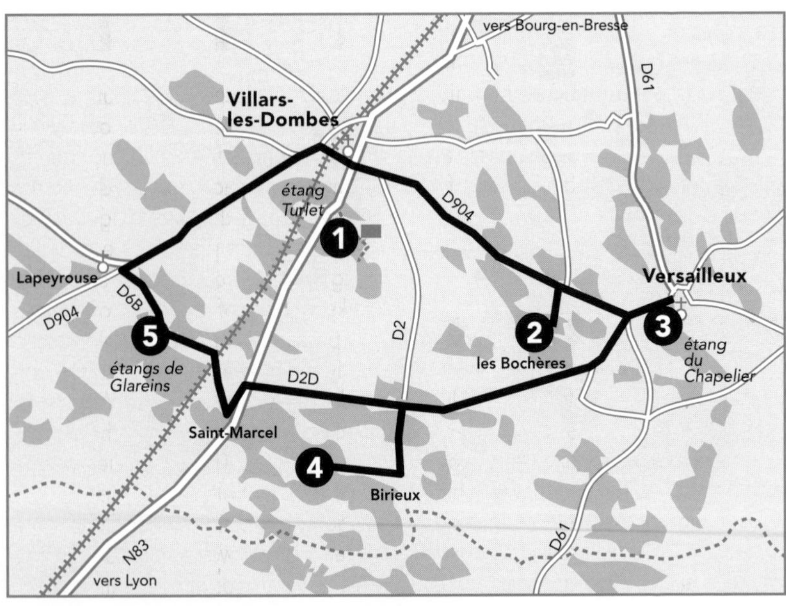

Birieux (4) can be seen from the road that runs west towards St.-Marcel. Species here include Purple Heron, Little Bittern, large flocks of duck and geese in winter, Whiskered Tern (with Black on passage), Reed and Great Reed Warblers and Penduline Tit. To the west of the N83, the Étangs de Glareins (5) can be seen from the D6B just to the south-east of Lapeyrouse; Great White Egret (winter visitor, but has bred), crakes, Short-toed Eagle, gulls and terns are often present here. One can complete this circuit to Villars via the D904. The whole area is criss-crossed by minor roads, and many of the lakes can be seen from the roadside. Remember that all the lakes are private property and that you should not venture off the road to view them.

CALENDAR

Spring and summer: Black-necked Grebe, Purple and Night Herons, White Stork, Whiskered Tern and Red-crested Pochard. *At times of migration*: various duck, waders, gulls and terns of all species, even coastal species at times of high winds. During April and May, Temminck's Stint, Marsh Sandpiper and White-winged Black Tern sometimes occur. In February and March there are large flocks of diving duck with a few Ferruginous Duck.

2. *Ceyzériat*

AIN (01) *IGN 44*

Situated in the first foothills of the Jura some 8 km to the east of Bourg-en-Bresse, the Roches de Cuiron (also known as Conches) is a good site for watching autumn migration, from September to November. Several thousand birds of prey pass each year and passerines are

CITRIL FINCH

often seen under excellent conditions. Twenty different species of raptor have been seen at Conches, and around mid-October Wallcreeper and Citril Finch are often observed. From Bourg-en-Bresse take the D979 east as far as Ceyzériat, then turn left on the D52 and immediately right along the 'Route des Crêts' for 2½ km. Then turn right to park 250 metres farther on, at the foot of the radio masts, above the rock-climbing site. Scan along the ridge and over the plain below for migrants on the move.

3. *Défilé de l'Écluse*

AIN (01) *IGN 44*

Strategically placed to the south-west of Lac Léman and Geneva, the gorge of the Défilé de l'Écluse forms a splendid funnel for migrants heading south during the autumn along the Jura ridges. Over 20,000 birds of prey pass each year, along with hundreds of Black and White Storks and tens of thousands of pigeons and passerines. Spotted Eagle is seen nearly every year in late autumn, and Golden Eagle occurs regularly. Wallcreeper often occurs on the walls of the old fort here in winter. The gorge lies on the D984 east of Bellegarde. Just east of Longeray the main road runs through a tunnel, and the lower fort can be scanned from here. In Longeray itself a minor road ('Route du Fort') runs to the north and leads to a spot from which you then have to walk to the upper fort. This provides an excellent vista of the gorge and any migrants moving past. A minor road on the south side of the Rhône provides another viewpoint; to reach this cross the river on the N206, continue eastwards and just before the bridge under the railway take the tarmac track to the right. Park after 300 metres.

4. Marais de Cormaranche-en-Bugey

AIN (01) *IGN 44*

This small marshy area lies to the south-west of the previous site, and is a quiet area in the limestone hills of the southern Jura. The marsh is next to a water-meadow, and is bordered with rushes and a small reedbed, although there is little standing water. It offers a refuge to some relatively rare species such as Great Grey Shrike, Marsh Warbler and a few pairs of Reed Warblers. The nearby beech and spruce wood has Black Woodpecker, Crossbill and Hazel Grouse. Peregrine, Raven and Nutcracker also occur in the area. From Bellegarde take the A40 west to exit 8, then head south on the D12 and then D8 to reach the village of Hauteville-Lompnes. From here follow signs for the 'Plan d'eau des Lésines'. There is a car park near the marsh, with information boards showing access along a way-marked trail. Spring is the best time for birds, and also the local flora.

CORNCRAKE

5. Marais de l'Étournel

AIN (01) *IGN 44*

This flood marsh lies in the valley of the River Rhône downstream of Geneva and just upstream of the Défilé de l'Écluse (see site 3 above). Here the Rhône, almost everywhere very much controlled, runs through one of its last wild areas before arriving in the Camargue right down by the Mediterranean. There is a wide range of habitats here, constantly changing, with the varying water levels (linked to activities at the Barrage de Génissiat downstream) often exposing sand or mudflats favourable for waders and gulls. The marsh itself provides habitat for various wetland passerines, a small population of Goosanders and many migrants, the latter including Goldeneye, crakes, Common Tern, Bluethroat and Penduline Tit. From Bellegarde, drive north-east to cross the Rhône on the N206 (Pont Carnot), and then take the first minor road left, to the north-east, to follow the left bank of the river. The marsh can be viewed from the roadside.

6. Val de Saône flood meadows

AIN (01) *IGN 43/44*

North of Mâcon, the River Saône regularly breaks its banks in winter and spring, the waters spreading out over the flood-meadows to the east. The area thus becomes of great value to wintering species and particularly to migrants heading north. Greylag Goose, Bewick's Swan, Merlin, Peregrine and Crane all occur. Once the fields have dried out they still provide valuable breeding habitat for birds such as Corncrake, Curlew, Lapwing, Black-tailed Godwit and Corn Bunting, particularly in evidence between May and July. The best area of meadows lie between Pont-de-Vaux (about 15 km north of Mâcon) and La Truchère. From Pont-de-Vaux take the D933 northwards and view the fields from any of the small roads westwards from Arbigny and Sermoyer or from the road to La Truchère to the north.

7. Col de l'Escrinet

ARDÈCHE (07) *IGN 52/59*

This pass, south of Privas and to the north of Aubenas, is situated at the limits of several different regions: the Cévennes to the south, the Boutières and high plateau of the Ardèche to the west, and the basalt plateau of Coiron to the east. The pass, at 787 metres, is much lower than other ridges in the immediate vicinity that rise to over 1,000 metres. The area's topography has made it an excellent place for watching spring migration; more than 160 species have been seen migrating north, with up to 10,000 birds of prey and hundreds of thousands of passerines each year. Buzzard, Stock Dove and Woodpigeon, Skylarks, thrushes and Starling are on the move from as early as February. During the first half of March it is the turn of Cormorant, White Stork, Black and Red Kites, Crane, White Wagtail and the largest numbers of Chaffinches. From mid-March and in April the next wave includes Black Stork, Osprey, Marsh Harrier, hirundines and a wide range of finches. In late April come Montagu's Harrier, Turtle Dove, Swift and Golden Oriole, with, finally, May being the best month for Honey Buzzard and Bee-eater. The col lies on the main N304 between Privas to the north (11 km) and Aubenas to the south (20 km), and a bus route runs along this road between the two towns, coming from Valence. The best place for watching is on the small mound overlooking the minor road which runs south onto the Coiron plateau. As a rule, the majority of passerines are observed in the early morning while raptors and other soaring species can be seen at almost any hour. A word of warning: there is a problem with illegal shooting in this area, particularly in February and March.

8. Vogüé

ARDÈCHE (07) *IGN 59*

The Ardèche valley, between Aubenas and Vogüé to the south-east, contains a wide variety of natural habitats – a river with numerous tributaries and nearby ponds plus some extensive and varied riverside woodland. There are also rocks suitable for cliff-dwelling species. This has led to the presence of a wide variety of bird species, even better because of the area's geographical position close to the Col de l'Escrinet migration route.

Particularly during the spring many migrants stop by the River Ardèche before continuing on their way north. Happily, a large part of the area has received protected status since 1994.

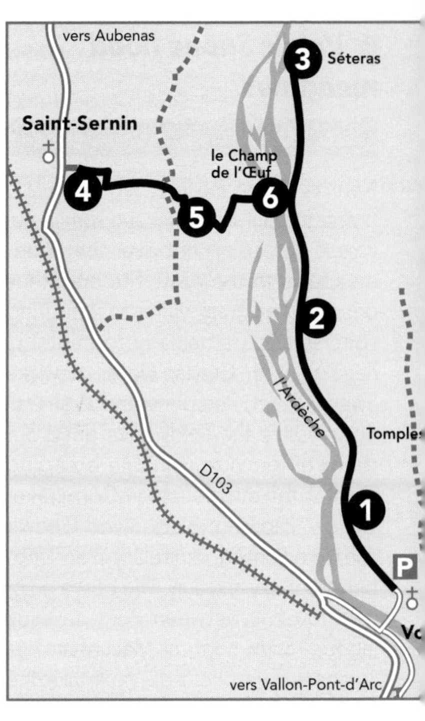

■ ACCESS

Vogüé is about 10 km south-east of Aubenas, and one possible route starts from here, affording good views over the Ardèche valley and its surrounding hillsides and is recommended for seeing birds of prey. In the village, park in the cemetery car park (follow signs to the château). From here walk north along a cul-de-sac which runs alongside the River Ardèche, to the north of the village. Under the cliff at Tomples (1), near the APPB sign, look for Crag Martin and Blue Rock Thrush in the breeding season, and for Wallcreeper in the winter. Keep checking the banks of the river; you should hear, even if you do not see, a Cetti's Warbler. Equally elusive are the beavers, although evidence of their presence is provided by their lodges close to the banks. Farther on (2) you get a good view over the Ardèche; this is a good spot to wait to see birds flying along the river – Cormorant, herons and birds of prey, for instance. A Hobby can sometimes be seen hunting overhead and on passage an Osprey may stop to fish. Continue as far as Séteras (3) where there is access to the riverside woodland, a good area for warblers, tits and other passerines, and a little further you come back to the river; look out for Dipper and Grey Wagtail anywhere here. Return to Vogüé by the same route. A second possibility starts from the village of St.-Sernin, 3 km to the north of Vogüé along the D103. This walk is better for passerines, going east though an area of crops and rough ground to the river and back again. Park near the church. Opposite the cemetery (4), the flat agricultural area is good for finches and buntings in the winter. There are fewer birds to be seen here in summer but is still worth a look; Fan-tailed Warbler has bred here in recent years, and there are usually Tree Sparrows to be seen. Near the Champ de l'Oeuf (5), look out for Kingfisher and Dipper along the River Auzon. The riverside woodland holds Lesser Spotted Woodpecker and, in summer, Spotted Flycatcher. During spring migration Penduline Tit and Wood Warbler often occur here. Once at the River Ardèche (6), check the gravel islands, a breeding site for Little Ringed Plover. Large numbers of hirundines may be seen along the river on migration, both in spring and autumn.

CALENDAR

All year: Grey Heron, Common Sandpiper, Kingfisher, Lesser Spotted Woodpecker, Crag Martin (irregular in winter), Dipper, Blue Rock Thrush, Cetti's Warbler, Raven.
Spring: on migration, Purple Heron, Black Stork, Shoveler, Marsh Harrier, Osprey, Green Sandpiper (and other waders in small numbers), Sand Martin, Blue-headed Wagtail, Penduline Tit.
Summer: Little Egret, Black Kite, Hobby, Little Ringed Plover, Alpine Swift, Bee-eater, Nightingale, Fan-tailed Warbler, Spotted Flycatcher, Golden Oriole.
Autumn: Tree Pipit, Pied Flycatcher and most of the migrants seen in spring.
Winter: Cormorant, Water Pipit, Goldcrest, Wallcreeper, Siskin, Rock and Reed Buntings.

9. Massif du Tanargue

ARDÈCHE (07) *IGN 59*

This range of hills lies 20 km due west of Aubenas, and in the breeding season holds a rich variety of birds. Montagu's Harrier, Short-toed Eagle and numerous passerines including Woodlark and Yellowhammer can be found on the grasslands and heaths. The more rocky areas, particularly along the southern slopes, provide breeding sites for Rock Thrush, while the forests have a good range of the species typical of the mountain woodlands of southern France such as Black Woodpecker, Common Treecreeper, Bullfinch and Crossbill. From Aubenas, take the N102 westwards as far as Lalevade-d'Ardèche, and then turn left on the D19 through Jaujac as far as the Col de la Croix de Bauzon. Park at the ski station and then follow the way-marked trails which lead south up onto the Tanargue plateau. A more detailed map (e.g. IGN 0838O and 0838E, 1:25,000) is useful here. One can also continue west on the D19 for another 3 km, then turn left on the D24 in the direction of Valgorge, in order to approach the hills from their southern side. Park at the Col de Meyrand pass and follow the way-marked trails onto the plateau.

10. Plateau de Jastre

ARDÈCHE (07) *IGN 59*

The Plateau de Jastre, a few kilometres east of Aubenas, on the east side of the River Ardèche, is a vast area of open and semi-open habitats, typical of the Mediterranean. Grassland with scattered clumps of broom alternates with garrigue and box trees, with some old almond orchards adding even more variety. This mixture is ideal for a whole series of species which are under threat and declining in much of Europe these days – Nightjar, Woodlark, Tawny Pipit, Dartford Warbler, Ortolan Bunting, and both Woodchat and Southern Grey Shrikes, the latter here at the northern edge of its range. The cliffs around the western edge of the plateau have Eagle Owl, Crag Martin, Blue Rock Thrush and Raven. Like site 8 above, this area is also close to the Col de l'Escrinet (site 7) spring migration route, and shares in the passage of many migrants each year, including many birds of prey. From Aubenas, take the N102 south-east towards Lavilledieu or alternatively the D259 via St.-Privat towards Lussas. The plateau lies north of the former road and south of the latter, and can be approached from both along minor roads and tracks. From the Lavilledieu industrial estate a road leads north towards the sports ground. Once there continue for 100 metres, turn left and park on a flat area some 500 metres farther on. A track from here goes uphill to the highest point, an ideal spot from which to watch spring migrants on the move. There are other tracks though the surrounding area to make a circuit of the various habitats.

11. Forêt de Saou

DRÔME (26) *IGN 52/59*

The Forêt de Saou lies 50 km south-east of Valence and 40 north-east of Montélimar. It is a densely-wooded mountain area, to the south of the valley of the River Drôme, surrounded by high cliffs. The range of altitude (between 400 and 600 metres), and the effect of the different orientations, has led to a great variety of vegetation types, and its oak, beech and spruce woodland is among the finest in the area. The extensive cliffs (a total length of 25 km) are much used by rock-dwelling birds.

ACCESS

From Valence, take the D111 south-east to Crest, then the D104 east to Aouste, and turn south on the D70 over the Pas de Lauzens. From Montélimar, take the D6 north-east to Puy-St.-Martin, then the D136 via Saou to enter the forest via the Défilé du Pertuis. The eastern part of the forest can be approached via Les Trois-Becs, on the D156 between Saillans (east of Crest on the D93) and Bourdeaux to the south, this route passing over the Col de la Chaudière. Two circuits are suggested here (IGN 3138OT, 1:25,000 covers this area). For the first, less strenuous one, take the D538 south-east from Saou and turn left to the farm at Lestang, and park nearby. A track north towards Le

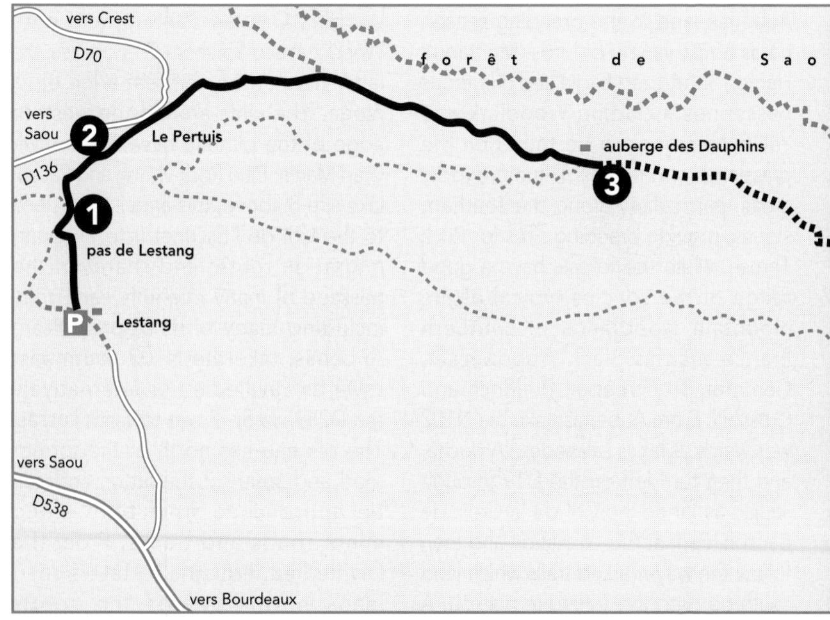

Pertuis crosses the Pas de Lestang (1) before dropping down to the River Vèbre (2). In the area around the pass look out for such Mediterranean passerines as Tawny Pipit and Subalpine Warbler. Raven and Crag Martin also occur here and you have a good chance of seeing Short-toed Eagle in the summer. Eagle Owls breed not far away, and can be heard calling at twilight, from late winter onwards. By the Vèbre, look for Kingfisher and Dipper. Black Woodpecker can be found in the forest and Golden Eagle and Peregrine often fly over. The path continues to Auberge des Dauphins (3), from where you can either return the same way, or continue on to the Refuge des Girards (4) – this should take another 2½ hours. The other route starts from the Col de la Chaudière, where there is a car park. It takes about 30 minutes to get to Les Trois-Becs (5) via the Pas de Siara. Honey

EAGLE OWL

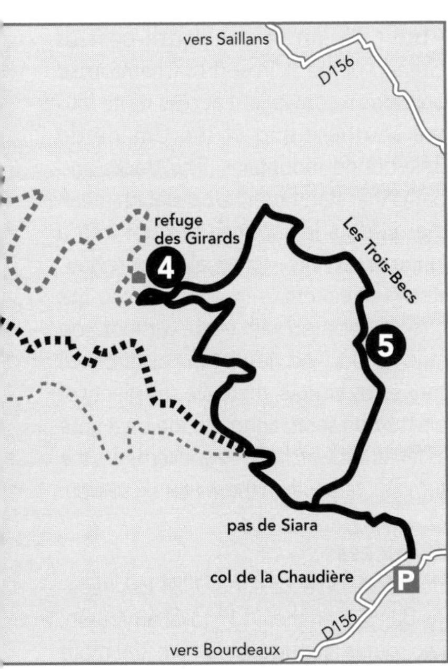

Buzzard and Goshawk can be seen over the woodland in spring and the edge of the forest is a good area to look for Ring Ouzel, Citril Finch and Willow Tit. Tengmalm's Owl can be heard calling in spring, but seeing them is a different matter. The circuit continues on up to the Refuge des Girards (4), about an hour's walk. Anywhere along the route, especially over the higher ground, Alpine Chough and Alpine Swift can be seen in flight, while Alpine Accentor, Wallcreeper and Water Pipit occur on the rocky areas and cliffs. One can make a circular route from the refuge to return to the Col de la Chaudière via the Pas de Siara. In general there is open access to the area, but cars are not allowed on the forest roads.

Calendar

Spring and summer: Golden Eagle, Short-toed Eagle, Peregrine, Eagle and Tengmalm's Owls, Tawny Pipit, Alpine Accentor, Subalpine Warbler, Alpine Chough.

12. Rémuzat

Drôme (26) *IGN 60*

Rémuzat is a village in the Eygues (or Aygues) gorges, about 26 km east of

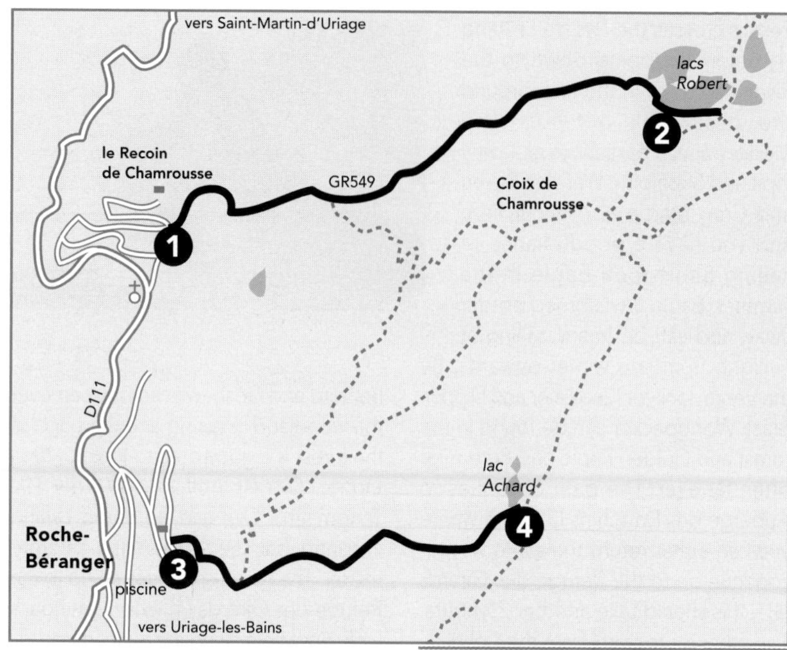

Nyons, in the Baronnies area of the south-east of the Rhône-Alpes region. Griffon Vultures were reintroduced here during the 1990s and have increased steadily ever since. There is a visitor centre – Maison des Vautours – in the village which has nformation about the birds of the area. There are two main observation points, either from the roadside in Rémuzat where it is possible to see the cliffs and birds in flight or alternatively from the St.-Laurent plateau, which is reached, to the west, via the village of St.-May and the Abbaye de Bodon. Other species to be seen on the plateau include Short-toed Eagle, Raven, Red-backed Shrike, Wheatear, Dartford and Subalpine Warblers and Whitethroat among others. With the build up of Griffon Vulture numbers a few Egyptian Vultures have arrived as a breeding bird in the area, and Black Vultures are also seen from time to time.

13. Chamrousse

Isère (38) *IGN 54*

About 15 km to the south-east of Grenoble, the ski resort of Chamrousse provides a convenient access route into the southern end of the Chaine de Belledonne mountains. The tracks and paths that start from the ski station mean that visitors in summer can get into a range of habitats – forest, alpine meadow, scree, lakes, etc. – in order to see the birds associated with each, without too much effort. And despite the disturbance caused by visitors, there are still plenty of birds to be seen, although the best time as far as birdwatchers are concerned is the summer, rather than the winter ski season.

Access

From Grenoble, take the D524 to Uriage-les-Bains, then the D111 to Chamrousse. Two routes are suggested here (the more detailed map IGN 3335OT, 1:25,000 is recommended), both leading to high mountain lakes. Starting from Recoin de Chamrousse (1), take the GR549 long-distance footpath to the Lacs Robert (2). Along the way look out for Golden Eagle, Ptarmigan, Black Woodpecker, Water Pipit, Rock Thrush and Alpine Accentor. Other paths lead to the Croix de Chamrousse, just to the south, an area where Snow Finches have been seen and may well breed. A second access route starts from Roche-Béranger (3), a short way to the south. From here take the track to Lac Achard (4). The areas along the edges of the forest and the alpine meadows are worth concentrating on for species such as Crested and Coal Tits, Nutcracker, Citril Finch and Crossbill.

CALENDAR

Summer: Golden Eagle, Ptarmigan, Black Woodpecker, Water Pipit, Rock Thrush, Wheatear, Crested Tit, Nutcracker, Crossbill, Citril Finch.

14. Barrage de St.-Égrève

ISÈRE (38) IGN 51

This dam on the River Isère, just below its confluence with the River Drac on the north-western outskirts of Grenoble can be accessed from either Noyarey or St.-Égrève, close to exit 14 on the A48. A cycle track runs along both sides of the reservoir, providing easy access and viewing opportunities. As there are no mudflats or reedbeds and, moreover, it suffers from disturbance from water sports, few species actually breed here. But it is always worth a look in winter, especially during and after spells of hard weather. Being close to Grenoble it can be easily visited. Species seen to date include Great Crested, Little and Black-necked Grebes, Cormorant, Grey Heron, Little Egret, Greylag Goose, Shelduck, Gadwall, Teal, Garganey, Pochard, Scaup, Tufted Duck, Velvet Scoter, Avocet, Yellow-legged, Herring and Lesser Black-backed Gulls.

15. Défilé de la Malsanne

ISÈRE (38) IGN 54

This area has some impressive cliffs about 40 km south-east of Grenoble. Birds using the rock faces as breeding sites include Kestrel, Crag Martin, Red-billed Chough and Raven. They are also worth checking in winter for Alpine Chough and Wallcreeper. The rocky south-facing slopes are favoured hunting grounds for Short-toed Eagles, present in the area from April to August. Look for Rock Buntings in the same habitat, while the river in the valley has both Dipper and Grey Wagtail. From Grenoble take the N85 south as far as La Mure, then turn east on the D526 through Valbonnais, as far as Entraigues. There is an information centre here, the Maison du Parc National des Écrins, with exhibitions, maps and leaflets available. From here the D526 continues north along the valley of the Malsanne as far as Le Bourg-d'Oisans. The easiest thing is just to stop at various spots along the road and scan both the rock faces and look down into the river valley.

16. Étang de Haute-Jarrie

ISÈRE (38) IGN 52/54

This small réserve naturelle (7 hectares) lies on a plateau overlooking the southern

BLACK GROUSE

outskirts of Grenoble, between the villages of Champagnier and Jarrie parish. A minor road runs along its southern edge, and it is easily reached at any season. Despite its small size, it is important both as a breeding site and as a migratory stop-over, particularly for aquatic species. There is a hide on the southern side of the lake, overlooking some reedbeds as well as open water. The whole reserve is of interest, including the meadows on the western side which flood when the water level is particularly high. At such times waders can be quite common, with Snipe, Ruff and the various *Tringa* species regularly being seen. In fact the site is of interest at any time of the year – in autumn for migrants, in winter for duck and buntings, although perhaps the best time is in the spring when any of the migrant species that pass through the area can be encountered. Little Bittern, Garganey, Water Rail and both Reed and Great Reed Warblers have all bred at the reserve, while Purple Heron and Marsh Harrier are regular spring migrants. Hoopoe and Wryneck also pass through here. During migration periods, check the ploughed fields and meadows to the north and south of the lake for migrants such as pipits (five species have been recorded), wagtails, chats, Ortolan and Cirl Buntings, Yellowhammer and even Red-footed Falcon.

17. Charmant Som

ISÈRE (38) *IGN 53*

This is a high point in the Massif de la Chartreuse just north of Grenoble, and easily accessible by car. The area is of interest throughout the year – Golden Eagle, Peregrine, Kestrel, Black Grouse, Tengmalm's Owl, Black Woodpecker, Tree Pipit, Alpine Accentor, Ring Ouzel, Wallcreeper, Citril Finch and Hazel Grouse can all be seen depending on the season. From Grenoble take the D512 north to the Col de Porte pass, and turn left along the D57D through the forest eventually to reach a car park. From here there is a path to the left that passes through a variety of habitats – spruce forest, dry alpine meadows, scree – and can be used to access the summit. By taking this and other walks in the area you should be able to locate some of the species mentioned above. The only inconvenience is the large number of walkers in the area on fine weekends.

18. Écopôle du Forez

LOIRE (42) *IGN 43/50*

The Écopôle du Forez visitor centre is a showcase for the wildlife of the Forez plain (see site 20 below for details of the area) and for the efforts made to re-establish wetland wildlife in the area. It should be the first port of call for anyone visiting this little-known part of the Loire valley, between St.-Étienne and Roanne.

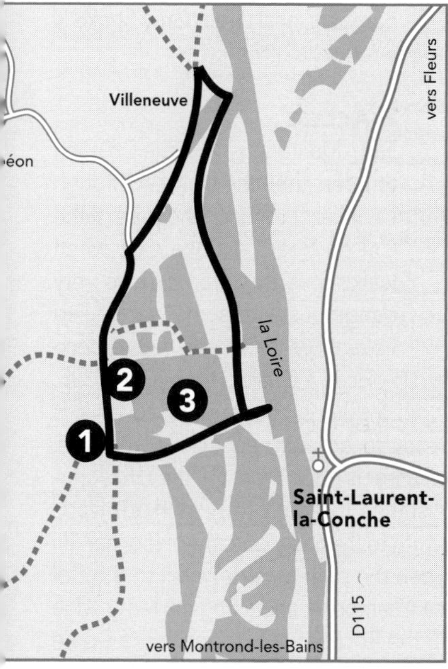

■ Access

From St.-Étienne, take the N82 north to Montrond-les-Bains, turn left on the D496 towards Montbrison, and then, having crossed the Loire, turn right on the D6 as far as Magneux-Haute-Rive. From here follow signs for the Écopôle du Forez visitor centre. The site is open to the public every afternoon from 14.00 to 18.00, and groups can be catered for by prior arrangement. There is a car park (1) (fee payable) at the centre, and the various access routes are signposted from here. In the main building (2) there is a video-camera link to a display screen showing direct images of a Kestrel's nest in a nearby nestbox, enabling you to watch the incubating adult or the young being fed. The centre itself also functions as an immense hide overlooking the immediate area. However, for the more energetic there is a nature trail, taking in several hides, and running alongside the River Loire. Stone Curlew, Lapwing and Curlew all breed on the cultivated land to the west of the car park. In the coppices along the water's edge look for Whitethroat and Melodious Warbler.

On the lakes, especially in front of the hide labelled 'La Bécassine' (3), there are often many ducks, and Common Terns nest on specially provided rafts. Marsh and Hen Harriers regularly come from the surrounding area to hunt over the site. Kingfishers can be seen along the Loire and around the lakes, and both Little Ringed Plover and even the odd Common Sandpiper breed. Being on a migration route, a few waders can be seen in spring and autumn on the more open areas of shore. In winter, as the site is free from hunting, it has the largest concentration of aquatic birds (several thousand) in the area.

■ Calendar

Spring and summer: Great Crested Grebe, Grey and Night Herons, Little Egret, Red-crested Pochard, Marsh and Hen Harriers, Stone Curlew, Curlew, Lapwing, Little Ringed Plover, Redshank, Black-headed Gull, Kingfisher, Sand Martin, Blue-headed Wagtail, Reed Warbler.
Autumn: White and Black Storks, Osprey, Crane, ducks and waders.
Winter: Cormorant, Wigeon, Pintail, Shoveler, Peregrine, Great White Egret, Willow Tit.

19. Monts du Forez

Loire (42) *IGN 43/50*

This chain of hills is some 60 km long, from north to south, and lies to the west of the previous site. The underlying geology is of crystalline rocks with some granitic incursions, the highest point,

COMMON SWIFT

Pierre-sur-Haute, reaching 1,634 metres. The northern part of these mountains (locally called 'Hautes-Chaumes') is the area of most interest to birdwatchers. This strip of high ground, about 20 km long and about 5 km wide, mostly lies above 1,300 metres. It is dominated by heather and bilberry moorland, and is dotted with peat-bogs that contain some rare and interesting plants. The area has a mountain climate, with plenty of snow between December and April, this sometimes lasting into June, and the subalpine vegetation and associated forest makes for an area with a varied bird population. Buzzard and Hen Harrier and in summer Montagu's Harrier, Honey Buzzard and Short-toed Eagle hunt over the heaths. The woodland edges attract Ring Ouzels and the forests have various tits (Coal, Crested and Marsh) as well as Crossbill. The area varies considerably from season to season, and even from day to day in autumn, when some quite unexpected species can turn up, including 'southern' species such as Bee-eater. During the autumn, finches, thrushes and larks migrate through in large numbers, and Great Grey Shrike is a regular visitor.

Access

From Montbrison, take the D8 north to Boën, then the D6 west through Chalmazel to reach the pass of the Col du Béal (1). Take care when walking as this area can be very dangerous with some water-filled holes more than seven metres deep in places; a detailed map (IGN 2732E, 1:25,000) is recommended as it is easy to get lost, especially when the weather is poor. From (1), the GR3 long-distance footpath (way-marked) leads south to the rocky outcrop of Procher (2). Then the path runs downhill to the Col de Chamboite, and along the rocky ridge of the Rocher Pavé, to reach the Dôme de Pierre-sur-Haute (3). Along the ridge look out for Rock Thrush, Wheatear and Black Redstart, while the coppices nearby have passerines such as Willow Warbler and Dunnock. Skylark and both Meadow and Tree Pipits can be found almost anywhere in the area. In spring, the high point of Pierre-sur-Haute is the best area for Water Pipit, Rock Thrush occurs here regularly and occasionally an Alpine Accentor can be seen feeding on the ground. A few Citril Finches sometimes remain through the summer, although more regular on passage. Birds of prey migrate through in autumn when Dotterel sometimes also turn up, particularly favouring the more open higher areas. From (3) it is possible to continue to Le Gros-Fumé (4) by skirting the réserve naturelle of Les Jasseries-du-Colleigne, and returning by the same route (18 km in all). Another path drops down from Le Gros-Fumé to reach the road at Sauvain, another point of access from the east. Alternatively, a little before Pierre-sur-

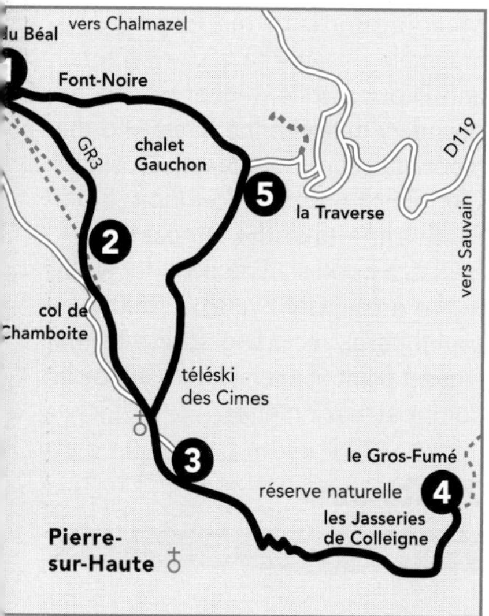

Haute, take the Cimes ski-lift track to La Traverse (5). Turn left towards the Chalet Gauchon, and get back to the Col du Béal via the ruins of Font-Noire (this making a circuit of 12 km there and back). The Col de Baracuchet, at the southern end of the hills, south-west of Montbrison, has been the site of an observation centre for several years, with watchers present from mid-September to early November, and is worth a visit at that time.

Calendar

Spring and summer: Buzzard, Honey Buzzard, Short-toed Eagle, Sparrowhawk, Montagu's and Marsh Harriers, Kestrel, Hobby, Quail, Woodcock, Swift, Black Woodpecker, Skylark, Water, Meadow and Tree Pipits, Black Redstart, Whinchat, Wheatear, Rock Thrush, Ring Ouzel, Willow Warbler, Crested Tit, Raven.
Autumn: Crane, raptors, Woodpigeon, thrushes, Hawfinch, Siskin, Citril Finch, Chaffinch and Brambling; sometimes Black Stork, Osprey, Peregrine or Dotterel.
Winter: many thrushes, including Fieldfare.

20. Étangs du Forez

Loire (42) *IGN 43/50*

The Forez plain, which lies in the valley of the Loire to the north of St.-Étienne, is notable for being well-watered by rainfall from the surrounding mountains (the Monts du Forez and the Monts du Lyonnais). It is an area with many lakes, set in a landscape of scattered coppices, a few areas of oak woodland and the agricultural land of the flood-plain. Along the River Loire are a series of gravel workings, some of which have been rehabilitated by local conservation societies, and which are also worth investigating, most notably at the Écoplôle du Forez (see site 18 above). A wide variety of species can be seen in this little-known area, including a breeding population of about 50 pairs of Red-crested Pochard. Spring is the best time to see these and the other wetland species nesting here – Great Crested and Black-necked Grebes, Mallard, Gadwall, Shoveler, Garganey, Pochard and Tufted Duck. In addition, Marsh Harrier, Hobby and Black Kite all nest in small numbers and there are colonies of Whiskered Terns and Black-headed Gulls. A few pairs of Stone Curlew occur on the drier sections. There are also migrants to be seen moving along the Loire valley, Ospreys for instance regularly passing through in spring and autumn. From St.-Étienne, take the N82 north to Andrézieux, which lies at the southern end of the Forez plain. The N82 continues north via Montrond-les-Bains and Feurs to provide access from the east, while the D8 via Montbrison and Boën runs along the western side. Although most of the lakes are private and entry is prohibited, it is nonetheless quite easy to obtain good views of the birds from the local roads.

21. Gorges of the upper Loire valley

Loire (42) *IGN 50*

Immediately to the west of St.-Étienne, the River Loire flows through a series of gorges that enjoy a warm, dry climate giving rise to Mediterranean-like vegetation. This is a good area for birds of prey such as Short-toed Eagle, Red Kite, Kestrel, Sparrowhawk and Eagle and Little Owls. Characteristic breeding species of the rocky broom-covered heathland are Nightjar, Melodious Warbler, Red-backed Shrike and Rock Bunting. In winter, the cliffs attract Wallcreepers and the rocky areas sometimes have a few Alpine Accentors. The riverside can be reached at St.-Victor-sur-Loire, due west of St.-Étienne along the D3, and at Le Pertuis/Unieux along the D25 a little further south. A footpath between the two makes for a walk of four hours there and back.

22. Le Pilat

Loire (42) *IGN 51/52*

The Parc Naturel Régional du Pilat lies immediately east of St.-Étienne, and the high ground here dominates the Rhône valley to the east and marks the start of the Massif Central. The area has a varied landscape, with moors on high ground, dense fir and beech woods in the valley bottoms, and Mediterranean-type vegetation on south-facing slopes between the two. The Short-toed Eagle hunts over the open areas and both Buzzard and Honey Buzzard are common breeding birds of the forests. The mountain streams have Grey Wagtail and Dipper while, higher up, at the boundary between the forest and the moorland, look for Linnet, Crossbill, Citril Finch and Meadow Pipit. From St.-Étienne take the D8 east to Le Bessat, a good starting point for walks in the area (IGN 2933E, 1:25,000 is useful here), including access to the highest point of the hills, the Crêt de la Perdrix at 1,432 metres.

23. Roanne

Loire (42) *IGN 43*

The main interest for the birdwatcher in the area around Roanne, in the north of the region, lies with the River Loire. To the south of the town the river has been dammed at Villerest, where it leaves the lowest section of its gorges, marking the transition from the fast mountain river upstream and the meandering lowland river below. In the valley north of Roanne, the river is marked by sandy islands covered with vegetation, and it is in this area that a good mixture of species can be found – Grey and Night Herons, Little Egret, Stone Curlew, Little Ringed Plover, Curlew, Common Sandpiper, and both Common and Little Terns, most of which breed here. There are gravel-pits next to the river in places (e.g., just east of Mably) and these are worth checking in winter for Pochard, Tufted Duck, Great Crested, Little and sometimes Black-necked Grebes. Goldeneye sometimes occurs at this time and the Great White Egret is becoming a more frequent visitor. Osprey often occurs on migration. To the north-west of Roanne, 15 km away, is the Forêt de Lespinasse, set in a landscape of

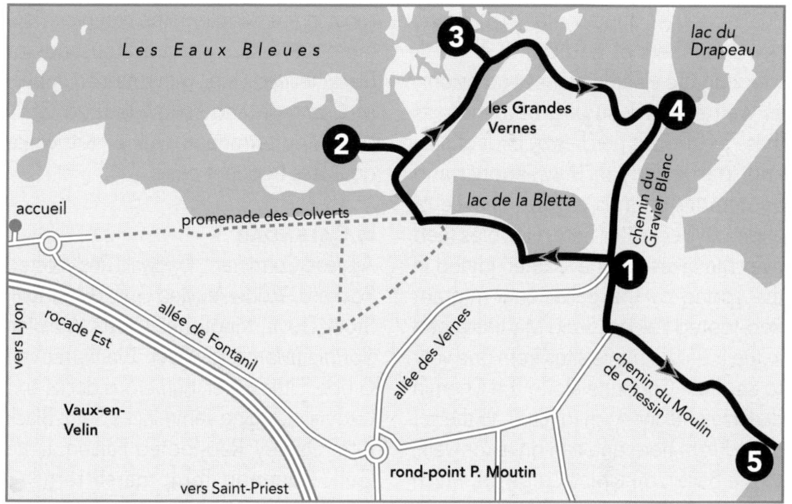

hedgerows and meadows. This can be explored along the woodland tracks and nearby roads, and its breeding population includes Goshawk, Booted Eagle, Middle Spotted Woodpecker, Wood Warbler and Red-backed Shrike.

24. Miribel-Jonage and Le Grand Large at Lyon

RHÔNE (69) *IGN 44*

Situated less than 15 km from the centre of Lyon, this area of ancient gravel-pits provides year-round birdwatching with a varied habitat comprising gravel islands, mudflats, the old meanders of the River Rhône, riverside woodland and dry meadows. Lying between the plateau of La Dombes to the north-east and the continuation of the Rhône valley to the south, the site attracts numerous migrants: gulls and terns, waders, herons, passerines.

■ ACCESS

The leisure centre of Parc de Miribel-Jonage lies immediately north-east of Lyon, and can be accessed from the ring road ('rocade') in a couple of places; it is well-signposted. All the gravel-pits can attract birds, so the whole area is worth exploring if you have time. Starting from the Allivoz car park (1) walk along the southern side of the Lac de la Bletta where, out of the breeding season, it is possible to find Red-crested Pochard, diving ducks and grebes. In the summer Stock Dove and Black Kite are often seen in this area. Continue to the viewpoint overlooking the Lac des Eaux Bleues (2). This is one of the best areas for flocks of wildfowl in winter, and it is worth checking through them carefully for rarer visitors such as Goldeneye, Velvet Scoter, Goosander or Smew. Also in winter, this is where a Cormorant roost usually builds up. Continue along the same track as far as Les Grandes Vernes (3). In late summer, when the water levels tend to be fairly low, this area attracts many waders – Curlew Sandpiper, Dunlin, Temminck's and Little Stints, sometimes Knot or Sanderling – plus various gulls and terns. Rarities turn up among the regular species on an annual basis. The path leads on to the Lac du Drapeau (4), another area that attracts good numbers of wildfowl. It is worth checking the electricity lines and pylons, as well as overhanging branches, as these are used as perches by birds of prey and, particularly in May, August and September there is a good chance of finding a Bee-eater here. Hobbies feed over the lakes and have been joined in the spring by the occasional migrant Red-footed Falcon. Sand Martins breed in the area but move sites from one year to another. Continue along the Chemin du Gravier Blanc track to return to the car park. From here one can drive (or walk) to the Bassin du Grand Large (5), which lies about 1 km away to the south-east. To the south of the car park, turn left at the cafe 'La Petite Camargue' along the Chemin du Moulin de Chessin which leads to Le Grand Large. Before getting there the track runs alongside a small reedbed, with many willows and alders, and this is a good place to find migrant Penduline Tits in March or April. In addition, both Reed and Melodious Warblers breed in this area. The Bassin du Grand Large is an old reservoir fed by the canalised River Rhône, and is of particular interest during the spring and autumn migration periods. Shooting is not allowed here, and so it forms a refuge for birds from the surrounding areas. On arriving on the embankment, walk southwards along the shoreline. In spring, Little Gull and Black and Whiskered Terns are regular migrants, late April and May being the best times. This is also the best period for rarities, which have included Arctic, Gull-billed, Sandwich and White-winged Black Terns and Slender-billed Gull, among many others. Osprey and Hobby are very frequent visitors here. On winter evenings large numbers of gulls can be seen coming to roost in the middle of the reservoir. The most numerous are the thousands of Black-headed Gulls, with smaller numbers of Common and Yellow-legged Gulls plus Mediterranean Gull or Kittiwake on a less frequent basis.

Calendar

All year: Cormorant, Gadwall, Red-crested Pochard, Yellow-legged Gull, Water Rail, Stock Dove, Kingfisher, Cetti's Warbler.
Spring (March to May): Black-necked Grebe, Little Egret, numerous ducks and waders including Temminck's Stint; Black Kite, Osprey, Red-footed Falcon, Little Gull, Common Tern, marsh terns (3 species) and Penduline Tit.
Summer: Little Egret, Night and Purple Herons, Black Kite, Hobby, Bee-eater, Nightjar, Sand Martin, Melodious Warbler, Spotted Flycatcher and Golden Oriole.
Winter: Red-throated and Black-throated Divers (annual), Red-necked Grebe (rare), Pochard, Tufted Duck, Scaup and Ferruginous Duck (annual between October and March), Velvet Scoter, Eider, sawbills (the three species), Black-headed, Yellow-legged, Common, Herring (rare but annual), Lesser Black-backed (uncommon), sometimes Little and Mediterranean Gulls.

25. Landes de Montagny

Rhône (69) IGN 51

This area of heathland, although only some 15 km to the south-west of the conurbation of Lyon, and popular with visitors, is of great interest from a natural history point of view, and the habitat now benefits from a degree of legal protection. To reach the area take the D42 south-west from Lyon towards St-Étienne or the N86 south towards Givors. The village of Montagny lies on the D105 just to the south of the intersection of these two roads. There is an information board with a map of the area in Sourzy, just south of Montagny, which is worth consulting to choose a circuit to walk. The main area of heathland lies between Montagny south to Chassagny. The Étang du Battoir, between these two villages, is one spot worth checking, as both Night Heron and the occasional Little Bittern have been seen. In general, to get the best from the area, one needs to walk the farm tracks that cross the crops and patches of wet meadowland, allowing much of the area to be covered easily. The hedges, meadows and crops shelter many passerines such as Nightingale, Whitethroat, Melodious Warbler and Skylark. Several waders rare in this part of France breed in the area, including Stone Curlew, Lapwing and Curlew. Hen and Montagu's Harriers, Short-toed Eagle and Hobby can all be seen hunting over the heathland and farmland. Quail and Nightjar also occur here, while Scops Owls breed around Mornant, just to the west. The whole plateau roughly delimited by the villages of Mornant, St.-Laurent-d'Agny, Montagny and St.-Andéol-le-Château, being close to the Rhône valley, is a stop-off point for many migrants. Species such as Tawny Pipit, Wheatear and Ortolan Bunting are sometimes found on the ploughed fields and among the market gardens, and the whole area has a reputation of being a good one for locally rare migrants. Two species that have recently started breeding in the area are Cattle Egret, usually found with the Charolais cattle almost anywhere on the plateau, and Sardinian Warbler, here at the very northern edge of its range, and to be looked for among the bushes along the road from Montagny to the Étang du Battoir.

26. Forêt de Bellevaux

SAVOIE (73) *IGN 53*

This forest lies in the Parc Naturel Régional du Massif des Bauges, between Chambéry and Albertville to the east. The woodland is dominated by beech and spruce, and contains some mature trees more than a hundred years old, and has a bird community typical of the high mountains of eastern France. Black Woodpecker, Hazel Grouse and Common Treecreeper can all be found in the woodland, and once one reaches the upper limit of the forest and moves into the alpine meadows one comes across yet more species such as Black Grouse, Raven, Alpine Chough, Alpine Accentor and Ring Ouzel. Both Peregrine and Golden Eagle can be seen hunting overhead almost anywhere. From the N6/N90 about half-way between Chambéry and Albertville, take the D911 north through St.-Pierre-d'Albigny to École-en-Bauges, and turn right towards Notre Dame de Bellevaux. It is possible to park along this road and explore on foot (IGN 3432OT, 1:25,000 covers this area).

27. Golfe de Coudrée on Lac Léman

HAUTE-SAVOIE (74) *IGN 45*

This bay on the southern side of Lac Léman between Geneva and Thonon-les-Bains is very shallow, and this makes it a particularly favourable section for diving duck in winter. In spring, the falling water

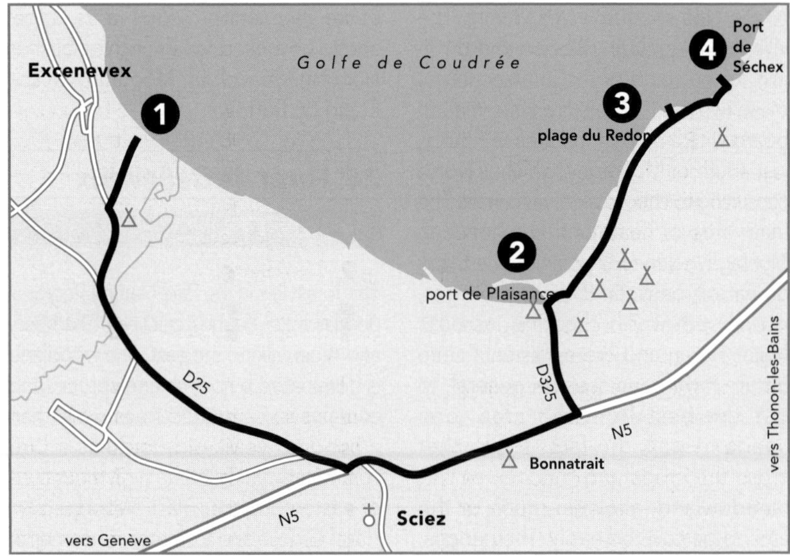

levels result in the appearance of sandy islands opposite the beach at Excenevex, and many migrants occur here between March and early June.

■ Access

From Geneva, take the N5 towards Thonon-les-Bains as far as the village of Sciez. Here turn left on the D25 towards Excenevex. At the first roundabout, turn right, then 500 metres farther on turn right again, just after the camp site. Park in the beach car park (1). From the lakeside one can scan both the lake itself, and the offshore sand banks in spring if they are exposed. Pochard and Tufted Duck are the most numerous species, but Scaup or Ferruginous Duck may well be present as well. Amongst the hundreds of Great Crested and Black-necked Grebes, check for Red-necked or Slavonian Grebe, as both species also winter here in small numbers. All three species of diver have been seen, Goosander are the most numerous sawbill, with Red-breasted Merganser and sometimes Smew also turning up. Of the scoters, Velvet Scoter is the most likely to be seen; Common Scoter is rarer, as are Long-tailed Duck and Eider. The bay can also be viewed from its eastern side. From Excenevex return along the D25 as far as Sciez, and then take the N5 towards Thonon-les-Bains. On leaving the village of Bonnatrait turn left towards the port (2) where there is a car park near the first roundabout. During periods of northerly winds many grebes and duck take shelter in the port – this is the place where many of the rarer visitors have been seen. Continue east along the lakeside road for another 700 metres to reach the beach at Redon (3) from where the lake can be scanned. There is a car park on the left just after the bridge over a small river here. Similarly, the landing stage at the port of Séchex (4) is also worth a stop.

■ CALENDAR

All year: Goosander, Black-headed and Yellow-legged Gulls.
Spring: Little Egret, Black Kite, Ringed and Little Ringed Plovers (Kentish Plover is rare), many smaller waders (particularly Dunlin, Little Stint, Ruff, Greenshank and Wood Sandpiper), Mediterranean Gull (rare), Common Tern, marsh terns (principally Black Tern), Water Pipit, Red-throated Pipit has been recorded on several occasions, wagtails.
Autumn: the same species as in spring in much smaller numbers.
Winter: divers, grebes, Cormorant, dabbling duck, diving duck, Goldeneye, Common Gull, sometimes Dipper and Common Sandpiper.

28. Alpage de Doran / Sallanches

HAUTE-SAVOIE (74) *IGN 45*

This part of the Chaine des Aravis, to the east of Annecy, is an area with a reintroduction programme for Lammergeier. You have a good chance of seeing adults overhead throughout the year, supplemented by young birds raised in captivity and released between late June and late August. All the released birds have differently coloured wing tags. Other typical mountain species can also be seen – Golden Eagle, Rock Partridge, Alpine Accentor, Rock Thrush, Wallcreeper, Alpine Chough and Raven. From Annecy the A41 then A40 runs eastwards towards Chamonix. Leave at exit 20 for Sallanches, from where a minor road leads west into the mountains towards the refuge of the Chalets de Doran. A walk into the alpine habitat of this area (IGN 3430ET, 1:25,000) should provide a good chance of seeing the various specialities of the area. There are other walks possible in this area. For more information on the reintroduction scheme, see www.gypaete-barbu.com (Tel: 04 50 93 08 48) or visit the Centre de la Nature Montagnarde at the Château des Rubins in Sallanches.

29. Le Hucel

HAUTE-SAVOIE (74) *IGN 45*

Le Hucel is a migration watch-point situated at the eastern end of Lac Léman, close to the Swiss border, just north of the village of Thollon-les-Mémises. It lies at an altitude of 966 metres, on the slopes between the high ground of the Pic de Mémise (altitude 1,674 metres) to the south and Lac Léman to the north. The site is of particular interest for birds of prey and other soaring species, the topography being such as to channel birds close to the viewpoint. It is particularly good in spring, between early February and early June. More than 15,000 birds of prey pass through each year, the numbers dominated by Buzzard, Black Kite and Honey Buzzard, but rarer species such as Booted or Spotted Eagles are also seen along with small numbers of Black Storks. From Thonon-les-Bains (see also site 27 above) take the N5 east to Évian-les-Bains and just after this turn right on the D24 at Neuvecelle. Continue to Thollon-les-Mémises and 300 metres after the village turn left at Nouy, towards Le Hucel. Park near the village and walk up a track to get to the observation site at the base of a relay antenna, obvious from a distance.

Glossary

Anse: a bay or cove, usually relatively enclosed.

Barrage: a dam, but sometimes also applied to the lake formed behind the dam itself.

Bac: a ferry, usually on a river.

Ballastière: excavation site for material needed for construction industry, similar to gravel-pits and sand-pits, and like those often resulting in wetland sites attractive to waterfowl and waders.

Barthe: name for riverside flood-meadow, particularly associated with south-west France.

Base de loisirs, Base nautique: leisure centre, often by an inland lake or reservoir.

Bassin: area of water, which may be large or small.

Bergerie: sheepfold.

Bocage: countryside with small fields, hedgerows and trees, particularly but not exclusively associated with Normandy.

Bois, Forêt: woodland, forest.

Boucle: a meander along the course of a river.

Causse: limestone plateau, particularly associated with the Cévennes area in Languedoc-Roussillon.

Château d'eau: water-tower.

Col: a mountain pass.

Coussous: dry steppe-like grassland, particularly associated with La Crau (site 18 in Provence-Alpes-Côte d'Azur).

Déchetterie: rubbish-tip or recycling centre.

Département: the name given to the 95 main administrative divisions of France, approximating roughly to the counties of the UK. They are grouped into 22 Régions.

Digue: a sea-wall or similar dike.

Étang, Lac: lake, pond or lagoon.

Estive: summer pastures in the mountains.

Falaise: cliff.

Garrigue, Maquis: areas of bushes and scrub found on Mediterranean hillsides. The latter term usually applies to the taller scrub found on less calcareous soils than the former.

Gravière: gravel-pit.

Gué: a river ford.

Lande: moorland.

Marais: marsh.

Mollières: local name in Picardy for salt-marsh habitat.

Observatoire: bird-hide.

Phare: lighthouse.

Plage: beach, either by the sea or an inland lake.

Plan d'eau: a stretch of smooth water, often a reservoir, but may be along a river.

Rocade: ring-road, usually associated with large towns.

Roselière: reedbed.

Réserve de chasse: an area free from hunting.

Sablière: sand-pit.

Sansouire: low salt-marsh vegetation found in the coastal marshes along the Mediterranean.

Sentier: footpath.

Station d'épuration, Station de lagunage: waste-water treatment plant ('sewage farm').

Tombolo: narrow strip of land, often sand or gravel, joining an offshore islet to the mainland.

Tourbière, Narse: peat-bog.

Vasière: mudflats, usually tidal on the coast, but may also occur by inland lakes.

Val, Vallée: valley.

Species Index

A

Accentor Alpine 24, 25, 48, 51, 52, 123, 127, 129, 135, 174, 176-77, 182, 183, 214, 216, 221, 329, 332, 334, 335, 339, 357, 367, 369, 370, 372, 374, 377, 379

Auk, Little 76, 237

Avocet 15, 33, 82, 83-84, 85, 163, 172, 173, 178, 179, 180, 181, 230, 242, 246-47, 252, 260, 274, 283, 286, 288, 290, 291, 299-300, 301, 310, 311, 316, 325, 342-43, 345, 352, 369

B

Bee-eater 15, 33, 39, 44, 45, 46, 55, 61-62, 64-65, 123, 125, 131, 139-40, 155, 173, 174, 179, 180, 181, 186, 187, 226, 239, 339, 341, 343, 350, 353, 354, 357, 363, 365, 376

Bittern 16, 59, 77-78, 93, 94, 96, 109, 113, 117, 157, 167, 177, 181, 185, 198-99, 202, 203, 206, 209, 242, 247, 249, 260, 264, 268, 282, 296, 300, 303, 335, 336, 341, 343, 346, 349, 377

Little 27, 46, 77, 93, 96, 109, 113, 117, 124, 131, 160-61, 167, 168, 177, 181, 185-86, 198-99, 200, 203, 209, 244-45, 247, 248-49, 264, 289, 295, 296, 303, 335, 344, 346, 349, 353, 355, 357, 360, 370

Blackbird 14, 16, 76, 141, 177, 198-99, 241

Blackcap 16, 88, 98, 131, 148-49, 161, 227, 274, 283, 307, 317, 332, 338

Bluethroat 30, 33, 40, 64-65, 78, 83-84, 85, 125, 137, 140, 232-33, 241, 244-45, 248-49, 254-55, 260, 268, 274, 286, 287, 288, 289, 290, 291, 295, 296, 298, 300, 303, 310, 311, 313, 316, 317, 319, 362

White-spotted 30

Brambling 15, 49, 76, 100, 149, 167, 175-77, 178, 215, 234, 241, 295, 303, 338, 373

Bullfinch 26, 27, 98, 149, 161, 195, 306, 333, 339, 365

Bunting

Cirl 39, 62, 90, 91, 98, 122-23, 129, 140, 141, 149, 180, 182, 219, 253, 255, 275, 280, 317, 29, 330, 336, 339, 370

Corn 59, 61-62, 65, 66, 110, 123, 140, 144, 207, 210, 253, 278, 283, 286, 324, 330, 336, 338, 349, 353, 363

Lapland 16, 76, 78, 241, 254-55, 257, 260, 261, 281, 283, 286, 299

Ortolan 33, 53, 61-62, 105, 142, 174, 176-77, 180, 182, 183, 184, 215, 286, 324, 330, 336, 338, 355, 357, 365, 370, 377

Reed 52, 59, 66, 77, 90, 99, 100, 104, 109, 117, 118, 131, 143-44, 155, 167, 179, 194, 195, 198-99, 210, 218, 226, 248-49, 253, 255, 260, 273, 278, 279, 283, 284, 286, 289, 295, 300, 307, 310, 313, 323, 328, 335, 336, 349, 365

Rock 24, 25, 51-52, 142, 191, 192, 195, 216, 329, 330, 338-39, 365, 369, 374

Snow 16, 25, 76, 78, 232, 237-38, 246-47, 252, 255, 256-57, 258, 260, 261, 281, 286, 300, 301, 302, 316

Bustard, Little 283, 289, 319, 320, 324, 330, 347, 349, 353, 357

Buzzard 14, 15, 31, 35, 36, 41, 44, 48, 53, 67, 93, 98, 100, 103, 119, 138, 140, 154, 156, 159, 164, 179, 183, 191, 192, 195, 219-20, 223-24, 231, 233, 234-35, 245, 249, 253, 266, 275, 281, 291, 300, 303, 306, 317, 323, 363, 373, 374, 379

Honey 15, 22, 24, 31, 40-41, 44, 46, 48, 49, 52, 53, 54, 55, 59, 85, 94, 96, 97, 98, 100, 114-15, 119, 124, 138, 141, 156, 159, 173, 174, 175-76, 181, 182, 183, 186, 187, 191, 192, 195, 199, 200, 202, 203, 209, 214-15, 216, 219, 224, 233, 235, 253, 266, 275, 280, 281, 96, 298, 303, 306, 317, 319, 324, 335, 339, 349, 353, 363, 367, 373, 374, 379

Rough-legged 16, 249, 300

C

Capercaillie 135, 221

Chaffinch 15, 41, 49, 76, 100, 161, 174, 175-77, 178, 215, 234, 241, 303, 363, 373

Chiffchaff 14, 16, 53, 60, 61-62, 76, 88, 91, 98, 114-15, 125, 131, 148-49, 153, 195, 227, 283, 306, 318, 328, 332, 336

Siberian 239

Chough

Alpine 127-28, 214, 221, 333, 335, 337, 339, 367, 369, 377, 379

Red-billed 76, 80, 84, 127, 175, 177, 183, 214, 215, 216, 221, 329, 333, 335, 338, 369

Coot 14, 16, 21, 27, 30, 50, 52, 59, 68, 76, 88-89, 108, 109, 119, 131, 135, 165, 166, 167, 168, 169, 173, 184, 185, 210, 217, 226, 230, 234, 242, 243, 245, 249, 275, 279, 284, 295, 309, 325, 328, 337, 338, 344

Cormorant 14, 15, 20, 21, 26, 27, 30, 32, 33, 34, 40, 45, 55, 59, 63, 65, 66, 68, 91, 100, 103, 105, 108, 110, 111, 113, 116, 118, 130-31, 144, 145, 152, 155, 161, 162, 163, 164, 165, 167, 174, 179, 180, 181, 185, 200, 202, 203, 209, 210, 215, 218, 222, 226, 227, 230-31, 232, 243, 247, 249, 252- 3, 254-55, 258, 264, 268, 278, 279, 286, 288, 295, 310, 325, 328, 338, 344, 349, 363, 365, 369, 371, 375, 376, 379

Corncrake 65, 101, 110, 144, 145, 199, 202, 207, 210, 253, 268, 269, 276, 277, 279, 298, 363
Crake
Little 124, 185, 203, 205, 209, 345, 349, 360, 362
Spotted 36, 46, 47, 124, 137, 167, 198-99, 203, 205, 209, 218, 269, 276, 278, 281, 289, 297, 317, 337, 338, 345, 349, 360, 362
Crane 16, 32, 35, 36, 40, 41, 45, 47, 50, 53-54, 59, 61, 63, 65, 66, 90, 96, 103, 110, 112-13, 115-17, 119, 144, 145, 187, 193, 199, 202, 203, 205, 206, 207, 208-9, 218, 222, 269, 286, 295, 306, 310, 321, 324, 335, 363, 371, 373
Crossbill 16, 24, 25, 49, 52, 54, 123, 124, 129, 135, 136, 149, 191, 211, 221, 280, 283, 332, 333, 336, 338, 339, 362, 365, 369, 372, 374
Cuckoo 14, 62, 76, 88, 98, 125, 140, 149, 154, 226, 230, 253
Great Spotted 39, 172, 173, 174, 177, 181, 344
Curlew 16, 22, 34, 35, 36, 45, 47, 50, 64, 65, 73, 74, 77-78, 79, 80, 81-82, 84, 85, 90, 99-10, 110, 112-13, 117, 119, 131, 137, 140, 143-44, 145, 185, 199, 200, 202, 207, 209, 210, 222, 238, 241, 257, 258, 259, 261, 274, 275, 277, 281, 283, 288, 298, 299, 301, 302, 310, 311, 315, 316, 319, 335, 336, 345, 353, 363, 371, 374, 379
Stone (see Stone Curlew)

D

Dipper 26, 27, 51-52, 60, 69, 98, 177, 183, 191, 192, 214, 221, 225, 234, 333, 339, 365, 367, 369, 374, 379
Diver
Black-throated 34-35, 40, 144, 158, 173, 174, 180, 185, 215, 217, 226, 238, 240, 243, 252, 256, 258, 260, 264, 268, 281, 302, 310, 325, 342, 344, 376, 377
Great Northern 34-35, 40, 158, 215, 217, 238, 240, 243, 258, 260, 264, 274, 310, 325, 344, 377
Red-throated 34, 40, 108, 144, 158, 180, 226, 238, 240, 243, 252, 256, 257, 258, 260, 264, 268, 274, 281, 310, 315, 376, 377
Dotterel 15, 25, 49, 76, 77, 129, 135, 187, 241, 259, 283, 310, 312, 372, 373
Dove
Rock 84, 126-27
Stock 32, 45, 49, 59, 60, 138, 141, 183, 187, 225, 253, 268, 279, 283, 296, 302, 303, 317, 323, 363, 375, 376
Turtle 76, 88, 123, 140, 248, 266, 269, 286, 329, 354, 363
Duck
Ferruginous 59, 89, 131, 168, 186, 194, 227, 264, 296, 306, 325, 341, 349, 361, 376, 378
Long-tailed 16, 23, 27, 231, 349, 378
Ruddy 157, 265, 349
Tufted 20, 21, 26, 27, 30, 40, 59, 60, 65, 66, 68, 78, 88-89, 91-92, 96, 100, 101, 102-3, 108, 113, 118, 131, 136-37, 144, 149, 150, 152-53, 155, 158, 161, 162, 163, 164, 165, 166, 168, 169, 179, 185, 186, 194, 199, 200, 204, 210, 226-27, 230-31, 245, 247, 249, 264, 284, 289, 295, 296, 300, 302, 306, 307, 314, 317, 325, 328, 341, 343, 349, 369, 373, 374, 376, 378
White-headed 130
Dunlin 34, 45, 62, 73, 80, 82, 83-84, 89, 99, 104, 110, 111-13, 117, 131, 137, 144, 161, 172, 180, 185, 222, 252, 255, 257, 259, 261, 274, 275, 277, 281, 283, 286, 288, 289, 301, 302, 310, 315, 316, 352, 375, 379
Dunnock 14, 24, 141, 221, 318, 372

E

Eagle
Bonelli's 180, 215, 346, 349, 357
Booted 44, 46, 49, 50, 89, 124, 174, 187, 192, 202, 220, 223-24, 226, 375, 379
Golden 41, 52, 123, 127, 128-29, 174, 180, 182, 183, 214, 216, 221, 329, 332, 335, 336, 337, 339, 357, 361, 367, 369, 370, 377, 379
Short-toed 15, 31, 33, 38, 49, 50, 51, 52, 53, 54, 58-59, 60, 94, 96, 97, 98, 173, 174, 176, 180, 182, 183, 187, 191, 192, 216, 220, 223-24, 225, 291, 306, 310, 318, 319, 324, 330, 338, 339, 346, 353, 357, 361, 365, 367, 368, 369, 373, 374, 379
Spotted 35, 181, 341, 343, 350, 361, 379
White-tailed 16, 21, 35, 36, 45, 111-13, 115-17, 130, 203, 205-6, 209, 215, 249, 318
Egret
Cattle 32, 33, 35, 36, 40, 44, 45, 65, 96, 131, 140, 174, 177, 185, 226, 227, 249, 279, 301, 311, 316, 328, 341, 343, 353, 377
Great White 21, 30, 35, 36, 45, 59, 61, 63, 65, 66, 68, 91, 96, 100, 102-3, 110, 111, 113, 116-17, 130-31, 137, 138, 177, 179, 181, 185, 193-94, 198-99, 202, 203, 205, 206, 207, 208, 209, 215, 217, 218, 222, 226, 260, 295, 296, 306, 335, 341, 343, 345, 349, 361, 371, 374
Little 32, 33, 36, 40, 44, 45, 46, 55, 61-62, 64, 65, 82, 84, 89, 91, 94, 96, 101, 111, 113, 117, 124, 130-31, 139, 140, 163, 174, 177, 178-79,

181, 185, 194, 217, 218, 226, 227, 232, 246-47, 249, 254-55, 261, 274, 279, 286, 301, 310, 311, 314, 316, 341, 343, 365, 369, 371, 374, 376, 379
Eider 16, 27, 35, 40, 60, 65, 82, 111, 113, 118, 152, 194, 238, 241, 252, 258, 265, 268, 272, 286, 299, 302, 317, 341, 344, 346, 350, 376, 378

F

Falcon
Eleonora's 173, 180, 181, 339, 354
Red-footed 47, 124, 131, 136-37, 180, 286, 300, 349, 353, 370, 376
Fieldfare 15, 26, 27, 32, 36, 52, 58-59, 65, 92, 101, 108, 110, 115, 118, 135, 137, 149, 166, 167, 195, 203, 209, 234-35, 373
Finch
Citril 24, 25, 52, 135, 178, 216, 221, 332, 333, 361, 367, 369, 370, 373, 374
Corsican 123, 127, 129, 131
Snow 15, 52, 183, 221, 334, 335, 357, 369
Trumpeter 124
Firecrest 16, 24, 27, 33, 53, 54, 63, 75-76, 85, 97, 98, 114, 127-28, 167, 224, 235, 267, 283, 339, 357
Flamingo
Chilean 254
Greater 15, 130-31, 173, 178-79, 180, 181, 184-85, 341-43, 344, 345-46, 352, 353
Flycatcher
Collared 15, 119, 199, 200-201, 202, 203, 205, 206, 208-9
Pied 76, 125, 137, 149, 156, 210, 211, 226, 295, 296, 298, 310, 317-18, 354, 365
Red-breasted 76, 85
Spotted 15, 76, 127, 129, 131, 135, 137, 142, 148-49, 158, 202, 275, 286, 317-18, 354, 365, 376
Fulmar 72-73, 76, 80, 85, 242, 253, 256-57, 268, 290, 302

G

Gadwall 26, 30, 32, 35, 40, 45, 59, 64-65, 68, 78, 89, 91, 96, 100, 102-3, 108, 110, 112-13, 136, 143, 155, 162, 164, 194, 199, 205, 206, 209, 217, 227, 230-31, 245, 249, 264, 284, 291, 295, 306, 317, 319, 325, 328, 337, 341, 344, 369, 373, 376
Gallinule, Purple 184-85
Gannet 15, 33, 35, 72-73, 76, 79, 81, 85, 123, 124, 173, 174, 185, 237-38, 240-43, 255, 256, 258, 260, 274, 299, 315, 316, 342, 346, 350, 351
Garganey 14, 50, 52, 59, 68, 78, 84, 89, 91, 96, 100, 102-3, 108, 110, 112-13, 117, 124, 136-37, 144, 145, 157, 167, 194, 198-99, 200, 202, 203, 205, 207, 209, 217, 226, 245, 247, 249, 260, 275, 277, 288, 289, 291, 300, 315, 317, 319, 328, 338, 344, 349, 369, 370, 373
Godwit
Bar-tailed 61, 73, 74, 78, 80, 84, 85, 179, 238, 241, 255, 259, 274, 281, 286, 288, 289, 299, 301, 310, 311, 315
Black-tailed 14, 15, 47, 61, 80, 82, 85, 100, 131, 137, 144, 145, 162, 163, 179, 207, 227, 238, 241, 255, 268, 274, 275, 277, 279, 281, 283, 286, 288, 289, 291, 299, 310, 311, 315, 63
Goldcrest 16, 24, 53, 54, 60, 63, 76, 85, 97, 98, 114, 127-28, 149, 167, 191, 221, 235, 267, 283, 323, 332, 333, 339, 365
Goldeneye 16, 20, 21, 26, 27, 59, 60, 63, 65, 68, 83-84, 88-89, 92, 100, 101, 102-3, 108, 111, 113, 117, 143-44, 157, 158, 168, 169, 194, 199, 201, 202, 203, 204-5, 209, 210, 231, 238, 243, 264, 274, 281, 297, 300, 302, 306, 308, 310, 341, 343, 345, 362, 374, 375, 379
Goldfinch 49, 161, 167, 241
Goosander 16, 20, 21, 26, 27, 63, 65, 68, 92, 100, 101, 104-5, 112-13, 117, 118, 152, 157, 168, 169, 199, 201, 203, 204, 206, 209, 210, 231, 232, 243, 264, 281, 284, 289, 295, 300, 302, 346, 362, 375, 376, 379
Goose
Barnacle 286
Bean 16, 21, 65, 66, 111, 113, 115, 117, 145, 205, 209, 210, 261, 279
Brent 16, 30, 73, 74, 81, 83-84, 85, 237, 240, 254-55, 257, 258, 274, 286, 288, 290, 301, 310, 312, 315, 316
pale-bellied 255, 259
Canada 55, 164
Greylag 14, 16, 21, 34, 35, 65, 66, 88, 91, 96, 99-100, 101, 110, 111-13, 115, 117, 144, 145, 161-62, 194, 202, 203, 205, 206, 207, 209, 218, 222, 227, 230, 245, 246-47, 261, 264, 276, 277, 279, 281, 283, 286, 288, 291, 298, 299, 301, 303, 310, 311, 315, 317-18, 324, 328, 349, 360, 363, 369
White-fronted 16, 66, 111, 113, 115, 117, 158, 261, 279, 286, 291, 311
Goshawk 14, 22, 46, 49, 53, 54, 59, 98, 113, 114-15, 119, 124, 127-28, 131, 135, 138, 141, 183, 191, 192, 195, 199, 200, 202, 203, 205, 209, 211, 223-24, 234-35, 275, 283, 298, 306, 319, 323, 336, 339, 367, 375
Grebe
Black-necked 23, 59, 83-84, 89, 94, 96, 100, 102, 103, 108, 113, 131, 144, 157, 174, 179-80, 185-86, 193, 199, 200, 209, 226, 237-38,

247, 257, 258, 264, 274, 284, 296, 308, 310, 315, 317, 345, 350, 361, 369, 373, 374, 376, 378
Great Crested 21, 27, 38, 45, 46, 59, 60, 63, 64, 65, 68, 82, 83-84, 89, 91, 96, 100, 101, 102, 104, 108, 109, 111, 113, 117, 118, 131, 136-37, 140, 144, 157, 160-61, 162, 163, 164, 165, 166, 167, 168, 169, 174, 179-80, 185-86, 199, 200, 202, 205, 209, 217, 226, 227, 231, 233, 234, 237-38, 243-45, 248-49, 252, 257, 258, 264, 274, 275, 284, 289, 295, 306, 308, 310, 315, 324, 325, 328, 335, 349, 369, 371, 373, 374, 378
Little 21, 27, 36, 40, 45, 46, 50, 52, 59, 60, 63, 65, 68, 83-84, 89, 92, 100, 101, 102, 108, 113, 131, 140, 157, 161, 166, 167, 194, 217, 225-26, 227, 231, 237-38, 243-45, 247, 252, 258, 264, 274, 275, 284, 289, 295, 307, 310, 314, 324, 335, 345, 349, 369, 374
Red-necked 23, 27, 59, 89, 108, 144, 152, 157, 194, 199, 205, 237-38, 243, 258, 264, 274, 310, 376, 378
Slavonian 27, 83-84, 89, 144, 152, 157, 205, 237-38, 257, 258, 274, 310, 315, 344, 350, 378
Greenfinch 49, 161, 167, 175, 178, 241, 258
Greenshank 45, 47, 80, 89, 92, 99, 105, 108, 111, 117, 143-44, 145, 163, 166, 167, 181, 185, 209, 222, 227, 274, 275, 286, 299, 370, 379
Grouse
Black 15, 332, 336, 337, 370, 377
Hazel 119, 135, 136, 362, 370, 377
Guillemot 73, 74, 76, 80, 238, 241, 243, 253, 255, 258, 268, 290, 302, 316, 317
Gull
Audouin's 124, 130-31, 351
Black-headed 15, 21, 23, 25, 27, 34, 40, 47, 50, 55, 59, 60, 63, 65, 66, 76, 77, 89, 91-92, 94, 99, 102, 103, 104-5, 108, 110, 116, 118-19, 130, 144, 149, 151-52, 155, 157, 158, 161, 162, 163, 165, 166, 167, 168, 169, 172, 180, 194, 200-201, 203, 204, 206, 209, 210, 226, 227, 233, 245, 246-47, 249, 264, 265, 274, 277, 281, 283, 286, 288, 290, 295, 307, 310, 325, 343, 371, 373, 376, 379
Caspian 23, 157, 158, 237, 258
Common 21, 34, 40, 66, 89, 105, 108, 113, 117, 144, 157, 158, 200-201, 204, 206, 209, 210, 227, 240, 274, 277, 286, 310, 376, 379
Glaucous 76, 237, 258
Great Black-backed 34, 73, 76, 77-78, 80, 84, 157, 158, 240, 249, 255, 256-7, 258, 268, 286, 290, 310, 313
Herring 34, 66, 73, 76, 77, 84, 89, 108, 157, 158, 240, 242, 246-47, 253, 255, 256-7, 258, 268, 286, 290, 302, 309, 369, 376
Iceland 258
Lesser Black-backed 34, 66, 73, 76, 77-78, 84, 89, 99, 108, 117, 158, 180, 227, 240, 253, 258, 268, 277, 279, 281, 283, 286, 290, 310, 344, 369, 376
Little 16, 21, 23, 34, 40, 59, 66, 77-78, 89, 103, 108, 109, 113, 117, 137, 144, 158, 164, 175, 178, 181, 185, 199, 200, 205, 209, 227, 230, 240, 252-53, 255, 260, 279, 289, 296, 300, 315, 317, 338, 343, 344, 376
Mediterranean 34, 40, 66, 77-78, 89, 103, 105, 151, 153, 157, 162, 172, 179-80, 200-201, 243, 245, 247, 252-53, 256, 261, 264, 268, 288, 290, 300, 301, 310, 315, 343, 346, 376, 379
Ring-billed 34
Sabine's 15, 34, 76, 79, 82, 237, 240, 243, 260, 274, 317
Slender-billed 172, 179, 342-43, 376
Yellow-legged 21, 23, 30, 34, 40, 47, 63, 66, 89, 99, 105, 108, 111, 113, 117, 122, 127, 130, 157, 158, 164, 172, 180, 194, 200, 210, 226, 227, 238, 258, 265, 266, 290, 310, 343, 369, 376, 379

H

Harrier
Hen 22, 33, 35, 36, 37, 44, 47, 48, 50, 51, 52, 53, 54, 59, 62-63, 64, 74, 78, 80, 96, 97, 98, 100, 103, 110, 117, 137, 138, 145, 161, 175, 180, 181, 183, 187, 190-91, 192, 194, 199, 203, 206, 209, 219, 224, 237-38, 244-45, 249, 255, 261, 275, 280, 281, 283, 286, 288, 300, 303, 306, 311, 317, 318, 319, 320-21, 324, 330, 335, 336, 349, 353, 371, 372, 379
Marsh 30, 32, 33, 35, 40, 41, 47, 48, 52, 54, 58-59, 64-65, 77, 78, 82, 84, 92, 93, 96, 100, 102-3, 109, 113, 117, 124, 131, 137, 138, 139-40, 145, 155, 162, 163, 173, 176, 177, 179, 180, 181, 185, 187, 193-94, 198-99, 200, 202, 203, 205, 206, 209, 210, 226, 230, 238, 241-42, 244-45, 247, 248-49, 254-55, 260, 261, 268, 274, 281, 283, 286, 288, 291, 295, 300, 303, 309, 310, 313, 314, 316, 319, 320, 328, 335, 338, 339, 343, 345, 353, 363, 365, 370, 371, 373
Montagu's 14, 33, 37, 44, 47, 48-49, 50, 52, 53, 59, 64, 80, 124, 138, 139-40, 145, 175, 180, 182, 183, 187, 190-91, 199, 210, 215, 220, 238, 283, 286, 288,

291, 300, 306, 310, 319, 320-21, 324, 330, 335, 353, 363, 365, 373, 379

Pallid 124

Hawfinch 53-54, 89, 98, 115, 158, 167, 224, 235, 267, 280, 296, 303, 306, 307, 323, 338, 373

Heron

Grey 21, 26, 27, 32, 33, 36, 40, 44, 45, 46, 47, 50, 55, 59, 61, 63, 64, 65, 68, 82, 84, 91, 99-100, 101, 103, 113, 119, 124, 130-31, 137, 138, 140, 143, 155, 160-61, 162, 163, 164, 165, 166, 167, 172, 174, 177, 178, 181, 183, 185, 194, 198-99, 203, 205, 209, 217, 218, 222, 225-26, 227, 230, 232, 234, 239, 243, 245, 249, 253, 254-55, 264, 277, 279, 286, 295, 301, 307, 310, 314, 323, 325, 328, 337, 338, 349, 365, 369, 371, 374

Night 31, 33, 36, 40, 44, 45, 55, 61-62, 64-65, 89, 90-91, 96, 101, 103, 117, 124, 131, 139-40, 142, 174, 181, 194, 217, 218, 226, 227, 288, 317, 324, 328, 337, 338, 341, 344, 349, 355, 361, 371, 374, 376, 377

Purple 31, 36, 64-65, 77-78, 93, 94, 96, 98, 100, 108, 111, 113, 117, 131, 137, 138, 139-40, 142, 172, 174, 177, 181, 185, 194, 198-99, 203, 209, 217, 218, 226, 227, 288, 299, 310, 316, 318, 324, 328, 336, 337, 338, 341, 346, 349, 361, 365, 370, 376

Squacco 124, 131, 181, 226, 328, 337, 341, 344, 349, 360

Hobby 22, 27, 32, 33, 36, 38, 40, 41, 46, 47, 51, 52, 53, 55, 58-59, 61-62, 64, 65, 89, 90, 94, 98, 100, 104-5, 109, 113, 118, 131, 136-37, 138, 140, 144, 145, 153, 155, 156, 157, 161, 163, 173, 174, 180, 199, 200, 202, 203, 205, 209, 216, 217, 219, 224, 225, 226, 227, 230, 233, 245, 253, 255, 260, 264, 266, 269, 275, 281, 283, 286, 291, 296, 298, 300, 303, 306, 309, 310, 317, 319, 324, 330, 335, 339, 349, 365, 373, 376, 377

Hoopoe 14, 46, 50, 53, 61-62, 119, 131, 140, 154, 172, 174, 176, 177, 179, 183, 184, 186, 211, 218, 226, 309, 310, 317, 330, 338, 343, 347, 357, 370

I

Ibis

Glossy 181, 341, 343

Sacred 81-82, 84, 274

J

Jackdaw 69, 183, 225, 231, 257, 268, 302

Jay 124

K

Kestrel 24, 31, 33, 35, 49, 52, 53, 59, 67, 89, 98, 119, 127, 135, 138, 140, 142, 167, 173, 183, 192, 225, 245, 253, 257, 274, 286, 288, 291, 300, 302, 317, 323, 324, 333, 349, 357, 369, 370, 373, 374

Lesser 124, 348, 349, 350

Kingfisher 21, 27, 30, 32, 44, 51, 59, 61-62, 64, 65, 68, 69, 84, 90-91, 101, 108, 109, 118, 123, 131, 139, 154, 164, 165, 177, 183, 187, 194, 198-99, 203, 208, 217, 226, 227, 230, 239, 245, 249, 264, 278, 307, 310, 311, 345, 353, 355, 365, 367, 371, 376

Kite

Black 15, 27, 28, 30, 31, 32, 33, 36, 39, 40, 41, 44, 46, 47, 48, 49, 50, 52, 53, 55, 59, 61-62, 63, 65, 67, 68, 84, 89, 96, 98, 101, 109, 111, 113, 117, 118-19, 137, 138, 140, 141, 144, 167, 174, 175-76, 180, 181, 182, 183, 186, 187, 192, 198-99, 200, 202, 203, 205, 209, 215, 216, 217, 219-20, 222, 225, 226, 227, 275, 281, 283, 291, 306, 309, 310, 316, 317, 330, 335, 339, 346, 348, 349, 353, 363, 365, 373, 375, 376, 379

Red 16, 33, 41, 45, 47, 48, 49, 50, 51, 52, 53, 54, 59, 67, 89, 109, 113, 117, 118-19, 137, 138, 141, 144, 174, 175-76, 181, 183, 186, 187, 191, 192, 198-99, 202, 203, 209, 216, 222, 283, 286, 310, 336, 339, 349, 363, 374

Kittiwake 15, 35, 76, 80, 85, 89, 240, 242, 253, 260, 268, 316, 317, 376

Knot 15, 73, 80, 84, 185, 255, 274, 286, 288, 289, 310, 311, 315, 352, 375

L

Lammergeier 41, 123, 127, 128-29, 214, 221, 336, 339, 379

Lanner 350

Lapwing 14, 15, 16, 31, 32, 35, 36, 40, 45, 47, 50, 59, 62, 64, 65, 67, 76, 78, 79-80, 81, 90, 99-100, 101, 103, 104-5, 108, 110, 111, 117, 119, 137, 143-44, 145, 161, 164, 187, 193-94, 199, 200, 203, 206, 207, 209, 210, 217, 222, 227, 230, 234-35, 247, 248-49, 259, 269, 275, 276, 277, 279, 281, 283, 286, 288, 290, 291, 295, 300, 307, 309, 311, 319, 320, 321, 324, 349, 363, 371, 377

Lark

Calandra 348, 353

Crested 88, 101, 168, 174, 180, 284, 286, 320, 348, 353

Shore 16, 236, 238, 246-47, 252, 260, 261, 300, 301, 302

Short-toed 64-65, 76, 105, 123, 173, 175, 184, 216, 285, 324, 348, 353

Sky (see Skylark)

Wood (see Woodlark)
Linnet 62, 76, 161, 167, 174, 175-76, 191, 195, 246, 258, 280, 286, 300, 321, 374

M

Mallard 26, 27, 32, 38, 40, 45, 47, 52, 55, 59, 60, 68, 79-80, 82, 89, 91, 96, 100, 102-3, 105, 108, 118-19, 155, 158, 161, 162, 164, 165, 166, 167, 168, 173, 179, 185, 194, 199, 202, 209, 217, 218, 226, 227, 249, 255, 264, 284, 286, 289, 291, 295, 302, 306, 310, 317, 323, 325, 337, 341, 344, 373
Martin
Crag 51-52, 55, 126-27, 135, 142, 176, 181, 183, 192, 216, 224-25, 333, 339, 357, 365, 367, 369
House 15, 45, 51-52, 74, 125, 149, 192, 230, 244-45, 248-49, 302, 333
Sand 44, 45, 64-65, 68, 69, 101, 104-5, 125, 139-40, 161, 163, 230, 264, 269, 274, 284, 289, 310, 335, 336, 365, 371, 376
Merganser, Red-breasted 16, 40, 65, 74, 83-84, 152, 157, 173, 180, 185, 231, 237-38, 241, 243, 252, 257, 258, 274, 281, 284, 295, 300, 302, 308, 310, 315, 316, 317, 335, 344, 346, 353, 376, 378
Merlin 33, 36, 47, 48-49, 61, 63, 65, 76, 78, 100, 137, 138, 173, 181, 199, 203, 206, 210, 216, 222, 245, 254-55, 257, 258, 260, 261, 274, 281, 283, 286, 288, 291, 300, 311, 319, 320, 321, 324, 335, 349, 353, 363
Moorhen 21, 50, 89, 108, 109, 167, 169, 217, 230, 243, 245, 248-49, 284, 307, 325, 328, 338

N

Nightingale 14, 27, 30, 46, 58-59, 88, 90-91, 98, 140, 149, 175, 182, 226, 232, 244-45, 248, 252, 266, 269, 291, 306, 317, 337, 365, 377
Nightjar 37, 46, 53, 54, 60, 74, 97, 98, 125, 131, 141, 154, 159, 191, 195, 216, 219, 266, 267, 275, 280, 282, 283, 306, 318, 321, 324, 346, 355, 357, 365, 374, 376, 377
Nutcracker 25, 52, 135, 332, 336, 337, 339, 362, 369
Nuthatch 16, 22, 88, 97, 114-15, 148-49, 218, 233, 303, 323, 356
Corsican 123, 124, 127-28, 129

O

Oriole, Golden 14, 27, 36, 58-59, 66, 76, 118, 140, 141-42, 149, 154, 199, 203, 218, 225-26, 239, 245, 247, 253, 275, 298, 306, 307, 349, 363, 365, 376, 281209
Osprey 21, 23, 27, 30, 33, 35, 40, 45, 49, 50, 54, 55, 59, 61, 63, 65, 68, 84, 85, 89, 91, 96, 100, 101, 103, 105, 109, 112-13, 117, 118-19, 123, 126-27, 130-31, 137, 138, 140, 142, 143-44, 145, 157, 161, 163, 173, 179, 180, 181, 183, 185, 193, 198-99, 200, 202, 203, 205, 206, 207, 216, 218, 222, 226, 227, 230, 233, 238, 245, 249, 264, 281, 284, 286, 291, 295, 296, 303, 306, 310, 318, 324, 325, 339, 344, 349, 363, 365, 371, 373, 374, 376
Ouzel, Ring 24, 25, 33, 48-49, 52, 55, 76, 90, 135, 154, 167, 183, 216, 221, 238, 242, 257, 280, 310, 321, 332, 333, 336, 367, 370, 373, 377
Owl
Barn 140, 183, 253, 283, 286
Eagle 16, 50, 51, 180, 183, 216, 225, 336, 357, 365, 367, 374
Little 32, 46, 50, 91, 140, 141, 177, 183, 187, 211, 226, 239, 253, 266, 269, 276, 285, 310, 316, 317, 319, 335-36, 346, 347, 357, 374
Long-eared 50, 61-62, 91, 98, 140, 163, 167, 177, 249, 252, 253, 275, 281, 283, 303, 306, 309, 310, 319, 323
Pygmy 336, 337, 339
Scops 123, 124, 131, 176-77, 180, 181, 183, 184, 187, 215, 216, 224, 319, 324, 335, 346, 354, 357, 377
Short-eared 237, 241-42, 253, 255, 268, 279, 281, 283, 286, 300, 311, 314, 319, 335
Tawny 16, 22, 50, 53, 61, 98, 141, 149, 183, 275, 281, 306, 323, 335-36
Tengmalm's 54, 119, 135, 137, 211, 336, 339, 367, 370
Oystercatcher 16, 73, 76, 80, 82, 84, 131, 179, 241, 246-47, 255, 257, 258, 261, 286, 288, 301, 302, 310, 311, 315, 316, 346

P

Partridge
Grey 140, 142, 276, 283
Red-legged 52, 140, 182, 183, 276, 283, 286, 324, 338, 357
Rock 332, 336, 379
Peregrine 24, 25, 26l, 30, 33, 35, 41, 45, 47, 48-49, 52, 55, 60, 61, 63, 69, 76, 79, 99-100, 111-13, 116-17, 124, 126-27, 129, 135, 142, 174, 183, 192, 194, 199, 200, 203, 205, 209, 210, 211, 216, 218, 222, 225, 237, 254-55, 258, 260, 268, 274, 281, 283, 286, 288, 291, 300, 302, 310, 313, 318, 319, 320, 329, 343, 349, 353, 354, 357, 362, 363, 367, 370, 371, 373, 377
Petrel
Leach's 76, 240

Storm 72-73, 76, 79, 237-38, 290, 317
Phalarope
Grey 16, 76, 237, 247, 317
Red-necked 130, 247, 351, 352
Pheasant 140
Pigeon see Woodpigeon
Pintail 26, 27, 35, 40, 59, 80, 82, 83, 89, 91, 96, 100, 102, 108, 110, 112-13, 131, 153, 173, 179, 181, 185, 186, 203, 205, 207, 217, 227, 230-31, 245, 249, 261, 274, 275, 277, 284, 286, 288, 291, 295, 298, 302, 306, 310, 315, 317, 319, 325, 328, 371
Pipit
Meadow 24, 25, 41, 53, 54, 55, 78, 79, 99-100, 110, 118, 137, 167, 191, 195, 199, 207, 210, 241, 255, 258, 278, 286, 295, 309, 311, 318, 323, 338, 339, 373, 374
Red-throated 15, 47, 124-25, 142, 175, 185, 200, 203, 209, 379
Richard's 76, 78, 85
Rock 73, 74, 79, 257, 258, 268, 300, 309, 310, 311
Tawny 53, 78, 97, 98, 123, 142, 154, 174, 175, 176, 180, 182, 184, 200, 224, 241, 283, 286, 289, 310, 311, 313, 314, 315, 320, 324, 330, 338, 348, 353, 355, 357, 365, 367, 377
Tree 25, 37, 53, 55, 61, 78, 141-42, 158, 191, 195, 215, 219, 241, 280, 281, 283, 303, 310, 321, 324, 339, 357, 365, 370, 373
Water 24, 25, 27, 48-49, 52, 55, 59, 68, 99-100, 103, 109, 117, 118, 123, 127-28, 129, 135, 181, 194, 199, 203, 214, 216, 218, 221, 226, 278, 282, 286, 307, 318, 328, 332, 334, 335, 337, 338, 339, 365, 367, 369, 373, 379
Plover
Golden 14, 16, 31, 32, 34, 47, 80, 99-100, 101, 110, 112-13, 117, 144, 145, 161, 164, 177, 187, 199, 203, 207, 210, 227, 275, 276, 277, 281, 283, 288, 291, 301, 311, 318, 319, 320, 324, 349, 353
Grey 15, 16, 62, 80, 84, 113, 117, 131, 172, 179, 199, 203, 257, 258, 259, 261, 274, 286, 288, 301, 310, 311, 315, 316, 352
Kentish 15, 74, 78, 80, 84, 172, 175, 179, 181, 237-38, 246-47, 255, 272, 289, 300, 301, 309, 310, 313, 315, 343, 345, 352, 379
Little Ringed 44, 45, 46, 61-62, 64-65, 68, 89, 91, 94, 101, 104-5, 108, 113, 117, 119, 123, 124, 137, 139, 140, 145, 155, 164, 165, 167, 169, 200, 215, 225-26, 230, 238, 246-47, 252, 255, 264, 275, 281, 283, 284, 289, 295, 300, 309, 310, 318, 338, 345, 349, 365, 371, 374, 379
Ringed 61, 74, 76, 78, 80, 82, 83-84, 89, 113, 117, 124, 137, 166, 173, 178, 186, 199, 200, 215, 230, 237-38, 245, 246-47, 252, 257, 258, 274, 275, 277, 281, 283, 286, 288, 289, 299, 300, 301, 310, 311, 314, 316, 345, 352, 379
Pochard 20, 21, 26, 27, 30, 38, 40, 59, 60, 64-65, 66, 68, 78, 88-89, 91, 96, 100, 101, 102-3, 108, 111, 113, 117, 118, 131, 136-37, 144, 149, 155, 158, 161, 162, 163, 164, 165, 166, 167, 168, 169, 173, 179, 185, 186, 194, 199, 200, 202, 204, 209, 210, 217, 226-27, 230-31, 245, 247, 249, 264, 275, 284, 295, 296, 300, 302, 306, 307, 314, 317, 319, 325, 328, 337, 341, 343, 349, 369, 373, 374, 376, 378
Red-crested 21, 23, 59, 60, 94, 113, 131, 136-37, 150, 179, 181, 186, 209, 210, 215, 227, 299, 306, 341, 343, 344, 349, 361, 371, 373, 375, 376
Pratincole, Collared 131, 177, 185, 341, 343, 345
Ptarmigan 15, 214, 332, 334, 369
Puffin 72-73

Q

Quail 53, 64, 65, 140, 176, 191, 207, 253, 255, 277, 283, 286, 324, 329, 330, 353, 373, 377

R

Rail
Water 20, 21, 47, 52, 59, 92, 96, 99, 100, 103, 109, 115, 123, 140, 145, 167, 177, 185, 194, 198-99, 202, 205, 206, 218, 230, 245, 249, 276, 279, 289, 296, 307, 330, 335, 337, 345, 370, 376
Raven 25, 49, 51, 52, 55, 73, 74, 80, 84, 127-28, 135, 137, 142, 174, 182, 183, 214, 215, 216, 224-25, 255, 257, 333, 338, 357, 362, 365, 367, 368, 369, 373, 377, 379
Razorbill 35, 73, 74, 76, 173, 185, 238, 243, 253, 255, 258, 268, 290, 302, 316, 317, 342, 346, 350, 351
Redpoll 15, 90, 92, 114-15, 136, 166, 167, 232, 280, 307
Lesser 332
Redshank 14, 32, 76, 80, 82, 84, 85, 89, 99, 108, 110, 119, 161, 163, 164, 178, 181, 185, 199, 202, 246-47, 252, 257, 259, 274, 275, 286, 288, 290, 291, 299, 302, 309, 310, 311, 352, 370, 371
Spotted 30, 80, 89, 96, 111, 117, 119, 144, 181, 185, 227, 274, 286, 310, 311, 352, 370
Redstart 76, 125, 149, 154, 156, 192, 211, 253, 269, 275, 283, 296, 298, 303, 306, 310, 317, 323, 354
Black 74, 76, 214, 221, 258,

268, 307, 318, 332, 333, 337, 373
Redwing 15, 32, 36, 53, 59, 92, 101, 115, 149, 166, 167, 195, 203, 209
Robin 16, 125, 131, 149
Roller 125, 177, 179, 180, 181, 187, 330, 343, 346, 347, 349, 350, 355
Rook 16, 88, 324
Ruff 14, 32, 80, 89, 110, 117, 145, 185, 193, 199, 202, 207, 210, 222, 226, 230, 275, 277, 283, 286, 291, 311, 352, 370, 379

S

Sanderling 15, 62, 74, 77, 78, 80, 83-84, 185, 237-38, 286, 310, 311, 316, 375
Sandgrouse, Pin-tailed 347, 349, 350
Sandpiper
Baird's 247
Broad-billed 66, 247, 351
Buff-breasted 15, 297, 317
Common 20, 21, 26, 27, 46, 51-52, 55, 61-62, 64, 68, 69, 80, 89, 91, 104, 108, 109, 117, 118-19, 124, 139, 140, 157, 161, 162, 163, 164, 168, 183, 186, 226, 243, 249, 281, 286, 307, 325, 333, 352, 365, 371, 374, 379
Curlew 62, 117, 137, 185, 274, 286, 289, 310, 312, 375
Green 15, 20, 21, 89, 96, 163, 226, 274, 281, 286, 295, 318, 333, 365
Marsh 66, 130, 177, 185, 247, 281, 310, 317, 345, 349, 352, 361
Pectoral 15, 66, 247, 317
Purple 73, 76, 78, 80, 256, 258, 261, 290, 310, 316, 317
Terek 130, 247
Wood 89, 124, 131, 163, 186, 227, 274, 281, 286, 352, 379
Scaup 23, 59, 60, 78, 81-82, 89, 108, 168, 194, 204, 210, 231, 264, 296, 300, 306, 349, 369, 376, 378
Scoter
Common 16, 73, 82, 118, 158, 168, 169, 238, 241, 243, 255, 258, 268, 272, 286, 302, 315, 316, 342, 344, 346, 350, 351, 378
Velvet 16, 111-13, 118, 158, 168, 169, 194, 204, 210, 238, 241, 243, 255, 258, 268, 272, 284, 302, 315, 325, 342, 344, 346, 350, 351, 369, 375, 376, 378
Serin 167, 174, 328, 333
Shag 73, 76, 80, 84, 174, 238, 252, 255, 257, 258
Mediterranean race 122-23, 124, 126-27
Shearwater
Balearic 33, 73, 76, 82, 185, 237-38, 243, 255, 260, 274, 285, 290, 315, 316-17
Cory's 33, 76, 122-23, 124, 290, 315, 354
Great 76, 290
Manx 72-73, 76, 237-38, 240, 243, 260, 273
Sooty 76, 237-38, 240, 243, 260, 273, 290
Yelkouan 122-23, 124, 337, 354
Shelduck 21, 30, 33, 59, 60, 61, 73, 80, 82, 83-84, 85, 103, 112-13, 117, 118, 144, 169, 175, 180, 181, 194, 200, 217, 230, 243, 247, 249, 252, 254-55, 257, 258, 259, 274, 283, 284, 286, 288, 290, 300, 301, 302, 310, 319, 325, 328, 342, 345, 353, 369
Shoveler 30, 32, 35, 40, 59, 78, 82, 83, 89, 91, 96, 102-3, 108, 110, 112-13, 118, 131, 136-37, 158, 161, 162, 164, 173, 179, 181, 185, 186, 194, 200, 205, 207, 209, 217, 226-27, 230-31, 245, 247, 249, 264, 275, 284, 286, 288, 291, 295, 299, 300, 302, 306, 310, 315, 317, 319, 325, 337, 344, 365, 371, 373
Shrike
Great Grey 50, 52, 53, 54, 58- 59, 96, 119, 137, 153, 203, 206, 207, 209, 210, 234-35, 253, 282, 362, 372
Lesser Grey 347
Red-backed 23, 31, 32, 44, 46, 50, 52, 53, 59, 61-62, 64, 66, 76, 90, 94, 96, 97, 98, 115, 116, 117, 119, 123, 140, 152-53, 155, 174, 175-77, 182, 199, 218, 219, 223, 225, 234-35, 253, 266, 269, 280, 282, 296, 298, 310, 312, 317, 319, 329, 336, 338, 355, 357, 368, 374, 375
Southern Grey 172-73, 175, 177, 180, 182, 329, 330, 348, 355, 357, 365
Woodchat 36, 46, 66, 90, 96, 119, 123, 173, 175, 177, 180, 182, 211, 218, 310, 317, 329, 330, 338, 354, 357, 365
Silverbill, Indian 338
Siskin 15, 49, 52, 59, 76, 89, 90, 92, 100, 114-15, 124, 131, 149, 166, 169, 178, 203, 209, 221, 232, 249, 307, 333, 339, 365, 373
Skua
Arctic 76, 82, 240, 243, 252, 260, 274, 285, 301, 316
Great 76, 82, 240, 243, 252, 260, 274, 285, 316
Long-tailed 237, 240, 243, 260, 342
Pomarine 76, 82, 240, 243, 260, 273, 316
Skylark 41, 62, 64, 65, 101, 110, 135, 167, 184, 199, 246, 255, 278, 286, 319, 330, 348, 353, 363, 373, 377
Smew 16, 59, 65, 68, 92, 101, 102, 104-5, 108, 112-13, 117, 118, 168, 201, 203, 204, 206, 209, 210, 231, 264, 276, 289, 306, 375, 376, 378
Snipe 14, 20, 21, 27, 31, 32, 36, 40, 47, 59, 62, 68, 76, 80, 90, 92, 96, 99-100, 103, 105, 110, 111-12, 117, 137, 143-44, 161, 164, 177, 191, 195, 198-99, 200, 206, 209, 210, 217, 218, 225-26, 230,

243, 248-49, 260, 269, 276, 277, 282, 283, 289, 291, 295, 302, 307, 310, 311, 314, 321, 324, 328, 349, 370
Jack 31, 36, 80, 110, 145, 199, 200, 206, 210, 225-26, 280, 297, 310, 311, 321, 324, 349
Sparrow
Italian 122-23
Rock 180, 181, 183, 184, 215, 216, 357
Spanish 122
Tree 110, 177, 269, 295, 364
Sparrowhawk 15, 22, 24, 35, 36, 41, 44, 48-49, 52, 53, 59, 60, 63, 67, 76, 92, 98, 100, 104-5, 113, 114-15, 119, 124, 127-28, 129, 131, 135, 138, 141, 149, 154, 156, 164, 167, 180, 182, 183, 187, 191, 192, 195, 202, 205, 219-20, 223-24, 231, 233, 234-35, 245, 248-49, 266, 275, 281, 286, 300, 303, 306, 317, 323, 336, 339, 373, 374
Spoonbill 30, 33, 34, 35, 40, 83-84, 85, 99-100, 131, 158, 222, 230, 237, 243, 246-47, 260, 261, 268, 274, 282, 283, 286, 289, 291, 301, 310, 316, 328
Starling 16, 49, 110, 139-40, 302, 339, 363
Rose-coloured 247
Spotless 122-23, 345
Stilt, Black-winged 15, 34, 40, 84, 85, 131, 163, 173, 177, 178-79, 180, 181, 185, 215, 226, 247, 274, 290, 291, 309, 310, 316, 341, 343, 345, 349, 352
Stint
Little 62, 104, 112-13, 131, 137, 161, 185, 274, 286, 289, 311, 352-53, 375, 379
Temminck's 62, 137, 177, 247, 281, 283, 286, 297, 299, 310, 311, 317, 349, 352, 361, 375, 376
Stone Curlew 44, 45, 55, 61-62, 64-65, 89, 104-5, 139, 140, 159, 163, 184, 216, 242, 264, 265-66, 276, 283, 319, 320, 324, 330, 347, 353, 357, 371, 373, 374, 377
Stonechat 52, 61-62, 97, 100, 115, 117, 140, 149, 154, 167, 182, 195, 199, 210, 241, 253, 257, 280, 286, 301, 307, 318, 321, 328, 330
Stork
Black 15, 40, 45, 53, 89, 90, 100, 109, 111, 113, 119, 124, 137, 138, 145, 173, 174, 181, 187, 193, 199, 202, 203, 206, 207, 209, 216, 218, 222, 235, 286, 291, 301, 318, 335, 336, 339, 361, 363, 365, 371, 373, 379
White 15, 31, 32, 33, 35, 36, 40, 45, 47, 66, 68, 89, 90, 119, 124, 137, 138, 173, 174, 181, 187, 203, 206, 207, 208, 209, 216, 218, 222, 253, 260, 269, 274, 283, 291, 298, 301, 310, 314, 335, 336, 339, 350, 361, 363, 371
Swallow 15, 41, 89, 91, 100, 149, 161, 173, 230, 244-45, 248-49, 274, 335, 336
Red-rumped 15, 123, 124-25, 174, 178-79, 180, 181, 338, 343, 349, 355
Swan
Bewick's 66, 111-13, 117, 203, 209, 237, 276, 341, 363
Mute 20, 21, 25, 27, 30, 59, 65, 66, 84, 88, 108, 117, 136-37, 155, 165, 209, 210, 245, 248-49, 276, 295, 344
Whooper 66, 76, 117, 145, 209, 210, 235, 276
Swift 14, 15, 27, 49, 91, 100, 124, 161, 162, 164, 167, 168, 173, 174, 179, 209, 230, 233, 244-45, 249, 295, 298, 310, 315, 339, 363, 373
Alpine 51-52, 123, 124, 126-27, 129, 142, 176, 182, 183, 216, 224, 225, 329, 333, 339, 357, 365, 367
Pallid 123, 124, 126-27, 339
White-rumped 124

T

Teal 27, 32, 35, 40, 45, 47, 52, 55, 59, 68, 78, 80, 82, 83, 89, 91, 96, 100, 102-3, 105, 108, 110, 113, 118, 131, 136-37, 143-44, 145, 155, 158, 161, 162, 164, 165, 173, 174, 179, 181, 186, 194, 198-99, 202, 206, 209, 217, 218, 222, 226-27, 234, 242, 245, 247, 249, 252, 255, 261, 274, 286, 289, 291, 295, 302, 306, 307, 310, 317, 319, 325, 328, 337, 338, 341, 344, 349, 369
Tern
Arctic 79, 240, 281, 286, 301, 317, 376
Black 21, 23, 47, 59, 61-62, 64, 66, 78, 89, 91, 94, 96, 101, 103, 108, 109, 111, 113, 117, 131, 137, 145, 161, 162, 164, 177, 179, 181, 194, 199, 200, 202, 203, 205, 218, 226, 227, 230, 244-45, 248-49, 252, 279, 281, 283, 284, 289, 291, 295, 296, 299-300, 303, 317-18, 328, 338, 341, 344, 352, 353, 361, 376, 379
Caspian 179, 281, 286, 345
Common 21, 23, 44, 45, 55, 61, 63, 64-65, 66, 68-69, 73, 74, 78, 84, 89, 99-100, 101, 104-5, 108, 111, 113, 116-17, 139-40, 144, 145, 150-53, 155, 161, 163, 164, 179, 194, 199, 200-201, 205, 227, 230, 240, 247, 249, 258, 264, 274, 279, 281, 284, 286, 288, 290, 295, 297, 301, 309, 315, 318, 338, 343, 345, 349, 352, 353, 362, 371, 374, 376, 379
Gull-billed 341, 343, 376
Little 44, 45, 61-63, 64, 66, 74, 78, 89, 101, 104-5, 150-51, 179, 181, 185, 230, 237-38, 247, 279, 286, 301, 343, 345, 352, 353, 374
Roseate 83-84
Sandwich 33-34, 78, 82, 130-31, 179, 245, 247, 256, 258, 274, 281, 286, 288, 301,

Species index

308, 310, 315, 316, 338, 343, 345, 376
Whiskered 47, 50, 59, 62, 64, 66, 89, 94, 96, 98, 101, 102-3, 113, 137, 164, 177, 179, 181, 194, 199, 200, 202, 205, 209, 218, 226, 279, 281, 284, 299-300, 317, 338, 341, 344, 352, 353, 361, 373, 376
White-winged Black 62, 66, 131, 137, 177, 179, 181, 205, 209, 317, 338, 341, 344, 352, 361, 376
Thrush
Mistle 31, 49, 53, 59, 129, 141, 218-19, 248, 332, 333, 339, 363
Rock 15, 25, 49, 52, 55, 174, 175, 176, 180, 183, 184, 214, 332, 335, 336, 338, 365, 369, 373, 379
Blue 123, 124, 126-27, 128, 174, 176, 180, 181, 183, 329, 330, 357, 365
Song 14, 16, 27, 32, 53, 59, 141, 195, 306, 339
Tit
Bearded 36, 77-78, 84, 173, 177, 179, 181, 185, 232, 234, 241, 254-55, 259, 268, 289, 298, 300, 314, 343, 345, 349, 350
Blue 97, 98
Coal 16, 24, 52, 53, 55, 60, 97, 123, 124, 127-28, 129, 141, 167, 191, 219, 221, 235, 275, 280, 322-23, 332, 333, 339, 369, 372
Crested 16, 24, 52, 53, 60, 97, 98, 141, 167, 191, 211, 216, 219, 221, 235, 275, 280, 322-23, 333, 339, 369, 372, 373
Great 129
Long-tailed 129, 148, 323
Marsh 98, 219, 224, 227, 275, 280, 372
Penduline 23, 36, 40, 131, 137, 167, 173, 177, 179, 181, 185, 198-99, 200-201, 205, 210, 226, 289, 312, 314, 328, 338, 341, 349, 361, 362, 365, 376
Willow 22, 65, 158, 244, 280, 298, 332, 333, 339, 367, 371
Treecreeper
Common 16, 54, 55, 124, 127-28, 129, 135, 199, 202, 203, 209, 211, 221, 267, 296, 332, 336, 365, 377
Short-toed 16, 22, 33, 58, 88, 97, 114-15, 124, 149, 177, 199, 202, 203, 209, 219, 224, 226, 233, 248, 267, 280, 302, 323
Turnstone 15, 73, 74, 78, 80, 82, 83-84, 131, 252, 257, 258, 286, 310, 311, 316, 352
Twite 236, 246, 300, 302

V

Vulture
Black 182-83, 215, 216, 368
Egyptian 41, 183, 215, 216, 329, 348, 349, 350, 357, 368
Griffon 41, 182-83, 215, 216, 221, 329, 368

W

Wagtail
Blue-headed 30, 32, 44, 47, 65, 80, 84, 137, 140, 142, 143-44, 185, 193-94, 199, 200-201, 203, 205, 207, 210, 226, 253, 255, 259, 260, 269, 275-76, 277, 279, 282, 283, 286, 288, 310, 313, 317, 343, 365, 371
Grey 52, 69, 98, 99-100, 109, 141, 203, 221, 234, 328, 339, 369, 374
Pied 238, 283
White 27, 44, 47, 53, 65, 99-100, 110, 140, 253, 258, 328, 339, 363
Yellow 64, 65, 78, 88, 110, 124, 137, 157, 179, 238, 241, 269, 277, 283, 288, 295
Wallcreeper 15, 51-52, 55, 60, 124, 129, 135, 174, 176-77, 182, 183, 215, 216, 221, 224-25, 329, 333, 335, 339, 357, 361, 365, 367, 369, 370, 374, 379
Warbler
Aquatic 77-78, 179, 274, 289
Bonelli's 46, 53-54, 60, 98, 135, 142, 153, 174, 184, 195, 220, 223, 224, 225, 275, 283, 306, 318, 323, 331, 332, 336, 354, 357
Cetti's 32, 44, 76, 78, 80, 93, 96, 123, 131, 161, 177, 227, 242-43, 248, 252, 264, 269, 274, 281, 284, 291, 295, 303, 307, 324, 328, 330, 337, 365, 376
Dartford 37, 76, 78, 80, 84, 98, 122-23, 126-27, 153-54, 172, 174, 180, 182, 216, 224, 253, 255, 257, 275, 280, 283, 311, 318, 320-21, 329, 330, 338, 339, 346, 357, 365, 368
Fan-tailed 30, 32, 78, 79-80, 82, 84, 90, 93, 96, 131, 180, 253, 259, 273, 278, 287, 301, 310, 313, 353, 365
Garden 65, 88, 104, 125, 148-49, 158, 161, 226, 275, 282, 283, 310, 317, 332
Grasshopper 46, 62, 65, 80, 90, 98, 103, 104, 109, 125, 137, 139-40, 145, 155, 162, 179, 194, 199, 201, 205, 209, 226, 235, 241, 249, 253, 257, 269, 278, 280, 283, 289, 296, 298, 303, 321, 324
Great Reed 59, 64-65, 96, 123, 125, 131, 139-40, 145, 179, 181, 198-99, 200-201, 205, 206, 209, 226, 243, 245, 314, 317, 335, 337, 343, 346, 349, 357, 361, 370
Icterine 15, 21, 22, 76, 88, 125, 239, 247, 338
Marmora's 122-23, 126-27, 129
Marsh 15, 22, 136-37, 165, 167, 198-99, 200-201, 202, 206, 209, 239, 243, 247, 248-49, 253, 264, 269, 281, 296, 298, 335, 336, 343, 362
Melodious 44, 49, 76, 88, 91, 104, 140, 141-42, 149, 219, 226, 234, 255, 266, 282, 286, 296, 303, 317,

338, 349, 353, 371, 374, 376, 377

Moustached 131, 173, 177, 179, 181, 185, 343, 345, 349, 350

Orphean 174, 175, 180, 182, 216, 329, 357

Pallas's 85, 239

Reed 15, 32, 46, 49, 59, 64-65, 77-78, 80, 84, 88-89, 90, 96, 99, 100, 102-3, 109, 123, 125, 131, 136-37, 139-40, 145, 153, 161, 167, 168, 179, 185, 194, 198-99, 205, 209, 226, 243, 248-49, 264, 269, 274, 278, 281, 284, 289, 295, 296, 303, 307, 314, 324, 335, 336, 337, 343, 346, 349, 361, 362, 370, 371, 376

Sardinian 14, 122-23, 126-27, 129, 172, 174, 176, 180, 182, 328, 329, 330, 338, 339, 346, 357, 377

Savi's 15, 59, 76, 93, 96, 109, 117, 145, 179, 185, 199, 200-201, 203, 209, 244-45, 248-49, 268, 274, 289, 296, 303, 314, 317, 335, 350

Sedge 15, 32, 59, 77-78, 84, 90, 93, 99, 102-3, 124, 137, 140, 143-44, 145, 155, 161, 179, 185, 194, 198-99, 203, 205, 209, 226, 249, 253, 274, 278, 281, 284, 289, 291, 296, 303, 307, 314, 317, 324, 336, 349

Spectacled 174, 180, 330, 342, 343, 346, 354

Subalpine 126-27, 172, 174, 176, 180, 182, 183, 216, 224, 225, 329, 338, 346, 354, 357, 367, 368

Willow 53-54, 60, 61-62, 76, 91, 114-15, 124, 148-49, 153, 158, 167, 195, 226, 232, 274, 280, 282, 283, 306, 318, 321, 336, 354, 373

Wood 46, 53-54, 60, 98, 114-15, 119, 125, 135, 142, 153, 158, 195, 200, 202, 224, 235, 275, 280, 281, 283, 296, 298, 303, 306, 318, 323, 336, 375

Yellow-browed 16, 76, 85, 239

Wheatear 24, 25, 47, 48, 50, 52, 62, 76, 77, 80, 90, 135, 137, 142, 154, 167, 176, 184, 198-99, 214, 221, 242, 257, 280, 282, 283, 286, 288, 300, 310, 314, 317, 320, 321, 332, 333, 337, 338, 354, 368, 369, 373, 377

Black-eared 15, 172-73, 176, 180, 182, 184, 357

Whimbrel 80, 82, 131, 137, 144, 185, 286, 288, 291, 299, 310, 345, 353

Whinchat 47, 49, 50, 52, 54, 64, 65, 76, 90, 101, 110, 115, 143-44, 154, 167, 190-91, 199, 202, 207, 210, 253, 260, 269, 276, 278, 282, 283, 286, 298, 310, 314, 317, 321, 333, 335, 354, 373

Whitethroat 30, 65, 88, 98, 100, 104, 125, 140, 149, 161, 165, 167, 176, 182, 248, 253, 255, 275, 280, 282, 286, 310, 317, 332, 338, 368, 371, 377

Lesser 65, 76, 90-91, 140, 152, 161, 167, 199, 205, 234-35, 239, 249, 253, 255, 266, 296, 298

Wigeon 26, 27, 30, 35, 40, 59, 78, 80, 83, 89, 91, 96, 100, 108, 112-13, 117, 131, 143, 164, 165, 173, 174, 179, 185, 194, 200, 205, 207, 209, 217, 222, 230-31, 245, 247, 249, 255, 261, 264, 274, 276, 279, 284, 286, 288, 291, 302, 306, 310, 317, 319, 325, 328, 341, 371

American 247

Woodcock 16, 52, 76, 97, 135, 136, 154, 167, 195, 202, 211, 223-24, 233, 235, 267, 280, 283, 296, 323, 373

Woodlark 39, 44, 53, 61-62, 119, 123, 154, 159, 174, 176, 182, 184, 211, 216, 219, 323, 353, 357, 365

Woodpecker

Black 21, 22, 24, 25, 26, 46, 52, 54, 55, 59, 65, 97, 98, 113, 114-15, 119, 135, 137, 141, 155, 156-57, 195, 199, 200-201, 202, 205, 209, 211, 215, 216, 221, 233, 235, 266-67, 275, 283, 296, 298, 303, 306, 318, 323, 332, 339, 362, 365, 367, 369, 370, 373, 377

Great Spotted 21, 22, 26, 46, 54, 55, 59, 61, 65, 98, 124, 129, 131, 141, 148-49, 155, 156, 167, 199, 200-201, 202, 209, 219, 230, 233, 275, 283, 303, 306, 323, 332, 339

Green 21, 26, 46, 59, 61, 65, 141, 149, 155, 156, 167, 199, 200-201, 202, 209, 219, 230, 233, 249, 266, 275, 283, 303, 306, 323

Grey-headed 21, 26, 46, 59, 65, 113, 119, 145, 199, 200-201, 202, 209, 211, 283, 306

Lesser Spotted 21, 22, 26, 46, 54, 55, 59, 61-62, 65, 98, 116, 140, 149, 155, 156, 167, 199, 200-201, 202, 205, 209, 219, 225, 235, 275, 281, 283, 303, 306, 307, 323, 355, 365

Middle Spotted 21, 22, 26, 46, 55, 59, 97, 98, 113, 114-15, 119, 141-42, 145, 155, 156-57, 199, 200-201, 202, 203, 205, 206, 208-9, 218, 223-24, 235, 266, 275, 281, 283, 295, 298, 306, 323, 375

Woodpigeon 32, 40, 41, 45, 49, 54, 59, 138, 141, 174, 203, 209, 303, 339, 363, 373

Wryneck 76, 115, 140, 159, 199, 211, 215, 295, 310, 338, 357, 370

Y

Yellowhammer 52, 59, 62, 90, 98, 117, 191, 195, 253, 255, 275, 317, 335, 336, 365, 370

Yellowlegs, Lesser 66, 247

Site Index

A

Adour (barthes de l') [40], 35-36
Agon-Coutainville (dunes de -) [50], 259
Aigle (barrage de l') [19], 192
Aiguillon (baie de l') [85], 284-286
Aiguillon [47], 38-39
Ailette (plan d'eau de l') [02], 294-295
Ain [01], 360-363
Aisne [02], 294-295, 297-298
Aisne, en amont et en aval d'Attigny (vallée de l') [08], 110
Aitone/Évisa (forêt d') [2A], 123-124
Albatre (falaises de la Côte d') [76], 267-268
Allier (val d') [63], 54-55
Allier [03], 44-46
Allier (river) [18], 89
Alpes-de-Haute-Provence [04], 328-330
Alpes-Maritimes [06], 337-339
Alsace, 18-27
Amagne [08], 109-110
Ambly-Fleury [08], 110
Amel (étang d') [55], 206
Ancenis [44], 275
Andelys (boucle des -) [27], 265-266
Andlau (bruch de l'-) [67], 22
Angers (lac de Maine) [49], 278-279
Anneville [76], 269
Anthy-sur-Léman [74], 377-378
Apremont-sur-Allier [18], 89
Aquitaine, 28-41
Arbigny [01], 363
Arche à Chémery (étang de l') [41], 103-104
Ardèche [07], 52, 363-366
Ardennes [08], 108-110
Argenton-sur-Creuse [36], 98
Argonne (étangs d') [51], 117
Ariège [09], 214-215
Arjuzanx [40], 36
Arme (col de l') [06], 339
Armentières [59], 230-231
Arre/Le Vigan (L') [30], 177-178
Ars (Fier d') [17], 307-310
Artix (Réserve de chasse du lac d') [64], 39-40
Asco [2B], 127-128
Aste-Béon [64], 41
Attigny [08], 109
Aube (réservoir -) [10], 111- 113
Aube [10], 110-113
Auberive (forêt d') [52], 119
Aude [11], 172-175, 180-181
Audenge [33], 30
Ault (falaises d') [80], 302
Ault (Réserve nationale de chasse du Hâble d') [80], 298-300
Aumelas (causse d') [34], 180
Aumône à Mantes-la-Jolie (île -) [78], 163-164
Auron (lac d') [18], 88-89
Auvergne, 42-55
Avaloirs (mont des -) [53], 279-280
Aveyron (gorges de l') [81/82], 224-225
Aveyron [12], 215-218
Axin (étang d') [57], 211
Ayes (Réserve biologique forestière du bois des -) [05], 336-337
Ayvelles (ballastières des -) [08], 108

B

Bagatelle (parc de -) [75], 149
Bagnas (étang du -) [34], 178-179
Baillies (prairies des -) [49], 277-278
Bairon (lac de -) [08], 109
Baleines (phare des -) [17], 316-317
Ballots [53], 281
Balloy (plan d'eau de -) [77], 152
Bannac (Réserve naturelle volontaire du lac du moulin de -) [12], 217-218
Barbey (plans d'eau de -) [77], 153
Barcaggio/Ersa [2B], 124-125
Bas-Rebourseaux, Vergigny/Saint-Florentin (lac de -) [89], 67-68
Bas-Rhin [67], 20-23
Bassée (Réserve naturelle de La -) [77], 150-153
Basse-Normandie, 250-261
Bassigny [52], 119
Battoir (étang du -) [69], 377
Baume-les-Messieurs (cirque de -) [39], 142
Bavella/Zonza (col de -) [2A], 123
Baye et Vaux (étangs de -) [58], 63
Bazoches-les-Bray (plan d'eau de -) [77], 153
Bazoches-les-Gallerandes [45], 105
Beauce aux alentours de Pithiviers (La -) [45], 105
Beauguillot (Réserve naturelle de) [50], 261
Beauvoir-sur-Mer (« terrains LPO » au sud de -) [85], 291
Bec de Dore [63], 55
Bellebouche [36], 96-98
Bellebranche (forêt de -) [53], 281-282
Belle-Henriette (lagune de la -) [85], 289-290
Belle-Île [56], 84-85
Bellevaux (forêt de -) [73], 377
Belval-en-Argonne [51], 117
Bercé (forêt de -) [72], 283
Berre (complexe des zones humides de l'étang de -) [13], 343-346
Bessin (falaises du -) [14], 252-253
Bessin (Parc naturel des marais du Cotentin et du -) [50], 260
Bielle-Bilhères [64], 41
Biguglia (étang de -) [2B], 130-131
Billy-sous-Mangiennes [55], 206
Blanc-Nez (cap -) [62], 241-242
Blandas (causse de -) [30], 175-177
Bois-de-Cise (Le -) [80], 302
Boisset [34], 182
Bonifacio et son plateau [2A], 122-123
Bonne Anse (baie de -) [17], 315
Boréon (Le -) [06], 339-340
Bouafles (carrière de -) [27], 266
Boucheries (étangs des -) [85], 289
Bouches-du-Rhône [13], 339-351

Bouconne (forêt de -) [31], 219-220
Boulogne (bois de -) [75], 148-149
Bourges [18], 88-89
Bourgneuf (Réserve maritime de la baie de -) [85], 286-288
Bourgogne, 56-69
Bournazel (étang de -) [12], 217
Bouverans (lac de -) [25], 137-138
Braconne (forêt de la -) [16], 306
Bray-Dunes [59], 239
Brayssou, [47], 38
Brenne (étangs de la -) [36], 92-96
Bretagne, 70-85
Brignogan [29], 78
Briqueville [14], 253
Brittany, 70-85
Brocottes [14], 253
Brotonne (forêt de -) [27], 266-267
Brouage (marais de) [17], 316
Bruges (Réserve naturelle des marais de -) [33], 30-32
Bruniquel [82], 224
Bruyères-le-Châtel (bassin de retenue de -) [91], 165

C

Calern (plateau de -) [06], 338
Calvados [14], 252-253
Camargue et alentours (Réserve nationale de -) [13], 339-343
Cambounet-sur-le-Sor (Réserve naturelle de -) [81], 225-226
Campet (forêt de -) [47], 37-38
Campignol (étang de -) [11], 172-173)
Canche (baie de -) [62], 249
Canet (étang de -) [66], 184-185
Cannes-Écluse (plan d'eau de -) [77], 152
Cantal [15], 46-50
Cap Ferret (pointe du -) [33], 33-34
Capbreton (port de -) [40], 34-35
Cap-Sizun [29], 80
Captieux [40], 36
Cardeilhac (forêt de la -) [31], 218-219
Carolles (falaises de -) [50], 253-255
Cattenom (lac et forêt de -) [57], 209
Causse Rouge [12], 216
Caussols et plateau de Calern [06], 338-339
Cayeux (Bas-Champs de -) [80], 298-300
Cébron (lac du) [79], 317-318
Celle-sur-Loire (La -) [58], 62
Centre, 86-105
Cergy-Neuville (étangs de -) [95], 169
Certes (domaine de -) [33], 30
Cévennes/Saint-Pierre-des-Tripiers et Le Rozier (Réserve de la biosphère du Parc national des -) [48], 182-183
Ceyzériat [01], 361
Champagne-Ardenne, 106-119
Chamrousse [38], 368-369
Chanfroy/massif des Trois-Pignons (Réserve biologique de la plaine de -) [77], 153-154
Chapelle-aux Naux (La -) [37], 101
Chapelle-sur-Loire (La -) [37], 101
Chardonnière (pointe de -) [17], 316
Charente [16], 306-307
Charente-Maritime [17], 307-317
Charette-Varenne [71], 64-65
Charité-sur-Loire (La -) [58], 62
Charmant Som (le tour -) [38], 370
Charmont-en-Beauce [45], 105
Charmoy [71], 67
Chassagny [69], 377
Chassiron (pointe de -) [17], 315
Châtel-de-Neuvre [03], 44
Châtillon-le-Roi [45], 105
Chaucre (pointe de -) [17], 316
Chaudefour (vallée de -) [63], 55
Chaume (La -) [85], 290
Chaussée-Tirancourt (La -) [80], 303
Cheire d'Aydrat [63], 54
Chémery [41], 104
Cher [18], 60-63, 88-90
Chevais (landes de -) [79], 318-319
Chiers et zone de confluence avec la Meuse (vallée de la -) [08], 110
Chingoudy/Hendaye (baie de -) [64], 40
Cité des Oiseaux [85], 289
Clairmarais [62], 247-248
Clapeyto (chalets de -) [05], 334
Combourg (étang de -) [86], 324
Compiègne (forêt domaniale de -) [60], 295-296
Compiègne [60], 296-297
Conches (Les -) [01], 361
Confluent/Aiguillon (pays du -) [40], 38-39
Conie (vallée de la -) [28], 92
Contres (marais de -) [18], 90
Coqueteaux (Les -) [03], 46
Cormaranche-Hauteville (marais de -) [01], 362
Corneilla del Vercol [66], 187
Corrèze [19], 190-191
Corse 120-131
Corse-du-Sud [2A], 122-124
Corsept (vasière de -) [44], 275
Corsica 120-131
Côte-d'Or [21], 58-60
Cotentin et du Bessin (Parc naturel des marais du -) [50], 260
Côtes-d'Armor [22], 72-74
Cotinière (La -) [17], 316
Coudrée/Lac Léman (golfe de -) [74], 377-379
Courcelles (carrière de -) [27], 266
Courcelles-en-Bassée [7], 152
Courneuve (Parc départemental de La -) [93], 167
Couyrac [81], 224
Crabec (anse de -) [50], 261
Cragous (Réserve des -) [29], 81
Crau (plaine de la -) [13], 347-349
Crécy-en-Ponthieu (forêt de -) [80], 303

Créteil (lac de -) [94], 168
Creuse (val de -) [36], 98
Creuse [23], 192-194
Croisic (traicts du -) [44], 272-274
Cuiron (roches de -) [01], 361
Curécy (étang de -) [53], 281-282
Cussac [15], 46-47

D

Dauges (Réserve naturelle de la tourbière des -) [87], 194-195
Der-Chantecoq et les étangs d'Outines et d'Arrigny (lac du) [51], 115-117
Desnes (sablières de -) [39], 142-143
Deux-Sèvres [79], 317-320
Dijon [21], 60
Dives (marais de la -) [14], 253
Dombes (La -) [01], 360-361
Dômes (chaîne des -) [63], 54
Doran (alpage de -) [74], 379
Dordives [77], 156
Dordogne (gorges de la -) [15], 49
Dordogne, entre le barrage de l'Aigle et le site de Saint-Nazaire (gorges de la -) [19], 191-192
Doubs à Charette-Varenne et Pierre-de-Bresse (le -) [71], 64-65
Doubs à Petit-Noir (basse vallée du -) [39], 138-140
Doubs [25], 134-138
Dourbie (gorges de la -) [12], 215-216
Drôme [26], 366-368
Dunkerque (port de -) [59], 235-238
Dunkerque (sites dunaires et zones vertes à l'est de -) [59], 239
Durance et gravières du Puy-Sainte-Réparade [13], 349-350

E

Écluse (défilé de l') [01], 361-362
Écluzelles-Mézières (plan d'eau et marais d') [28], 90-92
Écourt-Saint-Quentin (étangs et marais de -) [62], 243-245
Écrins (Parc national des -) [05], 331-332
Éguzon [36], 98
Engeville [45], 105
Épense [51], 117
Épisy (marais d') [77], 155-156
Ersa [2B], 124
Erstein (forêt d') [67], 22-23
Escale (lac de l') [04], 328
Escarcets (lac des -) [83], 355
Escrinet (col de l') [07], 363
Espinouse [04], 329
Essonne [91], 164-166
Étang-Vieux de Saclay (Réserve naturelle de l') [91], 164
Étournel (marais fluvial de l') [01], 362
Eure [27], 264-267
Eure-et-Loir [28], 90-92
Excenevex [74], 378
Eyne [66], 186-187
Ézerville [45], 105

F

Falkenstein (château de -) [88/57], 211
Fango/Galeria et Manso (vallée du -) [2B], 131
Faverois [90], 145
Ferté-sur-Chiers (La -) [08], 110
Fief d'Arblincourt [02], 298
Finistère [29], 74-81
Fleury-la-Tour (étang de -) [58], 63
Flicourt à Guernes (domaine régional de -) [78], 163
Fontainebleau (forêt de -) [77], 156-157
Font-de-l'Orme [84], 357
Forez (écopôle du -) [42], 370-371
Forez (étangs du -) [42], 373-374
Forez (monts du - [42], 371-373
Franche-Comté, 132-145
Frasne (petit étang et Réserve naturelle de -) [25], 135-137
Fréhel (cap) [22], 73-74

G

Galeria [2B], 131
Ganne, Brayssou (lacs de retinues collinaires) [47], 38
Gard [30], 175-178
Gattemare (cordon dunaire de -) [50], 261
Gatteville (phare de -) [50], 260-261
Gavarnie (cirque de -) [65], 221
Gâvre (forêt du -) [44], 275
Gelucourt (étang de -) [57], 211
Gevrey-Chambertin [21], 59-60
Gigondas [84], 356
Gironde [33], 30-34
Givry-sur-Aisne [08], 110
Goriaux (mare à -) [59], 232-234
Goulien [29], 80
Goulven (Réserve de chasse de l'anse de -) [29], 78-80
Gourde (lac de la -) [12], 217
Grand Large (bassin du -) [69], 375-376
Grande-Paroisse (plan d'eau de la -) [77], 151
Grand-Montmirail [84], 355-357
Gratte-Bruyère (belvédère de -) [15], 49
Grec (étang du -) [34], 179-180
Grée (marais de -) [44], 275-276
Grésigne (forêt domaniale de -) [81], 222-224
Grigny [91], 165
Gris-Nez (cap -) [62], 240-243
Grisy-sur-Seine [77], 153
Gron [89], 69
Gros-Banc (Réserve du -) [14], 252
Gros-Fouteau (Réserve biologique de -) [77], 157
Gruissan et l'étang de Campignol [11], 172-173
Gué-de-Selle (étang du -) [53], 281
Guérande (marais de -) [44], 272-274
Guernes (Moisson) [78], 158-159
Guernes (Seine) [78], 162-163
Guil (haute vallée de -) [05], 336

H

Hague (cap de la -) [50], 255-257
Haute-Corse [2B], 124-131
Haute-Garonne [31], 218-220
Haute-Jarrie (étang de -) [38], 369-370
Haute-Loire [43], 50-52
Haute-Marne [52], 113, 117-119
Haute-Normandie, 262-269
Hautes-Alpes [05], 331-337
Haute-Saône [70], 143-145
Haute-Savoie [74], 377-379
Hautes-Chaumes/monts du Forez [42], 371-373
Hautes-Pyrénées [65], 220-222
Haute-Vienne [87], 194-195
Haut-Rhin [68], 23-25
Hauts-de-Seine [92], 166
Hendaye [64], 40
Hérault [34], 178-182
Héron (lac du -) [59], 238-239
Herry [18], 62
Hoc (point du -) [14], 253
Hoëdic (île d') [56], 85
Hohneck (Le -) [68/88], 23-25
Hôpiteau (Bois, landes et étang de l') [79], 318
Horre (étang de la -) [10], 113
Hossegor et port de Capbreton (lac marin d') [40], 34-35
Hotot-en-Auge [14], 253
Houdancourt (bassins de décantation d') [60], 297
Hucel (Le -) [74], 379
Hures-la-Parade [48], 184
Hyères (îles d') [83], 354-355
Hyères et marais environnants (salins d') [83], 351-353

I

Île-de-France, 146-169
Indre [36], 92-98
Indre-et-Loire [37], 98-103
Isère [38], 368-370
Isle de Saint-Quentin (Réserve naturelle du marais d') [02], 295

J

Jablines [77], 157
Jargeau [45], 104
Jarrie [38], 369-370
Jastre (plateau de -), [07], 365-366
Joigny [89], 69
Jolivet [57], 202
Jumièges [76], 269
Jura [39], 138-143

K

Kembs [68], 25-27
Kir/Dijon (lac -) [21], 60
Krafft (plan d'eau de -) [67], 23

L

Lachaussée (étang de -) [55], 202-203
Lancosme et domaine de Bellebouche/Vendœuvres (forêt de -) [36], 96-98
Landes (étang des -) [23], 192-194
Landes [40], 34-36
Landes-Genusson [85], 289
Languedoc-Roussillon, 170-187
Larchant (marais de -) [77], 155
Lascols/Cussac [15], 46-47
Lasse (La -) [17], 316
Lassolas (puy de -) [63], 54
Latga [15], 50
Lautaret (col du -) [05], 335
Lavacourt (lac de -) [78], 158-159
Lavaud et de Mas-Chaban (barrage de -) [16], 306
Lavaux, Gevrey-Chambertin (la combe de -) [21], 59-60
Lavoûte-Chilhac [43], 51
Lécluse [62], 244
Leffrinckoucke [59], 239
Léman (lac -) [74], 377-379
Les Ponts d'Ouve [50], 260
Leucate [11], 174
Lezay [79], 319
Liamone/Coggia et Casaglione (embouchure du -) [2A], 123
Lilleau des Niges (Réserve naturelle de -) [17], 308-310
Limons [63], 55
Limousin, 188-195
Lindre (étang de -) [57], 207-209
Liozargue [15], 50
Locarn (landes de -) [22], 74
Loing (vallée du -) [77], 155-156
Loire (estuaire de la -) [44], 274-275
Loire amont (Gorges de la -) [42], 374
Loire de Jargeau à Orléans (la -) [45], 104-105
Loire en Touraine (la -) [37], 101
Loire entre Nevers et Neuvy-sur-Loire (vallée de la -) [58/18], 60-63
Loire [42], 370-375
Loire-Atlantique [44], 272-276
Loiret [45], 104-105
Loir-et-Cher [41], 101-104
Loix-en-Ré [17, 316
Londe (forêt de La -) [27/76], 266-267
Longéroux (tourbière du -) [19], 190-191
Longevialle [15], 50
Lorraine, 196-211
Lot-et-Garonne [47], 36-39
Louroux (étang du -) [37], 100-101
Lozère [48], 182-184
Luberon (Petit -) [84], 357
Lunéville [54], 200
Lussat [23], 193
Lyons (forêt de -) [27/76], 266-267

M

Madic [15], 49
Madine (lac de -) [55/54], 203-206
Maillys (gravière des -) [21], 59
Maine (lac de -) [49], 278-279
Maine-et-Loire [49], 276-279
Maleconche (anse de -) [17], 315
Malène (La -) [48], 183
Malo-les-Bains [59], 239
Malsanne (défilé de la -) [38], 369
Manche [50], 253-261

Manicamp [02], 298
Manso [2B], 131
Mantes-la-Jolie (île Aumône) [78], 163-164
Manteyer - La Roche-des-Arnauds (marais de -) [05], 335-336
Marainviller [54], 202
Marboué [28], 92
Marcenay (lac de -) [21], 58-59
Marchand (dune -) [59], 239
Marcilly-en-Gault [41], 102
Marnay [71], 66
Marne [51], 113-117
Marolles-sur-Seine (Réserve ornithologique de -) [77], 150, 152
Marquenterre (Parc ornithologique du -) [80], 300-302
Marsainvilliers [45], 105
Mas-Chaban [16], 306
Mas-Saint-Chély [48], 184
Maures (plaine et massif des -) [83], 355
Maxe (plan d'eau de La -) [57], 210
Mayenne [53], 279-282
Mazière-Villeton (Réserve naturelle de la -) [47], 36-37
Médoc (marais du Nord-) [33], 32-33
Méjean (causse -) [48], 184
Membrey [70], 145
Merry-sur-Yonne [89], 69
Mers-les-Bains [80], 302
Meurthe-et-Moselle [54], 198-202, 203-206, 211
Meuse (vallée de la Chiers et zone de confluence avec la -) [08], 110
Meuse [55], 202-207
Mézangers [53], 281
Mezenc (massif du -) [43/07], 52
Mézières-en-Brenne [36], 92
Michelbach (barrage de -) [68], 27
Midi-Pyrénées, 212-227
Migné [36], 95
Migron [44], 274
Minerve [34], 181-182
Mirebeau (plaine de -) [86], 324
Miribel-Jonage et le bassin du Grand Large (les îles de -) [69], 375-376
Mison (lac de -) [05], 335
Moëze-Oléron (Réserve naturelle des marais de -) [17], 310-313
Moisson et de Guernes (boucles de -) [78], 158-159
Moncharville [45], 105
Monieux, [84], 357
Monnerie (lac de la -) [72], 284
Montagny (landes de -) [69], 376-377
Montbel (lac de -) [09], 215
Montcourt-Fromonville (plan d'eau de -) [77], 156
Mont-d'Or (massif du -) [25], 134-135
Montescot [66], 187
Mont-Gros [06], 339
Montilly (secteur de -) [03], 46
Montlouis-sur-Loire [37], 101
Montmirail (Dentelles de -) [84], 355-357
Mont-Saint-Michel (baie du -) [50], 253-255
Morbihan et presqu'île de Rhuys (golfe du -) [56], 82-84
Morbihan [56], 81-85
Moret-sur-Loing [77], 156
Morieux (anse de) [22], 73
Mornant [69], 377
Moru [60], 297
Moselle [57], 207-211
Mosnes [37], 101
Moulière (forêt domaniale de -) [86], 320-324
Moulins [03], 44-45
Mouzay (prairies de -) [55], 206-207
Müllembourg (Réserve naturelle des marais de -) [85], 290-291

N

Néouvielle (Réserve naturelle du -) [65], 220-221
Nérizelec (étang de -) [29], 80
Neuvy-sur-Loire [58/18], 60-63
Nevers : pont de Loire au pied de la vieille ville [58], 61
Nevers [58], 63-64
Neyran [33], 33
Nez-de-Jobourg (Réserve du -) [50], 256-257
Nièvre [58], 60-64
Niort et ses plaines environnantes [79], 319
Noirmoutier-en-l'Île [85], 290-291
Nord [59], 230-239
Nord-Pas-de-Calais, 228-249
Nouvialle [15], 50
Noyarey [38], 369
Noyon [60], 297-298

O

Ognon (vallée de l') [70], 145
Oise en amont de Noyon (vallée inondable de l') [60/02], 297-298
Oise entre Creil et Compiègne (Plans d'eau de la vallee de l') [60], 296-297
Oise [60], 295-298
Oisy-le-Verger (étangs et marais de -) [62], 243-245
Oléron : autres sites (île d') [17], 315-316
Olonne (marais d') [85], 290
Onival (falaises d') [80], 302-303
Orbieu et le plateau de Bouisse (gorges de l') [11], 174
Organbidexka (col d') [64], 40-41
Orient : le barrage/réservoir Seine et le barrage/réservoir Aube (lacs de la forêt d') [10], 110-113
Orléans [45], 104-105
Orne (baie d') [14], 252
Ossau (vallée d') [64], 41
Ouessant (île d') [29], 74-76
Oye (Réserve naturelle du Platier d') [62], 245-247

P

Palluel [62], 244
Palud-sur-Verdon [04], 329
Pannesière (barrage de -) [58], 63
Parcé-sur-Sarthe (plaine de -) [72], 282-283
Pareloup (lac de -) [12], 217
Paris [75], 148-149

Parroy (étang et forêt de -) [54], 198-199
Pas-de-Calais [62], 240-249
Pays de la Loire, 270-291
Peau-de-Meau [13], 347-349
Pénestin [56], 81-82
Penne [81], 224
Perray-en-Yvelines [78], 160-161
Perros-Guirec [22], 72-73
Petit-Fossard (Réserve ornithologique du -) [77], 151
Petit-Noir [39], 138-140
Picardie, 292-303
Picquigny [80], 303
Pierre-de-Bresse [71], 64-65
Pierrefitte (plan d'eau de -) [15], 50
Pilat (Le -) [42], 374
Pinail [86], 320-324
Pincemaille [37], 98-100
Pissevaches [11], 175
Pithiviers [45], 105
Plobsheim [67], 23
Plomb du Cantal [15], 49
Plougonven [29], 81
Plovan [29], 80
Poiré-sur-Velluire (communal du -) [85], 288-289
Poitou-Charentes, 304-325
Pont-de-Roide (roches de -) [25], 138
Pont-de-Vaux [01], 363
Port-de-Lanne [40], 35-36
Port-la-Nouvelle (digue de -) [11], 173
Port-sur-Saône [70], 145
Porto [2B], 126-127
Poses (boucle de -) [27], 264-265
Pouilly-sur-Loire [58], 61-62
Prades (rocher de -) [43], 50-52
Prat-de-Bouc/Plomb du Cantal [15], 47-49
Pré-en-Pail [53], 279-280
Prés-du-Hem (lac des -) [59], 230-231
Prévost (étang du -) [34], 179-180
Privezac (étangs de -) [12], 217
Provence-Alpes-Côte d'Azur, 326-357
Puydarrieux (lac de -) [65], 222
Puy-de-Dôme [63], 52-55
Puy-Sainte-Réparade (gravières du -) [13], 349-350
Pyrénées-Atlantiques [64], 39-40
Pyrénées-Orientales [66], 184-187

Q

Queyras : zone nord-ouest - secteur des chalets de Clapeyto (Parc naturel régional du -) [05], 333-334
Queyras : zones est et sud - haute vallée de Guil ; secteur du mont Viso (Parc naturel régional du -) [05], 336
Quierzy [02], 298

R

Raismes [59], 232-233
Rambouillet (forêt de) [78], 159-161
Ré (île de -) [17], 307-310
Ré (phare des Baleines, île de -) [17], 316-317
Réaltor (bassin du -) [13], 349
Regnéville (havre de -) [50], 259
Reine (forêt de la -) [54], 201-202
Remilly-Aillicourt [08], 110
Remises d'Herneuse (gravières des -) [60], 297
Rémuzat [26], 367-368
Réthoville (marais de -) [50], 259-260
Revère (fort de la -) [06], 339
Rhin (les îles du -) [68], 25-27
Rhinau (île de -) [67], 20-21
Rhône [69], 375-377
Rhône-Alpes, 358-379
Rhuys (presu'île de -) [56], 82-84
Rillé (lac de -) [37], 98-100
Rincerie (étang de la -) [53], 281
Ristolas [05], 336
Rivière [40], 35
Roanne (plaine du -) [42], 374-375
Robehomme [14], 253
Roche-des-Arnauds (La -) [05], 335-336
Rochefort (station de lagunage) [17], 317
Rohrschollen (île du -) [67], 23
Romelaere (Réserve naturelle du -) [62], 247-249
Romersberg (forêt du -) [57], 207-209
Roquebrune-sur-Argens [83], 355
Rosières-aux-Salines [54], 200-201
Rosnay [36], 93
Rougon [04], 330
Roumare (forêt de -) [27], 266-267
Rozier (Le -) [48], 182-183
Rumaucourt (étangs et marais de -) [62], 243-245

S

Saclay [91], 164-165
Sacy-le-Grand (marais de -) [60], 296
Saint-Amand [84], 357
Saint-Andéol-le-Château [69], 377
Saint-Antonin [82], 224
Saint-Bonnet (étang de -) [03], 46
Saint-Brieuc (baie de) [22], 73
Sainte-Come-du-Mont [50], 260
Saint-Cyr (plan d'eau de -) [86], 324-325
Saint-Daumas (vallon de -) [83], 355
Saint-Denis-du-Payré [85], 291
Sainte-Énimie [48], 183
Saint-Egrève (barrage de -) [38], 369
Saintes-Maries-de-la-Mer [13], 350
Saint-Florentin [89], 67-69
Saint-Flour (planèze de -) [15], 50
Saint-Germain-Laval [77], 152
Saint-Gobain (forêt de -) [02], 298
Saint-Hubert/Le Perray-en-Yvelines (étangs de -) [78], 160-161
Saint-Julien-du-Sault [89], 69
Saint-Laurent-d'Agny [69], 377
Saint-Laurent-du-Var [06], 337-339

Saint-Léger-La-Montagne [87], 194-195
Saint-Loup-sur-Thouet [79], 319
Saint-Martin-de-Seignanx [40], 36
Saint-Michel-en-Brenne [36], 92
Saint-Nazaire (étang de -) [66], 184-185
Saint-Nazaire [19], 192
Saint-Nazaire [44], 274
Saint-Nicodème [22], 74
Saint-Nicolas-de-la-Grave (plan d'eau de -) [82], 226-227
Saint-Pierre-des-Tripiers [48], 184
Saint-Quentin [02], 295
Saint-Quentin-en-Yvelines (Réserve naturelle de -) [78], 161-162
Saint-Saturnin [63], 53-54
Saint-Vaast-la-Hougue (rade de -) [50], 257-258
Saint-Viâtre [41], 101-103
Salin-de-Giraud [13], 350-351
Sallanches [74], 379
Salles-Curan [12], 216-217
Saône (plaine de la -) [70], 145
Saône (prairies inondables du val de -) [01], 363
Saône à Marnay (la -) [71], 65-66
Saône-et-Loire [71], 64-67
Saou (massif de la forêt de -) [26], 366-367
Sarthe [72], 282-284
Sassey-sur-Meuse [55], 207
Saubusse [40], 35
Sault [84], 357
Saulx-les-Chartreux (Réserve de -) [91], 165-166
Saussois/Merry-sur-Yonne (rochers du -) [89], 69
Sauvetat (narces de La -) [43], 52
Savoie [73], 377
Scamandre (étang du -) [30], 177
Scandola/Osani (Réserve naturelle de -) [2B], 126-127
Sceaux (parc de -) [92], 166
Sciez [74], 378
Ségala (étangs du -) [12], 216-217
Seille (vallée de la -) [57], 210-211
Seine - rive droite (estuaire de la -) [76], 268
Seine (forêts de la vallée de la -) [27/76], 266-267
Seine (prairies humides de la vallée de la -) [76], 269
Seine (réservoir -) [10], 111-113
Seine entre Grigny et Vigneux (les « fouilles » de la -) [91], 165-166
Seine-et-Marne [77], 150-157
Seine et Yonne (Montereau) [77], 150-153
Seine-Maritime [76], 266-269
Seine-Saint-Denis [93], 167
Séné (Réserve naturelle des marais de -) [56], 85
Sens [89], 69
Sentzich (plaine de -) [54], 210
Sept-Îles (Réserve naturelle des -) [22], 72-73
Seriers (lac de -) [15], 50
Serre (massif de la -) [39], 140-142
Serre (La -) [63], 53-54
Serre (montagne de la) [63], 52-54
Sion (colline de -) [88/54], 211
Solférino [40], 36
Sologne (étangs de -) [41], 101-103
Somme (marais de la vallée de la -) [80], 303
Somme (Réserve naturelle de la baie de -) [80], 300-302
Somme [80], 298-303
Sorme (lac de la -) [71], 66-67
Sorques (plaine de -) [77], 155
Soulangy [58], 61
Spincourt (forêt de -) [55], 206
Suech (plateau de -) [04], 330
Sundgau [90], 145

T

Talbert (sillon de -) [22], 74
Tanargue (massif du -) [07], 365
Tarn (bords du -) [48], 183
Tarn [81], 222-226
Tarn-et-Garonne [82], 224-225, 226-227
Tassineta/Asco (vallée de la -) [2B], 127-128
Teich (Parc ornithologique du -) [33], 33
Territoire de Belfort [90], 145
Thollon-les-Mémises [74], 379
Thonon-les-Bains [74], 377-378
Thouars et ses plaines environnantes [79], 320
Tillaie (Réserve biologique de La -) [77], 157
Tombolo bianco, réserve naturelle de l'étang de Biguglia (vasière de -) [2B], 130-131
Tosny (carrière de -) [27], 266
Touraine [37], 101
Touvre (vallée de la -) [16], 306-307
Tréboul (pont de -) [15], 50
Tréchy (coteau de -) [77], 152
Trélon (massif forestier de -) [59], 234-235
Trois-Fontaines (forêt domaniale de -) [51], 113-115
Trois-Pignons (massif des -) [77], 153-154
Tronçais (forêt de -) [03], 46
Trunvel (Réserve biologique de -) [29], 77-78
Truyère (gorges de la -) [15], 50

V

Vache (puy de la -) [63], 54
Vaivre-Vesoul (lac et plaine inondable de -) [70], 143-144
Val d'Allier aux alentours de Moulins [03], 44-45
Val d'Oise [95], 169
Val de Marne [94], 168-169
Valensole (plateau de -) [04], 330
Valenton [94], 168-169
Var (embouchure du -) [06], 337-338
Var [83], 351-355
Varennes-le-Grand [71], 66
Varennes-sur-Seine [77], 151
Varesnes [60], 298
Varghello/Venaco (vallée du -) [2B], 128-129
Vaucluse [84], 355-357
Vaux [58], 63
Vebron [48], 184
Venaco [2B], 128-129
Vendée [85], 284-291
Vendœuvres [36], 97-98

Vendres (étang de -) [34/11], 180-181
Verdon (gorges du -) [04], 329-330
Verdon (lac du -) [49], 279
Vergigny [89], 67-69
Vesoul [70], 143-145
Vezouze (vallée de la -) [54], 202
Viabon [28], 92
Vicdessos (haute vallée du -) [09], 214-215
Vic-la-Gardiole (étang de -) [34], 181
Videlange (étang de -) [54], 210
Vienne [86], 320-325
Vigan (Le -) [30], 177
Vignes (Les -) [48], 184
Vigneulles (gravières de -) [54], 200-201
Vigneux [91], 165-166
Vigueirat (marais du -) [13], 350
Vilaine (estuaire de la -) [56], 81-82
Vilers-en-Argonne [51], 117
Villard-Saint-Pancrace [05], 336
Ville de Paris [75], 148-149
Villegusien, ou de la Vingeanne (réservoir de -) [52], 117-119
Villeneuve-d'Ascq [59], 239
Villeneuve-de-la-Raho [66], 185-186
Villeneuve-sur-Yonne [89], 69
Villepey (étangs de -) [83], 353-354
Vincennes (bois de -) [75], 149
Vingeanne (La -) [52], 117-119
Vinon-sur-Verdon (aérodrome de -) [83], 353
Viso (mont -) [05], 336
Vitrimont (forêt de -) [57], 200-201
Vogüé [07], 363-365
Voncq [08], 110
Vosges [88], 211
Vouziers [08], 110
Vrizy [08], 110
Villeneuve-sur-Yonne **[89]**, 69
Villepey (étangs de –) **[83]**, 353-354
Villerest (barrage de –) **[42]**, 372
Vincennes (bois de –) **[75]**, 148-149
Vingeanne (La –) **[52]**, 117-119
Vinon-sur-Verdon (aérodrome de –) **[83]**, 353
Viso (mont –) [05], 336
Vitrimont (forêt de –) [57], 200-201
Vogüé [07], 361-363
Voncq [08], 110
Vosges [88], 211
Vouziers [08], 110
Vrizy [08], 110
Vulbens [74], 360

Yffiniac (anse d') [22], 73
Yonne - de Joigny à Sens (gravières du Nord de la vallée de l') [89], 68-69
Yonne [89], 67-69
Yvelines [78], 158-164
Yves (Réserve naturelle du marais d') [17], 313-315

Zommange (étang de -) [54], 210
Zonza [2A], 123
Zuydcoote [59], 239

Illustrations

Éric Alibert:
pages 326 (illustration taken from *naturalistes en Provence,* Éditions Nathan, 2000); 358 (illustration taken from *Carnets naturalistes autour du Mont Blanc,* Nathan, 1996).

Denis Chavigny:
page 86 (illustration taken from *Carnets naturalistes au fil de la Loire,* Éditions Nathan, 1994).

Jean Chevallier:
pages 18, 28 (illustration taken from *Promenades naturalistes en France,* Éditions Nathan, 1992); 42 ; 106 (illustration taken from *Promenades naturalistes en France,* Éditions Nathan, 1992); 146 (illustration taken from *Voyages naturalistes en Île-de-France,* Éditions Nathan, 1993); 170 (illustration taken from *Promenades naturalistes en France,* Éditions Nathan, 1992); 196; 212; 228 (illustration taken from *Promenades naturalistes en France,* Éditions Nathan, 1992); 262; 304.

Denis Clavreul:
pages 70 (illustration taken from *Carnets naturalistes à la pointe de la Bretagne,* Éditions Nathan, 1995); 120.

François Desbordes:
pages 188; 292.

Alan Johnston:
page 250 (illustration taken from *Carnets d'un naturaliste en Normandie,* Éditions Nathan, 2001).

Serge Nicolle:
pages 21, 22, 24, 27, 33, 34, 37, 38, 41, 45, 47, 49, 50, 60, 61, 63, 67, 69, 74, 76, 82, 85, 88, 90, 92, 95, 97, 105, 110, 113, 115, 119, 123, 125, 126, 127, 129, 131, 135, 137, 138, 142, 143, 149, 152, 155, 158, 165, 173, 174, 177, 181, 182, 187, 191, 192, 194, 201, 204, 206, 207, 211, 215, 217, 218, 221, 222, 231, 236, 243, 245, 247, 249, 252, 255, 259, 261, 266, 276, 287, 297, 303, 307, 311, 313, 321, 325, 330, 332, 334, 340, 343, 344, 345, 346, 347, 351, 353, 354, 361, 362, 367, 370, 372.

Benoît Perrotin:
page 270 (illustration taken from *Carnets naturalistes en Vendée,* Éditions Nathan, 2004).

Patrick Vaucoulon:
pages 56 and 132 (illustrations taken from *Carnets naturalistes en Bourgogne,* Éditions Nathan, 1998).

Maps created by:

Pascal Langendorff